THE
MARKETING
RENAISSANCE

HARVARD BUSINESS REVIEW EXECUTIVE BOOK SERIES

Executive Success: Making It In Management

Survival Strategies for American Industry

Managing Effectively in the World Marketplace

Strategic Management

Financial Management

Catching Up with the Computer Revolution

Using Logical Techniques for Making Better Decisions

Growing Concerns: Building and Managing the Smaller Business

Business and Its Public

Sunrise . . . Sunset: Challenging the Myth of Industrial Obsolescence

The Marketing Renaissance

The Executive Dilemma: Handling People Problems at Work

THE
MARKETING
RENAISSANCE

DAVID E. GUMPERT
Editor

JOHN WILEY & SONS
New York • Chichester • Brisbane • Toronto • Singapore

Library of Congress Cataloging in Publication Data:

Main entry under title:

The marketing renaissance.

  (Harvard business review executive book series)
  Includes indexes.
  1. Marketing—Addresses, essays, lectures. I. Gumpert, David E. II. Series.

HF5415.M319 1985   658.8   84-26991
ISBN 0-471-81352-4

658.8
M3458

Printed in the United States of America

10 9 8 7 6 5 4 3 2 1

Foreword

For sixty years, the *Harvard Business Review* has been the farthest reaching executive program of the Harvard Business School. It is devoted to the continuing education of executives and aspiring managers primarily in business organizations, but also in not-for-profit institutions, in government, and in the professions. Through its publishing partners, reprints, and translation programs, it finds an audience in many languages in most of the countries in the world, occasionally penetrating even the barrier between East and West.

The *Harvard Business Review* draws on the talents of the most creative people in modern business and in management education. About half of its content comes from practicing managers, the rest from professional people and university researchers. Everything *HBR* publishes has something to do with the skills, attitudes, and knowledge essential to the competent and ethical practice of management.

The Marketing Renaissance consists of 39 articles dealing with the evolution of marketing strategy amidst rapidly changing environments, both externally and within companies. Neither abstruse nor superficial, the articles chosen for this volume are intended to be usefully analytical, challenging, and carefully prescriptive. Every well-informed businessperson can follow the exposition in its path away from the obvious and into the territory of independent thought. I hope that readers will find these ideas stimulating and helpful in making their professional careers more productive.

KENNETH R. ANDREWS, Editor
Harvard Business Review

Contents

Introduction, David E. Gumpert, 1

Part One Marketing Amidst Rapid Change

An Overview, 13
1. *The Globalization of Markets*, Theodore Levitt, 15
2. *Survival Strategies in a Hostile Environment*, William K. Hall, 32
3. *The Maturing of Consumerism*, Paul N. Bloom and Stephen A. Greyser, 51
4. *Antitrust Risk Analysis for Marketers*, Harry A. Garfield II, 68
5. *What Every Marketer Should Know About Women*, Rena Bartos, 82
6. *Over 49: The Invisible Consumer Market*, Rena Bartos, 104
7. *Beware of International Brand Piracy*, Jack G. Kaikati and Raymond LaGarce, 116
8. *The Health Care Market: Can Hospitals Survive?* Jeff C. Goldsmith, 124
9. *Gone Are the Cash Cows of Yesteryear*, Raymond Vernon, 144
10. *The Marketing of "Unmentionables,"* Aubrey Wilson and Christopher West, 153
11. *Counter-Competition Abroad to Protect Home Markets*, Craig M. Watson, 171

Part Two Planning Strategy for Today's Marketplace

An Overview, 177
12. *Market Success Can Breed "Marketing Inertia,"* Thomas V. Bonoma, 179

13. *The Surprising Case for Low Market Share*, Carolyn Y. Woo and Arnold C. Cooper, 191

14. *End-Game Strategies for Declining Industries*, Kathryn Rudie Harrigan and Michael E. Porter, 205

15. *Gateways to Entry*, George S. Yip, 220

16. *Marketing Success Through Differentiation—of Anything*, Theodore Levitt, 232

17. *How Global Companies Win Out*, Thomas Hout, Michael E. Porter, and Eileen Rudden, 246

18. *Is Vertical Integration Profitable?*, Robert D. Buzzell, 263

19. *Growing Ventures Can Anticipate Marketing Stages*, Tyzoon T. Tyebjee, Albert V. Bruno, and Shelby H. McIntyre, 280

20. *Match Manufacturing Policies and Product Strategy*, Robert Stobauch and Piero Telesio, 286

Part Three   The Growing Challenge of Implementation

An Overview, 299

21. *Making Your Marketing Strategy Work*, Thomas V. Bonoma, 301

22. *Taking Technology to Market*, David Ford and Chris Ryan, 315

23. *Quality Is More Than Making a Good Product*, Hirotaka Takeuchi and John A. Quelch, 331

24. *Successful Share-Building Strategies*, Robert D. Buzzell and Frederik D. Wiersema, 342

25. *Marketing Intangible Products and Product Intangibles*, Theodore Levitt, 359

26. *Three Essentials of Product Quality*, Jack Reddy and Abe Berger, 371

27. *Good Product Support Is Smart Marketing*, Milind M. Lele and Uday S. Karmarkar, 383

28. *Manage Risk in Industrial Pricing*, Barbara Bund Jackson, 399

Part Four   New Approaches for Reaching Customers

An Overview, 419

29. *New Ways to Reach Your Customers*, Benson P. Shapiro and John Wyman, 421

30. *Major Sales: Who Really Does the Buying?*, Thomas V. Bonoma, 436

31. *Get More Out of Your Trade Shows*, Thomas V. Bonoma, 452

32. *Nonstore Marketing: Fast Track or Slow?*, John A. Quelch and
    Hirotaka Takeuchi, 465

33. *Better Marketing at the Point of Purchase*, John A. Quelch and
    Kristina Cannon-Bonventre, 481

34. *It's Time to Make Trade Promotion More Productive*,
    John A. Quelch, 493

35. *Industrial Distributors—When, Who, and How?*, James D. Hlavacek
    and Tommy J. McCuistion, 503

36. *Nonprofits: Check Your Attention to Customers*,
    Alan R. Andreasen, 512

37. *Ads That Irritate May Erode Trust in Advertised Brands*,
    Rena Bartos, 521

38. *Plan for More Productive Advertising*, Malcolm A. McNiven, 526

39. *"Buying in" to Market Control*, Robert E. Weigand, 538

About the Authors, 553

Author Index, 563

Subject Index, 565

THE
MARKETING
RENAISSANCE

Introduction

DAVID E. GUMPERT

Back in 1960, when Theodore Levitt published his landmark *Harvard Business Review* article, "Marketing Myopia," the world was a fairly understandable and orderly place for marketing executives.

They could look forward with a high degree of confidence to economic growth and prosperity for the foreseeable future; such pressures as inflation and high interest rates were mainly of concern in foreign countries. Critical natural resources—especially oil and natural gas—were both plentiful and relatively inexpensive. Internationally, the United States was preeminent, both economically and militarily.

Although the emerging Civil Rights movement was challenging the old order in the South, the nation's social structure still relied heavily on the nuclear family. Such issues as product quality, consumer protection, and offensive advertising were only specks on a distant time horizon.

In such an environment of stability, "Marketing Myopia," with its emphasis on looking beyond narrow product categories and its focus on customer needs, opened a whole new vista of ideas and opportunities for many marketing managers. Newspaper, book, and magazine publishers, for instance, could all feel comfortable viewing themselves as being in the information business. The notion of designing products and services to fill customer needs rather than internal production or distribution structures took hold.

Much has happened on the national and international scene since 1960 to affect marketers. Perhaps the most significant difference is that the pace of change has quickened, whether from an economic, social, technological, cultural, or informational perspective.

If anything, the quickening rate of change has made "Marketing Myopia" more relevant than it was back in the 1960s. Those companies with the broadest view of their business expertise and most attuned to changing customer needs are best able to adapt by offering the most appropriate products and services.

1

But today's rapid changes also make it incumbent on managers to have additional tools at their disposal to enable them to cope with a constantly altered marketplace. That is where this volume of *Harvard Business Review* articles becomes important. It includes research and analysis by some of the nation's most prominent marketing experts to explain recent environmental and strategic changes executives must face. It also contains specific prescriptions for making effective use of the research and analysis in management decision making. Indeed, this collection might be viewed as a means of adapting the marketing concept Mr. Levitt articulated so well to today's circumstances.

The Most Challenging Areas of Change

What are the most significant environmental changes with which marketers must learn to deal? Broadly speaking, there are four that have combined to make the marketing manager's job increasingly challenging and complex:

1. *A rapidly changing national and international order.* This order is changing socially, economically, and in other respects. Just to cite one example on a national scale, the traditional family as we knew it not long ago has nearly vanished from the American scene. Supplanting the old family structure—a working husband and home-based wife taking care of the children—are new ones with working husbands and wives leaving children in daycare, unmarried couples with and without children, homosexual couples, and single-person households.

Such quick, radical changes in how people arrange their lives have marketing implications so profound that they haven't even begun to be fully digested and accounted for. What kinds of special products and services can companies offer to help working couples resolve their nagging daycare problems? How do advertisers appeal to the expanding homosexual market without offending heterosexuals? How do market researchers determine which single adults live alone and which live in couple or roommate situations?

Similarly, wide swings in the economy, from recession to growth and back to recession, accompanied by sharp changes in inflation and interest rates play havoc with long-term marketing plans. During one Christmas season consumers are extremely cautious in their buying habits, while the following year they spend as if there's no tomorrow. Auto makers have learned the unhappy lesson of fast-changing consumer moods as the companies switch back and forth between emphasizing large and small cars, usually just out of step with the consumer desires.

On the international scene, as well, rapid change has become the rule rather than the exception, with important implications for marketers. The fundamentalist Islamic revolution in Iran caught even American government analysts off-guard, and has led to growing instability throughout the Near and Middle East. Leftist guerilla movements have sprouted in Central America, with immense implications for our hemisphere. Added to all that has been the huge increase in international terrorism.

Marketers must thus be ready to enter and leave markets more quickly than ever before. They must also be prepared to alter their marketing tactics according to the changing social and political structures and attitudes in many countries, particularly those in the Third World. Nestlé certainly discovered that in its efforts to expand markets for baby formula; increased sensitivities to both the company's tactics and the needs of mothers and their infants in a number of underdeveloped countries forced the company to change its approach.

2. *An increasingly competitive marketing environment.* It wasn't too long ago that growth was everything, whether in industry trends, sales, market share, or profits. With the economy exhibiting the kind of sustained growth levels that were part of the 1960s, it was reasonable to expect most markets to simply continue expanding. And in many industries that's still the case, particularly in high-technology areas such as computers and medical equipment.

But the spiral of inflation, recession, unemployment, and high interest rates through the 1970s and 1980s are symptomatic of fundamental economic problems. For marketers in many industries, these problems have meant the same number or even increasing numbers of companies selling goods and services to fewer-than-expected potential customers. The inevitable result: heightened competition.

As some industries have declined—notably autos and steel—and others have been deregulated or otherwise changed radically—notably airline, financial services, and telecommunications—marketers accustomed to a familiar and comfortable marketing order have had to face up to new rules of competition.

Those companies in deregulated industries find themselves scouting out new marketing terrain. For instance, in the banking industry, where services and interest rates were just a few years ago clearly delineated by government regulations, marketers must now determine which factors are most important to customers. Should bankers emphasize convenience of service, interest rates, or a variety of products? Should they offer brokerage, credit card, and insurance services?

The same situation applies in the airline industry. Should airlines compete on fares, schedule convenience, or such extra services as meals and advance-boarding passes? Should either financial service companies or airlines be emphasizing mass-market appeal or be striving to lure specific market segments, even if that means losing certain segments?

Nor is the sharpened competition just a function of domestic developments. Whereas American companies 20 years ago had most key markets in this country nearly to themselves, competition with foreign companies is now an accepted part of life in many industries. And the pace of change in international competition is quite rapid; just as we become accustomed to the idea of the Germans and Japanese as the primary competitors, we suddenly discover that South Korea and Taiwan have become important factors.

Similarly, American international corporations, which not long ago dominated many overseas markets in certain product categories, now must compete head-on with rapidly expanding foreign companies in overseas markets. Whether in the United States or overseas, American companies face many of the same issues in competing with foreign competitors. Which sorts of differences—price, quality, technology, or some other—should be emphasized in promoting products or services? Which market segments should be pursued and which left to the foreign companies?

3. *Changing attitudes about what comprises effective management.* The difficulty many companies have had adapting to the quickened pace of environmental change has called into question their basic managerial approaches. When such seemingly impenetrable corporate giants as Chrysler and International Harvester stumble so badly, and many others stumble nearly as badly, its' not enough to simply ascribe the problems to a recessionary economy; indeed, it's clear that managers must absorb blame as well.

The *Harvard Business Review*, among other business publications, has raised several serious questions about the way American managers operate. For one thing, it's been charged that they tend to focus too much on short-term financial results and not enough on the longer-term financial commitments and strategies that are likely to affect ultimate business success. For another, American managers have been accused of not paying enough attention to employee productivity and ways to improve it.

But in a rapidly changing environment, it might be asked, how realistic is it to focus on the long term? Indeed, the new interest in entrepreneurship and arguments that large companies must learn to be more entrepreneurial can be interpreted to mean that attention to the long term can easily be at the expense of being entrepreneurial. Entrepreneurship, after all, suggests reacting quickly to rapidly developing opportunities and making financial and marketing commitments incrementally rather than all at once.

Similarly, measuring the productivity of marketing researchers or of mass media advertisements can be much more difficult than measuring the productivity of assembly line workers. And when something can't be measured, there's a tendency either to ignore it or else eliminate it out of frustration.

For marketing executives, the fast-changing attitudes about what comprises effective management can understandably be troubling. Should they focus on short-term or long-term issues? How should they approach the productivity issue? How do they organize their research, advertising, and distribution to account for the rapid environmental changes described previously?

4. *The technology-information revolution.* The much-publicized changes going on in the areas of personal computers, video technology, and

data bases, among others, have broad implications for rapid change in our society at large. Just to take one example, the advent of home computers has begun to foster social divisions according to those who are and aren't computer literate. It might even be argued that what is sometimes referred to as the information revolution—and the resulting data bases and varied information delivery systems (telephones, cable television, etc.)—is leading to divisions according to those adept and those unfamiliar with the rapidly increasing number and types of information tools.

This revolution, of course, also has special implications for marketers. First, such fundamental alterations in the way information is accumulated and received mean that marketers have new options for accumulating marketing research. It's no longer automatically necessary to go out and do lots of expensive primary research before a new product is introduced, because certain relevant information might be available easily and cheaply in some data base somewhere.

Second, the quick accumulation of information that the computer technology makes possible means that marketers can find out faster than ever before how well particular products are selling and which are in short supply. That enables managers to make quick changes in selling, advertising, or distribution strategies.

Third, marketers suddenly have a variety of new options for disseminating product and service information. These new options include cable television and home computer data networks. (Of course, there's also the danger video cassette recorders pose to users of television ads that they will be edited out before they're ever seen by viewers.)

Finally, the technology-information revolution offers the potential of new ways to distribute products. But if consumer products are bought via computer or telephone, what are the implications for retailers? And which types of products and services best lend themselves to electronic ordering or distribution?

These environmental trends, then, will not only affect our society in important ways, but will affect the marketing of all goods and services for many years to come. And the questions they post require specific answers.

The articles in this volume begin to provide ideas and practical suggestions for dealing with just the sort of fundamental change our society has been experiencing in recent years. The articles are arranged in four categories to correlate with the major trends just described:

1. *Marketing amidst rapid change.* The rapid pace of economic and social change and the resulting reordering of markets have played havoc with many companies' marketing plans. In part, this is because marketers have chosen to ignore important shifts affecting primary demand.

Yet one of the underlying themes from nearly all the articles in this section is that opportunities abound amidst, and sometimes because of the change. Conversely, danger lurks for those companies that don't take fundamental change seriously enough or else deal with it inappropriately.

Take the social and political upheaval occurring in many foreign countries. One could easily assume that marketers must diversify their product lines to account for rapidly changing tastes. But, as Theodore Levitt argues in "The Globalization of Markets," international tastes are in important respects becoming more homogenized and less differentiated than would seem likely at first glance. He notes, for instance, the irony of young Iranian revolutionaries at anti-American rallies dressed in fashionable Western European clothes.

Or consider the upheaval in domestic markets. During the early and mid-1970s, issues related to product safety, prices, and selling tactics became the focus of much organizational and media attention. But by the end of the decade, issues associated with consumerism appeared to have faded away, seemingly replaced by more hard-core economic concerns as unemployment and inflation.

Companies easily could be tempted to conclude that they don't have to pay as much attention as they once did to consumer-type issues. Not so, argue Paul N. Bloom and Stephen A. Greyser in their article, "The Maturing of Consumerism." They maintain that the consumerism issue merely entered a new phase in its development cycle and that companies can hasten its departure from the public consciousness by seeking to address as many customer concerns associated with consumerism as possible.

Similarly, while profound social and demographic changes conspired to nearly do away with the nuclear family, they have also combined to create important new markets. But the sudden appearance of large and potentially lucrative segments—working women and well-heeled older adults—has caught many companies unaware. They continue in the old patterns of catering to housewives and 18-to-49-year-olds, wondering why sales are declining and competition increasing; well-managed companies, meanwhile, are moving to exploit new opportunities, observes Rena Bartos in two articles, "What Every Marketer Should Know About Women" and "Over 49: The Invisible Consumer Market."

2. *Planning strategy for today's marketplace.* Few marketing managers have been able to escape the pressure of increasing competition. As they seek to formulate coherent strategies within such a pressure-cooker environment, they can easily feel as if they're torn in two different directions. On the one hand, they're well aware of the adage: once you find a workable strategy, stick to it. On the other hand, they must confront the notion that those who can't adapt their strategies to rapid changes in the marketplace will fall by the wayside.

How to deal with such conflicting approaches? As the pace of external change quickens and competition increases, marketers should give greater weight to the second consideration as they formulate strategy, suggests Thomas V. Bonoma in "Market Success Can Breed 'Marketing Inertia'."

He maintains that companies with successful marketing strategies can easily be lulled into a false sense of security. Such an unrealistic feeling can then color reactions to outside events that affect the marketing environment. Too often, the temptation is to simply ignore the external changes and continue on as before.

Another problem confronting marketers as they seek to formulate strategy amidst increasing competition is the so-called conventional wisdom about what comprises effective strategy. The conventional wisdom has it that marketers must be market-share leaders to reap the most attractive profits. That same wisdom has it that the best approach for companies in declining industries is the strategy known as harvesting—simply reaping whatever financial benefits still exist from products without making additional significant financial investments in them. Another part of the conventional wisdom suggests that vertically integrated companies can operate most cost effectively and best weather competitive challenges.

But, as authors of three articles maintain, the conventional wisdom doesn't always hold up as marketers face constantly changing external condition. In "The Surprising Case for Low Market Share" by Carolyn Y. Woo and Arnold C. Cooper, we learn that in certain kinds of industries under varying conditions, low market share can be not only a viable survival option, but an arguable strategic option for achieving financial success.

Similarly, Kathryn Rudie Harrigan and Michael E. Porter suggest in "End-Game Strategies for Declining Industries" that a simple harvesting strategy in industries with deteriorating markets may be inappropriate. Rather, managers can actually devise strategies either to increase their market shares within such declining industries and wind up in dominant positions or else to exit in ways that leave them unscathed financially.

And the notion of a strategy that relies on vertically integrating product lines and acquisitions as a way to realize financial economies and marketing consistency doesn't always work out in practice, argues Robert D. Buzzell in "Is Vertical Integration Profitable?" In certain situations, vertical integration actually imposes heavy capital requirements on companies and reduces their technological and marketing flexibility, among other potential problems, he notes. In the context of a rapidly changing environment, that can be risky.

Finally, marketers might easily wonder how they can keep coming up with new strategies in the face of frequent market changes. Theodore Levitt has an encouraging and no-holds-barred response to that worry, which he puts forth in "Marketing Success Through Differentiation—of Anything." In his view, no product is so mundane and no industry so crowded that marketers can't constantly find ways to distinguish their products or services from those of their competitors.

3. *The growing challenge of implementation.* The rising chorus of criticism of American management techniques may be traceable, at least in part, to the perception that this country's executives do an impressive job

of devising strategic approaches, but somehow fail to make it all work in the marketplace. That is, managers appear to pay an inordinate amount of attention to analyzing problems and coming up with potential solutions and not enough attention to the hands-on work that is required to make sure that strategic changes are put into practice within organizations.

Part of the problem, as Thomas V. Bonoma suggests in "Making Your Marketing Strategy Work," is determining whether marketing difficulty is a function of inappropiate strategy or of implementation. He points out that poor execution can mislead managers to alter perfectly appropriate strategy; therefore, he suggests that managers look to the implementation process before making major strategic changes.

Another, probably more challenging, aspect of the problem is making certain that the incentives and structure underlying a company's marketing organization are appropriate to the strategy being used, he suggests. Thus, managers must be sure that sales commissions on new products provide enough incentive to salespeople to ensure that such products aren't ignored at the expense of proven older products. And managers must also be certain that such organizational obstacles as rituals and politics don't sap the effectiveness of strategic changes, Mr. Bonoma argues.

Increasing competition and changing values mean that managers must be able to not only shift strategy quickly, but care for highly specific implementation issues. Two of the most important issues of recent years have related to product quality and the rising prominence of the service sector of the economy.

Quality, of course, turned into an important managerial issue as the perception grew among consumers that Japanese and German companies, in particular, were offering autos, stereos, cameras, and other products of better quality than were American companies. Consumer advocates and high-level executives alike began wondering how American companies could go about matching the high quality of foreign competitors.

That issue, not surprisingly, raised other questions. What, exactly, are the characteristics of high quality? How do producers go about conveying these characteristics to consumers? What happens to costs—and prices—when additional quality is built into products? By how much should a top-quality product improve over competitors' offerings?

The questions, of course, can continue, since quality is a very subjective property. But, as two articles observe, marketers can use the issue of quality to improve customer satisfaction. Using the quality issue effectively means changing and improving the way companies gather information, position their products, and deal with customers after the sale.

Hirotaka Takeuchi and John A. Quelch observe in "Quality Is More Than Making a Good Product" that marketers must first understand how consumers define quality for the product in question. That is usually much easier said than done, and typically involves closely monitoring and surveying customer attitudes and reactions to products. As if that isn't enough, they note that customer definitions of quality tend to change over time; in addition, consumers have different criteria for defining quality before the purchase, at the point of purchase, and after receiving and trying the product. For instance, the availability of effective customer service after the sale often becomes extremely important in determining perceptions of product quality.

The mechanics of building additional quality into products often aren't as onerous, or costly, as marketers tend to imagine, argue Jack Reddy and Abe Berger in their article, "Three Essentials of Product Quality." For instance, improved quality doesn't automatically mean higher costs, and can result in lower costs as reject rates and inspection costs decline. Nor does a product's quality level necessarily need to exceed that of competitors by a wide margin. What's extremely important, they argue, is gaining a commitment to improved quality throughout an organization so that certain quality-improving steps, such as obtaining relevant data and ensuring vendor quality, can be implemented effectively.

The implementation issue is also extremely important to the growing numbers of companies in the business of selling services. Because services incorporate such an inherently high degree of intangibility, marketers must be attuned to certain special obstacles they face in the sales process, suggests Theodore Levitt in his article, "Marketing Intangible Products and Product Intangibles."

Among the obstacles such marketers must be able to overcome are that services depend so heavily on the human factor in both production and delivery and also that customers often are unaware of the value and usefulness of their purchase. Mr. Levitt suggests that marketers of services make heavy use of technology to minimize the human factor and also make concerted efforts to remind customers—through such things as newsletters and surveys—that their purchases are important and that the service providers want very much to provide satisfaction.

4. *New approaches for reaching customers.* The technological-communications revolution currently under way has made certain marketing approaches less attractive than they once were while simultaneously opening up an array of new ones. Skyrocketing costs for such traditional tools as traveling salespeople and television advertising have become less tolerable as new options, such as telemarketing and national account management, have become viable.

Implicit in the new marketing approaches is that marketers have a clearly defined sense of who their customers are and how they can be reached most effectively. After all, it's not much help to use telemarketing if the real decision maker with regard to purchases isn't reached. Several articles in this section provide a sense of the challenge the new marketing approaches pose to executives.

Benson P. Shapiro and John Wyman suggest that many marketers can reach their customers more effectively at lower cost than at present by appropriately matching their needs with the developing new selling approaches. For instance, telemarketing allows marketers quick and immediate feedback from potential customers while simultaneously allowing specific information to be widely distributed. Industrial stores allow for personal selling by a sales force that doesn't incur the high expenses associated with traveling.

Similarly, Thomas Bonoma maintains in two articles—"Major Sales: Who *Really* Does the Buying?" and "Get More Out Of Your Trade Shows"— that marketers must correlate their products with the most viable selling techniques available. For big-ticket items such as corporate jets and sophisticated computer systems, the individuals with whom sellers must deal may not be those actually making the buying decision, he cautions. For sellers who aren't aware of that problem and don't get to the actual decision maker early enough, sales may be lost. Similarly, sellers who view trade shows as obligatory social events may lose significant sales and intelligence-gathering opportunities, he suggests.

Where will the changing approaches to reaching customers lead marketers in coming years? Certainly there is no lack of projections about the wonders sellers will see from the high-technology revolution currently under way. One of the most intriguing of these concerns the possible replacement of retail outlets by such high-tech, order-taking marvels as two-way cable television and computers.

But, as in many areas of marketing, the future isn't always what is seems, as John A. Quelch and Hirotaka Takeuchi point out in their article, "Nonstore Marketing: Fast Track or Slow." They note that technological developments aren't moving as fast as marketers sometimes think and that a number of cost, policy, and other barriers could inhibit growth of new marketing technologies. Moreover, the authors remain skeptical that consumers will easily give up the familiar retailing experience for unfamiliar technologically oriented shopping approaches.

Looking Ahead

It's clear, then, that marketers face dramatic, even explosive, changes in the external environment. Less clear is the impact those changes should have on strategy and tactics.

At the very least, marketers will need to pay closer attention than ever before to developing social, political, technological, and other trends. It's clear that the rapid pace with which trends develop is creating both marketing opportunities and dangers.

In addition, marketers will need to monitor their competitors quite attentively. The ever-sharpening competition shortens the amount of time companies have to react to actions by others in the marketplace.

The more troublesome challenge facing marketers will be formulating appropriate responses to the external changes. The number of possible strategic responses only increases as researchers challenge the conventional wisdom in such areas as market share and product–service differentiation.

The growing range of potential strategic responses similarly complicates the managerial task of implementing actions after they've been decided on. Managers charged with carrying out strategy must possess a growing degree of sophistication to make necessary changes speedily and to deal with uncharted approaches.

The growing array of selling techniques and approaches places a similar challenge on marketing executives. First they must familiarize themselves with the options and then decide which are appropriate to their product and service lines.

On top of all the changes and options, the marketer must not lose sight of one central point: that the marketing concept as articulated by Theodore Levitt back in 1960 is no less true today than it was then. It's just that the conditions under which it must be implemented have become more complex and demanding than they were back then. If nothing else, the developing conditions should make the marketing terrain an increasingly dangerous, and exciting, place in which to manage.

PART ONE
MARKETING AMIDST RAPID CHANGE

AN OVERVIEW

The articles in this section chronicle significant social, economic, and other trends which have had a special impact on marketing.

"The Globalization of Markets" by Theodore Levitt considers the effects of increasingly sophisticated communications and growing wealth on consumer aspirations worldwide. His conclusion: that consumers, when made aware of their options, aren't all that different across international, ethnic, and religious boundaries and that marketers must increasingly take into account similarities rather than differences in devising international marketing strategies.

Paul N. Bloom and Stephen A. Greyser trace the history of America's tumultuous consumer movement in "The Maturing of Consumerism" and conclude that it isn't fading away, but rather entering a new phase. Indeed, tracing the movement's history isn't unlike tracing a product's life cycle, they suggest.

Various substantive changes in certain aspects of antitrust law have combined to make analysis by marketers more practical than it used to be, suggests Harry A. Garfield II in "Antitrust Risk Analysis for Marketers." He offers guidelines for determining the possibilities of antitrust problems.

Rena Bartos describes and analyzes the emergence of two large and increasingly influential market segments in her two articles, "What Every Marketer Should Know About Women" and "Over 49: the Invisible Consumer Market." Marketers who ignore the growing influence of women and older consumers risk not only passing up significant selling opportunities, but of being left behind competitively, she suggests.

The rapidly increasing pace of international trade has not only created new overseas markets, but updated versions of skullduggery as well. Jack G. Kaikati and Raymond LaGarce in their article, "Beware of International Brand Piracy," assess the increasing tendency by unscrupulous entrepreneurs to produce cheap imitations of items bearing popular trademarks.

Rapid economic change has even affected the seemingly impregnable area of hospitals, and has made their managers increasingly aware of the dangers of failing to innovate. Jeff C. Goldsmith offers managers in this area advice for lowering costs so as to compete effectively, in his article "The Health Care Market: Can Hospitals Survive?"

Aubrey Wilson and Christopher West in their article "The Marketing of 'Unmentionables,'" consider the effects of rapid social change and the consequent disappearance of many taboos on marketing such products as birth control products and funeral services.

And finally, Craig M. Watson argues in his article "Counter-competition Abroad to Protect Home Markets," that American companies can upstage increasingly aggressive foreign competitors by grabbing market share on their home turfs.

1

The Globalization of Markets

THEODORE LEVITT

Many companies have become disillusioned with sales in the international market-place as old markets become saturated and new ones must be found. How can they customize products for the demands of new markets? Which items will consumers want? With wily international competitors breathing down their necks, many organizations think that the game just isn't worth the effort.

In this powerful essay, the author asserts that well-managed companies have moved from emphasis on customizing items to offering globally standardized products that are advanced, functional, reliable—and low priced. Multinational companies that concentrated on idiosyncratic consumer preferences have become befuddled and unable to take in the forest because of the trees. Only global companies will achieve long-term success by concentrating on what everyone wants rather than worrying about the details of what everyone thinks they might like.

A powerful force drives the world toward a converging commonality, and that force is technology. It has proletarianized communication, transport, and travel. It has made isolated places and impoverished peoples eager for modernity's allurements. Almost everyone everywhere wants all the things they have heard about, seen, or experienced via the new technologies.

The result is a new commercial reality—the emergence of global markets for standardized consumer products on a previously unimagined scale of magnitude. Corporations geared to this new reality benefit from enormous economies of scale in production, distribution, marketing, and management. By translating these benefits into reduced world prices, they can decimate

---

Published 1983.

competitors that still live in the disabling grip of old assumptions about how the world works.

Gone are accustomed differences in national or regional preference. Gone are the days when a company could sell last year's models—or lesser versions of advanced products—in the less-developed world. And gone are the days when prices, margins, and profits abroad were generally higher than at home.

The globalization of markets is at hand. With that, the multinational commercial world nears its end, and so does the multinational corporation.

The multinational and the global corporation are not the same thing. The multinational corporation operates in a number of countries, and adjusts its products and practices in each—at high relative costs. The global corporation operates with resolute constancy—at low relative cost—as if the entire world (or major regions of it) were a single entity; it sells the same things in the same way everywhere.

Which strategy is better is not a matter of opinion but of necessity. Worldwide communications carry everywhere the constant drumbeat of modern possibilities to lighten and enhance work, raise living standards, divert, and entertain. The same countries that ask the world to recognize and respect the individuality of their cultures insist on the wholesale transfer to them of modern goods, services, and technologies. Modernity is not just a wish but also a widespread practice among those who cling, with unyielding passion or religious fervor, to ancient attitudes and heritages.

Who can forget the televised scenes during the 1979 Iranian uprisings of young men in fashionable French-cut trousers and silky body shirts thirsting with raised modern weapons for blood in the name of Islamic fundamentalism?

In Brazil, thousands swarm daily from pre-industrial Bahian darkness into exploding coastal cities, there quickly to install television sets in crowded corrugated huts and, next to battered Volkswagens, make sacrificial offerings of fruit and fresh-killed chickens to Macumban spirits by candlelight.

During Biafra's fratricidal war against the Ibos, daily televised reports showed soldiers carrying bloodstained swords and listening to transistor radios while drinking Coca-Cola.

In the isolated Siberian city of Krasnoyarsk, with no paved streets and censored news, occasional Western travelers are stealthily propositioned for cigarettes, digital watches, and even the clothes off their backs.

The organized smuggling of electronic equipment, used automobiles, Western clothing, cosmetics, and pirated movies into primitive places exceeds even the thriving underground trade in modern weapons and their military mercenaries.

A thousand suggestive ways attest to the ubiquity of the desire for the most advanced things that the world makes and sells—goods of the best quality and reliability at the lowest price. The world's needs and desires have been irrevocably homogenized. This makes the multinational corporation obsolete and the global corporation absolute.

Living in the Republic of Technology

Daniel J. Boorstin, author of the monumental trilogy *The Americans*, characterized our age as driven by "the Republic of Technology [whose] supreme law . . . is convergence, the tendency for everything to become more like everything else."

In business, this trend has pushed markets toward global commonality. Corporations sell standardized products in the same way everywhere—autos, steel, chemicals, petroleum, cement, agricultural commodities and equipment, industrial and commercial construction, banking and insurance services, computers, semiconductors, transport, electronic instruments, pharmaceuticals, and telecommunications, to mention some of the obvious.

Nor is the sweeping gale of globalization confined to these raw material or high-tech products, where the universal language of customers and users facilitates standardization. The transforming winds whipped up by the proletarianization of communication and travel enter every crevice of life.

Commercially, nothing confirms this as much as the success of McDonald's from the Champs Elysées to the Ginza, of Coca-Cola in Bahrain and Pepsi-Cola in Moscow, and of rock music, Greek salad, Hollywood movies, Revlon cosmetics, Sony televisions, and Levi jeans everywhere. "High-touch" products are as ubiquitous as high-tech.

Starting from opposing sides, the high-tech and the high-touch ends of the commercial spectrum gradually consume the undistributed middle in their cosmopolitan orbit. No one is exempt and nothing can stop the process. Everywhere everything gets more and more like everything else as the world's preference structure is relentlessly homogenized.

Consider the cases of Coca-Cola and Pepsi-Cola, which are globally standardized products sold everywhere and welcomed by everyone. Both successfully cross multitudes of national, regional, and ethnic taste buds trained to a variety of deeply ingrained local preferences of taste, flavor, consistency, effervescence, and aftertaste. Everywhere both sell well. Cigarettes, too, especially American-made, make year-to-year global inroads on territories previously held in the firm grip of other, mostly local, blends.

These are not exceptional examples. (Indeed their global reach would be even greater were it not for artificial trade barriers.) They exemplify a general drift toward the homogenization of the world and how companies distribute, finance, and price products.[1] Nothing is exempt. The products and methods of the industrialized world play a single tune for all the world, and all the world eagerly dances to it.

Ancient differences in national tastes or modes of doing business disappear. The commonality of preference leads inescapably to the standardization of products, manufacturing, and the institutions of trade and commerce. Small nation-based markets transmogrify and expand. Success in world competition turns on efficiency in production, distribution, marketing, and management, and inevitably becomes focused on price.

The most effective world competitors incorporate superior quality and reliability into their cost structures. They sell in all national markets the same kind of products sold at home or in their largest export market. They compete on the basis of appropriate value—the best combinations of price, quality, reliability, and delivery for products that are globally identical with respect to design, function, and even fashion.

That, and little else, explains the surging success of Japanese companies dealing worldwide in a vast variety of products— both tangible products like steel, cars, motorcycles, stereo equipment, farm machinery, robots, microprocessors, carbon fibers, and now even textiles, and intangibles like banking, shipping, general contracting, and computer software. Nor are high-quality and low-cost operations incompatible, as a host of consulting organizations and data engineers argue with vigorous vacuity. The reported data are incomplete, wrongly analyzed, and contradictory. The truth is that low-cost operations are the hallmark of corporate cultures that require and produce quality in all that they do. High quality and low costs are not opposing postures. They are compatible, twin identities of superior practice.[2]

To say that Japan's companies are not global because they export cars with left-side drives to the United States and the European continent, while those in Japan have right-side drives, or because they sell office machines through distributors in the United States but directly at home, or speak Portuguese in Brazil is to mistake a difference for a distinction. The same is true of Safeway and Southland retail chains operating effectively in the Middle East, and to not only native but also imported populations from Korea, the Philippines, Pakistan, India, Thailand, Britain, and the United States. National rules of the road differ, and so do distribution channels and languages. Japan's distinction is its unrelenting push for economy and value enhancement. That translates into a drive for standardization at high quality levels.

Vindication of the Model T

If a company forces costs and prices down and pushes quality and reliability up—while maintaining reasonable concern for suitability—customers will prefer its world-standardized products. The theory holds, at this stage in the evolution of globalization, no matter what conventional market research and even common sense may suggest about different national and regional tastes, preferences, needs, and institutions. The Japanese have repeatedly vindicated this theory, as did Henry Ford with the Model T. Most important, so have their imitators, including companies from South Korea (television sets and heavy construction), Malaysia (personal calculators and microcomputers), Brazil (auto parts and tools), Colombia (apparel), Singapore (optical equipment), and yes, even from the United States (office copiers, computers, bicycles, castings), Western Europe (automatic washing machines), Rumania (housewares), Hungary (apparel), Yugoslavia (furniture), and Israel (pagination equipment).

Of course, large companies operating in a single nation or even a single city don't standardize everything they make, sell, or do. They have product lines instead of a single product version, and multiple distribution channels. There are neighborhood, local, regional, ethnic, and institutional differences, even within metropolitan areas. But although companies customize products for particular market segments, they know that success in a world with homogenized demand requires a search for sales opportunities in similar segments across the globe in order to achieve the economies of scale necessary to compete.

Such a search works because a market segment in one country is seldom unique; it has close cousins everywhere precisely because technology has homogenized the globe. Even small local segments have their global equivalents everywhere and become subject to global competition, especially on price.

The global competitor will seek constantly to standardize his offering everywhere. He will digress from this standardization only after exhausting all possibilities to retain it, and he will push for reinstatement of standardization whenever digression and divergence have occurred. He will never assume that the customer is a king who knows his own wishes.

Trouble increasingly stalks companies that lack clarified global focus and remain inattentive to the economics of simplicity and standardization. The most endangered companies in the rapidly evolving world tend to be those that dominate rather small domestic markets with high value-added products for which there are smaller markets elsewhere. With transportation costs proportionately low, distant competitors will enter the now-sheltered markets of those companies with goods produced more cheaply under scale-efficient conditions. Global competition spells the end of domestic territoriality, no matter how diminutive the territory may be.

When the global producers offer their lower costs internationally, their patronage expands exponentially. They not only reach into distant markets, but also attract customers who previously held to local preferences and now capitulate to the attractions of lesser prices. The strategy of standardization not only responds to worldwide homogenized markets but also expands those markets with aggressive low pricing. The new technological juggernaut taps an ancient motivation—to make one's money go as far as possible. This is universal—not simply a motivation but actually a need.

The Hedgehog Knows

The difference between the hedgehog and the fox, wrote Sir Isaiah Berlin in distinguishing between Dostoevski and Tolstoy, is that the fox knows a lot about a great many things, but the hedgehog knows everything about one great thing. The multinational corporation knows a lot about a great many countries and congenially adapts to supposed differences. It willingly accepts vestigial national differences, not questioning the possibility of their transformation, not recognizing how the world is ready and eager for the benefit of modernity, especially when the price is right. The multinational corporation's accommodating mode to visible national differences is medieval.

By contrast, the global corporation knows everything about one great thing. It knows about the absolute need to be competitive on a world-wide basis as well as nationally and seeks constantly to drive down prices by standardizing what it sells and how it operates. It treats the world as composed of few standardized markets rather than many customized markets. It actively seeks and vigorously works toward global convergence. Its mission is modernity and its mode, price competition, even when it sells top-of-the-line, high-end products. It knows about the one great thing all nations and people have in common: scarcity.

Nobody takes scarcity lying down; everyone wants more. This in part explains division of labor and specialization of production. They enable people and nations to optimize their conditions through trade. The median is usually money.

Experience teaches that money has three special qualities: scarcity, difficulty of acquisition, and transience. People understandably treat it with respect. Everyone in the increasingly homogenized world market wants products and features that everybody else wants. If the price is low enough, they will take highly standardized world products, even if these aren't exactly what mother said was suitable, what immemorial custom decreed was right, or what market-research fabulists asserted was preferred.

The implacable truth of all modern production—whether of tangible or intangible goods—is that large-scale production of standardized items is generally cheaper within a wide range of volume than small-scale production. Some argue that CAD/CAM will allow companies to manufacture customized products on a small scale—but cheaply. But the argument misses the point. (For a more detailed discussion, see Appendix 1, "Economies of Scope.") If a company treats the world as one or two distinctive product markets, it can serve the world more economically than if it treats it as three, four, or five product markets.

Why Remaining Differences?

Different cultural preferences, national tastes and standards, and business institutions are vestiges of the past. Some inheritances die gradually; others prosper and expand into mainstream global preferences. So-called ethnic markets are a good example. Chinese food, pita bread, country and western music, pizza, and jazz are everywhere. They are market segments that exist in worldwide proportions. They don't deny or contradict global homogenization but confirm it.

Many of today's differences among nations as to products and their features actually reflect the respectful accommodation of multinational corporations to what they believe are fixed local preferences. They *believe* preferences are fixed, not because they are but because of rigid habits of thinking about what actually is. Most executives in multinational corporations are thoughtlessly accommodating. They falsely presume that marketing means giving the customer what he says he wants rather than trying to understand exactly what he'd like. So they persist with high-cost, customized multinational products and practices instead of pressing hard and pressing properly for global standardization.

I do not advocate the systematic disregard of local or national differences. But a company's sensitivity to such differences does not require that it ignore the possibilities of doing things differently or better.

There are, for example, enormous differences among Middle Eastern countries. Some are socialist, some monarchies, some republics. Some take their legal heritage from the Napoleonic Code, some from the Ottoman Empire, and some from the British common law; except for Israel, all are influenced by Islam. Doing business means personalizing the business relationship in an obsessively intimate fashion. During the month of Ramadan, business discussion can start only after 10 o'clock at night, when people are tired and full of food after a day of fasting. A company must almost certainly have a local partner; a local lawyer is required (as, say, in New York), and irrevocable letters of credit are essential. Yet, as Coca-Cola's Senior Vice President Sam Ayoub noted, "Arabs are much more capable of making distinctions between cultural and religious purposes on the one hand and economic realities on the other than is generally assumed. Islam is compatible with science and modern times."

Barriers to globalization are not confined to the Middle East. The free transfer of technology and data across the boundaries of the European Common Market countries are hampered by legal and financial impediments. And there is resistance to radio and television interference ("pollution") among neighboring European countries.

But the past is a good guide to the future. With persistence and appropriate means, barriers against superior technologies and economics have always fallen. There is no recorded exception where reasonable effort has been made to overcome them. It is very much a matter of time and effort.

A Failure in Global Imagination

Many companies have tried to standardize world practice by exporting domestic products and processes without accommodation or change—and have failed miserably. Their deficiencies have been seized on as evidence of bovine stupidity in the fact of abject impossibility. Advocates of global standardization see them as examples of failures in execution.

In fact, poor execution is often an important cause. More important, however, is failure of nerve—failure of imagination.

Consider the case for the introduction of fully automatic home laundry equipment in Western Europe at a time when few homes had even semiautomatic machines. Hoover, Ltd., whose parent company was headquartered in North Canton, Ohio had a prominent presence in Britain as a producer of vacuum cleaners and washing machines. Due to insufficient demand in the home market and low exports to the European continent, the large washing machine plant in England operated far below capacity. The company needed to sell more of its semiautomatic or automatic machines.

Because it had a "proper" marketing orientation, Hoover conducted consumer preference studies in Britain and each major continental country. The results showed feature preferences clearly enough among several countries (see Exhibit I).

The incremental unit variable costs (in pounds sterling) of customizing to meet just a few of the national preferences were:

	£	s.	d.
Stainless steel vs. enamel drum	1	0	0
Porthole window		10	0
Spin speed of 800 rpm vs. 700 rpm		15	0
Water heater	2	15	0
6 vs. 5 kilos capacity	1	10	0
	£6	10s	0d

$18.20 at the exchange rate of that time.

Considerable plant investment was needed to meet other preferences.

The lowest retail prices (in pounds sterling) of leading locally produced brands in the various countries were approximately

U.K.	£110
France	114
West Germany	113
Sweden	134
Italy	57

Exhibit 1. Consumer Preferences as to Automatic Washing Machine Features in the 1960s

Features	Great Britain	Italy	West Germany	France	Sweden
Shell dimensions[a]	34 in. and narrow	Low and narrow	34 in. and wide	34 in. and narrow	34 in and wide
Drum material	Enamel	Enamel	Stainless steel	Enamel	Stainless steel
Loading	Top	Front	Front	Front	Front
Front porthole	Yes/no	Yes	Yes	Yes	Yes
Capacity	5 kilos	4 kilos	6 kilos	5 kilos	6 kilos
Spin speed	700 rpm	400 rpm	850 rpm	600 rpm	800 rpm
Water-heating system	No[b]	Yes	Yes[c]	Yes	No[b]
Washing action	Agitator	Tumble	Tumble	Agitator	Tumble
Styling features	Inconspicuous appearance	Brightly colored	Indestructible appearance	Elegant appearance	Strong appearance

[a]34 inch height was (in the process of being adopted as) a standard work-surface height in Europe.
[b]Most British and Swedish homes had centrally heated hot water.
[c]West Germans preferred to launder at temperatures higher than generally provided centrally.

Product customization in each country would have put Hoover in a poor competitive position on the basis of price, mostly due to the higher manufacturing costs incurred by short production runs for separate features. Because Common Market tariff reduction programs were then incomplete, Hoover also paid tariff duties in each continental country.

How to Make a Creative Analysis

In the Hoover case, an imaginative analysis of automatic washing machine sales in each country would have revealed that:

1 Italian automatics, small in capacity and size, low-powered, without built-in heaters, with porcelain enamel tubs, were priced aggressively low and were gaining large market shares in all countries, including West Germany.
2 The best-selling automatics in West Germany were heavily advertised (three times more than the next most promoted brand), were ideally suited to national tastes, and were also by far the highest priced machines available in that country.
3 Italy, with the lowest penetration of washing machines of any kind (manual, semiautomatic, or automatic) was rapidly going directly to automatics, skipping the pattern of first buying hand-wringer, manually assisted machines and the semiautomatics.
4 Detergent manufacturers were just beginning to promote the technique of cold-water and tepid-water laundering then used in the United States.

The growing success of small, low-powered, low-speed, low-capacity, low-priced Italian machines, even against the preferred buy highly priced and highly promoted brand in West Germany, was significant. It contained a powerful message that was lost on managers confidently wedded to a distorted version of the marketing concept according to which you give the customer what he says he wants. In fact the customers *said* they wanted certain features, but their behavior demonstrated they'd take other features provided the price and the promotion were right.

In this case it was obvious that, under prevailing conditions, people preferred a low-priced automatic over any kind of manual or semiautomatic machine and certainly over higher priced automatics, even though the low-priced automatics failed to fulfill all their expressed preferences. The supposedly meticulous and demanding German consumers violated all expectations by buying the simple, low-priced Italian machines.

It was equally clear that people were profoundly influenced by promotions of automatic washers; in West Germany, the most heavily promoted ideal machine also had the largest market share despite its high price. Two things clearly influenced customers to buy: low price regardless of feature preferences and heavy promotion regardless of price. Both factors helped homemakers get what they most wanted—the superior benefits bestowed by fully automatic machines.

Hoover should have aggressively sold a simple, standardized high-quality machine at a low price (afforded by the 17% variable cost reduction that the elimination of £6-10-0 worth of extra features made possible). The suggested retail prices could have been somewhat less than £100. The extra funds "saved" by avoiding unnecessary plant modifications would have supported an extended service network and aggressive media promotions.

Hoover's media message should have been: *this* is the machine that you, the homemaker, *deserve* to have to reduce the repetitive heavy daily household burdens, so that *you* may have more constructive time to spend with your children and your husband. The promotion should also have targeted the husband to give him, preferably in the presence of his wife, a sense of obligation to provide an automatic washer for her even before he bought an automobile for himself. An aggressively low price, combined with heavy promotion of this kind, would have overcome previously expressed preferences for particular features.

The Hoover case illustrates how the perverse practice of the marketing concept and the absence of any kind of marketing imagination let multinational attitudes survive when customers actually want the benefits of global standardization. The whole project got off on the wrong foot. It asked people what features they wanted in a washing machine rather than what they wanted out of life. Selling a line of products individually tailored to each nation is thoughtless. Managers who took pride in practicing the marketing concept to the fullest did not, in fact, practice it at all. Hoover asked the wrong questions, then applied neither thought nor imagination to the answers. Such companies are like the ethnocentricists in the Middle Ages who saw with everyday clarity the sun revolving around the earth and offered it as Truth. With no additional data but a more searching mind, Copernicus, like the hedgehog, interpreted a more compelling and accurate reality. Data do not yield information except with the intervention of the mind. Information does not yield meaning except with the intervention of imagination.

Accepting the Inevitable

The global corporation accepts for better or for worse that technology drives consumers relentlessly toward the same common goals—alleviation of life's burdens and the expansion of discretionary time and spending power. Its role is profoundly different from what it has been for the ordinary corporation during its brief, turbulent, and remarkably protean history. It orchestrates the twin vectors of technology and globalization for the world's benefit. Neither fate, nor nature, nor God but rather the necessity of commerce created this role.

In the United States two industries became global long before they were consciously aware of it. After over a generation of persistent and acrimonious labor shutdowns, the United Steelworkers of America have not called an industrywide strike since 1959; the United Auto Workers have not shut down General Motors since 1970. Both unions realize that they have become global—shutting down all or most of U.S. manufacturing would not shut out U.S. customers. Overseas suppliers are there to supply the market.

Cracking the Code of Western Markets

Since the theory of the marketing concept emerged a quarter of a century ago, the more managerially advanced corporations have been eager to offer what customers clearly wanted rather than what was merely convenient. They have created marketing departments supported by professional market researchers of awesome and often costly proportions. And they have proliferated extraordinary numbers of operations and product lines—highly tailored products and delivery systems for many different markets, market segments, and nations.

Significantly, Japanese companies operate almost entirely without marketing departments or market research of the kind so prevalent in the West. Yet, in the colorful words of General Electric's chairman John F. Welch, Jr., the Japanese, coming from a small cluster of resource-poor islands, with an entirely alien culture and an almost impenetrably complex language, have cracked the code of Western markets. They have done it not by looking with mechanistic thoroughness at the way markets are different but rather by searching for meaning with a deeper wisdom. They have discovered the one great thing all markets have in common—an overwhelming desire for dependable, world-standard modernity in all things, at aggressively low prices. In response, they deliver irresistible value everywhere, attracting people with products that market-research technocrats described with superficial certainty as being unsuitable and uncompetitive.

The wider a company's global reach, the greater the number of regional and national preferences it will encounter for certain product features, distribution systems, or promotional media. There will always need to be some accommodation to differences. But the widely prevailing and often unthinking belief in the immutability of these differences is generally mistaken. Evidence of business failure because of lack of accommodation is often evidence of other shortcomings.

Take the case of Revlon in Japan. The company unnecessarily alienated retailers and confused customers by selling world-standardized cosmetics only in elite outlets; then it tried to recover with low-priced world-standardized products in broader distribution, followed by a change in the comany president and cutbacks in distribution as costs rose faster than sales. The problem was not that Revlon didn't understand the Japanese market; it didn't do the job right, wavered in its programs, and was impatient to boot.

By contrast, the Outboard Marine Corporation, with imagination, push, and persistence, collapsed long-established three-tiered distribution channels in Europe into a more focused and controllable two-step system—and did so despite the vociferous warnings of local trade groups. It also reduced the number and types of retail outlets. The result was greater improvement in credit and product-installation service to customers, major cost reductions, and sales advances.

In its highly successful introduction of Contac 600 (the timed-release decongestant) into Japan, SmithKline Corporation used 35 wholesalers instead of the 1,000-plus that established practice required. Daily contacts with the wholesalers and key retailers, also in violation of established practice, supplemented the plan, and it worked.

Denied access to established distribution institutions in the United States, Komatsu, the Japanese manufacturer of lightweight farm machinery, entered the market through over-the-road construction equipment dealers in rural areas of the Sunbelt, where farms are smaller, the soil sandier and easier to work. Here inexperienced distributors were able to attract customers on the basis of Komatsu's product and price appropriateness.

In cases of successful challenge to prevailing institutions and practices, a combination of product reliability and quality, strong and sustained support systems, aggressively low prices, and sales compensation packages, as well as audacity and implacability, circumvented, shattered, and transformed very different distribution systems. Instead of resentment, there was admiration.

Still, some differences between nations are unyielding, even in a world of microprocessors. In the United States almost all manufacturers of microprocessors check them for reliability through a so-called parallel system of testing. Japan prefers the totally different sequential testing system. So Teradyne Corporation, the world's largest producer of microprocessor test equipment, makes one line for the United States and one for Japan. That's easy.

What's not so easy for Teradyne is to know how best to organize and manage, in this instance, its marketing effort. Companies can organize by product, region, function, or by using some combination of these. A company can have separate marketing organizations for Japan and for the United States, or it can have separate product groups, one working largely in Japan and the other in the United States. A single manufacturing facility or marketing operation might service both markets, or a company might use separate marketing operations for each.

Questions arise if the company organizes by product. In the case of Teradyne, should the group handling the parallel system, whose major market is the United States, sell in Japan and compete with the group focused on the Japanese market? If the company organizes regionally, how do regional groups divide their efforts between promoting the parallel vs. the sequential system? If the company organizes in terms of function, how does it get commitment in marketing, for example, for one line instead of the other?

There is no one reliably right answer—no one formula by which to get it. There isn't even a satisfactory contingent answer.[3] What works well for one company or one place may fail for another in precisely the same place, depending on the capabilities, histories, reputations, resources, and even the cultures of both.

The Earth Is Flat

The differences that persist throughout the world despite its globalization affirm an ancient dictum of economics—that things are driven by what happens at the margin, not at the core. Thus, in ordinary competitive analysis, what's important is not the average price but the marginal price; what happens not in the usual case but at the interface of newly erupting conditions. What counts in commercial affairs is what happens at the cutting edge. What is most striking today is the underlying similarities of what is happening now to national preferences at the margin. These similarities at the cutting edge cumulatively form an overwhelming, predominant commonality everywhere.

To refer to the persistence of economic nationalism (protective and subsidized trade practices, special tax aids, or restrictions for home market producers) as a barrier to the globalization of markets is to make a valid point. Economic nationalism does have a powerful persistence. But, as with the present almost totally smooth internationalization of investment capital, the past alone does not shape or predict the future. (For reflections on the internationalization of capital see Appendix 2, "The Shortening of Japanese Horizons.")

Reality is not a fixed paradigm, dominated buy immemorial customs and derived attitudes, heedless of powerful and abundant new forces. The world is becoming increasingly informed about the liberating and enhancing possibilities of modernity. The persistence of the inherited varieties of national preferences rests uneasily on increasing evidence of, and restlessness regarding, their inefficiency, costliness, and confinement. The historic past, and the national differences respecting commerce and industry it spawned and fostered everywhere, is now subject to relatively easy transformation.

Cosmopolitanism is no longer the monopoly of the intellectual and leisure classes; it is becoming the established property and defining characteristic of all sectors everywhere in the world. Gradually and irresistibly it breaks down the walls of economic insularity, nationalism, and chauvinism. What we see today as escalating commercial nationalism is simply the last violent death rattle of an obsolete institution.

Companies that adapt to and capitalize on economic convergence can still make distinctions and adjustments in different markets. Persistent differences in the world are consistent with fundamental underlying commonalities; they often complement rather than oppose each other—in business as they do in physics. There is, in physics, simultaneously matter and anti-matter working in symbiotic harmony.

The earth is round, but for most purposes it's sensible to treat it as flat. Space is curved, but not much for everyday life here on earth.

Divergence from established practice happens all the time. But the multinational mind, warped into circumspection and timidity by years of stumbles and transnational troubles, now rarely challenges existing overseas practices. More often it considers any departure from inherited domestic routines as mindless, disrespectful, or impossible. It is the mind of a bygone day.

The successful global corporation does not abjure customization or differentiation for the requirements of markets that differ in product preferences, spending patterns, shopping preferences, and institutional or legal arrangements. But the global corporation accepts and adjusts to these differences only reluctantly, only after relentlessly testing their immutability, after trying in various ways to circumvent and reshape them as we saw in the cases of Outboard Marine in Europe, SmithKline in Japan, and Komatsu in the United States.

There is only one significant respect in which a company's activities around the world are important, and this is in what it produces and how it sells. Everything else derives from, and is subsidiary to, these activities.

The purpose of business is to get and keep a customer. Or, to use Peter Drucker's more refined construction, to *create* and keep a customer. A company must be wedded to the ideal of innovation—offering better or more preferred products in such combinations of ways, means, places, and at such prices that prospects *prefer* doing business with the company rather than with others.

Preferences are constantly shaped and reshaped. Within our global commonality enormous variety constantly asserts itself and thrives, as can be seen within the world's single largest domestic market, the United States. But in the process of world homogenization, modern markets expand to reach cost-reducing global proportions. With better and cheaper communication and transport, even small local market segments hitherto protected from distant competitors now feel the pressure of their presence. Nobody is safe from global reach and the irresistible economies of scale.

Two vectors shape the world—technology and globalization. The first helps determine human preferences; the second, economic realities. Regardless of how much preferences evolve and diverge, they also gradually converge and form markets where economies of scale lead to reduction of costs and prices.

The modern global corporation contrasts powerfully with the aging multinational corporation. Instead of adapting to superficial and even entrenched differences within and between nations, it will seek sensibly to force suitably standardized products and practices on the entire globe. They are exactly what the world will take, if they come also with low prices, high quality, and blessed reliability. The global company will operate, in this regard, precisely as Henry Kissinger wrote in *Year of Upheaval* about the continuing Japanese economic success—"voracious in its collection of information, impervious to pressure, and implacable in execution."

Given what is everywhere the purpose of commerce, the global company will shape the vectors of technology and globalization into its great strategic fecundity. It will systematically push these vectors toward their own convergence, offering everyone simultaneously high-quality, more or less standardized products at optimally low prices, thereby achieving for itself vastly expanded markets and profits. Companies that do not adapt to the new global realities will become victims of those that do.

Notes

1. In a landmark article, Robert D. Buzzell pointed out the rapidity with which barriers to standardization were falling. In all cases they succumbed to more and cheaper advanced ways of doing things. See "Can You Standardize Multinational Marketing?" *HBR* November-December, 1968, p. 102.

2. There is powerful new evidence for this, even though the opposite has been urged by analysts of PIMS data for nearly a decade. See "Product Quality: Cost Production and Business Performance—A Test of Some Key Hypotheses" by Lynn W. Phillips, Dae Chang, and Robert D. Buzzell, Harvard Business School Working Paper No. 83-13.

3. For a discussion of multinational reorganization, see Christopher A. Bartlett, "MNCs: Get Off the Reorganization Merry-Go-Round," *HBR* March-April 1983, p.138.

Appendix 1

Economies of Scope

One argument that opposes globalization says that flexible factory automation will enable plants of massive size to change products and product features quickly, without stopping the manufacturing process. These factories of the future could thus produce broad lines of customized products without sacrificing the scale economies that come from long production runs of standardized items. Computer-aided design and manufacturing (CAD/CAM), combined with robotics, will create a new equipment and process technology (EPT) that will make small plants located close to their markets as efficient as large one located distantly. Economies of scale will not dominate, but rather economies of scope—the ability of either large or small plants to produce great varieties of relatively customized products at remarkably low costs. If that happens, customers will have no need to abandon special preferences.

I will not deny the power of these possibilities. But possibilities do not make prob. ilities. There is no conceivable way in which flexible factory automation can achieve the scale economies of a modernized plant dedicated to mass production of standardized lines. The new digitized equipment and process technologies are available to all. Manufacturers with minimal customization and narrow product-line breadth will have costs far below those with more customization and wider lines.

Appendix 2

The Shortening of Japanese Horizons

One of the most powerful yet least celebrated forces driving commerce toward global standardization is the monetary system, along with the international investment process.

Today money is simply electronic impulses. With the speed of light it moves effortlessly between distant centers (and even lesser places). A change of ten basis points in the price of a bond causes an instant and massive shift of money from London to Tokyo. The system has profound impact on the way companies operate throughout the world.

Take Japan, where high debt-to-equity balance sheets are "guaranteed" by various societal presumptions about the virture of "a long view," or by government policy in other ways. Even here, upward shifts in interest rates in other parts of the world attract capital out of the country in powerful proportions. In recent years more and more Japanese global corporations have gone to the world's equity markets for funds. Debt is too remunerative in high-yielding countries to keep capital at home to feed the Japanese need. As interest rates rise, equity becomes a more attractive option for the issuer.

The long-term impact on Japanese enterprise will be transforming. As the equity proportion of Japanese corporate capitalization rises, companies will respond to the shorter-term investment horizons of the equity markets. Thus the much-vaunted Japanese corporate practice to taking the long view will gradually disappear.

2

Survival Strategies in a Hostile Environment

WILLIAM K. HALL

How are such domestic manufacturing industries as steel, tire and rubber, auto-motive, heavy-duty truck and construction equipment, home appliance, beer, and cigarette evolving in the face of today's adverse external pressures? Given the lower growth, inflationary, regulatory, and competitive impacts, what business strategies are appropriate? Which strategic choices offer the best chances for survival, growth, and ROI in a hostile environment? This author investigates these issues and presents some preliminary findings from an ongoing research project which explores the strategic and structural changes that took place in the 1970s and that are expected to continue into the 1980s.

As economists, managers, and industry analysts pause to look back on the past decade, there remains little doubt that the business environment in the United States grew increasingly hostile during the 1970s. More important, there is now little doubt that this hostile environment will continue (and perhaps even worsen) during the decade ahead, reflecting the combined effects of:

☐ Slower, erratic growth in domestic and world markets.

☐ Intensified inflationary pressures on manufacturing and distribution costs.

☐ Intensified regulatory pressures on business conduct and investment decisions.

Published 1980.

☐ Intensified competition, both from traditional domestic competitors and also from the new wave of foreign competitors entering U.S. markets with different objectives and frequently lower ROI expectations.

As a result of these growing pressures, large U.S. manufacturing corporations are witnessing a major evolution in industry structures and competitive behaviors. Many structures that were stable and highly profitable during the "go-go" decade of the 1960s are now moving toward instability and marginal profitability.

Moreover, the broad range of corporate strategies and business "success formulas" which brought prosperity in those earlier years are no longer working. Instead, these are being replaced with a much narrower range of strategic choices that are becoming essential to survive in the hostile environment ahead.

The purpose of this article is to present some preliminary findings from an ongoing research project that my colleagues and I are conducting to explore these strategic and structural changes in more depth. This project is focusing on two broad questions:

1   How are industry structures in the mature markets evolving in the face of the adverse external pressures of the late 1970s?
2   Given this evolution, what business strategies are appropriate? Which strategic choices give the best chances for survival, growth, and return in the hostile environment ahead?

In-Depth Investigation

To examine these issues, I selected eight major domestic manufacturing industries for comprehensive study because of their importance to national and/or regional economic development and also because the adverse external trends of the 1970s have been especially severe in their impact on them. As a result, during the 1970s, all eight industries underwent a significant structural change which is expected to continue into the 1980s. Within these industries, I examined the strategies and evolving competitive positions of the 64 largest companies by using a combination of public data sources and field interviews.

In examining the impact of external pressures on these companies, I found that the eight industries either matured during the 1970s or will mature in the 1980s, resulting in lower growth records and growth expectations as shown in Exhibit 1. While the industries (on average) exceeded national economic growth rates in the 1950s and 1960s, they grew only slightly faster than the GNP in the 1970s, and they are projected to grow significantly more slowly than the U.S. economy in the 1980s.

During this maturation period, these eight industries, which are capital, raw material, and labor intensive, have been subjected to heavy inflationary

Exhibit 1.   Compound Annual Real Growth Rates in Demand for Eight Basic Industries—United States

	1950–1970	1971–1980	1980 Forecast[a]
Industrial goods			
Primary products			
Steel	4.0%	2.2%	1.5–2.5%
Tire and rubber	4.2	1.4	1.0–1.5
Intermediate products			
Heavy-duty trucks	7.0	2.8	2.5
Construction and materials handling equipment	7.8	3.6	2.3
Consumer goods			
Durable products			
Automotive	4.8	3.5	2.0–3.0
Major home appliances	6.2	2.9	2.3–2.8
Nondurable products			
Beer	3.1	2.5	2.3
Cigarettes	1.6	1.0	0
Average growth rates— eight industries	**4.8%**	**2.4%**	**1.9%**
Average growth rates— U.S. GNP	**3.7%**	**2.3%**	**2.5%**

[a]Based on economic forecasts and industry projections.

pressures that cannot easily be price recovered. All are being forced by regulatory agencies to make major investments to comply with new occupational safety and health regulations and with new product safety, performance, and environmental protection standards.

In addition to the domestic pressures, foreign competition has been harsh in the eight basic industries selected for study. Foreign competitors have achieved significant market shares in three of the industries—steel, tire and rubber, and automotive; moderate shares in two—heavy-duty trucks and construction and materials handling equipment; and entry positions in the other three—major home appliances, beer, and cigarettes.

Because many of these foreign competitors are either nationalized, quasinationalized, or highly salient in their own countries, they are frequently willing to accept lower returns in U.S. markets, offsetting these lower returns against unemployment, balance of payments, and capital gains at home. While these foreign approaches have been criticized as unfair, the results have altered U.S. domestic industry structures in all eight cases.

Needless to say, the net effect of these adverse trends has made life anything but pleasant for managers and companies in these basic industries. Profitability and sales growth levels have generally fallen to or below the average manufacturing returns in the U.S. economy (Exhibit 2). And industry spokesmen frequently speak out, urging either public assistance or some type of return to the simpler, less painful world of the 1960s.

As one senior executive I interviewed commented: "Maybe I should have accepted that job as an IBM systems engineer after graduation from college. It sure would be fun to look forward to going to work in the morning." Despite the outcries, the adverse external trends haven't gone away, and structural evolution continues at a slow, but inevitable, pace.

The heavy-duty truck manufacturing industry provides an excellent example of this evolution. In the early 1960s, spurred by rapid growth in the economy and by the completion of the U.S. interstate highway system, the industry grew at more than 8% per year. Eight major manufacturers—International Harvester, General Motors, Ford, Mack, White Motor, Diamond Reo, Chrysler, and Paccar—participated fairly equally in this growth, producing 60 truck models to serve the rapidly growing light-heavy and heavy-duty segments (19,000 pounds and greater gross vehicle weight).

However, by the late 1970s, annual growth had slowed to less than 3%. Emission regulations and inflation had raised unit costs. Investments for new truck model development had slowed to the extent that the number of models had dropped from 60 to 35 by 1979.

As a result of this movement toward a hostile environment, Chrysler closed its heavy-duty truck manufacturing operation. Diamond Reo was in

Exhibit 2. Financial Returns and Revenue Growth Rates, 1975–1979, for Eight Basic Industries

	Return on Equity	Return on Capital	EPS Growth	Revenue Growth
Steel	7.1%	5.7%	5.5%	10.4%
Tire and rubber	7.4	5.9	3.9	9.6
Heavy-duty trucks[a]	15.4	11.6	13.8	13.8
Construction and materials handling equipment	15.4	10.7	16.8	13.0
Automotive[a]	15.4	11.6	13.8	13.8
Major home appliances	10.1	9.0	3.2	6.8
Beer	14.1	10.2	6.2	12.4
Cigarettes	18.2	10.5	8.9	12.2
Average—eight industries	**12.9%**	**9.4%**	**9.0%**	**11.5%**
Average *Fortune* "1,000" company	**15.1%**	**11.0%**	**13.1%**	**13.1%**

[a]All vehicle manufacturers.

bankruptcy, and White lingered near receivership. Both Mack and International Harvester had lost significant market share and were searching for foreign assistance or major cost-cutting programs to maintain their viability. Of the eight healthy domestic competitors in the early 1960s, only three— General Motors, Ford, and Paccar—maintained free-standing, vibrant, competitive positions as they entered the decade of the 1980s.

Similar moves toward lower profitability and consolidation occurred in all eight industries as the hostile environment took its evolutionary toll. In steel, Bethlehem announced in 1977 the largest corporate quarterly loss in U.S. history up to that time (exceeded by Chrysler two years later and U.S. Steel in late 1979), Jones & Laughlin and Youngstown merged under the failing firm provision of U.S. antitrust laws in 1978, and Kaiser tried to sell its steel-making operation to the Japanese in 1979. In rubber, industry analysts waited impatiently for Uniroyal to exit the industry; and in automotive, Chrysler made front-page headlines in its race against time to achieve federal loan assistance. Words like "dinosaur" and "dog" were coined by industry observers to describe the evolving competitive profiles in all eight industries.

However, the profiles of basic industry problems and corporate failures tell only part of the story. These "disaster" tales need to be juxtaposed against some success stories to see how some companies have survived and even prospered in the same hostile environment. The resulting comparisons provide important insights into survival strategies and industry dynamics not only for general managers in the eight industries under study but also for managers in other industries as they lead their companies into the new decade. For example, a careful comparison of success and problem strategies in the eight industries in this study demonstrates that:

☐ Great success is possible, even in a hostile environment.

☐ Strategies leading to success share common characteristics.

☐ Successful strategies come from purposeful moves toward a leadership position.

☐ Problems come from failure to gain or defend a leadership position.

☐ For a deteriorating position, diversity may not be the proper recovery approach.

☐ Structural evolution moves toward a dynamic equilibrium as basic industries face a hostile environment.

I will amplify and discuss each of these insights in subsequent sections of this article.

Great Success Is Possible, Even in a Hostile Environment

When one looks at the eight industries in this study, as well as at other basic manufacturing industries facing the hostile environment of the 1980s, it is easy to slip into generalizations by extrapolating from aggregate industry problems to the individual companies within the industry.

Recent articles in the business press, asking "What Killed the U.S. Steel Industry?", "Is Chrysler the Prototype?", or proclaiming "Tire Industry Goes Flat" or "Last Chances for Cigarette Producers," are typical of those that tend to project adverse trends uniformly onto all competitors in the industry. In fact, however, nothing could be further from the truth. Some of the most vibrant, successful companies in the world reside and prosper in these seemingly hostile industry environments.

If one eliminates from my eight-industry sample of 64 companies all competitors who gain a majority of revenues and profits from diversification efforts outside their basic industry (e.g., Armco Steel and General Tire), then the most profitable remaining competitors (the industry leaders) in terms of corporate return on equity are those shown in Exhibit 3.

While some variation in returns exists among these leading competitors (Goodyear and Inland had significantly lower returns and growth rates than the other six), the corporate average return on equity earned over the last half of the 1970s easily places these companies in the top 20% of the *Fortune* "1,000" industrials and well ahead of the median *Fortune* company on return on capital and annual growth rate.

Moreover, the average returns on both equity and capital in my sample of industry leaders are well ahead of those earned by the leading international oil company (Phillips Petroleum). These average returns are also well ahead

Exhibit 3.   Financial Returns and Growth Rates, 1975–1979, for Leading Companies in Eight Basic Industries[a]

	Average Return on Equity	Average Return on Capital	Annual Revenue Growth Rate
Goodyear	9.2%	7.0%	10.0%
Inland Steel	10.9	7.9	11.4
Paccar	22.8	20.9	14.9
Caterpillar	23.5	17.3	17.2
General Motors	19.8	18.0	13.2
Maytag	27.2	26.5	9.1
G. Heileman Brewing	25.8	18.9	21.4
Philip Morris	22.7	13.5	20.1
Average	**20.2%**	**16.3%**	**14.7%**
Median *Fortune* "1,000" company (same time period)	**15.1%**	**11.0%**	**13.1%**

[a]Excluding those companies which gained a majority of their returns from diversification efforts.

of those earned by companies heralded by the business community as technology leaders (Xerox, Eastman Kodak, Texas Instruments, and Digital Equipment), and these returns are likewise well ahead of those earned by corporations singled out as models of progressive diversification and acquisition planning (General Electric and United Technologies).

In fact, as Exhibit 4 shows, the industry leaders shown in Exhibit 3 outperformed all of the highly touted companies during the most recent five years. In addition, the industry leaders grew faster than premier corporations like 3M and IBM, and they returned only slightly less to their shareholders and capital investors than these same "blue chip" competitors in high-growth industries.

In retrospect, perhaps the much publicized article, "TI Shows U.S. Industry How to Compete in the 1980s,"[1] should have been written about one of the leading companies in my sample instead of about Texas Instruments, because 75% of the leaders in the basic industries I studied outperformed TI during the latter half of the 1970s. Moreover, they outperformed TI in industries that averaged only 2.4% real growth during the past decade, significantly less than the 15% to 20% compound growth rates of the semiconductor industry during this same period.

Exhibit 4.   Financial Returns and Growth Rates, 1975–1979, for Leading Companies in Other and More Rapidly Growing Industries

	Average Return on Equity	Average Return on Capital	Annual Revenue Growth Rate
International oil			
Phillips Petroleum	19.5%	14.7%	16.6%
Technology leaders			
Xerox	17.8	14.4	15.5
Eastman Kodak	18.8	17.7	11.8
Texas Instruments	17.2	16.3	14.6
Digital Equipment	17.0	15.5	37.4
Diversification leaders			
General Electric	19.4	16.9	10.5
United Technologies	18.3	12.6	19.0
Average of these "high performance" leaders	**18.3%**	**15.4%**	**17.9%**
Average (leading companies in basic industries from Exhibit III)	**20.2%**	**16.3%**	**14.7%**
"Blue chip" competitors			
IBM	21.9	21.2	13.5
3M	20.7	17.7	13.1

Thus even a cursory analysis of leading companies in the eight basic industries leads to an important observation: survival and prosperity are possible even when the business environment turns hostile and industry trends change from favorable to unfavorable. In this regard, the casual advice frequently offered to competitors in basic industries—that is, diversify, dissolve, or be prepared for below-average returns[2]—seems oversimplified and even erroneous. A hostile environment offers an excellent basic investment opportunity and reinvestment climate, at least for the industry leaders insightful enough to capitalize on their positions.

Strategies Leading to Success Share Common Characteristics

A more detailed, in-depth examination of the business strategies employed by the top two performing (nondiversified) companies in each of the eight industries sampled reveals that these success strategies share strong common characteristics, irrespective of the particular industry. Indeed, throughout their modern history, all 16 of these leading companies have demonstrated a continuous, single-minded determination to achieve one or both of the following competitive positions within their respective industries:

☐ Achieve the lowest delivered cost position relative to competition, coupled with both an acceptable delivered quality and a pricing policy to gain profitable volume and market share growth.

☐ Achieve the highest product/service/quality differentiated position relative to competition, coupled with both an acceptable delivered cost structure and a pricing policy to gain margins sufficient to fund reinvestment in product/service differentiation.

A rough categorization of the strategies employed by these 16 companies, based on selective field studies and observed behavior over time, is shown in Exhibit 5. In most cases, the industry growth and profit leaders chose only one of the two strategic approaches, on the basis that the skills and resources necessary to invest in a low-cost position are insufficient or incompatible with those needed to simultaneously invest in a strongly differentiated position.

The rudiments of this strategic trade-off can be found as early as the 1920s in Alfred P. Sloan's statements regarding General Motors' selection of a cost-reduced strategy:

"Management should now direct its energies toward increasing earning power through increased effectiveness and reduced expense. . . . Efforts that have been so lavishly expended on expansion and development should now be directed at economy in operation. . . . This policy is valid if our cars are at least equal to the best of our competitors in a grade, so that it is not necessary to lead in design."[3]

However, in at least three cases, the leading companies in my sample chose to combine the two approaches, and each has had spectacular success.

Exhibit 5.   Competitive Strategies Employed by Leading Companies for Eight Basic Industries

Industry	Achieved Low Delivered Cost Position	Achieved "Meaningful" Differentiation	Simultaneous Employment of Both Strategies
Steel	Inland Steel	National	
Tire and rubber	Goodyear	Michelin (French)	
Heavy-duty trucks	Ford	Paccar	
Construction and materials handling equipment		John Deere	Caterpillar
Automotive	General Motors	Daimler Benz (German)	
Major home appliances	Whirlpool	Maytag	
Beer	Miller	G. Heileman Brewing	
Cigarettes	R.J. Reynolds		Philip Morris

Caterpillar has combined lowest cost manufacturing with higher cost but truly outstanding distribution and after-market support to differentiate its line of construction equipment. As a result, Caterpillar, ranking as the 24th largest and 39th most profitable company in the United States, is well ahead of its competitors and most of the *Fortune* "500" glamour companies.

Similarly, the U.S. cigarette division of Philip Morris combines the lowest cost, fully automated cigarette manufacturing operation in the world with highest cost, focused branding and promotion to gain industry profit leadership, even without the benefit of either the largest unit volume or segment market share in both domestic and international markets.

And finally, Daimler Benz operates with elements of both strategies but in different segments, coupling the lowest cost position in heavy-duty truck manufacturing in Western Europe with an exceptionally high quality, feature differentiated car line for European and North American export markets.

A more complete picture of the strategic and performance profiles of all major competitors in these eight hostile environments can be obtained by positioning on a matrix those businesses whose axes reflect the relative delivered cost position and the relative product/service differentiation with respect to other competition. The result is a conceptual diagram like that shown in Exhibit 6.

While the quantification of competitive profiles in this format is typi-

Exhibit 6. Strategic Profile Analysis: Basic Mature Industries

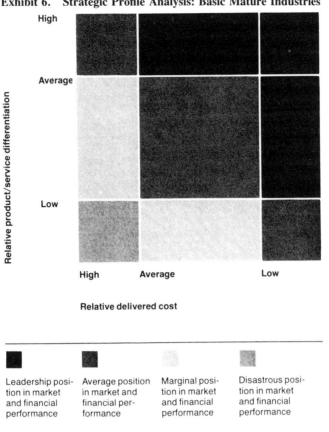

Leadership posi-
tion in market
and financial
performance

Average position
in market and
financial per-
formance

Marginal posi-
tion in market
and financial
performance

Disastrous posi-
tion in market
and financial
performance

cally inexact—because of the proprietary nature of relevant cost, sector, and performance data—a qualitative attempt to perform this analysis for the heavy-duty truck manufacturing industry is presented in Exhibit 7. This representation, based on analysis of industry interviews and public records, is imprecise, yet it correlates perfectly with the industry performance profiles over time.

For example, from Exhibit 7, it is clear why Ford and Paccar continually lead the heavy-duty truck industry in growth and financial performance. It is equally clear why White lingers near bankruptcy and also why Freightliner and International Harvester are rethinking their strategies for heavy-duty trucks. (Freightliner recently entered into a distribution agreement with Volvo in an attempt to differentiate its distribution system in the light-heavy segment, and International Harvester initiated a major cost-reduction effort in truck design and manufacturing in an attempt to improve its weak relative cost position.)

Exhibit 7.   Strategic Profiles in U.S. Heavy-Duty Truck Manufacturing

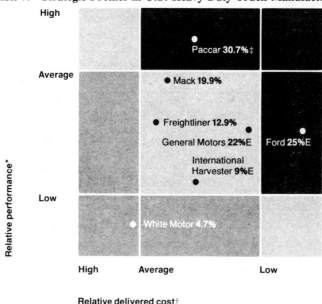

*Based on customer and industry interview data.

†Based on manufacturing and distribution cost analysis, evaluating economies of scale, and vertical integration profiles.

‡ Operating return on assets; E = Estimated from industry sources.

A similar analysis of business-level returns for all 16 leading competitors in the eight industries (Exhibit 8) indicates some interesting aspects of the respective strategies, as the following comparison reveals:

1.   The *lowest delivered cost* leader typically grows more slowly, holding price increases and operating margins down to gain volume, fixed-cost reductions, and improved asset turnover. In addition, this competitor will typically have a lower sales turnover than the differentiated producer, reflecting the higher asset intensity necessary to gain cost reductions in production and distribution.

2.   The *differentiated position* leader typically grows faster, with higher prices and operating margins to cover promotional, research, and other product/service costs. At the same time, this competitor typically operates with lower asset intensity (higher sales turnover), reflecting both higher prices and a lower cost, "flexible" asset base.

Exhibit 8. Business Level Returns and Revenue Growth Rates

	Operating Margins	Sales Turnover	Operating ROA	Revenue Growth Rates, 1975–1979
Leading industrial goods producers[a] **1978**				
Steel				
Inland Steel	8.3%	1.3	10.8%	11.4%
National	12.0	1.5	18.0	12.0
Tire and rubber				
Goodyear	8.6	1.5	12.9	10.5
Michelin	10.0(est.)	N.A.	N.A.	N.A.
Heavy-duty trucks				
Ford	11.0(est.)	2.3	25.0(est.)	12.7
Paccar	12.7	2.4	30.5	15.5
Construction and materials handling equipment				
Caterpillar	15.5	1.8	27.9	14.9
John Deere	10.0	1.3	13.0	17.5
Leading consumer goods producers[a] **1978**				
Automotive				
General Motors	9.6%	2.0	19.2%	13.2%
Daimler Benz (automotive)	11.0	2.4	26.4	15.1
Major home appliances				
Whirlpool	8.4	1.0	8.4	5.3
Maytag	21.8	1.8	39.2	9.1
Brewing				
Miller	8.2	1.5	12.3	29.2
G. Heileman Brewing	9.5	3.5	33.3	32.2
Cigarettes				
R.J. Reynolds	17.1	2.3	39.3	15.0
Philip Morris	17.7	1.4	24.8	20.1

[a]Lowest delivered cost producer listed first, followed by most differentiated producer.

Successful Strategies Come from Purposeful Moves
Toward a Leadership Position

In examining the business strategies and subsequent performance of the
leading competitors, it becomes clear that purposeful movement toward and
defense of a "winning" strategic position—either lowest cost and/or superior, price-justified differentiation—has been the fundamental long-term objective of all 16 high performance companies. There is little doubt that consistency and clarity of purpose have helped to mobilize and coordinate internal
resources in gaining and defending a leadership position.

It is important to note that the time-phased pattern of investment decisions used to attain and hold these winning positions was based on "doing
the right things" to gain leadership in lowest costs and/or differentiation. As
a result, all the high performers in my sample used careful strategic analysis
to guide their investments, avoiding simplistic adherence to doctrinaire approaches toward strategy formulation which come from the naive application
of tools like:

   ☐ Share/growth matrices—planning models which suggest that mature market segments should be "milked" or "harvested" for cash
   flows.
   ☐ Experience curves and PIMS[4]—planning models which suggest
   that high market share and/or lowest cost, vertically integrated production are keys to success in mature markets.

Instead, based on a case-by-case analysis, the performance leaders made
investment decisions which frequently conflicted with these doctrinaire
theories:

   1. The leadership positions in mature markets were not being milked
by any of the 16 competitors, contrary to the advice of consultants who
emphasize the portfolio approach to asset management. In fact, the top
managers in two of the leading companies I interviewed laughed when they
discussed this concept. They pointed out that their future success and growth
opportunities were far greater if they aggressively reinvested in their base
business than if they redeployed assets into other (diversified) industries.
   2. Low-cost production is not essential to prosper in mature markets,
contrary to the belief of strong proponents of the experience curve. Instead,
high sustainable returns also come from reinvesting in an average cost, highly
differentiated position, as the data of the previous section and Exhibit 8
demonstrate, and as the ongoing track records of companies like Paccar and
Maytag clearly illustrate.
   3. High market share and accumulated experience are not essential
for cost leadership in a mature market, as indicated by proponents of the
experience curve and some large-sample empirical studies like PIMS. In
fact, four of the eight low-cost producers in this study—Inland Steel, Whirl-

pool, Miller, and Philip Morris—have achieved their lowest cost positions without the benefit of high relative market shares.

Rather, these producers have focused their plants by emphasizing modern, automated process technology, and they have heavily invested in their distribution systems to gain scale economies and other cost reductions in their delivery systems.

4. Vertical integration is not necessary to exploit cost leadership in mature markets, as suggested by a number of empirical and economic studies. In fact, all of the low-cost producers in the industries under study were less vertically integrated into upstream and downstream activities than at least one other major competitor in their industry.

Instead of emphasizing vertical integration as a policy, all looked for selective integration into high value-added, proprietary componentry, following the type of integration policy first delineated by General Motors in the 1920s of "not investing in general industries of which a comparatively small part of the product is consumed in the manufacture of cars."

Instead of fully integrating, the low-cost leaders invested to have the most efficient process technology in at least one selective stage of the vertical chain. Consider, for example, Ford in truck assembly and Inland in order entry-distribution. The result in all cases is focus—the ability to orient management attention to gain low costs in a partially integrated operation. As one of Ford's major competitors observed:

"Ford is the least integrated of any of the high-volume, heavy-duty truck manufacturers in the world, yet it is still the low-cost producer and gains one of the highest ROIs in the industry. In retrospect, Ford's strategy was brilliant; they let the rest of us learn to manufacture componentry while they learned to manufacture profits."

Problems Come from Failure to Gain or Defend a Leadership Position

A more detailed examination of the marginal or failing competitors in each of the eight basic industries (Exhibit 9) also reveals some interesting observations:

1. The historical strategies and policies pursued by these companies have placed them in an unstable position. All are the high-cost producers in their segments, and all have a product that not only is largely undifferentiated in any meaningful sense but also in many cases is below average in quality and performance.

2. The external pressures that these companies complain about—unwarranted regulation and unfair foreign competition—are simply the final blows, sealing a fate that was predestined by improper strategic positioning or repositioning in the 1950s and 1960s, a period when there was still growth and time to maneuver.

3. Many of these marginal producers held low-cost or differentiated

Exhibit 9.   Marginal or Failing Companies in U.S. Markets

Steel	J&L-Youngstown
	Kaiser
Tire and rubber	Uniroyal
	Mohawk
	Cooper
Heavy-duty trucks	White Motor
Construction and materials handling equipment	Massey Ferguson
	Allis Chalmers
Automotive	Chrysler
Major home appliances	Tappan
Beer	Most regional breweries
	Schlitz
Cigarettes	Liggett & Myers

positions in these earlier years, and made strategic errors in their reinvestment decisions which contributed to their marginal or failing positions today, as the following examples show.

International Harvester led the U.S. heavy-duty truck manufacturing industry in 1965 with a market share of 30%. However, over the next decade, IH failed to reduce costs as rapidly as Ford and GM. As a result, the IH truck division is now a high-cost low-margin producer.

White Motor, a strong number-two truck producer in the mid-1960s, invested in backward integration into cabs, frames, axles, and engine manufacturing, assuming that this would reduce costs. Unfortunately, these investments, all made at suboptimal capacities for efficient scale economies, resulted in a relative high-cost position, adding momentum to White's deteriorating situation.

Tappan, the technology leader in ranges in the early 1960s, chose to broaden that product line, to diversify, to reduce R&D expenditures, and to out-source certain key engineering activities. As a result, it failed to gain the low-cost position in ranges (today held by GE). And by failing to reinvest in technology, it lost its differentiated position in ranges to Caloric (gas), Jenn-Air (electric), and Raytheon (microwave).

Chrysler, the technology leader in the U.S. automotive market in the early 1950s with a 25% market share, chose to make questionable international expansion decisions while adopting a "me too" participatory strategy in the domestic market. The subsequent decline in Chrylser's position and returns was predictable, and this disaster trajectory was certainly accelerated in the early 1970s when its management team announced a revised (but highly inappropriate) strategy to "try to be a General Motors in whatever segments of the market we choose to compete in."

For a Deteriorating Position, Diversity May Not Be
the Proper Recovery Approach

Over the past several years, it has become fashionable to recommend product/market diversification as a way out of an unstable or failing position for mature companies in hostile environments. Unfortunately, in the 64 companies I examined in this research, diversification has "helped" overcome major competitive/performance problems in only three—B.F. Goodrich, General Tire, and Armco Steel (now Armco Group). These three competitors recognized the tenuous nature of their positions early in the maturity cycle and took steps to resegment their base businesses into more advantageous positions by redeploying assets in carefully chosen diversification moves.

Goodrich moved into high-margin, specialty segments of the tire industry while diversifying to attain a low-cost position in PVC and other basic chemicals.

General shifted into low-cost production of tires for commercial vehicles while diversifying to attain a participatory position in very high-growth, fragmented industries such as communications and aerospace.

Armco proceeded into low-cost steel production in selected regional segments like oil country pipe, while diversifying into high-growth markets like oil-field equipment, oil and gas exploration, and financial services. (A recent public relations release from Armco announced that most of its new capital investment would go toward growing these diversification ventures, while maintaining only current capacity levels in steel making.)

These early efforts to resegment and to gain meaningful diversification have paid off. General and Armco lead all competitors in the rubber and steel industries in return on capital and growth, while Goodrich has moved into a stable third place among the surviving tire and rubber producers.

On the other hand, efforts to gain meaningful economic diversification have eluded most of the other problem competitors in the eight industries. By waiting too long to begin diversification efforts, most lack the capital and managerial skills to enter new markets and/or to grow businesses successfully in these markets. Thus their diversification efforts to date have been too small or have been managed in too conservative a fashion to obtain sustainable performance improvements, as witnessed by the very minor performance contribution of U.S. Steel's diversification program into chemicals and the continuing problems of Liggett & Myers despite a 43% diversification program out of the tobacco industry.

As a result of these modest, participatory efforts, some of the marginal performers in the eight industries have even divested diversified assets to gain capital and "hang on" for a few years in the base business. Two notable examples are White Motor's recent sale of its construction equipment operation and Uniroyal's sale of its consumer goods division.

On the whole, it would appear that diversification comes too little and too late for most companies caught in a hostile environment. However, for a courageous few, continued managerial commitment and refocus on the base business to provide a steady flow of capital for promoting meaningful positions in diversified businesses may work to ensure ongoing growth and vitality.

Structural Evolution Moves Toward a Dynamic Equilibrium as Basic Industries Face a Hostile Environment

A summary of the underlying data in my study suggests that basic industries in mature, hostile environments are moving through a structural evolution, leading ultimately to four industry and performance subgroups (Exhibit 10):

1. *Leadership position.*   Competitors who achieve the lowest delivered cost and/or the highest differentiated position. These positions are gained either on a full product line (Caterpillar) or on an economically viable segment (Whirlpool in washers and dryers). At maturity these competitors will

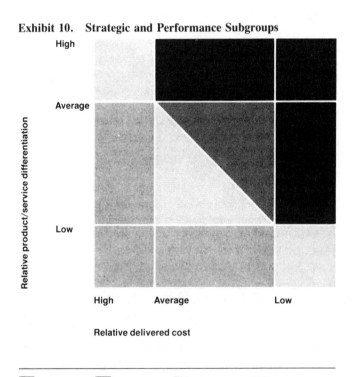

Exhibit 10.   **Strategic and Performance Subgroups**

| Leadership position: survival and prosperity possible given appropriate strategy for reinvestment. | Next best position: company existence and survival possible unless leader aggressive. | Next worst position: instability leads to failure unless company resegments and/or diversifies. | Marginal or failing position: company must fail or be subsidized in perpetuity. |

have the highest growth rates and returns in the industry, the best rein-vestment prospects, and they should be able to prosper and coexist in dy-namic equilibrium even though external pressures continue.

2. *Next best position.* Competitors who attain the second best po-sition in either cost or differentiation (again on either a full or partial line basis). These companies will have moderate but generally acceptable growth rates and returns, and reinvestments can (and will typically) be made at return levels slightly above the cost of capital. For these companies, vul-nerability to strategic and performance deterioration occurs mainly when the industry leaders or a set of externally subsidized competitors choose to aggressively attack. (For example, the recent problems of Ford in the U.S. automotive market can be directly traced to GM's more aggressive market share strategy, coupled with the European and Japanese attacks on U.S. small car markets.)

3. *Next worst position.* Competitors who finish in third place as the industry matures. Given a hostile environment, growth rates and return prospects for these companies are bleak unless they resegment into uncov-ered niches and gain a sustainable leadership position in these segments (AMC in utility vehicles, Goodrich in performance tires), or unless they can make major asset redeployment into meaningful diversified markets (like Armco and General). Without the ability to resegment or diversify, com-petitors in this class ultimately will move toward a marginal or failing po-sition. (Chrysler in automotive, Uniroyal in tires, and Schlitz in brewing are examples of companies currently going through such a transition.)

4. *Marginal or failing position.* Competitors who end up last in ma-ture, hostile environments ultimately must fail or be subsidized, either through government ownership or aid (Chrysler) or through cash infusions from a diversified parent (Kaiser in steel, Allis Chalmers in construction equip-ment). Despite efforts to use such subsidies to resegment and refocus their operations, the survey data shows no successful efforts in such turnaround attempts among the 64 competitors in the eight basic industries, raising a fundamental question as to whether there is any real possibility of strategic turnaround. Consequently, a society or a company subsidizing this type of marginal competitor should expect the worst—perpetual subsidies, perhaps slightly offset by infrequent operating returns during high peaks in basic economic cycles.

In Summary

The strategic and performance data from this eight-industry study suggest that both great successes and failures are occurring as basic, mature indus-tries move into a hostile business environment created by slower growth, higher inflation, more regulation, and intensified competition. Uniformly, the successes come to those companies that achieve either the lowest cost or most differentiated position. Simultaneously, survival is possible for those companies that have the foresight to downsize their asset commitments into niches in their basic industry and to use their incremental capital for meaningful diversification moves. For the weaker companies, the inability to achieve a lowest cost or most differentiated position results in high vulnerability and ultimate failure or perpetual subsidy.

For general managers guiding their companies into the economic environment of the 1980s, the implications of these findings are clear. The laws of the jungle change as maturity comes and hostility intensifies. In such a jungle, the range of strategic options narrows, requiring both an early warning of the coming hostility and an early strategic repositioning for a company to survive and prosper.

Hence intensified efforts must be made to create internal administrative structures and mechanisms to recognize and efficiently manage this repositioning. (GM's effective organizational restructuring in the early 1970s to respond to the down-sizing imperative stands as a brilliant case study in the use of such an administrative effort to create strategic change.)

For public policymakers monitoring and attempting to influence the business environment, these results suggest that failures will be inevitable as industry structures evolve in the face of maturity and hostility. The currently popular attempts at forced consolidation and subsidies are one way of dealing with these failures. However, these actions should be taken with full knowledge that they will not stop the driving market forces.

The question that remains in the decade ahead is whether the short-run employment, balance of payments, and fiscal stability provided by such public policy actions is worth the long-run cost of maintaining an inefficient industry structure that conflicts with the driving market forces created by a hostile environment.

Notes

1. *Business Week*, September 18, 1978, p. 66.

2. See, for example, Theodore Levitt, "Dinosaurs among the Bears and Bulls," *HBR* January-February 1975, p. 41; also the section on basic industries in Richard P. Rumelt, *Strategy, Structure, and Economic Performance* (Boston: Division of Research, Harvard Business School, 1974), pp. 128–139.

3. Alfred P. Sloan, Jr., *My Years with General Motors* (New York: Doubleday, 1964), pp. 65–66, 172.

4. PIMS (Profit Impact of Market Strategies) is a multiple regression model which relates profitability to a number of associative variables. See Sidney Schoeffler, Robert D. Buzzell, and Donald F. Heany, "Impact of Strategic Planning on Profit Performance," *HBR* March-April 1974, p. 137.

3

The Maturing of Consumerism

PAUL N. BLOOM and STEPHEN A. GREYSER

What lies ahead for the American consumer movement? Or, to put it another way, how will the consumer movement follow up on its accomplishments of the 1970s? If examined in a marketing context—with the consumer movement viewed as a product and the public as its potential customers—consumerism could be seen as entering an important new stage of its product life cycle. Shifting political and social attitudes along with fragmentation of consumerist organizations have heightened competition within the movement for supporters.

The authors break down the existing consumer movement into eight distinct categories according to the sorts of changes sought for society. They then examine the likely future of the competing groups and discuss the implications their projections hold for business.

During the early and middle 1970s, consumerism was a hot topic. Consumer protection legislation and regulations were being pursued, and indeed some activists joined the government as regulators. Ralph Nader and his adherents gained high public visibility, and others in political and social arenas who advocated proconsumer positions received strong public support. Observers concluded that consumerism would not only endure but would continue to play an important role in marketing.[1]

But now consumerism seems to have been shunted aside as a major issue of controversy. The movement experienced several setbacks at the end of the decade—for instance, legislation to establish a federal consumer protection agency was defeated. Now, particularly in the wake of the 1980 elections and the nation's politically conservative bent, some see consumerism rapidly fading as an issue.

Published 1981.

We disagree with this assessment of the movement's future. We believe that consumerism will continue to have a significant impact, albeit a less dramatic one, on business—especially marketing—in the years ahead.

What has happened to consumerism over the last decade can be compared to what frequently happens to products: it has moved through stages of its life cycle. Consumerism has now entered the mature stage of its product life cycle and, like breakfast cereals or detergents, has experienced a considerable degree of market fragmentation. (Before continuing our discussion, let us note here that our use of life cycle terminology is consistent with current thinking, in both the sociology and the political science literature, about the evolution of social movements.[2])

Many organizations, institutions, and individuals now offer what we view as a wide variety of "brands" of consumerism to different segments of American society. These brands are competing with one another for funds, workers, media attention, and public opinion—just as businesses compete for capital, managerial talent, retailer support, and customer loyalty. How this competition evolves and how the entire consumerism "industry" adapts to outside changes will determine consumerism's future.

Although it is in the mature stage of its life cycle, consumerism is not, we believe, in a declining or faltering stage. We reached this conclusion after considering the results of several recent public opinion surveys which point to continuing strong, though latent, public demand for actions that help consumers obtain a better deal. We also believe that certain aspects of consumerism—redress assistance, education, cooperative buying, and deregulation—are still well accepted, although some older offerings (such as consumer protection legislation) have fallen on hard times.

In this article we analyze and predict likely directions for consumerism in the 1980s. We build on our premise that the life cycle represents the movement's evolution reasonably well. But before we pry further into consumerism's current and future status, let us review more of its history.

Filling a Marketing Void

A new wave of consumerism emerged during the 1960s. While a wave in the 1930s had been primarily economic in orientation, the 1960s resurgence was largely social. It stemmed from a perceived need to redress the imbalance in the marketplace between seller and buyer. Manifested in John Kennedy's 1962 statement of consumer rights, the new consumerism was symbolized by the efforts of the nation's largest corporation (General Motors) to discredit an individual (Ralph Nader) who sharply criticized that company.

Combining to create strong "consumer demand" for ideas and actions that would help people get satisfaction in the marketplace were the increased complexity of products, the broadening of self-service channels and depersonalized shopping, the growth of consumer services (whose quality is difficult for customers to judge), and increases in consumers' discretionary buying power.

Initially the few consumer oganizations active in the 1960s sought to cultivate this latent demand by "selling" consumer protection via legislation. Ralph Nader, Betty Furness, and several others were highly successful at getting legislators and the public to support laws designed to bring safer products and better information to the public. The success of the Truth in Packaging, Truth in Lending, and Consumer Product Safety Acts naturally pulled other, more specialized groups—including environmental, health and nutrition, and senior citizens organizations—into the business of selling consumer protection legislation.

But these organizations and their leaders soon recognized the limitations of legislation as the sole means of achieving change in the marketplace. They needed other means of persuasion to attract the funds and supporters required to keep their organizations viable. Consequently, the organizations expanded their "product lines" and began to promote such offerings as institutional reform, consumer representation, redress assistance, consumer education, and vigorous enforcement of the new buyer protection laws. While these processes had no doubt interested such organizations all along, they had received negligible promotion compared with legislation.

Thus, Nader and his associates began to call for reform of regulatory agencies such as the Federal Trade Commission and for improved consumer representation in government and industry. They used publicity-generating devices such as research reports from "Nader's Raiders," proxy fights (e.g., Campaign GM), and major lawsuits to generate public interest in their new offerings.

In a more quiet way, leaders like Esther Peterson called for businesses to exhibit enlightened self-interest and establish active, influential internal units to monitor consumer affairs and to undertake consumer education efforts.[3] Groups such as Consumers Union and "Banzhaf's Bandits" (a team of George Washington University law students led by Professor John Banzhaf) petitioned federal agencies and took other legal actions designed to strengthen and expand consumer protection legislation and regulation.

In their desire to get a better deal from the marketplace, the American public apparently accepted the initiatives and philosophies of these reformers and supported the development of a burgeoning bureaucratic infrastructure to aid and abet the newly minted laws. The huge number of federal, state, local and corporate consumer affairs offices created in the 1970s, as well as the stepped-up activity of such agencies as the FTC and the FCC, were testimony to the success of the consumerism industry.

Consumerism's Own Watchdogs

The new consumerists eventually discovered, however, that Americans would not accept everything that was pushed at them. The industry, in fact, ran into a form of consumerism of its own. In the late 1970s, many responsible individuals began challenging the need for consumer protection initiatives such as seat-belt interlock systems and bans on advertising during children's TV shows.

Even the credibility of Nader himself was challenged. He was sharply criticized in 1977 for publicly castigating a former colleague, Joan Claybrook, after she became head of the National Highway Traffic Safety Administration and approved a delay on requirements for auto air bags. Moreover, his group's efforts to organize Fight to Advance the Nation's Sports (FANS), a consumer group for sports fans, raised questions about the seriousness (or overseriousness) of consumer activists.[4]

Perhaps the strongest signal of the public's reservations came in 1978 when Congress voted down a long-standing proposal to establish a federal agency that supporters said would represent the interests of consumers within the federal bureaucracy.

The events of 1977 and 1978 clearly indicated a fundamental problem facing consumer organizations: only when the populace didn't feel greatly inconvenienced but did feel endangered would the "consumer interest" label sell. In the case of seat-belt interlocks, many people apparently found the personal inconvenience costs too high; in the case of a consumer protection agency, many people apparently saw public costs of these initiatives as outweighing public benefits.

At the same time, many consumer activist groups came to be viewed more accurately as special interest organizations than as public interest groups. Even though they were promoting consumer's special interests, the obvious antibusiness nature of some activist initiatives and positions tarnished their image somewhat.

Of course, increased counterefforts by businesses and business associations accelerated this closer consideration of the price of consumerism. Using advocacy advertising, intensive congressional lobbying, highly publicized research reports, and the like, individual businesses—as well as groups like the Business Roundtable, Consumer Issues Working Group, and American Enterprise Institute—entered the consumerism industry and attempted to sell such concepts as deregulation and industrial growth.

To a public becoming disenchanted with the offerings of consumerism, these business-oriented groups seemed attractive. The 1980 elections further indicated a shift in popular attitudes toward these groups.

Over the past decade, then, the consumerism industry has evolved from a few organizations selling primarily legislation into an enormous web of organizations and institutions, each trying to serve the interests of the purchasing public with its own distinctive set of offerings. (A recent compilation titled *Contacts in Consumerism* describes 101 national organizations and 630 state and local groups with activities designed to serve consumer interests.[5])

As the life cycle of the industry has peaked and leveled off, the friendly and not-so-friendly competition among these entities for donors, supporters, clients, media attention, and public opinion has heated up.

The Current Scorecard

The results of several national opinion polls suggest that the public still appreciates the benefits of consumerism. Public dissatisfaction with the marketplace has remained strong in recent years, and positive attitudes toward various reform measures have not diminished.

Five studies conducted by Hiram C. Barksdale and William Perreault between 1971 and 1979 provide evidence of the public's continued dissatisfaction with the marketplace and its desire for reform. The authors summarize their findings this way: "In general, there were no drastic shifts in consumer attitudes during the 1970s. While there were some important gradual changes, the major areas of consumer discontent were substantially the same at the end as at the beginning of the decade. Furthermore, the level of consumer apprehension at the beginning of the 1980s appears to be about the same as in 1971."[6]

In 1979 a Marketing Science Institute survey showed that Americans saw the balance in the marketplace between "buyer beware" and "seller beware" philosophies as more tilted toward the former than it had been two years before—when the Sentry study of public attitudes toward consumerism had captured proconsumerist views on a broad range of issues at their apex.[7]

A 1979 study sponsored by Union Carbide and a 1980 study sponsored by the Food Marketing Institute also suggest that strong latent demand for consumerism continues.[8] The Union Carbide study found that a substantial majority of its respondents wanted stricter health and safety regulations and were concerned about the power of corporations (45% of the respondents stated that corporate power hurts our economy, while only 27% said it helps). The FMI study found that a higher percentage of respondents (52%) considered themselves "consumer activists" or "potential consumer activists" than was found in four similar surveys conducted since 1974.

Finally, a recent Yankelovich, Skelly, and White survey showed that only 19% of the public agrees with the statement: "Business tries to strike a fair balance between profits and the interests of the public."[9]

How the "Industry" Is Organized

Mass discontent and public support for social change do not necessarily produce an active social movement. To maintain vitality, social movements must be led by well-managed organizations that can mobilize resources and support. We have identified eight different, though somewhat overlapping, types of consumerist organizations.

In discussing the various organizations and their approaches, we follow the lead of sociologists John O. McCarthy and Mayer N. Zald, who argue that the "products" of social movement groups can be described by examining each organization's "conceptions of the extremity of solutions required" and "strategies of goal accomplishment."[10] (See Exhibit 1.) Our comments refrain from reaching any firm conclusions about the overall effectiveness of each type of organization because we lack information on organizational goals and financial conditions.

The "Nationals."   These organizations include (1) large broad-based groups like the Consumer Federation of America, the National Wildlife Federation, and Common Cause; (2) smaller multi-issue organizations like the National Consumer's League and Ralph Nader's Public Citizen; and (3) national special interest groups like Action for Children's Television, the American Association of Retired Persons, and GASP (Group Against Smoking and Pollution).

Linking these groups is their concern for protecting consumers from abuses in interstate commerce and their active participation in the Washington political arena. They can generally be characterized as moderate to liberal in terms of the amount of social change they seek to achieve. They typically focus on legislation, institutional reform, consumer representation, enforcement of consumer protection laws, and consumer education.

Many of the nationals' products—especially legislation—haven't been selling well recently. Some groups have had fund-raising problems as a result. For example, Ralph Nader's Public Citizen reportedly raised $1.3 million in 1977 but only a little less than $1 million in 1978.[11] As Exhibit 2 suggests, the legislative victories of these groups have diminished in recent years. They have lost battles over the consumer protection agency, automobile air bags, the powers of the FTC, and other issues.

These losses, coupled with cutbacks in federal funds for public participation in rule making (and for rule making in general), indicate that institutional reform, consumer representation, and consumer protection law enforcement have not been particularly successful products for the nationals. Recent court decisions restricting the filing of consumer class action suits have created additional problems for them.[12]

The "Feds."   This category includes all the federal agencies with programs designed to enhance the purchasing public's welfare—the FTC, FDA, Consumer Product Safety Commission, Office of Consumer Affairs, Office of Consumers' Education, and others. As government institutions which purport to serve the masses, they generally cannot promote major structural reforms and must remain reasonably moderate—although critics of FTC initiatives in recent years might view this agency as having been ultraliberal or even radical in its outlook.

These organizations have primarily been selling consumer protection

Exhibit 1. Positioning of Organizations in the Consumerism Industry

Type of Organization	Conceptions of Extremity of Solutions Required[a]	Strategies of Goal Accomplishment (Products Sold)[b]
Nationals	Moderate to liberal	Legislation Consumer representation Law enforcement Consumer education
Feds	Moderate	Law enforcement Consumer education Redress assistance
Deregulators	Conservative	Deregulation
Locals	Moderate to liberal	Legislation Law enforcement Consumer education Redress assistance
Coops	Conservative to radical	Information services Buying services
Corporates	Moderate	Top management advising Consumer education Redress assistance
Anti-industrialists	Radical	Citizen control of corporations Slow growth and conservation Controlled technology
Reindustrialists	Conservative	Deregulation Tax reform Industrial growth

[a] This dimension ranges from "conservative" to "moderate" to "liberal" to "radical," with conservative indicating a desire for major structural changes that would reduce government's role in U.S. society and moderate, liberal, and radical indicating desire for increasing amounts of structural changes that would add to government's role.

[b] This dimension ranges from strategies that tend to focus on achieving institutional changes (i.e., selling legislation, deregulation, consumer representation, and law enforcement) to strategies that tend to focus on achieving changes in people (i.e., selling consumer education, redress assistance, and information and buying services).

Exhibit 2. Selected House of Representatives Votes on Consumer Issues

Congress	Purpose of Bill	Proregulation	Antiregulation
92nd	To establish a consumer protection agency	344	199
93rd	To establish a consumer protection agency	293	84
94th	To establish a consumer protection agency	208	199
95th	To establish a consumer protection agency[a]	189	227
95th	To strike major class action provision from FTC bill	139	279
96th	To reauthorize the FTC with a congressional veto	63	321

Source. U.S. Chamber of Commerce as published in the *Washington Post*, January 13, 1980.
[a]A bill to establish a consumer protection agency never passed both houses of Congress and received presidential approval.

law enforcement, consumer education, and redress assistance. Recently they have encountered difficulty selling enforcement to the public and to Congress, but they have been reasonably successful at obtaining support for their educational and complaint-handling programs.

The "Deregulators."   Much of the resistance the federal agencies have encountered when encouraging enforcement can be attributed to the deregulators. Although certain nationals and the FTC were the original enthusiasts for deregulation of the airlines, railroads, trucking industry, and legal and other professions, groups such as the American Enterprise Institute, U.S. Chamber of Commerce, Business Roundtable, and Consumer Alert—along with companies like Mobil and R. J. Reynolds—have taken the lead in advocating deregulation for many more sectors.

The deregulators are among the most conservative competitors in the consumerism industry. They seek major structural reforms that would cause a sharp turn in the federal government's role—back to the less intrusive position it held before the recent resurgence of consumerism. And currently their efforts seem to be paying off.

The "Locals."   This category includes public and private organizations that focus on local issues and serve relatively small constituencies or memberships. Groups range from the largely campus-based, Nader-inspired Public Interest Research Groups (PIRG) to active local consumer protection offices in places like Dade County, Florida, and Montgomery County, Maryland. Also in this category are the numerous "action line" operations of local newspapers and broadcasters.

In the framework of "solutions required" (see Exhibit 1) most of these groups tend to be moderate or perhaps liberal in outlook, only occasionally seeking major structural changes. They tend to promote legislation, consumer protection law enforcement, consumer education, and redress assistance.

Many of the locals have been more successful lately than their counterparts among the nationals or feds, in part because they concentrate on and serve a much more homogeneous market than other organizations. Stronger protection legislation than what exists on the federal level is on the books in Massachusetts, New York, New Jersey, and other states because of successful selling by the locals. Active consumer education and complaint-handling programs in these jurisdictions are further evidence of their power. Whether these activities can continue in the wake of local tax-reduction efforts such as California's Proposition 13 and Proposition 2½ in Massachusetts remains to be seen.

The "Coops." These organizations (whether legally organized cooperatives or not) provide mechanisms through which people can pool their resources to obtain better information and/or better buys than they could otherwise. Some coops are national (Consumers Union—the publishers of *Consumer Reports*—is one and the national for-profit buying service Compucard, another). However, most coop retail organizations are local—for example, Chicago's Hyde Park Cooperative, Cambridge's Harvard Cooperative Society, and the Greenbelt Cooperative in Maryland.

Inflation has spurred the growth of local coops (especially food coops where members volunteer working time), since many people have become willing to trade their time for lower prices. The coop movement has also spread in the form of small local operations like neighborhood babysitting networks or day-care centers.

These organizations range from the conservative to the liberal. Some promote cooperative activity as a way to inject increased competition into a market, while others promote it as a vehicle for circumventing or challenging the power of big business.

In general, the coops seem to be doing reasonably well in selling their services. One recent report estimates that one in three Americans belongs to a cooperative of some type. And the 1980 opening of the National Consumer Cooperative Bank—a quasi-government institution that can receive up to $300 million in federal funds over the next five years to lend out to various sorts of coops—gives the cooperatives a base from which to expand their market share.

The "Corporates."   Many corporate consumer affairs offices sprouted during the past decade. They aim to resolve consumer complaints, conduct consumer education efforts, and serve as advisers to top management in making decisions about product safety features, advertising claims, and so forth.

Although consumer affairs offices in companies such as Giant Food and JC Penney have apparently had considerable influence on the policies and actions of their companies, several recent studies suggest that most of these offices owe allegiance to their companies first and their customers second.[13] (Indeed, where should the hearts of corporate consumer affairs personnel lie? Some conflicts of interest seem inevitable.)

Whatever their formal mission, many consumer affairs specialists believe that it's their responsibility to keep the company out of trouble via complaint-handling and educational activities. In a sense, these personnel have had difficulty selling consumer representation to corporate executives. They have, however, been reasonably successful at selling redress assistance and consumer education to the public.

For instance, a recent Conference Board study found that the use of corporate complaint-handling services has increased markedly in the last few years.[14] Although this surge could be a sign that customers have become less satisfied with products and services, we think it more likely that improved complaint-handling processes have made it easier for people to voice complaints and have elevated public expectations about the likelihood of getting results.

(Alan R. Andreason and Arthur Best, however, reported in 1977 that less than half of customers they surveyed who had complaints about products took their objections to the seller or maker. And of those who did, about one in three considered the outcome of such efforts unsatisfactory.[15])

The "Anti-Industrialists."   The groups and individuals in this category are the most radical members of the consumerism industry. Organizations such as Congress Watch (part of the Nader network), the Institute for Policy Studies, and the Interfaith Center on Corporate Responsibility comprise this sector, along with writers Mark Green, Richard Barnet, Timothy Smith, and others. They are selling citizen control of corporations (through federal chartering), controlled use of technology (e.g., "no nukes"), slower economic growth, stronger environmental protection, and several other causes that are somewhat difficult to label (e.g., demarketing of infant formula in less developed nations).

Recent setbacks—for instance, the lukewarm reception of "Big Business Day" in April 1980 and the defeat of an antinuclear referendum in Maine in the same year—suggest that the products of the anti-industrialists are not selling. However, one must keep in mind that more than 40% of the voters supported the Maine antinuclear proposition, while millions showed their support for stopping nuclear power following the Three Mile Island accident.

Furthermore, public opinion surveys such as the 1979 Union Carbide study cited earlier continue to show significant public concern about the extent of corporate power in the United States. Clearly, the ideas of the anti-industrialists are well received by many.

The "Reindustrialists."   Scholars like sociologist Amitai Etzioni and companies like Union Carbide have begun selling reindustrialization as somewhat of a competitor to anti-industrialization. These more conservative voices are calling for increased industrial growth, wider investment in technologically advanced production facilities, more emphasis on hard work and productivity, and less reliance on regulation. (There is a lot of overlap between the reindustrialists and the deregulators.)

The results of the 1980 elections and of a 1980 Union Carbide survey on growth both suggest that the public is ready to accept tax incentives and other growth policies to make reindustrialization happen.[16]

Considering the Future

Serious observers of the consumer movement differ widely in their predictions of where consumerism is headed. Futurist Graham Molitor, former Washington representative for General Mills and a longtime careful analyst of consumer protection activities throughout the world, sees pressures welling up for the U.S. government to adopt many of the liberal consumer protection measures enacted in the Scandinavian countries and in liberal states like Massachusetts.[17] On the other hand, consumer economists Robert O. Herrmann and Rex H. Warland, who have written extensively on the subject, believe that the movement has entered a long, slow decline in its life cycle.[18]

Our own view lies between these two positions. We see consumerism remaining in a mature, active stage—experiencing neither substantial growth nor serious decline—throughout the 1980s if not longer. In sharp contrast to the situation ten years ago, we sense that *consumerism is no longer the exclusive domain of the traditional movement.*

As we noted, the number of suppliers of consumerism's products has increased, and brands and offerings have fragmented. Further, many once-innovative ideas like improved redress have become institutionalized within businesses and through local governments and consumer organizations.

We should add that these changes are not necessarily unhealthy for the spirit of consumerism. We see this fragmentation as something that will help the movement endure and overcome the failures of some of its individual organizations. In the same way that companies seek to extend the life cycles of their products and brands, the consumer movement can find creative strategies for remarketing its products.

Our prediction is influenced greatly by current thinking on social movements. To maintain their vitality, social movements require organizations capable of mobilizing resources rather than just mass discontent. In this light we will now examine the prospective staying power of the consumer organizations discussed earlier.

Managing "Free Riders"

All social-movement organizations must deal with what economist Mancur Olson has labeled the "free rider" problem.[19] They must find a way to get the support and funding of people who would reap—without paying—many of the benefits such organizations might spur. For example, an organization pushing product safety legislation must convince people to support it even though the public will benefit from passage of such legislation without contributing anything to the organization.

In marketing terms, the free rider problem becomes one of formulating attractive products or offerings for which people will pay a price. Generally, products that provide direct, personal benefits (such as services or assistance) sell better than those that merely provide indirect, collective benefits (such as promises to fight for legislation or stricter law enforcement.)

Social movement organizations usually find this to be true, though for a long time many of the national consumer organizations got around the free rider problem without providing direct, personal benefits. Using publicity-generating devices such as lawsuits, boycotts, congressional testimony, and controversial research studies, many organizations were able to spark enough interest in their activities to get large numbers of people to donate small sums or to pay nominal dues. They also used direct-mail solicitation with considerable success. These organizations were able to get people to buy promises because the price was very low and because the promises were usually kept.

At that earlier stage of consumerism's life cycle, broad generic benefits were still rather distinctive—and there were few organizations promoting such services and activities. As fragmentation occurred, the nationals became less able to keep their promises about such issues as new legislation or court cases and consequently were less successful in raising funds. Further, with more and more organizations using direct mail, consumers are less likely to donate to any single cause.

Assessing the Brands

To use the marketing analogy, more narrowly segmented brands focusing on specific consumer benefits have supplanted some of the more broadly oriented early entrants.

Unless the nationals begin selling more than promises, they may find the 1980s to be a bleak period. Although a few of these groups could experience a short resurgence as the conservative Reagan administration provides a target against which to rally support, we think that many of them are due for hard times if not extinction.

On the other hand, locals and coops appear to have a reasonably bright future in the 1980s. These groups can overcome the free rider problem by selling redress assistance, education, information, and services from which people receive direct, personal benefits. People are willing to exchange tax dollars, membership dues, subscription fees, and the like for these benefits.

We believe that the 1980s will see the growth of many more organizations like the Washington Center for the Study of Services, which publishes the quarterly *Washington Consumers' Checkbook* report on the attributes of local auto repair dealers, plumbers, roofers, doctors, and other providers of consumer services.

The fate of the remaining types of consumerist organizations is more difficult to predict. Forecasts are shaky about the deregulators and reindustrialists, though business support is likely to keep them out of severe financial difficulties. Whether these groups can continue to attract strong public support for their ideas will depend on a host of factors, including the ability of deregulation to fulfill its promise of reducing prices and increasing productivity. If not, there may be calls for "reregulation."

Difficulties also arise in predicting the status of the feds, corporates, and anti-industrialists. The redress assistance and consumer education activities of the feds and corporates should by themselves help support most of these organizations, but how successful these groups will be in rallying support for their other activities (like law enforcement and top-management advising) is harder to project.

It is also hard to predict what the anti-industrialists will achieve, though we think that they too will be able to stay in business. Most of these groups are built around single issues about which some segment of the public will probably remain (or become) strongly agitated. These organizations should be able to obtain financial support from church groups and from small donors aroused by crises like "Three Mile Island" or "Love Canal."

Evolution and Survival

Ultimately, the future of each consumerist organization depends on how well it adapts and responds to certain trends in America's society and economy.

Key among these are inflationary pressure and the depletion of energy resources. Both of these worries tend to increase consumer dissatisfaction with the marketplace and therefore to aid the cause of consumerism. If inflation and energy shortages cannot be stemmed, then coops will prosper (to help people obtain scarce goods at lower prices) and the conservation-oriented anti-industrialists will gain appeal.

Under inflationary, energy-scarce circumstances, the anti-industrialists might call for structural reforms in marketing, promoting them as devices to lower consumer costs and conserve resources. Such reforms would be designed to force less product differentiation, less advertising and promotion, and less use of other marketing approaches that they believe encourage inflation and wasteful consumption.

At the same time, if inflation becomes a way of life, "pocketbook consumerism" will become central. All consumer-related organizations will have to concentrate on demonstrating that their proposals translate into money or time savings for the purchasing public.

If, however, the supply-side policies of the Reagan administration—with their emphasis on deregulation and tax incentives for reindustrialization—prove effective in squelching energy shortfalls and inflation, Americans might see a different trend. Latent demand for consumerism would likely remain, because a victory over inflation would probably raise people's expectations about what they should receive from the marketplace.

We would expect some consumers, freed of the need to spend their time and energy developing inflation-survival skills, to pursue the causes of improved product safety and durability, environmental protection, and so forth. Other consumers would likely continue to use the services of the locals, corporates, and coops to get the best deals possible or to pursue redress from deceptive and unfair sellers. And, of course, the ideas of the deregulators and reindustrialists would be in vogue; one could expect these groups to push proposals such as the elimination of corporate income taxes or the removal of many antitrust laws.

In sum, we foresee a quieter but still active consumer movement during the 1980s. We think the public will shift from its past role as largely cheering spectators to one of active participants. We envision *participative consumerism* as a major characteristic of the marketplace.

The daily behavior of many people will be influenced by consumerist issues; we expect consumerism to entail a great deal of activity by people on their own—like comsumer education, consumer information, redress assistance, cooperative buying, and home-grown products. On the other hand, we anticipate much less activity propelled by national organizations and their leaders.

The only reasons, in our opinion, for the protest aspect of consumerism to reach the intensity it achieved in the past would be either via dramatic near-disasters (such as Three Mile Island) or if deregulation and reindustrialization fail miserably at checking inflation and energy problems. If these ugly events occur, then—we believe—the slow-growth and conservation-oriented views of those we have labeled anti-industrialists will be heard frequently.

What Can Business Do?

Business has three strategies available to it for coping with the mature, fragmented consumerism of the 1980s. It can:

1 Try to accelerate the decline stage of the movement by attempting to *reduce demand* for consumerism.
2 *Compete* in the consumerism industry.
3 *Cooperate* with nonbusiness competitors in the consumerism industry.

Of course, each of these strategies has strengths and weaknesses. Attempting to reduce demand would lead a business to concentrate on improving product quality, expanding services, lowering prices, toning down advertising claims, and taking other actions to reduce the causes of consumer dissatisfaction. Such a strategy is consistent with the marketing concept, and at least some of the public would respond positively to this strategy. But if pocketbook concerns dominate, improved product quality and expanded services may find only limited consumer support.

Furthermore, a company that relies solely on the good efforts and intentions of its marketing program to cope with the consumer movement is flirting with trouble. One can never tell when unanticipated events like a computer breakdown in customer services or the discovery of unethical activities on the part of a competitor (and consequent tainting of the industry) can make a business the target of customer complaints, consumer agency investigation, or other actions. Nor is it possible to be certain how high customer expectations may have been elevated by a company's previous fine performance.

If a business chooses to compete in the consumerism industry, it can follow one of two routes. (1) An active consumer affairs department can offer redress assistance and consumer education. This approach will work as long as buyers believe in the department and do not see it merely as a public relations gimmick. At this stage of consumerism's development, "cosmetic consumerism" is unlikely to be successful. (2) A business can fund and/or coordinate activities designed to sell deregulation, reindustrialization, and other probusiness causes. Companies can donate to the American Enterprise Institute or run advertisements to publicize survey data showing that Americans favor economic growth (as Union Carbide has done). While this type of effort can be effective, it can also annoy and anger some members of the public.

If following a strategy of cooperating with nonbusiness competitors, a company might assist government agencies, nonprofit organizations, and coops in selling the latter groups' consumerist offerings. A business can give financial assistance, provide access to facilities, or lend managerial and creative talent to consumer education and other programs. This approach can improve relations with consumerists and generate favorable low-cost publicity but may also generate suspicion that the company is trying to co-opt the organization it is supporting. And obviously there are some organizations whose views may be so opposed to those of a particular company that it could not cooperate with them.

We believe that, for most businesses, the optimal approach involves elements of all three of the strategies we cite. A good approach entails a combination of purchase-oriented marketing, reliable and sincere consumer affairs departments, and selected cooperative ventures with external organizations.

In conclusion, let us suggest that businesses monitor, understand, and be sensitive to trends in public attitudes, particularly public responses to consumerist offerings. Businesses should recognize the difference between serving the public interest and pursuing their own narrower interests. Corporations should also work to present their own viewpoints on relevant consumer issues (as General Foods did in a recent campaign on national nutritional policy).

A gap still exists between promises and performance—a gap that fuels proconsumerist sentiment. But, for companies working to narrow that gap, consumerism remains an opportunity rather than a threat.

Notes

1. Philip Kotler, "What Consumerism Means for Marketers," *HBR* May-June 1972, p. 48; and Stephen A. Greyser, "Marketing and Responsiveness to Consumerism," *Journal of Contemporary Business*, Autumn 1973; "Marketing and the Future: The Response to Consumerism," *Advertising Quarterly*, Autumn 1974; and preface and epilogue, *Understanding and Meeting Consumerism's Challenges*, *HBR* reprint series, 1975.

2. See Mayer N. Zald and John O. McCarthy (eds.), *The Dynamics of Social Movements* (Cambridge, Mass.: Winthrop Publishers, 1979); and see Joel F. Handler, *Social Movements and the Legal System* (New York: Academic Press, 1978).

3. See Esther Peterson, "Consumerism as a Retailer's Asset," *HBR* May-June, 1974, p. 91.

4. See Marc Leepson, "Consumer Protection: Gains and Setbacks," *Congressional Quarterly*, 1978, p. 123 (editorial research report, 1978, vol. 1, no. 7).

5. Ann P. Harvey (ed.), *Contacts in Consumerism: 1980-1981* (Washington, D.C.: Fraser/Associates, 1980).

6. Hiram C. Barksdale and William D. Perreault, "Can Consumers Be Satisfied?" *MSU Business Topics*, Spring 1980, p. 19.

7. Opinion Research Corporation "caravan studies" for MSI; Louis Harris survey for Sentry Insurance Company.

8. *The Vital Consensus: American Attitudes on Economic Growth* (New York: Union Carbide, 1979); and *Supermarket Trends: 1980 Update* (Washington, D.C.: Food Marketing Institute, 1980).

9. See "purview," *PR Reporter*, January 1981, p. 1.

10. John O. McCarthy and Mayer N. Zald, "Resource Mobilization and Social Movements: A Partial Theory," *American Journal of Sociology*, May 1977, p. 1230.

11. See Timothy B. Clark, "After A Decade of Doing Battle, Public Interest Groups Show Their Age," *National Journal*, July 12, 1980, p. 1139.

12. See *Consumer Class Actions* (Washington, D.C.: American Enterprise Institute, 1977).

13. See Richard T. Hise, Peter L. Gillett, and J. Patrick Kelley, "The Corporate Consumer Affairs Effort," *MSU Business Topics*, Summer 1978, p. 17; see also Claes Fornell, *Consumer Input for Marketing Decisions: A Study of Corporate Departments for Consumer Affairs* (New York: Praeger, 1976).

14. See E. Patrick McGuire, "Consumerism Lives! . . . and Grows," *Across the Board*, January 1980, p. 57.

15. See "Consumers Complain: Does Business Respond?" *HBR* July-August 1977, p. 93.

16. *Adversaries or Allies? American Attitudes on Business, Government and Growth* (New York: Union Carbide, 1980).

17. Graham T.T. Molitor, "Consumer Policy Issues: Global Trends for the 1980s," in Kent Monroe (ed.), *Advances in Consumer Research*, vol. 8 (Ann Arbor, Mich.: Association for Consumer Research, 1981).

18. See their paper, "Does Consumerism Have a Future?" in Norleen M. Ackerman (ed.), *The Proceedings of the 26th Conference of the American Council of Consumer Interests* (Columbia, Mo.: ACCI, 1980), p. 12.

19. Mancur Olson, *The Logic of Collective Action* (Cambridge: Harvard University Press, 1965).

4

Antitrust Risk Analysis for Marketers

HARRY A. GARFIELD II

When product distribution issues suddenly take on antitrust significance, the typical reaction of marketing managers is to call for legal help. Until recently, that was an appropriate response. But the changing attitudes of law enforcement officials toward antitrust law, along with new court rulings, have made it possible for executives to do some legal analysis of their own. It doesn't require legal training; rather, managers can use familiar analytic techniques to screen their marketing decisions for the amount of antitrust risk they entail. This screening process involves three steps: determining the degree of antitrust risk along a chain of possible distribution restraints, pinpointing the business motives of distribution decisions, and doing elementary economic analysis of the markets. A final issue to be considered is the likelihood of challenge by law enforcement officials, customers, and competitors.

A new day is dawning in antitrust. The new environment raises important questions for the marketing manager who must make pricing decisions and maintain relationships with customers and distributors. Is it safe to tie distributors up through exclusive arrangements, to fortify good customer relations with special pricing deals, or to cut off dealers who cause trouble down the distribution line? Did someone say that even resale price maintenance may be O.K.—under some circumstances?

This article examines this new environment in distribution antitrust and concludes that some important changes are at hand. Indeed, the time appears to have arrived when marketing managers, with a less than overwhelming

Published 1983.

amount of background and understanding, are able to make intelligent assessments of antitrust risk without continually resorting to expensive legal advice. They will also find that the antitrust rules now favor good management techniques. This article describes a framework for providing "yes–no" answers to questions concerning antitrust restraints in the distributive process and minimizing the gray area of "maybe."

New Rules in Distribution Antitrust

Antitrust law concerning distribution has matured so much that intelligently selected distribution arrangements—even those restrictive in some sense—are recognized as having justification in sound economics and good business practices. A company moving into a new market can select loyal distributors, make exclusive arrangements, create profit incentives for good dealer performance, and refuse to sell to anyone it doesn't like without incurring significant antitrust risks—if it plays the game right. A seller facing market erosion and an inadequate dealer network can revise its distribution system, cut off unsatisfactory dealers, take over exclusive control of big national accounts, and generally improve its marketing structure without fear of undue reprisals—if it proceeds with care and wisdom.

A few years ago this would not have been the case. As recently as the late 1970s, the Department of Justice's Antitrust Division was vigorously pursuing distribution restraint cases and even pressing criminal charges for resale price fixing. The Federal Trade Commission cranked up a test case against Russell Stover Candies challenging classic legal doctrine that a seller is free to select its distributors and to require them to maintain suggested prices at pain of being cut off, so long as the act is unilateral. It seemed as if every disgruntled dealer and distributor who was severed from a company for whatever reason was able to find a lawyer willing to sue for treble damages.

Recently much of this has changed. The present head of the Antitrust Division, Assistant Attorney General William Baxter, has indicated a reluctance to bring vertical restraint cases; indeed he has withdrawn several that were already in court and has even indicated a desire to intervene against treble damage claimants when he thinks their suits are economically unsound. The following is a statement of the division's new policy by one of Baxter's deputies:

"Distributional practices may, under some circumstances, be used to adversely affect horizontal competition. But practices adopted independently by a firm (i.e., company) that restrict in some way the freedom of firms purchasing from it may be intended simply to increase the efficiency of the distribution process. For example, a manufacturer may attempt to limit competition among its retailers by restricting the territories that each may serve. Such vertical restrictions may be designed by the manufacturer to encourage retailers to provide services to consumers and to intensify their sales efforts in order to enhance the position of that manufacturer's product and allow it to compete more effectively in the market. Similarly, a firm's choices with respect to the granting of franchises or the grouping of goods and services for sale may simply reflect the firm's judgment about the most efficient way to structure a marketing effort. Consumers may benefit substantially from resulting intensified interbrand competition among products and services."[1]

The picture from the Federal Trade Commission is a little confusing because it is a collegial body, but the agency has also indicated little interest in vertical cases.

The courts are still listening to treble damage complainants, but indications are that the average dealer, cut out of a manufacturer's distribution network, will receive little court attention unless the plaintiff can marshal economic evidence not merely that he or she lost some business but that competition was hurt.[2]

The Law's Development

The antitrust laws are mostly judge-made—judicial decisions about legal cases over a long period of time. The laws are otherwise established only in very general terms by the underlying legislation. This means there are many areas as well as periods of uncertainty, and the strictures on business behavior are unclear.

So it has been with the development of the antitrust laws concerning distribution restraints. In the early days of antitrust the courts tended to recognize a seller's almost absolute right unilaterally to determine how it wished to market its products and what restrictions it wished to place on its distributors and dealers. This is the doctrine of the famous *Colgate* case decided by the Supreme Court in 1919. At the same time, the courts recognized that a seller who creates a horizontal network of price arrangements among its dealers through policing of a rigid resale price maintenance program has cartelized the distribution process. In an era when distribution systems remained simple, this dichotomy—freedom of a seller unilaterally to determine its distribution policies and prohibition of cooperative efforts to maintain resale prices—presented a workable environment for carrying out the distribution function.

One other aspect of distribution restraints of concern in the early development of the antitrust laws was exclusivity of distributorships. Here again, two clear rules emerged—that the appointment of an exclusive distributor having defined territorial or customer responsibility was not unlawfully restrictive, and that an agreement by a distributor not to deal in the goods of a competing seller could be illegal if such a decision was likely to injure the competition. The concern was not that dealers could be coerced into captive positions but that competitors of powerful sellers would be foreclosed from access to markets.

For many years the areas of much distribution antitrust uncertainty were geographic and customer allocation restrictions. Generally, antitrust experts subjected such restrictions to a rule of reason test, but worried about them if they were imposed by a manufacturer to prevent natural competition among distributors. In 1967 the Supreme Court clarified the situation in the *Schwinn* case by holding simply that all customer and territorial restraints were per se unlawful, with a possible exception of restrictions imposed by newcomers in the business or by a failing company.

(Under the antitrust laws a violation is said to be per se if the behavior involved is in itself unlawful. When illegality depends on further inquiry about the economic or business effect of the behavior, it is said to be subject to a "rule of reason" test.)

Thus by 1967 the judicial closing of the door on distribution restraints was nearly complete, to the point that most marketers knew they had to avoid any direct restrictions involving prices, customers, or territories. If the client was a seller, the legal adviser tried to keep him or her out of trouble; if the client was a distributor, the lawyer's ploy was to sue the seller for treble damages, claiming mistreatment.

In 1977 all this changed again because of the Supreme Court's decision in the *GTE Sylvania* case, which reversed the *Schwinn* decision and re-opened customer and territorial restraints to a rule of reason analysis. Now, instead of preparing for litigation, the legal adviser was more likely trying to develop distribution arrangements that were consistent with good business practice and that ran few risks of landing the client in court.

The Marketing Manager's Role

The manager's day-to-day decisions can either give rise to intense antitrust exposure or smooth out potentially serious distribution problems. The safe course is to consult legal counsel at every turn, but that is expensive and time consuming and tends to restrict distribution innovation. The knowledgeable manager can come up with his or her own assessment of the risks.

The risk analysis is not in terms of the chances of "getting caught," for one objective is to avoid any deceitful or hidden practices that help establish antitrust guilt. Actually, it may be advisable to document the risk analysis, even to make the documentation available to any would-be challenger (law enforcer or private party) as evidence that the marketing decisions were made reasonably and in accord with acceptable business procedures. That way, a formal legal challenge would likely fall on its face.

The initial stage of the analysis has the following three parts:

1 Identification and ranking of distribution restraints.
2 A definition of marketing objectives and strategy that are to be furthered by the particular restrictions chosen, and the seller's motives in choosing them.
3 A cursory analysis of the economics of the market.

Analysis of the information required for each of these three areas should enable the marketing manager to evaluate the antitrust risks against such questions as who is likely to challenge and what is the likelihood of a successful challenge. In a surprising number of instances, marketing managers can determine, without resort to formal legal advice, that the antitrust risks of a particular proposed course of action are slight, or that, through modifications that will not hinder the overall business objectives, a set of distribution restraints can be made relatively risk free. At the very least, the marketing manager should have a better idea as to when to call for formal legal advice.

Structuring a Hierarchy

Lawyers tend to put distribution problems in antitrust categories; that is to say, in terms of types of restraint such as vertical price fixing, customer and territorial allocations, and exclusive dealing. Then the lawyer ranks the categories according to the degree of danger or severity of violation, from highest to lowest.

Businesspeople, on the other hand, may find it more useful to consider a continuous hierarchy ranging from no restraints to full control of the distribution system. The marketing manager's objective, after all, is not to argue legal niceties; it is to determine the most effective distribution methods.

The marketing manager ought to view each possible mechanism for control as a means to some end in the distribution process. If there were no question of illegality, the marketing manager might freely consider whether maintaining resale prices is a good way to win dealer loyalty or to ensure dealer support by guaranteeing a profit level that permits servicing or providing some form of downstream marketing assistance. Maybe this would be effective or maybe not, but the manager's objective, not the means selected, would determine the preference. For example, the same result might be achieved by working closely with the dealer to develop a new market area or by simply taking the dealer regularly to lunch!

We can set out a series of possible distributor arrangements that exhibit ever closer seller-distributor ties and greater control of the distributive function. We can represent the main categories of antitrust restraints within that hierarchy by simply ranking them in terms of the amount of distributor control. Such a ranking system is laid out in Exhibit 1, starting with what we might call a "mail order" situation. The seller simply receives and fills orders without regard to the identity of the buyer or what the buyer does with the goods. This is obviously a no-antitrust risk situation.

As the first restrictive step in the heirarchy, we can rank a simple refusal to sell. The mail-order house mindlessly fills every order as it comes in. The marketing manager may determine, as an arbitrary first step in a

Exhibit 1. Hierarchy of Distribution Restraints

Complexity of distribution restraints and requirements

Least						Most
"Mail order" selling to all comers	Unilateral refusals to sell	Appointment of exclusive distributors	Requiring distributors not to deal in rival sellers' goods	Controlling distributors' market activity: resale price maintenance	Controlling distributors' market activity: customer and territorial allocation	Requiring image, service or technical support, or distributor feedback
None	Low	Low	High	High or *per se*	Medium	Low

Antitrust risk of restraints and requirements

limited distribution system, to deal with some buyers and refuse to deal with others. In this simplest case, from an antitrust viewpoint, the seller normally may refuse to sell to anyone for whatever reason. There may be exceptions to this where the seller is a monopoly or near-monopoly, but generally, a simple refusal to sell, based on the seller's *unilateral* decision, does not expose the seller to antitrust liability.

(Antitrust risks are classified throughout this article in three basic categories—low, medium, and high—and two extremes—none and per se unlawful. This is decidedly simplistic from a legal viewpoint but seems to be sufficient for the functions proposed here.)

Moving on from the simplest distribution situation, the seller begins to choose particular buyers and exclude others by designating only one or a few distributors as exclusive. This is just an extension of the refusal-to-sell situation and is equally unobjectionable, so long as the seller is unilaterally choosing distributors. Again, antitrust risk is low, perhaps nil. Obviously, the law recognizes business reality.

If the seller moves along the risk scale and tries to exact an agreement that the distributor will be exclusively loyal, a potential for trouble arises. As previously noted, the law seeks to protect the seller's rivals, especially in the cases of sizable sellers seeking to lock up the best outlets by contractual agreement. There are plenty of other ways to provide dealer encouragement and gain loyalty. This approach, then, runs a substantial risk of antitrust action.

(Accomplishing foreclosure by indirect means, such as through requirements contracts or tying arrangements that force customers to buy unwanted products in order to obtain desired ones, presents special problems for which legal advice is appropriate. They are not covered in this article.)

Further along the hierarchy, we encounter additional restrictions that affect the marketing functions of the distributor. For whatever reason, the seller wishes to influence how the distributor will resell the goods, either by controlling some element of the transaction, such as the price charged, or by limiting the freedom of the distributor concerning where, to whom, and under what conditions to resell.

The law tends to look with suspicion on such restrictions. To be sure, there is some judicial sentiment that distributors ordinarily should be free to do whatever they want once title to the goods has passed to them—to sell to whomever they wish and at whatever price they wish. As previously noted, the law has now shifted to the point that the courts are recognizing business reasons why customer and territorial restrictions should be permitted in some circumstances. It is not safe to assume similar leniency with respect to resale price maintenance.

Perhaps the courts will look with greater favor on unilaterally announced and enforced resale price maintenance requirements than on price-policing systems involving distributors, but there is still a good deal of sentiment that resale price maintenance should be per se unlawful. In any event we are assessing risks and not trying to decide antitrust cases. Therefore, it is appropriate to assign a high level of risk to resale price maintenance restrictions, and a lower level of risk to nonprice restrictions that will likely be subject to a rule of reason test as to their business justification.

Resale price maintenance entails, then, a high risk and customer and territory allocations entail a medium risk. The restrictions are ranked in this order in the hierarchy because distribution agreements to maintain prices are a less powerful way of commanding or controlling the distributor function than customer and territorial allocations. Telling a distributor not to sell to particular customers or across territorial lines may be more restrictive, in marketing terms, than dictating his or her pricing.

Finally, at the extreme of the hierarchy, are distribution restrictions that in some respects are more confining than those previously discussed, but at the same time are more likely to be tolerated under the antitrust laws. These restrictions are firmly based on a seller's need to preserve and foster a distinctive marketing attribute in the distribution process. The attribute may range from a quality image to some high-technology aspect requiring a high degree of dealer service or communication with the consumer. Or the seller may require some form of market information from the distributor, perhaps to determine consumer preference for model options. These kinds of restrictions, if properly justified, rank fairly low in antitrust risk.

Rocking the Legal Boat

While the hierarchy's structure should be quite comfortable for the marketing manager, it may be less so for the antitrust lawyer since it does not conform to traditional antitrust analysis. That tradition is most severely critical of agreements that control resale prices and inhibit other sellers' access to the market. Those restraints are not logically ordered in the scheme just described.

Antitrust lawyers may also be uncomfortable because the analysis omits one of the most important high-risk areas of antitrust—cutting off dealers. They will point out that when you terminate price-cutting dealers you are most likely to arouse the interest of enforcement authorities.

That may be true, but cutting off dealers is not part of a hierarchy of distributional controls. It is something that a seller may do to alter, and presumably improve, a distribution system, whether because of bad credit experience or because the dealer has been shading prices. In a sense, the restraint is a refusal to sell, which presents a high antitrust risk because the seller's motive may be the elimination of a price-cutting dealer or the policing of a price maintenance system.

If the motive is merely to eliminate a bad credit risk, the antitrust risk is nil—assuming the seller's motive is believed. For these reasons, terminations of dealers should be considered not according to a hierarchy of restraints but according to the underlying business objectives—the subject of the next part of the analysis.

Assessing Motivation

How does one evaluate the seller's motives? Again, we can construct a hierarchy in terms of the extent to which the presence of particular marketing objectives can enhance or diminish the antitrust risk. And remember, we are looking for risk assessment factors, not support for legal arguments.

Start from the proposition that antitrust law is currently giving greater recognition to good business practice in assessing distribution restraints. The more a statement of objectives demonstrates strong business justification or distributional efficiency, the more it will diminish the antitrust risks of particular restraints. Yet if the only objectives that can truthfully be stated are to prevent price erosion or to prevent transshipment of goods to unauthorized dealers, the risks identified with particular restraints will be increased. A marketing manager can thus have some confidence that the antitrust dangers have been minimized if good business practices and marketing efficiencies are identifiable as motivating and supporting the restraint.

Exhibit 2 lists a series of possible distribution objectives in a rough order of their antitrust justification, descending from least satisfactory to most satisfactory in terms of providing business justification.

Several additional points should be noted about determining the risk effect of objectives and motivation. First, objectives to prevent *intra*brand competition for its own sake are risk-enhancing. Those clearly bent on improving *inter*brand competition diminish the risk. Since the law now recognizes a trade-off of benefit to interbrand competition against detriment to intrabrand competition, the risk analysis should fairly state how these objectives lie. If the goal of obtaining dealer loyalty is to enhance dealer effectiveness against rival brands, the analysis should recognize both the plus and minus factors, and weigh them appropriately.

Next, examining motives and objectives may permit the marketing manager to reassess them and possibly to restate them so as to reduce risk. This may also lead to an alteration of the distribution restraints in order to reduce risk. A marketing manager may ask, "Why do we really want to maintain resale prices?" If the answer is, "Because we want to prevent dealers from competing on price and to promote orderly marketing," a red flag should go up. This is a high-risk restraint and a risk-enhancing motive. It also is probably symptomatic of a poor marketing approach, since it implies both restricting output and lack of aggressiveness against competing brands. Such analysis might cause some rethinking of marketing strategy to focus on effective interbrand competition by encouraging more aggressive dealer marketing.

Perhaps a different dealer setup with different restrictions would be better suited to achieving the resale price objective and simultaneously reducing antitrust risk. Similarly, a dealer support system focusing on presale provision of technical information and postsale servicing could be made virtually risk free by shifting from territorial and customer restrictions to contractually specified obligations.

Exhibit 2. Antitrust–Marketing Motives and Effects

Motive	Effect on Competition	Effect on Risk
Force dealers to conform to price maintenance policy	**Hindering intrabrand competition** ↑	**Risk-enhancing objectives and motives** ↑
Appease dealers complaining of price cutters		
Protect loyal dealers from price competition		
Prevent erosion of resale prices		
Prevent boot-legging to discounters		
Maintain dealer profit margins		
Prevent dealers from crossing territorial lines		
Stop "free rider" benefits to discounting dealers		
Increase market share by enhancing brand recognition		
Establish market by developing loyal dealer network		
Maintain quality image		
Provide essential postsale service		
Encourage presale transfer of technical information		
Ensure feedback of essential market information	↓	↓
	Enhancing interbrand competition	**Risk-diminishing objectives and motives**

77

Finally, there is always the problem of credibility. Some legitimacy exists for controlling distribution in order to preserve a product quality image. If this truly results in more effective interbrand competition, the antitrust authorities probably would approve, but the question can always be raised as to whether a quality image is really justifiable. The marketing manager must appraise such motivation and objectives while avoiding bias.

Economic Mini-Analysis

The third step in the marketing manager's antitrust risk evaluation is a mini-analysis of market economics. While such an analysis does not require a deep understanding of economics, any marketing manager assessing antitrust risks must recognize that a company's position in its industry along with its products' positions in defined markets can add to or subtract from the risks.

Marketing managers know their competitors and the competing products that can reasonably be expected to fill a particular customer need. It is fairly safe for the knowledgeable marketing manager to rely on experience to draw up a list of competing products, the companies that manufacture them, and an estimate of the sales of each, thereby providing a usable set of data for a first attempt at rough economic analysis.

Quite simply, if the industry exhibits a significant concentration of control, the antitrust risks are increased for those companies that are among the controlling group and are reduced for those that are struggling against large competitors. Where the industry is not concentrated, risks for all companies are usually reduced.

There are two other factors that need to be taken into account in the rough analysis of the economics of any market. One is the difficulty of entering a market. Managers might ask what would be likely to happen if the members of the industry were able to raise prices significantly. Would a number of companies be likely to come into the industry to take advantage of the profit potential? Would they be deterred from doing so because of some technological or capital cost, or by any other factor making competition against existing companies and entry difficult? To assess the effect on antitrust risks, we need only determine the answer to these questions on a relative basis. If businesses can enter and leave the industry freely, the risks are low. If entry is difficult, the risks for companies with large market shares are higher.

Another factor is the dynamics of the market. Is the industry new and growing or is it mature or even in the dying phase of its life cycle? While less clear than some other areas of this analysis, the antitrust risks here follow the same curve as an industry's life cycle. When an industry is young and dynamic, reasonable economic arguments can be made that the achievement of distribution efficiency should render tolerable some degree of control over the distribution system. As a product cycle advances, sensitivity to antitrust increases. On the waning side, government antitrust officials should have less interest in preserving dying competition.

Finally, economic and antitrust analysts are placing increasing emphasis on the relationship between interbrand and intrabrand competition. Vertical restraints always lessen the vitality of intrabrand competition to some extent. Is that detriment to intrabrand competition outweighed by the accompanying enhancement of interbrand competition? Again, the marketing manager is in the best position to judge.

Who Cares?

Finally, it is important to consider the question of whether anyone will complain about behavior that arguably or technically violates the antitrust law.

That may sound like heresy to the traditional antitrust lawyer and clearly in certain antitrust areas such an attitude would be foolhardy. The obvious example is price fixing among direct competitors. That would be a per se offense, carrying criminal liability. In regard to distribution restraints, however—with the possible exception of systematic resale price maintenance—there appear to be no areas where a company is subject to either criminal responsibility or per se liability. So if a legal test results, business justification and arguments based on economic efficiencies will be considered.

The likelihood of challenge may present the largest variable in the risk analysis. Significantly, it is exactly this variable that the marketing manager, not the attorney, may be best able to judge, for the marketing manager is well acquainted with the players in the market—competitors and customers who are likely to make challenges.

The legal adviser may be better able to assess the likelihood of government challenge. Because antitrust enforcement is subject to pendulum swings, the marketing manager would be well advised to watch out for changes. In the meantime, with very few exceptions, it should be easy to minimize the risk that federal enforcement authorities will challenge any set of distribution restraints.

State antitrust enforcement authorities are also a source of potential challenge, but they do not usually have the resources to put together a complex economic case against a company. Again, a well-done risk analysis will permit the marketing manager to demonstrate economic and business justifications that should persuade the state authorities to direct their meager enforcement resources elsewhere.

The larger area of concern, of course, is whether competitors or customers will want to mount a legal challenge. Competitors do engage in such challenges, but they are highly unlikely to do so unless they can argue that the practice in question is so harmful to their ability to compete as to be considered predatory. In all probability, the existence of distribution restraints by themselves is not likely to result in competitor challenge. Competitors can expect to successfully challenge restraints only if they are used by a dominant company as part of a scheme to keep others out of the market, or with intent to monopolize.

Customers who are cut off or who think they receive unfavorable treatment are the prime source of antitrust suits; these are far more numerous than all state and federal enforcement actions combined. The dollar exposure in verdicts, settlements, legal fees, and corporate displacement has been astronomical. Among the most serious mistakes a marketing manager can make is to miscalculate whether a disgruntled customer will sue.

If the marketing manager's analysis shows some high-risk or problem areas, the likelihood of customer retaliation requires close assessment. Here also, the marketing manager knows best. Are there a lot of customers out there who are energetic price discounters or transshippers and who are likely to cause trouble if they are cut off or disfavored? If so, managers should proceed with caution in revamping the distribution system.

On the other hand, if existing customers are generally a fickle lot who require constant cultivation to maintain loyalty, they may be disinclined to cause trouble. The risk assessment of real life situations largely involves judging human behavior, not legal analysis.

Assessment of customer response is particularly important when a seller finds it necessary to rework an unsatisfactory distribution system. This can occur when a company has outgrown its original distribution setup. Suppose a seller achieves initial success through a small network of loyal retail dealers by pushing a quality image with strong presale support. Later, the seller sees opportunities for expanding through mass merchandising and goes to a national account system that serves high-volume distributors. Then a secondary market that uses industrial distributors for OEM accounts opens up. The company may have created a distribution monster with potential for antitrust disaster if the seller tries to control these different channels of distribution.

How can such a distribution system be reworked to make it more efficient? Assume that business analysis shows that the small-dealer network described previously is no longer desirable because individual volume is too low. It also shows that "boot-legging" into the national retail market by some industrial distributors—who receive favorable prices for the OEM market—has undermined the secondary market. The seller decides to cut off the small dealers and the industrial distributors, fortify the national distributors, and take over the OEM market itself.

Analysis shows great risk in the system as it stands, particularly if the company has had problems with pricing and transshipping or selling across distribution channels. The proposed setup, however, seems well justified for business reasons if the seller is not in a monopoly or near-monopoly position: the inefficient, direct-buying retailers are to be eliminated; stronger selling responsibilities will be placed on the national distributors, supported by appropriate incentives; and control of the OEM channel will eliminate boot-legging and improve direct service to that customer class. The restraints incorporated in the proposed revision would be thus fairly low-risk.

The question of whether anyone cares now becomes paramount. If the small network of dealers and terminated industrial distributors are not likely to squawk, there is no point in agonizing over the antitrust niceties. It would still be a good idea to document the analysis and the decision to make the required changes, as previously outlined, but there really is no antitrust obstacle to doing the job that needs to be done. But if the marketing manager identifies dealers or distributors who are likely to challenge their termina-tions, the changes still may proceed—but at greater risk. At this point it might be wise to call in an antitrust specialist to prepare legal strategy and help accomplish the legitimate business objectives.

In all of this, then, the marketing manager performs the analysis without the need for legal counsel until the analysis shows that the risks are high enough to warrant incurring the legal costs.

Notes

1. Richard J. Favretto, "Antitrust Division Enforcement Priorities," Department of Justice news release (Washington, D.C.: September 18, 1981).

2. See for example, Valley Liquors, Inc. v. Renfield Importers, Ltd. 678 F2d 742 (7th Cir. 1982).

5

What Every Marketer Should Know About Women

RENA BARTOS

The dramatic rise in the number of working women in the United States, says Eli Ginzberg, is "the single most outstanding phenomenon of our century." Paradoxically, marketing leaders, who like to think of themselves as experts on changing social trends, seem to have been looking the other way. They not only have underestimated the numbers of working women and overestimated the numbers of full-time housewives, they also have missed the *qualitative* changes that have occurred among both. As this article shows, there are four distinct segments in the women's market. These groups shop differently, favor different brands, and use the media differently. They have different motivations and are committed to different lifestyles. They are having a profound impact on the U.S. marketing picture. Indeed, changes in women's lives may be the missing factor in many marketing programs and may result in unrealized potential and lost opportunities. What is needed is more realistic assumptions with which to begin analyzing and planning.

Marketing procedures and tools have never been more sophisticated and complex than they are today. Yet there is a curious gap between the realities of social change and the picture of society reflected in most marketing plans and advertising campaigns. Many marketing specialists who pride themselves on their pragmatism and realism have not related their day-to-day marketing activities to the facts of social change.

The potential contribution of these sophisticated marketing tools may

---

Published 1978.

be limited by the social perspective of the marketing specialists who use them.

Most marketing plans start with the definition of "target groups," that is, the type or types of consumers who represent the best prospects for the brand, the product, or the service. The more specifically the targets are defined, the more likely it is that any research study or market analysis that assesses them will reaffirm the assumptions of the definers. The reality gap cannot be closed after the marketing process is begun. We need to challenge the basic assumptions that underlie marketing planning before any planning gets under way.

The unspoken assumptions behind many marketing plans suggest that all of the United States lives in the kind of split-level pattern that emerged in the 1950s, with most women engaged in "home making," keeping house, shopping, drinking endless cups of coffee with their neighbors, critically eyeing the state of their laundry or the shine on their kitchen floors, and driving their kiddies to and from scout meetings, birthday parties, and Little League games.

Hubby, in the meantime, is off in the city striving for success—to get a bigger office (a Bigelow on the floor), a promotion, a title. Hubby's secretary is working only until she snags a beau who will propose ("she's lovely, she's engaged") and carry her off to her very own suburban ranch. There the pattern starts all over again.

When this view of society is expressed in marketing terms, the world is neatly divided into separate markets, one set for males and one set for females. Let us take a look at the familiar target groups that mirror these underlying assumptions about society. Most definitions of marketing targets are usually expressed in demographic terms. However, the attitudinal assumption about what motivates the demographic groups may be observed in the advertising that is often the visible end product of the marketing process. The advertising is beamed at these audiences:

Any Housewife, 18 to 49. The key customer for all household products and foods is the housewife, who is the prime purchaser for the family. Her motivations are to win the husband's/children's approval of her competent, good housewifery; to do a better/faster job than her neighbor; to fool her husband/mother-in-law into thinking she's done something the hard way when she has taken a shortcut.

Any Male Head of Household, 24 to 49. The key customer for all big-ticket items—cars, business travel, financial services—is a man (husband and father). His motivations? Status, that is, keeping up with/ahead of the Joneses; achievement; and protection of his dependents.

Any girl, 18 to 25. The key customer for cosmetics, perfume, fashion is the young, single girl. Her motivation, naturally, is to get a man.

Any man, 18 to 34.   The key customer for sports cars, beer, liquor, toiletries is the young bachelor before he settles down. His motivation? To have fun, to get girls.

The one characteristic that all these marketing targets have in common is that no one is ever over 49 years of age. In addition, marketers take for granted the conventional wisdom that brand choices are formed early and that younger families represent higher volume potential. Therefore, the most desirable customers are under 35, though in some cases the age target may go up as high as 49.

Is this set of assumptions an accurate reflection of the way most people live? If so, only in part. It is a static and monolithic view of our society that assumes that everyone is cut out of one of a few cookie-cutter patterns and that nothing really changes. Marketing programs built on this kind of perspective cannot reflect the diversity of different life-style groups in our country. Nor can they be responsive to the dynamics of changing attitudes and value systems, which, in turn, lead to changing behavior in the marketplace.

Recognizing the Realities of the Women's Market

Let's think of the different life-style groups in our country as representing a mosaic of targets that differ in their product wants and needs and in their value potential to the marketer. The key to unlocking this jigsaw puzzle lies in a combination of old and new demographic facts and in changing attitudes and value systems. This information provides clues to recognizing change and keeping up with it.

The demography is so basic it is almost simplistic. It consists of such straightforward facts as marital status, presence of children, age, sex, and occupation. These simple demographic facts are intertwined with changing attitudes and philosophies of life that influence the responsiveness of consumers to different products.

Most of the keys to keeping up with change are available to all. It is my contention that any practical-minded marketer can challenge the underlying assumptions on which past definitions of the market are based, learn whether the assumptions are out of date, and, if needed, bring his or her marketing procedures in step with the realities.

I have selected the traditional target group, "Any housewife, 18 to 49," to illustrate this discussion. However, this basic approach can be applied equally well to other kinds of ethnic or lifestyle groups, such as men, unmarrieds, and consumers over that cutoff age of 49. What assumptions about the women's market are commonly reflected in marketing plans? Consider the following:

1   Most women in the United States are full-time housewives, usually with a few children at home.

2 The number of women who work may be increasing, but they are usually unmarried women. They are mostly single girls working for a few years before they are married or some poor unfortunates who have to work because they are divorced or widowed.
3 If a married woman works, her husband can't support her (and she probably isn't a very valuable customer).
4 No married woman would work if she could afford to stay at home.
5 Women with young children won't go to work.
6 All nonworking women are full-time housewives.
7 All homemakers are married.
8 Working women and housewives are sisters under the skin. They want the same things from products and they respond to the same strategies.

How valid are these assumptions? Let us look at the realities. Here are some simple demographic and attitudinal facts about women and the implications of those facts for marketers.

The Quiet Revolution

The number of working women is rising dramatically. The flood of women entering the work force is not only a demographic trend; it could be a manifestation of a profound social change. Eli Ginzberg, chairman of the National Commission for Manpower Policy, calls it "the single most outstanding phenomenon of our century."

Even well-informed marketers tend to understate the number of women in the work force. They say: "It's around 30% to 40%, isn't it?" In 1970 and 1971 the number was actually 43%. Our most recent data from the Bureau of Labor Statistics show that in 1976 of all females in the United States 16 years of age and over, 47% were in the work force. And the preliminary figures for 1977 are mind boggling. In its June 1977 report, the Bureau of Labor Statistics tells us that 49% of all women 16 years of age and over are at work.

What are the other women doing? "Keeping house" would be the stock answer of most marketers. Actually, in 1976 only 39% of U.S. women were full-time housewives. This means that 8% more women are working out of the house than are staying home and keeping house. The remaining 14% were out of the mainstream. They were either still in school or they were retired and/or disabled (see Exhibit 1). Once we remove the schoolgirls and the grandmothers from the picture, we see that the ratio of working women to housewives is 55% to 45%. This balance has shifted swiftly since the early 1970s. In each succeeding year the proportion of working women has increased and the proportion of housewives has decreased (see Exhibit 2).

It is not enough for the marketer to say that the market for a product or service is housewives—or working women. Neither is a well enough defined target group. Approximately three out of five working women are

Exhibit 1. Occupational Profile of American Women in 1976

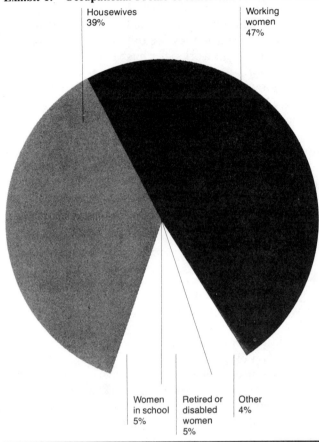

Housewives
39%

Working
women
47%

Women
in school
5%

Retired or
disabled
women
5%

Other
4%

Source: Bureau of Labor Statistics, January 1977. The base used is all women age 16 and over (81,198,000 women).

married and, therefore, they are housewives as well as working women. We can no longer assume that every bride automatically becomes a full-time housewife. "Living happily ever after" does not necessarily mean staying barefoot and pregnant.

Another assumption to challenge is that married women are the only ones who keep house. Some 13% of all women are unmarried working women who are also heads of their own households. While they may represent a smaller volume of buying because of the size of their households, they represent an additional increment to the "housewife" market.

Thus the housewife market is far greater than the size assumed by marketers who define housewives only as full-time housekeepers (45% of all women age 16 or more are housewives versus 55% who are working

Exhibit 2. Ratio of Working Women to Housewives, 1971–1976

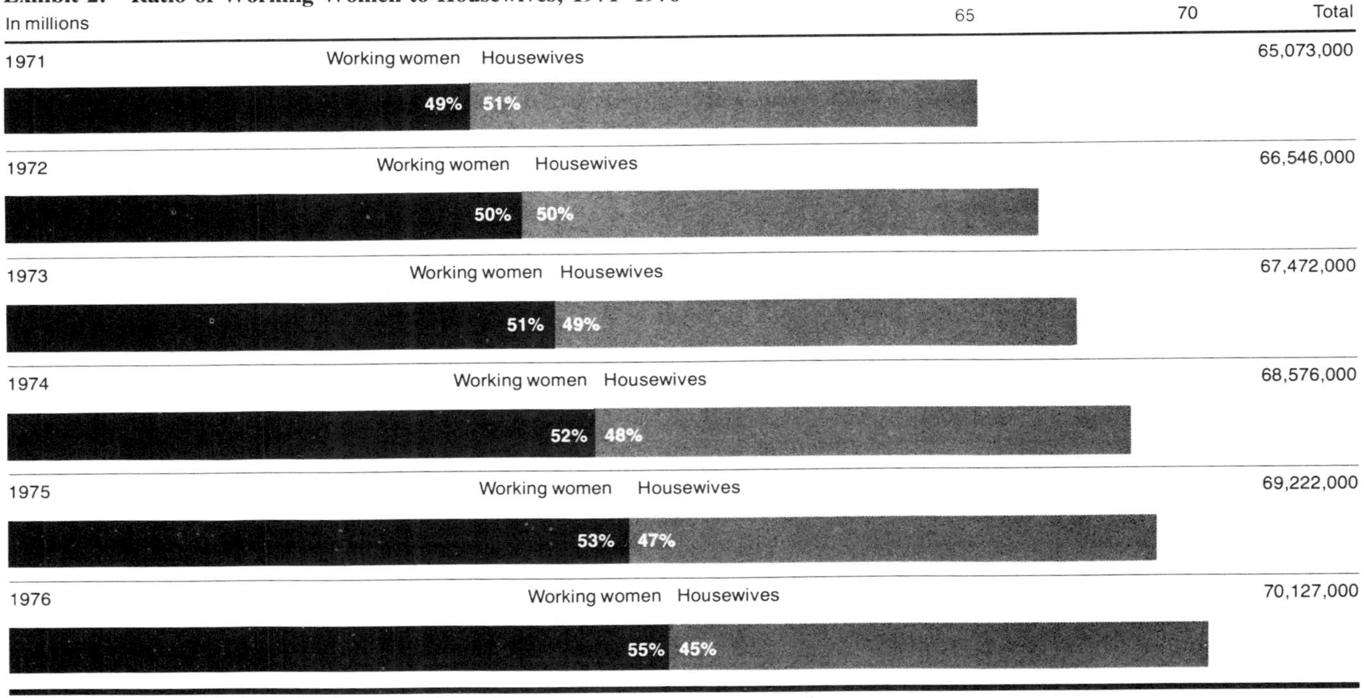

In millions

	65	70	Total
1971			65,073,000
1972			66,546,000
1973			67,472,000
1974			68,576,000
1975			69,222,000
1976			70,127,000

1971 — Working women 49% / Housewives 51%
1972 — Working women 50% / Housewives 50%
1973 — Working women 51% / Housewives 49%
1974 — Working women 52% / Housewives 48%
1975 — Working women 53% / Housewives 47%
1976 — Working women 55% / Housewives 45%

Source: Bureau of Labor Statistics, *Employment and Earnings*, 1972 to 1977. These statistics include all women age 16 and over in the labor force or keeping house.

women). It includes another 31% of American women who are working and married; it also includes the 13% of women, unmarried and working, who are household heads (see Exhibit 3).

The Changing Life Cycle

While recognizing the importance of working women as a market, we do not want to invent a new set of working women stereotypes to match those of housewives. One way to close the reality gap between women as they really are and cookie-cutter stereotypes is to recognize their diversity.

Women change as consumers as they move through different stages of life. The way they buy and use products and the way they read or watch or listen to media is affected by whom they live with or without. Is there a

Exhibit 3. The Real Size of the "Housewife" Market

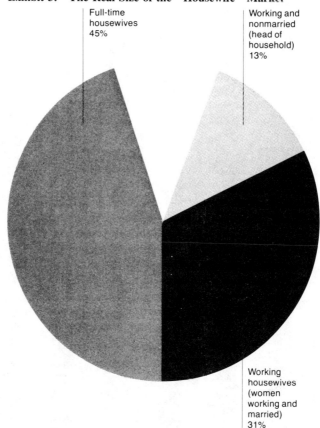

Full-time
housewives
45%

Working and
nonmarried
(head of
household)
13%

Working
housewives
(women
working and
married)
31%

Source: Bureau of Labor Statistics, *Employment and Earnings,* January 1977, and unpublished data, March 1976. Base used is all women age 16 and over who are in the labor force or keeping house (70,127,000 women).

man around the house? Are there any children at home? These two demo-graphic facts are basic clues to women's marketplace behavior.

Exhibit 4 shows the extent of the life-cycle patterns of women who work and who do not. The patterns are remarkably similar. If we want to learn how working women differ from nonworking women as consumers, we should compare their marketing behavior *within* stages of the life cycle. This is a game that any number can play because the information is available to all. It just requires some straightforward crosstabs to decide how the targets differ from each other, how they are alike, and where to reach them.

The life cycle is also crucial to understanding the changes in the quality of the women who have flooded into the labor market. The major influx of women into the work force comes from an unexpected source: the married women we had assumed were happily engaged in keeping house. Apparently, marketers are not the only ones whose assumptions about life have colored their professional judgments. Earlier in the 1970s government forecasters under estimated the current rise of women in the work force because they assumed that women with very young children under six years of age would not go to work. In fact, as Exhibit 5 shows, these young mothers have entered the labor force to a greater degree than any other group.

Why Women Work

What accounts for the exodus of wives from the kitchen to the work place? Are their husbands unable to support them? Are they driven to go to work out of sheer necessity?

There are no definitive answers to the question of why women work. Synthesizing observations from a number of sources, however, reveals four basic motivations for women's employment. Two of them are economic, and two of them are attitudinal.

Economic Necessity.   Some women must work if they or their families are to survive. Sheer economic necessity is a motivation that has always been with us, but one that tends to be ignored when we talk about the "new women" and their reasons for entering the work force. This group includes the unmarried women with no husbands or fathers to support them; some of them have never married and have always had to work for a living. Others have had their marriages interrupted by death or divorce and were suddenly thrust into the working world. Still others included are those married to men whose incomes simply cannot support their families.

The Second Paycheck.   Another motivation is that a second paycheck, while not needed for survival, may enable a wife to maintain or improve her family's standard of living. Many women are working for conveniences of life that have begun to seem like necessities—the second car, the washing machine, the color TV set, the family vacation. They also appreciate the

Exhibit 4. Life Cycle Profiles of American Women in 1976

Nonworking women

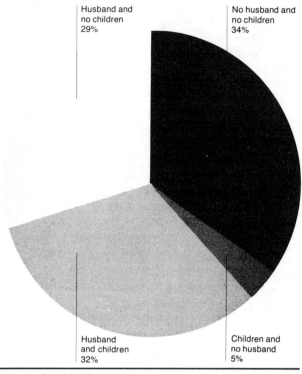

Husband and
no children
29%

No husband and
no children
34%

Husband
and children
32%

Children and
no husband
5%

Working women

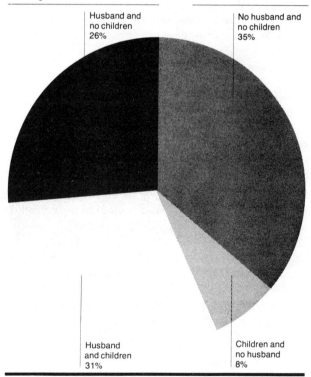

Husband and
no children
26%

No husband and
no children
35%

Husband
and children
31%

Children and
no husband
8%

Source: Bureau of Labor Statistics, March 1977.

Exhibit 5. Who the Working Wives Are, 1950–1975

Percentage of each group in labor force

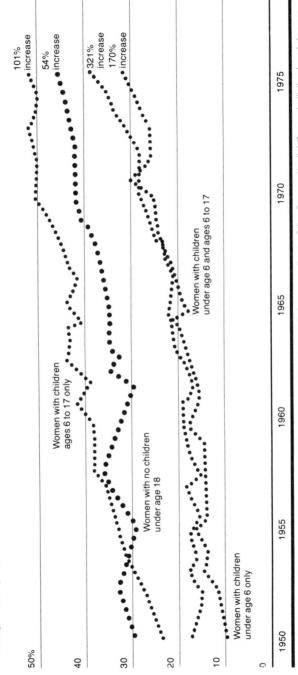

Source: *Employment and Training Report of the President, 1977*, Table B-4, published by the U.S. Government Printing Office. Base used is all civilian, noninstitutional married women, with a husband present, in the labor force.

independence of having "my money, I earned it," which enables them to indulge their yearning for clothes, cosmetics, and personal luxuries.

"Something More than the Kitchen Sink." The second paycheck motivation for working is intertwined with a craving for broader horizons. This is what might be called the "there must be more to life than the kitchen sink" reason for working. It is not so much a reaching out for professional achievement or personal fulfillment as it is a yearning for the social stimulation and sense of identity that comes with going to work.

The evidence of this comes from several sources. In a study conducted by the Bureau of Advertising of the American Newspaper Publishers Association, with a national probability sample of 1,000 women, the working women were asked: "Suppose you could receive just as much money as you earn now without going to work?" A surprising six out of ten respondents indicate that they would rather go on working than receive their paychecks and stay at home. Obviously, something beyond economic necessity drives these women out of the house.

The Yankelovich Monitor reports that in answer to a question on the *primary* reason why women work, fewer than one in five cite income as their main motivation. More than half say that their main reason for working is a "source of enjoyment"; three in ten say a "desire for independence."

In an opinion poll conducted in the early 1970s, although economic motivation was the single most frequently cited reason for going to work, a constellation of "broader horizons" reasoning dominates the responses. These women say, "I need an interest outside the home," "I work for companionship during the day," "I prefer working to staying at home," or "Most of my friends are working."

Professional Achievement. The data also pinpoint the fourth reason for working. This is the motivation for personal fulfillment and professional achievement that career-minded men have always known. Although only 8% of the women say their reason for working is "my career," this motivation seems to be growing.

The Yankelovich Monitor has asked working women whether they think the work they do is "just a job" or "a career." These are not definitions of the kind of work they do, but rather how they feel about that work. In the six years since Yankelovich first asked this question, the proportion of working women who describe themselves as career-minded has risen steadily. A generation ago there were only a handful of women who carved out careers because they were really motivated to do so. Today, according to Yankelovich, about one in three women who work are strongly committed to careers. These women are motivated by the work itself. They equate working with an opportunity for self-realization, self-expression, and personal fulfillment.

Will this trend continue? Career-oriented working women are much more apt to be college educated than are women who perceive their work as just a job. Better educated women are more likely to work.

Of all women who have graduated from college, 65% go to work as compared with only 24% of the women who did not go past grade school. Therefore, it seems likely that achievement will become even more important as a motivation.

An increasing proportion of women go to college. More important, they seek training in professions that used to be considered the exclusive provinces of men. This is a far cry from the image of a coed going to college in order to major in catching a husband.

Changing Values

As we look to the future, it seems clear that we cannot assume that all young women will marry, settle down, and turn into traditional wives or mothers as their mothers did before them. Some may not marry at all. Many may live in a nontraditional lifestyle arrangement, which may not culminate in marriage. Indeed, according to the Yankelovich Monitor, more than half of the American public think there is "nothing wrong with a couple living together (without marriage) as long as they really care for each other." This new kind of household arrangement has a higher level of endorsement from men and unmarried adults.

Other women may decide against embarking on motherhood, even if they should get married eventually. While only a few years ago we might have assumed that all newly married couples were in a state of transition between the honeymoon and parenthood, there is a real possibility that, from now on, many of these women will not undertake the responsibility of bringing children into the world.

The acceptance of childlessness as an option is a major attitudinal change that presents a profound challenge to our assumptions about society. In turn, this could have a major impact on the way people live and their behavior in the marketplace. Almost nine out of every ten people in this country—89%, according to the Yankelovich Monitor—feel there is nothing wrong with a married couple deciding not to have any children. What is more, both men and women hold this opinion to the same extent.

The campus debates about marriage versus career that dominated our attention a generation ago would amaze these young women. They may marry later than their mothers, and they may opt to delay having children (or have no children at all), but for these women the question of whether to work is not even an issue.

Meanwhile, Back at the Ranch House . . .

But what about the 39% of all adult women who are at home keeping house? Apparently, not all housewives are equally committed to the housewife's role. In 1971 the Yankelovich Monitor began asking housewives if they ever planned to go to work (or back to work). Obviously, answers to this kind of question in an interview situation are not predictive of behavior. However, the housewives who say "yes" would seem to have a different kind of "mind set" or predisposition than do those housewives who say they prefer to stay at home.

Yankelovich did a special analysis of the social values of these four types of women. The results are dramatic. "Plan to work" housewives have much more in common with working women (those who look at work as a career as well as those who consider it just a job) than with "stay at home" housewives. The stay at homes appear to be out of step with the majority of other women. This leads to some disquieting questions:

☐ Have we been building our marketing strategies and directing our advertising to only a limited segment of the female audience?

☐ Have all those marvelous marketing tools that aid decision makers been applied to a limited corner of the market?

Until recently there was no way to confirm or deny these questions. We at J. Walter Thompson could not tell which housewives in our research studies or in our audiences plan to work and which ones want to stay at home. Nor could we differentiate between just a job and career-minded working women.

In order to translate these attitudinal insights from Yankelovich into marketing actions, we asked our research organization, Target Group Index, to add these "new demographic" questions to their questionnaire. (The index is an annual trend study of market and media behavior; it is produced by Axiom Market Research Bureau, a subsidiary of J. Walter Thompson.) The questions are simple. It's just that we had not thought of asking them before. The answers enable us to analyze working women and housewives from a new perspective.

What is the size of the four segments of American women (see Exhibit 6)? If we play a retrospective game here and apply the proportions of the new demographic groups reported by Yankelovich each year to the Bureau of Labor Statistics's ratios of working to nonworking women in each of those years, it becomes clear that the plan to work segment actually put their intentions into practice and swelled the ranks of working women as they departed from their homemaker roles.

Demographic Differences

What about the qualitative differences among the segments? An important one is education. The housewives who would rather stay at home than go to work have the lowest educational level of any of the four groups, while the career-oriented working women have the highest. The plan to work housewife is somewhat better educated than the working woman who says it's just a job.

Exhibit 6. Size of the Segments

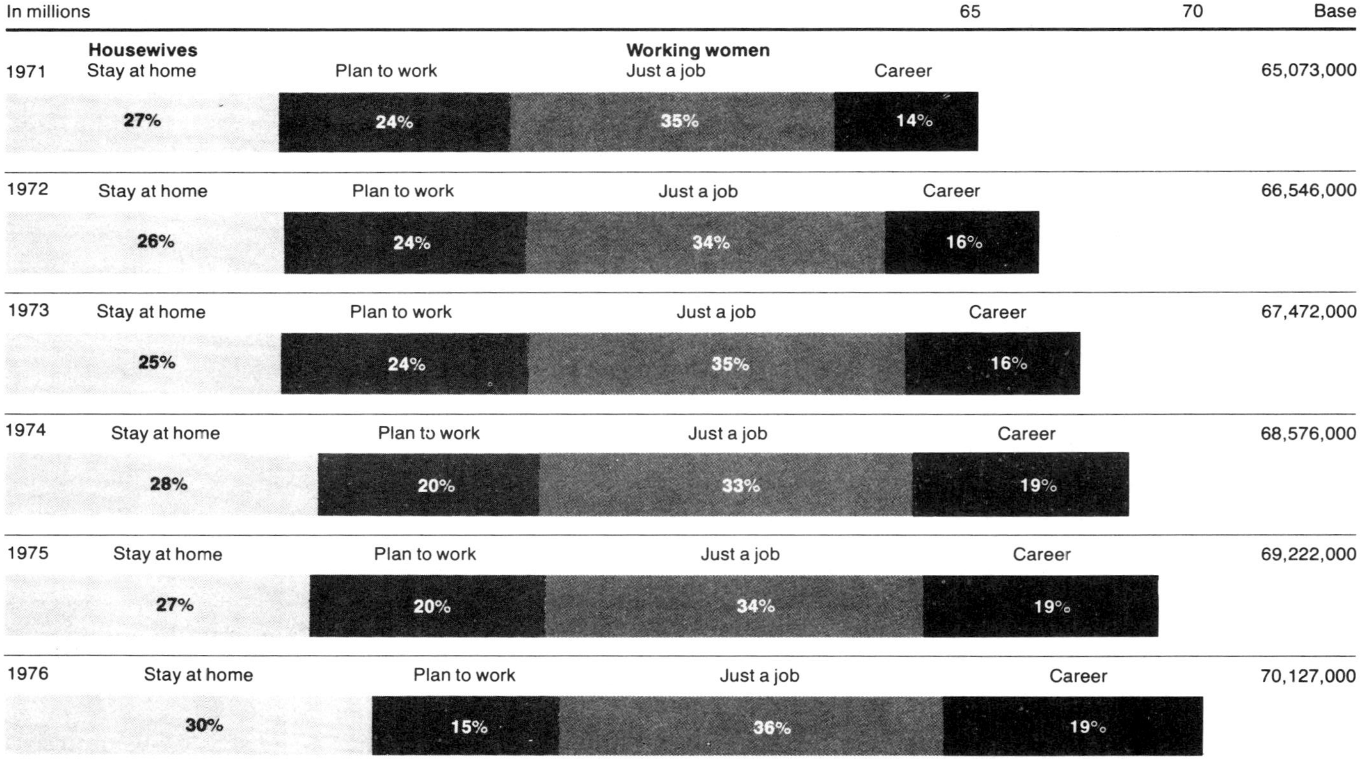

In millions

							65	70	Base

	Housewives		**Working women**			
1971	Stay at home 27%	Plan to work 24%	Just a job 35%	Career 14%		65,073,000
1972	Stay at home 26%	Plan to work 24%	Just a job 34%	Career 16%		66,546,000
1973	Stay at home 25%	Plan to work 24%	Just a job 35%	Career 16%		67,472,000
1974	Stay at home 28%	Plan to work 20%	Just a job 33%	Career 19%		68,576,000
1975	Stay at home 27%	Plan to work 20%	Just a job 34%	Career 19%		69,222,000
1976	Stay at home 30%	Plan to work 15%	Just a job 36%	Career 19%		70,127,000

Source: Bureau of Labor Statistics, *Employment and Earnings*, 1972 to 1977, and Yankelovich Monitor, 1972 to 1977. The base used is all women age 16 and over in the labor force or keeping house.

Age is another important difference. The plan to work housewife is the youngest of the lot. There is not too much age difference between the just a job and career-oriented working women, but the stay at home housewives are the oldest of the groups by far.

What has been keeping the young, plan to work housewives at home? Not surprisingly, it is the children. The plan to work wives are most likely to have children under 18 years of age; also, they have more very young children in their households than do the other groups of women.

Some marketers might still assume that those housewives who want to go to work obviously need the money. Maybe so, but it is interesting that the plan to work housewife is more affluent than her stay at home neighbor. This checks with the fact that the housewives who do not want to go to work are the least educated and the oldest. Career-oriented working women live in the most affluent households of all.

Women's Self-Concepts

You may say, "This is all very interesting, but they are really all sisters under the skin when it comes to how they look at life and how they buy products." Is this true? When one examines the self-perceptions of the group, they emerge as distinctly different. Specifically:

□ Career women have the strongest positive self-images. They see themselves as more broad-minded, dominating, frank, efficient, and independent than the others. They are the only ones of the four types of women who describe themselves as self-assured and very amicable.

□ The just a job working women are quite different from working women who perceive themselves as career-oriented. They are closer to the norm than any of the other three groups.

□ The plan to work housewife is far different from her stay at home neighbor, towering above the others in being tense, stubborn, and feeling awkward. However, she echoes many of the self-perceptions of the career woman, describing herself as creative. Both career women and plan to work housewives are more apt than the others to think of themselves as affectionate.

□ The stay at home housewife thinks of herself as kind, refined, and reserved. She is strikingly below the norm in feeling brave, stubborn, dominating, or egocentric. Incidentally, all women, including the supposedly self-assured career types, have a very low sense of ego when compared with the male population.

Media Behavior

When it comes to reaching women through the media, marketers tend to think they are a homogeneous audience. The unwritten assumption may be that "most of them watch the same programs" or that "women read magazines in such-and-such a way." However, the realities are quite different from these views.

Television. Both types of housewives watch more prime time TV than do the working women. The career-oriented working woman is least likely to watch TV during the evening. As for daytime TV, it is no surprise that both of the housewife groups watch it more than working women do. What is surprising is that the plan to work housewife has her set turned on even more than the stay at home housewife does.

Radio. Marketers have known that working women listen to radio more than housewives do. However, the new facts tell us that career women are the heaviest listeners. They use radio more intensely than do working women who say their work is just a job. The real insight is that the plan to work housewife has her radio turned on more than does her stay at home neighbor. The plan to work housewife seems to be a more active user of all media and a more active consumer. Actually, this is not surprising when we consider her age and educational level as compared with her stay at home neighbor.

Magazines and Newspapers. Marketers long have known that the habit of reading correlates closely with educational level. Therefore, it is no surprise that career-oriented working women are the heaviest users of magazines, and the plan to work housewives are second in magazine readership. Also, as might be expected, career women are more likely than are any of the other three groups to read newspapers.

However, the stay at home housewives are slightly more active in their use of newspapers than are their plan to work neighbors.

Translating the Data into Marketing Behavior

How do the four groups of women compare as consumers and prospective consumers?

Buying Style

Career women are most likely to plan ahead, to be cautious, and to be brand loyal when they go marketing. On the other hand, they admit to being impulse buyers. I suspect that this apparent conflict between planning and impulse is a matter of the type of purchase to be made. Conversely, the just a job working woman says she is experimental when she goes shopping.

The stay at home housewife is the only one who is not an impulse buyer, and she describes herself as more persuasible than do the others. She is the only one who is above the norm in conformity. Both she and the plan to work housewife are more economy-minded than are working women.

While all women are style conscious, the career woman is the most style conscious of all.

Assumptions about Purchasing

"The traditional housewife is house proud; the working woman wants convenience." The realities of women's purchasing behavior challenge many of our assumptions about women. For example, many marketers assume that the stay at home housewife exemplifies traditional pride in housewifery and in housewifely skills. They are sure she is most "house proud" and most concerned with cleaning, polishing, and grooming her home. Also, they assume that to the extent that working women engage in housework, they give it minimal attention and are more concerned with product convenience than with any other considerations. The facts challenge such assumptions.

The data show that the stay at home housewife is slightly *below* the norm in her use of floor wax and rug shampoo and barely above the norm in her use of furniture polish. Surprisingly, it is the plan to work housewife who is the most active consumer of these products. The career-oriented working woman is also above the norm in her use of them.

When one examines frequency of use, the importance of the plan to work housewife begins to emerge. She is not only more likely to buy these products, she also uses them far more often than do women in any of the other groups. An exception is that career women seem to shampoo their rugs almost as frequently as the plan to work housekeepers, while the stay at home is below the norm in the frequency with which she shampoos her rugs or waxes her floors.

Air fresheners are also a mass household product. There is very little difference in the extent to which the four types of women buy them. However, the stay at home housewife is the only one who is above the norm in using them *frequently*. She may not polish the floors much, but she apparently sprays the air a lot.

"Women may pick the color of the upholstery, but men make the car purchase decision." Is there anyone who still believes that the only role that women play in the car market is to pick the color of the upholstery? An examination of the facts shows that while women are not, as yet, equal to men in their importance to auto marketers, their importance is growing fast. They now account for about 40% of the automotive purchase decisions. However, not all women are equally valuable in this market. Life cycle and new demographic values should be considered if we are to identify the most promising female prospects for cars.

The households of married women, both working and not, are more likely to contain two or more cars than are those headed by unmarried women. Among married women with and without children, the career-oriented working woman is most likely to live in a two-car household. Where there are no kiddies at home, the plan to work housewife is far more likely to have two cars than her stay at home neighbor, and somewhat more likely to drive that second car than the just a job working woman.

Another cliche is exploded when it comes to actual car use. The common assumption that women drivers are primarily housewives who drive the kiddies to the supermarket and to scout meetings is denied by the facts. Working women rack up more miles on their cars than do housewives. Among all life-cycle groups, the career-oriented working woman—married or not, with or without children—does the most driving.

The role of life cycle becomes apparent when we consider the purchase decision. It is not surprising that married women are far more likely to share in the purchase decision than are unmarried women.

On the other hand, unmarried women are more likely to have made the decision themselves—but only if they are working.

The career-oriented working woman emerges as the heroine of the car advertiser. She is far more likely to have shared in the purchase decision than the average woman in any of the other three groups. Both types of unmarried working women are above the norm of the total population in having selected and purchased a car on their own. However, career-oriented working women without husbands tower above the other groups in making automotive purchase decisions for themselves.

"The business traveler is a man." Both their situation in the life cycle and new demographic dimensions affect women's travel behavior. For example, the data show that, in general, women who work are far more likely to travel than those who are full-time housewives. As might be expected, women with children at home are far less likely to travel than are their childless neighbors. In addition, the career-oriented working woman is far more likely to own luggage, to use traveler's checks, to have a valid passport, and to have traveled outside the United States in the past year. She is also far more likely to have flown on a scheduled airline and to have stayed in a hotel when she took her trip.

The career woman is not just a desirable customer when compared with other women. She is anywhere from 50% to 70% above the norm when compared with the total population. So, by any measure, she is a desirable customer for travel. Yet there is little evidence that her business has been cultivated by the travel marketer.

Travel marketers have always known that a small number of business people are heavy users of travel services. Most marketers have assumed that the business traveler is a man. This assumption holds up if business travel is analyzed on sex alone; for example, 17% of all men as compared with only 5% of women have traveled on business in the United States. But the assumption does not hold up if career women are distinguished from other women. As travel customers, career women are somewhere between 70% and 94% as important as men in their business travel activities (see Exhibit 7).

100

Exhibit 7. Business Travelers

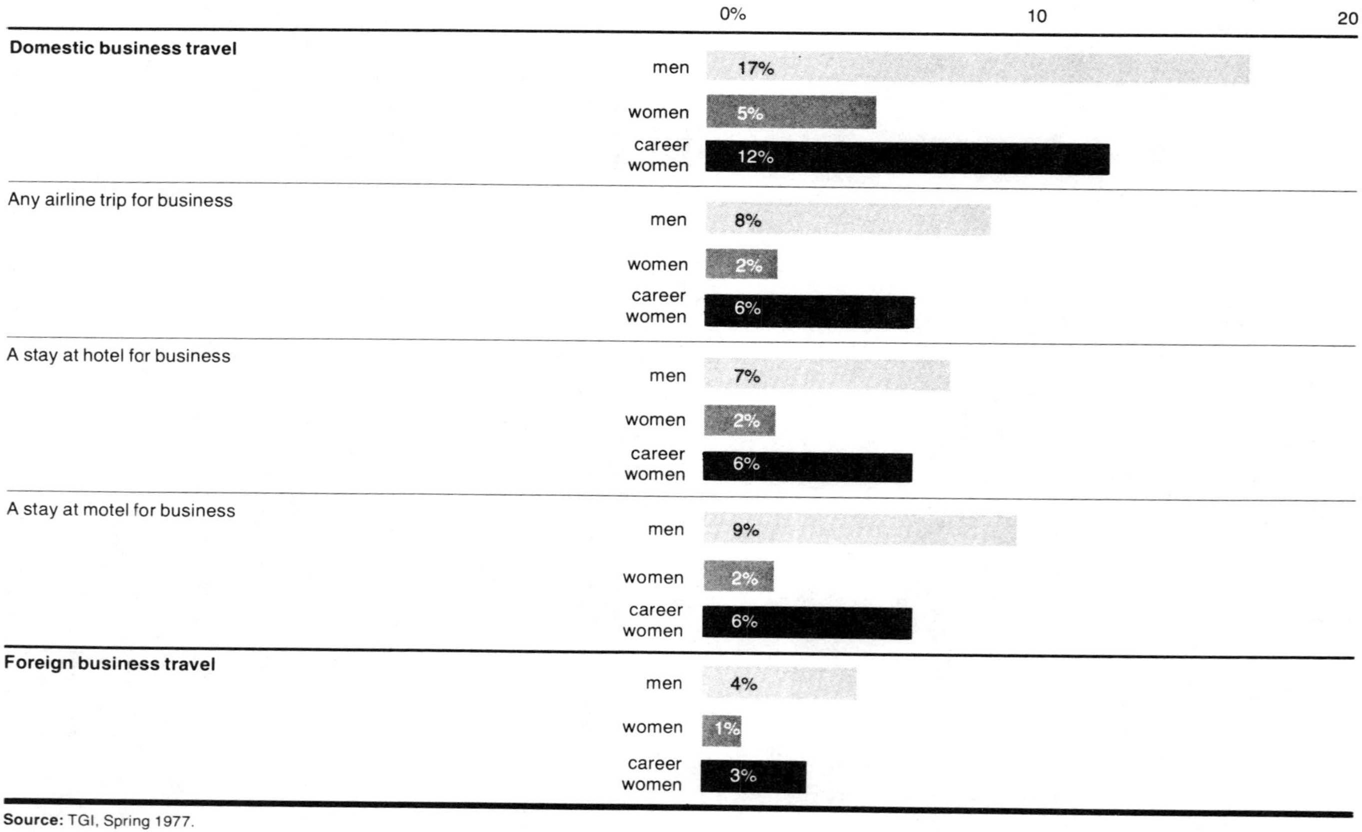

Domestic business travel

men	17%
women	5%
career women	12%

Any airline trip for business

men	8%
women	2%
career women	6%

A stay at hotel for business

men	7%
women	2%
career women	6%

A stay at motel for business

men	9%
women	2%
career women	6%

Foreign business travel

men	4%
women	1%
career women	3%

0%   10   20

Source: TGI, Spring 1977.

Changing Role from Supermom to Partner

These patterns suggest a redefinition of that traditional target, "Any housewife, 18 to 49." As we redefine the target, we also need to understand the context within which women use products and services. Do the traditional motivations of pleasing their husbands and competing with the neighbors still apply?

It is not enough to know what the consumers do; marketers need to know how they *feel* about what they do. Therefore, I have explored the lifestyle context within which the four groups buy and use products. One surprise is the shift in women's tone of voice toward their role as housewives—from "woman's work is never done" and "it's all on my shoulders" to a sense of partnership and family teamwork. This is particularly true of working women, both the job and career types. However, the attitude of partnership also is evident among the plan to work housewives. The stay at home women are least likely to expect to receive help from their husbands and children.

These attitudes are confirmed by new data on the extent to which husbands actually participate in household chores:

☐ More than half of the husbands in the United States are apt to participate in marketing chores, while three out of four men married to just a job working women are in the supermarket. This fact alone challenges our assumptions about who should be the target for household products.

☐ Caring for young children is the next level at which husbands are apt to participate. Here there is a strong difference among the men married to stay at home housewives and those whose wives plan to work. The latter are much more likely to have their husbands help with the children than are the stay at homes. Also, the career-oriented working women are far more likely to get help with the children than are their just a job counterparts.

☐ For almost every other chore, the husbands of working women are far more likely to help or participate than are husbands of housewives. However, the men who are married to the plan to work housewives are more likely to help around the house than are the husbands of the stay at home housewives. Machismo still lives in the houses of the stay at homes. Their husbands are far less likely to help with cooking, mopping floors, cleaning bathrooms, or ironing.

We Have Nothing to Lose But Our Assumptions

The keys to keeping up with change in the marketplace are available to all of us. If marketers use them, they can, in fact, link social change to their marketing procedures. Any practical-minded marketer can challenge the underlying assumptions on which past target definitions are based and, if needed, bring marketing procedures into step with present realities. The process is simple:

1. *Reexamine the assumed target.* Examine the facts. The size and composition of particular groups or segments of consumers are available from the Census or Bureau of Labor Statistics. Professional journals, the daily newspapers, and the popular press are constantly full of reports on changing attitudes, values, and life-styles. Many companies have access to continuing sources of public opinion poll data that track social beliefs and attitudes. Does a review of both the hard and soft data suggest that some groups within our society are changing or represent departures from the monolithic norm? (In the case of women, as we have seen, the answer is a resounding "yes.")

2. *Evaluate the market potential of new target groups.* We can learn whether new or changing groups represent differing market opportunities by reanalyzing existing market data. An objective appraisal of the market behavior of newly identified consumer groups can tell us whether they buy or use products differently from their neighbors and whether their media behavior is distinctive. An equally objective appraisal of their incidence or volume of product use can tell us the kind of potential each group represents for a particular category or brand.

3. *Develop a fresh perspective.* The reanalysis of existing data is possible only if the key demographic questions are built in as a matter of course. When they are not, and when new insights suggest the need for new questions, these should be included in all ongoing and future studies. (As explained, a series of "new demographic" questions is necessary to keep up with changes among women customers.)

If some of the life-cycle groups are underrepresented in copy tests and other studies using small samples, it may be necessary to set quotas or "weight up the cells" in order to represent each constituency in its true proportion.

4. *Explore the attitudes and needs of the new groups.* It is classic research procedure to begin a study with a review of the available data and to use qualitative explorations to develop general hypotheses that ultimately can be quantified. I suggest reversing this sequence. Hypotheses about potential targets are identified through a review of masses of data and verified through a reanalysis of existing data in order to determine whether their marketing and media behavior is unique. In order to understand why these redefined targets behave as they do, we need to return to qualitative exploration. The newly identified opportunity groups define the sample to be studied.

This approach proceeds from quantified evidence of marketing behavior to seek qualitative understanding of the reasons for that behavior. Because marketers know the size of each group, exactly which products and brands it buys, and how much, the results are actionable. It will be clear how to reach the groups, whether women or other customers, through the media.

5. *Redefine marketing targets.* If the foregoing examination of data suggests that the newly identified segments represent useful markets, it should be possible to revise planning readily to meet the need. No new tools or methodology are required. If the facts suggest untapped opportunities, the kinds of marketing procedures that have worked so well in the past can be put to work in approaching the new target groups.

The first marketers who meet the challenge and close the gap between the realities of social change and their procedures will reap the benefits of discovering new marketing opportunities. The tools are available to all.

6
Over 49
The Invisible Consumer Market

RENA BARTOS

One does not need to be a marketing expert to know that marketers are enchanted, some might say obsessed, with young consumers. Concentrating nearly exclusively on this marketing group may be costly, though, because it means marketers are failing to adequately exploit a consumer market consisting of about 40% of American adults—those past age 49. The over-49 market is a potentially lucrative one that can be segmented into a number of different groupings. Such segmentation suggests that those over 49 vary in their lifestyles, media preferences, and buying habits. The author offers guidance for marketers seeking to further analyze this market to sell their own particular products.

In these days of escalating marketing costs and intense product competition, every market share point gained or maintained represents a hard-won marketing achievement. Yet most major marketers limit their efforts to only three out of five of their potential customers by directing their marketing activities to consumers under the age of 49. They cross that age barrier only for such items as denture cleansers, laxatives, tonics, arthritic remedies, and other products that are clearly designed to relieve the aches and pains of old age. In effect, two out of every five American adults are invisible consumers.

Recently, some advertisers have begun to address older consumers. The over-49 market seems to be in a discovery stage analogous to the early 1970s when some marketers "discovered" the working woman market. The pundits who discuss the older-age market talk about it in monolithic terms, as though people in this age group were all cut out of the same mold.

In fact, the invisible consumer market is not a monolithic market at all. The greatest mistake any marketer can make is to generalize about

---

Published 1980.

"senior citizens" or "older Americans" as a group. The paradox of the over-49 market is that, although marketers have overlooked this age group, age by itself is not differentiating enough to reveal the marketing opportunities that exist within it.

Several keys can help unlock this market. The socioeconomic conditions that shape peoples' lives are far more differentiating than age alone. Peoples' needs as consumers change as they move through the life passages of the empty nest, retirement, loss of a spouse, and ill health. The potential adjustment of people over 49 to the watershed events is dependent on a multifaceted balance of *time, money,* and *health.*

The watershed events that occur after 49 and the time-health-money relationship are clues to six segments that exist within this invisible market (see Exhibit 1). Three segments are of little interest to marketers. They are the disadvantaged, those in poor health, and so-called others.

The disadvantaged. These are people below the poverty level, who account for 17% of those over 49. We refer to them as the disadvantaged

Exhibit 1.   Profile of People over 49 Years of Age.

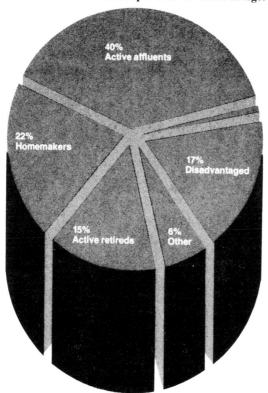

because they truly are. Their needs and problems are more appropriately dealt with by policymakers than by marketers.

Those in poor health. Less than 1% of those over 49 are defined by the census takers as ill or disabled. Their special needs and problems are relevant to the medical profession and other health care specialists, but not to marketers of general products.

Others. The 6% of those over 49 mysteriously labeled by the Bureau of the Census as others are people who do not fit into any preconceived occupational or situational designations. We honestly do not know anything about them.

Three segments have significant potential as customers for advertised products and brands. I have designated these as the active affluents, the active retireds, and the homemakers.

The Active Affluents

About 40% of over-49s are still at work and in the mainstream of life. Thus they have limited free time, are in relatively good health, and have significant disposable income. Their family time tends to be more flexible than when they were younger because their children are usually grown and on their own. Because they are at the height of their careers and no longer have family responsibilities, these over-49s have more discretionary money available than they did during the years of family formation. They are also more likely than the total population to be professionals and managers.

Almost 90% of the active affluents are under age 65, and the majority are in their 50s. About 60% are men and 40% women. The majority are married, and 75% of these are empty nesters with no children under age 18 at home. Surprisingly, in 57% of the marriages, both husband and wife work.

Active careerists in this group cannot escape the nagging realization that retirement is not far off. Their financial goals have changed from providing for their children to anticipating their own futures. They are thus good prospects for annuities and investment and financial planning programs.

The shift from family life to the empty nest may create emotional traumas, but it also means new living patterns for suddenly childless couples. They now have the money and the opportunity to indulge in luxury travel, restaurants, and theater. They want comfort and luxury when they travel, not backpacking. Their increased travel and entertainment mean they have more need for fashionable clothing and jewelry.

Active affluents are usually in relatively good health but concerned with the incipient ills of aging. They watch their waistlines and diets and are thus good prospects for spas, health clubs, cosmetics, and beauty parlors. Perhaps one reason over-49s are invisible is that very often only their hairdressers know for sure!

Although their chronological age moves them past the traditional marketing cutoff age of 49, active affluents don't feel or act old. They have adopted many of the new values of living for the moment and not deferring gratification until some unspecified time in the future. They are less likely than previous generations to assume that, because they have reached a certain age, they should adopt restrictions in the way they live.

The Active Retireds

Another key consumer group, comprising 15% of the over-49 segment, is the active retireds. They are people above the poverty level who retired while they were still in good health.

Though active retireds include people who took early retirements, fewer than 1 in 5 active retireds are under age 65, and most of these are in their early 60s; half are 65 to 75; and almost 1 in 3 is over 75.

Because men have tended to be the sole wage earners, 4 out of 5 active retireds are men. The percentage of women in the group can be expected to increase as active affluents retire from the work force. Among active retireds 2 out of 3 are married, and the majority of the wives are full-time housewives. As a group, active retireds are somewhat less well educated than the active affluents; only about 20% have some college education.

Rejecting the Age Ghetto

Generally speaking, active retireds do not want to be isolated from other people. In spite of all the merchandising of retirement communities, most retired people prefer to live among people of all ages, according to a survey by The Roper Organization.[1] Only 5% say they would like to live among people of their own age.

Nor are all retired people fleeing to condominiums in the Sun Belt. According to a study on retirement issued by the Conference Board, only 4% of retirees moved out of their own regions after they stopped working.[2] Another 20% moved to another dwelling in the same neighborhood or to a nearby community.

What is the key to successful retirement? Given enough money to live comfortably and in reasonably good health, time seems to be the crucial issue. When people are working, time is at a premium, so they tend to pay for convenience, services, and speed. At retirement, time is open-ended. They have a need to develop a structure to replace that imposed by working.

How active retireds use their new-found time is critical to their potential as consumers. Are they, in fact, the new pioneers of leisure? They have the time to take more leisurely trips than their working counterparts. They can take cruises rather than compress their holidays into one- or two-week long-distance plane trips. They have the time for exploring off-beat experiences, such as traveling by freighter rather than by conventional luxury liner or plane.

A study of retirement conducted by the *Los Angeles Times* found that more than half of the retirees sampled began planning for their retirement almost 10 years before it started and some began their retirement planning 15 years in advance. The more affluent and better-educated retirees and pre-retirees were most apt to anticipate the leisure activities they could pursue after retirement.

The Homemakers

Twenty percent of over-49s are women above poverty level who are full-time homemakers. About 70% of these women are married; nearly 40% are married to active affluents, and just under 30% are married to active retireds. Almost 25% are widowed.

The great majority of housewives whose husbands are still actively working are at the lower end of the age spectrum: 84% are under 65, and less than 2% are over 75. The unmarried women in this segment are the oldest of all. Almost 40% are over 75, and only 20% are under 65.

The wives of active affluents are somewhat better educated than the wives of retired men. The widows, who are the oldest homemakers, are also most likely to have limited educations.

Not surprisingly, the housewives whose husbands are still in the work force also live in the most affluent households. The income patterns of the unmarried homemakers run to extremes. At the upper end, they are slightly more affluent than the wives of retired men. However, the unmarried home-makers are more likely than any other group to have household incomes under $5,000 a year.

The most important events for married housewives are their children leaving home, their adjustment to the empty nest, and the changes that occur in their husbands' lives when they move from work to retirement. The wives of the active affluents in particular can experience the shock of no longer being needed when children leave home. But with good health and enough money, these housewives can overcome their shock by joining their hus-bands in the fun of luxury restaurants and travel. The empty nest also allows them time for other personal indulgence and pampering.

When Does a Homemaker Retire?

Probably less difference exists in the lives of full-time housewives after their husbands retire than in the lives of men and women who retire from jobs because the routines of housekeeping remain much the same. Margaret Mead has said: "One reason that women live longer than men is that they continue to do something they are used to doing, whereas men are abruptly cut off—whether they are admirals or shopkeepers."[3]

Nonetheless, since women tend to live longer than men and may marry men who are somewhat older than themselves, they are more likely than men to experience the loss of a spouse. The emotional trauma of the loss then becomes an abrupt situational change not unlike that of involuntary retirement. To the extent that their life patterns have run along traditional lines, their husbands and children have been the focal points of their lives. Their identities and satisfactions have come from being wives and mothers. When they become widowed, they also in a sense become unemployed.

Widows resemble other retired people in that their time is open-ended. Like other retired people, their ability to cope with this change probably started long before their husbands' deaths. If they had hobbies and interests and active social lives when their husbands were alive, they were probably able to continue and expand some of these activities after their husbands died. Another factor that determines how well they adjust is the extent to which they participated in family decision making while their husbands were alive. I would speculate that the finances and health of such women are most important in determining the kinds of lives they lead. A world of difference exists between the blue-haired dowagers traveling on the QE II and isolated old women living on meager incomes.

The bottom-line marketing questions are whether any evidence exists that people over 49 are viable consumers and whether they use media or buy products differently from anyone else. These questions can be answered by examining both the media and marketplace preferences of these over-looked consumers.

How Do Over-49s Use Media?

People over 49 are more likely than the general population to be heavy readers of newspapers and also to be interested in news reports from all other media. They watch television news programs and listen to radio news at all times of the day. They are also above the norm in reading news magazines. Interestingly, the *Christian Science Monitor* elicits more relative readership from this age group than any other single publication. They also respond to magazines related to travel, health, business, and the home.

They are less interested in non-news television and radio programs than the general population. Still, they watch more golf, baseball, and bowling on television than average. They also listen to sports broadcasts on radio.

Of the nonsports television they watch, the situation comedies, variety shows, and dramatic programs rate highest. A small group is devoted to police and detective dramas. When listening to the radio, they prefer talk shows and soft or classical music.

This brief overview indicates that people over 49 have distinctive media preferences. However, enormous variations exist in the media patterns within this total market.

Active Affluents

Men are the heaviest newspaper readers among the active affluent over-49s. Although they watch television news in the evening, they are more likely than the others in the market to tune into radio news. They also watch all types of television sports programs from auto racing to tennis; however, they are not intrigued by bowling. They listen to sports stations on their radios and are active readers of all the sports magazines.

Their magazine reading reflects a wide range of interests; active affluent men are heavy readers of business, travel, and science and mechanics magazines. They are also strong fans of *Esquire* and moderately heavy readers of *Playboy*, but they tend not to read the other so-called skin books like *Oui* and *Penthouse*.

Active affluent women are also avid followers of current events through magazines, television, and radio. They tend to watch dramatic programs more than situation comedies. They are devoted readers of a spectrum of magazines including home, health, women's service, fashion, and movie magazines. Their magazine reading extends, however, beyond the confines of conventional women's interests. They also love to read about travel and are very responsive to a number of selective publications such as the *New Yorker, Saturday Review, Smithsonian,* and *Town & Country*.

The media patterns of active affluent women vary with their marital status. Working wives are more likely than any other segment to read newspapers. And they are particularly heavy magazine readers. In addition to the types of magazines discussed previously, they read *Cosmopolitan, Ms.,* and (surprisingly for this age group) *Parents* magazine. These married working women are also intrigued by television police dramas.

Unmarried working women are more likely than any other over-49 segment to listen to the radio, and they are the only group in this market with a strong interest in *Bride's* magazine!

Active Retireds

Retired men have more leisure time than active affluents and spend much of it watching television. They are somewhat more likely to watch television during the day than the evening, particularly if they are married. The reverse is true for unmarried retired men. Overall, retired men watch news programs morning, noon, and night. They are also a significant part of the daytime television audience, particularly for talk shows, game shows, and situation comedies. However, they do not appear to have succumbed to soap operas.

While they are more likely than the active affluent men to listen to radio sports programs, active retired men are less likely to watch sports on television. In particular, they watch less football, though they watch more baseball and bowling. Golf also gets their strong attention.

Retired men are slightly more likely than the active affluent men to read news magazines, but less likely to read anything else. Although retirement gives them more leisure time, they do not appear to spend as much of that time reading as watching television.

Retired women not only watch daytime television, they also read magazines, particularly if they are married. Unmarried retired women do not read very much, but they are devoted to daytime television. All retired women are enthusiastic viewers of news programs at all times of the day. They are also fans of talk shows, game shows, soap operas, and situation comedies. They are more likely than retired men to listen to radio talk shows as well. While they are far above the norm in reading women's service, health protection, and home and garden magazines, they are less involved than active affluent women in reading any of these. They have also lost interest in fashion magazines.

Household Managers

Although the structure of a housewife's day may not change very much after her husband retires or when she is widowed, the focus of her personal interests shifts with each change in her situation. The housewives who are married to active affluent men are active users of more types of media than any other group in the over-49 market. They are the heaviest viewers of daytime television and the heaviest readers of magazines. They are above average in newspaper readership, and they are the only segment among the over-49s who watch more than an average amount of evening television. They watch all types of daytime television programs with great intensity. They are particularly enthusiastic viewers of soap operas, game shows, and situation comedies.

The housewives whose husbands are retired also watch television during the day and read magazines, but at a lower level of intensity. And those housewives who are not married are strong fans of daytime television, but below the norm for all other media. Though the unmarried homemakers are not involved with soap operas, they are more likely to watch news and game shows than the wives of retired men. The latter enjoy talk shows more than their unmarried counterparts.

A similar pattern of declining interest is apparent in homemakers' magazine tastes. The housewives whose husbands are still working read general interest magazines such as the *Reader's Digest, National Geographic,* and *People*; selective magazines such as *Town & Country, Natural History, Smithsonian,* and *Saturday Review*; and travel magazines. They are more likely than any other segment to read the women's service and home magazines, and they are almost as enthusiastic as their neighbors in the working world about fashion magazines. They are also more likely than any other group to read the movie and romance publications.

The wives of retired men are somewhat responsive to news magazines, but thereafter their interest falls off sharply. They read the same categories of women's magazines as their more active neighbors, but all at a far lower level of intensity.

The unmarried homemakers do the least reading of all. They are moderately responsive to women's service magazines and home-oriented publications. However, they are more likely than any other segment among the over-49s to read *Atlantic Monthly* and the *Christian Science Monitor*.

How They Spend Their Time . . .

From their media use patterns we can see that people over 49 have distinctive interests. Marketers must next consider how this group's particular demographics and interests affect the way these consumers buy and use products and services. We can gain insight into this issue by examining how those over 49 use their time and what this tells us about them as consumers.

Community Participation.   Over 49s are active participants in a broad range of community and charitable clubs and organizations. Active affluent men are important supporters of community groups. While retired men do not participate to the same degree, they are well above the norm in their support of fraternal orders, veterans' clubs, local government committees, and hospital and church boards. Active affluent women are most likely to support religious clubs and regional development committees, while unmarried homemakers channel their energies into local school and hospital boards.

Country Clubs.   Over-49s as a group are above the norm in belonging to country clubs, with the main support coming from active affluent men. Their wives and active retired men are also country club members, but to a lesser degree.

Golf.   Active affluent men are the only segment of the over-49s to include a sizable number of golfers. However, those people in each of the other segments (including all homemaker groups) who do play golf are apt to play very often. This is one way in which the nonworking homemakers and retired men and women use their leisure time. Few among the over-49s are likely to play tennis.

Gardening.   Active affluent men and women along with homemakers are the most apt to garden, and they do so intensively. Retired men garden in smaller numbers, but they are the most active gardeners. They are followed in frequency by nonworking over-49 women, the three types of homemakers, and the retired women.

Needlework.   All segments of over-49 women—employed, retired, and homemakers—are very involved with sewing and needlework. But the frequency with which they indulge in these hobbies increases with their available leisure time. Active affluent women and the homemakers who are married to active affluent men seem to have other demands on their time. However, retired women, the wives of retired men, and the unmarried homemakers seem to be sewing up a storm. Incidentally, a small number of retired men are very devoted to both sewing and needlework.

Keeping House.   Over-49 housewives appear to be proud and fastidious about the way they keep house. They frequently polish their silver and brass.

As a group, they are far more likely than all homemakers to buy metal polish and use it often. They are above the norm in buying such cleaning products as kitchen cleansers, toilet bowl cleaners, bathroom cleaning products, and drain cleaners. They use scouring powder somewhat more often than the average homemaker.

Their patterns of housekeeping seem to shift with changes in their life situations. Active affluent women and wives of active affluent men are most lavish in their purchases of housecleaning products. The wives of retired men are also good customers, but at a slightly lower level. The unmarried buy a narrower range of household products and don't use them as frequently.

Travel. People over 49 are active domestic and international travelers. They are particularly apt to use travel agents and to take overseas cruises and domestic bus tours, to have valid passports, and to have bought travelers checks in the past year.

Domestically, active affluent men are frequent business travelers and more likely than any other group to use hotels and motels when they travel. Active affluents of both sexes often travel by plane. The over-49 women also ride on trains and buses. They are especially good customers for cruises and bus tours. Retired women are more apt than retired men to travel by plane. However, both retired men and women take cruises and travel or tour by bus. Housewives whose husbands are employed love cruises and bus tours. Housewives whose husbands are retired are less apt to travel. The unmarried homemakers are less apt to take cruises but are devoted to bus tours.

Active affluent women are the best customers for foreign travel. They are most likely to travel by plane, both scheduled and charter. Foreign cruises appeal to all segments of the over-49s except the unmarried home-makers. Both the active affluent and retired women are particularly responsive to cruises. Retired men and their wives are also likely to travel by train when they are overseas. Retired women are generally more active travelers than retired men.

. . . and Money

We might also ask how those over 49 handle their money and how they spend it.

Investments. The over-49s are relatively affluent and financially sophisticated, and their investment behavior shows it. While only 18% of all adults invest in stocks, bonds, or in securities other than savings bonds, more than 25% of over-49s are likely to make such investments.

Active affluents of both sexes are the heaviest investors. The change to retirement brings a lower level of investment activity, although active retireds are substantially above the total population norm in this area. Retired men are almost twice as likely as retired women to be active investors.

Credit Cards.   The total group of over-49s is also more likely than all adults to own credit cards, either the travel and entertainment (T&E) variety or bank cards, thanks almost entirely to the active affluents. Active affluent men are especially heavy subscribers to T&E cards, and they own bank cards as well. Active affluent women are more likely to own bank cards than T&Es. And housewives who are married to active affluent men are more likely than the population as a whole to say "charge it" with either type of card.

Luxuries and Cars.   Active affluent men constitute a unique market within the total over-49 group. They not only invest in stocks and bonds, they are the only segment above the norm for buying diamond rings, and they are slightly above par in collecting coins.

They are also active drivers. They drive more miles than average and are more likely to own two or three cars, compared with the overall population. Not surprisingly, they are good customers for tires and car wax.

Active affluent women, however, are unlikely to buy diamonds, but they do buy costume jewelry. They are more likely to own only one car. They are also especially good customers for luggage.

Beyond the Rocking Chair

The over-49 market represents a wealth of opportunities for those marketers who are willing to challenge their own assumptions about age. Marketing procedures that have succeeded with the usual target groups can be applied just as effectively to these relatively undiscovered consumers. This article is not intended as an exhaustive inventory of all the products and services of possible interest to those over 49. Not is it intended as a blanket recommendation that every advertiser of every product category automatically concentrate on consumers over 49.

Judgments as to products' potential should be made on a case-by-case basis. Those marketers who conclude that outdated assumptions about age may have deprived them of valuable customers can take action. The potential market for various products and services among the over-49 segments can be determined. Practical-minded marketers must challenge the underlying assumptions on which past target definitions have been based. The process for doing that is as follows:

1. *Reexamine the assumed target.*   Information about particular groups or segments of consumers is available from the U.S. Census Bureau or Bureau of Labor Statistics. Professional journals, daily newspapers, and the rest of the popular press are constantly full of reports on changing attitudes, values, and life-styles. Many companies have access to public opinion polls that track social beliefs and attitudes. Does a review of the data suggest that some groups within our society are changing or in need of being segmented?

2. *Evaluate the marketing potential of new target groups.* An objective appraisal of the market behavior of newly identified consumer groups can indicate whether they buy or use products differently from their neighbors and whether their media behavior is distinctive. An appraisal of their product use can tell us the potential each group represents for a particular category or brand.

3. *Develop a fresh perspective.* When new insights suggest the need for new demographic questions, they should be included in all ongoing and future studies. In the case of the over-49 market, occupational status, sex, income, marital status, and occupation of spouse are required to identify the relevant market segments described.

4. *Explore the attitudes and needs of the new groups.* Hypotheses about potential targets can be identified by reviewing masses of data and then can be verified by reanalyzing existing data to determine whether the targets' marketing and media behavior is unique. To understand why these redefined targets behave as they do, we need to make use of qualitative exploration.

5. *Redefine marketing targets.* If the facts suggest untapped opportunities, the kinds of marketing procedures that have worked well in the past can be used to go after the new target groups.

We have the know-how. We have the data. The relationship of time, health, and money and water-shed events can help us to segment this monolithic mass into meaningful markets. The challenge for marketers is to break away from their absolute fixation with the 18 to 49 age group.

If we get off the comfortable rocking-chair way we have always defined our targets, we might discover significant opportunities within the invisible consumer market.

Notes

1. *The Roper Reports* (New York, N.Y.: The Roper Organization, 1977), vol. 77-7, p. Q.

2. *Retirement: Reward or Rejection* (New York, N.Y.: Conference Board, 1977), p. 23.

3. "Challenging the Sixty-five Barrier," *Time*, August 8, 1977, p. 68.

7
Beware of International Brand Piracy

JACK G. KAIKATI and RAYMOND LaGARCE

Identification of brands was not dreamed up by some enterprising American ad agency. Ancient wine caps have been uncovered that bear impressions used to show the high quality of Greek and Roman wine-makers' products.

In the Middle Ages, trademarks were used more to determine liability than anything else. The English Parliament in 1266 passed a law requiring bakers to mark their bread so that: "If any bread be faultie in weight it may bee then knowne in whome the fault is."

In those days, penalties for infringement were severe. In Flanders, for example, a tapestry worker who failed to mark his work correctly could lose his right hand. While sanctions are not as severe today, the law still provides civil remedies for infringement, and society continues to attach considerable importance to trademarks.

Foreign countries, however, are adopting increasingly lenient attitudes toward counterfeiting—especially when U.S. companies are the plaintiffs. Local laws favor national goods over imports, and multinational corporations (MNCs) are becoming concerned about expansion in the fake goods market:

☐ Japanese pirates have blanketed foreign countries with out-and-out duplicates of Singer sewing machines, down to the big S and distinctive logo on the base.

☐ Taiwan and other countries play host to brand pirates and mete out only light fines to brand counterfeiters.

Published 1980.

☐ In Mexico, Cartier has been involved for seven years in a lawsuit involving a chain of stores operating freely (in major hotels) under the Cartier name and selling jewelry bearing the same label.

The objectives of this study are four-fold. We shall (1) focus on the major economic, political, and cultural factors that currently favor brand piracy; (2) discuss various forms of brand piracy; (3) present reactions from and strategies implemented by MNCs to combat the problem; and (4) outline various international conventions established to protect trademarks and brand names.

Contributing Factors

The recent wave of counterfeiting can be attributed to at least four major components:

☐ *Consumer goods shortages.* Counterfeiting did not erupt as an international abuse until after World War II, when it was stimulated by the heavy, pent-up demand for consumer goods caused by continuing production shortages.

☐ *Status symbols.* The growing taste for wearing status symbol emblems on the outside of clothing and accessories has encouraged brand piracy. For example, it spurred counterfeiters in Brazil to put "Cartier" on bookjackets, dresses, pencils—products that are not even made by the genuine Cartier.

☐ *Narrowing technological gap.* Recent improvements in technology in Europe and Japan have made it easier for many foreign countries to produce credible counterfeits of American products. (Sharper images in offset printing, for example, have made it simple for almost anyone to duplicate product labels.)

☐ *Increased interest in foreign markets.* With the increased activity of multinationals in markets outside the United States, specific brand names are becoming more recognizable, and thus more attractive, to consumers around the world.

Forms of Piracy

Famous trademarks are abused in various ways, running the gamut from outright piracy to legal imitation. And, as can be expected, there is a lot of gray area in between.

Outright Piracy. Japanese stores are flooded with counterfeit big-name items. In fact, it was once reported that Mitsukoshi, Tokyo's most prestigious department store, had unknowingly sold a fake Hermes necktie to the emperor!

Some counterfeiters vie to become authorized dealers for the very manufacturers whose products they have chosen to counterfeit. Then they make a great show of publicity materials furnished by the manufacturers to promote their fake products.

When a drop in sales begins to worry the manufacturers, counterfeiters reply that the slowdown is caused by imitations which have been released on the market. The manufacturers ask the authorized dealers to investigate, which they promise to do—all too willingly.

"Palming Off" Fakes. This is the practice of adopting a mark similar in appearance, phonetic qualities, or meaning to the original product's. In the watch industry, for example, Omega, Hamilton, Longines, and Bulova have been copied by "Cimega," "Hormilton," "Longune," and "Bulovia." Packages and other outward features of products such as these are duplicated so meticulously that often even experts cannot spot fakes without laboratory tests.

Recently, McDonald's filed a request for a temporary injunction against McDavid's, a Tel Aviv hamburger outlet. The restaurant looks distinctly American—from the plastic counters and beeping digital cash register to the Uncle Sam hat atop the McDavid's symbol. The owner of McDavid's was quoted as saying that he had had McDonald's 120-page manual for its franchise owners translated into Hebrew.

Imitation. Some countries tend to distinguish between imitation and piracy. For example, no Mexican legislation protects the foreign manufacturer if the product in question is termed an "imitation" as opposed to a "counterfeit," for which there is legal recourse in Mexico as well as in most other countries.

Some Mexican businesspeople buy local sparkling wine, duplicate the "Moët and Chandon" label, and add Spanish words to that label, all to avoid being found guilty of counterfeiting. This legal gray area has permitted some entrepreneurs to build a healthy trade specializing in false Hennessy brandy, false Bordeaux wines, and false scotch whisky.

Wholesale Piracy. In some countries, unscrupulous individuals can make a living registering foreign trademarks and selling them back to the international company when it wants to sell in that market.

In 1966, Dr. Robert S. Aries apparently found a loophole in Monaco's law against counterfeiting: registration of trademarks for services and products is permitted. He registered about 300 brand names, including some of the best-known names in the United States: Chase Manhattan, Bankers Trust, Du Pont, Sears, Texaco, NBC, CBS—even the *New Yorker* and *Harper's*. Although not illegal, such actions are of course ethically questionable.

How Companies React

In some cases, groups of companies have taken collective action against international brand piracy; in other instances, companies have acted alone.

Since France has long been a leader in the luxury goods field, it has suffered more than other countries from the expanding market in imitation goods. The French formed an association to fight counterfeiting as far back as 1954. Known as the Comité Colbert, it was sponsored by owners of famous French brand names to protect their goods against copiers.

Nevertheless, the problem in France seems to be getting worse— the Comité estimates that imitations cut at least 1% annually from profits in the luxury goods market, which total approximately $6.6 billion each year.

The multinational business community is also becoming anxious about international brand piracy. In April 1978, 25 U.S. and European businesses, with Pierre Cardin as spokesman, formed the International Anticounterfeiting Coalition.

Though many of the members of the coalition (including representatives from Samsonite, Helene Curtis, and Munsingwear) have not had serious difficulties in the U.S. marketplace, nearly all are fighting counterfeiting abroad. Most are concerned that the pirates will soon land on America's shores.

The coalition has already pushed an amendment through the U.S. Senate Finance Committee that would allow U.S. customs officials to confiscate counterfeit goods.

Until recently, the U.S. government treated counterfeiting offenses lightly. If counterfeit goods were discovered at customs, the importer was either forced to remove the bogus labels or permitted to reexport the goods. (The fakes then became someone else's problem.)

Under the new U.S. law, customs officials will seize questionable goods. If the importer protests that the goods are genuine, the trademark owners must post a bond and then prove the products fake.

If the merchandise is finally proved phony, it can be turned over to the government, given to a charitable institution, or auctioned off after one year. American representatives are pressing for passage of similar laws at the 1979 Tokyo Round of trade negotiations in Geneva.

Apart from the collective actions by French business people and the International Anticounterfeiting Coalition, companies generally act on their own. The reactions of individual companies to international brand piracy can be classified into at least four major strategies:

1. *Hands-off strategy.* Some of the offended companies hesitate to prosecute the counterfeiters vigorously, partly because they are afraid customers would switch to competing brands if they knew the products were being faked.

Also, getting conclusive evidence against counterfeiters is a difficult and expensive proposition that often entails hiring private investigators and lawyers for long periods of time. Moreover, if a multinational corporation loses a case, it is wide open to a countersuit for malicious prosecution.

The problem is compounded by the difficulties of dealing with foreign police, foreign courts, and inadequate laws.

Civil action against counterfeiters frequently takes more time than criminal cases to come to trial; and often when the company does win damages, the pirates turn out to be broke. Criminal action is better, provided the company catches the culprits just as they are applying the bogus labels.

Loopholes and shortcomings in many local laws frustrate MNCs. While local authorities are usually willing to help out, laws are sometimes worded so that a captured counterfeiter gets off scot-free or is merely fined a small amount.

For example, numerous Hong Kong exporters benefit from local laws which imply that sale of a counterfeit product is legal as long as the exporter does not participate in actual application of the labels. Thus a manufacturer of counterfeit Arrow labels had his case thrown out of court because the police raiders had detected no one actually sewing the labels on shirts.

Even though the hands-off strategy seems ineffective in most countries, it has actually worked in Taiwan. Cut-throat price competition among Taiwanese book pirates is forcing them to go legitimate.

The publication of H.R. Haldeman's *The Ends of Power* shows why: the Imperial Bookstore, a notorious pirater of trade books, priced the $12.95 book at $1.84. A rival started retailing it for the same price but discovered that a neighboring bookstore was selling it for $1.32, so he felt forced to reduce his tag to the same ruinous $1.32.

This fierce competition gives pirates an incentive to seek local reprint rights to protect themselves against the ravages of price wars. Taiwan is not a signer of the Universal Copyright Convention, so only locally copyrighted works are protected there.

2. *Prosecuting strategy.*   Despite the legal booby traps and the expense, a few companies decided to go all out against fakers because they were losing not only goodwill but also sales. Consequently, these U.S. and European companies have set up elaborate security forces, with former FBI and Secret Service agents serving as internal detectives.

In 1977, Levi Strauss & Co. broke an international scheme to counterfeit the company's jeans. The counterfeiting activities were discovered after an extensive investigation (costing more than $200,000) by Levi Strauss that resulted in the seizure of more than 125,000 pairs of bogus Levi's in Switzerland, Belgium, the Netherlands, and Taiwan and short jail sentences for the parties involved.

3. *Withdrawal strategy.*   Even though Levi Strauss used the prosecution strategy successfully, the French luggage company Louis Vuitton did not. It hired private detectives to track down manufacturers of faked

bags, but the combination of wily crooks and legal loopholes proved too much for the company.

Consequently, Vuitton decided to withdraw its much-imitated pebbled plastic LV "Speedy" travel bag from the Italian market. The withdrawal was announced in ads appearing in Rome and Milan dailies as well as in newsweeklies and fashion monthlies. No other company has gone that far.

The strategy of withdrawing the bag was to transform a serious problem into an image builder; a snob-appeal campaign read: "Louis Vuitton is at least as upset as you are that such a bag won't be sold anymore in Italy. But Louis Vuitton is as sure as you are that those who buy his luggage want, above all, an exclusive article."

4. *Warning strategy.* Imitation might be the sincerest form of flattery, but some companies have repaid the compliment by warning the public of imitations.

Cartier claims it is useless to complain to the Mexican government about the waves of forgeries bombarding the Mexican market; consequently, all Cartier ads in Mexico include addresses of stores in which consumers can be sure to get the real thing.

Other companies are playing up the flattering side of the problem. Harley-Davidson motorbikes tout a 12-month and/or 12,000-kilometer guarantee in Italy, and their ads proclaim: "Harley-Davidson gives the competition yet another chance to imitate." Dr. Scholl's is advertising its anatomical sandals with such headlines as "Once you climb to a Dr. Scholl's, you will never sink to an imitation."

International Agreements

While governments have held conventions and arrived at various agreements to address the problems of brand piracy, the individual company has usually had to rely on itself. International agreements provide guidelines for the setting of policies by responsible companies, but such agreements often lack means to enforce them.

No world court exists for handling trademark disputes, and intranational legal systems vary greatly. And since a company cannot always depend on a foreign country's legal system for protection, the burden for effective brand protection rests on company-initiated actions.

In the United States, a common-law country, whoever can establish first use is usually considered the rightful owner of a trademark. In fact, before brand names and trademarks can be registered, they must actually be in use.

In many code-law countries, however, ownership is established by registration rather than by prior use. International conventions have been formed to reconcile the differences that exist among the users of trademarks, designs, and commercial names, and the United States is a party to some of these treaties:

1. The International Union for the Protection of Industrial Property is the major intergovernmental agreement to protect against piracy. Commonly referred to as the "Paris Union," it was established in Paris in 1883 and is adhered to by the United States and 80 other countries.

Present membership is divided about equally between developed and developing countries and includes the U.S.S.R. as well as five Soviet satellites.

In substance, the convention deals with patents and industrial designs as well as commercial names and trademarks, all of which constitute industrial property rights.

Under this convention the signatory countries agree to:

1   Register and protect the trademarks of other signatory states to the extent that national trademarks are protected.
2   Register trademarks of other signatory states in the form in which they are registered in the country of origin.
3   Acknowledge the property rights associated with trade names without the formality of registration.
4   Grant that a company which files for registration in its native country be given a six months' priority period to file in a signatory state. (Thus if a U.S. business files first in the United States and within six months in another member country, the second filing is given the same status as the first.)

2. The General Inter-American Convention for Trademark and Commercial Name Protection includes most of the Latin American nations plus the United States and provides protection similar to that of the Paris Union.

3. The Madrid Agreement Concerning the International Registration of Trademarks provides centralized protection in about 23 countries by means of an international registration.

Even though the United States is not a participant of the Madrid Convention, if a subsidiary of a U.S. company is located in one of the member nations it can file through the membership of its host country and thereby provide protection in all member countries for that company.

The basic advantage of international registration is that it saves money, a company can obtain multiple-country protection for about $100 (the average fee). The period of protection for an internationally registered trademark is the same for all contracting countries—20 years—and is renewable for further periods of 20 years each.

4. The Trademark Registration Treaty (TRT) has been proposed by delegates to the Vienna Diplomatic Conference on Property and will take effect as soon as five countries have ratified it. The TRT would allow for a single-fee filing of a trademark application with the World Intellectual Prop-

erty Organization in Geneva and would have the effect of a filing in each country designated by the applicant.

5. Other regional arrangements for the registration of patents and trademarks are gradually coming into existence. The Benelux countries have already adopted a trademark convention that introduces a unified trademark law (supplanting national laws).

An accord for the creation of an African and Malagasy Industrial Property Office was signed in September 1962 by 12 member states of the African and Malagasy Union. It establishes a common system for maintenance of a patent and trademark rights, with a single deposit and centralized administration.

Trademark experts from European Common Market countries have also drafted a trademark convention. Certain questions of policy have not yet been decided, including whether U.S. corporations will be eligible for full or at least partial participation in the Common Market patent and trademark system.

No Easy Answer

It is obvious that the problem of brand piracy is becoming more acute. Also, the prognosis is for increased abuses unless additional measures are taken.

One such action that may assist companies is the International Anti-Counterfeiting Coalition's move to grant customs officials the power to confiscate goods suspected of being counterfeit. If a majority of the industrialized nations would develop standardized customs control for trademark protection, this step would at least give some added protection to the import market. Unfortunately, it would do little to regulate false goods produced domestically.

In the short run, the best protection a company can exercise is close observation and control of its markets, channels, and products. However, even a high level of scrutiny will not provide total protection.

The Health Care Market

Can Hospitals Survive?

JEFF C. GOLDSMITH

Does it sound familiar? Resources are scarce, competition is tough, and government regulations and a balanced budget are increasingly hard to meet at the same time. This is not the automobile or oil industry but the health care industry, and hospital managers are facing the same problems. And, maintains the author of this article, they must borrow some proven marketing techniques from business to survive in the new health care market. He first describes the features of the new market (the increasing economic power of physicians, new forms of health care delivery, prepaid health plans, and the changing regulatory environment) and then the possible marketing strategies for dealing with them (competing hard for physicians who control the patient flow and diversifying and promoting the mix of services). He also describes various planning solutions that make the most of a community's hospital facilities and affiliations.

The hospital industry in the United States is big business. During 1978, more than 7,000 U.S. hospitals employed 3.2 million workers and expended over $71 billion. Because the costs of hospital care have risen far more rapidly than the rate of inflation during the past 15 years (see Exhibit 1), local, state, and federal governments have escalated regulatory efforts to contain them. These efforts have heightened competition among hospitals for increased use of their facilities. At the same time, new health care delivery forms have presented hospitals with significant external competition. For these reasons, marketing is now a major management concern in the health care field.

Conventional wisdom about the health care industry says that com-

Published 1980.

Exhibit 1. Selected Components of the Consumer Price Index, 1967–1979 (All urban consumers)

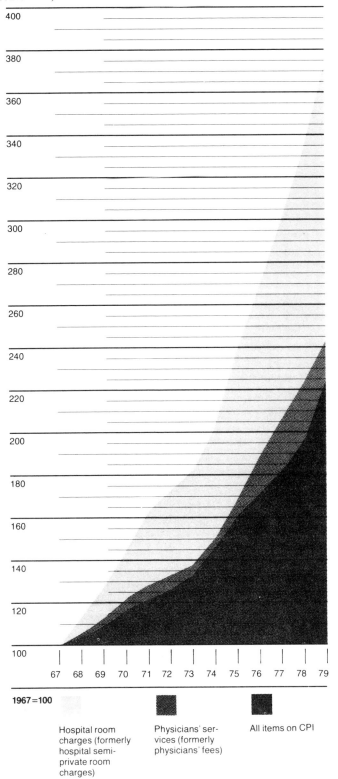

1967=100

Hospital room charges (formerly hospital semi-private room charges)

Physicians' services (formerly physicians' fees)

All items on CPI

petition is minimal among health care providers. This is certainly true of price competition for inpatient hospital services. Because health insurance has anesthetized the consumer against rising hospital costs, those costs have increased in a hyperinflationary way.[1] Hospitals do compete intensely, however, for physicians and patients, and new forms of delivering health care may compete with hospitals for health care business based on both increased convenience to the consumer and lower costs. And the more rapidly hospital costs escalate, the more rapidly these alternative methods of delivering care will grow. Hospitals that do not respond to these changes by broadening their mix of services and by developing more flexible distribution systems to bring in patients are likely to experience difficulties competing in this new environment.

Before examining some of the marketing tools hospital managers are bringing to bear on their competitive problems, it might be helpful to look at some of the changes taking place in the health care field that are making these strategies so important.

Changing Health Care Environment

The hospital is the core institutional provider of health care. Yet, for the reasons that follow, as their costs increase, hospitals will be in an increasingly vulnerable position within the health care market. Much like the urban department store, which faces major competition from alternative outlets (drugstore chains, discount houses, direct mail, boutiques and specialty shops, and so forth), hospitals face threats from emerging alternative forms of health care.

Increasing Economic Power of Physicians

Hospital managers labor under some unique managerial constraints in mobilizing their resources. They have almost no ability to control the use of hospital services directly. And physicians, who determine how and how much the hospital is used, exert enormous power in allocating resources—but the physicians, too, are often beyond managers' control.

Existing health insurance plans, including Medicare, pay many physicians' fees regardless of where they hospitalize their patients. Thus in most cases the hospital manager has no control over physician income. Recruitment retention and management of physicians—who, like a "sales force," bring in patients—are the key marketing issues for hospital managers. Physicians also have the financial resources to compete in their own offices with many hospital services. Since the overhead in an office setting is much lower than in a hospital, they can frequently undersell hospitals for the same services and will do so increasingly in the future.

New Forms of Health Care Delivery

Because of advances in drug therapy (for many mental disorders, for example) and in technology (in kidney dialysis, for instance), many patients can now receive health care without being hospitalized on a long-term basis. Standards of medical practice are changing as well. Many types of emergency (short of massive trauma) can now be managed outside the hospital. Also, many types of surgery can now be performed on an outpatient basis.

All the new forms of care have in common the substitution of outpatient for inpatient care, with both lowered costs and increased convenience for patients. As such, they threaten to reduce use of the hospital's key inpatient services. The extent of the shift to alternative forms of health care was revealed by a recent Blue Cross study that showed an 18.6% decline in inpatient days of care and a 137.6% increase in outpatient visits among Blue Cross subscribers between 1968 and 1978.[2]

Prepaid Health Plans

More than 6.3 million Americans are now enrolled in health maintenance organization (HMO) plans. Patterned after the successful corporate health plan sponsored by Kaiser Industries, HMOs provide all their members' health care for a fixed, predetermined fee. Because HMOs can effectively reduce hospitalization rates for their members below the level of the general U.S. population, they present a competitive problem for hospitals.[3]

Changing Regulatory Environment

As public concern over the high costs of health care mounts, the hospital industry is rapidly emerging as one of the country's most heavily regulated: in 1976, New York hospitals alone spent more than $1 billion coping with government regulation.[4] While much of this regulation has had little or no impact in reducing health care costs, some regulatory policies have enormously complicated the life of the hospital manager.[5]

1. *Certificate of need.* Since 1964, 46 states have enacted certificate of need laws that require health facilities to obtain approval from state health departments before proceeding with building programs. With the enactment of the National Health Planning and Resource Development Act of 1974, the federal government threw its weight behind these state laws and devoted itself to restricting further growth in hospitals and reducing excess bed capacity (estimated at between 68,000 and 83,000 beds).[6]

In late May, the Carter administration accelerated these efforts by proposing that no federal funding, whether direct (through grants) or indirect (through tax exemptions for hospital beds), be provided for projects in "overbedded" areas.

These restrictions have created incentives for hospital managers to compete more aggressively with neighboring facilities. The 1977 National Guidelines for Health Planning set a target occupancy rate of 80% for all nonfederal, acute care hospitals in the United States (though many states use a target of 85% or 90%). Under continued cost pressures, states may deny hospitals permission to renovate, replace, or equip themselves unless they meet occupancy standards. Hospitals that do not meet occupancy standards would then have difficulty keeping up with changes in medical technology, altering their mix of services, and recruiting or retaining medical staffs.

2. *Health manpower policy.* During the 1960s, Congress instituted loan programs for students pursuing health careers and grant programs for medical, dental, and other health profession schools to increase student enrollment. But federal policymakers in the Department of Health and Human Services (HHS)—formerly Health, Education, and Welfare (HEW)—and the Office of Management and Budget are now convinced that the demand for physician services is virtually limitless and increases proportionately to the supply of physicians.[7] Accordingly, they believe that there are too many physicians and that they are maldistributed by specialty and geographic area. Based largely on this thinking, the Carter administration proposed in its fiscal year 1980 budget to discontinue capitation grants to medical, dental, and other health profession schools.

Also, in the Health Professions Educational Assistance Act of 1976, Congress restricted sharply the further entry into the United States of foreign-trained physicians who come for residency training and who, as a rule, remain to practice here.

Reductions in the total number of new physicians will present managers of hospitals in the rural Midwest, West, and South and some inner-city areas—which have very low ratios of physicians to population—with problems in attracting staff if their share of the physician market remains constant. Efforts of these institutions to substitute nurses and other allied health professionals for the lost foreign-trained physicians are likely to founder in an increasingly tight nursing and paraprofessional marketplace.

3. *Federal Trade Commission.* While Congress and HHS want to cap the growth in physician supply, the FTC has conducted an investigation to determine whether the medical profession's control over medical school accreditation constitutes a "conspiracy in restraint of trade," apparently believing that *more* physicians would mean *lower* health care costs.

Under the theory that increased advertising would encourage price competition among physicians and reduce the costs, the FTC also acted in October 1979 to lift medical society restrictions on physician advertising. This explicitly countered HHS's prohibition against institutional providers—such as hospitals, nursing homes, and home health care agencies under the medicare program—engaging in advertising and other marketing practices that might artificially stimulate use of their services.

4. *Cost containment.* The Carter administration's frontal attack on rising hospital costs was blunted last fall by a decisive defeat in the House of Representatives. If passed, the Carter bill would have regulated hospital revenue increases *per admission* without simultaneously capping hospital admissions. This regulation could create heightened competition for patients who would not have entered the health care system otherwise, unintentionally *increasing* overall health outlays.

In a regulatory environment as confused as the present health policy arena appears to be, the consequences of regulatory strategies often have an effect exactly opposite to that intended.

Regulatory approaches to hospital cost containment have, perhaps unwittingly, focused too much managerial attention on increasing or maintaining levels of hospital use and market share. By making certificate of need and rate review decisions contingent on those levels, overall health outlays may actually increase. Regulatory pressures have intensified to the point where some health care executives argue that takeover of the industry by large health corporations is inevitable.[8] Ultimately, the problem of hospital costs may be solved by substitution rather than by capping or other direct regulatory action.

The message to hospital managers is unambiguous: analyze and adapt to the changing health care markets or face financial difficulties or absorption. Now let us look at some strategies for dealing with the changes.

Strategic Response to the New Environment

Many of the strategies hospital managers can use to confront the new environment are easily recognizable as those corporations use for protecting an enterprise's position in a maturing market. But these strategies represent a departure from conventional methods of hospital management. They include:

1 Compete aggressively for physicians.
2 Diversify out of acute inpatient care into a broader mix of medical services.
3 Develop captive distribution systems to control patient flow.
4 Promote the institution's services.

In what follows I discuss these strategies as well as some emerging new forms of organizational structure that may also represent creative responses to the new competitive environment.

Compete for Physicians

Since the key to hospital use is an active, committed medical staff, recruiting and retaining physicians are the most important marketing issues facing hospital managers. Because it frequently involves commitments to program changes or acquisition of facilities or equipment, physician recruitment is expensive. Administrators may have to guarantee compensation regardless of direct productivity—for example, to physicians beginning their practices. In some academic health centers, the cost of a single recruitment (a department chairperson or service chief) may exceed $10 million. To attract physicians to more conventional hospital settings, administrators may have to purchase new equipment, hire nursing staff, construct or finance physicians' office buildings, provide parking facilities convenient to the hospital, pay for recreational facilities, or offer financial assistance in purchasing homes.

Hospitals are often affiliated with medical schools, many of which have special appointments and positions (e.g., clinical professorships) that are given to physicians in the community who are not full members of the medical school faculty but who may participate in teaching. Such affiliations give hospitals prestige in the community, a place to refer complex medical cases, and preferential access to the residents and medical students who may rotate through the hospitals as part of their training.

Many hospitals have developed medical education programs at the post-MD level to provide a captive market of potential recruits to the medical staff. By establishing residency programs, with or without medical school affiliation, hospitals secure licensed physicians who are training in a medical specialty. Major efforts are made•to encourage those who are completing their training at the hospital to practice there later.

Some larger hospitals in Chicago and elsewhere now offer financial, legal, and other kinds of assistance in setting up medical practices to graduates of their residency programs who offer some assurance they will remain linked to the hospital. Because a stable patient population generates a predictable annual amount of fee income and hospital revenue, a medical practice is much like an annuity. Further, as patients grow older, their demand for health services obviously increases. Practices can actually be bought and sold by physicians who move into exclusively administrative activities or who retire or move away.

The federal government is increasingly interested in encouraging the growth of residency programs in primary-care specialties such as pediatrics, family practice, obstetrics, and gynecology. Because physicians trained in these specialties must depend heavily on consultation from colleagues on the medical staff, they are doubly attractive to the hospital administrator. Patients requiring surgery or complex diagnostic procedures are referred to others on the medical staff—cardiologists, neurologists, neurosurgeons, and so forth—thus ensuring a flow of patients to these specialists.

Recruiting strategies for hospital-based physicians, such as pathologists, radiologists, and anesthesiologists, often focus on sharing profits on a volume basis from the medical diagnoses and tests they perform, which tend to be profitable for the hospital. Federal policymakers have cited this practice as encouraging unnecessary tests or procedures, however, and Congress is considering outlawing it.

In an increasingly litigious environment, it is not surprising that some physicians themselves are beginning to view hospital privileges as a property right that cannot be abridged without due legal process. Accordingly, the ability of the administrator or chief of medical staff to terminate staff members who do not use the hospital actively or who do not meet ethical or other professional standards may be compromised, making it essential that recruitment efforts yield quality recruits.

The growth in aggregate supply of physicians predicted between now and 1990 may help tip the economic power balance back into the hands of the hospital manager. However, even though many areas of the country—including rural and inner-city areas—will probably continue to have serious difficulty recruiting medical staff, local conditions of over-supply will present hospital managers with another problem. Medical staffs may close ranks and refuse to grant privileges to young physicians moving into a community. This may create further litigation and affect a hospital's vitality and use of its services. In Illinois, the age (i.e., the youth) of the medical staff is a key variable in determining whether hospitals can finance long-term debt for capital projects and is considered an indicator of the overall health of the hospital.

Diversify into New Services

Because inpatient hospitalization costs have escalated drastically, the search for substitute methods of rendering care will intensify. Inpatient care will be increasingly rationed, whether through overt action by the insurance industry or the government in altering health care reimbursement policies or through demands by consumers. Hospital managers can confront this problem by diversifying the services they offer to patients.

Outpatient Care. Because much prehospital care is rendered in physicians' offices, most hospitals do not assume corporate responsibility for it. The hospital's "feeder" or distribution system includes all the office practices of physicians on the medical staff.

For many teaching hospitals, and for larger hospitals that have a mixture of volunteer and full-time salaried medical staff, a portion of prehospital care is rendered in captive outpatient facilities operated by the hospital, such as hospital-based clinics or emergency rooms. At the University of Chicago, which has a full-time salaried medical staff, the hospitals and clinics deliver more than 220,000 outpatient and 80,000 emergency room visits annually. These two systems account for over 95% of hospital admissions.

Captive, hospital-based outpatient facilities, however, have significant problems. Because the current federal reimbursement regulations for Medicaid and Medicare authorize payment for whichever is *lower,* cost or charges, and because full hospital overhead must be allocated to outpatient cost centers if *cost* is used as the basis for reimbursement, the cost of outpatient care in hospitals has soared in tandem with that of inpatient care. Currently, many hospital-based outpatient clinics are increasingly unable to compete with office practices in urban areas. Because many health insurance plans provide incomplete coverage for outpatient care or large deductibles, outpatient care tends to accumulate significant bad debt, and hospitals lose money on it.

The incentives to segregate outpatient activity in office buildings adjacent to the hospital are obvious. Medical services in these facilities are not only convenient to the hospital but occur outside the hospital's cost base. Patient fees can compete with those of other providers of outpatient facilities that are linked to the hospital by common medical staff under a separate corporate umbrella.

Excellent examples of both strategies as part of an institution's master plan can be found at Rush-Presbyterian-St. Luke's Hospital and Medical Center in Chicago. Rush constructed offices that house more than 200 physicians adjacent to the hospital. Though Rush owns the building, it leases it to the group practices; the lease costs are part of the physicians' fees. The private practices of many of its voluntary staff are carried out in the building, which has its own ancillary laboratory and radiology facilities, as well as facilities for outpatient surgery.

Rush also developed a network of community-based outpatient facilities under separate incorporation from the parent hospital. The Mile Square Health Center, Inc., named for the mile square area of inner city around the hospital, delivers 125,000 visits of care annually. The center is affiliated with the Medical College at Rush, which provides academic appointments and teaching opportunities for the center's salaried medical staff.

Having put these two structures in place, Rush closed its hospital-based outpatient department, relying on these two captive but corporately independent distribution systems, its emergency room, and extensive referrals from physicians in the Chicago area to fill its hospital. One drawback to these strategies is that, under cost reimbursement, closing an outpatient department means inpatient overhead costs cannot be spread over as many cost centers, and they inflate artificially.

Outpatient Surgery.   Another major development in outpatient care is the growing acceptance of outpatient, or day, surgery. As many as 20% to 40% of all surgical procedures can be performed this way, saving one to three days of high-cost hospitalization.[9] And many patients prefer day surgery because it minimizes time away from work and is more convenient than a longer hospital stay.

Both hospitals and private physicians have established day surgery programs that provide all the logistical support for surgery. Patients are prepared in their physicians' offices in advance of the visit. They come in the morning for surgery, spend the day recuperating in the facility—frequently with friends or family present—and go home in the evening.

Shifts within the hospital to day surgery programs may radically reduce a hospital's inpatient use. Hospitals with less than peak surgical bed occupancy or without a waiting line for elective surgical procedures should proceed with extreme caution in developing such programs. In some cases, however, the institution may not have a choice. For example, the creation of an outpatient surgical program in a physician's office across the street from the Good Samaritan Hospital of Phoenix forced the hospital to develop a similar program.

It is likely that regulators and insurers will accelerate the rapid development of such programs by refusing to reimburse hospitals for inpatient costs for surgical procedures that could be performed on an outpatient basis. Ultimately, hospitals may have no choice but to create their own day surgery programs to preserve their shares of the surgical market.

Freestanding Emergency Rooms.   Yet another significant innovation in health care delivery could threaten a key feeder system for many hospitals—the hospital emergency room, which typically provides from 15% to 30% of hospital admissions. Many patients who are not acutely ill but who have no physician or other means of getting care use emergency rooms. In many underserved areas, as many as two-thirds of the visits may be nonemergency cases. Emergency rooms are the health system's current answer to the need for episodic health care.

For reasons of both high cost and potential substitution, hospital emergency rooms are vulnerable to replacement by innovative alternative methods such as the freestanding emergency room. According to a study conducted for the Robert Wood Johnson Foundation, 55 such facilities existed in the United States in late 1978.[10] They can provide most of the services of a hospital-based emergency room except for full-scale surgery that requires general anesthesia. Most of them have their own laboratory and radiology facilities, though some contract with others for these services if rapid turnaround on tests is available nearby. They bill as if they were either emergency rooms (if corporately linked to a hospital) or doctors' offices, usually at half or less of the prevailing emergency room visit charge.

In the Chicago area, a fresh entry into this market is the brainchild of a former partner of Arthur Young & Company, Dr. Bruce Flashner. Its name, the Doctor's Emergency Officenter, expresses cogently its hybrid private physician/emergency room nature. It is, however, reimbursed by Blue Shield as a doctor's office. (Ironically, Blue Shield refuses to reimburse the facility for itemized charges for patient care, despite the fact that the total charges per patient are lower than a typical physician's fee for the same type of care, which it does reimburse. But it reimburses all lump-sum expenses as long as they are called "professional fees.")

The Officenter operates on a no-appointment basis and, six months after opening, receives an average of 50 visits a day. Dr. Flashner encountered difficulties with anxious physicians in the Arlington Heights community, where the facility is located, until it became clear that he did not intend to build a practice through the center. Instead, its physicians return patients to their family doctors for continuing care or refer them to specialists for complex conditions. In addition to a single doctor per shift, the center has two paraprofessionals who are trained to handle billing, laboratory and radiology work, and other matters. The Officenter required almost no initial capital outlay; facility and equipment were leased, and the capital cost of the leases was less than $100,000.

Bridging the gap between the expensive, frequently impersonal hospital emergency room and the private physician's office, facilities like this represent a competitive threat to both. Hospitals that are competing for patients will offer preferential admitting privileges for patients coming from them. It may actually be easier to be admitted through a freestanding facility than through the hospital's own emergency room.

In Phoenix, the Samaritan Health Service, one of the nation's most successful voluntary multihospital systems, established a captive freestanding emergency facility in the far eastern suburbs. The facility feeds the easternmost satellite hospital in the Samaritan group with emergency cases requiring hospitalization. It was established in a developing area to provide Samaritan with a medical presence that could form the nucleus of a hospital if population growth were to continue at the current rate. Captive facilities give the hospital control over the geographic origins of patients coming into its facility and a low-cost method of entering new or developing markets.

Health Maintenance Organizations. Freestanding emergency rooms occupy one end of a continuum of medical treatment that runs from acute episodic care to continuing primary care. The HMO—of which there are approximately 165 in the United States—occupies the other end.[11] HMOs provide complete health care to a stable population of enrolled patients for a fixed arrival fee. They are integrated vertically, offering preventive and acute care, outpatient and inpatient care.

Paul M. Ellwood, Jr., the executive director of Interstudy of Minneapolis and one of the main figures in the development of HMOs, and Michael E. Herbert described HMOs' underlying principles as risk sharing and enrollment of consumers.[12] The risk-sharing feature means that to the HMO, sickness is a cost. Since HMOs assume the cost of treating illness, they and their patients share an economic incentive to minimize it. The enrollment procedure ensures that the organization, not consumers or doctors, will control the resource allocation process required to meet the health care needs of its members.

The HMOs embody a mechanism and incentives to ration expensive services such as inpatient care. This rationing can reduce levels of use of hospital services from 10% to 40% below those of traditional fee-for-service treatment.

Health maintenance organizations reduce health costs through programs, including an initial screening and periodic physical examinations, to prevent or avoid illness. Just as the HMO is a competitive threat to conventional office practice, it is a threat to the hospital, since its interests run directly counter to the hospital manager's imperative to maintain his or her level of use.

A few progressive larger hospitals, such as Rush-Presbyterian-St. Luke's Hospital and Medical Center and Michael Reese Hospital and Medical Center in Chicago, have established HMOs based at their institutions. The Reese HMO grew out of demands by hospital labor unions for a more progressive health care system. While the HMO (which has almost 15,000 members) uses Reese for its hospitalization, the relatively expensive 1,000-bed teaching hospital setting has created major economic incentives for the HMO to hospitalize patients for routine illness in less expensive community-based institutions.

If a captive HMO is to successfully meet its economic objectives and minimize its fee levels, powerful incentives to lessen reliance on the parent hospital are created. The inherent conflict of interest for the hospital has caused HHS to discourage captive HMOs through its regulations governing federal subsidies. The development of an HMO is a risky undertaking that places a premium on accurate estimates of the market and on rates of enrollment. Achieving federal accreditation is a major bureaucratic hurdle. But certification opens up access to federal funding and market opportunities (e.g., federal requirements that qualified HMOs be listed as employee-benefit alternatives).

While the HMO holds tremendous promise for reducing health care costs in an open market, it is a questionable growth strategy for the hospital manager. Ellwood and Herbert's estimate—that an HMO must enroll 100,000 people before it can generate a high enough level of use to support a 200-bed hospital—is still reasonable. The size of the necessary enrollment base suggests that HMOs may not be an effective way to increase or sustain levels of hospital use.[13]

Screening Programs. Many hospitals now offer screening programs through schools and employers or to the general community for a variety of illnesses—such as diabetes, cancer, glaucoma, hypertension, and vision and hearing deficiencies—that may introduce new patients to their systems. These programs, staffed by physicians or by a combination of physicians and nurses, can be located in schools, shopping centers, or in the hospitals themselves. The latter approach is useful for exposing the public to new facilities or programs. Sponsorship of screening programs also gives hospitals access to public service announcements—in effect, free advertising of their services.

Develop Distribution Systems

Many hospitals have gone further than diversifying their mix of services to ensure a more effective distribution system and have developed transportation services to bring in patients. One of the most elaborate of these serves the University of Iowa Hospitals and Clinics, a 1,100-bed facility in Iowa City, a town of approximately 60,000 people. To survive, the hospital cannot rely on patients from Iowa City alone but must reach out to the entire state and region. The hospitals developed a fleet of Checker limousines that can be dispatched from Iowa City to any location in the state to bring patients to the hospital.

This service has made it more convenient for Iowa's physicians to use the tertiary facilities (open-heart surgery, cancer therapy, kidney transplant, and so forth) at the University of Iowa, which is the tertiary medical center for the state. In addition, the hospitals own and operate an emergency helicopter service that is linked to the trauma center, which can dispatch a helicopter and put paramedical personnel into remote accident sites within minutes.

Another institution that has made a considerable investment in transportation systems is the Samaritan Health Service of Phoenix. Samaritan operates a fixed-wing air ambulance that brings patients in from the isolated regions of northern Arizona and New Mexico. The plane is equipped with life-support equipment and carries a critical care nurse in radio contact with the hospital so he or she can consult about and monitor the patient's condition. In addition, Samaritan operates several mobile intensive care vans that transport patients requiring sophisticated diagnostic procedures from the service's community-based facilities to Good Samaritan Hospital in central Phoenix. Patients are then sent back to their own hospitals with the test results. This system has increased the use of Good Samaritan's CAT (computerized axial tomographic) scanner as well as other complex diagnostic equipment. Though the mobile vans are operated at a small net subsidy by the hospital, the charges from the increased use of ancillary hospital services more than cover the cost of operation.

Hospitals contemplating development of transportation services may expose themseslves to common carrier regulation and require special licenses from city agencies. They may also face some political problems from taxi and ambulance companies, which have considerable leeway in where they take a critically ill patient and may retaliate. For these reasons, Samaritan explicitly links its mobile vans to its network on facilities and does not pick up patients at other hospitals or at their homes. Nevertheless, diversification into transportation services is an imaginative approach to escaping the geographic constraints of a physical plant and holds much promise.

Promotion of Services

In August 1977, when the American Hospital Association issued standards for responsible use of advertising by hospitals, the hospital industry entered a new era. The guidelines state:

> . . . Advertising may be looked upon as an investment that provides significant returns in community support of hospitals and knowledge of better health care opportunities. Advertising that has as its goal a better informed public or improved patient care is always acceptable—if it is consistent with acceptable content as outlined in these guidelines.[14]

The guidelines themselves warn against political advertising, comparative references to other institutions, claims for performance, or promotion of individual physicians. While these guidelines discourage some of the more agressive promotional strategies used in private industry, they do give hospitals considerable latitude in promoting their services.

Many of the larger institutions in the Chicago area have placed in the Sunday *Chicago Tribune* expensive, full-color supplements that stress the range and depth of their services. The supplements are supposed to either highlight new services and new facilities or enhance the institution's community image. To avoid difficulties with the federal government over the reimbursement of these costs under Medicare and Medicaid, hospital administrators financed their promotional efforts through voluntary contributions from affiliated charitable foundations.

Michael Reese Hospital and Medical Center pursued another, better-focused promotional strategy. Reese arranged with utility and insurance companies in Chicago to include health education brochures developed by the hospital in their billings and other mailings. The brochures were low-key, tasteful, and humorous, and focused on such specific medical problems as stress, hypertension, smoking, and lack of physical fitness.

Sometimes including self-rating scales to interest readers, as well as suggestions about when it might be advisable to seek medical attention, the brochures usually referred to the appropriate clinical department one should visit at the hospital but stopped considerably short of directly soliciting business.

Both these promotional strategies are, nonetheless, indirect methods of increasing levels of hospital use. Though they may generate patient inquiries, promotional campaigns will never replace the physician as the principal pathway to the hospital's services. It is exceptionally difficult to measure the impact of broadly based promotions on levels of use, and such approaches may not be the most cost-effective way of reaching specific markets. However, the less tangible benefits of assisting in health education and community service should not be overlooked in a regulatory climate that is generally hostile to institutional providers.

A more focused promotional strategy has recently been employed by Northwestern Memorial Hospital in Chicago. It has developed a direct patient inquiry line staffed by a registered nurse who responds to patient complaints about medical problems and directs patients to medical specialists on Northwestern's staff. The inquirers are sent literature that promotes the specialty sections of the medical staff and lists the members of the section and their office telephone numbers. Although this direct marketing of tertiary services may bring in more patients to see specialty physicians, it does have the drawback of bypassing the family physician who generally mediates between the patient and specialists in complex medical matters.

To encourage physicians to refer patients to the specialty medical staff, a critical problem in teaching hospitals, the University of Chicago is developing an incoming WATS line that area physicians can use to contact the university's specialists. A detailed directory of the medical specialties represented on the medical staff and the disease categories where the staff is particularly strong will be distributed through the university-organized, continuing medical education programs conducted in community hospitals. In all of these efforts, the promotional appeal is targeted to reach the decision makers who govern the flow of patients into the health care system.

A more controversial approach to advertising hospital services attracted national attention in 1977. Because neither patients nor physicans choose to use hospitals during weekends if they can avoid it, many hospitals have wide swings in their levels of use. In television, radio, and local newspaper advertising, Sunrise Hospital of Las Vegas offered a 5.25% cash rebate to patients who entered the hospital on Friday or Saturday. The program produced more than a 30% increase in admissions during the period. When insurance companies began deducting the 5.25% from their reimbursement of the hospital, however, Sunrise withdrew the rebate promotion and instead advertised a contest—a Mediterranean cruise for two—for weekend patients. This approach drew a sharp rebuke from the secretary of HEW as an example of profligate hospital spending.[15]

The growing use of commercial advertising by health care facilities has attracted the attention of the federal government. In the spring of 1979, the Health Care Financing Administration of HEW reinforced earlier rulings in a letter to its "fiscal intermediaries," the corporations that process Medicare claims and audit providers of Medicare services. The clear intention of the regulations is to avoid underwriting an expense "which seeks to increase patient utilization of the providers' facilities," thereby increasing the costs of Medicare and Medicaid programs.[16] The regulations are so rigorous they even forbid reimbursement for larger typeface listings in local telephone directories.

Hospitals are newcomers to the advertising world. Yet as competitive pressures intensify, managers are likely to use advertising ever more heavily as a marketing tool. Since most hospitals are small, it is unlikely that individual institutions will be able to support significant advertising expenses, and so they should concentrate on the most effective use of their limited funds. Promotional approaches that introduce new services or promote specific existing services are likely to prove the most fruitful. The national proprietary hospital chains will probably begin to advertise their hospitals nationally to establish product differentiation in the mass market.

Structural Innovation

Seven years ago, Ellwood and Herbert characterized the health care industry as a poorly organized collection of 150,000 separate units of production that lacked both horizontal and vertical integration. Many of the approaches I have suggested advocate strategies of vertical integration through diversification into nonacute health care and of capturing and controlling more of the hospital's patient flow. At the same time, however, major changes are taking place in the hospital industry itself.

Horizontal integration is occurring at an explosive pace. The number of voluntary, not-for-profit hospitals in the United States has remained stable, while large proprietary hospital chains have acquired more isolated local institutions by direct ownership or through management contracts. Since 1975, the number of hospitals managed or owned by chains has increased from 469 to 765. The management and financial controls installed by the chains can, at least in the first few years, significantly reduce the rates of increase in those hospitals' costs, partly because the acquired institutions are generally smaller community-based hospitals and are relatively simple to manage. Because the financial and staffing controls in hospitals are often weak, they can be strengthened through systems imposed by the chain.

While the initial period of highly profitable growth of the proprietary chains has demonstrated that management of smaller institutions can be standardized and that tighter controls can reduce costs and improve net revenues, it remains to be seen how effectively the chains can cope with the competitive pressures I have discussed. There is no *national* market for health services. The chains are acquiring hospitals over a wide area, but they are not usually linked together clinically at the local level.

If they are to preserve their market shares in local communities, the chains will have to develop marketing expertise and performance standards to match their successes in financial management. The chains can minimize pressures (at the present time) by selling quickly unprofitable or troubled institutions, but this may change when they have saturated the market and must still generate profits from an enlarged base. If competing chains expand to the point of saturating local or regional markets, they may have to diversify through direct ownership or franchises into ambulatory health services to protect their inpatient volume against competition from allied local hospitals.

Many of the emerging forms of health care delivery are eminently adaptable to the standardization of financial and management controls and of facilities employed in franchise arrangements. The parent company could dictate terms of patient referral or follow-up to ensure that any inpatients coming from the outpatient system flowed to hospitals it owned. Whether the chains will invest the resources needed to take this next step remains to be seen.

At the same time, new forms of health care organization are merging that are deeper vertically and more complex structurally than the national chains; they can, if properly organized, exercise control over a regional health care market. Over a decade ago, under the leadership of Dr. James Campbell, a forceful, articulate health care entrepreneur, Rush-Presbyterian-St. Luke's Hospital and Medical Center embarked on an ambitious organization strategy like that of a multidivisional corporation. Located in an inner-city area on the West Side of Chicago adjacent to the University of Illinois Medical Center and Cook County Hospital, the core hospital contains approximately 840 beds.

The Campbell strategy stratifies the health care system where primary- and secondary-level health resources are organized around the tertiary-care teaching hospitals in a metropolitan area. Dr. Campbell felt that through multi-institutional agreements, Rush should own, control, or link up with sufficient health resources to meet the needs of 1.5 million people. The organization strategy contains the following elements:

1.   *Backward integration into supply of health manpower.*   In 1969, Dr. Campbell reactivated the long-dormant Rush Medical College, formerly linked to the University of Chicago. Using state and federal aid to health education programs as building blocks, he built the medical school into a university for the health sciences with three divisions—medicine, nursing, and allied health. By 1979, the medical school had an enrollment of 497 students. In addition, at the post-MD level, 341 MDs are engaged in medical education. Of this group, approximately 40% are retained within the Rush system when their training ends.

The students in the nursing and the allied health profession programs also form a substantial captive market of potential recruits into the Rush system. The prestige of academic programs, including substantial research activities, has helped Rush attract and retain a first-rate clinical faculty and recruit top-quality residents to its specialty training programs. The ability to grant academic appointments made it easier for Rush to affiliate with community-based institutions.

2.   *Vertical integration with community hospitals.*   Using the medical school as its base, Rush affiliated or associated with a network of 11 community-based hospitals in the Chicago area. The medical staffs of these institutions received faculty appointments in the Rush Medical College. The medical staff at these affiliated institutions have been encouraged to use the expensive tertiary services available at Rush and to refer patients requiring subspecialty consultation or care to the central Presbyterian-St. Luke's Hospital. As a result, Rush has a medical/surgical occupancy rate of 91% and a waiting list for elective surgery.

3.   *Diversification into ambulatory and chronic care.*   During the late 1960s, under separate incorporation, Rush launched two health care systems, the Mile Square Health Center (discussed earlier) and the Anchor Health Plan (an HMO). With a current enrollment of more than 32,000, the Anchor Health Plan uses the facilities of affiliated institutions as well as the central hospital to keep its costs down. Patients from the center may be hospitalized either at community-based facilities or at Rush. In 1976, Rush opened the 176-bed Johnston R. Bowman Geriatric Facility for Chronic Disease on its own campus. Although it was intended to care for older individuals who are undergoing lengthy recuperation from illness, it can also serve as a skilled nursing facility.

The resulting structure has effectively achieved Dr. Campbell's ambitious objective of providing health resources for the large population and a solvent, successful core hospital. As federal funds for medical education begin to level off, the clinical operations of the Rush system will be sufficiently strong to absorb an increasing share of the burden of financing health education.

The system is not without problems—relationships with neighboring and affiliated institutions have not always gone smoothly, and some of its operations have lost money—but the overall system is healthy. The Rush system represents a model of cooperative multi-institutional relationships that link health resources to ensure the survival of all the various parts. Because it does not own all the elements but rather works with them through cooperative planning, Rush is protected financially from major shifts in the market or from vulnerability of individual elements of the system.

What Is a Hospital?

More than 20 years ago, in "Marketing Myopia," Theodore Levitt argued that the price of a static definition of an organization's business may be its extinction.[17] This is nowhere more true than in the hospital industry today. After a postwar period of explosive growth in activity, aggregate employment, and economic power, it is confronting major changes that threaten its key inpatient services. Hospital costs have risen to the point where they are a national political issue, and regulatory and planning bodies have proliferated in an effort, as yet unsuccessful, to control them.

The challenge to hospital managers is to deliver new forms of health care. By diversifying beyond acute inpatient care into a broader mix of medical services, managers accomplish two things. First, if the activities take place under the same corporate umbrella, they generate revenue that does not depend directly on inpatient use of their facilities. And second, they build pathways that can ultimately bring in additional inpatients and open facilities to new patients.

Hospitals augment their principal source of patients—the network of office practices of their medical staffs—through their emergency rooms and through organized, hospital-based outpatient services. The expansion and diversification of outpatient services hold the key to a hospital's future financial solvency. In many cases, peculiarities of the hospital reimbursement system will dictate corporate separation of some outpatient services from the hospital proper. However, as long as there is central organization and direction, through administration or medical staff loyal to the hospital, the separate corporate entities can serve the same objectives.

The effort to capture some of the new forms of health care delivery is not free of risk. High overhead, problems of estimating patient volume and start-up costs and phasing, potential damage to existing hospital programs, and additional hiring of scarce physicians and managers all suggest that, at least initially, diversifying away from acute inpatient care will involve financial commitments and careful planning. It should be obvious, however, that the alternative to hospital control of these new health care forms is the net loss of patient volume, both outpatient and inpatient. The higher inpatient hospital costs rise, the riskier it is to keep the definition of a hospital's business as acute inpatient care.

Both vertical integration and horizontal combination are taking place in the structure of the health care system. It is possible that in 15 or 20 years, most hospital care in the United States will be controlled, directly or through multi-institutional planning, by a few dozen organizations. The not-for-profit, voluntary hospital will be significantly challenged by proprietary institutions that have demonstrated in their initial forays into the market that they can generate significant profits at reduced rates of cost escalation. Structural changes will eliminate duplication of services in many areas and result in multi-institutional planning where government regulation may not succeed. The consumer, who will find the hospital and other health care providers increasingly concerned with meeting consumer needs, will ultimately benefit the most.

Notes

1. Martin Feldstein, "The High Cost of Hospitals and What to Do About It," *The Public Interest,* Spring 1975, p. 40.

2. "Blue Cross Plans Experience Sharp 10 Year Decline in Hospital Utilization Rates," Blue Cross and Blue Shield Associations, January 18, 1980.

3. Walter McClure, "Reducing Excess Hospital Capacity," a report prepared for the Bureau of Health Planning and Resources Development, Department of Health, Education, and Welfare by Interstudy, Inc., October 1976, p. 22.

4. *Hospitals,* October 16, 1978, vol. 52, p. 17.

5. Regina Herzlinger, "Can We Control Health Care Costs?" *HBR* March-April 1978, p. 102.

6. McClure, p. 19.

7. See Uwe E. Reinhardt, *Physician Productivity and the Demand for Manpower* (Cambridge, Mass.: Ballinger, 1975) for a full explication of this theory.

8. Thomas Frist, Jr., in "Drug Research Reports" (*The Blue Sheet*), vol. 22, no. 36, pRN-3, May 16, 1979.

9. James E. Davis and Don E. Detmer, "The Ambulatory Surgical Unit," *Annals of Surgery,* vol. 175, no. 4, June 1972.

10. "Preliminary Survey of Freestanding Emergency Centers," (Silver Spring, Md.: Orkand Corporation, February 1979).

11. John Iglehart, "HMOs—An Idea Whose Time Has Come," *National Journal,* vol. 10, no. 8, February 28, 1978, p. 311.

12. Paul M. Ellwood, Jr. and Michael E. Herbert, "Health Care: Should Industry Buy It or Sell It?" *HBR* July-August 1973, p. 99.

13. Ellwood and Herbert, p. 107.

14. "Advertising by Hospitals—Guidelines" (Chicago: American Hospital Association, 1977).

15. "Unique Ad Strategy Increases Use of Sunrise Hospital on Weekends," *Federation of American Hospitals Review,* vol. 10, no. 3, June 1977, p. 47.

16. Health Care Financing Administration Intermediary Letter No. 79-20, "Costs Incurred for Patient Solicitation (Unallowable Cost of Advertising)" (Washington, D.C.: Department of Health, Education, and Welfare, May 1979).

17. *HBR* July-August 1960, reprinted as HBR Classic, September-October 1975, p. 26.

9

Gone Are the Cash Cows of Yesteryear

RAYMOND VERNON

Here is one note of optimism in the overwhelmingly negative chorus of criticism currently aimed at American industry. This author argues not only that critics rail against the wrong thing but also that their hue and cry helps obscure some of the real possibilities and opportunities U.S. companies still enjoy. By using their foreign subsidiaries as conduits, American businesses can obtain information on the latest competitive developments in product, process, and market. Then they can realistically begin to assess the needs and wants of the world market.

Suddenly, we are told, the great American juggernaut has run out of steam. No longer can the United States generate the supply of Edisons, Fords, and Salks who for a century or more had given the country its formidable worldwide technological lead. The United States is the newest victim of the English disease—too much government, too little incentive, too little commitment. American industry, which only yesterday could think of the world as its succulent oyster, must now respond to the mounting tide of competitors from newer, more energetic lands.

Those who worry that the United States is drifting downhill in its innovative or productive capacities base their case on more than surmise. They point to figures on the decline in the nation's output per worker, the number of patents issued to American inventors, and the amount spent on R&D. But those figures, studied in detail, convey a complicated and uncertain message. We cannot say that American workers have grown lazier over the past 10 years or that American engineers and scientists have lost their creative capabilities (see the ruled insert on the facing page). But U.S.

Published 1980.

companies *are* losing competitive ground. To reverse the trend, we must first understand why.

To that end, it helps to explore the origins of our vaunted role—dating back to the second half of the nineteenth century—as the world's leader in industrial technology. That role did not result from an unusual abundance of skills. Although the Americans of that period were relatively literate and skilled, so were the British, the French, and the Germans. Indeed, outstanding scientists and engineers were more commonly found in Europe than in the United States. Americans, however, had other advantages: cheap and abundant raw materials, a large internal market, and almost no governmental restraints on the pursuit of profits.

How Did It All Begin?

Only one fly contaminated the economic ointment of the American entrepreneurs. Because opportunities in the United States were so rich, labor was scarce; farming, lumbering, and mining drew off some of the available skilled labor, including immigrant carpenters and metalworkers who had made their way to America from Europe. America's businessmen therefore faced a tantalizing opportunity. With a market there for the taking, they had to find new production methods that could overcome both the scarcity and high cost of skilled workers in the United States.

Driven by the extraordinary challenge, proprietors of textile plants, iron foundries, glass factories, and machine shops produced such devices as sewing machines, glass-blowing machines, automatic woodworking and metalworking machines, and automatic railway signaling devices. Having broken the skilled labor bottleneck, they went on to develop and market a new generation of products, including the electric light, the telephone, the low-priced automobile, and the vacuum cleaner—all appropriate to the tastes of the richest mass market in the world.

Americans have not monopolized industrial innovations over the past century. But their innovations have differed from those of the Europeans in some important respects. In industrial goods, Europeans tended to stress innovation that would conserve capital and raw materials, such as the use of oxygen in blast furnaces and fuel injection in automobile motors. Americans tended to concentrate on labor-saving innovations and were profligate with energy and raw materials. In consumer goods, the United States ground out a stream of new products that could satisfy an apparently unlimited appetite for novelty and comfort. On the other hand, Europe (and later Japan) concentrated on smaller, cheaper, and more durable versions of the same dishwashers and television sets that had first been produced in the United States.

American innovations continued to exhibit their labor-saving, income-serving characteristics during the three decades following World War II (see

Exhibit 1.   Perceived Advantages of Innovations Introduced in the United States, Europe, and Japan, 1945–1974[a]

Perceived Advantage	United States		Europe Including Britain		Japan	
	No.	Percent	No.	Percent	No.	Percent
Labor saving	331	40.1	120	12.7	6	6.4
Material saving	175	21.2	444	46.9	32	34.1
Capital saving	58	7.0	104	11.0	7	7.4
Novel function	106	12.8	83	8.8	12	12.8
Safety	50	6.1	60	6.3	7	7.4
Other	106	12.8	135	14.3	30	31.9
	826	100.0	946	100.0	94	100.0

[a]Based on a sample of 1,916 innovations.

Source: Adapted from W.H. Davidson, ''Patterns of Factor-Saving Innovation in the Industrialized World,'' *European Economic Review,* vol. 8, 1976, p. 214.

Exhibit 1). Through the end of the 1960s, many American enterprises felt secure and well entrenched. Here and there, some industries like automobiles and steel evidenced a certain amount of uneasiness. But by and large, American companies were contentedly herding and milking their cash cows, convinced that they were the most innovative and efficient producers on the face of the earth.

Thinning the Herd

The 1970s began to obliterate features that had distinguished the United States from other industrialized countries. For one thing, European and Japanese income levels were rising rapidly and no longer trailed far behind those of the Americans. Accordingly, foreign consumers' demands in food, household goods, transportation, recreation, safety, and health drew abreast of those in the United States. These foreign markets were no longer small or fragmented, and with the strengthening of the European Community, they began to rival the United States in size and buying power.

Gone, too, were the differences in cost structures that had distinguished the United States from the other countries. Labor was almost as expensive in Europe as in the United States. Capital, thanks partly to the burgeoning Euromoney market, was plentiful on both sides of the Atlantic. And as Americans began to rely increasingly on imported raw materials, their historic advantage in the prices of such materials was also evaporating. Therefore, American business no longer had the unique advantage of operating in the environment of the future in its home markets. For once, it was obliged to start off even with its European and Japanese competitors.

Indeed, in one critical respect, the conditions of the 1970s gave the rivals of the United States an edge. Long-time trends in production costs were reversed: for once, raw materials and capital became more expensive all over the world, outdistancing increases in labor costs. Now European and Japanese innovations were in demand, with their emphasis on conserving capital, raw materials, and fuel. Italian oil burners designed for fuel economy found markets in American homes and factories; and the cast-aluminum engines of the Japanese and Europeans, designed to reduce overall automobile weight, found American markets as well.

Alas for America's cash cows. The size and productivity of the herd had largely depended on America's technological lead. With good luck and the advantages of the experience curve, American innovators had been able to ride the crest of growing world demand, profiting from a product well into its senescence. Now, however, the experience curve offers Americans little advantage; indeed, in some cases, the advantage lies with their rivals. So the cash cows, we can be reasonably sure, will be fewer and not quite so plump.

What of Our Calving Rates?

America is losing its competitive edge partly because it can no longer count on the advantages of an experience curve. But the deeper worry is that the country may also be suffering from a falling off in the ability of its scientists and engineers to innovate as well as in the willingness of its business community to underwrite those innovative efforts. For instance, a larger proportion of the total patents issued each year by the U.S. patent office goes to foreigners, and a smaller proportion of the patents issued by foreign patent offices goes to U.S. inventors. Moreover, R&D expenditures in the United States, calculated as a percentage of the country's GNP, have drifted downward over the past five years or more, whereas the same ratios for other key countries such as Germany and Japan have remained more or less constant for the same period.

Nevertheless, it is not at all clear that America's scientists and engineers have lost their creative abilities (see Appendix 1). True, we have been diverting some of our innovative efforts in various ways: our capacity to make better battle tanks is increasing more rapidly than our ability to make better automobiles. Moreover, some U.S. companies have transferred their efforts to other countries, with some U.S. drug companies moving their laboratories to England to escape FDA regulations and IBM shifting some of its development work to Europe to keep French ministers happy. But the most important difference in the position of U.S. companies is the increase in the relevance of the technological work being done in Europe and Japan.

Look to Foreign Markets

Americans need to practice what the Japanese and Europeans have been doing all along—that is, making both cheaper and more durable goods to appeal to the tastes of foreign markets. In fact, the emphasis on the amount and quality of U.S. R&D threatens to be a red herring, diverting attention from more important factors that could boost U.S. industrial performance. History shows repeatedly that countries with an oustanding record in science and technology are not necessarily those that shine in productivity and competitiveness.

The United Kingdom is the outstanding case in point. Surrounded by industrial decay, British scientists continue to perform remarkably. And although Japan's scientific and technological efforts have been increasing, these efforts are still not very impressive when measured by normal quantitative yardsticks.

Clearly, the United Kingdom does not use effectively all the information it generates, while Japan manages to apply a lot of the world's information which it had no hand in generating. A good example of Japan's integrative capability is the Nikon camera. Nikon has absorbed technology from all over the world: it uses—imaginatively and well—shutter electronics developed by a Minneapolis company and a single lens reflex mechanism copied from the Germans.

In addition, we must consider that about half the world's present industrial output is generated by MNCs with widespread productive facilities. Accordingly, the flashes of genius produced by an engineer in Morristown, New Jersey could show up on an assembly line in Jakarta as readily as in nearby Newark. By the same token, the ideas first expressed in a laboratory in Fontainebleau can swiftly be brought across the Atlantic provided, of course, that American business has both the antennas to learn about those ideas and the wit to recognize their value.

Therein lie the basic lessons: no longer can we either suppose that the innovations of other countries are irrelevant to American needs or expect that American innovations will hold a lead for any length of time over foreign competition. The biggest challenge for U.S. business is to create a scanning capability to survey the advances taking place in other countries and a managerial capability to incorporate those advances wherever they are relevant to our needs.

Scanning Our Neighbors' Pastures

A visitor from a distant planet observing the great network of U.S. subsidiaries in foreign lands might readily assume that Americans already had a highly developed capability for scanning their foreign markets. These subsidiaries number in the thousands, carry millions of employees on their payrolls, and account for a substantial proportion of the profits of their

American parents. No other country's overseas contingent amounts to more than a fraction of America's establishment.

There are signs, however, that these networks are wired mostly for one-way transmission—the center issues commands, but the periphery has trouble transmitting unsolicited data back to the center. Most U.S.-owned subsidiaries operating abroad manufacture a range of products conceived in Toledo or Kankakee. The main task of the subsidiaries is to convince the local populace that these products are exactly what it needs.

Here and there, to be sure, U.S.-owned subsidiaries have adapted successfully to the foreign markets in which they operate. The special skills and knowledge of such subsidiaries, however, are rarely allowed to penetrate the main network of the company. Each of America's big three automobile companies, for example, contains in its network at least one European subsidiary that has long mastered the technology of small-car construction. But Detroit has been remarkably slow to absorb those hard-won skills.

Why Not Listen?

Several factors explain the American propensity for one-way transmission over its multinational networks. Most important, these subsidiaries were created during a period in which U.S.-based companies characteristically enjoyed a technological lead over their competitors, generating and selling products that would represent the market of the future. As long as U.S. companies were secure in their innovative leads, there was no great need to use foreign subsidiaries as listening posts.

A second factor has been the premature obliteration of international divisions in many U.S. companies. As the foreign interests of American companies grew and flourished in the postwar period, the international divisions were often the star performers. But their success was eventually their undoing. By the middle 1960s, one American company after another reorganized itself to acknowledge the increased importance of its foreign business. According to one study undertaken in the early 1970s, the typical pattern consisted of abolishing the international division and setting up a series of so-called global product divisions to do the worrying about foreign markets.

In a recent study covering a group of 57 large U.S.-based multinationals, a colleague and I ran into some disturbing indications suggesting that some of these reorganizations may have been wildly counterproductive. A subset of our sample, organized along global product lines, exhibited rather striking characteristics. This group of companies seemed to show decidedly less interest in its foreign operations than those with an international division. Ten years after they had introduced their new products into the United States, the global product companies were only producing about 50% of those products in overseas locations. By contrast, the other companies in the sample were manufacturing more than 80% of their new products in foreign plants. At least in the case of this sample, the demise of the international division and the creation of a global product division suggested a sharp decline in interest in foreign operations.[1]

That result may not be as surprising as it first seems. When managers of domestic product divisions in the United States assume responsibility for global product divisions, the change in perspective may go no deeper than the title on their business cards. In training and outlook, they may still be as American as the Dallas Cowboys and apple pie. And unlike the international specialists that they have replaced, these managers may shrink from confronting unfamiliar problems, which can range anywhere from transacting business in pesos to wrestling with Belgian labor laws.

Some companies have recognized the danger in the newer organizational form and are returning to the old way of doing things. A prime example is Westinghouse, which went from an international to a global product division and back to an international division again.

Getting Out of Dairying

It may seem paradoxical at first that the country with the world's most extensive network of foreign manufacturing subsidiaries should be so parochial in its approach to foreign environments. But the explanation for the apparent contradiction is obvious: very few U.S. companies actively study or understand the particular needs of their foreign markets.

Most U.S. companies were swept into those markets either on the strength of their domestic industrial innovations or by the desire to best their American competitors. Many European and practically all Japanese managers, on the other hand, have always believed that they must export to survive. That difference in viewpoint has produced a change in attitude toward studying the surprises and uncertainties of foreign markets.

But American manufacturers no longer have a choice of entering foreign markets or leaving them alone. Whether they go to foreigners or not, foreigners will come to them—if not through imports then through the output of manufacturing subsidiaries located in the United States.

When citizen band radios suddenly grew popular in the United States, the Japanese built better, cheaper models and now have almost captured the leadership in that market. Volkswagen's little Pennsylvania plant cannot keep up with the demand. Honda will soon be a prime competitor on these shores. And Hitachi also plans to conquer the color television market from a new manufacturing base in the West. There is no longer a place where American business can hide.

Responding to the Challenge

That ineluctable fact is just beginning to dawn on many U.S. managers. Once it becomes crystal clear, American companies may also realize that they still operate from a position of considerable strength. Their foreign subsidiaries are grossly underused sources of such strength. U.S. business can turn those subsidiaries into two-way conduits, relaying back to the parent information about the latest developments in product, process, and market that bear on America's competitive position. And the challenge for headquarters is to learn how to listen, to incorporate the foreign advances that are succeeding, and to try to improve on those advances.

A few companies already are rising to the challenge. Du Pont is one enterprise adept at scanning its foreign subsidiaries and using the results in other parts of its organization. A miniplant in Argentina, for instance, generates process innovations that can be used for other small plants in Africa.

For most companies, developing the new capability will take some time, but it will be worth it. The efforts of Ford and General Motors to develop a "world car," for instance, reflect their realization that what other markets want may really matter. There are, to be sure, certain inherent dangers—for example, the so-called world model could turn out to be a sham effort to dress up the preferred U.S. product in another guise. Nevertheless, some part of the world product response will be worthwhile, especially if it represents a genuine effort to respond to the tastes and needs of other markets.

Another strength on which U.S. business can draw is its formidable scientific and technological establishment, still by all odds the world's largest and best. Some of its current efforts seem misdirected, and those developments that are on target are unlikely to provide the same degree of technological lead as in the past. But it remains a formidable resource, unmatched in total strength by any other country.

In the end, U.S. business will have to accept the fact that its competitive position in world markets has changed profoundly. After American businesses have carefully studied the world's markets, after they have absorbed and incorporated the best that can be gleaned from the rest of the world, that effort will do no more than keep them abreast of their nearest competitors.

At that point, the race will be won by those enterprises with the best price, the best quality, and the best after-sales service. This emphasis will be new to many Americans—accustomed to offering the newest, most unusual products and hoping to turn a few of them into the proverbial cash cow. Changes in attitude come slowly, but I am betting that many U.S. enterprises will be able to make the shift.

Notes

1. Raymond Vernon and W. H. Davidson, "Foreign Production of Technology-Intensive Product by U.S.-Based Multinational Enterprises," Working Paper 79–5, Harvard Business School, 1979.

Appendix 1

The Meaning of Productivity

What is so difficult about interpreting the meaning of *productivity*, especially in terms of output per worker?

Until about 10 years ago, industrial plants increased their measured otuput while destroying the recreational value of lakes, rivers, and open spaces, reducing the potability of water, and increasing the health hazards from befouled air. Should we have reduced measured output in the past to reflect those unmeasured uses of our natural resources? Should we regard U.S. workers as less productive if some of their efforts are now used to reduce these hitherto unmeasured costs?

Next there is the problem of defining a worker. Over the past decade, untrained youths and women of all ages have augmented the work force in unprecedented numbers. Does the entry of this untrained contingent mean that U.S. workers, as a whole, should be regarded as less productive?

Finally, there is the problem of combining different kinds of output in an overall measure that makes sense. The output of the United States increasingly takes the form of services, including contributions to health, safety, recreation, and education. Most of these services do not come in measurable units; many have no market price. We measure this part of U.S. output in ways that say little or nothing about the diligence or energy of U.S. workers.

Importance of Patents

If U.S. inventors are getting fewer patents relative to foreigners both at home and abroad, why is this not conclusive evidence of declining innovative capabilities? There are two main factors to consider:

1. Inventors take out patents in a foreign country only if they plan to exploit the invention there. Formerly, many of the European and Japanese innovations had little application to the U.S. market; meanwhile, U.S. innovations had strong promise in the markets of Europe and Japan. More recently, however, the characteristic lines of innovation stressed by the Europeans and Japanese have become more relevant to the U.S. market, while U.S. lines of innovation have lost some of their uniqueness in foreign markets. These trends could well be producing the observed shifts in patenting.

2. The number of patents issued is probably losing its value as an indicator of innovation. With a speeding up in technological change, some companies prefer to keep their innovations to themselves rather than publish their results. Moreover, the shift in innovation from creating novel products to developing cost-reducing products and processes also tends to reduce the innovators' willingness to patent. Another major change is the tendency to create innovations by putting together familiar systems in new configurations—for instance, attaching microchips and electric circuits to electric ovens or washing machines. Innovations of this sort, useful though they may be, are commonly not patentable.

10
The Marketing of "Unmentionables"

AUBREY WILSON and CHRISTOPHER WEST

As times change, the old taboos drop away and what was unthinkable becomes commonplace. Once it was considered unladylike to drink gin, unmanly to go to a psychiatrist, and unheard of to advocate abortion. Now all of these things in one place or another are accepted as almost normal, but others are not. How does a marketer promote his or her product, service, or concept when it is unmentionable, even though the marketer is convinced that ultimately the product has social value? The authors of this article do not try to define for the reader what is good or what is bad—that issue is forever debatable. They simply describe what is currently considered unmentionable and illustrate what marketing approaches and strategies would work for various degrees of unmentionability.

In the early 1920s Marie Stopes, the English scientist, was vilified for her open advocacy of birth control. Her writings were banned in many quarters, and public hostility toward her built up almost to the point where she was seen as the Antichrist. At that time, the subject of birth control was unmentionable, the products involved were unmentionable, and very soon Marie Stopes herself was unmentionable. In today's climate of opinion, to some the reaction may seem laughable—for example, to the millions of Asians who have been offered transistor radios, watches, calendars, and T-shirts as inducements to curb their procreative activities.

Was it only fifty-five years ago that Rhea High School in Dayton, Tennessee, was the scene of a legal battle where fundamentalists fought, at first successfully, the teaching of Darwin's evolutionary theory in state-supported schools? In the sense that Philip Kotler writes of marketing philosophies and concepts,[1] John Scopes was marketing the Darwinian theory, which was most certainly an unmentionable subject to some at that time.

Published 1981.

In 1963, charges were brought against the publishers of D.H. Lawrence's *Lady Chatterley's Lover* under Britain's ancient prurience laws. The judgment that the publication was not "calculated to deprave" unleased a tidal wave of literature far from the excellence of Lawrence's. Today, just 18 years later, it is difficult to understand the cause célèbre of a book with limited erotic content or the frisson of excitement that occurred among both the intellectuals and the pornography merchants who realized that the floodgates had been opened.

Samuel Britten, the eminent economics journalist, stated in an obituary of Fred Hirsch that "[he] was the first to advocate the devaluation of sterling, two years before it occurred and *at a time when the subject was supposed to be unmentionable.*"[2] Certainly today devaluation lacks the emotive power of fundamentalist teaching, but the change in opinion about it exemplifies that what is unmentionable at one moment in time can soon become commonplace and unremarkable.

Birth control, radical evolutionary theories, pornography, and exchange rate adjustments have nothing in common except that in various places and at various times they are or have been unmentionable subjects. In fact, such unmentionability unites them with a host of other products, services, and ideas. Weaponry, hard and soft drugs, hygiene products, prostitution, abnormal or even moderately unusual sexual practices, and sanitation services are all to varying extents disagreeable either to prospective customers or society at large. In extreme cases, these products, services, and ideas are unmentionable because their use cannot be openly advocated; more commonly, discussion of them is constrained in deference to the possibility that offense be given or legal penalties invoked.

The marketing process relies heavily on a flow of information on customer requirements, levels of satisfaction, image and credibility of suppliers, and availability and benefits of products, services, or ideas. Any degree of unmentionability, which inhibits the flow of information, therefore frustrates the marketing process. Although marketing departments may well be used to dealing with unwilling or unconvinced customers, the existence of unmentionability means that some of the marketers' most effective weapons be rendered ineffective or unusable.

Clearly, some unmentionables cannot or should not be marketed, while others should be demarketed. As we will show, however, a significant number of unmentionables derive their low status from the inhibitions of the purchaser or society at large rather than from the nature of the products, services, or ideas themselves. In such cases, any frustration of the marketing process may in the long run severely disadvantage customers, suppliers, and society.

Few would shed any tears over the inability of suppliers of hard drugs to benefit from the latest marketing techniques (not that they need them), but customers and public health inspectors of restaurants would certainly like to be assured that the suppliers of sanitation services are doing an effective job of marketing to restaurant operators. In this article, we consider the nature of unmentionability, its effect on the marketing process, and the means by which desirable unmentionables can be marketed.

What Are Unmentionables?

Unmentionables are products, services, or concepts that for reasons of delicacy, decency, morality, or even fear tend to elicit reactions of distaste, disgust, offense, or outrage when mentioned or when openly presented (see Exhibit 1).

We can discern two groups of unmentionables. First, some are unpalatable to society at large but are, nevertheless, tolerated—indeed often highly sought after—by a limited number of customers. Suppliers of socially condemned products (which include pornography and prostitution and could include armaments) generally have little need for the panoply of marketing techniques: availability, distribution, and pricing suffice. The success of these products amply illustrate how demand can create its own supply, often against substantial adversity.

The second group of unmentionables includes products or services that are by all standards acceptable to society but that the buyer is reluctant to acknowledge or discuss. The barriers in these instances have been raised by the buyers themselves, often despite manifest need. Purchases are made

Exhibit 1. Unmentionables

Category	Example
Products	Personal hygiene articles
	Birth control products
	Some "defense" products, e.g., napalm, germ and chemical warfare
	Drugs for terminal illnesses
Services	Abortion
	Vasectomy and sterilization
	Veneral disease treatment
	Treatment for mental illness
	Material preparation for death (funeral arrangements, wills)
	Artificial insemination
Concepts	Extreme political ideas
	Emotional preparation for death
	Unconventional sexual activities
	Racial or religious prejudice
	Terrorism

only when the need is sufficiently acute to overcome the threshold of embarrassment, disgust, or fear. Unmentionables in this category include a wide range of goods and services such as personal hygiene products, burial arrangements and other death-related services, and certain types of medical treatment or supplies. In these markets, it can be argued that marketers need to be hyperactive to overcome the resistance threshold and, in addition, must develop specialized techniques to circumvent the problems caused by unmentionability.

One can argue, however, that what constitutes an unmentionable product, service, or idea is a matter of personal opinion, and there can be little agreement within any random group about what is good or bad. After all— to take our first example of birth control—the marketing of any form of population control may represent the highest desideratum to the followers of the Club of Rome and the soup of the Devil's cauldron to the Roman clergy.

Furthermore, as our introductory examples show, the existence or degree of unmentionability can vary according to both place and time. As the principal character in *Teahouse of the August Moon* wisely states, "Pornography is a question of geography!" At the height of the miniskirt fashion in Europe and North America, its wearers would have rated and would still rate a prison sentence in Zambia. The child pornography openly sold in California and Sweden is strongly condemned in most other places. Changes over time can be even more striking. Not only do standards alter rapidly, as with Sweden's sexual mores, but they also oscillate. Note, for example, the swing of the morality pendulum from Cromwellian puritanism to racy Regency acceptance to the incredibly inhibited and straitlaced Victorian ethos that formed the mores under which many Western people still live.

That the pace of such change is accelerating is illustrated by recent interpretations of the strict Code of Practice imposed on commercial radio and television advertising by the Independent Broadcasting Authority, a British government body. Under clause 12 in the code, a blanket exclusion is possible under the rather imprecise statement: "No advertisement should offend against good taste or decency or be offensive to public feeling." Offensiveness is judged partly by common sense but also by the number of protests received.

Among the products and services the IBA banned for advertising were hemorrhoid cures, pregnancy testing, sanitary napkins, and contraceptives. In 1972, it permitted a limited trial of tampon advertising, which produced such a volume of complaints that tampons remained on the banned product list. After seven years, feeling the climate of public opinion had changed, the IBA permitted a six-month trial of sanitary napkin advertising in two distinct geographical areas in Britain. Using the criteria of both pre- and post-campaign research, as well as public protest, the IBA decided that results were inconclusive, although it did observe greater acceptability after six months.

A further six-month trial is currently being undertaken, again with pre-

and post-campaign public research and protest as criteria, but advertising conditions remain stringent. No showing of the actual unwrapped product, no screening before 9:00 P.M., no impression of professional advice and support, no celebrity testimonials, no potentially offensive words to be used (e.g., odor), no undermining of an individual's confidence in his or her personal hygiene standards, and of course no implications of sex are allowed.

If the example of toilet paper advertising is anything to go by, time may erode objections. Once banned, toilet paper advertisements—even displaying the product—are now frequently seen.

Interestingly enough, radio advertisements for sanitary protection products were always coupled with a public service announcement informing the public of its right to complain about advertisements and of how to do so. (IBA could not be accused of an unfair test!) Radio advertisements, however, do not generally bring in as many complaints as television advertisements when unmentionables are promoted. This may be because radio listening tends to be solitary, while watching television is more a family activity; it may also be proof of the adage "seeing is believing."

The status of contraceptives is different. If the current preliminary research into public attitudes finds that the majority would accept such advertising, a limited advertising campaign may be permitted. The present code requires that advertisements for contraceptives be through official or officially sponsored family planning centers and also include a reference to these as well as doctors as a source of advice. The advertisements may not promote branded products but may refer to contraceptive methods and devices provided it is clear that advice about alternatives is available and should be sought. Advertisements—provided that they do not condone premarital sex—may address unmarried as well as married people.

All these caveats, of course, are supposed to protect the public, who might find the subject of sanitary protection or contraception or hemorrhoids unmentionable *in public;* but what is unmentionable in this context is probably mentioned all the time in private. Thus the marketing of unmentionables has to contend with the dual standards of the individual, as well as an ambiguous public situation.

Desirable and Undesirable Unmentionables

If the list of unmentionables worthy of marketing consideration is long, the list of unmentionables that ought not to be promoted is infinitely longer. Many governments' relatively mild attempts to demarket smoking and the United Nations' intensive antislavery work are the polarities in demarketing campaigns. As Kotler says, "There are many products or services for which the demand may be judged unwholesome from the viewpoint of the customer's welfare, the public's welfare, or the supplier's welfare. Unwholesome demand is a state in which any positive level of demand is felt to be excessive because of undesirable qualities associated with the offering."[3] But by whose standards should unwholesomeness be judged? The majority of people have little problem judging what can be called "vice" products—alcohol, tobacoo, prostitution, and drugs (although even these have their advocates)—but there is no majority around such issues as birth control, abortion, and weapons.

Customs, religious and social mores, and personal inhibitions create many unmentionable products, services, or ideas for which it is obvious that, if the emotive issues and taboos could be removed, promotion and increased use would contribute to the public good. Nevertheless, ever since Jeremy Bentham wrote his philosophy of utilitarianism—"the greatest happiness of the greatest number"—every petty tyrant has used it as a juggernaut to suppress the minority view. The danger still exists that in the promotion of unmentionables, the views of the minority will be ridden over roughshod.

The philosophic arguments for and against censorship in any form and on the boundary between freedom and license make fascinating polemics. But they add nothing to the discussion of how (and if) to market or demarket unmentionables and rarely get beyond the argument of what is and what is not good or an unmentionable.

We take no attitude—indeed, in what follows we might be said to have adopted a totally amoral approach. Our essential concern is: How do you market or demarket the unmentionable? The decision as to what is good and bad must be left to the reader.

Strategic Considerations in Marketing Unmentionables

Before considering strategy and technique, we want to look first at the kind and extent of marketing appropriate for certain degrees of unmentionability. The wide range of unmentionable products, services, and ideas can be meaningfully classified on a matrix, the two axes of which relate to buyers' and society's attitudes (see Exhibit 2A).

On both axes the scale ranges from acceptance of the products, services, or ideas through indifference to rejection. Each square on the matrix therefore defines whether the need is for marketing or demarketing and the extent of the task to be undertaken. Demarketing is normally undertaken by public authorities or by government, but hyper- or extra-effort marketing is undertaken by either suppliers or public authorities, or by both.

Demarketing is required strongly in segment 1 and perhaps moderately in segment 2. Hypermarketing is called for in segments 4 and 5. The buyer's acceptance or rejection defined in segments 3, 6, and 7 is of no concern to society, and products in these categories are promoted actively in varying degrees by suppliers.

In segment 3, however, manufacturers may encourage the use of products, while public authorities and organizations simultaneously engage in their demarketing. Tobacco products, for example, would fall into segment 3; the advertisement on page 98 shows one side of the conflict, and any well-known cigarette ad illustrates the other. Exhibit 2B provides examples of unmentionables in each segment of the scale.

Exhibit 2A.   The Unmentionable Matrix

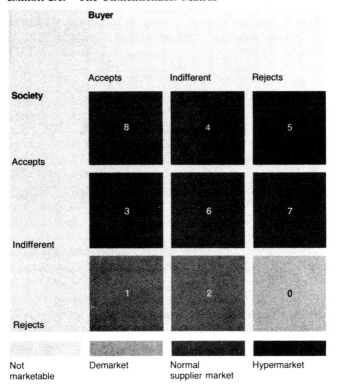

Exhibit 2B.   The Scale of Unmentionability

Segment	Classification	Examples
0	Not marketable	Murder for hire
1	Hard-core socially condemned	Hard drugs
2	Moderately socially condemned	Soft drugs
3	Moderate supplier marketing	Personal hygiene items
4	Active public encouragement	Venereal disease treatment
5	Major public promotion	Racial tolerance
6	Strong supplier marketing	Contraceptives
7	Hypersupplier marketing	Sanitary napkin disposal services
8	Normal marketing	Toothpaste

   Products in segment 8 represent normality, and segment 0 products would find few, if any, buyers.

   The intensity of marketing effort required is determined by the position of a product, service, or idea on the unmentionable matrix and the extent of its use (see Exhibit 3). The degree of demarketing required for hard drugs, backed up by stiff legally enforced penalties, is comparable to the positive marketing effort required to promote venereal disease treatment or high standards of personal hygiene.

   If the need or lack of it for a product, service, or idea is sufficiently great, when peaceful persuasion fails, the law will take over. But marketing should be able to cope on its own. Surely the system that can persuade American youth that its teeth are worth straightening and that countless useless products are worth chewing or sucking can also ensure that hygiene standards are worth adhering to.

   Back to Basics

To begin, we return to the first principles of marketing, which do not differentiate between what is being marketed or demarketed. That is, need

Exhibit 3.   Intensity of Marketing Effort

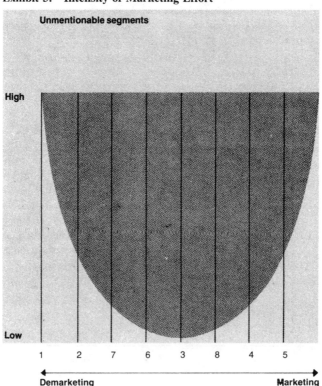

must be identified. In this context, "need" is two-dimensional and could either be a need for the product, service, or idea or a need to remove it from use.

Here the major difference occurs between mentionables and unmentionables: the buyer in a demarketing process is not the ultimate user of the product, service, or idea but is the person, organization, or society that seeks to remove it. Despite an organizational buying situation, neither the "buy phase" nor "buy class" concepts as developed by Patrick Robinson, Charles Farris, and Yoram Wind would seem to have any practical relevance.[4] In demarketing unmentionables, the interaction of buying and selling cannot be viewed in their somewhat mechanistic way, if only because of the extraordinarily high level of emotion that unmentionables generate—both for and against.

When an organization purchases a product or service, normally there would be at one end of the continuum the recognition of a need that results either from an internal or external stimulus. For unmentionables in the unacceptable class, the recognition of a need for demarketing is inherent in the unmentionable itself. Similarly, the steps that represent the second and third stages of the buy phase—namely, determining the character and quantity of the needed item and then the detailed specification—are rarely, if ever, logically developed. The passion with which the end is pursued totally overwhelms the means by which it is to be achieved. This is substantially true of all the stages of the buy phase.

On the buy class, the demarketer is always the "outside supplier" in the marketing sense. While his or her objectives in purely theoretical terms are no different from those of a commercial marketer—that is, changing the buying task from a straight rebuy to a new buy where all legitimate options are considered—in practice few of the tactics normally used are practical: for example, offering an innovative alternative for the unmentionable that gives as many real and perceived benefits as the unmentionable itself or outbidding the unmentionable supplier in price, quality of product or service, reliability, and image.

The ground rules must change because in demarketing there can be no similar product or service to meet the socially unacceptable unmentionable need, only a substitute that might give other but not comparable benefits. The moral self-approval that chastity may provide offers little in the way of an acceptable alternative to the prostitute's customer, any more than the certainty of a rapid and nasty death will convince a drug addict undergoing the agony of withdrawal that life without drugs is better than death with them.

Marketers can follow the conventional three-part strategy only for commercial services and products. For noncommercial marketing of products, services, and concepts, the normal divisions—market segmentation, marketing mix, and product mix—are applicable only with varying emphasis. In noncommercial marketing, the emphasis switches strongly from sophisticated development of segmentation criteria to the marketing mix and the strength and nature of its message. The product mix also seems to have little relevance unless, in a somewhat tortured way, the "product" of the marketing campaign is the message itself.

Market Segmentation

Having established need and benefit, the marketer's next stage must be to locate precisely where they exist. Some segments are clearly identifiable, while others are difficult or impossible to define even in vague terms. At this stage, the methodology for marketing unmentionables again diverge from conventional approaches, to investigate the cause of unmentionability. These causes are many and may stem from social or religious mores, conventional and current concepts of morality, acceptance or legality of certain practices, emotion, and deep psychological roots. However, it is certain—as with benefits—that unless a marketer understands why a product, service, or idea is unmentionable, its marketing must largely depend on luck.

The market segments where unmentionability is least pronounced must be identified. As with conventional products, marketing should commence where markets are "softest." What factors make a product, service, or idea less unmentionable to one group than to another—education, position in the family life cycle, or exposure to alternative cultures and ways of thought? The answers are important since knowing them may provide the clue for accelerating acceptance of the product in other groups.

Marketing Mix. A wide range of marketing tools exists, and it is illogical and inefficient not to use those that can be adapted to the marketing of what may be unmentionable because of the coyness of some media and the lingering fastidiousness of society. The illustrations and text of transit posters on the London Underground are still rigorously controlled by standards of an earlier decade. But not all tools are equally relevant in any market, regardless of their availability; it may be just as unwise to advertise certain types of professional services (such as law and medicine) as other types (such as prostitution). A direct mail campaign could be as inappropriate for marketing steel-making equipment as for marketing venereal disease treatment.

Given all the sensitivities and the need to identify appropriate marketing tools, all the usual methods of marketing could be introduced efficiently. The attempts that have been made to market desirable unmentionables or demarket undesirable ones have certainly not hesitated to use the full range of modern marketing methods. The difficulty lies not in the availability of tools but in the attitudes of their users and the media in which the marketing messages appear. Poster site owners (particularly of transit sites), newspapers, and radio and television networks have strict advertising codes that, to say the least, have a cognitive dissonance with the standards of some show business advertising material—the content of which is far more explicit and the purpose of which is more doubtful.

Therefore, although a wide range of marketing tools may be available, the concept of marketing and demarketing unmentionables may first have to be marketed to those who either control the marketing media or who are involved in marketing activities personally—such as demonstrators, exhibitors, salespeople, and others. "War," it is said, "is much too important to be left to generals." The statement also applies to marketing and marketing managers. It seems then that the first task in establishing the marketing mix is to ensure that the communication channels are open and clear. Then and only then can the mix be set appropriately.

Two key marketing tools that are beyond the censorship of the media owners but that may also be eliminated are market research and personal selling. Both can be rendered ineffective by the refusal of customers to discuss unmentionable topics. Equally, salespeople may prove difficult or impossible to recruit. How one company turned this factor to its advantage will be shown shortly.

The other principal difference between the marketing of unmentionables and other marketing lies in the *intensity with which the marketing mix is applied* and its *message or theme*. The marketing of legitimate unmentionables is, by definition, more difficult than marketing conventional products and services. The mix may need intensive application and—once the tools, media, message, and purpose of the message have been selected—will require careful planning and thought.

It has been argued that improved knowledge—and marketing is a communication process—of many unmentionables would benefit society as a whole. But many desirable unmentionables would not suffer in the intensity of their use by the fact that they are not talked about or marketed. Burial arrangements will be made and sanitary protection used whether people and providers talk about or promote them. The question marketers need to ask is whether society would benefit by less inhibited marketing. Would people suffer less if they could face the prospect of their own or loved ones' deaths and the attendant product or service implications?

Because history can only be recorded in words and pictures, people rarely stop to consider that over most of time man and his environment have smelled objectionably and that perhaps the greatest achievement of the rough-and-tumble advertising of the late Victorian era was to make the use of soap and other products socially desirable. Being smelly and dirty was possibly not unmentionable at the time; but if it was, then it should provide hope for the marketer that unmentionables can be marketed in the face of social taboos.

Product Mix. Since the product, service, or idea is unchangeable or undesirable in the first place, the third segment of the marketing strategy seems hardly applicable. Nevertheless, it may be easier to sell the basic product by adopting a wider but linked "product." For instance, if the idea is zero population growth, a marketer might sell products that go at least some way to meet the deprivations (emotional, physical, or financial) which occur if childbearing is limited. For example, marketers could promote the ultimate social value of birth control by stressing the improved housing, bigger pensions, and better educational facilities and opportunities for existing children that result from its practice. These incentives are as much a part of the product as the basic product itself.

In some marketing efforts it seems wise to move away from the basic approach of selling the benefits of the product, service, or idea to selling the benefits of the inducement. Lower birth rates and healthier children and mothers may be the benefit the sponsors of a birth control program would think of offering, but recipients may be far more interested in the benefits of more immediate and tangible incentives—whether a transistor radio or a watch—than in the impact a lower birth rate might have on their family, community, or country.

History cannot lightly be set aside. Who will provide for the Indian peasant in his old age if there is either no nuclear or a small nuclear family? In many countries children are not, after all, the result simply of sexuality; they are an insurance policy. Thus the question in the example chosen may be: What benefits do people seek from children (or a lot of children) rather than from lack of children?

Marketing Desirable Unmentionables

The principal problems managers encounter in marketing desirable unmentionables relate to the communication process. The problems arise when either the normal channels or media refuse to carry the advertisement or when buyers are unwilling to receive the message. In both cases, marketers have an uphill struggle; and although we have shown that time and marketing effort *can* change attitudes and practices sufficiently to normalize the marketing approach, manufacturers of desirable unmentionables cannot always wait. Nor can they afford to turn their backs on the marketing process; their need for what marketing has to offer is greater than that of suppliers of conventional commercial products. So what do they do? The answers are disarmingly simple:

☐ Be sure of the ultimate social value of the product.

☐ Seek to accelerate the process of change that reduces the unmentionability of the product or service.

☐ Seek new communication channels that do not suffer from the impediments unmentionability imposes.

☐ Confine the marketing efforts to those customers or intermediaries who do not find the product or service unmentionable and thus avoid the censure of society at large.

To take the last point first, armaments are widely regarded as an unmentionable product; they are certainly capable of inducing mass demonstrations against their use from a broad spectrum of the population. Yet marketing of armaments is effectively carried out by industry and government representatives in the closed rooms of defense departments and at private demonstrations of hardware organized on national military proving grounds. Employing brochures, catalogs, and audiovisual presentations as well as the equipment itself, armaments suppliers make surprisingly sophisticated contact with their buyers. By the subtle tactic of referring to defense rather than attack equipment, more broad-based use of the media could be employed, but the norm is a secretive, narrow-based, personal selling campaign. A supplier's credibility is enhanced by user endorsements and official test reports and his success guaranteed by a high degree of involvement with officialdom.

In what follows we go into two examples in detail to show not only how suppliers of unmentionables have sought to change public attitudes, but also how, in one case, unmentionability was neatly sidestepped through the use of an unconventional communications mix and, in the second, how unmentionability itself was used as a central platform for the marketing effort.

The Contraceptive Sheath

The contraceptive sheath is a classic unmentionable product. Available in various forms since Roman times, its use during the most intimate of human activities has led to high unmentionability. The Victorian era alone produced a strong and lingering association between the sheath and other unmentionables such as illicit premarital sex, surrounding it with an aura of sin and guilt. Its very prophylactic properties of preventing venereal infection added to its unmentionability, since venereal disease was not a risk in marital sex, and reinforced the sheath's connotation of clandestine sex. On top of all this, the distribution channels of back-street shops and surreptitious sales to men in dirty raincoats produced total unmentionability.

By the mid-twentieth century, responsible birth control had become an acceptable subject within a large part of society; yet the sheath, the major mechanical method of contraception, retained its unmentionability. The sheath was still widely associated with random sexual gratification rather than with the needs of parents to limit the size of their families.

The problems facing the marketing department of the London Rubber Company, the leading supplier of sheaths in the United Kingdom, were formidable. No research data were available or could be acquired on the use of contraceptives. Despite the apparent success of clinical researchers such as Kinsey in studying sexual behavior, market researchers did not believe that they could acquire accurate data on the purchase or use of sheaths. Distribution channels were confused and far from ideal. Pharmacies were not allowed to display the products openly, and many—such as Boots, the largest chemist chain—refused to stock them altogether.

Despite a substantial trade through back-street outlets where salesmen had a penchant for describing their wares as "surgical appliances," the main channel was the barbershop. Media advertising was banned and point-of-sale material was limited to display of the brand name without reference to what the product was or its benefits. The company did produce brochures that family planning clinics distributed along with advertising that contained a coupon with which readers could request literature.

Nevertheless, London Rubber achieved substantial market dominance, and its leading brand, Durex, became a generic name for sheaths. Given the sheath's unmentionable status, the prominence of the trade name could have been as much a disadvantage as an advantage but, regardless, it provided a most effective substitute to brand advertising. Every schoolboy had a high level of awareness dating from his first dirty joke, and the brand was impossible to forget.

Prior to 1973, London Rubber's marketing program relied on the promotion of the sheath as a technique for family planning. It took (and still takes) a very responsible attitude toward its product, refusing to associate it with the gratification aspects of sexual activity. But in the 1960s, the pill entered the scene and captured a high proportion of the family-oriented contraceptive market. In contrast to the sheath, the pill became the modern, clean, reliable, and unobtrusive contraceptive method. Moreover, it had the advantage of allowing more spontaneity and romance because preparation took place long before, not during, the sexual act.

More important, however, from London Rubber's viewpoint, contraceptive purchasing responsibility shifted from the man to the woman and reduced the effectiveness of its traditional distribution channels. Seeing the erosion of its market, London Rubber made a policy decision to change its marketing approach from promoting the concept of sheath contraception alone to a heavy promotion of the Durex brand name and of the acceptability and security of the sheath. The strategy was to disassociate the brand as well as the technique from the smutty aspects of sex.

Because, whatever the message might be, unmentionability still barred the sheath from the most common and possibly most effective marketing channels, London Rubber—which had by then changed its name to LRC International—began a search for alternatives. It chose sports sponsorship as its promotional vehicle and commenced with Formula One motor racing, which was seen as a modern, clean, nongambling, but glamorous activity. It had little to do with sex but could help establish Durex as a mentionable name in the market. Not many motor-racing stables were interested in accepting LRC money, but eventually the Surtees team did, and the Durex-Surtees Formula One race car rolled onto the circuits.

Sponsorship gave LRC the opportunity to promote the name Durex almost without offense or problem. In fact, threatened withdrawal by the

British Broadcasting Corporation of television coverage of a race provided a bonus of favorable publicity. The slogans used in the sponsorship campaign—"The Small Family Car" and "The Crowd Stopper"—were sufficiently ambiguous (without being obscure) and were thought witty, so they did not arouse controversy.

For a relatively small budget, then, LRC achieved a high level of visibility. Furthermore, the sponsorship provided text for other acceptable, below-the-line promotions—principally poster campaigns but also display cards, T-shirts, hats, and umbrellas.

With considerable success, LRC's sports sponsorship supported by poster campaigns was extended to include production car motor racing, powerboating, and motorcycle racing. But the problems of unmentionability continued to frustrate LRC's marketing approach. Many sports groups would not accept LRC sponsorship and many would have been inappropriate, e.g., horse and dog racing. A number of media owners refused to accept LRC advertising, and some newspaper editors proved surprisingly coy—notably the Sunday *News of the World,* which is otherwise noted for its prurient reporting of the sexual proclivities of the population.

Nevertheless, during the 1970s attitudes were changing, and LRC was able to broaden its use of the media. More overt advertising promoting the advantages of the sheath to women who began to worry about the medical dangers of using the pill after the age of 35 became possible in specialized journals. In deference to public sensibilities, the advertising theme remained informative, contained factual test results, and continued to revolve around family planning—though this copy did not suit such media as *Playboy* and *Penthouse,* from which LRC also found it was barred!

Along with the loosening of restrictions on publicity, LRC also saw improvements in distribution. In 1974, the prohibition on the open display of contraceptives in pharmacies was lifted, and even Boots' shops began stocking them. Unmentionability still plays a strong part in merchandising, however, since the products are usually displayed next to the cash register where purchasers can be as discreet as possible and do not have to ask for them by name or product type. Purchases can be handed to the clerk, who quickly and unobtrusively wraps them (with luck!).

Family planning clinics emerged as dispensing points for all contraceptives—including sheaths—thereby providing a sample distribution service for LRC. The company also developed a strong vending machine division so the products were available at the late hours when user decisions are sometimes made. It must be said, though, that the company does not favor this method of sales, largely because of the location of the machines and the image they create. Mail-order sales continue to prosper, but the general trend in distribution is toward more open channels.

A constant objective in LRC's marketing program for contraceptive sheaths has been the search for and use of uncommon channels that do not impose the restrictions generated by unmentionability elsewhere. Accept-

ability by the owners or controllers of these channels may come because
they need the income or because they are less constrained by external regulations or internal moralizing. A surprising number of such channels exist.
In addition to the vast army of specialized journals that are well known to
cater to minority interests, LRC has used Poster Motors (the British equivalent of the U.S. use of Volkswagen Beetles as roving advertising boards),
specialist exhibitions, customer competitions, and informational films (largely
for showing in schools and women's clubs).

Throughout its new marketing program, LRC has used the liberalization
of public attitudes to increase the visibility of its product. It has, nevertheless, resisted associating itself with loose sexual morals (as Swedish suppliers
of competitive products have done) but has maintained the theme of responsible family planning.

The Sanitary Napkin Disposal Service

Our second example has a quite different sexual connotation. The Rentokil
Company operates a very successful service, called Sanitac, within its hygiene division. This service chemically neutralizes used sanitary napkins and
removes them physically. The service sprang from a different section of the
company whose business was drain maintenance. Over a period of time
people in that division found that one of the principal causes of drain block-
ages in companies where no incineration equipment existed was sanitary
napkins disposed through toilets. The service developed almost naturally
out of an obvious, if unexpressed, need.

Within Rentokil there was intense internal opposition to its development, and it took considerable persuasion by a committed and eloquent
manager to obtain top management's agreement to at least try the service.
Management had to be convinced that the hygiene division—and Rentokil—
would not be hurt in any way by the introduction of what was seen as an
activity with offensive implications, that such a service would not only be
acceptable to companies but would also have social and industrial relations
value, and that the service would be profitable.

Thus the first marketing target was not corporate customers but Rentokil's internal management. Agreement was achieved to initiate the service
but with constraints that might have daunted most managers. The Sanitac
service was to be wrapped up in a range of other services as an "add on";
there was to be no internal mention of the service, and its operations were
not to appear in any company reports. In other words, Sanitac was to have—
internally at least—what would be described in modern parlance as a "low
profile." The decisions limiting the service to a trial introduction and im-
posing constraints were, it should be noted, all made by men.

When the marketing effort started, it was undertaken by an all-female
sales force selling personally to businesses employing female staffs. Britain's
Sex Discrimination Act, which normally makes illegal any sexual discrimination in recruitment, in fact permits certain activities to be carried out by

single-sex staff. Sanitac was able to exploit these exclusion clauses in the act.

The reaction of the substantially male-populated buying units was total distaste and an obvious desire not to discuss the matter. The female sales force of Sanitac quickly discovered that the greater the unmentionability, the more quickly and directly the discussion and decision were pushed away, generally to the buyer's or plant manager's secretary who—as a beneficiary of the service—gave a much more sympathetic hearing.

Thus the sales approach, perhaps accidental at first but then deliberate, enhanced the unmentionable aspects of the service to male buyers by the use of words and phrases that deliberately aroused feelings of revulsion. Words such as "bleeding," "menstruation," and "soiled napkins" were aggressively pushed by an aggressively female sales force. The obvious benefits of the service could be expounded on to the buyer, now usually female, without embarrassment or resentment on her part. The sales argument was strongly feminist and wholly successful: "If men menstruated, women would not have to put up with the squalid or embarrassing conditions that they endure in most plant and office lavatories and rest rooms."

The sales force was supported by direct mail campaigns, some media advertising in professional and trade papers, public relations, and audiovisual presentations. Direct mail produced only a 25% response compared with that of other more mentionable hygiene activities, and thus it can be concluded that unmentionability frustrated the promotion process. Nevertheless, despite a low response, direct mail achieved enough sales to justify its use.

A comparison of overall results shows that while it required something like 15 months of business with a customer for Sanitac to recover its selling costs to that customer, other divisions reached the break-even point on individual accounts in about half that time. By 1975 Sanitac broke even and by 1979 was showing a profit with a growth rate of 25%.

The Sanitac strategy has been to retain and enhance the service's unmentionability, both to force the decision into the hands of the actual users and, interestingly, to limit competition. Sanitac managers reasoned that if internal opposition to the service occurred at Rentokil it would occur for the competition as well. Sanitac figured that highlighting unmentionability would make it more difficult for protagonists of the service to convince their managements to enter the market.

In comparing the Durex and Sanitac cases, one can see that the strategies appear to be polar opposites. LRC attempted to remove or reduce unmentionability while Sanitac sought to increase it. Both strategies were successful. However, it is apparent if one looks closely that their approaches were in fact identical—namely, making the product and the service acceptable to women, who were the real marketing targets. For both, traditionally, the decision makers were men. Making Durex mentionable to women and generally respectable increased its visibility and acceptability. Making Sanitac's service unmentionable to men pushed the buying decision toward women, to whom it was mentionable and a matter of concern. In both cases, the companies succeeded in reducing unmentionability where it counted, at the point of sale.

A Litmus Test

One of the fundamental ingredients of marketing is the ability of the seller to communicate with the buyer. Unmentionability affects the flow of information in both directions: sellers are not easily able to define buyers' requirements or receive information about their products and services.

The marketing response to unmentionability should be either to seek uncommon communication channels or to make exceptionally creative use of conventional ones. This response involves primarily the selection of a marketing mix that avoids the constraints imposed by unmentionability and exposure to or contact with those who are offended by the product or service. Finally, the marketers of unmentionables can seek to accelerate the change that will reduce unmentionability.

Although we have refrained from making judgments about what is good or bad, we think it is important to add a final caveat. Many people, including us, *do* have opinions about what is unmentionable and whether one should market that which society rejects. The views and values of the minority need to be protected. But change also cannot be denied. Perhaps the litmus test of whether a product, service, or idea is a desirable unmentionable and ought to be marketed is the free market. If it is useful and functional, change will occur; if not, it probably won't survive.

Notes

1. Philip Kotler, *Marketing for Non-Profit Organizations* (Englewood Cliffs, N.J.: Prentice-Hall, 1975).

2. *Financial Times*, January 12, 1978 (emphasis added).

3. Philip Kotler, p. 89.

4. P.J. Robinson, C.W. Farris, and Y. Wind (contributor), *Industrial Buying and Creative Marketing* (Boston: Allyn & Bacon, 1967).

11
Counter-Competition Abroad to Protect Home Markets

CRAIG M. WATSON

A strategy for meeting foreign competition in domestic markets is an important component of the strategic package of major U.S. manufacturers, and it will continue to grow in importance as foreign companies gain a broader and deeper hold in these markets. To meet this threat, some American companies have taken a new look at some basic business considerations:

☐ The relative importance of domestic and international markets.

☐ The effectiveness of worldwide export, sourcing, and production practices.

☐ The appropriateness of each product line to its markets.

☐ The content and focus of strategies designed to offset the competition at home.

It might appear that attending to the last item on the list would entail efforts focused on domestic activity, but experience points in quite a different direction. Indeed, pursuit of a foreign competitor's domestic markets can help protect the threatened company's own home market share.

Foreign Competition in the United States

Penetrating a foreign market from the home base is an expensive and complex undertaking. The multinational company invading the U.S. market (or any large foreign market) must think through certain critical matters, such as:

Published 1982.

1. *The product and technology strategies with which to capture and hold market share.* Given the signal importance of demand in the home market, the foreign competitor pursuing overseas markets standardizes its domestic and export products as much as possible, employing the same manufacturing facilities and minimizing the costs of modification.

Product innovation will be necessary later for the penetrator to retain the growth segment of the market. We can expect, then, that "old" products will be replaced by new ones that become rapidly standardized in both domestic and overseas markets.

2. *An integration program to coordinate and administer rapid and sustained growth in market share.* A successful penetration program demands an extraordinary degree of coordination and management. Manufacturing planning for continual increases in capacity, costly R&D programming for ongoing product innovation, and extensive promotion to generate demand must all be tightly integrated.

3. *The nature and source of the cash flows to fund the cost of aggressively expanding the business base to overseas markets.* As experience-curve analysis has shown, companies successful in this effort establish high-volume base markets capable of generating high net cash flow while adding to their production and marketing experience.[1] Aggressive manufacturers are willing to trade off short-term profit for longer-term market share because market share increases ultimately lead to reduced production costs, lower prices, and increased demand. Then these companies enjoy high cash flows—related to economies of scale—that can fund additional manufacturing capacity, promotional programs, and product innovations.

In most instances, the domestic markets of foreign competitors provide the base volume of demand that triggers this process.

Counter-Competition

Often, of course, U.S. companies facing such serious threats at home have already entered foreign competitors' domestic markets. While this activity is at first a by-product of international competition, it can be developed into an effective tool for protecting domestic market share from foreign penetration. Effective counter-competition has a destabilizing impact on the foreign company's cash flows, product-related competitiveness, and decision making about integration. Direct market penetration can drain vital cash flows from the foreign company's domestic operations. This drain can result in lost opportunities, reduced income, and limited production, impairing the competitor's ability to make overseas thrusts.

IBM moved early to establish a position of strength in the Japanese mainframe computer industry before two key competitors, Fujitsu and Hitachi, could gain dominance. Now holding almost 25% of the market, IBM is denying its Japanese competitors vital cash and production experience needed to invade the United States. They have lacked sufficient resources to develop the distribution and software capabilities essential to success in America. So the Japanese have finally entered into joint ventures with U.S. companies having distribution and software skills (Fujitsu with TRW, Hitachi with National Semiconductor). In an ironic reversal of the counter-competition strategy, a TRW vice president was quoted as saying, "Fujitsu . . . was eager to expand abroad to increase its economies of scale for the fight with IBM back home."[2]

General Electrtic (U.S.), by licensing its advanced gas turbine technology to foreign producers that were potential major competitors, created a captive market for its technology among such heavyweights as AEG (West Germany), Hitachi (Japan), Nuovo Pignone (Italy), and Alsthom Atlantique (France), in their respective countries. This move has eliminated competition for the huge U.S. market from these sources.

Innovative product differentiation may create such dramatic changes in domestic preferences that previously dominant foreign products suffer setbacks in their home markets. Such an occurrence may influence the foreign company to refocus its resources toward protecting the once-secure domestic market share.

Intel leads the American effort to produce and market a range of standard microprocessor chips augmented by application software that is designed to instruct the chip to perform in certain task settings. Enjoying less software capability, European chip makers rely on customized chips with designed-in application instructions. There are advantages and drawbacks to both approaches.

European custom chip makers like Philips hope to score in the U.S. market. But Intel, by licensing the electrical giant Siemens to compete with Philips, has moved aggressively to market its standard chip and the associated software in Europe. Philips has yet to make an effective entry into the U.S. market.

Cincinnati Milacron's highly articulated T^3 robot system enjoys manipulative advantages over several key competitors in international markets. As these units are marketed overseas, they will challenge manufacturers in Europe, such as ASEA, and Japan, such as Fanuc Fujitsu, in their home markets. These manufacturers will be forced either to accelerate innovation to keep up or to confine their efforts to less sophisticated industrial markets in America.

Nonproduct competitive tactics—in such aspects as distribution networks, manufacturing capacity, commercial terms, and R&D—can alter the competitive balance in foreigners' previously secure home markets.

In Japan and its other world markets, IBM has created such a vaunted place for its systems products that competition extends beyond mainframe hardware to software as well. This strategy has been so successful that competitors must make sure that IBM software is adaptable to their systems.

In nonproduct competition, IBM has a bevy of techniques to stall foreign opponents in their own home markets (and in U.S. markets). One of them is advance-notice advertising of new computer models to dry up demand for competitors' models. Another technique is locking in customers by including modernization and system-modification options in lease agreements, thus foreclosing this segment of the business to the competition.

Texas Instruments established semiconductor production facilities in Japan "to prevent Japanese manufacturers from dominating their own market." Even after much development work, the Japanese producers could muster neither the R&D resources nor the manufacturing capacity to compete at home or overseas with an acceptable product in sufficiently large quantities.

It stands to reason that a company already established in a foreign competitor's home market can use counter-competition more effectively than a company that has yet to enter that market. This reasoning does not always hold, however. On occasion the rate of growth of penetration from a low or nonexistent base has been so stunning that the foreign company could not effectively counter.

This rule-of-thumb may also be invalid when the market segment selected for penetration is unique or sufficiently specialized that the potential suppliers are known, if not established, in the target market. In the electric utility repair and supply market, for example, live-wire handling and repair equipment is the preserve of a handful of companies worldwide that serve only national or municipal utility customers.

What Makes It Work?

There is no question that counter-competition has had visible, though limited, success in some industries (industrial robots) and extraordinary success in others (computers, semiconductors). The pivotal question, then, is not whether it works but what product or industry characteristics favor its success. Experience underscores the positive contribution of the following factors:

1   Ability to gain significant market share rapidly in competitors' markets, enabling the defending company to deny home markets to these competitors. The earlier, swifter, and deeper the penetration, the more effective the strategy.

2   Capacity to differentiate the product continually or permanently, making it difficult for the foreign company to compete effectively at home in the market segment. Properly managed, product innovation can simultaneously redefine product applications, refocus market segments, and generate demand—outcomes that otherwise may be impossible to achieve.

3   The resources to extend competition to areas in which the foreign company will be at a disadvantage. Building on strength in R&D,

manufacturing capacity, or aftermarket support (to name a few areas) can change the key requirements for success in favor of the defending company.

Industries in which such opportunities can be exploited are excellent candidates for the use of counter-competition. It can be a highly effective strategy for protecting home markets from foreign invasion.

Notes

1. Boston Consulting Group, *Perspectives on Experience* (Boston, 1976).

2. TRW: Fujitsu's Key to the U.S.,'' *Business Week*, May 19, 1980, p. 123.

PLANNING STRATEGY FOR TODAY'S MARKETPLACE

AN OVERVIEW

It's one thing to be aware of important social and economic trends; it's another to recognize the strategic implications of a changing environment. The articles in this section seek to assist managers in formulating appropriate strategies based on significant marketplace changes.

In his article, "Market Success Can Breed 'Marketing Inertia,'" Thomas V. Bonoma warns managers of the danger of relying only on previously successful strategies and failing to pay heed to important environmental changes. Such an approach can make managers inflexible during periods when flexibility is all-important, he maintains.

One situation in which prior experience might dictate inappropriate strategy is that in which companies hold a relatively small percentage of market share, argue Carolyn Y. Woo and Arnold C. Cooper in "The Surprising Case for Low Market Share." They describe situations in which low market share isn't necessarily dangerous and may even turn into an asset.

Kathryn Rudie Harrigan and Michael E. Porter make a not totally dissimilar argument in their article, "End-Game Strategies for Declining Industries." They see various approaches, and even opportunities, for companies marketing products in industries that are experiencing deteriorating sales.

The notion that vertical integration is the most effective overall organizational and marketing strategy comes under close scrutiny by Robert D. Buzzell in his article, "Is Vertical Integration Profitable?" He concludes that the approach usually pays off for companies in strong market positions, but not necessarily for others.

As competition in most industries grows increasingly fierce, existing companies must give increasing attention to the likelihood that newcomers will enter the fray. George S. Yip offers an approach for analyzing barriers and opportunities created by virtue of marketing incumbency in his article, "Gateways to Entry."

The challenge of increasing competition can easily convince managers that they have exhausted possible ways of differentiating their products from others in their industry. Actually, the opportunities for differentiation are essentially endless, suggests Theodore Levitt in his article "Marketing Success through Differentiation—of Anything."

"How Global Companies Win Out," by Thomas Hout and Michael Porter suggests that managers who view their products and markets from a worldwide strategic perspective can compete more effectively than if they try simply to exploit individual international opportunities. Indeed, such a strategy may involve accepting little or no return on investment on certain investment projects, they maintain.

For fast-growing companies, the strategic marketing challenge may be more internally than externally based, suggest Tyzoon T. Tyebjee, Albert V. Bruno, and Shelby H. McIntyre in their article, "Growing Ventures Can Anticipate Marketing Stages." They offer advice for moving smoothly between stages.

Finally, in addition to maintaining extraordinary marketing flexibility, companies must be able to integrate product lines and manufacturing approaches to achieve greater synergy than ever before. Robert Stobaugh and Piero Telesio, in their article "Match Manufacturing Policies and Product Strategy," offer a strategic approach for meshing these often conflicting demands.

12

Market Success Can Breed "Marketing Inertia"

THOMAS V. BONOMA

Marketing is an inexact discipline. Understanding why one particular marketing strategy produces success while another does not may be impossible. Not surprisingly, then, managers are frequently reluctant to tamper with marketing strategies that have been successful in the past, even when market conditions have changed. Instead, managers frequently persist with old marketing strategies, even as profits and other indicators suggest the need for change. The author labels the inability of management to adapt to market changes "marketing inertia." He argues that managements possessing a certain rigidity in values are most inclined toward marketing inertia. To counter this inability to adapt, he advises managers to improve their understanding of market practices and conditions through such means as auditing their markets and closely monitoring their customers' attitudes.

In *Zen and the Art of Motorcycle Maintenance*, Robert Pirsig describes a number of "gumption traps," which are situations that can blind individuals to actions that seem to be in their self-interest. One trap, the "South Indian Monkey Trap," consists of a hollowed-out coconut chained to a stake. The coconut has rice inside, which can be reached through a small hole. The hole is big enough for a monkey's hand to go through but too small for his rice-filled fist to come out of. The monkey reaches in and is trapped—by nothing more than his own value rigidity. As Pirsig puts it, the monkey cannot see that "freedom without rice is more valuable than capture with it."[1]

Published 1981.

179

A similar value rigidity can affect a company's approach to marketing. This rigidity is a gumption trap that can be called "marketing inertia." It is the failure of management to react appropriately or at all to changed market conditions, as in the following examples:

1. The U.S. auto industry has frequently been accused of seeking short-term profits rather than long-term strength amid early signals that consumers were moving toward small, fuel-efficient cars.[2] Even so, General Motors still reacted to the changing market forces between two and four years earlier than did Ford. It can be argued that its strong cash position and large size helped GM adjust, but a close reading suggests that factors internal to the managements of these companies were most important. When Ford recognized the trend, the company "opted to let GM familiarize the public with shrunken cars."[3]

2. None of the seven largest oil companies was ready for the upheaval the 1973 oil embargo caused. Yet six of the companies quickly adapted and thrived, while the seventh, Texaco, Inc., experienced a near disaster. Texaco's long-range marketing strategy in the 1960s was similar to that of the other big oil companies in its central assumption that oil would remain cheap and plentiful. Companies concentrated their dollars and marketing efforts on expanding volume through additions to refinery and retail gasoline distribution capacity.

During and after the 1973 embargo, Texaco's competitors changed their emphasis from refining to exploring and from increasing the sale of refined products to diversifying. Texaco, however, remained committed for at least five additional years to increasing refining and distribution.

As a consequence, it fell from first place in profits to seventh. According to company observers, management's "introverted" style and its "overcentralization" of decision making were largely responsible. "Texaco's failing was that it had built up so much inertia in its system that it could not move off the course it had been following," stated a *Business Week* article.[4]

3. A much smaller company—a $100-million heavy equipment manufacturer—has been suffering from consistently small market shares and low profits from its line of machines. Its dominant, engineering-oriented CEO himself chooses major design projects for his development engineering staff and insists that the company produce machines of the highest quality. The company has been the last to market in four recent major industrial machine introductions. In one case, the corporation introduced a specialized rig for a large segment of the market four years after the market leader.

Unfortunately, the company's entries have been unable to command a significant price premium or to capture a significant market share. When questioned prior to the latest product introduction about product policy, the CEO admitted some concern about the company's low market share and almost nonexistent profits. Yet he remained convinced that being early to market was not essential, since customers would "eventually come around" to the superior quality of his company's entries in difficult application environments.

As these examples illustrate, marketing inertia develops in both large and small companies. Its presence is clearly evident in many industries, including steel, office copiers, telecommunicatins, and mainframe computers. Why are some companies unable to alter their marketing strategies in response to market changes, while others, when confronted with the same conditions, quickly modify their behavior to achieve continued marketplace success?

The Precondition of "Market Drift"

Inertia can develop as a successful company lets itself get out of touch with its customers, sales force, or distributors.

Usually a gradual but substantial shift in customer preferences, competitive behavior, or, increasingly, government directives precedes marketing inertia. The corporate market for telecommunications services, for example, has shown all three kinds of change in the last few years. Services are being deregulated, innovative competitors are entering the market with specialized services and, what is most important, customers' preferences have shifted from using voice communication to using a combination of voice

Exhibit 1.   Marketing Inertia and Market Drift

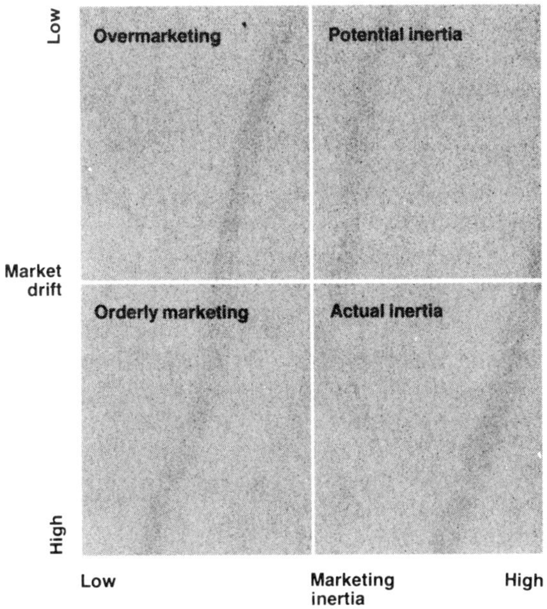

and data communication. Such changes in customer preference and marketplace structure might be termed "market drift."

The rate of market drift can vary. The market for vacuum tubes, for example, followed a very orderly textbook life cycle of rise, maturity, and gentle decline. With the introduction of the transistor, the vacuum tube market gracefully died. But when substantial market drift occurs over a short time, it can pose a serious threat to strategies that have worked well in the past. The automobile market, for example, has changed greatly in only 20 years.

When market drift is insignificant and marketing inertia the opposite, the inflexibility of a company's marketing approach is usually harmless. (See Exhibit 1.) But when both inertia and market drift are extensive, the consequences are almost always harmful. Market conditions have slipped away from the strategies designed to deal with them. Management has either failed to see or has ignored the warning signals. When eventually the company must rework its strategy, its marketing muscles are likely to be stiff from disuse.

When muscle market drift is occurring in the face of little inertia, management will quickly alter its marketing strategies and actions.

Beware the Danger Signs

The main cause of marketing inertia, given market drift, is management's value rigidity, which leads managers to prize things the way they *have* been done over the way they must *now* be done. Several conditions and practices seem to contribute to such rigidity.

Past Success

A company much enamored of its own marketing success is in the grip of its own history, corporate culture, and management psychology; it does not find changing easy.

A marketing strategy successfully introduced long ago by people still in positions of power can acquire the status of dogma. Managers may resist calls to abandon or change the strategy when conditions change. One striking example is Montgomery Ward, a company that several generations of family management drove to disarray by sticking to outdated products, store locations, and merchandising policies.

A company's perceptions can also restrict its response. Texas Instruments, for example, has encountered marketing difficulties stemming from its overriding belief that low prices lead to market share dominance. As a consequence, the company aggressively marketed its low-end office calculators at discount prices through large retail department stores and other mass merchandisers. In the process TI lost the allegiance of specialty office supply outlets, which had been selling most of the company's high-priced, high-margin machines.

In a different vein, both Smucker's the jam and jelly maker, and Coors, the brewer, encouraged a company strategy stressing product superiority. In both companies, top management was unresponsive to marketers' well-founded admonitions that quality is determined more by customers' preferences than by family formulas. Smucker's failure to capitalize on its name in developing a new product (ketchup) and Coors's failure to expand the distribution of its existing product are traceable to the dominance of company beliefs over change.

Finally, managers of successful businesses are often conditioned to avoid risk and seek quick payoffs. A company that made zinc, for example, responded to the triple threat of foreign competition, domestic production overcapacity, and narrow product line with a grand program of trade promotions and advertising. This marketing response, grossly inconsistent with the nature of the market threat, was low in risk, but it avoided the problems needing solution.

Similarly, when management runs scared of the reward system, price cuts to obtain quick volume may be recommended instead of price increases to weed out marginal accounts and return high long-term profits from remaining customers.

Others' Success

Imitating other companies can also lead to marketing inertia. The attractions of imitation are powerful, especially when a company is entering a new line of business or trying to rescue an existing one. While much can be said for the virtues of imitation over innovation,[5] copying can result in overlooking relevant new options. Moreover, competitive circumstances can change so that what is imitated is no longer appropriate.

Philip Morris's recent failure to follow R.J. Reynolds's entry into the low-tar cigarette market with its Cambridge brand cost the company more than $100 million. By taking so long to study the Reynolds product and strategy—more than four years—Philip Morris allowed Reynolds to build strong loyalty. In this narrow market segment, such a delay prevented Philip Morris's look-alike from succeeding.

Thoughtlessly following "generally accepted" industry rules is another form of imitation that can encourage marketing inertia. The old maxim that complex industrial products require personal selling instead of media advertising has caused many unnecessary selling expenses, especially in smaller companies. One small manufacturer of candy-making machines defied that maxim, though. Dissatisfied with its distributors' efforts and lacking money to hire people to sell its candy-making machines, the W.C. Smith Company ran an advertisement offering the customer what was in effect a $4,000 discount coupon for placing an early order for a machine. Sales of the machine nearly doubled in less than a year. Total incremental marketing expenses did not even equal the cost of one salesperson.

Taking On All Comers

Another dangerous practice is indiscriminately accepting "found" business. This practice leads to such problems as unprofitable products and customers, inadequate market feedback, and uncontrolled marketing expenses.

Almost every business, regardless of its marketing sophistication, finds refusing found business difficult. Once such business is acquired, management usually feels obligated to continue serving the accounts. But selling marginally profitable products to loyal customers outside a company's target segment creates costs that prevent a company from pursuing more attractive business. In such situations, management may find itself forever seeking business, any business, at the expense of margins and profits. Marketing inertia, in short, is likely to be felt when management is unable to turn away customers.

Companies that have uneven and unpredictable cash flows are especially susceptible to the lure of over-the-transom business. A prestressed concrete company, for example, recently analyzed its job-bidding practices in times of small and large work backlog. The company discovered that it was bidding too aggressively for marginally profitable or even unprofitable jobs to increase its backlog. This larger backlog was in turn influencing the company to bid too conservatively on jobs with much higher profit potential. Management was too busy delivering on promises that proved to be not very profitable.

The Difficulty of Making Changes

In its textbook form, marketing offers the manager several ways to tune company response to market demand. Changes can be made in the following areas:

1 The product or service offered.
2 Price policies.
3 Distribution channels.
4 Sales force.
5 Advertising or other ways of communicating with customers.

Marketing inertia can be thought of as a restriction on the range of these options. The nature of the restriction is usually toward choices that have helped produce past marketing successes. If the marketing mix is pictured as a set of adjustable valves between producer and consumer, marketing inertia freezes those valves in positions found appropriate in the past.

Exhibit 2 suggests in simplified form how inertia affects various marketing variables. It uses the number of years a company has experienced unchanging and successful practice as a proxy for management's value rigidity and the ease of altering different marketing mix elements to pinpoint

Exhibit 2. Inertia According to Marketing Variable

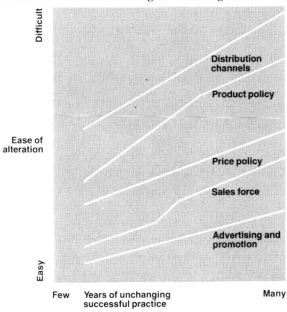

the effects of inertia. Changing marketing communications such as advertising is easier than changing pricing practices, which is in turn easier than
changing product policies or distribution channels. Marketing variables lock
in more or less tightly with time, and hence marketing inertia affects them
to varying degrees.

Distribution decisions are made early in a product line's history. Since
they involve economic dependence and require the cooperation of many
different outlets to work, they are usually complex and sensitive choices
that quickly become difficult to change. Management is likely to alter distribution only when serious trouble arises, especially when a single-purpose,
tightly controlled channel is used. The spate of gasoline service station
bankruptcies during shortages in the 1970s provided petroleum companies
with a degree of distribution flexibility that they had contemplated for years
but had found difficult to implement.

Marketing inertia affects product and price policies to a lesser degree
than distribution, but these policies can still be tough to change. Product
lines often acquire lives of their own, while cost- or competition-based price
strategies often persist long after inflation has rendered them harmful. Certainly part of the early ossification of products and prices comes from the
creation of customers' expectations. One major glass company is convinced
it cannot discontinue an unprofitable line because major users of its other
goods demand this one as well.

Similar expectations develop with prices, as the shrinking size of candy bars illustrates. Companies have reduced the bars' size to avoid exceeding some threshold price above which they think consumption will fall.

The variable least affected by marketing inertia is communications, including advertising, promotion, and, to a lesser degree, sales force decisions. Communications options often remain flexible, while other marketing valves stay frozen because (excepting sales force manning) these are short-term decisions, often involving less than a year's commitment. The advertising budget or sales force can also be changed more easily than prices and product lines.

On occasion a marketing problem needs a communications remedy, but oftentimes such "least-resistance marketing" only encourages management to make repeated tactical fixes until the problem is so severe it cannot be masked.

The Treatment

Relieving serious marketing inertia requires a resolute management effort. Usually a high-level champion winds up advocating a total reexamination of what is being done. One feasible way of making such a reexamination is through the marketing audit.[6] As in a financial audit, outside experts can be brought in to review the company's marketing practices. Ordinarily, marketing audits involve not only the evaluation of quantitative marketing data but interviews with management, distributors, and customers as well. The objectivity that these analyses bring to the audit helps to provoke action instead of denial.

When an audit is not possible or when immediate action is necessary, certain general remedies can be tried. The first step in treating especially serious cases of marketing inertia is to redirect attention toward the market. Simultaneously, the root of the problem—value rigidity—needs to be attacked.

One way of redirecting management's attention to the market is to collect information about marketing productivity, the sales force, and account controls. Marketing productivity measures, like the number of staff members per dollar of generated revenue, help focus attention on marketing return on investment. When controls are used to identify customer segments, wasted effort and merchandising failures can be pinpointed. Such information can promote flexibility to exploit opportunities for improving the use of marketing assets.

In some cases of inertia, existing controls may be ineffective because of management's value rigidity. The control system that collects sales force feedback to help formulate marketing strategy is the most vulnerable to corruption. As one manager for a major trailer manufacturer put the problem: "I can't even give you an estimate of how much I cost the company by not listening to what my salespeople learn from customers. Our system isn't set up to get information anyway—we hold back monthly expense checks until call reports are completed. As a result, they are filled out on the 30th of every month, half from memory and half from fiction. We have taught all our salespeople that call reports are just one more Mickey Mouse harassment that management sadistically imposes. We don't really want to hear what they know.''

Because qualitative monitoring methods may be unreliable gauges in companies with serious marketing inertia, I recommend sticking to simple quantitative measures to redirect management's attention to the market. What are sales by product line, market segment, and account? What are marketing expenses for the same categories? What about market share and profits? Are the trends over quarters or years positive or negative? Measures like these are not easily ''reinterpreted'' or ignored. They can be summarized on a single sheet of paper, and they serve as reliable indicators of performance.

Another way to redirect management's attention to the market is simply to encourage contact between customers and managers. As managers move up the corporate ladder, they become increasingly isolated from customers, distributors, and the small field problems that indicate trouble is brewing. One company regularly schedules a day per month for top marketing managers to take a ''roving tour'' of both important and average accounts. Managers in this company are also known to roll up their sleeves and man a distributor's counter for a morning or to ride around with salespeople. Value rigidity tends to dissipate out in the field.

Field visits may be insufficient, however, in situations where years of such rigidity have frozen attitudes. It is too easy to return to the comforts of bureaucracy and agreeable subordinates.

Two approaches can help thaw attitudes. One is to bring in a strong and aggressive outsider, either for a key management position or temporarily as a consultant. AT&T's recruiting of Arch McGill as a ''manager in charge of shaking things up'' is an example.

Another way to loosen value rigidity is to change the marketing organization itself, through restructuring. An organization that mirrors major market groups rather than just the company's product lines, for example, can help focus managerial values on consumers' preferences.

Handling Potential Inertia

When inertia has not seriously affected financial results, only a potential problem exists. The company has been fortunate because the market has not changed. Should it change, the flexibility necessary for modifying strategy would be absent. In such cases, some clear rethinking of product, price, and distribution policies can improve flexibility before it is needed.

Theodore Levitt has repeatedly argued for product differentiation as a key step in improving market performance in the face of competition. Differentiation also has a very important side effect. It entails the continual gathering of accurate knowledge of competitive moves. Then the market cannot slip away from management's grasp of customers' preferences and competitive moves.

Levitt distinguishes among "the expected," "the augmented," and "the potential" forms a product or service may take. He suggests that managers move beyond the minimal set of "extras" customers demand (what he calls "the expected product") to an analysis of whether market share and profits might be increased in return for augmented or potential benefits.

A sulfuric acid manufacturer, for example, noticed during the 1960s that its customers had difficulty convincing salvagers to remove used acid even for a fee. The acid manufacturer offered to remove spent acid without charge and reconditioned the acid for resale to other companies at prices substantially below that of the virgin product. A much-valued new benefit was offered to existing customers, the manufacturer expanded its market share, and the reconditioned acid was used to tap a new segment.

To stay flexible and prepared for change, management must regularly ask itself what "augmentations" of existing product or service lines might be added for competitive purposes.

Pricing policies can be a thorny area because the most frequently used strategies—pricing to cover costs and pricing vis-à-vis the competition—are producer rather than consumer oriented. Such strategies leave companies vulnerable to the danger that consumers will not pay the price asked and, possibly worse, that the sellers may leave significant amounts of money on the table.

One remedy for management's inattention to the market is value-based pricing. This sort of pricing involves making the starting point for determining price the benefits customers expect from the product and the economic value they place on those benefits. Looking at the cost of substituting other less effective products for the one in question is often a good way to estimate customer value.

When prices are based on anticipated customer judgments rather than on producer costs or competitive ceilings, management remains flexible to tailor its pricing strategy to market changes and to keep its tactical pricing moves consistent with its strategy objectives.

A maker of agricultural drainage tile, for instance, recently developed a new pipe system 180% as efficient as its own or competitors' systems for removing surface water. Because of materials savings, the product's manufacturing costs were only two-thirds those of the existing line. Several mangers thought that customers would not believe the efficiency claims if the savings were passed on to them, so after much debate the company decided to differentiate the benefits of the new system by pricing it 20% higher per foot. Concerned, however, about getting initial customers for its system, management was tempted to set the price low during the introductory phase and then raise the price later. Realizing that these tactics violated its value-pricing logic, management decided instead to encourage adoption, while maintaining the benefits logic, by offering distributor rebates and a money-back guarantee to early buyers.

A continuing reexamination of the adequacy of distribution channels can also help restore management flexibility. Conflict frequently characterizes these channels when inertia has set in. Distributors complain that they are being hurt by manufacturers being out of touch with the market. Manufacturers retort that they cannot keep doing their job and much of the distributors' as well. In such cases, arguments often focus more on issues of power and control than on the benefits of cooperation and joint profit making.

If current distribution outlets are no longer adequate for contemplated line extensions, the market may be moving away from its old habits. A major manufacturer of machine tools, for example, has found its distributorships unable to sell or service a low-priced robot manipulator and controller. Since the company expects to continue introducing similar products over the next five years, it is considering not only alternative methods of distribution for this product but also the needs of customers and the methods required to reach them.

The Monkey's Tale

We can now return to our monkey in midtrap, as it were, and to Pirsig:

The monkey reaches in and is suddenly trapped—by nothing more than his own value rigidity. . . . The villagers are coming to get him and take him away. They're coming closer . . . closer! . . . now! What general advice— not specific advice but what *general* advice—would you give the poor monkey in circumstances like this?

> Well, I think you might say exactly what I've been saying about value rigidity, with perhaps a little extra urgency. There is a fact this monkey should know: if he opens his hand he's free. But how is he going to discover this fact? . . . Well, he should somehow try to slow down deliberately and go over the ground that he has been over before and see if things he thought were important really *were* important and, well, stop yanking and just stare at the coconut for a while.

The essential problem of market success is that it can lead to contentment, legitimization of current practices, and rigidity in values. The danger is that companies will not accommodate small changes in customers, competitors, or environments over time with useful adjustments in marketing strategy because management has lost the ability to see and the will to respond.

What worked before can become a trap that causes failure in current marketing endeavors. The first task of every marketer is to take a very slow and deliberate look at that coconut.

Notes

1. Robert M. Pirsig, *Zen and the Art of Motorcycle Maintenance* (New York: Bantam Books, 1975).

2. See Jack Honomichl, "Consumer Signals: Why the U.S. Auto Makers Ignored Them," *Advertising Age,* August 4, 1980, p. 43.

3. "Ford After Henry II," *Business Week,* September 22, 1980, p. 62.

4. See "Texaco—Restoring Luster to the Star," *Business Week,"* December 22, 1980, p. 54.

5. See Theodore Levitt, "Innovative Imitation," *HBR* September–October 1966, p. 63.

6. See Phillip Kotler, William Gregor, and Will Rogers, "The Marketing Audit Comes of Age," *Sloan Management Review,* Winter 1977, p. 25.

13

The Surprising Case for Low Market Share

CAROLYN Y. WOO and ARNOLD C. COOPER

Conventional wisdom has it that companies with low market shares are doomed to marginal profits, at best, while market-share leaders show the best returns on investment. If the conventional wisdom is correct, though, most companies would be candidates for harvesting or liquidation. However, many companies with low market shares survive and even prosper. What characteristics enable the highly profitable low-share company to succeed? The authors contend that companies in industries with slow growth and few product changes and those that make frequently bought items are among businesses that prosper with low market share. Similarly, low-share businesses that pursue a specific focused competitive strategy, often emphasizing quality and cost, seem to do best.

Can businesses with small market shares be successful? If so, what strategies characterize such businesses? This article seeks to answer these questions by using research on 126 businesses, 40 of which have demonstrated superior performance despite low market shares.

Strategies tend to place much importance on having high-market-share positions. Bruce Henderson of the Boston Consulting Group observed, "In a competitive business, it [market share] determines relative profitability. When it does not seem to do so, it is nearly always because the relevant product market sector is misdefined or the leader is mismanaged."[1] One study, based on analysis of data at the Strategic Planning Institute in Cambridge, Massachusetts, concluded that "a difference of ten percentage points in market share is accompanied by a difference of about five points in pretax ROI."[2]

Published 1982.

High market share is frequently seen as offering businesses a number of attendant advantages, including economies of scale, brand-name dominance, and greater bargaining power with suppliers, distributors, and customers.

These correlations have often been interpreted to mean that businesses with low market shares inevitably have poor long-term prospects. Accordingly, analysts usually advise such businesses to build market share or reposition themselves so that they dominate some market segment. And, they contend, if neither action is feasible, the small-share business should be harvested or divested. Since only a few businesses are market-share leaders, presumably such dismal prognoses apply to most companies.

Each of these alternatives can cause serious problems. Building market share is a risky, costly activity that can ignite retaliatory actions by competitors. For low-share businesses in particular, share building may not even be possible because of limitations of resources or market influence. To reposition in an effort to dominate a market segment, a company must have product- and market-development capabilities. Harvesting or divestiture may be especially difficult in the multibusiness corporation because facilities, distribution channels, or customers are shared with other units in the company. Legal or social pressures may make it difficult to leave a business, and finally, those companies that lack attractive investment alternatives may realize little benefit from harvesting funds.

All of these concerns suggest that simple prescriptions do not apply to low-share businesses. Moreover, recent research suggests that pessimism about the prospects of low-share businesses is not always warranted. In 1978, Richard G. Hamermesh and associates reported on three companies they had studied—Burroughs, Union Camp, and Crown Cork & Seal—which had all been highly successful despite low-share positions.[3] They concluded that the strategies of these companies were characterized by the following: creative market segmentation, efficient research and development expenditures, controlled growth, and strong leadership. A subsequent study by William K. Hall identified companies in eight mature industries that had exhibited outstanding performance despite nonleadership positions.[4] The experiences of these companies demonstrates that market leadership is not always necessary to attain the lowest cost position. They also show that the lowest cost position is not required to achieve high margins.

Both studies show that long-run competitive success is feasible despite low-market-share position.

A New Approach

This article reports findings from a research project that examines a much larger number of businesses than the studies just mentioned and that looks at a number of factors associated with strategy. We have focused on two sets of broad questions, both relating to high-performing, low-share companies:

1   What kinds of industry settings do these businesses enter? What types of products do they offer?

2   How do these businesses compete? Do they allocate resources in distinctive ways to achieve a competitive advantage?

For a given business, performance might be expected to depend both on the product, market, and industry characteristics that determine its competitive environment and on its business strategy, that is, the way it competes within that environment.

The businesses in this sample were chosen from the PIMS data base.[5] Each business is defined as "a division, product line or other profit center within its parent company, selling a distinct set of products or services to an identifiable group or groups of customers, in competition with a well-defined set of competitors." We studied a total of 649 domestic manufacturing companies for the period 1972 through 1975. From this group, we sought to identify low-share businesses that achieved superior returns without diminishing their market shares. To qualify, businesses had to show a pretax return on investment of at least 20%. Their market shares could not exceed 20% of the combined share of their three largest competitors. Of the 649 businesses, 40 met these requirements.

It should be noted that the managements of these businesses estimated their own market shares, defining the market in terms of the customers they sought to serve. It is clear that the market definitions used directly affect a company's market share; however, these are the market definitions used by managements in their own planning. It should also be noted that, because of the nature of the PIMS data base, most of these were divisions of large corporations, not free-standing small businesses.

For contrast, we compared these high-performing businesses with two control groups: effective high-share businesses and ineffective low-share businesses. The definitions of those groups and the number of businesses in each category are shown in the ruled insert.

The Best Circumstances

For proprietary reasons, the names of the companies or the industry segments they serve are not given in the data base. However, we do know the characteristics of their industries, as reflected by 13 different factors. These factors are the nature of the product, the degree of product standardization, the importance of auxiliary services, the stage of product life cycle, purchase frequency by both immediate and end users, geographic scope, industry value added, industry concentration, number of competitors, industry growth, market growth, and frequency of product changes (see Exhibit 1). In examining these environmental characteristics, we can determine whether high-performing, low-market-share businesses sell in markets with distinctive characteristics.

Exhibit 1. Dimensions of Market Environment and Competitive Strategy

Market
environment:

Elements of
a competitive
strategy:

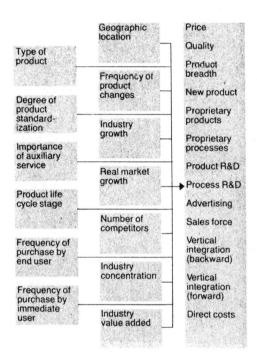

Market environment		Elements of a competitive strategy
Type of product	Geographic location	Price
		Quality
	Frequency of product changes	Product breadth
Degree of product standard-ization		New product
	Industry growth	Proprietary products
Importance of auxiliary service		Proprietary processes
	Real market growth	Product R&D
Product life cycle stage		Process R&D
	Number of competitors	Advertising
		Sales force
Frequency of purchase by end user		Vertical integration (backward)
	Industry concentration	Vertical integration (forward)
Frequency of purchase by immediate user	Industry value added	Direct costs

Using a statistical technique called "cluster analysis," we could classify the environments of the 126 businesses into six groups.[6] These six groups, shown in Exhibit 2, differ in a number of dimensions but particularly in the nature of the products and their market growth rates. These six groups do not describe all possible environments but do include the settings of the 126 businesses we studied. Bear in mind that businesses within a group do not necessarily compete with each other; rather, they compete in environments with common characteristics.

The distribution of effective low-share businesses and the two control samples in these six groups is displayed in Exhibit 3. Most of the effective low-share businesses are found in three environments: those designated as groups three, four, and six. Group four contains almost 50% of these high performers; this is an environment characterized by businesses offering standardized industrial components and supplies in low-growth markets.

Exhibit 2.   Characteristics and Composition of Market Groups

Group one   Group two

3 businesses   11 businesses

Consumer nondurable and industrial components	Consumer nondurable and industrial components
Very high-growth market	Declining market
Regular product changes	Frequent product changes
Nonstandardized products	Standardized products
High degree of auxiliary services	Low degree of auxiliary services
Purchased moderately often	Purchased often
Low value added	High value added

Another 25% are included in group six, an environment also characterized by slow market growth but which has industrial components that are less standardized and that are experiencing some product changes. Group three, which contains 15% of these high-performing businesses, includes mature consumer durables and capital goods in slow-growth markets.

The environments where we found most of the high-performing, low-share businesses share certain characteristics, some of which are very different from the environmental characteristics often thought to be most promising for smaller businesses:

1. *Profitable low-market-share businesses exist in low-growth markets.*   Groups four and six, which account for 72.5% of profitable low-share businesses, are characterized by real (inflation adjusted) growth rates of zero to 1%. This may seem surprising because limited opportunities and low profits are often thought to be associated with low-growth markets. High-growth markets, however, are turbulent arenas where competitors try to grab share leadership before the market stabilizes. During this period, competition can be intense. Rapid product and process changes add to the un-

Exhibit 2. *(Continued)*

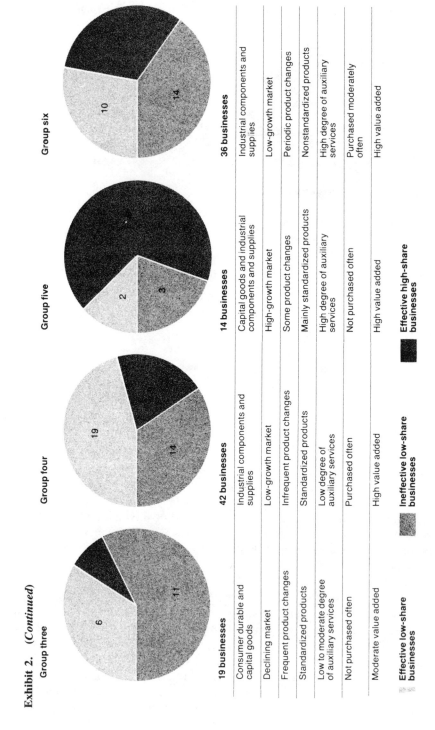

	Group three	Group four	Group five	Group six
	19 businesses	42 businesses	14 businesses	36 businesses
	Consumer durable and capital goods	Industrial components and supplies	Capital goods and industrial components and supplies	Industrial components and supplies
	Declining market	Low-growth market	High-growth market	Low-growth market
	Frequent product changes	Infrequent product changes	Some product changes	Periodic product changes
	Standardized products	Standardized products	Mainly standardized products	Nonstandardized products
	Low to moderate degree of auxiliary services	Low degree of auxiliary services	High degree of auxiliary services	High degree of auxiliary services
	Not purchased often	Purchased often	Not purchased often	Purchased moderately often
	Moderate value added	High value added	High value added	High value added

■ Effective low-share businesses

▨ Ineffective low-share businesses

■ Effective high-share businesses

Exhibit 3. Distribution of Effective Low-Share Businesses and Two Control Groups Across Six Market Groups

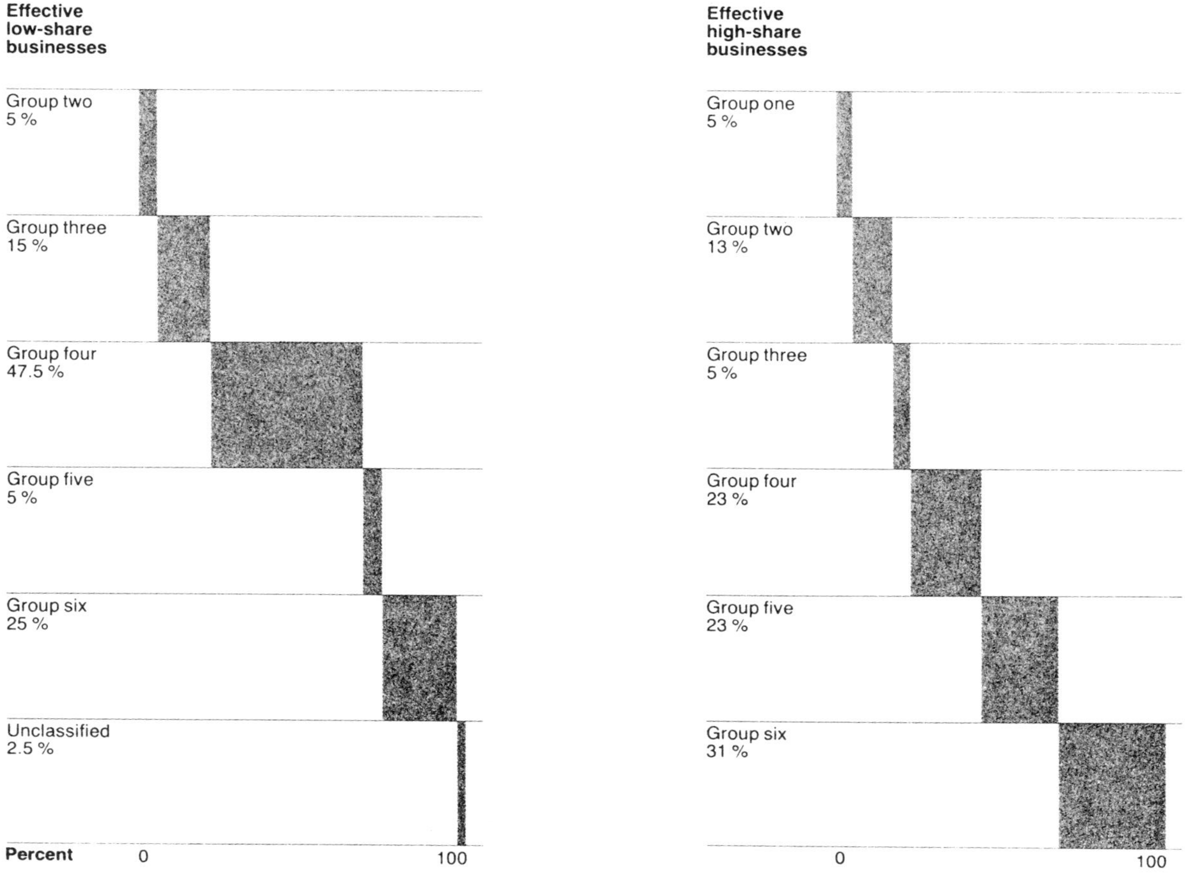

Effective low-share businesses

Group two 5 %
Group three 15 %
Group four 47.5 %
Group five 5 %
Group six 25 %
Unclassified 2.5 %

Percent   0   100

Effective high-share businesses

Group one 5 %
Group two 13 %
Group three 5 %
Group four 23 %
Group five 23 %
Group six 31 %

0   100

Exhibit 3.   (*Continued*)

**Ineffective
low-share
businesses**

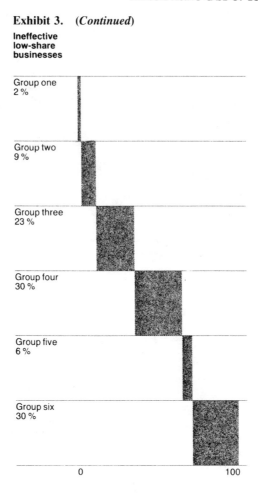

certainty. Often a shakeout period follows, when weak competitors are forced
to exit. This turbulence is repeated when the market reaches a stage of
negative growth.

Profitable low-share businesses thrive between these two stages. Most
of them seek mature though nondeclining markets with low real growth.
Such markets seem to provide a more stable environment, in which there
is less elbowing to gain market share. Hence, this structure makes it easy
for all players to define and protect their positions.

2.   *Their products don't change often.*   The mature markets mentioned previously also have low levels of product and process change. The
concentration of profitable low-share businesses in this environment is sur-

prising. High rates of change benefit companies that can move quickly as well as those seeking product differentiation opportunities. Low-market-share companies are often expected to benefit from such environmental changes.

Frequent changes may, however, force all members of an industry to spend heavily on product introduction as well as on research and development, which is difficult for smaller businesses that have less revenue to support these activities. High rates of change may also force smaller producers to scrap production tools and dies before their useful lives run out. By contrast, the greater production volumes of businesses with large market shares may mean that tools and dies are depreciated and ready for replacement sooner. Moreover, frequent changes also reduce the stability of markets and may be a reflection of greater competitive intensity.

3. *Most of their products are standardized and they provide few extra services.* Smaller businesses are often viewed as having the flexibility that permits them to cater to customers' special needs. They might be expected to avoid direct competition with large corporations' standardized products. They are often advised to choose fields in which competition is based on custom products or auxiliary services such as engineering consultation, frequent on-site visits, or maintenance and repair.

Contrary to expectations, 72.5% of successful low-share performers competed in markets characterized by standard products (groups two, three, four, and five). Moreover, the markets were not heavily supported by auxiliary services.

Competing in such markets permits focused strategies, in which companies need not incur the costs of providing custom products or special services. These market characteristics may stem from the nature of industrial components and supplies, which (as we discuss next) are the main products of successful low-share businesses. These products often require little subsequent servicing or technical support.

4. *Most of them make industrial components or supplies.* All businesses in groups four and six and some in two and five manufacture industrial components and supplies. These represent 70% to 80% of successful low-share performers in our sample. Purchase decisions for industrial products are based largely on performance, service, and cost. In industrial markets, it may be possible for small-share businesses to develop strong relationships with selected customers through emphasis on performance variables important to them. Advertising, normally thought to have high economies of scale, is usually less important for industrial products; therefore, small-share businesses are at only a minor competitive disadvantage.

In addition, purchases of industrial products are frequently governed by contracts. This guarantee of a market puts the sellers in a better position to project sales volume, capital spending, and costs.

5. *These products and supplies are purchased frequently.* Market share appears to be less important for products that need to be bought often.

More than half the low-share businesses studied produced such items (groups two and four). For such products, customers tend to rely more on experience and less on the brand name of market leaders for indications of reliability and performance. Thus, the share advantage of market leaders is less pronounced in these markets.

In addition, the rate of product purchases is likely to affect the requirement for working capital. High purchase frequency usually leads to faster turnover of inventory and receivables, allowing for quicker recovery of capital. Indeed, in our study, businesses making frequently purchased products had lower working-capital ratios than others.[7]

6. *Profitable low-share businesses are in industries with high value added.* Companies in these industries often enjoy margins wide enough to absorb cost increases from suppliers or price declines in the markets they serve. High-value-added industries are less likely to invite forward integration by suppliers or backward integration by customers. When the value-added factor is high, many opportunities exist for differentiation according to product characteristics and cost structures. In this study, 82.5% of successful low-share businesses are in such industries (groups two, four, five, and six).

Which Strategies Work Best

How do high-performing, low-share businesses compete in particular environments? Competitive strategy is reflected by the emphasis organizations place on such variables as relative prices, quality, product-line breadth, emphasis on new products, and advertising and selling efforts. (A more complete listing of factors comprising competitive strategy is contained in Exhibit 1.)

Examining market groups three, four, and six, where nearly 90% of these successful low-share businesses are clustered, we find distinctive patterns of competitive strategy in each environment:

1. *A strong focus tailored to environmental differences.* These successful businesses are distinguished by highly focused strategies. They do not try to do everything. They compete in carefully selected ways with the competitive emphasis differing according to the market environment.

Effective low-share businesses had similar strategies in groups four and six, both of which involve the sale of components and supplies. In group four, where products are standardized and undergo little change, successful low-share businesses are distinguished from the two control groups by their orientation toward low costs, low prices, and high quality. Though these characteristics are also present in group six, the high-performing, low-share businesses in this group are notable for their lower product R&D allocations and lower levels of backward integration. Products in group six undergo frequent changes. Hence, careful monitoring of product R&D is important to achieve a balance between long-term competitive position and short-term profitability.

In this market environment, we found that successful low-share businesses adopted a very conservative posture toward R&D spending yet achieved ROIs exceeding 20% over four years. Though the long-term success of this approach has not been proved, a lower R&D emphasis did not reduce the competitiveness of these businesses in the four-year period we observed. The lower vertical integration policy also contributed to success by providing these low-share businesses with greater flexibility to respond to changes, which minimized the disadvantage of their lower volumes.

In the mature consumer durables and capital goods area (group three), which contains 15% of our sample, effective low-share businesses adopt an aggressive marketing strategy and place less emphasis on quality, competitive prices, or research and development. The heavy emphasis given to marketing, particularly in the use of their sales forces, compensates for the other shortcomings of these businesses. Their reputations for quality were lower than competitors', and their product lines were not as broad. Yet these businesses command high prices. They sustain higher direct costs and have less forward and backward integration than do competitors. Despite weaker positions in cost, quality, and product value, a targeted marketing focus enables these businesses to derive rather strong margins from a low-share position in a declining market environment.

2. *A reputation for high quality.* Except for those businesses in group three, effective low-share performers consistently turned out high-quality products. Superior performance and reliability may be particularly important competitive weapons in the sale of industrial components and supplies. Knowledgeable buyers and frequent use lead to constant evaluation of tangible product characteristics.

3. *Medium to low relative prices complementing high quality.* The majority of successful low-share performers had lower prices than competitors (72.5% in groups four and six). Like product quality, competitive prices are particularly important in the environments in which these businesses compete. Buyers of industrial products are well informed and often enjoy strong bargaining positions in dealing with suppliers. When switching costs are low, buyers can solicit bids from eager suppliers. Within these mature, technologically stable markets, price might be expected to be an important consideration in purchase decisions. Note that the combination of high product quality and lower price means that those businesses offer their customers exceptionally good value.

4. *Low total cost.* Relatively low costs presumably permit low-share businesses to offer high-quality products at low prices and still show high profits. It follows that effective low-share businesses have lower unit costs than do ineffective low-share businesses. How do they achieve low costs? (After all, they do have higher unit costs than the market-share leaders

because of smaller production volumes and less vertical integration.) In part, by concentrating on a narrow line of standardized products. These high-performing, low-share businesses also spend less on product R&D, advertising, promotion, sales force support, and new product introduction.

Strategies of Poor Performers

Interestingly, there are no substantial differences in the environment chosen by effective and ineffective low-share businesses. Both have more than 80% of their businesses in groups three, four, and six. The differences between these two groups of companies relate more to how they compete in each environment.

By contrast, low-performing, low-share businesses compete aggressively along many fronts; they might emphasize broad product lines, advertising, selling expenses, product R&D, and process R&D. They also have considerable vertical integration, which requires still more resources. Their price-quality performance is below that of their competitors.

The 126 companies we studied

Type of business	Pretax return on investment	Relative market share	Number of businesses
Effective low-share	20% or higher	20% or lower	40
Effective high-share	20% or higher	125% or higher	39
Ineffective low-share	5% or lower	20% or lower	47

We observed the absence of a clear focus in all three market groups (three, four, and six) where we compared these low-performing, low-share businesses with high-performing, low-share businesses.

In general, the resource allocation patterns of ineffective low-share performers are similar to those of effective large-share businesses. The latter offer a broad line of products complemented by aggressive marketing, selling, R&D, and new product introduction. They are also highly integrated vertically. While both groups emphasize a large number of competitive weapons, small-share businesses lack the sales volume to support such broad-scale aggressive strategies.

Implications for Success

First, low market share does not inevitably lead to low profitability. Despite the well-accepted correlation between market share and profitability, market share is not a necessary condition for profitability. The dismal prospects often foreseen for low-share businesses do not always come to pass—certainly not to this sample of 40 businesses, all very profitable despite low-share positions.

Since these businesses have low market shares and are positioned in low-growth markets, they would usually be classified as candidates for harvesting or divestiture. The performance of these 40 businesses demonstrates that such blanket recommendations should be considered with care.

Second, a stable market environment contributes to low-share success. The performance of effective low-share businesses depends on both the characteristics of their industry settings and their business strategies. The successful businesses tend to concentrate in competitive environments somewhat different from those of effective large-share businesses but similar to those of ineffective low-share performers. These environments are not characterized by an absence of large-market-share businesses, as might be expected if "niche" strategies were followed. Rather, the overriding feature is stability. Low market growth, infrequent product and process changes, high value added, and high purchase frequency all contribute to more predictable and less turbulent environments. These markets are unlikely to attract new competitors. As such, competitors' divisions may receive less top management attention and staff support, and they may be staffed by less able and creative managers.

Third, selectivity is a key to low-market-share success. Effective low-share businesses compete in distinctive ways. They normally offer superior products at prices lower than competitors. This supports the traditional wisdom that success in any business ultimately depends on the benefits provided customers.

The most distinctive features of these strategies is selective focus. They do not copy the strategies of market leaders (unlike ineffective low-share businesses). These high-performing, low-share businesses choose particular bases of competition, such as product quality and price. They then limit their expenditures in other areas of competition, such as product R&D, product-line breadth, or marketing expenditures, so that they can achieve high performance despite relatively limited sales volume.

The specific strategy of any business must be tailored to its capabilities and the requirements of its competitive environment. Small-share businesses clearly vary widely in their possibilities. But the experience of these 40 companies demonstrates that success is possible for well-positioned and well-managed small-share businesses.

Notes

---

1. Bruce D. Henderson, *Henderson on Corporate Strategy* (Cambridge, Mass.: Abt Books, 1979), p. 94.

---

2. Robert D. Buzzell, Bradley T. Gale, and Ralph G.M. Sultan, "Market Share—A Key to Profitability," *HBR* January-February 1975, p. 97.

3. Richard G. Hamermesh, M. Jack Anderson, Jr., and J. Elizabeth Harris, "Strategies for Low Market Share Businesses," *HBR* May-June 1978, p. 95.

4. William K. Hall, "Survival Strategies in a Hostile Environment," *HBR* September-October 1980, p. 75.

5. PIMS (Profit Impact of Market Strategy) is a research program sponsored by the Strategic Planning Institute in Cambridge, Massachusetts and includes more than 1,000 member businesses.

6. For a detailed discussion of the methodology, refer to Carolyn Y. Woo and Arnold C. Cooper, "Strategies of Effective Low Share Businesses," *Strategic Management Journal*, July-September 1981, p. 301.

7. A correlation coefficient of + .26 was obtained between purchase frequency and working-capital-to-revenue. Based on the definition of the purchase frequency variable, the coefficient indicated that longer time periods between purchases (infrequently purchased products) were correlated with higher working-capital-to-revenues ratios.

14
End-Game Strategies for Declining Industries

KATHRYN RUDIE HARRIGAN and MICHAEL E. PORTER

During the last year or so you watched the demand for one of your business's products decline and noted that the same decline hit your competitors. Searching for a reason, you realize that your product may be becoming technologically obsolete. It looks as if it's just a question of time. Can you be profitable if you stay in and invest? What should your end-game strategy be?

> **End game** *n* **1**: the last stage (as the last three tricks) in playing a bridge hand **2**: the final phase of a board game; specifically the stage of a chess game following serious reduction of forces.[1]

As early as 1948, when researchers discovered the "transistor effect," it was evident that vacuum tubes in television sets had become technologically obsolete. Within a few years, transistor manufacturers were predicting that by 1961 half the television sets then in use would employ transistors instead of vacuum tubes.

Since the 1950s, manufacturers of vacuum tubes have been engaged in the industry's end game. Like other end games, this one is played in an environment of declining product demand where conditions make it very unlikely that all the plant capacity and competitors put in place during the industry's heyday will ever be needed. In today's world of little or no economic growth and rapid technological change, more and more companies are being faced with the need to cope with an end game.

Because of its musical chair character, the end game can be brutal. Consider the bloodbath in U.S. gasoline marketing today. Between 1973 and

Published 1983.

1983, in response to high crude oil prices and conservation efforts by consumers, the output from petroleum refineries declined precipitately. Uncertainty concerning supply and demand for refined products has made predicting the speed and extent of decline difficult, and an industry consensus has never evolved. Moreover, the competitors in this end game are very diverse in their outlooks and in the tactics they use to cope with the erratic nature of decline.

As in the baby food industry's end game, where a ten-year price war raged until demand plateaued, gasoline marketers and refiners are fighting to hold market shares of a shrinking pie. As industry capacity is painfully rationalized and companies dig in for the lean years ahead in their end game, a long period of low profits is inevitable.

In the vacuum tube industry, however, the end game was starkly different. Commercialization of solid-state devices progressed more slowly than the transistor manufacturers forecast. The last television set containing vacuum tubes was produced in 1974, and a vast population of electronic products requiring replacement tubes guaranteed a sizable market of relatively price-insensitive demand for some years. In 1983, several plants still produce tubes. Where obsolescence was a certainty and the decline rate slow, the six leading vacuum tube manufacturers were able to shut down excess plant capacity while keeping supply in line with demand. Price wars never ruined the profitability of their end game, and the companies that managed well during the decline earned satisfactorily high returns, particularly for declining businesses.

To recoup the maximum return on their investments, managers of some declining businesses are turning with considerable success to strategies that they had used only when demand was growing. In the past, the accepted prescription for a business on the wane has been a "harvest" strategy—eliminate investment, generate maximum cash flow, and eventually divest. The strategic portfolio models managers commonly use for planning yield this advice on declining industries: do not invest in low- or negative-growth markets, pull cash out instead.

Our study of declining industries suggests, however, that the nature of competition during a decline and the strategic alternatives available for coping with it are complex (see the appendix for a description of this study). The experiences of industries that have suffered an absolute decline in unit sales over a sustained period differ markedly. Some industries, like vacuum receiving tubes, age gracefully, and profitability for remaining competitors has been extremely high. Others, like rayon, decline amid bitter warfare, prolonged excess capacity, and heavy operating losses.

The stories of companies that have successfully coped with decline vary just as widely. Some companies, like GTE Sylvania, reaped high returns by making heavy investments in a declining industry that made their businesses better sources of cash later. By selling out before their competitors generally recognized the decline, and not harvesting, other companies, like Raytheon and DuPont, avoided losses that competitors subsequently bore.

In this article we discuss the strategic problems that declining demand poses, where decline is a painful reality and not a function of the business cycle or other short-term discontinuities. Sometimes, of course, innovations, cost reductions, and shifts in other circumstances may reverse a decline.[2] Our focus here, however, is on industries in which available remedies have been exhausted and the strategic problem is coping with decline. When decline is beyond the control of incumbent companies, managers need to develop end-game strategies.

First, we sketch the structural conditions that determine if the environment of a declining industry is hospitable, particularly as these affect competition. Second, we discuss the generic end-game strategy alternatives available to companies in decline. We conclude with some principles for choosing an end-game strategy.

What Determines the Competition?

Shrinking industry sales make the decline phase volatile. The extent to which escalating competitive pressures erode profitability during decline, however, depends on how readily industry participants pull out and how fiercely the companies that remain try to contain their shrinking sales.

Conditions of Demand

Demand in an industry declines for a number of reasons. Technological advances foster substitute products (electronic calculators for slide rules) often at lower cost or higher quality (synthetic for leather). Sometimes the customer group shrinks (baby foods) or buyers slide into trouble (railroads). Changes in life-style, buyers' needs, or tastes can also cause demand to decline (cigars and hatmaking equipment). Finally, the cost of inputs or complementary products may rise and shrink demand (recreational vehicles). The cause of decline helps determine how companies will perceive both future demand and profitability of serving the diminished market.

Companies' expectations concerning demand will substantially affect the type of competitive environment that develops in an end game. The process by which demand in an industry declines and the characteristics of those market segments that remain also have a great influence on competition during the decline phase.

Uncertainty. Correct or not, competitors' perceptions of demand in a declining industry potently affect how they play out their end-game strategies. If managers in the industry believe that demand will revitalize or level off, they will probably try to hold onto their positions. As the baby food industry example shows, efforts to maintain position despite shrinking sales will probably lead to warfare. On the other hand, if, as was the case of synthetic sodium carbonate (soda ash), managers in different companies are all certain that industry demand will continue to decline, reduction of capacity is more likely to be orderly.

Companies may well differ in their perceptions of future demand, with those that foresee revitalization persevering. A company's perception of the likelihood of decline is influenced by its position in the industry and its difficulty in getting out. The stronger its stake or the higher its exit barriers, the more optimistic a company's forecast of demand is likely to be.

Rate and Pattern of Decline.   Rapid and erratic decline greatly exacerbate the volatility of competition. How fast the industry collapses depends partly on the way in which companies withdraw capacity. In industrial businesses (such as the synthesis of soda ash) where the product is very important to customers but where a substitute is available, demand can fall drastically if one or two major producers decide to retire and customers doubt the continued availability of the original product. Announcements of early departure can give great impetus to the decline. Because shrinking volume raises costs and often prices, the decline rate tends to accelerate as time passes.

Structure of Remaining Demand Pockets.   In a shrinking market, the nature of the demand pockets that remain plays a major role in determining the remaining competitors' profitability. The remaining pocket in cigars has been premium-quality cigars, for example, while in vacuum tubes it has been replacement and military tubes.

If the remaining pocket has favorable structure, decline can be profitable for well-positioned competitors. For example, demand for premium-quality cigars is price insensitive: customers are immune to substitute products and very brand loyal. Thus, even as the industry declines, companies that offer branded, premium cigars are earning above-average returns. For the same reasons, upholstery leathers are a profitable market segment in the leather industry.

On the other hand, in the acetylene industry, ethylene has already replaced acetylene in some market segments and other substitutes threaten the remaining pockets. In those pockets, acetylene is a commodity product that, because of its high fixed manufacturing costs, is subject to price warfare. The potential for profit for its remaining manufacturers is dismal.

In general, if the buyers in the remaining demand pockets are price insensitive, for example, buyers of replacement vacuum tubes for television receivers, or have little bargaining power, survivors can profit. Price insensitivity is important because shrinking sales imply that companies must raise prices to maintain profitability in the face of fixed overhead.

The profit potential of remaining demand pockets will also depend on whether companies that serve them have mobility barriers that protect them from attack by companies seeking to replace lost sales.

Exit Barriers

Just as companies have to overcome barriers in entering a market, they meet exit barriers in leaving it. These barriers can be insurmountable even when a company is earning subnormal returns on its investment. The higher the exit barriers, the less hospitable the industry is during the industry's decline. A number of basic aspects of a business can become exit barriers.

Durable and Specialized Assets.   If the assets, either fixed or working capital or both, are specialized to the business, company, or location in which they are being used, their diminished liquidation value creates exit barriers. A company with specialized assets such as sole-leather tanneries must either sell them to someone who intends to use them in the same business, usually in the same location, or scrap them. Naturally, few buyers wish to use the assets of a declining business.

Once the acetylene and rayon industries started to contract, for example, potential buyers for plants were few or nonexistent; companies sold plants at enormous discounts from book value to speculators or desperate employee groups. Particularly if it represents a large part of assets and normally turns over very slowly, specialized inventory may also be worth very little in these circumstances. The problem of specialized assets is more acute where a company must make an all-or-nothing exit decision (e.g., continuous process plants) versus a decision to reduce the number of sites or close down lines.

If the liquidation value of the assets is low, it is possible for a company to show a loss on the books but earn discounted cash flows that exceed the value that could be realized if management sold the business. When several companies perform this same analysis and choose to remain in a declining industry, excess capacity grows and profit margins are usually depressed.

By expanding their search for buyers, managers can lower exit barriers arising from specialized assets. Sometimes assets find a market overseas even though they have little value in the home country. But as the industry decline becomes increasingly clear, the value of specialized assets will usually diminish. For example when Raytheon sold its vacuum tube-making assets in the early 1960s while tube demand was strong for color TV sets, it recovered a much higher liquidation than companies that tried to unload their vacuum facilities in the early 1970s, when the industry was clearly in its twilight years.

High Costs of Exit.   Large fixed costs—labor settlements, contingent liabilities for land use, or costs of dismantling facilities—associated with leaving a business elevate exit barriers. Sometimes even after a company leaves, it will have to supply spare parts to past customers or resettle employees. A company may also have to break long-term contracts, which, if they can be abrogated at all, may involve severe cancellation penalties. In many cases, the company will have to pay the cost of having another company fulfill such contracts.

On the other hand, companies can sometimes avoid making fixed investments such as for pollution control equipment, alternative fuel systems, or maintenance expenditures by abandoning a business. These requirements promote getting out because they increase investment without raising profits, and improve prospects for decline.

Strategic Considerations.   A diversified company may decide to remain in a declining industry for strategic reasons even if the barriers just described are low. These reasons include:

1. *Interrelatedness.*   A business may be part of a strategy that involves a group of businesses, such as whiskey and other distilled liquors, and dropping it would diminish overall corporate strategy. Or a business may be central to a company's identity or image, as in the case of General Cigar and Allied Leather, and leaving could hurt the company's relationships with key distribution channels and customers or lower the company's purchasing clout. Moreover, depending on the company's ability to transfer assets to new markets, quitting the industry may make shared plants or other assets idle.

2. *Access to financial markets.*   Leaving an industry may reduce a company's financial credibility and lessen its attractiveness to acquisition candidates or buyers. If the divested business is large relative to the total, divestment may hurt earnings growth or in some way raise the cost of capital, even if the write-off is economically justified. The financial market is likely to ignore small operating losses over a period of years buried among other profitable businesses while it will react strongly to a single large loss. While a diversified company may be able to use the tax loss from a write-off to mitigate the negative cash flow impact of exit decisions, the write-off will typically still have an effect on financial markets. Recently the markets have looked favorably on companies who take their losses on businesses with little future, an encouraging sign.

3. *Vertical integration.*   When companies are vertically integrated, barriers to exit will depend on whether the cause of decline touches the entire chain or just one link. In the case of acetylene, obsolescence made downstream chemical businesses, using acetylene as a feedstock, redundant; a company's decision whether to stay or go had to encompass the whole chain. In contrast, if a downstream unit depended on a feedstock that a substitute product had made obsolete, it would be strongly motivated to find an outside supplier of the substitute. In this case, the company's forward integration might hasten the decision to abandon the upstream unit because it had become a strategic liability to the whole company. In our study of end-game strategies, we found that most vertically integrated companies "deintegrated" before facing the final go/no go decision.

Information Gaps.   The more a business is related to others in the company, and especially when it shares assets or has a buyer-seller relationship, the more difficult it can be for management to get reliable information about its performance. For example, a failing coffee percolator unit may be part of a profit center with other small electrical housewares that sell well, and the company might not see the percolator unit's performance accurately and thus fail to consider abandoning the business.

Managerial Resistance. Although the exit barriers we've described are based on rational calculations, or the inability to make them because of failures in information, the difficulties of leaving a business extend well beyond the purely economic. Managers' emotional attachments and commitments to a business—coupled with pride in their accomplishments and fears about their own futures—create emotional exit barriers. In a single-business company, quitting the business costs managers their jobs and creates personal problems for them such as a blow to their pride, the stigma of having "given up," severance of an identification that may have been longstanding, and a signal of failure that reduces job mobility.

It is difficult for managers of a sick division in a diversified company to propose divestment, so the burden of deciding when to quit usually falls on top management. But loyalty can be strong even at that level, particularly if the sick division is part of the historical core of the company or was started or acquired by the current CEO. For example, General Mills's decision to divest its original business, flour, was an agonizing choice that took management many years to make. And the suggestion that Sunbeam stop producing electric percolator coffee makers and waffle irons met stiff resistance in the boardroom.

In some cases, even though unsatisfactory performance is chronic, managerial exit barriers can be so strong that divestments are not made until top management changes.[3] Divestments are probably the most unpalatable decisions managers have to make.[4]

Personal experience with abandoning businesses, however, can reduce managers' reluctance to get out of an industry. In an industry such as chemicals where technological failure and product substitution are common, in industries where product lives are historically short, or in high-technology companies where new businesses continually replace old ones, executives can become used to distancing themselves from emotional considerations and making sound divestment decisions.

Social Barriers. Because government concern for jobs is high and the price of divestiture may be concessions from other businesses in the company or other prohibitive terms, closing down a business can often be next to impossible, especially in foreign countries. Divestiture often means putting people out of work, and managers understandably feel concern for their employees. Workers who have produced vacuum tubes for 30 years may have little understanding of solid-state manufacturing techniques. Divestiture can also mean crippling a local economy. In the depressed Canadian pulp industry, closing down mills means closing down whole towns.[5]

Asset Disposition.   The manner in which companies dispose of assets can strongly influence the profitability of a declining industry and create or destroy exit barriers for competitors. If a company doesn't retire a large plant but sells it to a group of entrepreneurs at a low price, the industry capacity does not change but the competition does. The new entity can make pricing decisions and take other actions that are rational for it but cripple the competition. Thus if the owners of a plant don't retire assets but sell out instead, the remaining competitors can suffer more than if the original owners had stayed on.

Volatility of End Game

Because of falling sales and excess capacity, competitors fighting in an end game are likely to resort to fierce price warfare. Aggression is especially likely if the industry has maverick competitors with diverse goals and outlooks and high exit barriers, or if the market is very inhospitable (see Exhibit I).

As an industry declines, it can become less important to suppliers (which raises costs or diminishes service) while the power of distributors increases. In the cigar business, for example, because cigars are an impulse item, shelf positioning is crucial to success, and it's the distributor who deals with the retailer. In the whiskey trade too, distillers hotly compete for the best wholesalers. Decline has led to substantial price pressures from these powerful middlemen that have reduced profitability. On the other hand, if the industry is a key customer, suppliers may attempt to help fight off decline as, for example, pulp producers helped the rayon industry fight cotton.

Perhaps the worst kind of waning-industry environment occurs when one or more weakened companies with significant corporate resources are committed to stay in the business. Their weakness forces them to use desperate actions, such as cutting prices, and their staying power forces other companies to respond likewise.

Strategic Alternatives for Declining Businesses

Discussions of strategy for shrinking industries usually focus on divestment or harvest strategies, but managers should consider two other alternatives as well—leadership and niche. These four strategies for decline vary greatly, not only in their goals but also in their implications for investment, and managers can pursue them individually or, in some cases, sequentially:

Leadership

A company following the market share leadership strategy tries to reap above-average profitability by becoming one of the few companies remaining in a declining industry. Once a company attains this position, depending on

Exhibit 1. Structural Factors that Influence the Attractiveness of Declining Industry Environments

Structural Factors	Environmental Attractiveness	
	Hospitable	Inhospitable
Conditions of demand		
Speed of decline	Very slow	Rapid or erratic
Certainty of decline	100% certain predictable patterns	Great uncertainty, erratic patterns
Pockets of enduring demand	Several or major ones	No niches
Product differentiation	Brand loyalty	Commodity-like products
Price stability	Stable, price premiums attainable	Very unstable, pricing below costs
Exit barriers		
Reinvestment requirements	None	High, often mandatory and involving capital assets
Excess capacity	Little	Substantial
Asset age	Mostly old assets	Sizable new assets and old ones not retired
Resale markets for assets	Easy to convert or sell	No markets available, substantial costs to retire
Shared facilities	Few free-standing plants	Substantial and interconnected with important businesses
Vertical integration	Little	Substantial
"Single product" competitors	None	Several large companies
Rivalry determinants		
Customer industries	Fragmented, weak	Strong bargaining power
Customer switching costs	High	Minimal
Diseconomies of scale	None	Substantial penalty
Dissimilar strategic groups	Few	Several in same target markets

the subsequent pattern of industry sales, it usually switches to a holding position or controlled harvest strategy. The underlying premise is that by achieving leadership the company can be more profitable (taking the investment into account) because it can exert more control over the process of decline and avoid destabilizing price competiton. Investing in a slow or diminishing market is risky because capital may be frozen and resistant to retrieval through profits or liquidation. Under this strategy, however, the company's dominant position in the industry should give it cost leadership or differentiation that allows recovery of assets even if it reinvests during the deline period.

Managers can achieve a leadership position via several tactical maneuvers:

☐ Ensure that other companies rapidly retire from the industry. H.J. Heinz and Gerber Products took aggressive competitive actions in pricing, marketing, and other areas that built market share and dispelled competitors' dreams of battling it out.

☐ Reduce competitors' exit barriers. GTE Sylvania built market share by acquiring competitors' product lines at prices above the going rate. American Viscose purchased—and retired—competitors' capacity. (Taking this step ensures that others within the industry do not buy the capacity.) General Electric manufactured spare parts for competitors' products. Rohm & Haas took over competitors' long-term contracts in the acetylene industry. Proctor-Silex produced private-label goods for competitors so that they could stop their manufacturing operations.

☐ Develop and disclose credible market information. Reinforcing other manager's certainty about the inevitability of decline makes it less likely that competitors will overestimate the prospects for the industry and remain in it.

☐ Raise the stakes. Precipitating the need of other competitors to reinvest in new products or process improvements makes it more costly for them to stay in the business.

Niche

The objective of this focus strategy is to identify a segment of the declining industry that will either maintain stable demand or decay slowly, and that has structural characteristics allowing high returns. A company then moves preemptively to gain a strong position in this segment while disinvesting from other segments. Armira followed a niche strategy in leather. tanning, as Courtaulds did in rayon. To reduce either competitors' exit barriers from the chosen segment or their uncertainty about the segment's profitability, management might decide to take some of the actions listed under the leadership strategy.

Harvest

In the harvest strategy, undergoing a controlled disinvestment, management seeks to get the most cash flow it can from the business. DuPont followed this course with its rayon business and BASF Wyandotte did the same in soda ash. To increase cash flow, management eliminates or severely curtails new investment, cuts maintenance of facilities, and reduces advertising and research while reaping the benefits of past goodwill. Other common harvest tactics include reducing the number of models produced; cutting the number of distribution channels; eliminating small customers; and eroding service in terms of delivery time (and thus reducing inventory), speed of repair, or sales assistance.

Companies following a harvest strategy often have difficulty maintaining suppliers' and customers' confidence, however, and thus some businesses cannot be fully harvested. Moreover, harvesting tests managers' skills as administrators because it creates problems in retaining and motivating employees. These considerations make harvest a risky option and far from the universal cure-all that it is sometimes purported to be.

Ultimately, managers following a harvest strategy will sell or liquidate the business.

Quick Divestment

Executives employing this strategy assume that the company can recover more of its investment from the business by selling it in the early stages of the decline, as Raytheon did, than by harvesting and selling it later or by following one of the other courses of action. The earlier the business is sold, the greater is potential buyers' uncertainty about a future slide in demand and thus the more likely that management will find buyers either at home or in foreign countries for the assets.

In some situations it may be desirable to divest the business before decline or, as DuPont did with its acetylene business, in the maturity phase. Once it's clear that the industry is waning, buyers for the assets will be in a strong bargaining position. On the other hand, a company that sells early runs the risk that its forecast will prove incorrect, as did RCA's judgment of the future of vacuum tubes.

Divesting quickly will force the company to confront its own exit barriers, such as its customer relationships and corporate interdependencies. Planning for an early departure can help managers mitigate the effect of these factors to some extent, however. For example, a company can arrange for remaining competitors to sell its products if it is necessary to continue to supply replacements, as Westinghouse Electric did for vacuum tubes.

Choosing a Strategy for Decline

With an understanding of the characteristics that shape competition in a declining industry and the different strategies they might use, managers can now ask themselves what their position should be:

☐ Can the structure of the industry support a hospitable, potentially profitable, decline phase (see Exhibit 1)?

☐ What are the exit barriers that each significant competitor faces? Who will exit quickly and who will remain?

☐ Do your company's strengths fit the remaining pockets of demand?

☐ What are your competitors' strengths in these pockets? How can their exit barriers be overcome?

In selecting a strategy, managers need to match the remaining opportunities in the industry with their companies' positions. The strengths and weaknesses that helped and hindered a company during the industry's development are not necessarily those that will count during the end game, where success will depend on the requirements to serve the pockets of demand that persist and the competition for this demand.

Exhibit 2 displays, albeit crudely, the strategic options open to a company in decline. When, because of low uncertainty, low exit barriers, and so forth, the industry structure is likely to go through an orderly decline phase, strong companies can either seek leadership or defend a niche, depending on the value to them of remaining market segments. When a company has no outstanding strengths for the remaining segments, it should either harvest or divest early. The choice depends, of course, on the feasibility of harvesting and the opportunities for selling the business.

When high uncertainty, high exit barriers, or conditions leading to volatile end-game rivalry make the industry environment hostile, investing to achieve leadership is not likely to yield rewards. If the company has strengths in the market segments that will persist, it can try either shrinking into a protected niche, or harvesting, or both. Otherwise, it is well advised to get out as quickly as its exit barriers permit. If it tries to hang on, other companies with high exit barriers and greater strengths will probably attack its position.

This simple framework must be supplemented by a third dimension of this problem—that is to say, a company's strategic need to remain in the business. For example, cash flow requirements may skew a decision toward harvest or early sale even though other factors point to leadership, as interrelationships with other units may suggest a more aggressive stance than otherwise. To determine the correct strategy a company should assess its strategic needs vis-à-vis the business and modify its end-game strategy accordingly.

Exhibit 2.   Strategies for Declining Businesses

	Has competitive strengths for remaining demand pockets	Lacks competitive strengths for remaining demand pockets
Favorable industry structure for decline	Leadership or niche	Harvest or divest quickly
Unfavorable industry structure for decline	Niche or harvest	Divest quickly

Usually it is advantageous to make an early commitment to one end-game strategy or another. For instance, if a company lets competitors know from the outset that it is bent on a leadership position, it may not only encourage other companies to quit the business but also gain more time to establish its leadership. However, sometimes companies may want to bide their time by harvesting until indecisive competitors make up their minds. Until the situation is clear, a company may want to make preparations to invest should the leader go, and have plans to harvest or divest immediately should the leader stay. In any case, however, successful companies should *choose* an end-game strategy rather than let one be chosen for them.

The best course, naturally, is anticipation of the decline. If a company can forecast industry conditions, it may be able to improve its end-game position by taking steps during the maturity phase (sometimes such moves cost little in strategic position at the time):

☐   Minimize investments or other actions that will raise exit barriers unless clearly beneficial to overall corporate strategy.

☐   Increase the flexibility of assets so that they can accept different raw materials or produce related products.

☐   Place strategic emphasis on market segments that can be expected to endure when the industry is in a state of decline.

☐   Create customer-switching costs in these segments.

Avoiding Checkmate

Finding your company's position in Exhibit 2 requires a great deal of subtle analysis that is often shortchanged in the face of severe operating problems during decline. Many managers overlook the need to make strategy in decline consistent with industry structure because decline is viewed as somehow different. Our study of declining industries revealed other factors common to profitable players:

They Recognize Decline.   With hindsight, it is all too easy to admonish companies for being over-optimistic about the prospects for their declining industries' revitalization. Nevertheless, some executives, such as those of U.S. oil refineries, fail to look objectively at the prospects of decline. Either their identification with an industry is too great or their perception of substitute products is too narrow. The presence of high exit barriers may also subtly affect how managers perceive their environment; because bad omens are so painful to recognize, people understandably look for good signs.

Our examination of many declining industries indicates that the companies that are most objective about managing the decline process are also participants in the substitute industry. They have a clearer perception concerning the prospects of the substitute product and the reality of decline.

They Avoid Wars of Attrition.   Warfare among competitors that have high exit barriers, such as the leather tanning companies, usually leads to disaster. Competitors are forced to respond vigorously to others' moves and cannot yield position without a big investment loss.

They Don't Harvest Without Definite Strengths.   Unless the industry's structure is very favorable during the decline phase, companies that try to harvest without definite strengths usually collapse. Once marketing or service deteriorates or a company raises its prices, customers quickly take their business elsewhere. In the process of harvesting, the resale value of the business may also dissipate. Because of the competitive and administrative risks of harvesting, managers need a clear justification to choose this strategy.

They View Decline as a Potential Opportunity.   Declining industries can sometimes be extraordinarily profitable for the well-positioned players, as GE and Raytheon have discovered in vacuum tubes. Companies that can view an industry's decline as an opportunity rather than just a problem, and make objective decisions, can reap handsome rewards.

Notes

---

1. *Webster's Third New International Dictionary* (Springfield, Mass: G.&C. Merriam, 1976). The term has also been used for an existentialist play by Samuel Beckett.

---

2. See Michael E. Porter, *Competitive Strategy* (New York: Free Press, 1980), Chapter 8. The book also contains a treatment of exit barriers and other industry and competitor characteristics discussed in this article.

3. See, for example, Stuart C. Gilmour, "The Divestment Decision Process," DBA dissertation, Harvard Graduate School of Business Administration, 1973; and Kathryn Rudie Harrigan, *Strategies for Declining Businesses* (Lexington, Mass: D.C. Heath, 1980).

4. See Michael E. Porter, *Interbrand Choice, Strategy and Bilateral Market Power* (Cambridge: Harvard University Press, 1976).

5. See Nitin T. Mehta, "Policy Formulation in a Declining Industry: The Case of the Canadian Dissolving Pulp Industry," DBA dissertation, Harvard Graduate School of Business Administration, 1978.

Appendix

Study of Strategies for Declining Businesses

Compiling 20-year histories of industry competition and company departures, we studied the strategies of 61 companies in eight declining industries. We interviewed key competitors in the rayon and acetate, cigar, baby food, electric percolator coffee maker, electronic vacuum receiving tube, acetylene, synthetic soda ash, and U.S. leather tanning industries. (Follow-up studies examined the petroleum refining and whiskey distilling industries and attained consistent results). Leaving their industries, 42 companies were profitable or did not suffer significant losses. Thirty-nine of the 42 successful companies followed the prescriptions of the strategy matrix shown in Exhibit 2. Sixteen of the 19 unsuccessful companies acted contrary to the recommendations of the strategy matrix. In short, if companies followed the matrix recommendations, their chances for success were better than 92%, while if they did not follow them, their chances of success were about 15%.

15

Gateways to Entry

GEORGE S. YIP

The entry of new competitors into established markets is a strategic issue for both entrants and existing competitors. The incumbents may be comforted by the thought that their profitable markets are protected by what marketing managers call barriers to entry—whether they be economies of scale, product differentiation, absolute cost advantages, access to distribution channels, superior skills and resources, the threat of retaliation, or any combination of these. On the other hand, potential entrants may worry about the barriers they have to avoid or surmount and whether they can develop strategies that will work to their advantage. However powerful a defense weapon these may be, they are not impregnable. In this article, the author offers a framework for identifying and evaluating the different types of barriers and discusses a new concept for turning them into gateways to entry.

Managers today, increasingly interested in long-term planning, are achieving corporate growth by selecting new markets to enter and developing the appropriate entry strategies. The other two sources of corporate growth— present markets and acquisitions—are far less attractive today for many companies than a decade ago. Some companies participate in growth markets, but many others languish in stagnant ones. Moreover, as companies have struggled to manage their newly adopted, fully grown, and intractable "children," acquisition has lost much of the luster it used to hold.

Despite its increasing popularity, direct entry is elusive. Newcomers must penetrate that first line of market defense—barriers to entry. Why do some companies succeed and others fail? Entry is one of the supreme tests of competitive ability. No longer is the company proving itself on familiar ground; instead it has to expose its competencies in a new area.

Entry is also a trial for incumbent competitors. The efforts of new-comers to establish themselves frequently render the market less profitable

---

Published 1982.

for all. Even worse for the incumbents, the new players often possess superior skills, greater resources, and new ways to compete.

The concept of barriers, developed by industrial organization economists, was introduced into the business world decades ago. Some incumbents may take comfort in thinking that they have erected impregnable barriers to protect their profitable markets. Potential entrants may worry about the heights they have to scale. Yet there has been no systematic approach for managers to use in determining the effectiveness of entry barriers—or to devise ways of overcoming or sustaining them.

This article offers such a framework by building on Michael E. Porter's pioneering work in integrating industrial organization economics with business strategy. The "threat of new entrants" is one of the five forces Porter identified as governing competition in an industry.[1]

On the basis of my two-year study of barriers to entry, which includes collection and analysis of new data, I will provide a framework for evaluating the different types of entry barriers and how they work. At the same time, I will describe the concept of "gateways to entry," which shows that the same factors giving rise to barriers can be exploited to an entrant's advantage. One crucial conclusion, which I shall elaborate on, is that potential entrants are far less deterred by barriers than marketing managers might think.

Types of Barriers

What constitutes entry depends on the definition of the particular market. The entries I will concentrate on are limited to products, assets, and activities developed internally for new markets. Likewise, the barriers described are those that apply to direct entry. Another route that many large companies prefer—acquisition—faces a different set of problems that I will discuss later.

The disadvantages that entrants face relative to incumbents arise from the fact of direct entry and are separate from the disadvantages of size or general inferiority in skills and resources. Smaller-company entrants face the usual size, skill, and resource handicaps common to most existing small competitors. Entry against established incumbents creates additional problems.

Barriers are, therefore, an inherent feature of the market and can exact a cost from all entrants crossing them. The six major classes of barriers— economies of scale, product differentiation, absolute cost, access to distribution, capital requirement, and incumbent reaction—are well known and require no elaboration here.

How They Work
Barriers protect markets in two ways: they can deter some potential entrants at the outset, and they can prevent or dampen the success of those who do

enter. In my study of nearly 800 markets I found that, contrary to traditional economic theory and marketing managers' beliefs, most types of barriers seldom deter entrants. For example, high-barrier markets are no less likely to be entered than those with low barriers. (See the accompanying ruled insert for my study methodology.)

On the other hand, many entrants are not particularly well qualified to achieve success. From my subsample of 31 representative markets, the 45 most successful direct entrants typically had a worse position than the leading incumbents on most of the important strategic dimensions: product quality; price; cost; production, sales force, and distribution effectiveness; advertising and promotion expenditure; and reputation or brand name.

The weak strategic position of the 45 direct entrants resulted in poor performance on the most important measure—market share. Two-thirds of the entrants, even six years after entry, had failed to capture a share level that the incumbents estimated as the minimum required for a major competitor in a particular market. Unfortunately for incumbents, even the weak share performance of the new entrants reduced the existing competitors' profit margins on sales by an average of 7%.

Reducing or Avoiding Barriers

Barriers often produce disadvantages for both parties. Ignoring barriers, newcomers rush in—with kamikaze results for themselves as well as incumbents. Using a two-step process, direct entrants can evaluate barriers and their chances of success. First, potential entrants should examine the extent of each type of roadblock. (I will not elaborate on this step since it is the easier one; what is difficult is having the discipline to do it, explicitly and thoroughly.) The much harder second step is a determination of whether and how they can reduce or avoid the barriers.

The key to the second step lies in one of two strategic approaches: (1) whether the entrants can reduce barriers by using the same competitive strategy as the incumbents or (2) whether the entrants can avoid them by using a different strategy.

Barriers are obviously most effective when entrants challenge incumbents at their own game with fewer skills and resources. A successful strategy consists, of course, of many elements spanning all business functions: marketing, production, financial, and so forth.

The more mature the market, the more likely it is that customer, channel, and supplier practices and expectations have drastically curtailed any challenger's range of strategic choice. Thus, it is doubly tempting for entrants to use a clone strategy: incumbents have demonstrated how to execute it and customers have shown that they accept it. My evidence cited earlier— that newcomers have worse strategic positions than incumbents—strongly suggests that most entrants do use clone strategies that they execute with less experience and fewer assets.

Using the Same Strategy

If they deploy sufficient skills and resources, direct entrants using the same strategy as incumbents can minimize barriers. Challengers who already operate in other markets can transfer capabilities to the new market to reduce the effect of the barriers they face. Most entrants already have other markets; of the U.S. entrants in my study, only eight were new companies.

Indeed, even newly created entrants have abundant skills, and perhaps resources, if they are founded by executives breaking away from an incumbent in the same market. Witness the spawning of many such companies in the computer industry. And the airline industry is also demonstrating this phenomenon—as Southwest Airlines has given birth to Muse Air and Texas International Airlines to People Express.

The existing talents and assets of new entrants can reduce barriers in many ways:

1. Required *economies of scale* may already be met. For example, huge economies are possible in R&D if the entrants develop many products from one set of laboratories. On the other hand, even the incumbents may find the required scale too great for them. Recently, Richardson-Merrell, Inc. divested its ethical drug business mostly because its sales could not support the minimum necessary size in R&D.

2. The *product differentiation* disadvantage may be offset if the entrant uses a well-known brand name from one of its existing markets. An entrant's name in other fields may even be stronger than existing brands in the entered market. In its incipient all-fronts assault on the total market for financial services, American Express will doubtless benefit from a name recognition and prestige greater than that of almost all incumbents in the markets it attacks.

3. Entrants may already have access to the labor or raw material sources that give an *absolute cost advantage* to incumbents. They may even have access to cheaper labor or raw materials, an advantage enjoyed by many new competitors from the Far East.

4. Entrants may already possess *distribution* networks to serve the new market. For example, the preferred diversification strategy of consumer products marketers is to develop new products for distribution through their existing channels. Dart & Kraft recently announced its entry into the wine market, using the Kraft sales force to obtain rapid distribution. Conversely, Komatsu, the Japanese entrant in the U.S. earth-moving equipment market, has been limited to a 10% segment share and a 3% total market share, primarily because the U.S. incumbents had already tied up the best dealers. In particular, market-leading Caterpillar has twice as many (and mostly exclusive) high-capitalized dealers as Komatsu's nonexclusive, low-capitalized dealers.

5. Existing companies that have no problems in raising the *capital required* for direct entry often enter markets to reinvest surplus funds. IBM

and Xerox dominate the market for electronic office equipment, which needs a great deal of capital for basic R&D and product development. A recent entrant, Exxon, has not found capital to be a barrier (as might be expected).

6. Incumbents may be less eager to *retaliate* against an entry launched by an existing company with a deep pocket or a reputation as a tough competitor. Even better than a rich parent company is a generous government or two. Airbus Industrie was able to enter the U.S. market by offering financing provided by European governments to Eastern Airlines, which Boeing could not match.

If barriers are a wall, existing skills and resources are a platform. Thus, entrants can go beyond reducing the height of barriers and can, in fact, obtain an advantage over incumbents. For example, if the barrier is product differentiation created or maintained by high advertising expenditures, an entrant more adept at advertising or with more resources to spend on it can turn this barrier against incumbents. Thus, advertising becomes a quick way to get into the market, and the product differentiation issue becomes a gateway to entry.

Procter & Gamble is a master of the higher-platform gateway. Its entry strategies are seldom radically new. Instead, they combine incremental advantages on many dimensions with overwhelming marketing support. P&G took such an approach in its entry into the tampon market with Rely. The results were disastrous for competitors, who were saved only by the toxic shock crisis, which prompted P&G's reluctant retreat.

Advantages of Lateness. Often, direct entrants need not even have superior skills and resources to benefit from a higher platform. There can be a number of advantages in lateness:

1. Entrants can feature the latest technological improvements in their products, while incumbents are committed to their current investments. Prestel in Britain, the world's first commercial system in view-data/videotext, has been surpassed in technological capabilities by a later German entrant. The West German Bundespost built its superior Bildschirmtext system on Prestel software and know-how. A game of leapfrog will no doubt continue in this market.

2. Entrants can achieve greater economies of scale than incumbents. Usually the optimal size of plant continually increases, with corresponding cost decreases.

3. Entrants can obtain better terms from suppliers, employees, or customers. In many markets, older companies are locked into higher labor costs. For example, new airlines such as New York Air and People Express enjoy big cost advantages because they employ younger and less expensive crews and also because they are generally less encumbered by contracts, union agreements, and route-system obligations.

4.   Entrants can offer lower prices that incumbents find costly to match. An entrant offering lower prices to part of the market poses an unpleasant dilemma for incumbents: Should they forego all of the margin on some of their customers by not matching the entrant's cut, or should they forego some of the margin on all of their customers by matching the cut?

5.   Entrants can attack the particular weak link of a business strategy, while incumbents cannot fully respond without upsetting their entire system. In the tight-knit world of oil field services, SWECO invaded the market for "mud cleaners"—that is, the equipment for cleaning and recycling drilling fluid—and captured a large share of it. SWECO sold only the cleaners while incumbents sold the cleaners and the mud. Whereas the mud had furnished the greater portion of incumbents' revenues, SWECO's more efficient cleaners reduced mud consumption. Thus, the incumbents were constrained in defense of the equipment portions of their drilling-fluid systems.

In markets where lateness offers advantages, incumbents are riding a down elevator relative to future entrants.

Using a Different Strategy

The higher-platform gateway holds for direct entrants using essentially the same, but stronger, competitive strategies as incumbents. The only qualitative differences are in incremental improvements such as more up-to-date plant and equipment. Even a markedly superior product is a clone strategy when the product provides the same customer benefits as existing products.

Another major gateway involves using a different strategy from incumbents. Such a strategy need not be stronger to create a gateway. And entrants need not be strategic clones of incumbents.[2]

The three sources of different strategies are: (1) radical opportunities to exploit technological or environmental changes, (2) opportunities to avoid direct competition, and (3) opportunities to negate barriers by changing the accepted business structure.

Exploit Technological Change.   Radical technological or environmental changes usually offer the widest gateway for most entrants, and such changes tend to be the most dangerous for incumbents. When incumbents are unwilling or unable to adapt, they magnify the entry opportunities posed by technological change. In cardiac pacemakers, for example, market leader Medtronic invited a breakaway entrant in the early 1970s when it failed to switch to a new lithium-based technology. Medtronic wanted to milk its existing product lines rather than to invest in new ones. The entrant, CPI, had no such constraint, thereby using a product innovation to offset the incumbent's reputation and distribution barriers.

Technological and environmental changes can also easily destroy the scale barrier to entry. The entrenched companies' commitments to large-scale but obsolete facilities become their feet of clay—both fragile and immobile.

Legal and regulatory changes have frequently removed or lessened the barrier imposed by law. Such changes should not be equated with the creation of gateways. The removal of the legal or regulatory barrier merely allows entry, which can be sufficient for successful follow-through if the legal barrier had restricted satisfaction of demand. Where no great imbalance of supply and demand exists, entrants must still find gateways via superior skills and resources, the advantages of lateness, or some strategy different from that of incumbents.

The recent deregulation of the airline industry provides examples of entry into both situations of unsatisfied demand and supply-demand balance. Some new airlines have simply created new routes between previously unserved destinations: a me-too strategy has been sufficient in such cases. Others, such as New York Air, have entered existing routes but with some areas of advantage over incumbents.

Avoid Direct Competition.   Entrants cannot rely on technological or environmental changes to create gateways, nor can incumbents rely on their absence as surety of protection. Entrants can also sidestep barriers by avoiding direct competition with incumbents—that is, by offering a product or service that satisfies another need or customer group. Obviously, a sufficiently different offering may consitute a separate market. Yet incumbents should be wary. American and British motorcycle manufacturers have learned to their sorrow that what they considered a different but contiguous market— small motorcycles—was to the Japanese a beachhead in the same market.

Such flank-attack entries post two types of danger for incumbents, as well as corresponding opportunities for entrants. The flank position can be used as a base to gain experience and credibility for invading the core market, or—often more dramatic—the flank position itself becomes the core market. Michelin's push into the United States with steel-belted radial tires greatly accelerated the shift of the core market from bias-ply to radial.

How does a flank entry avoid barriers? A product appealing to a somewhat different need or customer group obviously avoids some of the differentiation barrier. For example, entrants selling liquid soaps are assailing the hitherto monolithic toilet-soap oligopoly. In one year, the number of competitors offering liquid soap for domestic use jumped from 0 to 40.

The liquid-soap example also shows how the flank strategy can reduce scale barriers. To achieve comparable costs, entrants have not needed to build huge plants similar to those of incumbents. Their differentiated entry also reduces the distribution barrier. Obtaining shelf space is much easier than with a me-too product.

Reduction of the scale, differentiation, and cost barriers can obviously lower the capital barrier. Versatec made a successful low-capital entry into the computer peripheral-plotter-machine market by minimizing all facets of the scale of its operation. This approach was sound because Versatec focused on a narrow and untargeted market segment.

Perhaps the most dramatic aspect of avoiding direct competition is its impact on the retaliation barrier. If incumbents keep to their existing product lines, an indirect entry avoids the full rigors of direct retaliation, which requires matching the entrant's product. Frequently, however, incumbents are constrained from such direct retaliation. Cannibalization of existing sales intervenes. So does the fear of giving the entrant a stamp of approval. For the past decade, U.S. automobile manufacturers have faced this dilemma concerning smaller imports. Traditional soap companies feel similarly constrained about the new entrants. As yet, only Procter & Gamble has decided to copy them. Facing the same situation in the United Kingdom, neither of the market leaders (Lever Brothers and P&G) has responded.

Negate the Barriers. The third flank gateway is to change the accepted business structure and thus avoid the barriers, while still offering competitive products. The soft-drink industry, for example, poses huge distribution barriers since there are a limited number of bottlers, most of whom have highly lucrative contracts with Coca-Cola or Pepsi. Shasta negated this problem by distributing its product in a different way—directly to supermarkets. And Japanese manufacturers of many consumer durables have overcome service network barriers in the United States by building more reliability into their products.

Entrants who choose this approach benefit most in terms of the retaliation barrier. That is, incumbents have built barriers via their existing business structure, and these commitments become their own barriers to response. A radically new business structure can also provide marketing, as well as production and delivery, advantages. Federal Express uses an uncommon production system—delivering packages in its own planes—as its own marketing tool.

All three differentiated strategies—exploiting technological or environmental changes, avoiding direct competition, and negating the barriers—rely on incumbents' responses being restrained by their own commitments. Given the absence of such constraints, however, entrants—even the me-too's—can benefit from the lethargy of those already in the market.

An earlier study by Ralph Biggadike found that entrants faced little direct reaction from incumbents;[3] the fear may be greater than the reality. Large, established parent companies seem the most feared, since their markets are among the least likely to be entered.

The Acquisition Route

Acquiring a competitor is another gateway to entry that of course avoids the barriers altogether: this strategy does not add a competitor but does introduce a new one. These new owners may have more ambitious plans than the previous owners, and they may also have the resources to back those plans. Such a new competitor may also play the game differently. Thus, acquisition entry may be the prelude to a blitzkrieg on incumbents, without any initial barriers to slow the assault.

Acquisition entry is a frequently exercised option. My subsample of 31 markets reveals that there is one acquisition entry made for every two attempted directly. Acquisition's advantages over direct entry arise to the extent that the acquiring of immediate share, assets, and skills allows the new owners to avoid not only entry barriers but also the uncertainty of high-risk new ventures.

A classic example of the dangers to incumbents of acquisition entry is Philip Morris's acquisition of Miller Brewing Company. Philip Morris entered the beer market with the intention of converting Miller from a minor competitor with a 4% market share into a major one. Ten years later, Miller is now second in the market with more than a 20% share. Philip Morris had both the financial resources and competitive skills to exploit its 4% entry base fully.

Incumbents should therefore be aware of the threat of acquisition entry as a potential Trojan horse—dangerous new competitors may pass right through the front gate. For example, Bausch & Lomb, which had been so successful in the contact lens market that it drove weaker competitors to sell out to large and aggressive acquisition entrants, in recent years has found itself competing with Revlon, Schering-Plough, Johnson & Johnson, Ciba-Geigy, SmithKline, and Nestlé.

Reasons for Caution

Despite its advantage in avoiding barriers, for the following reasons entrants should not automatically choose the acquisition mode:

1. The acquisition route is not always available, since the supply of candidates in a market at any time is usually limited. In addition, antitrust constraints may come into play.

2. There are differing financial and managerial implications between direct entry and acquisition. The financial differences in terms of both the balance sheet and the profit-and-loss statement are obvious. Less evident are the differing risks and opportunities faced by the managers responsible. Direct entry is usually the more risky gateway since no guarantee exists that there will ever be an ongoing business of the required size and profitability. The generally long period of start-up losses imposes many strains and career risks on managers.

On the other hand, acquisition entry normally imposes different risks and demands on managers. To justify the price paid, those responsible for operating the new business may be expected to make rapid turnaround improvements or to quickly achieve synergy with the new owner. The two modes may therefore require different styles of management—a more entrepreneurial approach for direct entry and a more organization-conscious and cost-conscious approach for acquisition entry.

    3. Perhaps most important, to the extent that capital markets are efficient, the price of an acquisition includes a premium representing what it would have cost an entrant to breach the barriers directly. An entrant that can reduce or avoid barriers in the ways I have described would therefore be paying too much to achieve entry via acquisition. Thus, acquisition should be a fallback choice for those seeking to enter high-barrier markets without the time, skills, or resources to penetrate those barriers. My study findings confirm that markets with high barriers are more likely to be entered via acquisition than directly.

Some Caveats

While the foregoing framework for evaluating the different types of barriers and how they work offers several paths for potential entrants to explore—gateways to entry that involve both reducing and avoiding barriers—some caveats are in order.

    In using existing skills and resources to reduce entry problems, these assets must really be transferable to the new market. A realistic assessment of ways of lowering barriers requires a clear specification of how these various capabilities will be applied. A general sense of synergy is not enough. Anheuser-Busch, which has many apparent skills and resources to apply to the soft-drinks business, has failed twice in entry attempts.

    In using a differentiated strategy to avoid barriers, entrants have to ensure that they deliver real advantages in cost or customer appeal. Many companies have been lured into setting up operations to deliver a different product that customers supposedly crave. Even economists have fallen into this trap. Encouraged by the grumblings of clients, the field of commercial economic forecasting has recently spawned breakaways. These entrants have found the grumblings to be mostly just that.

    Potential entrants face many barriers but they also have a range of options—from a me-too strategy applied with fewer capabilities to combinations of multiple advantages via both resource superiority and strategic differentiation. The strongest entry strategy, however, is not automatically the best choice because it is also usually the most costly, difficult, and time consuming. Entrants need to balance the increased chance of success from stronger strategies against their increased cost of implementation and delay.

Notes

1. See Michael E. Porter, "How Competitive Forces Shape Strategy," *HBR* March-April 1979, p. 137.

2. The reader might argue that there is always *some* basis for competitive difference. See Theodore Levitt, "Marketing Success Through Differentiation—of Anything," *HBR* January-February 1980, p. 83.

---

3. See Ralph Biggadike, "The Risky Business of Diversification," *HBR* May-June 1979, p. 103.

Appendix 1

Study Methodology

I studied 793 U.S. and Canadian consumer and industrial product markets drawn from the PIMS (profit impact of market strategy) research base. I observed each market for one five-year period, with the periods ranging from 1972 to 1979. This sample represents at least 60% of all four-digit SIC-defined manufacturing industries in the United States. I designated an entrant, a new competitor that had obtained a minimum of 5% market share. My results are from multiple regression, with entry as the dependent variable and the indicators of barriers as the independent variables.

The negative results on the deterrence effect of barriers contradict much previous research by economists. See my book *Barriers to Entry: A Corporate-Strategy Perspective* (Lexington, Mass.: D.C. Heath, 1982). For more information about the PIMS data base, see Sidney Schoeffler, Robert D. Buzzell, and Donald F. Heany, "Impact of Strategic Planning on Profit Performance," *HBR* March-April 1974, p. 137.

Appendix 2

Antitrust Intervention

The theory of entry barriers has made an impact on U.S. antitrust policy, which has as a major goal the maintenance of easy market-entry conditions. The theory has been invoked to support two major types of government intervention.

The first type alters market structures to reduce barriers to entry. The most recent example was the Federal Trade Commission's lengthy investigation of the breakfast cereals market. The FTC argued that a combination of brand proliferation and high market concentration created insurmountable entry barriers. Its proposed remedy was the mandatory licensing of existing trademarks to new competitors. Finally, last January the FTC abandoned its ten-year effort to alter that market structure and dismissed the cereals case.

The second type of intervention encourages direct entry by discouraging acquisition entry—that is, it encourages the introduction of a new competitor but discourages an entrant from buying an existing competitor.

This policy is based on three major assumptions underlying the theory of entry barriers:

1   That the presence of potential direct entrants would constrain incumbents from reaping "excess" profits. An acquisition entry by a potential entrant would reduce such constraints.
2   That potential entrants would enter directly if denied the acquisition route.
3   That direct entry promotes competition but acquisition entry does not.

In 1979, the Federal Trade Commission forced Exxon to partially operate at arm's length its new acquistion, the Reliance Electric Company. The FTC argued that Exxon could and would have entered the drives industry on its own had it not acquired Reliance.

These two types of antitrust intervention are now seriously questioned by the Reagan administration and by James C. Miller III, chairman of the FTC.

16

Marketing Success Through Differentiation—of Anything

THEODORE LEVITT

On television we see product differentiation all the time, whether the subject of the commercial is a distinguishable good like an automobile or an indistinguishable good like laundry detergent. These are packaged products. How does the marketer differentiate a so-called commodity like isopropyl alcohol, strip steel, commercial bank services, or even legal counsel? The author describes the attributes of products that give the marketer opportunity to win customers from the competition and, having won, to keep them. Finally, the author describes the alert, imaginative state of mind that characterizes good management of product differentiation. "The way in which the manager operates becomes an extension of product differentiation," he says.

There is no such thing as a commodity. All goods and services are differentiable. Though the usual presumption is that this is more true of consumer goods than of industrial goods and services, the opposite is the actual case.

In the marketplace, differentiation is everywhere. Everybody—producer, fabricator, seller, broker, agent, merchant—tries constantly to distinguish his offering from all others. This is true even of those who produce and deal in primary metals, grains, chemicals, plastics, and money.

Published 1980.

Fabricators of consumer and industrial goods seek competitive distinction via product features—some visually or measurably identifiable, some cosmetically implied, and some rhetorically claimed by reference to real or suggested hidden attributes that promise results or values different from those of competitors' products.

So too with consumer and industrial services—what I call, to be accurate, "intangible." On the commodities exchanges, for example, dealers in metals, grains, and pork bellies trade in totally undifferentiated generic products. But what they "sell" is the claimed distinction of their execution—the efficiency of their transactions in their clients' behalf, their responsiveness to inquiries, the clarity and speed of their confirmations, and the like. In short, the *offered* product is differentiated, though the *generic* product is identical.

When the generic product is undifferentiated, the offered product makes the difference in getting customers and the delivered product in keeping them. When the knowledgeable senior partner of a well-known Chicago brokerage firm appeared at a New York City bank in a tight-fitting, lime green polyester suit and Gucci shoes to solicit business in financial instrument futures, the outcome was predictably poor. The unintended offering implied by his sartorial appearance contradicted the intended offering of his carefully prepared presentation. No wonder that Thomas Watson the elder insisted so uncompromisingly that his salespeople be attired in their famous IBM "uniforms." While clothes may not make the man, they may help make the sale.

The usual presumption about so-called undifferentiated commodities is that they are exceedingly price sensitive. A fractionally lower price gets the business. That is seldom true except in the imagined world of economics textbooks. In the actual world of markets, nothing is exempt from other considerations, even when price competition rages.

During periods of sustained surplus, excess capacity, and unrelieved price war, when the attention of all seems riveted on nothing save price, it is precisely because price is visible and measurable, and potentially devastating in its effects, that price deflects attention from the possibilities of extricating the product from ravaging price competition. These possibilities, even in the short run, are not confined simply to nonprice competition, such as harder personal selling, intensified advertising, or what's loosely called more or better "services."

To see fully what these possibilities are, it is useful first to examine what exactly a product is.

What's a Product?

Products are almost always combinations of the tangible and the intangible. An automobile is not simply a machine for movement visibly or measurably differentiated by design, size, color, options, horsepower, or miles per gallon. It is also a complex symbol denoting status, taste, rank, achievement, aspiration, and (these days) being "smart"—that is, buying fuel economy rather than display. But the customer buys even more than these attributes. The enormous efforts of the auto manufacturers to cut the time between placement and delivery of an order and to select, train, supervise, and motivate their dealerships suggest that these too are integral parts of the products people buy and are therefore ways by which products may be differentiated.

In the same way, a computer is not simply a machine for data storage and processing; it is also an operating system with special software protocols for use and promises of maintenance and repair. Carbon fibers are chemical additives that enhance flexuous stiffness, reduce weight, fight fatigue and corrosion, and cut fabrication costs when combined with certain other materials. But carbon fibers have no value for an inexperienced user without the design and applications help that only the experienced seller can provide.

In thousand-page contract proposals by government contractors or five-page consulting proposals to industrial clients, the product is a promise whose commercial substance resides as much in the proposer's carefully curried reputation (or "image") and in the proposal's meticulous packaging as it does in its physical content.

When the substantive content of the products of competing vendors are scarcely differentiable, sales power shifts to differentiating distinctions by which buyers may be influenced. In this regard, there is scant substantive difference among all that's done by Morgan Stanley & Co., Lockheed, McKinsey & Co., and Revlon. Though each will vigorously proclaim commanding generic distinctions vis-à-vis competitors, each is profoundly preoccupied with packaging—that is, with representing itself as unique. And, indeed, each may be unique, but its uniqueness resides most powerfully in things that transcend its generic offerings.

Take investment banking. Underwriters promise money to issuers and suggest similar promises to buyers. But how these promises are packaged profoundly influences both issuers and buyers. Consider this quotation from a close observer of the industry: "One eminent [U.S. investment banking] house has entrances on two streets, with different stationery printed for each entrance. One door is intended to be more exclusive than the other, and a visitor supposedly can tell the firm's assessment of his importance by the entrance indicated on the letterhead of the stationery he receives."[1] Obviously, the distinctions being made are selling devices based on the assumption that VIP treatment of certain visitors at reception will persuade them of VIP results later in actuality.

To the potential buyer, a product is a complex cluster of value satisfactions. The generic thing is not itself the product; it is merely, as in poker, table stakes—the minimum that is necessary at the outset to give its producer a chance to play the game. It is the playing that gets the results, and in business this means getting and keeping customers.

Customers attach value to a product in proportion to its perceived ability to help solve their problems or meet their needs. All else is derivative. As a specialist in industrial marketing has expressed it, "The 'product'. . . is the total package of benefits the customer receives when he buys."[2]

Consider the pragmatism of the Detroit auto manufacturers in buying sheet steel. Detroit buys to exceedingly tight technical specifications, but it specifies much more than the steel itself. It also demands certain delivery conditions and flexibilities, price and payment conditions, and reordering responsiveness. From year to year, the Detroit companies shift the proportions of steel they buy from their various suppliers on the basis of elaborate grading systems that measure each supplier's performance on the specified conditions, including the kind and quality of unsolicited help on such matters as new materials ideas, ideas for parts redesign, and even purchasing procedures.

Clearly, Detroit buys a bundle of value satisfactions of which the generic product is only a small portion. If, say, the delivery conditions and flexibilities are not fulfilled—or if they are fulfilled erratically, grudgingly, or only partially—the customers are not getting the product they expect. If, moreover, one supplier is more effectively active with new facilitating ideas, that "product" is better than the competitors'. Detroit sees with supreme clarity that No. 302, 72-inch, hot-rolled strip carbon steel is not a commodity. It is a measurably differentiated product.

The customers never just buy the "generic" product like steel, or wheat, or subassemblies, or investment banking, or aspirin, or engineering counsultancy, or golf balls, or industrial maintenance, or newsprint, or cosmetics, or even 99% pure isopropyl alcohol. They buy something that transcends these designations—and what that "something" is helps determine from whom they'll buy, what they'll pay, and whether, in the view of the seller, they're "loyal" or "fickle."

What that something is in its customer-getting and customer-satisfying entirety can be managed. To see how it can be managed, it is helpful to look at the process graphically. Exhibit 1 does this by suggesting that a product consists of a range of possibilities, which I shall now describe.

The Generic Product

The fundamental, but rudimentary, substantive "thing" that's the table stakes of business—what's needed for a chance to play the game of market participation—is the *generic product*. It is, for the steel producer, the steel itself—or, in the Detroit example, No. 302, 72-inch, hot-rolled strip, or somebody's technical equivalent. For a bank, it's loanable funds. For a realtor, it's for-sale properties. For a retailer, it's a store with a certain mix of vendables. For a lawyer, it's having passed the bar exam.

Not all generic products are the same. Having passed the New York bar exam is not the same as having passed the Colorado exam. Because of slight differences among automobile company manufacturing processes, one

Exhibit 1.   The Total Product Concept

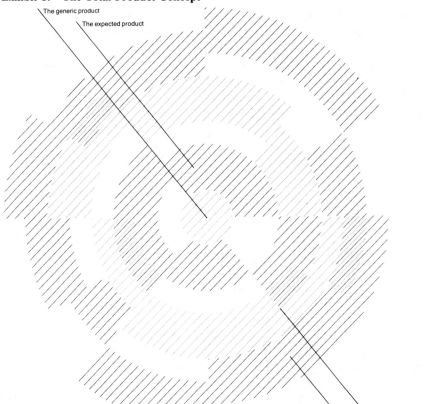

supplier's "302" may, in fact, be "better" than another's. One mill's 302 may take certain coatings more easily or quickly than another's. One supplier may fill orders from a single mill, and another from several. In the latter case, the sheen or hue of the generic product may vary slightly from mill to mill, which makes considerable difference in the case of stainless steel that is used for decorative trim.

In most cases, these differences are not salient. More important are the characteristics of the expected components of the product.

The Expected Product

In Exhibit 1, the *expected product* is everything within the outer and inner gray circles, including the generic product. It represents the customer's minimal purchase conditions. What, for example, does the customer consider absolutely essential in strip steel?

1. *Delivery.* At what plants? When? Not just on what day, but at what hours of each day, so as to minimize valuable space for backup stock and to reduce inventory costs? The supplier has to be "logistically even" with the buyer. The proper quantity and flexibility—that is, quick and hassle-free responsiveness to snags in delivery quantities and times—are also expected. Finally, preferential treatment may be specified in case of shortages.

2. *Terms.* Specific prices for specific quantities for specific lengths of time. In the case of a change in list prices, the terms contain negotiable parameters, perhaps linked to such indexes as moving price averages of scrap and other steel-making ingredients over specified periods. The terms may also be reflected in discount structures related to the promptness of payment and add-on provisions for extended payment periods.

3. *Support efforts.* Depending on what the uses of the product are, the purchaser may expect special applications advice and support.

4. *New ideas.* A normal expectation may include suppliers' ideas and suggestions for more efficient and cost-reducing ways of using the generic product in its various intended forms, such as fabrication, coating, and fastening.

All this may be well known, but the underlying principles encompass much more. The failure to fulfull certain more subtle expectations may reflect unfavorably on the generic product. A shabby brokerage office may cost a realtor access to customers for her for-sale properties. Even though the lawyer performed brilliantly in the bar exam and occupies offices of prudential elegance, his personality may clash with a potential client's. A manufacturer's competitively priced machine tools might have the most sophisticated of numerical controls tucked tightly behind an impressive panel, but certain customers may refuse to buy because output tolerances are more precise than necessary or usable. The customer may actually expect and want less.

The generic product can be sold only if the customer's wider expectations are met. Different means may be employed to meet those expectations. Hence differentiation follows expectation.

The Augmented Product

Differentiation is not limited to giving the customers what they expect. What they expect may be augmented by things they have never thought about. When computer manufacturers implant diagnostic modules that automatically locate the source of failure or breakdown inside the equipment (as some now do), they have taken the product beyond what was required or expected by the buyer. It has become an *augmented product*. When a securities brokerage firm includes with its customers' monthly statements a current balance sheet for each customer and an analysis of sources and disposition of funds, that firm has augmented its product beyond what was required or expected by the buyer. When a manufacturer of health and beauty aids offers warehouse management advice and training programs for the employees of its distributors, that company too has augmented its product beyond what was required or expected by the buyer.

These voluntary or unprompted "augmentations" to the expected product are shown in Exhibit 1 by the irregular band that surrounds the expected product.

In every case, the supplier has exceeded the normal expectations of the buyer. In the case of our steel example, it can be done by developing better ways of fabricating and coating the product or by reducing thickness to cut weight. The seller may provide other unexpected but moderately helpful aids, such as new delivery scheduling ideas, more "interesting" terms, different ways of delivering batches so as to reduce the buyer's handling problems and costs, and invoicing systems that give the buyer more information about the use patterns of the generic product by his various plants, divisions, or brands.

Not all customers for all products and under all circumstances, however, can be attracted by an ever-expanding bundle of differentiating value satisfactions. Some customers may prefer lower prices to product augmentation. Some cannot use the extra services offered. Steel users, for instance, once dependent on mills for applications help and engineering support, gradually grew sufficiently sophisticated to free themselves of that dependence—a freedom which, incidentally, led to the rapid growth of independent steel distribution centers in competitions with the mills.

(Now the centers, which have distinguished themselves from the mills by faster delivery on standard grades and sizes, a wider item mix, and ability to handle small orders, have augmented *their* product by doing more minor fabricating and adding certain specialty steel applications services.)

As a rule, the more a seller expands the market by teaching and helping customers to use his product, the more vulnerable he becomes to losing them. When a customer no longer needs help, he gains the flexibility to shop for things he values more—such as price.

At this point, it makes sense to embark on a systematic program of customer-benefiting, and therefore customer-keeping, product augmentation. The seller should also, of course, focus on cost and price reduction. And that's the irony of product maturity: precisely when price competition heightens, and therefore when cost reduction becomes more important, is when the seller is also likely to benefit by incurring the additional costs of new product augmentation.

The augmented product is a condition of a mature market of relatively experienced or sophisticated customers. Not that they could not benefit from or would not respond to extra services; but when a customer knows or thinks he knows everything and can do anything, the seller must test that assumption lest she be condemned to the purgatory of price competition alone. The best way to test the customer's assumption that he no longer needs or wants all or any part of the augmented product is to consider what's possible to offer that customer.

The Potential Product

Everything that might be done to attract and hold customers is what can be called the *potential product*. For the steel user, the offering may include:

☐ Suggested technical changes, such as redesign of a component to reduce weight, add strength or durability, cut lateral flex, improve adhesion and desirability of coatings, or enhance safety.

☐ Market research findings regarding customers' attitudes toward, and their problems with, the various alternatives to steel (plastics and aluminum, for example).

☐ New methods and technologies for shaping, forming, and fastening steel to steel, steel to plastics, and the like.

☐ New ideas for lubricants, noise-reducing materials, buffers, and gaskets.

☐ Tested proposals for easier, faster, and cheaper assembly systems.

☐ New ideas for varying product characteristics for various user segments, such as commercial fleets, taxi fleets, and rental companies, each of which has its own buying criteria.

☐ Concrete, tested suggestions for combining materials like steel and fiberglass.

Only the budget and the imagination limit the possibilities. But what the budget is and ought to be is often a function of what is necessary to being competitive in all the dimensions of the potential product.

Things will vary with conditions—economic conditions and competitive conditions. Competition may be a function not simply of what other steel suppliers offer but also of what suppliers of substitute materials offer. Reordering responsiveness is not nearly as important to buyers in good times as in bad—except when a competitor strategically uses the good times (that is, when demand is high and supply short) to accommodate a large prospective customer in order to get a foot in the door.

Economic conditions, business strategies, customers' wishes, competitive conditions, and much more can determine what sensibly defines the product. Nor are the ingredients of the described classifications fixed. What's "augmented" for one customer may be "expected" by another; what's "augmented" under one circumstance may be "potential" in another; part of what's "generic" in periods of short supply may be "expected" in periods of oversupply.

As with most things in business, nothing is simple, static, or explained very reliably by textbook taxonomies. One thing is certain: there is no such thing as a commodity—or, at least, from a competitive point of view, there need not be. Everything is differentiable, and, in fact, usually is differentiated. (See the Appendix.)

Role of Management

The way a company manages its marketing can become the most powerful form of differentiation. Indeed, that may be how some companies in the same industry differ most from one another.

Brand management and product management are marketing tools that have demonstrable advantages over catchall, functional modes of management. The same is true of market management, a system widely employed when a particular tangible or intangible product is used in many different industries. Putting somebody in charge of a product that's used the same way by a large segment of the market (as in the case of packaged detergents sold through retail channels) or putting somebody in charge of a market for a product that's used differently in different industries (as in the case of isopropyl alochol sold directly to manufacturers or indirectly to them via distributors) clearly focuses attention, responsibility, and effort. Companies that organize their marketing this way generally have a clear competitive advantage.

The list of highly differentiated consumer products that not long ago were sold as undifferentiated or minimally differentiated commodities is long: coffee, soap, flour, beer, salt, oatmeal, pickles, frankfurters, bananas, chickens, pineapples, and many more. Among consumer intangibles, in recent years brand or vendor differentiation has intensified in banking, insurance of all kinds, credit cards, stock brokerage, travel agencies, beauty parlors, entertainment parks, and small-loan companies. Among consumer hybrids, the same thing has occurred: theme restaurants, opticians, food retailers, and specialty retailers are burgeoning in a variety of categories—jewelry, sporting goods, books, health and beauty aids, pants and jeans, musical records and cassettes, auto supplies, and home improvement centers.

In each of these cases, especially that of consumer tangibles, the presumption among the less informed is that their competitive distinction resides largely in packaging and advertising. Even substantive differences in the generic products are thought to be so slight that what really counts is the ads and the packages.

This presumption is palpably wrong. It is not simply the heavy advertising or the clever packaging that accounts for the preeminence of so many General Foods and Procter & Gamble products. Nor is it their superior generic products that explain the successes of IBM, Xerox, ITT, and Texas Instruments. Their real distinction lies in how they manage—especially, in the cases of P&G, General Foods, IBM, and Xerox, in how they manage marketing. The amount of careful analysis, control, and field work that characterizes their management of marketing is masked by the visibility of their advertising or presumed generic product uniqueness.

The branded food products companies advertise heavily, and they work as hard and as closely with their wholesale and retail distributors as do the auto companies. Indeed, often these food companies work with distributors even harder because their distributors handle many competing brands and the distribution channels are longer and more complex. Most grocery stores, of course, handle a number of more or less competing brands of the same generic (or functionally undifferentiated) product. There are more than two dozen national brands of powdered laundry detergent. The stores get them from a supermarket chain warehouse or from the warehouse of a cooperative wholesaler, a voluntary wholesaler, or an independent wholesaler. Each of these warehouses generally carries a full line of competing brands.

Though the national brands try via advertising and promotion to create consumer "pull," they also try to create retailer and wholesaler "push." At retail they regularly seek more advantageous shelf space and more advertising support from the retailer. At wholesale they do other things. Some years ago General Foods did a massive study of materials handling in distribution warehouses. Then the company made its results and recommendations available to the trade through a crew of specialists carefully trained to help implement those recommendations. The object, obviously, was to curry favor with the distributive trades for General Foods products.

The company did something similar for retailers: it undertook a major study of retail space profitability and then offered supermarket owners the opportunity to learn a new way of space-profitability accounting. By helping retailers manage their space better, General Foods presumably would gain retailers' favor for its products in their merchandising activities.

Another company, Pillsbury, devised a program to help convenience stores operate and compete more effectively. The object was, of course, to obtain preferential push treatment for Pillsbury products in these stores.

Similar examples abound in branded food marketing:

☐   The form in which goods are delivered—pallets, dollies, bulk—is often customized.

☐   When Heinz sells, delivers, and packages ketchup to institutional purveyors who supply hospitals, restaurants, hotels, prisons, schools, and nursing homes, it not only operates differently from the way it deals with cooperative wholesalers, but it also seeks to operate in some advantage-producing fashion different from the way Hunt Foods deals with the same purveyors.

☐   Some years ago the Institutional Food Service Division of General Foods provided elaborate theme-meal recipes for schools—"safari" meals that included such delectables as "groundnut soup Uganda" and "fish Mozambique." General Foods provided "decorations to help you go native" in the cafeteria, including travel posters, Congo face masks, pith helmets, lotus garlands, and paper monkeys.

Case of Isopropanol

Four of the companies I have mentioned before (General Foods, P&G, IBM, Xerox) are organized along product or brand-management lines for their major generic products. IBM and Xerox also have market managers and geographic managers. What differentiates them from others is how well they manage marketing, not merely what they market. It is the *process*, not just the product, that is differentiated.

To see the importance of the process, let's consider the lost opportunities of a company lacking the right process. Take the case of a large manufacturer of isopropyl alcohol, commonly called isopropanol. It is a moderately simple, totally undifferentiated generic product chemically synthesized via a well-known process from gas recovered in petroleum refining. It comes in two grades: crude, which is 9% water, and refined, which is 1% water. In 1970, 1.9 billion pounds were produced in the United States. Of that amount, 43% was bought as a feed stock to make acetone (principally a solvent), and most of the remainder was bought for use in chemicals, lacquers, and protective coatings.

With the introduction of the new cumene process, isopropanol was no longer needed in the manufacturing of acetone. Hence in 1970 isopropanol was in vast oversupply. Prices were deeply depressed and expected to remain so for some five years until demand caught up with supply. One of the larger isopropanol companies employed a substantial proportion of its output to make acetone. In 1970 the company sold 310 million pounds of both products to the "merchant market"—that is, directly to manufacturers.

Although the prevailing prices per pound for both acetone and isopropanol were exceedingly low (as low as $.04 for acetone and $.067 for isopropanol), later analysis of this producer's invoices showed wide variations around these prices for sales made to different customers even on the same days. Two possible conclusions follow: (1) not all buyers were identically informed about what, indeed, were the "prevailing" prices on each of those days, and (2) not all buyers were equally price sensitive.

Analysis showed further that these price variations tended to cluster by industry category and customer size but not by geographical location. Another breakdown of industry categories revealed still other price segments: manufacturers of various kinds of coatings exhibited different clusterings of prices they had paid. Substantial differences in prices paid also showed up between agricultural chemical producers and biochemical producers. A category called "other" showed a great variety of price clusterings.

All this, however, is a matter of hindsight. No such analysis was made at the time. Had the marketing process been managed well, a product manager would have known these facts. The revealed differences in invoice prices and price clusterings would have led an intelligent and inquisitive product manager to ask:

1 Who are the least price-aware or price-sensitive among the industry users to whom we sell? What is their size distribution? Exactly which companies are they?
2 Who are the most and the least vendor-loyal—that is, who buys regularly from us, regardless of price fluctuations? Why? And who buys from us only occasionally, largely on considerations of price?
3 Who can use our applications help most? Who least?
4 Who would respond most to our offer for help?
5 Where and with whom could we selectively raise prices? Should we selectively hold prices?
6 How should we communicate all this to the sales organization and employ it in managing the sales forces?

Suppose that by astute management, the sales force had sold largely to the less informed or less price-sensitive industry sectors or customers. Suppose that each customer segment had yielded higher prices of as little as $.001, $.002, or $.005 per pound. What would have been the immediate cash contribution to the company? Exhibit 2 gives an answer.

If only 10% of total sales had been made for only one-tenth of a penny more than they were, the pretax contribution would have been an extra $155,000; if 50% had been raised by two-tenths of a penny, the yield would have been $310,000 extra.

Exhibit 2. Presumed Results of Improved Sales Distribution

Industry and Use	Millions of Pounds	Additional Cash Contributions of Incremental Price Points by Price Increments per Pound		
		$.001	$.002	$.005
Acetone	124	$124,000	$248,000	$ 620,000
Other intermediates	20	20,000	40,000	100,000
Agribiochemical	31	31,000	62,000	155,000
Coatings	86	86,000	172,000	430,000
Other	49	49,000	98,000	245,000
Total	310	$310,000	$620,000	$1,550,000
If 50% had been sold at the premiums		$155,000	$310,000	$ 775,000
If 10% had been sold at the premiums		$ 31,000	$ 62,000	$ 155,000

Given the analysis of markets and users that I outlined, such increases seem to have been well within reach. To get them, how much would it have been worth to expand the market analysis function into an on-the-spot, on-line differentiating activity guiding the sales organization? Obviously, a lot.

It is this and related kinds of attention to marketing details that characterize the work of product managers and market managers. Among producers of generically undifferentiated products—particularly of products sold as ingredients to industrial customers—the management of the marketing process can itself be a powerful differentiating device. This device is constantly and assiduously employed in the better-managed branded, packaged consumer goods companies.

It is a matter of staying aware of exactly what's going on in the market, of how people use, misuse, or modify their products, of how and where they buy, of who makes buying decisions and how these get modified, and the like. It is a matter of looking continuously for gaps in market coverage that the company can fill, of looking continuously at new ways of influencing buyers to choose one's product instead of a competitor's. In this unceasing effort of the managers, *the way in which they operate* becomes an extension of the idea of product differentiation itself.

While differentiation is most readily apparent in branded, packaged consumer goods, in the design, operating character, or composition of industrial goods, or in the features or "service" intensity of intangible products, differentiation consists as powerfully in how one operates the business. In the way the marketing process is managed may reside the opportunity for many companies, especially those that offer generically undifferentiated products and services, to escape the commodity trap.

Notes

1. Samuel L. Hayes, III, "Investment Banking: Power Structure in Flux," *HBR* March-April 1971, p. 136.

2. E. Raymond Corey, "Key Options in Market Selection and Product Planning," *HBR* September-October 1975, p. 119. For an elaboration, see his *Industrial Marketing: Cases and Concepts* (Englewood Cliffs, N.J.: Prentice-Hall, 1976), pp. 40-41; also, see Benson P. Shapiro, "Making Money Through Marketing," *HBR* July-August 1979, p. 136.

Appendix

The Complexity of a Generic Product

Durum is a variety of wheat produced in rather small quantities and almost exclusively in three counties in eastern North Dakota. Its main use is in pasta. Farmers generally deliver the durum in truckload quantities to country elevators, from which it is shipped to processors. In recent years, however, many large farm operations have built their own storage elevators. Using very large trailer trucks, they make direct shipments to the elevators of large users. Thus they not only avoid middleman storage discounts, but they also obtain access to premiums paid by the purchasers for high-quality wheat.

Similarly, country elevator operators in the Great Plains have increasingly organized to take advantage of unit-train shipments to the Gulf Coast and thereby qualify for substantial rail tariff discounts. These arrangements affect the quantities and schedules by which country elevators prefer to buy and take delivery from growers, which in turn affect how the growers manage their delivery capabilities and schedules.

The prices that elevator operators and processors pay vary substantially, even for identical grades of durum wheat. The elevator operators will pay premiums above, or take discounts from, prices currently quoted or prices previously agreed to with farmers, depending on the results of protein and moisture tests made on each delivery. Wheat users, like Prince Spaghetti Company, make additional tests for farina and gluten content. Premiums and discounts for quality differences in a particular year have been known to vary from the futures prices on commodity exchanges by amounts greater than the futures price fluctuations themselves during that year.

17

How Global Companies Win Out

THOMAS HOUT, MICHAEL E. PORTER, and EILEEN RUDDEN

International competition. Citizens from most of the older industrialized countries have become obsessed with it since the first Japanese cars started selling well. Vulnerability has replaced invincibility as the word many would use to describe once firmly established international companies. But this disquiet obscures the steady achievements a number of corporations have made against competition from companies based outside their countries.

These companies rely on global strategies to succeed in today's world. That calls on a company to think of the world as one market instead of as a collection of national markets and sometimes requires decisions as unconventional as accepting projects with low ROIs because of their competitive payoff. An orgnization with such a global focus formulates long-term strategy for the company as a whole and then orchestrates the strategies of local subsidiaries accordingly.

The power of global strategies is illustrated here by the histories of three companies (one American, one European, and one Japanese) that have what the authors think it takes to win the new competitive game. These case studies should help managers decide whether a global strategy is appropriate for their companies.

Hold that obituary on American manufacturers. Some not only refuse to die but even dominate their businesses worldwide. At the same time Ford struggles to keep up with Toyota, Caterpillar thrives in competition with another Japanese powerhouse, Komatsu. Though Zenith has been hurt in consumer electronics, Hewlett-Packard and Tektronix together profitably control 50% of the world's industrial test and measurement instrument market. American

Published 1982.

Authors' Note. We acknowledge that this article is based in part on a paper co-authored by Eric Vogt.

forklift truck producers may retreat under Japanese pressure, but two U.S. Chemical companies—Du Pont and Dow—dramatically outperform their competitors.

How do these American producers hold and even increase profitability against international competitors? By forging integrated, global strategies to exploit their potential; and by having a long-term outlook, investing aggressively, and managing factories carefully.

The main reason is that today's international competition in many industries is very different from what it has been. To succeed, an international company may need to change from a multidomestic competitor, which allows individual subsidiaries to compete independently in different domestic markets, to a global organization, which pits its entire worldwide system of product and market position against the competition. (For a more complete discussion of this distinction, see the Appendix.)

The global company—whatever its nationality—tries to control leverage points, from cross-national production scale economies to the foreign competitors' sources of cash flow. By taking unconventional action, such as lowering prices of an important product or in key markets, the company makes the competitors' response more expensive and difficult. Its main objective is to improve its own effectiveness while eroding that of its competitors.

Not all companies can or should forge a global strategy. While the rewards of competing globally are great, so are the risks. Major policy and operating changes are required. Competing globally demands a number of unconventional approaches to managing a multinational business to sometimes allow:

☐ Major investment projects with zero or even negative ROI.

☐ Financial performance targets that vary widely among foreign subsidiaries.

☐ Product lines deliberately overdesigned or underpriced in some markets.

☐ A view of country-by-country market positions as interdependent and not as independent elements of a worldwide portfolio to be increased or decreased depending on profitability.

☐ Construction of production facilities in both high and low labor-cost countries.

Not all international businesses lend themselves to global competition. Many are multi-domestic in nature and are likely to remain so, competing on a domestic-market-by-domestic-market basis. Typically these businesses have products that differ greatly among country markets and have high transportation costs, or their industries lack sufficient scale economies to yield the global competitors a significant competitive edge.

Before entering the global arena, you must first decide whether your company's industry has the right characteristics to favor a global competitor. A careful examination of the economies of the business will highlight its ripeness for global competition.[1] Simply put, the potential for global competition is greatest when significant benefits are gained from worldwide volume—in terms of either reduced unit costs or superior reputation or service—and are greater than the additional costs of serving that volume.

Identifying potential economies of scale requires considerable insight. Advantages to increased volume may come not only from larger production plants or runs but also from more efficient logistics networks or higher volume distribution networks. Worldwide volume is also particularly advantageous in supporting high levels of investment in research and development; many industries requiring high levels of R&D, such as pharmaceuticals or jet aircraft, are global. The level of transport or importing costs will also influence the business's tendency to become global. Transport is a relatively small portion of highly traded optical goods, for example, while it is a barrier in trading steel reinforcing bars.

Many businesses will not be able to take the global step precisely because their industries lack these characteristics. Economies of scale may be too modest or R&D spending too closely tied to particular markets. Products may differ significantly across country boundaries, or the industry may emphasize distribution, installation, and other local activities. Lead times may be short, as in fashion-oriented businesses and in many service businesses, including printing. Also, transportation costs and government barriers to trade may be high, and distribution may be fragmented and hard to penetrate. Many consumer nondurable businesses or low-technology assembly companies fall into this category, as do many heavy raw-material processing industries and wholesaling and service businesses.

Our investigation into the strategies of successful global companies leads us to believe that a large group of international companies have global potential, even though they may not know it. Almost every industry that is now global—automobiles and TV sets, for example—was not at one time. A company must see the potential for changing competitive interaction in its favor to trigger a shift from multidomestic to global competition. And because there is no guarantee that the business can become global, the company must be willing to risk the heavy investment that global competition requires.

A company that recognizes its business as potentially global but not yet so must ask itself whether it can innovate effectively and must understand its impact on the competition to find the best answers to these three questions:

☐ What kind of strategic innovation might trigger global competition?

☐ Is it in the best position among all competitors to establish and defend the advantages of global strategy?

☐   What kind of resources—over how long a period—will be required to establish the leading position?

The Successful Global Competitor

If your industry profile fits the picture we've drawn, you can better judge your ability to make these kinds of unconventional decisions by looking at the way three global companies have succeeded. These organizations (American, European, and Japanese) exemplify the global competitor. They all perceive competition as global and formulate strategy on an integrated, worldwide basis. Each has developed a strategic innovation to change the rules of the competitive game in its particular industry. The innovation acts as a lever to support the development of an integrated global system but demands a market position strong enough to implement it.

Finally, the three companies have executed their strategies more aggressively and effectively than their competitors. They have built barriers to competitive responses based on careful assessment of competitors' behavior. All three have the financial resources and commitment needed to compete unconventionally and the organizational structure to manage an integrated system.

We will take a careful look at each of these three and how they developed the strategic innovation that led, on the one hand, to the globalization of their industries and, on the other, to their own phenomenal success. The first company's innovation was in manufacturing; the second, in technology; and the third, in marketing.

The Caterpillar Case: Warring with Komatsu

Caterpillar Tractor Company turned large-scale construction equipment into a global business and achieved world leadership in that business even when faced with an able Japanese competitor. This accomplishment was difficult for a variety of reasons. For one thing, specifications of construction equipment varied widely across countries. Also, machines are expensive to transport, and field distribution—including user financing, spare parts inventories, and repair facilities—is demanding and best managed locally.

Navy Seabees who left their Caterpillar equipment in other countries following World War II planted the seeds of globalization. The company established independent dealerships to service these fleets, and this base of units provided a highly profitable flow of revenue from spare parts, which paid for inventorying new units. The Caterpillar dealers quickly became self-sustaining and to this day are larger, better financed, and do a more profitable parts business than their competitors. This global distribution system is one of Cat's two major barriers against competition.

The company used its worldwide production scale to create its other barrier. Two thirds of the total product cost of construction equipment is in heavy components—engines, axles, transmissions, and hydraulics—whose manufacturing costs are capital intensive and highly sensitive to economies of scale. Caterpillar turned its network of sales in different countries into a cost advantage by designing product lines that use identical components and by investing heavily in a few large-scale, state-of-the-art component manufacturing facilities to fill worldwide demand.

The company then augmented the centralized production with assembly plants in each of its major markets—Europe, Japan, Brazil, Australia, and so on. At these plants Cat added local product features, avoiding the high transportation cost of end products. Most important, Cat became a direct participant in local economies. The company achieved lower costs without sacrificing local product flexibility and became a friend rather than a threat to local governments. No single "world model" was forced on the customer, yet no competitor could match Caterpillar's production and distribution cost.

Not that they haven't tried. The most recent—and greatest—challenge to Caterpillar has come from Komatsu (see Exhibit 1 for a financial comparison). Japan's leading construction equipment producer forged its own global strategy based on exporting high-quality products from centralized facilities with labor and steel cost advantages. Over the last decade Komatsu has gained some 15% of the world construction-equipment market, with a significant share of sales in nearly every product line in competition with Cat.

Caterpillar has maintained its position against Komatsu and gained world share. The two companies increasingly dominate the market vis-à-vis their competitors, who compete on a domestic or regional basis. What makes Caterpillar's strategy so potent? The company has fostered the development

Exhibit 1. Financial Comparison of Caterpillar and Komatsu

1980 estimated sales of construction equipment	$7.2 billion	$2.0 billion
1974–1979 averages:		
Return on capital employed	13.6%	4.0%
Debt/equity	0.4 times	2.1 times
Return on equity	19.1%	12.2%
Percent of earnings retained	69%	65%
Spare parts as percent of total revenue (estimated)	30% to 35%	15% to 20%
Cash flow available from operations	$681 million	$140 million

Source: Financial statements.

of four characteristics essential to defending a leading world position against a determined competitor:

1. *A global strategy of its own.* Caterpillar's integrated global strategy yields a competitive advantage in cost and effectiveness. Komatsu simply plays catch-up ball rather than pulling ahead. Facing a competitor that has consciously devised a global strategy, Komatsu is in a much weaker position than were Japanese TV and automobile manufacturers when they took off.

2. *Willingness to invest in manufacturing.* Caterpillar's top management appears committed to the kind of flexible automated manufacturing systems that allow full exploitation of the economies of scale from its worldwide sales volume.

3. *Willingness to commit financial resources.* Caterpillar is the only Western company that matches Komatsu in capital spending per employee; in fact, its overall capital spending is more than three times that of the Japanese company. Caterpillar does not divert resources into other businesses or dissipate the financial advantage against Komatsu by paying out excessive dividends. Because Komatsu's profitability is lower than Caterpillar's, it must exhaust debt capacity in trying to match Cat's high investment rates.

4. *Blocking position in the Japanese market.* In 1963, Caterpillar formed a joint venture in Japan with Komatsu's long-standing but weaker competitor, Mitsubishi. Operationally, the venture serves the Japanese market. Strategically, it acts as a check on the market share and cash flow of Komatsu. Japan accounts for less than 20% of the world market but yields over 80% of Komatsu's worldwide cash flow. The joint venture is number two in market position, serving to limit Komatsu's profits. Japanese tax records indicate that the Cat-Mitsubishi joint venture has earned only modest profits, but it is of great strategic value to Caterpillar.

L.M. Ericsson: Can Small Be Beautiful?

L. M. Ericsson of Sweden has become a successful global competitor by developing and exploiting a technological niche. Most major international telephone-equipment producers operated first in large, protected home markets that allowed the most efficient economies of scale. The additional profits helped underwrite R&D and provided good competitive leverage. Sweden's home market is relatively small, yet Ericsson translated the advent of electronic switching technology into a powerful global lever that befuddled competitors in its international market niche. In the electromechanical era of the 1960s, the telephone switching equipment business was hardly global. Switching systems combine hardware and software. In the electromechanical stage, 70% of total installed costs lay in hardware and 70% of hardware cost was direct labor, manufacturing overhead, and installation of the equipment.

Each country's telephone system was unique, economies of scale were low, and the wage rate was more important than the impact of volume on costs. In the late 1960s, major international companies (including Ericsson) responded by moving electroswitching production to LDCs not only to take advantage of cheaper labor but also to respond to the desire of government telephone companies to source locally.

Eventually, each parent company centrally sourced only the core software and critical components and competed on a domestic-market-by-domestic-market basis. For its part, Ericsson concentrated investment in developing countries without colonial ties to Europe and in smaller European markets that lacked national suppliers and that used the same switching systems as the Swedish market.

The telecommunications industry became global when, in the 1970s, electronic switching technology emerged, radically shifting cost structures and threatening the market position Ericsson had carved for itself. Software is now 60% of total cost; 55% of hardware cost is in sophisticated electronic components whose production is highly scale sensitive. The initial R&D investment required to develop a system has jumped to more than $100 million, which major international companies could have amortized more easily than Ericsson. In addition, the move to electronics promised to destroy the long-standing relationships Ericsson enjoyed with smaller government telephone companies. And it appeared that individual electronic switching systems would require a large fixed-cost software investment for each country, making the new technology too expensive for the smaller telephone systems, on which Ericsson thrived.

Ericsson knew that the electronic technology would eventually be adapted to small systems. In the meantime, it faced the possibility of losing its position in smaller markets because of its inability to meet the ante for the new global competition.

The company responded with a preemptive strategic innovation—a modular technology that introduced electronics to small telephone systems. The company developed a series of modular software packages that could be used in different combinations to meet the needs of diverse telephone systems at an acceptable cost. Moreover, each successive system required fewer new modules. As Exhibit 2 shows, the first system—Södertalje in Sweden—required all new modules, but by the third year, the Åbo system in Finland required none at all. Thus the company rapidly amortized development costs and enjoyed economies of scale that steepened as the number of software systems sold increased. As a result, Ericsson was able to compete globally in small systems.

Ericsson's growth is accelerating as small telephone systems convert to electronics. The company now enjoys an advantage in software cost and variety that continually reinforces itself. Through this technology Ericsson has raised a significant entry barrier against other companies in the small-system market.

Honda's Marketing Genius

Before Honda became a global company, two distinct motorcycle industries existed in the world. In Asia and other developing countries, large numbers

Exhibit 2. Ericsson's Technology Lever: Reduction of Software Cost Through Modular Design

	Representa- tive Systems	New Modules Required	Existing Modules used
Year 1	Södertalje, Sweden	57	0
Year 2	Orleans, France	22	57
Year 3	Åbo, Finland	0	77

Source: Boston Consulting Group, *A Framework for Swedish Industrial Policy* (Uberforlag, Stockholm, 1978).

of people rode small, simple motorcycles to work. In Europe and America, smaller numbers of people drove big, elaborate machines for play. Since the Asian motorcycle was popular as an inexpensive means of transportation, companies competed on the basis of price. In the West, manufacturers used styling and brand image to differentiate their products. No Western market exceeded 100,000 units; wide product lines and small volumes meant slight opportunities for economies of scale. Major motorcycle producers such as Harley-Davidson of the United States, BMW of West Germany, and Triumph and BSA of the United Kingdom traded internationally but in only modest volumes.

Honda made its industry global by convincing middle-class Americans that riding motorcycles could be fun. Because of the company's marketing innovations, Honda's annual growth rate was greater than 20% from the late 1950s to the late 1960s. The company then turned its attention to Europe, with a similar outcome. Honda invested for seven full years before sustaining profitability in Europe, financing this global effort with cash flows earned from a leading market position at home and in the United States.

Three crucial steps were decisive in Honda's achievement. First, Honda turned market preference around to the characteristics of its own products and away from those of American and European competitors. Honda targeted new consumers and used advertising, promotions, and trade shows to convince them that its motorbikes were inexpensive, reliable, and easy to use. A large investment in the distribution network—2,000 dealerships, retail missionaries, generous warranty and service support, and quick spare-parts availability—backed up the marketing message.

Second, Honda sustained growth by enticing customers with the upper levels of its product line. Nearly half of new bike owners purchased larger, more expensive models within 12 months. Brand loyalty proved very high. Honda exploited these trends by expanding from its line of a few small motorcycles to one covering the full range of size and features by 1975. The result: self-sustaining growth in dollar volume and a model mix that allowed higher margins. The higher volume reduced marketing and distribution costs and improved the position of Honda and other Japanese producers who invaded the 750cc "super bike" portion of the market traditionally reserved for American and European companies. Here Honda beat the competition with a bike that was better engineered, lower priced, and whose development cost was shared over the company's wide product line.

The third step Honda took was to exploit economies of scale through both centralized manufacturing and logistics. The increasing volume of engines and bike assemblies sold (50,000 units per month and up) enabled the company to use less costly manufacturing techniques unavailable to motorcycle producers with lower volumes (see Exhibit 3). Over a decade, Honda's factory productivity rose at an average annual rate of 13.1%—several times higher than European and American producers. Combined with lower transportation cost, Honda's increased output gave it a landed cost per unit far lower than the competition's. In turn, the lower production cost helped fund Honda's heavy marketing and distribution investment. Finally, economies of scale in marketing and distribution, combined with low production cost, led to the high profits that financed Honda's move into automobiles.

What Can We Learn?

Each of these successful global players changed the dynamics of its industry and pulled away from its major competitors. By achieving economies of scale through commonality of design, Caterpillar exploited both its worldwide sales volume and its existing market for parts revenues. Competitors could not match its costs or profits and therefore could not make the in-

Exhibit 3.   The Effect of Volume on Manufacturing Approaches in Motorcycle Production

Cost Element	Low Volume	High Volume
Machine tools	Manual, general purpose	Numerical control, special purpose
Changeover time	Manual, slow (hours)	Automatic positioning, fast (minutes)
Work-in process inventory	High (days of production)	Low (hours of production)
Materials handling	Forklift trucks	Automated
Assembly	Bay assembly	Motorized assembly line
Machine tool design	Designed outside the company, available throughout industry	Designed in-house, proprietary
Rework	More	Less

Source: Strategy Alternatives for the British Motorcycle Industry, a report prepared for the British Secretary of State for Industry by the Boston Consulting Group, July 30, 1975.

vestment necessary to catch up. Ericsson created a cost advantage by developing a unique modular technology perfectly adapted to its segment of the market. Its global strategy turned electronics from a threat to Ericsson into a barrier to its competitors. Honda used marketing to homogenize worldwide demand and unlock the potential for economies of scale in production, marketing, and distribution. The competition's only refuge was the highly brand-conscious, small-volume specialty market.

In each case, the industry had the potential for a worldwide system of products and markets that a company with a global strategy could exploit. Construction equipment offered large economies of scale in component manufacture, allowing Caterpillar to neutralize high transportation costs and government barriers through local assembly. Ericsson unlocked scale economies in software development for electronic switches. The modular technology accommodated local product differences and governments' desire to use local suppliers. Once Honda's marketing techniques raised demand in major markets for products with similar characteristics, the industry's economies of scale in production combined with low transportation costs and low tariff barriers to turn it into a global game.

In none of the cases did success result from a "world product." The companies accommodated local differences without sacrificing production costs. The global player's position in one major market strengthened its position in others. Caterpillar's design similarities and central component facilities allowed each market to contribute to its already favorable cost structure. Ericsson's shared modules led to falling costs each time a system was sold in a new country. Honda drew on scale economies from the centralized production of units sold in each market and used its U.S. marketing and distribution experience to succeed in Europe.

In addition to superior effectiveness and cost advantages, a winning global strategy always requires abilities in two other dimensions. The first is timing. The successful global competitor uses a production cost or distribution advantage as a leverage point to make it more difficult or expensive for the competitor to respond. The second is financial. The global innovator commits itself to major investment before anyone else, whether in technology, facilities, or distribution. If successful, it then reaps the benefits from increased cash flows from either higher volume (Honda and Ericsson) or lower costs (all three companies). The longer the competitor takes to respond, the larger the innovator's cash flows. The global company can then deploy funds either to increase investment or lower prices, creating barriers to new market entrants.

A global player should decide against which of its major competitors it must succeed first in order to generate broad-based success in the future. Caterpillar located in the Far East not only to source products locally but also to track Komatsu. (Cat increasingly sources product and manufacturing technology from Japan.) Ericsson's radical departure in technology was aimed squarely at ITT and Siemens, whose large original market shares would ordinarily have given them an advantage in the smaller European and African markets. Honda created new markets in the United States and Europe because its most powerful competitors, Yamaha and Kawasaki, were Japanese. By exploiting the global opportunity first, Honda got a head start, and it remained strong even when competitors' own international ambitions came to light.

Playing the Global Chess Game

Global competition forces top management to change the way it thinks about and operates its businesses. Policies that made sense when the company was multidomestic may now be counterproductive. The most powerful moves are those that improve the company's worldwide cost position or ability to differentiate itself and weaken key worldwide competitors. Let us consider two potential moves.

The first is preempting the leading positions in major newly industrializing countries (NICs). Rapid growth in, for example, Mexico, Brazil, and Indonesia has made them an important part of the worldwide market for many capital goods. If its industry has the potential to become global, the company that takes a leading position in these markets will have made a decisive move to bar its competitors. Trade barriers are often prohibitively high in these places, and a company that tries to penetrate the market through a *self-contained* local subsidiary is likely to fall into a trap.

The astute global competitor will exploit the situation, however, by building a specialized component manufacturing facility in an NIC which will become an integral part of a global sourcing network. The company exports output of the specialized facility to offset important complementary components. Final assembly for the domestic and smaller, neighboring markets can be done locally. (Having dual sources for key items can minimize the risk of disruption to the global sourcing network.)

A good illustration of this strategy is Siemen's circuit breaker operation in Brazil. When the company outgrew its West Germany capacity for some key components, it seized the opportunity presented by Brazilian authorities seeking capital investments in the heavy electrical equipment industry. Siemens now builds a large portion of its common components there, swaps them for other components made in Europe, and is the lowest-cost and leading supplier of finished product in Brazil.

Another move that can be decisive in a global industry is to establish a solid position with your largest customers to block competitors. Many businesses have a few customers that dominate the global market. The global competitor recognizes their importance and prevents current or prospective competitors from generating any sales.

A good example is a British company, BSR, the world's largest producer of automatic record changers. In the 1970s, when Japanese exports of audio equipment were growing rapidly, BSR recognized that it could lose its market base in the United States and Europe if the Japanese began marketing record changers. BSR redesigned its product to Japanese specifications and offered distributors aggressive price discounts and inventory support. The Japanese could not justify expanding their own capacity. BSR not only stalled the entry of the Japanese into the record-changer market but it also moved ahead of its existing competitor, Garrard.

A global company can apply similar principles to block the competition's access to key distributors or retailers. Many American companies have failed to seize this opportunity in their unwillingness to serve large, private-label customers (e.g., Sears, Roebuck) or by neglecting the less expensive end of their product line and effectively allowing competitors access to their distributors. Japanese manufacturers in particular could then establish a toehold in industries like TV sets and farm equipment.

The decision on prices for pivotal customers must not be made solely on considerations of ROI. Equally important in global competition is the impact of these prices on prospective entrants and the cost of failing to protect and expand the business base. One way to control the worldwide chess game in your favor is to differentiate prices among countries.

Manage Interdependently

The successful global competitor manages its business in various countries as a single system, not a portfolio of independent positions. In the view of portfolio planning theory, a market's attractiveness and the strength of a company's position within it determine the extent of corporate resources devoted to it. A company should defend strong positions and try to turn weak ones around or abandon them. It will pursue high-profit and/or high-growth markets more aggressively than lower-profit or lower-growth ones, and it will decide on a stand-alone basis whether to compete in a market.

Accepting this portfolio view of international competition can be disastrous in a global industry. The global competitor focuses instead on its ability to leverage positions in one country market against those in other markets. In the global system, the ability to leverage is as important as market attractiveness; the company need not turn around weak positions for them to be useful.

The most obvious leverage a company obtains from a country market is the volume it contributes to the company's overall cost or effectiveness. Du Pont and Texas Instruments have patiently won a large sales volume in the sophisticated Japanese market, for example, which supports their efforts elsewhere. Winning a share of a market that consistently supports product innovation ahead of other markets—like the United States in long-haul jet aircraft—is another leverage point. The competitor with a high share of such a market can always justify new product investment. Or a market can contribute leverage if it supports an efficient scale manufacturing facility for a region—like Brazil for Siemens. Finally, a market can contribute leverage if a position in it can be used to affect a competitor's cash flow.

Organization: The Achilles Heel

Organizational structure and reporting relationships present subtle problems for a global strategy. Effective strategic control argues for a central product-line organization; effective local responsiveness, for a geographic organization with local autonomy. A global strategy demands that the product-line organization have the *ultimate* authority, because without it the company cannot gain systemwide benefits. Nevertheless, the company still must balance product and area needs. In short, there is no simple solution. But there are some guidelines to help.

No one organization structure applies to all of a company's international businesses. It may be unnecessarily cumbersome, for example, to impose a matrix structure on all business. Organizational reporting lines should probably differ by country market depending on that market's role. An important market that offers high leverage, as in the foregoing examples, must work closely with the global business-unit managers at headquarters. Coordination is crucial to success. But the manager of a market outside the global system will require only sets of objectives under a regional reporting system.

Another guideline is that organizational reporting lines and structures should change as the nature of the international business changes. When a business becomes global, the emphasis should shift toward centralization. As countries increase in importance, they must be brought within the global manager's reach. Over time, if the business becomes less global, the company's organization may emphasize local autonomy.

The common tendency to apply one organizational structure to all operations is bound to be a disadvantage to some of them. In some U.S. companies, this approach inhibited development of the global strategy their industries required.

Match Financial Policies to Competitive Realities

If top management is not careful, adherence to conventional financial management and practices may constrain a good competitive response in global businesses. While capital budgeters use such standard financial tools as DCF return analysis or risk profiles to judge investments and creditors and stock analysts prefer stable debt and dividend policies, a global company must chart a different course.

Allocating Capital

In a global strategy, investments are usually a long-term, interdependent series of capital commitments, which are not easily associated with returns or risks. The company has to be aware of the size and timing of the total expenditures because they will greatly influence competitors' new investment response. Most troublesome, however, is that revenues from investments in several countries may have to build up to a certain point before the company earns *any* return on investment.

A global strategy goes against the traditional tests for capital allocation: project-oriented DCF risk-return analysis and the country manager's record of credibility. Global competition requires a less mechanical approach to project evaluation. The successful global competitor develops at least two levels of financial control. One level is a profit and cost center for self-contained projects; the other is a strategy center for tracking interdependent efforts and competitors' performance and reactions. Global competitors operate with a short time frame when monitoring the execution of global strategy investments and a long time frame when evaluating such investments and their expected returns.

Debt and Dividends

Debt and dividend policies should vary with the requirements of the integrated investment program of the whole company. In the initial stages, a company with a strong competitive position should retain earnings to build and defend its global position. When the industry has become global and growth slows or the returns exceed the reinvestment needed to retain position, the company should distribute earnings to the rest of the corporation and use debt capacity elsewhere, perhaps in funding another nascent global strategy.

Honda's use of debt over the last 25 years illustrates this logic (see Exhibit 4). In the mid-1950s, when Honda held a distant second place in a rapidly growing Japanese motorcycle industry, the company had to leverage its equity 3.5 times to finance growth. By 1960, the Japanese market had matured and Honda emerged dominant. The debt-equity ratio receded to 0.5 times but rose again with the company's international expansion in motorcycles. In the late 1960s, Honda made a major move to the automobile market, requiring heavy debt. At that time, motorcycle cash flows funded the move.

Which Strategic Road to Take?

There is no safe formula for success in international business. Industry structures continuously evolve. The Caterpillar, Ericsson, and Honda approaches will probably not work forever. Competitors will try to push industrial trends away from the strengths of the industry leaders, and tech-

Exhibit 4. Honda Motor Company's Financial Policy from 1954 to 1980

Period	Interest-Bearing Debt-to-Equity Ratio	Strategic Phase
1954–55	3.5 times	Rapid growth in domestic motorcycle market; Honda is low-margin, number two producer
1959–60	0.5	Domestic motorcycle market matured; Honda is dominant, high-margin producer
1964–65	0.7	Honda makes major penetration of U.S. motorcycle market
1969–70	1.6	Honda begins major move in domestic auto market
1974–75	1.3	Investment pause due to worldwide recession; motorcycle is major cash generator
1978–80	1.0	Auto exports are highly profitable, as are motorcycles

Source: Annual reports.

nological or political changes may force the leading companies to operate in a multidomestic fashion once again.

Strategy is a powerful force in determining competitive outcomes, whether in international or domestic business. And although adopting a global strategy is risky, many companies can dramatically improve their positions by fundamentally changing the way they plan, control, and operate their businesses. But a global strategy requires that managers think in new ways. Otherwise the company will not be able to recognize the nature of competition, justify the required investments, or sustain the change in everyday behavior needed.

If the company can successfully execute a global strategy, it may find itself joining the ranks of the truly successful international companies. Whether they be Japanese, American, European, or otherwise, the strategic thread that ties together companies like IBM, Matsushita, K. Hattori (Seiko), Du Pont, and Michelin clearly shows that the rules of the international competitive game have changed.

Notes

1. For a more detailed look at globalization, see Michael E. Porter, *Competitive Strategy*.

2. For more on this subject, see Craig M. Watson, "Counter-Competition Abroad to Protect Home Markets," *HBR* January–February 1982, p. 40.

Appendix

What is a Global Industry?

The nature of international competition among multinationals has shifted in a number of industries. *Multinational* generally denotes a company with significant operations and market interests outside its home country. The universe of these companies is large and varied, encompassing different kinds of organizations operating in different types of industries. From a strategic point of view, however, there are two types of industries in which multi-nationals compete: *multidomestic* and *global*. They differ in their economics and requirements for success.

In *multidomestic* industries a company pursues separate strategies in each of its foreign markets while viewing the competitive challenge independently from market to market. Each overseas subsidiary is strategically independent, with essentially autonomous operations. The multinational headquarters will coordinate financial controls and marketing (including brand-name) policies worldwide and may centralize some R&D and component production. But strategy and operations are decentralized. Each subsidiary is a profit center and expected to contribute earnings and growth commensurate with market opportunity.

In a multidomestic industry, a company's management tries to operate effectively across a series of worldwide positions, with diverse product requirements, growth rates, competitive environments, and political risks. The company prefers that local managers do whatever is necessary to succeed in R&D, production, marketing, and distribution but holds them responsible for results. In short, the company competes with other multinationals and local competitors on a market-by-market basis. A large number of successful U.S. companies are in multidomestic industries, including Proctor & Gamble in household products, Honeywell in controls, Alcoa in aluminum, and General Foods in branded foods.

A *global* industry, in contrast, pits one multinational's entire worldwide system of product and market positions against another's. Various country subsidiaries are highly interdependent in terms of operations and strategy. A country subsidiary may specialize in manufacturing only part of its product line, exchanging products with others in the system. Country profit targets vary, depending on individual impact on the cost position or effectiveness of the entire worldwide system—or on the subsidiary's position relative to a key global competitor. A company may set prices in one country to have an intended effect in another.

In a global business, management competes worldwide against a small number of other multinationals in the world market. Strategy is centralized, and various aspects of operations are decentralized or centralized as economics and effectiveness dictate. The company seeks to respond to particular local market needs, while avoiding a compromise of efficiency of the overall global system.

A large number of U.S. multinationals are in global industries. Among them, along with their principal competitors, are: Caterpillar and Komatsu in large construction equipment; Timex, Seiko, and Citizen in watches; General Electric, Siemens, and Mitsubishi in heavy electrical equipment.

The multidomestic and global labels apply to distinct industries and industry segments, not necessarily to whole industry groups. For example, within the electrical equipment industry, heavy apparatus such as steam turbine generators and large electric motors is typically global while low-voltage building controls and electrical fittings are multidomestic in nature.

18

Is Vertical Integration Profitable?

ROBERT D. BUZZELL

On the face of it, vertical integration seems a sensible strategy. Managers can assume that their transaction costs will go down, that they will be guaranteed necessary supplies, that internal coordination will improve, and that they'll reap the benefits of the technological capabilities of other units. In a study of 1,649 manufacturing-processing units, the author of this article discovered, however, that in more cases than not, the minuses outweigh the pluses. Because vertical integration requires managers to pump quite a bit of capital into new operations, the strategy may not be worth it unless a company gains needed insurance as well as cost savings from the acquisition.

Vertical integration, or the lack of it, can have a significant impact on business performance. While some observers claim that adequate vertical integration can be crucial to survival, others blame excessive integration for causing corporate failure. Examples of the reasons behind moves toward integration and of their success or failure aren't hard to find:

☐   In mid-1981, Du Pont acquired Conoco Inc. in a $7.3 billion transaction. Edward Jefferson, chairman of Du Pont, stated that the merger would give the company "a captive hydrocarbon feedstock source" and would "reduce the exposure of the combined companies to fluctuations in the price of energy and hydrocarbons."[1]

Published 1983.

☐   In the early and mid-1970s, producers of integrated circuits and finished electronic product manufacturers made a flurry of vertical integration moves into each other's industries. Texas Instruments integrated forward into calculators, watches, and other products. Bowmar, the early leader in hand-held calculators, made a desperate effort to integrate backward into integrated circuit production. (The move ultimately failed, and Bowmar withdrew from the business.) The president of Commodore, another calculator producer, argued that backward integration was neither necessary nor desirable. "It's well worth it [to spend more for chips]," he claimed, "and to be able to get into and out of a technology when you want to."[2]

☐   Some observers have blamed the U.S. automobile industry's woes, in part, on excessive vertical integration. According to Robert H. Hayes and William J. Abernathy, "In deciding to integrate backward because of apparent short-term rewards, managers often restrict their ability to strike out in innovative directions in the future."[3]

As these cases illustrate, vertical integration moves sometimes involve big commitments of resources and can make or break the fortunes of even a large corporation. Managers of smaller businesses, too, often face "make versus buy" and "use versus sell" choices for certain materials, components, products, or services. Should a manufacturer operate a company-owned trucking fleet or use independent owner-operators? At what point can a small supermarket chain afford to own and operate its own warehouse? Is it wise for Coors to manufacture all of its own beer cans and bottles, or is Anheuser-Busch's approach—buying about half its requirements from suppliers—a better strategy?

These alternatives, and countless others that managers select affecting the vertical scope of a company's (or a business unit's) activities, define a business's vertical integration strategy.

Despite the importance of decisions about vertical integration, managers have few guidelines for this aspect of strategy. Consultants and academic authorities on strategic planning and management have offered numerous prescriptions for success in designing corporate portfolios and for market segmentation, pricing, and product development strategies. But beyond suggesting lists of possible advantages and risks, researchers have little to say about vertical integration. Nor does economic theory offer much in the way of guidance.

In this article I summarize the results of some analyses based on the PIMS (profit impact of market strategies) data base. I undertook the investigation to determine how vertical integration relates to business profitability. To shed some light on the following questions, I analyzed PIMS data for business units with varying degrees of vertical integration:

1   In general, are highly integrated businesses more or less profitable than those that are less integrated?

2   Under what conditions does a high or a low degree of vertical integration appear to be most beneficial?

Before presenting the results of the analyses, I want to give attention to the potential benefits and drawbacks of being vertically integrated that previous studies have identified.[4]

Pluses and Minuses

According to the traditional economic definition, vertical integration is the combination, under a single ownership, of two or more stages of production or distribution (or both) that are usually separate. In the oil industry, for example, the process that takes the oil from the well to the service station is divided into four stages—crude oil production, transportation, refining, and marketing. Some companies specialize in just one of these—Buckeye Pipe Line Company, for instance, focuses on the transportation stage. Other companies combine two or three stages, and the fully integrated major oil companies are involved in all four.

The Pluses

What are the benefits of vertical integration in the oil industry or in any industry that has several distinct production stages?

Transaction Costs.   In many cases, a major objective of vertical integration is to eliminate, or at least greatly reduce, the buying and selling costs incurred when separate companies own two stages of production and perhaps the physical handling costs as well. Thus, a company that manufactures integrated circuits as well as finished products can operate with little or no sales force, advertising, sales promotion, or market research. Another producer selling to independent customers would need all these activities.

Supply Assurance.   Vertical integration may also be essential to assure a supply of critical materials. Certainly, this aspect of vertical integration has been a major attraction of that strategy to the petroleum industry, both in its early days and more recently in the OPEC-dominated 1970s.[5] During the crisis of 1973–1974, with little warning, some companies found their supplies sharply reduced and prices doubling or tripling. Apart from the impact they have on materials costs, shortages of materials in industries with high fixed costs are extremely damaging because they lead to low usage of expensive facilities.

Improved Coordination.   Even when supplies of materials are certain, vertical integration may permit cost reductions through improved coordination of production and inventory scheduling between stages. Some argue that an in-house supplier can schedule production more efficiently when it has firm commitments from a "downstream" manufacturing or distribution facility than when it deals with independent customers.

Technological Capabilites.   Some claim that, in general, businesses and companies that are vertically integrated, especially backward, are best equipped to innovate because they participate in many of the production and distribution activities in which change can occur. This argument rests in part on the notion that a critical requirement for successful innovation is adequate coordination of marketing and technical functions and that integration improves coordination.[6]

Higher Entry Barriers.   The more vertically integrated a business, the greater the financial and managerial resources required to enter and compete in it. Established companies in an industry may combine their operations as a way of raising the stakes and discouraging potential new entrants. Of course, this gambit is effective only if vertical integration becomes necessary for competing.

The Minuses

If this strategy offers so many potential gains, why don't more managers employ it? Operating on an integrated basis brings offsetting costs and risks, the most important of which are increased capital requirements, unbalanced throughput, reduced flexibility, and loss of specialization.

Capital Requirements.   When a business integrates either backward or forward, it must provide the capital that the newly integrated operations require. Studies based on the PIMS data base and other evidence show that high investment intensity usually leads to low profitability.[7] The implication is that unless the operating cost savings of vertical integration are substantial, investment intensity will make integration strategies unprofitable.

Unbalanced Throughput.   A problem inherent in combining various stages of production or distribution is the varying scale of operation that each stage may require for efficient functioning. For example, to achieve costs competitive with those of independent suppliers, a manufacturer may have to produce integrated circuits at a very high volume. But if the manufacturer integrates forward into minicomputers, say, it could be that the "minimum efficient scale" of operation for integrated circuits may be much greater than the volume needed for efficient production of minicomputers.

The fact that scale requirements differ among vertically linked activities suggests that integrated businesses must either operate on a scale large enough to satisfy the requirements of the most volume-dependent production stages or suffer the penalties of operating on inefficient scales at one or more stages. An implication of this line of reasoning is that vertical integration is probably more feasible for businesses with high market shares, which, relative to competitors in that market, involve large-scale operations. The experience of the automobile industry illustrates this point. According to one estimate, General Motors buys 10% to 15% of its standard components from outsiders, while Ford buys 40% to 50%.[8]

Reduced Flexibility.   Because vertical integration implies commitment to a particular technology or way of operating, it can be an extremely risky strategy. If technology or market changes make the products or methods of one stage in a vertically integrated system obsolete, the integrated company may find adjusting very difficult. In the 1960s, Jonathan Logan, a women's apparel producer, committed itself to double-knit fabrics by investing in a textile mill. Later, when double-knits had gone out of fashion, Jonathan Logan continued to manufacture them, principally to accommodate the mill's production. In 1981, when it finally closed the mill, the company reported a $40 million write-off.

Loss of Specialization.   A somewhat hard to pinpoint, but often important, danger of vertical integration is the very distinct managerial approaches that the various stages of production or distribution may require. For instance, retail or wholesale distribution operations seem to need forms of organization, control systems, and management styles that are quite different from those for manufacturing and processing. Up to the mid-1930s, the major U.S. oil companies were expanding their ownership of service stations. Then the companies began to phase out their ownership positions in favor of franchising. A prime reason for this shift was the inflexible way in which companies operated their service stations and priced their products.[9] This approach may work for manufacturing, but it doesn't for retailing.

   Other industries have had problems similar to those of the oil refiners when they attempted to integrate forward into retailing. For instance, in the 1960s the inner-city stores owned and operated by the major tire producers suffered severely when mass merchants started competing with them and consumers moved to the suburbs. Integrated manufacturers such as Robert Hall and Bond, the men's clothing producers, and Sherwin-Williams, the paint producer, all had similar difficulties during the 1970s. While other reasons may also account for these companies' troubles, it appears that their efforts to run geographically dispersed retail chains were handicapped by a "manufacturing mentality."

Is It Profitable or Isn't It?

Since vertical integration entails both benefits and risks, it is reasonable to expect the payoff of a strategy of increased integration to vary according to the market and competitive conditions in which a business operates. To explore the profit impact of variations in vertical integration, I have used the PIMS data base.

   The PIMS research program has been described in several published accounts.[10] Consequently, only a very brief discussion of this data base is necessary here.

The data used in the analysis are for "businesses," not companies. Each business is a subdivision of a company, usually a product division or a product line that is distinguished from other parts of the company by the customers it serves, the competitors it has, and the resources it employs. The use of business unit data is of particular importance in the analysis of vertical integration. A company can be vertically integrated and treat the linked segments either as a single, combined business or as separate units. The PIMS data include some measures of the extent of vertical integration that go beyond the business unit level. But profitability and other perform- ance measures are confined to the reporting business units. Hence, the data base allows us to explore the effects of vertical integration strategies that are implemented *within* single business units. Only to a very limited extent, however, can we examine the impact at a company level.

As of early 1982, the PIMS data base contained financial, market, and strategic data on 1,742 business units over four or more years. In the analysis reported here, I have excluded service and distribution businesses both because the samples of these kinds of operations are small and because the meaning of vertical integration in service and distribution industries is less clear than in manufacturing. The sample used here therefore consists of 1,649 manufacturing-processing industry businesses. They cover consumer products, industrial goods and components, and raw and semifinished ma- terials. The data for each business unit are for four-year periods during the 1970s; only the most recent four years of this information are used.

PIMS Measures

The PIMS data base includes two types of vertical integration measures— absolute and relative. The absolute measure is value added as a percentage of sales for each business unit. *Value added* is defined as sales revenue minus all purchases (materials, components, supplies, energy, and services) by one business from other businesses. (Purchases from another business in the same parent corporation are treated as "outside" purchases.) Thus, value added as a percentage of sales is simply

$$\frac{\text{Sales} - \text{purchases}}{\text{Sales}} \times 100$$

To explore how differences in this ratio are related to profitability, one has to make an adjustment. Because each business unit's value-added mea- sure includes net profit, increases in profitability arising from many sources other than vertical integration will also increase value added and thus create an apparent positive relationship between the two factors.

To eliminate the tautological relationship between the ratio of value added to sales ratio and profitability, I have constructed an adjusted ratio in which *reported* net profit is replaced by an *average* rate of return on each business unit's invested capital. The appendix shows the method of calculation used.

In the analysis that follows, I use adjusted value added as a percentage of adjusted sales (as defined in the appendix) as the primary measure of each business unit's degree of vertical integration (I use "VA/S" to refer to this measure). The businesses in the data base vary greatly in VA/S, from a low of around 20% to a high of 90%. The average for the 1,649 businesses is 56%, half of them being clustered between 45% and 65%.

Business units' VA/S differ, no doubt, because they operate in different industries or product markets, where norms vary . To supplement the VA/S measure of vertical integration, I use an additional measure of *relative* vertical integration. This relative measure is based on PIMS participants' responses to the following question: In comparing the degree of backward vertical integration of this business with that of each of its leading competitors, do you find this business's less, about the same, or greater? Responses to this question indicate that more than 60% of the PIMS businesses integrated to about the same extent as their competitors.

Finally, the businesses reported whether their parent companies were vertically integrated (backward *and* forward) to a greater or lesser extent than others in the industry. Where a business was integrated to the same degree as competitors but the company was more (or less) so, either the company or one or more of its competitors had carried out a vertical integration strategy but organized the component activities into separate business units. While we can compare businesses that vary in terms of overall company vertical integration, our measures of performance, including profitability, are limited to those of the reported business unit itself. Because transfer prices among vertically linked businesses may be distorted in one direction or another, performance at this level may or may not be a reliable indicator of the total effect of integration on the company.

To test the general propositions about vertical integration strategies listed earlier, then, we can compare the profit and other performance results that business units varying in degree of integration have achieved. As I indicated, I use both absolute and relative measures.

Vertical Integration and Profitability

Exhibit 1 shows average pretax profit margins, investment-to-sales ratios, and returns on investment for businesses with differing levels of vertical integration as measured by VA/S percentages. As expected, profit margins expressed as percentages of sales rise as VA/S increases. The differences in profit margins are modest up to a VA/S of 60%, but from that point, profits rise consistently with increasing integration.

Investment intensity, however, rises along with VA/S over the whole range of the data. As a result, the pretax rate of return on investment declines

Exhibit 1.   Vertical Integration and Profitability

Vertical Integration Measured by Adjusted VA/S	Net Profit as Percent of Sales	Investment as Percent of Sales	Net Profit as Percent of Invest- ment (ROI)	Number of Businesses
Under 40%	8%	38%	26%	267
40%–50%	8	45	22	341
50%–60%	9	54	20	389
60%–70%	10	56	22	338
Over 70%	12	65	24	314

up to the point where VA/S is between 50% and 60%. Beyond an integration level of 60%, investment intensity increases more slowly than profit margins, and ROI consequently rises with increasing vertical integration.

The "V-shaped" relationship between VA/S and ROI suggests that profitability is highest at the two opposite ends of the spectrum. Either a very low or a very high level of integration yields an above-average rate of return, while earnings are lowest in the middle. This pattern is identical to one reported by Edward Bowman in a study of minicomputer and computer peripherals manufacturers. Bowman interpreted the pattern to mean that a company "can do most of its work itself, such as research and development, production, and service, and be relatively successful. On the other hand, it can be low on value added, essentially a purchased-component assembler, and also successful. The middle ground is apparently a questionable strategy."[11]

The data in Exhibit 1 suggest that what Bowman found in a single industry also applies to manufacturers in general. (Supplementary analyses show the same V-shaped pattern for consumer and industrial products manufacturers. The only exceptions were producers of raw and semifinished materials, for which ROI declined consistently over the whole range from low to high VA/S.)

The figures in Exhibit 1 demonstrate clearly how rising investment requirements offset the higher profit margins associated with intensified vertical integration. If integration can somehow be achieved without the penalty of a proportionally higher investment base, then increasing vertical integration should be extremely beneficial. Exhibit 2 shows that this is, indeed, the case. Here the PIMS businesses are sorted into nine groups on the basis of both VA/S and investment intensity. The data indicate that when investment intensity is constant, ROI steadily increases as levels of VA/S rise.

The lesson seems clear: if a company's management can carry out a strategy of increasing integration without greater investment intensity, this strategy usually leads to higher profitability. But the data also show that the winning combination of high VA/S and low investment intensity is uncom-

Exhibit 2. Vertical Integration, Investment Intensity, and Return on Investment

	Investment as Percent of Sales		
Adjusted VA/S	Under 40% Average ROI	40%–60% Average ROI	Over 60% Average ROI
Under 50%	31% (322)[a]	19% (196)	8% (90)
50%–65%	35 (165)	19 (233)	10 (182)
Over 65%	38 (91)	26 (180)	12 (190)

[a]The number of businesses in each cell is shown in parentheses.

mon. Of the 461 businesses in the highest VA/S group (over 65%), fewer than one fifth also had low levels of investment intensity.

Relative Vertical Integration and Profitability

As noted earlier, cross-sectional differences in the VA/S among businesses are mainly due to differences in the nature of the markets or industries in which they operate. To the extent that this is true, one might conclude that the main implication of the data in Exhibit 1 is that it pays to be in the kinds of businesses in which VA/S is inherently very low or very high. In many cases, however, managers have to make strategic choices about a business unit's relative degree of vertical integration. Is it profitable to be more highly integrated than the industry norm?

Exhibit 3 shows the average ROI performance for PIMS businesses whose relative vertical integration varied. These data are given separately for consumer and industrial products businesses; as I mentioned earlier, the feasibility of forward integration, backward integration, or both depends on where a business is located in a production-distribution system. Exhibit 3 shows measures of relative integration at both the business unit level and the company level.

The data in Exhibit 3 suggest that for both consumer and industrial product manufacturers, backward vertical integration slightly enhances ROI. For consumer products manufacturers, ROI is also higher when the parent company is more forward integrated than competitors are. This result is somewhat surprising; forward integration in consumer goods industries presumably means, in most cases, operation of company-owned wholesale and retail distribution facilities or both, which (as I argued earlier) often require different management systems and styles than manufacturing does. The ROI figures shown in Exhibit 3 are of course for the manufacturing components of the companies involved. Possibly these businesses earn above-average rates of return at the expense of their captive downstream customers.

Scale and Profitability

As I have said, large businesses should more often be able to use vertical integration strategies than their smaller competitors because large companies

Exhibit 3. Relative Vertical Integration and Profitability

	Type of Business	
Relative Vertical Integration[a]	Consumer Products Average ROI	Industrial Products Average ROI
At business unit level:		
Backward integration		
Less	20% (106)[b]	21% (316)
Same	22 (277)	22 (730)
More	23 (58)	26 (162)
At company level:		
Backward integration		
Less	23 (115)	20 (302)
Same	21 (255)	23 (678)
More	24 (71)	24 (228)
Forward integration		
Less	19 (64)	23 (208)
Same	22 (343)	22 (822)
More	27 (34)	22 (178)

[a]In each case, the degree of vertical integration is compared with that of leading competitors in the market that the business unit services.
[b]The number of businesses is shown in parentheses.

are more likely to be able to operate at efficient scales at each stage of activity. Of course, sometimes a company can integrate backward or forward on the basis of the shared requirements of two or more businesses that operate in separate product markets. For example, Texas Instruments produces semiconductors and other components that go into end products such as calculators, watches, and microcomputers. In other words, ways exist to achieve efficient scale other than by having a large share in a single market. Nevertheless, other things being equal, large market share businesses should derive greater benefit from increasing vertical integration.

Exhibit 4 shows that these effects do, indeed, depend on size. Here I've grouped the PIMS businesses according to relative market share, defined as the ratio of a business unit's market share to the combined shares of its three largest competitors. For businesses with small relative shares—less than 25% of those of their three largest competitors combined—ROI is significantly lower when a business is highly vertically integrated. This relationship applies both to the absolute level of integration, measured by VA/S, and to relative backward integration at the business unit level. For businesses with relative market shares over 25%, ROI is highest for the high and low extremes of integration based on the VA/S measure. When relative share

Exhibit 4. Vertical Integration, Relative Market Share, and Profitability

Vertical Integration	Relative Market Share[a]		
	Under 25% Average ROI	25%–60% Average ROI	Over 60% Average ROI
Adjusted VA/S			
Under 50%	14% (255)[b]	26% (202)	33% (171)
50%–65%	14 (188)	19 (204)	29 (188)
Over 65%	9 (113)	22 (150)	31 (198)
Relative backward integration			
Less	14 (193)	24 (139)	30 (90)
Same	13 (293)	21 (351)	31 (363)
More	11 (50)	23 (66)	34 (104)
Relative forward integration at company level			
Less	14 (110)	27 (84)	29 (78)
Same	13 (361)	22 (396)	31 (408)
More	15 (65)	19 (76)	34 (71)

[a]Relative market share is a business unit's market share, expressed here as a percentage of the combined share of its three largest competitors.
[b]The number of businesses is shown in parentheses.
Note:
The differences among the three market-share groups are statistically significant at the 99% probability level. In a multiple regression model that includes all major PIMS profit determinants, the coefficient of VA/S is negative but insignificant for small-share businesses. For businesses with relative shares above 25%, VA/S has a significant negative coefficient (p > 0.99) and $(VA/S)^2$ has a significant positive coefficient (p > 0.99).

exceeds 60%, however, ROI rises consistently with increasing relative backward integration.

Relative forward integration is analyzed in Exhibit 4 on the basis of comparisons among each business unit's parent company and competing companies. The relationship between this kind of integration and ROI is irregular. For businesses with small market shares, the extent of forward integration seemingly makes no difference; for high-share businesses, operating in a vertically integrated company helps profitability. For those in between—namely, those with relative shares between 25% and 60%—ROI is highest when the parent company is less integrated than competitors.

The figures in Exhibit 4, then, provide some support for the idea that the net effects of vertical integration vary according to the size of the business unit. The data also show that competitors with large market shares are more likely to pursue vertical integration strategies. For instance, more than 35% of the businesses with relative shares greater than 60% reported VA/S over 65%, whereas just 20% of the business units with small market shares reported this figure.

Market Stability

To test the proposition that vertical integration strategies are more effective when market conditions and technology are stable, I compared the relationship between ROI and VA/S for businesses in very stable and not very stable conditions. I divided the data base according to high and low real-growth rates, maturity of markets, degree of technological change, and rates of new product introduction. None of these analyses showed significant differences in the impact of vertical integration on profit. Apparently, integration strategies can be successful in both stable and unsettled markets.

Materials Costs

As mentioned earlier, some observers have advanced the notion that companies make integration moves like the Du Pont-Conoco merger because they find integrated organizations less vulnerable to increases in raw materials costs. If this is a valid theory, then a high VA/S should have the biggest impact on profitability when materials costs are growing most rapidly. To test this hypothesis, I separated the PIMS businesses into groups with high and low inflation in materials costs and set the dividing line at 10% annual rate of increase (see Exhibit 5).

The results are the opposite of the prediction. Among businesses that experienced rapid materials-cost inflation, ROI was highest when vertical integration was low, and vice versa. Possibly this situation reflects the greater capital intensity and fixed costs of highly vertically integrated business units. Whatever the explanation, the data certainly cast doubt on the notion that integration provides insurance against the effects of inflation.

Product Innovation

The final hypothesis that I tested concerns the relationship between vertical integration and product innovation. Are highly integrated businesses more

Exhibit 5. Vertical Integration, Cost Inflation, and Profitability

	Adjusted VA/S		
Rate of Inflation in Materials Costs	Under 50% Average ROI	50%–65% Average ROI	Over 65% Average ROI
Under 10% per year	21%	21%	24%
Over 10% per year	27	21	20

Note:
The difference between the two groups is statistically significant. In a multiple regression equation in which ROI was the dependent variable and all the major PIMS profit determinants were independent variables, the coefficient of VA/S was positive for businesses whose materials costs rose by less than 10% annually ($p > 0.97$). For businesses with cost growth above 10%, the coefficient was negative ($p > 0.975$).

innovative? Exhibit 6 shows the percentages of sales that new products generated for businesses with low, medium, and high VA/S. (Here "new products" are items introduced during the preceding three years.) The exhibit shows separate figures for businesses competing in mature versus growth markets, for businesses in which major technological change had occurred recently versus those where it had not, and for businesses with small, medium, and large market shares.

The results indicate that highly integrated businesses do generate more new products. In Exhibit 6, I use a cutoff of 50% to separate high from low VA/S because the data were essentially the same for all businesses beyond the 50% level. In both mature and growing markets, high levels of integration correspond to high rates of new product introduction. The same pattern holds regardless of whether technology is changing or whether the business has a small market share or a strong competitive position. Thus, the experience of the PIMS businesses lends support to the notion that vertical integration facilitates product innovation. In some instances, the need to innovate might justify a vertical integration strategy even if the move exacted some penalty in short-term profitability.

Evaluating Vertical Integration Strategies

Is vertical integration profitable? Sometimes yes, sometimes no. The statistical analyses reported here do not, of course, provide any formula for determining just how a particular integration strategy will affect performance. But the experiences of the PIMS businesses, together with other evi-

Exhibit 6. Vertical Integration and Product Innovation

	Adjusted VA/S	
	Under 50%	Over 50%
	Average Percent of New Products	
Product life cycle stage		
New and growing markets	16%	19%
Mature and declining markets	5	8
Recent technological change		
No	5	8
Yes	12	18
Market share		
Under 15%	8	12
15%–30%	8	10
Over 30%	4	10

dence drawn from various industries, do suggest some guidelines for evaluating the possible benefits and risks of integration.

1. *Beware heightened investment needs.* When a high level of vertical integration hurts ROI, it is usually because investment intensity is rising. An ideal strategy is one in which value added increases but the investment base does not. No doubt, the best way to ensure the investment base is to develop proprietary products or processes whose value derives from superior performance rather than from extensive in-house manufacturing or processing. Successful producers of cosmetics and other personal care products, for example, often enjoy ratios of value added to sales of 70% or more without heavily investing in plant and equipment. In much the same way, some companies in the computer industry have modest in-house manufacturing operations but very high VA/S. These companies add value through technical skills in design and customer service or both, not through production of standardized components.

Unfortunately, far more often, rising capital requirements accompany rising vertical integration. Many businesses seem to follow the path from "northwest" to "southeast" in Exhibit 2. When they do, the return on investment tends to fall. Are most decisions to increase vertical integration, then, mistakes? No doubt many of them are. Managers probably often underestimate the investment needed to support moves into their suppliers' or customers' businesses.

They may also view vertical integration moves as means of defending profitable core businesses. This reasoning is no doubt often valid, and accepting modest profits in one part of a business if it promises high rates of return elsewhere is perfectly sensible. The question is, how much is this kind of insurance worth? The data in Exhibit 2 indicate that the cost is often excessive.

2. *Consider alternatives to ownership.* In the traditional sense of the term, vertical integration is an arrangement based on ownership of activities linked up and down. In some cases, at least, manufacturers can reap some of the benefits of integration without owning all the stages. A manufacturer might, for example, reduce transaction costs via long-term contracts with independent suppliers. This approach is apparently more common in Japanese than in American industry. Hayes and Abernathy say that "long-term contracts and long-term relationships with suppliers can achieve many of the same cost benefits as vertical integration without calling into question a company's ability to innovate or respond to innovation."[12]

3. *Avoid "part-way" integration.* The V-shaped relationship between vertical integration and profitability (see Exhibit 1) suggests that some businesses may suffer because they don't carry their linking strategies far enough. Recall that the most profitable businesses are those at the extremes of the vertical integration spectrum. In general, the least profitable position is an intermediate one. The implication is that, on this dimension of strategy,

a clearly defined position is most likely to succeed. In the vertical scope of a business, managers should be wary of taking gradual, piecemeal steps that can lead to the unrewarding middle ground.

4. *Carefully analyze scale requirements.* A significant risk in many vertical integration strategies is that a production or distribution stage has too small a scope to be run competitively against independent suppliers or customers. Presumably for this reason, the PIMS data show that integration is much more likely to pay off for businesses with quite large market shares.

Just what scale of operation makes a given integration strategy effective depends, of course, on the technologies available in the situation. The conclusion I draw from the statistical data, however, is that mistakes are fairly common. Quite a few small-share businesses are highly integrated and, on average, unsuccessful. Some of them, at least, suffer from what Peter Drucker calls "being the wrong size." Excessive vertical integration is not the only route to becoming wrong sized, but it may well be one of the usual ones.

5. *Be skeptical of claims that integration reduces raw materials costs.* Economists have long questioned the idea that vertically integrated businesses or companies are somehow insulated from fluctuations in the costs of key raw materials. Unless it monopolizes materials supply, they ask, why should a vertically integrated enterprise be able to supply itself at anything less than open market prices? The data in Exhibit 5 indicate that skepticism about cost advantages is often well-founded.

All of these guidelines may seem unduly negative. Each points to possible dangers or illusions associated with increased vertical integration. Given that integration strategies often involve big investments, caution does seem advisable. On the other side, however, vertical integration is often a highly successful strategy. Especially for businesses and companies that enjoy strong market positions, increased integration can pay off in both profitability and greater product innovation.

Notes

1. "Du Pont's Costly Bet on Conoco," *Business Week*, July 20, 1981, p. 52.

2. "Why They're Integrating into Integrated Circuits," *Business Week*, September 28, 1974, p. 55.

3. Robert H. Hayes and William J. Abernathy, "Managing Our Way to Economic Decline," *HBR* July–August 1980, p. 72.

4. For a more extensive discussion of the potential benefits and limitations of vertical integration, see Michael E. Porter, chap. 14, *Competitive Analysis* (New York: Free Press, 1980).

5. David J. Tecce, "Vertical Integration in the U.S. Oil Industry," in *Vertical Integration in the Oil Industry*, ed. Edward J. Mitchell (Washington, D.C.: American Enterprise Institute, 1976), p. 105.

6. Edwin Mansfield and Samuel Wagner, "Organization and Strategic Factors with Probabilities of Success in Industrial Research and Development," *Journal of Business*, April 1975, p. 180.

7. Bradley T. Gale, "Can More Capital Buy Higher Productivity?" *HBR* July–August 1980, p. 78.

8. Robert A. Leone, William J. Abernathy, Stephen P. Bradley, and Jeffrey Hunker, "Regulation and Technological Innovation in the Automobile Industry," report to the Office of Technology Assessment (Washington, D.C., July 1981), p. 43.

9. Gale, ibid.

10. See Sidney Schoeffler, Robert D. Buzzell, and Donald F. Heany, "Impact of Strategic Planning on Profit Performance," *HBR* March–April 1974, p. 137, and Robert D. Buzzell, Bradley T. Gale, and Ralph G.M. Sultan, "Market Share: A Key to Profitability," *HBR* January–February 1975, p. 97.

11. Edward H. Bowman, "Strategy, Annual Reports, and Alchemy," *California Management Review*, Spring 1978, p. 70.

12. Hayes and Abernathy, p. 73.

Appendix

Adjustment of Ratio of Value Added to Sales as a Measure of Vertical Integration

Many companies use value added—or, specifically, its ratio to sales—as a measure of the extent of vertical integration. The logic of the measure is straightforward: the more that stages of production and distribution are combined within an enterprise, the higher the ratio of value added to sales. At the limit is the business that is completely self-contained—it makes no purchases from outside suppliers, and the ratio of value added to sales is 100%. At the opposite extreme is the business that performs only a single, narrowly defined function—for example, the broker who sells a commodity on a commission basis.

While the ratio of value added to sales (VA/S) clearly rises with increasing vertical integration, VA/S is not a good measure of vertical integration. As defined, value added includes a business unit's pretax profits. Suppose that profits increase for some reason totally unrelated to vertical integration. Then VA/S will also rise, but clearly it would be incorrect to treat such a change as an increase in vertical integration.

The same reasoning applies to differences among businesses. If businesses A and B are identical in all respects except that A has a profit of 20%

of sales while B has one of only 10%, treating the resulting ten-point spread in their VA/S as a difference in degree of vertical integration would be inappropriate.

The fact that value added includes net profits poses an especially difficult problem for an analysis of the relationship between vertical integration and profitability. If no adjustment is made in the VA/S measure, then both VA/S and measures of profitability such as ROI will reflect many things that affect profits. The result will inevitably be a high—but spurious—positive relationship between the two. Some way must therefore be found to adjust VA/S to eliminate, or at least minimize, the tautological relationship between it and profitability.

I derived the adjusted measure of VA/S used in this analysis as follows:

1 I subtracted net profit from each business unit's reported figures for value added. (For businesses reporting net losses, I do not add losses back to the reported value-added amount.) For businesses that earned positive profits, I also subtracted net profit from reported sales.
2 A "normal" profit, amounting to 20% of investment at book value, is added to value added and to sales. (The 20% figure is approximately the average pretax, preinterest rate of return for the businesses in the PIMS data base.)
3 The adjusted VA/S, used as a measure of vertical integration, is simply

$$\frac{\text{Value added } - \text{ net profits } + \text{ 20\% of investment}}{\text{Sales } - \text{ net profits } + \text{ 20\% of investment}}$$

19

Growing Ventures Can Anticipate Marketing Stages

TYZOON T. TYEBJEE, ALBERT V. BRUNO, and
SHELBY H. McINTYRE

One outstanding characteristic of many new fast-growing ventures is near chaos as they struggle with such matters as monitoring cash flow and setting production schedules. Because they are so busy putting out fires, owners of such companies can easily lose sight of developments in the outside world, where they must do their marketing. The authors conclude, as a result of interviews with top managers of several rapidly growing high-technology manufacturers, that each company passes through a four-stage marketing development process. In the initial stage, entrepreneurs sell customized products to friends and contacts. They must then exploit a larger marketplace, build appropriate internal communications, and diversify. Companies that successfully negotiate the subsequent stages wind up with well-organized marketing departments that effectively oversee sales, research, and other functions. The key to building an effective marketing organization, the authors conclude, is planning for all the stages rather than reacting to them haphazardly.

The theory of evolution suggests that an organism can flourish only if it adapts to environmental changes. No doubt, a business can expect to succeed only if it changes in response to altered external circumstances.

It is through the marketing function that companies must do the bulk of their adjusting to the outside world. Above all, the growing company's marketing apparatus must evolve in an orderly fashion if the company is to

Published 1983.

Authors' Note: This article is based on research funded by the Marketing Science Institute and the National Science Foundation.

avoid a traumatic transition from one growth stage to another. In this article, we identify the important marketing issues for businesses in transition and advise them how to cope with key problems. A premise of our analysis is that top management must not simply react to new situations created by growth but rather that while operating successfully in the present stage, management must take the initiative in planning for the next one. A marketing organization and strategy that are appropriate for one stage can become liabilities as the company passes into its next phase.

Rapidly growing businesses seem to pass through four evolutionary stages, as Exhibit 1 shows. The marketing effort in each stage takes some time to have an impact, and the growth rate during each stage eventually slows as that arrangement becomes constraining.

Stage 1: Entrepreneurial Marketing

Fast-growing high-technology companies are often founded by people who have left larger companies to start their own businesses. These entrepreneurs

Exhibit 1. The Evolution of a Marketing Organization

Problem	Diagnosis	Prescription
Top management suddenly finds itself unable to provide needed attention to marketing.	Stage 1 business is ready for transition to Stage 2.	Hire a sales manager. Continue to hold management responsible for product planning and pricing and for providing sales support in initial contact with new customers.
There are too many products or markets for top management to coordinate all business functions for each.	Stage 2 company is ready for transition to Stage 3.	Hire product managers and give them support in sales, advertising, and market intelligence. Delegate all marketing responsibility to product managers. Put top management in charge of strategic planning.
Growth opportunities are limited in current product-market scope.	Stage 3 business is ready for transition to Stage 4.	Decentralize marketing activities to divisional level. Establish a corporate marketing group that: Reviews division marketing plans. Furnishes specialized skills in planning and research. Manages corporate level marketing communication.

frequently have a wealth of technical expertise and a fund of innovative ideas but little marketing experience.

During the earliest phase of the young ventures' operations, the founders usually rely on a network of personal relationships built up during their previous employment. Early marketing successes are often in the form of sales to friends and acquaintances, and the products specially designed for these customers.

For example, Robert Buzzard, president of the rapidly growing Lexel Corporation (it had $50 million in sales in its sixth year), recalls that "during the first few years we built hardware for a few specialized companies. Our first customer, Varian, where we knew several people, wanted a particular type of laser, and we supplied it. I did a lot of engineering on the laser head and the optics, and I also did most of the marketing."

The company in this stage is simply trying to get its foot in the door of the market. It tries to identify customers whose needs are not being met by established competitors—"the elephants." The low production volume at this point cannot support much overhead, so the venture can ill afford a formal marketing organization.

The entrepreneurial marketing approach does furnish the new business with at least one powerful selling point: buyers are assured the undivided attention of top management. Eventually, however, personal attention becomes a drag on the company's growth.

Thus, entrepreneurial marketing helps to establish the business and generate early growth, but its effectiveness diminishes with the overextension of key people. The customer base is too small, the company's product line is too customized, and the founding managers are spread too thin to meet all their responsibilities effectively.

Stage 2: Opportunistic Marketing

The companies that continue to grow past Stage 1 do so by changing their operating objective from merely getting a foot in the door to seeking new customers. By the time they reach Stage 2, their credibility and products' technical feasibility have been established. A more standardized product line capable of appealing to a wider set of potential buyers replaces the customized product strategy of Stage 1. This expansion means that the business begins to compete directly with established companies. Successful Stage 2 businesses usually concentrate on introducing economies of scale and improving their internal reporting systems and financial controls. At the same time, an infant marketing department emerges that is often staffed exclusively by salespeople. Since it is tactical in orientation, product planning and pricing become the responsibility of top management.

The narrow tactical focus tends to create conflicts as new channels of distribution open to serve the broadening customer base. The case of Stoneware, a microcomputer software company, illustrates this point.

In its early days, Stoneware sold its products directly to retail dealers because of the more attractive profit margins available when it bypassed the wholesaler. It grew so rapidly (it had $2 million in sales in its first year) that it began to recruit wholesale distributors. It also continued to sell directly to the dealers with whom it had established relationships. Naturally, the company's new wholesale distributors objected, and since the broad distribution provided by wholesalers was important to Stoneware's growth goals, the company decided to stop selling directly to its original customers and to guarantee its wholesalers exclusive distribution rights. Thus, Stoneware eliminated the last vestige of Stage 1's entrepreneurial handholding so as to realize the high volume it needed to achieve economies of scale.

As a company such as Stoneware completes Stage 2, it should be poised for explosive growth. Its narrow customer base and specialized product line have been broadened and standardized, and its manufacturing capability is in place. Many companies at this point, however, fail to organize adequately for the next phase of marketing.

Stage 3: Responsive Marketing

By Stage 3, the company is usually expanding so fast that managers face serious problems of poor organization and division of responsibility. Often they have to make the difficult decision to delegate day-to-day responsibility for key products that have been their pet projects. Relinquishing responsibility is inescapable, but it has a great benefit—it often initiates a process that ends with the creation of a sophisticated marketing department.

Naturally enough, the new product managers emerge as champions for the marketing needs of their wares. Their energetic efforts are rewarded with more people and larger budgets for promotion, customer service, and, ultimately, market research. When the company has integrated such functions, a modern marketing organization emerges.

At this point, effective internal communication is vital to rapidly growing businesses, whose various units risk losing touch with one another and whose customers are becoming so numerous that informal monitoring is unworkable. Successful businesses appear to rely largely on marketing research and their field sales forces for intelligence on customers.

Whereas marketing goals in previous stages are formulated in terms of the needs of the venture, Stage 3 marketing goals are driven by customer needs. One company requires key technical personnel to accompany sales personnel periodically on calls to customers. Another company, which sells diagnostic test kits to medical laboratories, has organized an in-house lab to simulate customer use of the products; any new product has to be "sold" to this internal group before it can be put onto the market.

Eventually, market saturation may slow growth, or competitive forces may make additional gains in market share economically infeasible, or the prospect of antitrust action may make further dominance in a single business unattractive. Thus, the Stage 3 company must seek other product-market positions to sustain growth.

Stage 4: Diversified Marketing

As a business diversifies, it must reorganize, usually by creating divisions, to cope with increased complexity. As a company progresses into Stage 4, a marketing reorganization also takes place. Depending on the degree of decentralization, each division may operate as a quasi-independent Stage 3 unit within a larger portfolio. Each division has a group of product managers with total marketing responsibility for products in the line. Supporting marketing functions such as sales, advertising, and customer research provide the necessary resources to product managers.

The major marketing change in the transition to Stage 4 is the emergence of a marketing function at the corporate level. Regardless of the titles on the organizational chart, the marketing function has the responsibility for monitoring the company's divisions and for maintaining a favorable image of the company with customers and the general public. By providing specialized skills in market research and planning, the corporate-level marketing staff acts as an in-house consultant to the division's marketing staff. Marketing also plays a key role in setting the strategic direction for the company, particularly in identifying new growth opportunities.

Building a Marketing Organization

During Stage 1, management should carve out identifiable domains of responsibility that it can gradually delegate to the growing staff of specialists. This staff's control over day-to-day operations then expands to incorporate all duties the founding entrepreneurs once performed.

Toward the end of Stage 2, a mature marketing organization is needed to coordinate the product line and monitor the market. Finally, as a company outgrows the narrow focus of product-market coordination and evolves into Stage 4, each division spawns its own product organization. Supporting functions such as advertising and research are decentralized among the divisions into autonomous marketing groups. Exhibit 2 outlines the evolution of a marketing organization.

At the corporate level, a strategic marketing group reviews division plans, manages corporate-level marketing communications, and provides help in marketing research and planning.

What happens after Stage 4? Products and technologies eventually become obsolete, whereas basic market needs generally endure. A slide rule manufacturer will go out of business when the electronic calculator is invented unless it defines itself as a business to meet calculation needs, not to make slide rules.

Exhibit 2. The Evolution of the Marketing Function

	Stage 1 Entrepreneurial Marketing	Stage 2 Opportunistic Marketing	Stage 3 Responsive Marketing	Stage 4 Diversified Marketing
Marketing strategy	Market niche	Market penetration	Product-market development	New business development
Marketing organization	Informal, flexible	Sales management	Product-market management	Corporate and divisional levels
Marketing goals	Credibility in the marketplace	Sales volume	Customer satisfaction	Product life cycle and portfolio management
Critical success factors	A little help from your friends	Production economies	Functional coordination	Entrepreneurship and innovation.

The typical Stage 4 business has a highly bureaucratized organization that can easily encounter marketing problems. For the Stage 4 company, a key issue is whether it can continue to foster a spirit of seeking new venture opportunities, the same spirit that gave birth to the business.

20

Match Manufacturing Policies and Product Strategy

ROBERT STOBAUGH and PIERO TELESIO

As American industry begins to redress its long neglect of manufacturing, there is a danger that top management's renewed enthusiasm for operational mastery will outrun the bounds of strategic control. The important point to remember is that skill in production, like any other valuable corporate asset, must be carefully and purposefully deployed if it is to serve as a fulcrum for competitive leverage. That is, it must be richly and deliberately integrated—both in its appointed tasks and in the ends toward which it is directed—with the product strategies it is to support. Because the work of international manufacturing faces special difficulties in achieving this level of integration, the authors use it to illustrate their central argument: at all levels of business, as strategies shift, so must the mission of production.

☐ Deere & Company acquired subsidiaries in Germany in 1956 and in France in 1960 to serve European markets with low-horsepower tractors. Not until the mid-1960s, however, did the company adopt manufacturing policies for its production facilities in Europe that suited its strategy for competing in worldwide tractor markets. The delay cost Deere valuable market share.

☐ Warwick Electronics was at one time the only supplier of color televisions to Sears, Roebuck and Co. and depended on Sears for close to 75% of its sales. As technology changed and price competition increased, Warwick initially proved unable to manufacture good quality products at low cost. Its corrective actions—product redesign and the

Published 1983.

transfer of production to a Mexican facility—were too little and too late. Sears had lost confidence and turned elsewhere for suppliers. Warwick's losses increased, and it finally sold its television business to Sanyo, a Japanese manufacturer.

Both Deere and Warwick got into trouble because they too slowly realized that a change in product strategy alters the tasks of a manufacturing system. These tasks, which can be stated in terms of requirements for cost, product flexibility, volume flexibility, product performance, and product consistency, determine which manufacturing policies are appropriate. As the tasks shift over time, so must the policies covering:

- [ ] The location and scale of manufacturing facilities.
- [ ] The choice of manufacturing process.
- [ ] The span, or degree of vertical integration, of each manufacturing facility.
- [ ] The use of R&D units.
- [ ] The control of the production system.
- [ ] The licensing of technology.

In this article we draw on the results of a research project at the Harvard Business School to provide a conceptual framework with which managers can closely match manufacturing policies with product strategies. (See the ruled insert for the details of that project.) Although this framework, which we outline in Exhibit 1, has relevance for all companies, we focus on organizations operating in the international environment because of the many added complexities such operations entail.

Four notes of caution. First, as we explain Exhibit 1, we talk as if each of a company's major products had a separate manufacturing system with its own production tasks and policies. This is often, but not always, the case. Second, we identify product strategies by their dominant thrust (technology, for example) even though other considerations (marketing, say, or cost) are also important. Third, we do not consider divestment as an explicit strategy but as a response either to a strategy gone wrong or to the maturing of a product. Finally, the various policies recommended in Exhibit 1 are no substitute for a sound and detailed analysis of each company's situation. Our aim here is to provide a tool to guide a decision maker's thinking, not a list of all-purpose answers.

Technology-Driven Strategy

A strategy based on product technology (the first column in Exhibit 1) involves serving high-income markets with a flow of new, preferably unique,

Exhibit 1. Manufacturing Policies for Product Strategies

	Technology-Driven Strategy	Marketing-Intensive Strategy
	Key manufacturing task: To manufacture high-technology products and to be flexible enough to change products and processes quickly.	Key manufacturing task: To operate marketing programs with good product quality and prompt delivery.
Manufacturing policies		
Establishing facilities abroad		
Location	Large market, high-income countries, but invest only when the company cannot serve a market by importing from another company plant.	Local markets to be able to respond to marketing needs.
Scale	Small scale at first, then larger as markets grow.	Heterogeneous mix of sizes, depending on local market size.
Choice of process	Little incentive to adapt technology to local factor costs.	Little incentive to adapt technology to local factor costs.
Span	First, assembly; then simple fabrication; finally, full-scale manufacture.	From contract manufacturing to fully integrated production.
Managing technology		
Research and development	Establish facility to aid technology transfer and to adapt products to local market specifications and processes to local raw materials.	Establish facility to adapt products to local market's tastes and local raw materials.
Controlling the system	Parent heavily influences major manufacturing decisions; local control of other decisions unless transshipment among subsidiaries is large.	Parent has little influence.

288

	Scale Economies	Low-Cost Strategies	
		Low-Cost Labor	Other Low-Cost Inputs
Licensing technology	Some technologies are suitable for licensing; in some industries, licensing for reciprocal access to technology of other innovators is also desirable.		Little incentive to license.
	Key manufacturing task: To operate large-scale plants so as to keep costs at a minimum.	Key manufacturing task: To minimize cost by using low-cost labor for labor-intensive mature products and components.	Key manufacturing task: To keep costs low by using low-cost resources.
	Large national or large regional markets.	Countries with low-cost labor.	Countries with low-cost inputs.
	Large-scale plants.	Small-scale plants.	Depends on nature of key input.
	Little incentive to adapt technology to local labor costs.	Much incentive to adapt manufacturing technology to making use of low-cost labor.	Much incentive to adapt manufacturing to the use of low-cost inputs and to ensure product quality.
	Facilities specialized; limited number of components for which manufacturing scale economies are important.	Manufacturing of labor-intensive products or components.	Manufacturing limited to process steps using low-cost resources.
	R&D facility occasionally needed to improve process.	Little need for local R&D.	Little need for local R&D.
	Parent has tight control	Parent has tight control.	Parent has tight control if system is integrated; less need for tight control on operations otherwise.
	License if company is not a dominant producer.	Licensing unlikely.	Licensing likely for some technology.

289

high-performance and high-technology products. Industries like engineering plastics and biogenetics, for example, rely on manufacturing systems that are sufficiently flexible to accommodate frequent changes in products as well as their rapid introduction to the market. Because accurate sales projections are difficult to make, volume flexibility is important; because the product itself is the major competitive weapon, manufacturing costs are not of primary importance.

These manufacturing tasks have a major impact on the location of plants. Good communications with, and swift response to, a changing market for high-technology products ordinarily means locating the initial plant in a high-income country with a large market—that is, in one of the industrialized nations. Plants have usually first been built in the home market of the innovating company—often in America, but sometimes in Europe or Japan, where the necessary pool of skilled labor exists. And since process flexibility and product performance are more important than low costs, that skilled labor is affordable. This pattern is slowly changing, as modern technology allows rapid communication with distant markets and the proliferation of foreign subsidiaries permits the simultaneous introduction of products in a number of markets.

Establishing Facilities Abroad

Exports from the home-market plant can open markets abroad; but as demand grows and as imitators appear, some foreign markets become large enough to require local production. At first, the spread of manufacturing units abroad is usually limited to countries with high-income markets; as sales rise elsewhere, production facilities eventually follow. In size, the initial foreign plant must be able to handle the rapid growth that often comes early in a product's life. Until needed for the local market, this extra capacity can serve the markets in neighboring countries. In some instances, of course, scale economies are sufficiently important that the initial plant can serve the world market for an indefinite period; in other cases, low wages and high productivity in the innovating country—Japan, for example—are reason enough to keep manufacturing at home.

The need for great flexibility in a technology-driven strategy often limits the span of these manufacturing activities. Purchasing components from other companies—or other manufacturing facilities of the parent company— passes on to them some of the risks of rapid change in products and volumes. Early in the life of a product, foreign investment might merely involve assembly; but as output grows, so does the need for other production steps, which lead to full-scale manufacture. The production network that results will include a number of facilities, varying in size, location, and span of operations.

IBM's choice of manufacturing policies nicely illustrates these points. Market considerations determined the order in which the company established its foreign operations (1925 in Germany, 1935 in Italy, and 1950 in

Brazil) and the type of products each turns out (the more advanced goods being produced first in the larger, higher-income markets). In the mid-1970s, for example, IBM used half the capacity of its German facility to build central processing units but only a quarter of its Italian facility and none of its Brazilian facility.

IBM plants that serve local or regional markets have assembly operations only and thus relatively small capacity, but most overseas operations (about 80%) serve worldwide needs. In Europe, plants cover virtually all production steps, although some specialize in making semifinished parts in order to achieve scale economies. In developing countries in Asia and the Pacific, plants import raw boards and cards from IBM facilities elsewhere but do the rest themselves. In Latin America, they are mostly devoted to assembly work.

Driven by product technology, IBM does not attempt to substitute labor for capital in its plants abroad. Because most of its foreign facilities are located in high-wage countries and because new products do not usually compete on the basis of price, small reductions in manufacturing costs are unlikely to boost sales and profits. IBM keeps to this policy even in countries with low labor costs—that is, it chooses to rely on virtually identical processes, tooling, and equipment throughout the world, save where there is a need to accommodate variations in the grade of local raw materials.

Managing Technology

When R&D units are associated with plants abroad, they often assist in the transfer of complex technology, the adjustment of processes to local raw materials, and the adaptation of products to local markets. These units sometimes produce major modifications in products or even completely new products—for world, as well as local, markets. When, for example, IBM established its first foreign R&D units in the 1930s in the United Kingdom, Germany, and France, their purpose was to transfer technologies to IBM's European subsidiaries. Eventually, these three units, plus another five added between 1964 and 1970 in Europe, Canada, and Japan, began to serve the needs of IBM worldwide.

Because careful nurturing of process technology is essential to an effective technology-driven strategy, policy decisions are properly the responsibility of headquarters. Day-to-day manufacturing decisions, however, can be left to local managers. With the growth of manufacturing facilities abroad, shipments among international subsidiaries increase, and a more formalized control function becomes necessary. At IBM headquarters, personnel in international manufacturing, who numbered only about 10 at the end of the 1950s, grew to more than 200 by the mid-1970s. In the words of one IBM manager, "We are much more procedure oriented than we were, and of course procedures require administration."

And what of the many technologies that an innovation-based strategy generates? Licensing the more important of them is often unwise since it may stimulate price competition in some of the licenser's markets or create barriers to the establishment of a worldwide manufacturing network. In industries like chemicals, pharmaceuticals, and electronics, however, companies often exchange licenses, not to supplement foreign investment income but to maintain the technical dynamism of the industry. Indeed, IBM's policy is quite liberal: it licenses freely to unaffiliated companies.

Of course, no strategy that relies on a flow of new high-technology products within a product line can last forever. Sooner or later, markets and technologies mature. At times, a major change in the product may retard the maturation process, but price competition almost inevitably becomes important and competitive emphasis shifts to process changes that lower manufacturing costs. When this happens, licensing technology as a source of revenue takes on greater appeal. Maintaining flexibility, though still important, gradually takes a backseat to achieving economies of scale through larger, more automated plants and greater specialization of both work force and equipment. And these developments, in turn, lead to heightened control of operations by headquarters. Increased specialization and automation of manufacturing facilities, along with greater intracompany flows of components, make a manufacturing system more predictable, hence more susceptible to—as well as more needful of—centralized control.

Marketing-Intensive Strategy

With products like soft drinks, detergents, and over-the-counter drugs, a marketing-intensive strategy (the second column in the Exhibit) relies on heavy advertising and selling expenditures to distinguish a company's offerings from those of its competitors. Although marketing, not low-cost production, provides the competitive edge for such product lines, manufacturing has vital support to provide. At a minimum, it must ensure that the right mix of dependable-quality products is available as each market requires.

A manufacturing presence in these markets permits a company to respond quickly to changes in the nature or volume of demand. One manufacturer of canned soup, for example, adjusts recipes to the tastes of local markets and adapts the manufacturing process to make use of locally available ingredients. The risk of not being responsive to such changes outweighs any cost benefits of centralizing production into one large-scale facility designed to serve several markets. In fact, cost reductions usually have little effect either on profit margins (because most differentiated, or branded, products are priced well above manufacturing costs) or on sales (because the volume of such products is relatively insensitive to price).

Not surprisingly, both the scale and the span of foreign plants grow with the size of local markets. As these markets expand, otherwise limited activities give way to complete operations requiring little outside sourcing of intermediate goods. This pattern—product flexibility in the early stages of market penetration leading to increased dependability of supply as operations approach full integration—is clearly evident in the development of Colgate-Palmolive Company's manufacturing plants in more than 40 foreign countries.

Since most of the output of these facilities is sold in local markets, the first facility to be built in each country is usually for the production of toothpaste, for the minimum economic plant size is small. Next follows a larger investment for the manufacture of detergents. Over time, as the local markets grow, fully integrated production systems replace contract manufacturing.

Companies that follow a strategy of product differentiation have little need to do R&D abroad—save to adapt products to local tastes and specifications. Nor is licensing technology an issue. Companies with this kind of strategy do not often possess technologies that are attractive to potential licensees. More to the point, experience shows that they would rarely be willing to accept the risk, which is inherent in licensing to outsiders, of losing some control over marketing. Colgate, in fact, has virtually no licensing agreements.

Furthermore, since intracompany shipments are low, centralizing the control of the manufacturing system is not necessary. To be sure, major decisions about location and capacity should receive the attention of headquarters management, but day-to-day operating decisions are best left to local managers. When, however, the quality of a product in one market affects sales in another—as is the case with, say, pharmaceuticals—then strong central control of product quality is imperative.

Low-Cost Strategies

With a mature product that is unsuitable for a marketing-intensive strategy, a manager must either divest the business or manufacture the product at the lowest possible cost for a given level of quality.

Several approaches to this low-cost strategy are available: using large-scale plants to achieve scale economies, locating facilities in countries with low labor costs, and placing facilities so as to guarantee them access to critical inputs other than labor, such as cheap and abundant energy. (See the three right-hand columns in Exhibit 1.)

Scale Economies

When achieving scale economies is important, plants should, as a rule, be sited in large national markets or in countries with access to them. (Of course, it is possible for a small-market country, if protected by trade barriers, to be an attractive location.) The need for scale should also limit the span of manufacturing in any country to the items needed in large volumes.

In the late 1960s, for example, Otis Elevator Company, now a division of United Technologies, started a program of plant specialization within the European Common Market. As Otis explained in an annual report, its low-

cost strategy required it to place greater emphasis on "standardized models
. . . and on mass production of components in specialized plants." German
and Italian facilities specialized in producing motor units and control mechanisms; the French, in cabin components and foundry parts. High freight
costs on assembled elevators and the need to tailor the elevator cabins to
the needs of each customer led the company to do final assembly in the
markets where the elevators were sold.

Another effect of a scale-driven strategy is to discourage the substitution of labor for capital, not least because in high-volume operations the
proportion of labor costs to total costs is usually low. Substitution may
actually reduce scale economies and increase costs. Capital-intensive methods are preferable when reliable delivery and consistent quality are important
and when components are regularly transhipped for further assembly—a
common state of affairs under a low-cost strategy.

Common, too, is the minimal need such companies have for local R&D
facilities in their overseas operations. Standardized products allow little
scope for product R&D. Occasionally process R&D is needed in an effort
to lower costs.

Companies following a low-cost strategy need the tight control of headquarters to ensure that costs are indeed being kept low. And when there are
transshipments among a company's plants, sufficient control must be exercised over shipping schedules and product quality to guarantee smooth
operations in the various facilities. Otis's European headquarters in Paris
sets the quantities and prices on intracompany shipments and issues instructions for production scheduling, quality, cost standards, inventory, transportation of products, and materials storage. Under such conditions, it makes
sense to license technology only when the technology owner does not enjoy
a dominant position in the industry and when competing technologies have
a number of sellers.

Otis, for example, has no licensing agreements with other companies.
"It is the policy of the company," Otis reports, "not to license competitors
or potential competitors in areas that are open to company sales. Since we
have sales operations, either through subsidiaries or agents, in practically
all countries outside the Communist bloc, this policy effectively precludes
licensing to outsiders."

Low-Cost Labor

Companies seeking low labor costs should, of course, locate manufacturing
facilities in countries with low wage rates. Other relevant considerations
include transportation costs, the presence of an industrial infrastructure, the
availability of trainable workers, the level of political risk, and, of course,
the outlook for growth in wage rates. The size of local markets is less
important, for the products are not usually sold in the country where they
are produced. Nor must the scale of operations be large or its span extensive.
Investments should be in the labor-intensive steps of the production process,

which do not usually enjoy the economies of scale of the more capital-intensive steps.

With its home radios, General Electric follows a low-cost strategy based on manufacture in low-wage countries. In response to a threat to its domestic market for radios by foreign-label imports, the Audio Electronics Department opened foreign plants, first in Ireland and then in Hong Kong and Singapore. These supplied both finished radios and consumer electronics components for import into the United States. GE engineers made a number of process adaptations in these plants to expand their use of labor—among them, the cutting, sanding, finishing, transfer, and packaging of parts by hand instead of by machine.

As with all low-cost strategies, company headquarters should ordinarily exert tight control on the integration of manufacturing operations. Quality standards must correspond with the needs of the system and with delivery schedules; manufacturing costs must be kept at a minimum. For example, all major operating decisions for the Audio Electronics Department's overseas activities were made in the United States. The critical tasks were to ensure good quality, delivery, and cost. In the words of one manufacturing manager, "If you cannot hit those pricing points with a dependable product delivered on time, you're dead in this busines."

A word of caution about the low-cost labor strategy: a company should not neglect developments in the technology of automation. Rapidly increasing wage rates abroad might make automation attractive, especially given the swift advances now being made in that technology. Indeed, the Audio Electronics Department found that automation became necessary in Hong Kong and Singapore as wage rates rose.

Other Low-Cost Inputs

Here, the key task for a manufacturing system is to extract the maximum cost advantage from a critical resource such as raw materials or energy. Access to a secure and low-cost supply of raw material is an important reason why Exxon, Mobil, and Celanese, for example, are investing in petrochemical facilities in Saudi Arabia. Their facilities will produce commodity petrochemicals, most of which will be processed into end products outside Saudi Arabia.

As a rule, it is often desirable to locate such facilities in countries containing the critical resource, whether to save freight costs or to obtain a dependable supply. It also makes sense to limit the span of operations to the stages of production that make use of the low-cost input—unless the final market for the products is in the same country. Plant size will follow an industry's economies of scale, much as the choice of technology will follow the varying quality of raw materials. To the extent that local facilities are to be closely integrated with other plants in the system, important decisions about technology and operations will flow from headquarters; but if output is to be sold primarily in the local market, the need for centralized control diminishes.

Lessons for Managers

As we have tried to show, various manufacturing policies are appropriate for different product strategies. Perhaps the example of several domestic operations will help drive this point home. Apple Computer, which has a technology-driven strategy, initially selected the span of its manufacturing to include only an assembly operation; it has not yet moved into simple fabrication. Mohasco, a carpet manufacturer, adopted a marketing-intensive strategy for the West Coast and located a manufacturing facility in California to respond better to the styling changes required by West Coast markets. Gulf Oil follows a strategy of low-cost raw materials for its ethylene business. Its U.S. manufacturing facilities are on the Gulf Coast, where the raw material (ethane) is cheap.

Failure to match manufacturing policy and product strategy can have disastrous results in a domestic business. The construction of nuclear pressure vessels involves a technology-driven strategy, yet Babcock & Wilcox located a new manufacturing facility in a cornfield in a southwestern Indiana in order to tap "an unspoiled labor market." In spite of a massive training program to turn farmers into skilled welders and machinists, B&W suffered for years from the lack of a skilled, disciplined work force. As a result, poor quality and slow delivery forced customers to look to competitors.

Strategies, remember, must function in dynamic settings: a product based, for example, on a technology-driven strategy of innovation often matures. As a result, managers must be ever alert to the possibilities of change as they go about the work essential to the formulation of manufacturing policies. In practice, they should:

☐ Define a product strategy.

☐ Identify the critical tasks of a manufacturing system geared to serve that strategy.

☐ Set up, adapt, and control the manufacturing system so as to perform these tasks.

☐ Periodically reevaluate the ability of the manufacturing system to perform the required tasks.

☐ Stay abreast of changes in product strategy so as to modify the manufacturing policy accordingly.

Appendix

Research on International Technology Transfer and Production
This article is based on an extensive research project at the Harvard Business School on international technology transfer and production in more than 100

multinational enterprises. This project, directed by Mr. Stobaugh, has led to a number of studies, including:

☐ Michael A. Amsalem, Technology Choice in Developing Countries: The Impact of Differences in Factor Costs. DBA thesis, Harvard Business School, 1978 and his book, *Technology Choice in Developing Countries: The Impact of Differences in Factor Costs* (Cambridge: M.I.T. Press, forthcoming).

☐ Henri de Bodinat, Influence in the Multinational Corporation: The Case of Manufacturing. DBA thesis. Harvard Business School, 1975.

☐ Dong Cho, International Facility Planning: Regarding the Application of Scientific Approaches. DBA thesis, Harvard Business School, 1977.

☐ Richard W. Moxon, Offshore Production in the Less Developed Countries by American Electronics Companies. DBA thesis, Harvard Business School, 1973, and Offshore Production in the Less Developed Countries—A Case Study of Multinationality in the Electronics Industry. *The Bulletin*, Institute of Finance, New York University, Nos. 98–99, July 1974.

☐ Claude L. Pomper, International Facilities Planning: An Integrated Approach. DBA thesis, Harvard Business School, 1974 and his book, *International Investment Planning: An Integrated Approach* (New York: North-Holland Publishing, 1976).

☐ Robert C. Ronstadt, R&D Abroad: The Creation and Evolution of Foreign Research and Development Activities of U.S.-Based Multinational Enterprises. DBA thesis, Harvard Business School, 1975 and his book, *Research and Development Abroad by U.S. Multinationals* (New York: Praeger Publications, 1977).

☐ Piero Telesio, Foreign Licensing Policy in Multinational Enterprises. DBA thesis, Harvard Business School, 1977 and his book, *Technology Licensing and Multinational Enterprises* (New York: Praeger Publications, 1979).

☐ Brent D. Wilson, The Investment of Foreign Subsidiaries by U.S. Multinational Companies. DBA thesis, Harvard Business School, 1979 and his book, *Disinvestment of Foreign Subsidiaries* (Ann Arbor, Michigan: UMI Research Press, 1980). See also Robert B. Stobaugh and Louis T. Wells, Jr., editors, *International Technology Flows*, for several forthcoming articles based on some of these and related studies, including

☐ G. James Keddie, Adoptions of Production Technique by Industrial Firms in Indonesia. Ph.D. thesis, Harvard University, 1975. Donald Lecraw, Choice of Technology in Low Wage Countries: The Case of Thailand. Ph.D. thesis, Harvard University, 1976.

PART THREE

THE GROWING
CHALLENGE OF
IMPLEMENTATION

AN OVERVIEW

The most logical and well thought out strategy can easily go for naught if it isn't implemented effectively. That seemingly obvious observation has only recently become an issue of importance to many marketing managers.

Thomas V. Bonoma lays the groundwork for understanding the differences between effective strategy and implementation in his article, "Making Your Marketing Strategy Work." He argues that, more often than not, marketing problems stem from weaknesses in implementation rather than strategy; implementation difficulties result from organizational as well as interpersonal problems, in his view.

For companies that rely on technology as the basis of their products' appeal, David Ford and Chris Ryan present an approach for assisting managers in deciding how to get the most marketing mileage. Their article, "Taking Technology to Market," stresses reliance on the technology life cycle—a derivative of the product life cycle—as a basis for altering marketing approaches.

The notion of high quality as a necessary component of effective marketing implementation gets support from Hirotaka Takeuchi and John A. Quelch in their article, "Quality Is More Than Making a Good Product." They see quality as being linked particularly strongly to changing customer values and after-sale servicing.

Jack Reddy and Abe Berger also see quality as an important aspect of improving marketing strength and offer insights into organizing for better quality, in their article "Three Essentials of Product Quality." They see high quality resulting largely from appropriate organization, data collection, and controls on vendor quality.

High quality, new products, and increasing marketing budget outlays get much credit for improving market share in an article by Robert D. Buzzell and Frederik D. Wiersema, "Successful Share-Building Strategies." They also reaffirm the positive correlation between market share and return on investment.

Understanding and exploiting the intangible aspects of products in the marketing effort can aid both sales and postsales efforts, maintains Theodore Levitt in his article, "Marketing Intangible Products and Product Intangibles." Sellers of services must be especially attuned to making customers aware of intangibles, he notes.

Companies should build an effective program of product support into their marketing efforts to continue competing effectively, maintain Milind M. Lele and Uday S. Karmarkar in their article, "Good Product Support Is Smart Marketing." Implementing such a strategy involves appropriately defining customer needs and then designing the most effective support systems possible, they suggest.

Barbara Bund Jackson concludes this section with a framework for adjusting prices to take account of major commodity price fluctuations, in her article, "Manage Risk In Industrial Pricing."

21
Making Your Marketing Strategy Work

THOMAS V. BONOMA

Should we emphasize price or quality? Do we want to stay with smaller, upscale retailers or seek market expansion through large discount chains? Will our proposed new product take sales away from our existing line? These are the kinds of questions—ones of strategy—that marketers agonize over. But what happens once a particular strategy is agreed to? Will marketers effectively turn drawing-board strategy into marketplace reality? Too often a seemingly effective strategy fails to do what it is supposed to do, and marketing executives immediately assume that the strategy is at fault. The author argues that more often than not it is the implementation that goes awry. Implementation difficulties can result from a variety of organizational and structural problems as well as from inadequate personal skills. The author offers guidelines for identifying the most common difficulties as well as suggestions for remedying them.

The marketing literature is replete with research and analysis to help managers devise marketing strategies tailored to the marketplace. Yet when it comes to implementing those strategies, the literature is silent and the self-help books ring hollow. What top management needs in the 1980s is not new answers to questions about strategy but increased attention to marketing practice, to the signposts of good marketing management that direct clever strategies toward successful marketplace results.

The purposes of this article are to explain and help in diagnosing and solving marketing implementation problems, to catalog common problems

Published 1984.

of translating marketing strategies into management acts, and to recommend tactics for increasing the effectiveness of marketing practices. The examples and conclusions are drawn from a three-year clinical research program I conducted to initiate a course on marketing implementation at the Harvard Business School (see the Appendix for details of the study).

It is invariably easier to think up clever marketing strategies than it is to make them work under company, competitor, and customer constraints. Consider a pipe company that invented a new kind of triangular pipe 180% more efficient than the existing line, needing only two-thirds as much material. On the basis of value to users, the new marketing vice president wanted to price the new pipe high. He feared, however, that lack of support from other top managers, the company's marketing systems, and the sales force would hamper his strategy. "Everything three generations of managers have learned about doing business in this market, everything the company *is*," he complained, "seems to conspire against my being able to introduce this innovation properly."

What to do—the marketing strategy—is clear to this vice president: price according to value, encourage cannibalization of existing lines, and reap the profits. *How* to accomplish the strategy—the marketing implementation—is problematic.

This family-owned company customarily produced pipe in large quantities and sold it in a nongrowing market at low margins. The company started every year with high margins, but because of competitive pressure and the need to keep its plants at capacity, it wound up cost cutting in the heat of the selling season. Plant managers were paid on the basis of pipe produced per minute. The sales force thought in terms of cutting list prices to stimulate orders and ensure commissions.

Top management encouraged this commodity-oriented culture by setting budgets with high fixed costs and maintaining a measurement system designed to track the selling price of each unit of raw material rather than of the pipe itself. The vice president rightly worried that simply declaring a high price on the new pipe by fiat or even constructing a marketing program for the innovation would be ineffective in combating the entrenched and commodity-focused way of doing business.

As this example suggests, problems in marketing practice have two components: structural and human. The structural one includes the company's marketing functions, like pricing and selling, as well as any program based on these functions, any control systems, and policy directives. The second component is the people themselves, the managers charged with getting the marketing job done.

Strategy or Implementation?

Marketing strategy and implementation affect each other. While strategy obviously affects actions, execution also affects marketing strategies, especially over time. Despite the fuzzy boundary between strategy and execution, it is not hard to diagnose marketing implementation problems and to distinguish them from strategy shortfalls. When a 50-person computer terminal sales force sells only 39 of the company's new line of "smart" microcomputers during a sales blitz in which sales of more than 500 units were forecast, is the problem with sales force management or with the strategy move to the smart machines? The question is answerable.

Intense competition is eroding margins on sales of its old "dumb" terminals. Additionally, the smart terminals category is expected to grow by over 500% during the 1980s. The new product, a portable microcomputer with built-in printer and memory, has many benefits that the target market values. But because sales representatives already earn an average of more than $50,000 a year, they have little incentive to struggle with an unfamiliar new product. Management also inexplicably set sales incentive compensation on the new machines lower than on older ones. Finally, the old terminals have a selling cycle one-half as long as the new ones and require no software knowledge or support. Here is a case where poor execution stifles good strategy.

Exhibit 1 shows how marketing strategy and implementation affect each other. The computer example falls in the lower left cell of the matrix and illustrates an important rule about strategy and implementation: poor implementation can disguise good strategy. As the exhibit indicates, when both

Exhibit 1.   Marketing Strategy and Implementation Problem Diagnosis

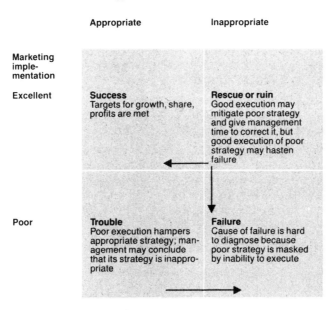

	Strategy	
Marketing implementation	**Appropriate**	**Inappropriate**
Excellent	**Success** Targets for growth, share, profits are met	**Rescue or ruin** Good execution may mitigate poor strategy and give management time to correct it, but good execution of poor strategy may hasten failure
Poor	**Trouble** Poor execution hampers appropriate strategy; management may conclude that its strategy is inappropriate	**Failure** Cause of failure is hard to diagnose because poor strategy is masked by inability to execute

strategy and implementation are on target, the company has done all it can to ensure success. Similarly, when strategy is inappropriate and implementation poor, implementation shortcomings may mask problems with the strategy; not only is failure the probable result, but such failure will be especially intractable because of the difficulty in identifying the cause of the problem.

When strategy is appropriate but implementation is poor or vice versa, diagnosis becomes tricky. Poor marketing execution may cause management to doubt even sound strategies because they are masked by implementation inadequacies (the lower left cell of the exhibit). As the foregoing computer company example suggests, management may hasten marketplace failure if it then changes its strategy. I have labeled such a situation the "trouble" cell on the matrix because poor execution hampers confirmation of the strategy's rightness and can provoke unnecessary change.

When strategy is inappropriate and execution excellent (the upper right cell), management usually winds up with time to recognize and fix its strategic mistakes. Good branch office heads, for instance, have been known to modify potentially disastrous headquarters directives. Indeed, some companies that are noted for excellent marketing execution, like Frito-Lay, expect such modifications from their managers. But at other times, good execution of bad strategy acts as the engine on a plane in a nose dive—it hastens the crash. Because it is hard to predict the result of inappropriate strategy coupled with good execution, I label this cell "rescue or ruin."

From this analysis two points stand out to help managers diagnose marketing implementation problems. First, poor execution tends to mask both the appropriateness and the inappropriateness of strategy. Therefore, when unsure of the causes of poor marketing performance, managers should look to marketing *practices* before making strategic adjustments. A careful examination of the *how* questions, the implementation ones, often can identify an execution culprit responsible for problems that are seemingly strategic.

Structural Problems of Marketing Practice

In his book *Zen and the Art of Motorcycle Maintenance*, Robert Pirsig proposes a catalog of traps that can sap the mechanic's resolve to do quality work. He tells, for instance, how a five-cent screw holding an access cover in place can, if stuck, render a $4,000 motorcycle worthless and the mechanic a frustrated wreck headed for truly grave mistakes. Like mechanics, managers need a catalog of the traps in marketing practice.

In the following sections I take up the problems and pitfalls of each level, or "place," in the structural hierarchy of marketing practice: functions, programs, systems, and policy directives. I then discuss the implementation skills required of those who are doing the marketing.

Functions: The Fundamentals
Marketing functions include selling, trade promotion, and distributor management. These low-level tasks are the fundamentals, the "blocking and

tackling" of the marketer's job. Yet I have observed that most companies and their managers have great difficulty with these tasks. Often the difficulty stems from a failure to pursue marketing's fundamentals in any determined way, as when one CEO doubted that his trade show expenditure was a good marketing communications device but continued to authorize $1 million every year because he thought the company had to be there.

Although the pitfalls peculiar to each function are worthy of a separate article, there are some management problems common to all.

Problems with marketing functions generally outnumber problems at the marketing program, systems, and policy levels. Managers most often have trouble with sales force management, distributor management, or pricing moves. When functions go awry, it is often because headquarters simply assumes that the function in question will get executed well by someone else, somewhere else, and thus ignores it until a crisis intervenes.

In one company, for instance, management decided to offer low list prices with correspondingly low discounts from list prices. In making what it thought was a sound pricing move for its line of graphics computers, however, management failed to take into account how pricing got implemented. The pricing shceme that resulted satisfied no one because the buyers proved their effectiveness by the size of the discounts received.

Thus, implementation problems at the functions level are caused primarily by faulty managerial assumptions or, as they say in the sports world, by not keeping your eye on the ball. As might be expected, this "disease" is more prevalent in large operating units, where administrators have functional specialists to rely on, than in small ones.

A second cause of marketing function problems is structural contradiction. A highly promising start-up business with $600,000 in revenues decided after careful deliberation to expand its domestic distribution network by setting up—at great expense—its own sales offices. The purpose was to control its distribution channels. For international distribution, though, management was torn between its need for control and its unfamiliarity with international markets. The conflict was heightened when a potential foreign partner said it would guarantee $30 million in sales.

Management was stumped. Its policy dictated that it should own foreign channels, but implementation was beyond its capabilities. Cash flow needs eventually seduced the company into deciding on indirect foreign distribution, with a different partner and arrangement in each country. The overall result was a complicated patchwork of direct and indirect distribution, which the thin ranks of executives could not handle. Management's attempts to balance the contradiction between desired control policies and functional-level distribution structure were ineffective and led to conflicts among company executives and foreign distributors.

And a third cause of problems is when the head office fails to pick one marketing function for special concentration and competence and instead takes satisfaction in doing an adequate job with each—what I call "global mediocrity." Officials thereby spread resources and administrative talent democratically but ineffectively. Typically, the pricing, advertising, promotion, and distribution functions are satisfactory, but no one function is outstanding.

The best companies have a facility for handling one or two marketing functions and are competent in the remainder. No marketers are good at everything, but the most able concentrate on doing an outstanding job at a few marketing functions. Frito-Lay is an example of a company that has refined two functional skills—selling and distribution—to such heights that they serve as the company's marketing basis. Gillette's Personal Care Division makes a science of advertising. Both these companies allocate resources, often unequally, to maintain competitive preeminence in the "showcase" functions.

Programs: The Right Combination

A marketing program is a combination of marketing and nonmarketing functions, such as sales promotion and production, for a certain product or market. Marketing programs are a basic reference point for marketing practice analyses; from them, it is possible to look down at the functions comprising the programs or up at the systems and policies directing the programs' execution.

At the program level, management seeks to blend marketing and nonmarketing functions in an attempt to sell a particular product line or penetrate a target segment. Managing all aspects of the Silkience hair conditioner line is an example of a marketing program; so is managing a company's key accounts and their special needs. If functions are the blocking and tackling of execution, marketing programs are the playbook showing how customers will be courted and the competition confounded.

A computer vendor, for example, wished to install a national account program to better serve its small but growing number of key accounts. The vendor recruited a highly regarded national account manager from another company, gave him a secretary, and issued a presidential mandate to put a key account program together.

Exactly how was this to be done? Perhaps the manager should try to create a headquarters-based dedicated national account sales force despite the attendant risks that competition with the sales vice president, his superior, implied. Or was he better off working in a dotted-line capacity through the company's sales managers, attempting no sales or service coordination beyond simple interfunctional persuasion, and running different risks with the customer base? The art of blending functions into programs is a poorly understood one at best, often left to on-the-job learning by trial and error.

One common program problem stems from what I call "empty promises" marketing, which results from instituting programs that either are contradicted by the company's identity or are beyond its functional capabilities. The computer graphics company alluded to previously made a generalized piece of computer equipment that served all the industry's segments, but most purchasers were small single-site users. Indeed, with the exception of its national account manager, every implementation action and policy directive geared the company to small customers. Unlike many businesses that obtain 80% of revenues from the largest 20% of customers, this company received only 30% of its revenues from its large accounts. In short, the business's national account program ran counter to what the company was set up to do in marketing. The program was an empty promise internally and to the marketplace.

In another case, the country's largest producer of private-label light bulbs decided it had to give its bulbs a brand name and place them on the grocery shelves to preempt others from an attack on its profitable main business. The company, which specialized in industrial lighting products, had no experience in consumer marketing or advertising and only a little in important retailing areas like trade promotion. Nonetheless, it created "Project Shopping Cart." After spending several million dollars for the design of a new display and packaging for the bulbs and even more to sponsor athletic events and recruit a host of brokers to place the bulbs, management accrued a 0.3% share of the market in two years. The marketing functions in this industrially and generically oriented company were unable to supply the retail blocking and tackling that headquarters simply assumed would be there to implement its well-conceived program.

A second program-level execution error is one I term "bunny marketing." It arises not from functional inability to execute program plans but from a lack of direction from top management's execution policies. One heavy manufacturing company was continually frustrated because it came out late with new products in an industry in which spare parts inventories and operator loyalties give the first-in vendor a significant advantage. One of its products, a machine for special mining conditions, came out almost two years after the competition's entry. Headquarters had kept its thin developmental engineering staff busy with a torrent of engineering projects, some to rework machines already in the field, one to come up with an automatic machine prototype under government grant, and another to design the new machine. In short, the profusion of programs lacked focus because it stemmed from a poor sense of what the company was and what it did.

The presence of many clever marketing programs—a great playbook—is often associated with implementation problems. This is so because when a strong sense of marketing identity and direction are absent, programs tend to go off in all directions. Such bunny marketing results in diffusion of effort and random results.

Systems: Bureaucratic Obstacles

Marketing systems include the formal organization, monitoring, budgeting, and other "overlays" that foster or inhibit good marketing practice. Systems can be as simple as voice telecommunications or as complex as profit accounting.

Of the systems at lower organizational levels, the most problematic is sales force reporting and control. Of the pervasive systems, those concerned with the allocation of marketing resources and those that help management monitor results are bugbears in all but a few companies. Especially in smaller companies, allocation systems cause many problems; in larger ones, control systems do more damage. Other kinds of systems as well as personnel and the formal organizational structure can also be problematic, but managers usually can get around these obstacles by exercising their execution skills.

Three problems that commonly occur at the systems level are errors of ritual, politicization, and unavailability. Errors of ritual arise when the company's systems drive it down habitual pathways, even when good judgment dictates a different course. At one concrete producer, the marketing control system relied on a plant backlog measure. When backlogs were low, the sales force beat the bushes for jobs no matter how marginal, the estimators (who control pricing in construction companies) shaved the margins, and everyone from the CEO on down got nervous. When backlogs were high, reactions were the opposite. As a consequence, the low-margin business taken in bad times hindered the company when it sought high-margin business in better times. When the president accepted suggestions for a new sales control system to remedy the problem, he instituted new forms and reports but refused either to modify backlog management or to approach profitability by job as a means toward more effective segmentation and selling.

The problem of politicization is never more evident than when observing sales force reporting and control systems and, in particular, call reports. Sales managers often weed out their call reports to fit their preconceptions. Even more dangerous, call reports can lose their intelligence function altogether and become instead a device with which to punish sales representatives who submit "inappropriate" ones.

The politicization of systems is in no way limited to sales controls, however. In one case, division management in an equipment rental company chose to report to headquarters that its new pricing scheme would increase unit revenues by 11% and margins by 13%. It neglected to note, unfortunately, that the rental equipment would be obsolete a year sooner than headquarters had planned!

The final, and most pervasive, systems problem is unavailability. That is, some systems designed to make line officers' lives easier just don't do so. In all but a handful of the companies I studied, for example, the financial accounting and sales accounting systems can only be called perverse in failing to meet marketing's requests.

One would expect that in today's data-oriented companies managers could make projections based on detailed analysis of results. Few executives, however, have any idea of profitability by segment, to name one element. Rarer still are good numbers on profitability by product, and only once have I seen a system that allowed profitability to be computed by individual account. Instead, managers either are treated to incomprehensible, foot-thick printouts of unaggregated data or else are told in response to their requests that "accounting won't give it to us that way." The inevitable result is a kind of bell-jar environment in which it is impossible to make sound decisions.

Policies: Spoken and Unspoken

At the broadest structural level of marketing practice are policy directives. While policies cover the spectrum of administrative activity, I focus here on two especially important marketing implementation policies: identity policies—those relating to what the company is—and direction policies—those conerning what it does. By policies I do not mean only verbal or written statements; indeed, some of the policies most central to good marketing practice are unspoken.

Identity problems are the most common policy difficulties and, paradoxically, occur more often in mature than in young business units. *Marketing theme* and *marketing culture* are two terms I use to capture the powerful but often unspoken feeling of common purpose that the best implementers have and others do not. Theme and culture transmit the company's identity policies.

Marketing theme is a fuzzy but significant term that refers to management's shared understanding of marketing's purpose. In one company, some executives perceived themselves as heading a commodity vendor with the only hope for the future being blue-sky R&D projects. Others believed that the company's key attribute was in differentiating its basic lines. The managers consistently functioned according to their different understandings, and the result was a confused and ineffective marketing effort—a sales force that thought headquarters gave it contradictory signals, a divisive trade, and unhappy customers.

By contrast, another company's management and entire 10,000-plus person sales force could recite (with conviction): "We are the premier vendor of snack foods in this country. Our products are great. But we have only two seconds to reach the supermarket shopper, so we live or die on service." Management's shared understanding and continual reinforcement (through compensation, training, and the like) of this theme, simple though it sounds, promoted exceptionally effective sales performance and consistent customer reactions.

It is tempting to dismiss the notion of fostering a common understanding of the company's marketing theme as a vague and insignificant idea. A test of your company executives' perceptions of that theme may stir up some concern. To conduct this test, write a single sentence describing your company's marketing essence. Then have your key people do so as well. The results are usually as instructive as they are shocking.

Marketing culture is a broader notion than theme. Whereas themes often can be verbalized, culture is the underlying and usually unspoken "social web" of management. It subtly but powerfully channels managers' behavior into comfortable ruts. Culture can be observed clearly from such things as lunchroom conversations and mottoes management puts on the walls.

For example, when I asked managers in one company why they were planning a $700-million plant addition to support a new product line that market research suggested would require only one-half that capacity, the marketing vice president responded, "We don't see much sense around here in chinning ourselves on the curb."

Direction policies refer to both marketing strategy and leadership. While marketing strategy is outside the realm of this article, leadership deserves attention as a key aspect of implementation. It has become fashionable in corporations to blame shortcomings in practice on culture. It is undeniably true, however, that some top marketing managers are top-notch leaders and others are not. The former inspire us with their eagerness to get out into the field; they are clever at designing simple and effective monitoring methods, and their understanding of customers is powerful. Others are much less effective as leaders, being immersed in complex conceptualizing or unwilling to leave their leather chairs for the marketplace; they are inspirational only as models of what their juniors hope not to become.

The quality of marketing leadership has a far-reaching effect on the quality of marketing practice. Indeed, of the business units I observed that had low-caliber leaders, not one had high-quality marketing practices overall.

Whether a strong theme and culture are brought about by the charisma of the person on top or orchestrated through memoranda is irrelevant. The critical question is whether these intangibles of identity, or "who we are," and direction, or "what we are about," exist as powerful though unquantifiable forces that impose themselves on an observer in the same way they permeate the company.

Gap Bridging: Execution Skills

Up to this point I have analyzed the motorcycle without much attention to the mechanic. Indeed, the primary reason good marketing practice occurs is that managers often use their personal skills to supplant, support, and sometimes quietly overthrow inadequate practice structures. I call this substitution of personal skills for weak structure a "subversion toward quality." Poorly functioning formal marketing systems are frequently "patched up" when the managers using them exercise informal organizing skills. Similarly, informal monitoring schemes often are created to get data the control system can't, and budget "reallocations" often are designed to subvert formal policy constraints. Managers bring four execution skills to the marketing job: interacting, allocating, monitoring, and organizing.

Interacting

The marketing job by its nature is one of influencing others inside and outside the corporation. Inside, there is a regular parade of peers over which the marketer has no power to impose preferences; instead he has to strike horse trades. Outside, the marketer deals with a plethora of helpers, including ad agencies, consultants, manufacturers' reps, and the like, each with an agenda and an ax to grind. I observed that those managers who show empathy, that is, the ability to understand how others feel, and have good bargaining skills are the best implementers.

Allocating

The implementer must parcel out everyone's time, assignments, and other resources among the marketing jobs to be done. Able managers have no false sense of egalitarianism or charity but are tough and fair in putting people to mature programs and too few to riskier and amorphous programs.

Monitoring

It is by using monitoring skills that a manager can do the most to reconstruct degraded corporate information and control systems. Good implementers struggle and wrestle with their markets and businesses until they can simply and powerfully express the "back of the envelope" ratios necessary to run the business, regardless of formal control system inadequacies. Poor implementers either wallow blissfully in industry clichés or else get mired in awesome and often quantitative complexity that no one understands. The general manager of a company with 38 plants and 300,000 customers, for instance, ran everything he considered crucial according to notations on two three-by-five-inch index cards. By contrast, the sales manager of a company some one-one hundredth that size generated hand-truckfuls of computer printouts monthly in his monitoring zeal, then let them age like cheese.

Organizing

Good implementers have an almost uncanny ability to create afresh an informal organization, or network, to match each problem with which they are confronted. They "know somebody" in every part of the organization (and outside too) who, by virtue of mutual respect, attraction, or some other tie, can and will help with each problem. That is, these managers reconstruct the organization to suit the marketing job that needs to be done. They customize their informal organization to facilitate good execution. Often, their organization and the formal one have little in common.

Good Practice in Marketing

The administration of marketing is problematic in all but a few companies, and management's adeptness often is restricted to a few functions or programs within the marketing discipline. Yet, some of the businesses in my sample showed truly excellent marketing implementation, and it is from them that some simple but important characteristics that differentiate good marketing practice emerge:

1. In the best companies, a strong sense of identity and of direction in marketing policies exists. There is no confusion and little disagreement among managers over "who they are." Further, the leaders are strong and able. There is, indeed, clarity of theme and vision.

2. The best implementers continually appeal to the customers, including the trade or distributors, in several unusual ways. Customer concern is an ingrained part of the culture and is always prominent in the theme of the best implementers. Interestingly, the distributors are also viewed as customers, and management has as a main objective the maintenance of a partnership with them and with end-users. I call this behavior "profit partnership with wide definition."

I did not find that the good implementers are less profit oriented than the poor ones; quite the opposite. Yet, managers best at execution take special care to see that the end-users also profit in terms of true value for the money they spend. The trade profits in more traditional ways, with dollar margins, but also benefits from having good implementers consider them as key accounts. The companies less competent at implementation never form a partnership with these two key marketing constituencies or, worse, lose a focus they once had.

3. In the best organizations, management is able and willing to substitute its own skills for shortcomings in the formal structure. At United Parcel Service, the story is told with some pride of the regional manager who took it on himself to untangle a misdirected shipment of Christmas presents by hiring an entire train and diverting two UPS-owned 727s from their flight plans. When top management learned of his actions, it praised and rewarded him. The culture suppported the manager's substitution of skill for structure, but the regional manager was also "combat ready" to defend his judgment.

4. Finally, in the companies that handle execution best, top management has a distinctly different view of both the marketing structure and the managers than do bosses in other companies. In the best companies, without exception, the importance of the executives dominates the importance of the execution structure. That is to say, marketing (and other) managers are top management's "key accounts" and are treated with a latitude not found in other corporations. Top executives in companies that are good at marketing encourage their followers to challenge and question them because it is not always possible for those at the top to be right. Those who are poor at following continually thwart the tendency for policies and structure to become religion, which would cause management to lose its flexibility in

times of change. This process can be characterized as a "good leaders, poor followers" common theme.

Top managers in the best companies also view the marketing structure differently. They tend to foster a philosophy of "allocation extravagance with program pickiness" in marketing investments. It is not always easy to get new programs approved by these managers, but the plans that are endorsed are staffed, funded, and otherwise fully supported to maximize their chances of success.

The full endorsement of fewer sound marketing programs seems to give these officers the critical mass they need to make the programs work in good times and bad and limits the risk to the company. This approach worked well for one business-jet distributor I studied, which weathered the recession in much better shape than its more programmatically prolific peers.

Again, in the best companies, management concentrates on one or a few marketing functions that it fosters and nurtures into a competitive distinction through expertise. When strong theme and culture, program pickiness, and functions-level concentration ae combined, the composite that emerges is that the businesses best at marketing execution encourage soundness at the top (policies) and the bottom (functions), rather than flashiness in the middle (programs).

When all is said and done, quality in marketing practice is not a guarantee of good marketplace results. There's just too much luck, competitive jockeying, and downright customer perverseness involved to hope for that sort of predictive accuracy. Rather, good marketing practice means using skill artfully to cope with the inevitable execution crises that blur the strategies for managing customers and middlemen. Individually, such threats are not much to fear. Taken collectively, they are strategy killers.

Appendix

The research project

The data for this article originated with a course development and research project into marketing implementation. Although I am still conducting the research, I have compiled 35 case studies on marketing practice problems to date. All the examples in the article, with one exception, are drawn directly from these cases. They cover a variety of company sizes and types.

The cases fall into the four structural categories I have outlined in the article. Some cases illustrate low-level *functional* marketing problems, such as how Hertz can retreat from its "no mileage, ever" pricing scheme, should that become appropriate. Others show problems at the *programs* level, concerning the synergistic combination of marketing functions to bring to market a particular product or sell a special segment. Key account management cases are a major concern here. There are *marketing systems* cases, in which management is troubled or concerned by the information it has (or doesn't have) available to direct and control the marketing effort. And, there are cases on *marketing policy directives*, the formal or informal policies by which management attempts to direct all marketing's execution. I have collected many such cases on marketing theme and leadership.

One of the reasons I initiated a course on marketing implementation was that top executives frequently complained to me that newly minted MBAs generally are great strategists but ''can't organize a three-car funeral'' when it comes to executing marketing plans in the field. The results of teaching the course for three years indicate that effective execution in marketing *can* be taught. The results of the research project indicate that marketing practice is as worthy of detailed management attention and academic study as is strategy formulation.

22

Taking Technology to Market

DAVID FORD and CHRIS RYAN

For many years, the concept of the product life cycle has helped managers maximize their return on product sales. But according to the authors of this article, using a technology solely in product sales is no longer enough. Today, companies face high R&D costs, competitive pressures from low-cost producers, capacity limitations, antitrust laws, financial difficulties, and foreign trade barriers. This means that they must improve the rate of return on their technology investments by marketing their technology as completely as possible during all phases of its life cycle. The technology life cycle—derived from the product life cycle—pinpoints the changing decisions companies face in selling their know-how.

The authors also discuss both the competitive dangers of transferring technology to low-cost foreign producers and the growing role of intermediaries in technology sales. They stress the importance of having a highly specialized staff to plan a company's technology marketing, a responsibility that should be assigned neither to the part-time attention of top management nor simply to marketers or strategic planners.

Corporate management of technology requires careful planning of the relationships among a company's technologies, its markets, and its development activities. It requires coordination of R&D activities to ensure an optimum research level—depending on a company's available resources, competitive pressures, and market requirements. And it requires systematic linkage between a company's product and process technologies: the products developed must also be produced efficiently.

Current management wisdom says that a company invests its skills and resources in developing products or services that are of value to its customers. However, we argue that, to maximize the rate of return on its

Published 1981.

technology investment, a company must plan for the fullest market exploitation of all its technologies. These technologies may, but need not necessarily, be incorporated into that company's own products or services. In fact, the growth of low-cost Third World producers will make it increasingly difficult for Western companies to exploit fully their technologies through their own production alone.

Thus, a company's marketing strategy may—and probably should— provide for the sale of technologies for a lump sum or a royalty. (By *sale*, we mean either the direct sale of a technology or the sale of a license to use it.)

The marketing literature, however, provides little help for the manager who wishes to exploit fully his or her company's technologies. Many critical questions remain unanswered, among them:

☐ What problems are involved in selling a technology?

☐ Is a company that sells a technology giving away its "seed corn" and thus prejudicing its future?

☐ How, to whom, and when should a technology be sold?

☐ What is the relationship between the sale of a technology and the sale of a product based on that technology?

In this article we draw on our own research to examine these important questions within the conceptual framework of the technology life cycle (TLC), which traces the evolution of a technology from the idea stage through development to exploitation by direct sale. In particular, we examine the relationships between product and technology sales and describe the important choices and strategies open to management throughout the TLC. Specifically, we examine the value of shifting from managing a product portfolio to managing a portfolio of technologies. We also consider the impact of the TLC positions of technologies in the portfolio and the significance of a company's level of dependence on individual technologies. (See the Appendix for information on the derivation of the TLC.)

Why Sell Technologies?

Let us look at some of the reasons that even a successful company cannot fully exploit its technologies through product sales alone:

1. The ever-increasing costs and risks of R&D, especially of basic research, mean that companies must be certain to get the most of the technologies they develop—including those that do not have immediate relevance to their own lines of business. For example, General Electric in the United States developed a microorganism that destroys spilled oil by digesting it. However, after winning a well-publicized patent case in the U.S. Supreme

Court, GE is now offering this technology for sale because it does not fit into the company's major lines of business.

2.   Some technologies may not fit into a company's overall strategy. Their application may be in markets that are too small or undesirable, or a company may have ethical objections to their use. Technologies may even cease to fit with a corporate strategy after they have been in use for some time. For example, GE sold off its mature Fluidics technology (which uses pressure changes in gas streams for measurement purposes and has wide application in textiles and metalworking) because it no longer fitted the company's major strengths or strategy.

3.   Producers of products based on new technologies frequently rely on patents as a protection against competitive pressures, but patent rights offer only limited protection. After all, most technology can be copied by other producers, given time. These producers have cost advantages in not having to amortize the high R&D costs incurred by the originator. And Third World producers, in particular, have the benefits of lower labor costs. The recent battle between Eastman Kodak and Polaroid over instant-picture technology is an extreme case of heavy reliance on patents that were unable to prevent competitive entry into a market.

4.   Similarly, a company may refuse to sell a technology to an overseas producer because it fears competition at home or in other markets. If, however, a competitor agrees to sell that technology, then the first company will face the same competition without any compensating royalty payments or any control over the technology's diffusion.

5.   A company may develop a new technology and then, because of financial woes or restrictions on its own production capabilities, may not be able to exploit it fully in the market. Sinclair Radionics, a small British company in the consumer electronics industry, claims to have made a breakthrough in the technology of flat-screen color TVs. The screens, measuring several feet in length and width and three-quarters of an inch in thickness, would render obsolete hundreds of millions of dollars of investment in conventional cathode-ray tube plants. The first company to succeed in producing them at a competitive cost would have a decisive advantage in a market worth more than $20 billion a year. But Sinclair's past marketing problems have made it impossible for the company to find further risk capital. Thus, it has sought joint venture arrangements with large multinational electronics companies as a way of combining resources.

6.   A company may not be able to capture through its own production all the world markets for a given technology. For one thing, sophisticated import restrictions on direct sales of manufactured products are common in Third World countries. For example, American Motors—which produces jeeps through subsidiaries in South Korea, India, and Australia and through license agreements in the Philippines, Pakistan, Sri Lanka, Thailand, and Bangladesh—is trying to penetrate the Chinese market. It is doing this through a license arrangement with the Beijing Automotive Industrial Corporation.

Beijing has produced a line of four-wheel drive vehicles since 1964 and now wants to acquire the technology to produce certain jeep models in an existing plant.

7. Finally, a company may be restricted in its direct exploitation of technology by antitrust legislation. One well-documented example is the Federal Trade Commission's complaint against Xerox. The FTC charged Xerox with using its patent position to acquire a complete monopoly over the paper copier market. The proceedings were terminated in 1975 when the court entered a consent decree under which Xerox offered its competitors nonexclusive licenses on a number of its patents at either no royalty or a minimal royalty.

The Technology Life Cycle

Given these restrictions on the direct embodiment of technology in products, a company that wants to get the most out of its technology must plan carefully to realize the full market value of that technology at all stages of its TLC evolution.

In developing the concept of the TLC from the more familiar notion of the product life cycle,[1] we examined technology development, application, and degradation in such diverse industries as electronics components, consumer electronics, automobiles, shoe manufacturing, construction, mining equipment, and air conditioning.

Exhibit 1 shows the complete TLC for a major technology application. It is equivalent to the product life cycle for an entire industry for a generic product. Included are the proportion of the total use of the technology accounted for by the originator's technology sales and the product or, more accurately, the *production* life cycle of the original manufacturer.

We now turn to the particular issues in marketing and selling a technology that face an originating company in each of the stages of the TLC.

Stage 1: Technology Development
This stage begins long before any production, when research indicates a potentially valuable technology. The major issue the company faces here is whether further development of the technology should take place. Normally, development continues if:

☐ The technology has an obvious application in a readily identifiable market that fits with the company's overall strategy.

☐ The company has the financial resources to develop the technology, and the technology is compatible with that company's production and marketing skills.

☐ The projected rate of return on development is favorable when compared with alternative investments.

Exhibit 1.   The Technology Life Cycle

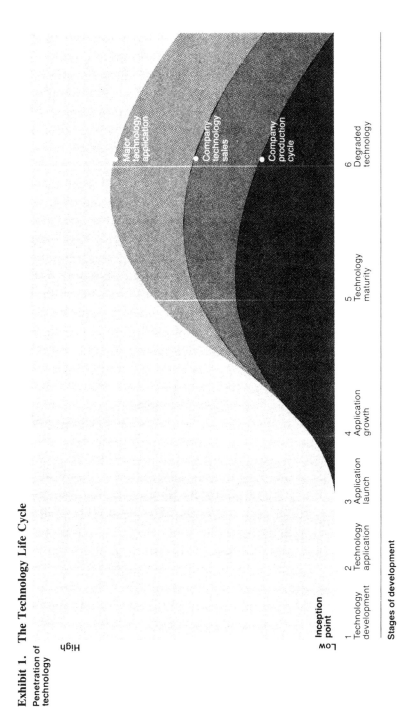

Penetration of
technology

High

Major
technology
application

Company
technology
sales

Company
production
cycle

Inception
point

Low

1	2	3	4	5	6
Technology	Technology	Application	Application	Technology	Degraded
development	application	launch	growth	maturity	technology

Stages of development

The situation is often less clear-cut. The technology may have several potential—but unclear and possibly unrelated—applications. Say a pharmaceutical company were to make a breakthrough in the technology surrounding the complex group of chemicals known as prostaglandins, which have wide applications in medicine, agriculture, and bioengineering. Early on, it might not be clear which application had the most potential or was most capable of realization. And even if the best application were readily identifiable, it might not match the company's strategy or resources.

Under these circumstances, the company would face more complex questions:

☐ Should it find a partner with whom to develop the technology further, especially if related technologies or additional financial resources were required?

☐ Should it try to sell the technology if it did not have immediate application within present markets or strategy?

Technology Sales at GE.   GE in the United States has formalized the latter approach by "packaging" for sale technologies that are too small or that lie outside its areas of interest. Since 1968 it has sold "surplus" technologies through a technology marketing operation, which is staffed by five technically trained people with experience in business planning, product sales, product planning, or market research, as well as by a licensing counsel. In each case, the technology marketing operation, after being approached by the operating division involved, seeks potential buyers on the basis of the data file that it maintains on known customer needs, which it cross-references with GE technologies available for sale.

This operation is also responsible for *Selected Business Ventures*, a monthly publication based on potentially useful and salable technologies. Ninety-eight percent of the ideas in it do not emanate from GE but are collected by it for the 400 to 600 companies that subscribe to the publication. In addition, the unit updates and sells to subscribers technical manuals, such as those on heat transfer and fluid flow, developed by the company. It does not, however, involve itself in major licensing decisions, which remain the responsiblity of the individual product divisions.

Benefits of Hanging On.   Even if a company wished to sell a technology this early in the TLC, it might have difficulty doing so; potential applications or the costs of developing marketable applications might be too uncertain. There is, however, an alternative at this stage that companies frequently ignore: their technology might be marketable but not in its present form. If developed further and incorporated into a product, it might then be salable to other companies. Frequently, technologies are ditched when they do not immediately fit into a company's product strategy, despite the fact that further development might lead to a marketable technology for someone else. Of course, this alternative also preserves a company's own option to produce products based on the technology.

Importance of Staffing. Companies face still another major issue in the early stage of the TLC: they must have staff who are as sophisticated in the marketing of technologies as in the marketing of products. Unfortunately, this is rarely the case.

The people who make decisions early on about a technology's future are frequently nonmarketing staff. Decisions to kill development of a technology often take place before a company's marketing staff are involved. On the other hand, when marketers are involved, they will more likely see the future of a technology solely in terms of its translation into a company's own products. They are often unable either to think about selling a technology or to analyze the potential market for a technology. More important, the market for a new technology may lie among a company's product competitors, and marketing staff may often have difficulty in dealing with these competitors as potential customers.

Stage 2: Technology Application

After a company has decided to apply a technology to a new product—whether for its own production or for production by others—it incurs its first major costs. These costs are likely to be the primary factor in the company's decision either to continue with development or to sell the technology during this stage.

Few stockholders of a public corporation will tamely allow the development of technologies that even at the outset involve both high costs and high risks.[2] For instance, the Pilkington Company's successful development of the float glass process was brought to fruition only because of the support of the privately held company's board and because of the determination of the entrepreneur involved.

Further, when embodying technology in a product, a company is likely to face heavy costs in other areas—for example, in developing associated process and product technologies. The company may find it necessary to buy into these associated technologies either by licensing or on a risk-bearing basis. Perhaps the largest recent example is the design for the European A300 Airbus, whose initial success led to the production consortium that included such companies as British Aerospace.

At this stage of the TLC, regardless of the high costs involved or the possibility of buying into related technologies, a company must not base its development decisions on the projected returns from product sales alone. Instead, it should consider potential returns from the technology as a whole—including product sales, license revenues, and perhaps turnkey deals.

Burroughs, for example, has put its computer technology to work in a network that allows some 700 of the world's largest banks to make transactions anywhere in the world in a matter of seconds. The banks run the network as a nonprofit organization, but it is staffed by Burroughs's people using Burroughs's equipment. A similar computer system, Ethernet, is being launched by Xerox in conjunction with Digital Equipment and Intel. This system allows participating companies to set up total communications networks within single buildings or closely built clusters of buildings. The three companies have made a special point of allowing other manufacturers to license their network system—in this case, as a way of encouraging use of their protocols and equipment.

Sell or License?   Possible applications of a technology become clearer and financing is more likely to be forthcoming when the technology has progressed beyond the idea stage to the point of practical demonstration. Similarly, potential licensees are likely to become more interested in a technology after it has been brought to the prototype or preproduction stage.

Nevertheless, decisions on the sale of technology at the end of stage 2 are primarily determined by the development costs incurred and by the projected initial revenues from licenses or product sales or both.

Dolby Laboratories provides an example of the problems created by high development costs and the need to ensure an adequate return. Ray Dolby initially saw his company as a research laboratory that would sell its noise reduction technology for tape equipment to the professional electronics industry. He wished to sell to this market first to gain a quality reputation among recording engineers. But, having invested $25,000 of personal savings and loans from friends, he quickly found that to survive he needed the income which could come only from product sales. Thus, he decided to make and sell noise reduction units initially for the professional music recording market.

The professional market in the electronics field is small, and any attempt to exploit it through the licensing of technology would not have provided sufficient revenue to justify Dolby's initial investment. On the other hand, the smallness of the market made it possible for a new company such as Dolby's to exploit the technology without major investment capital and without attracting overwhelming competition from large rivals. Once Dolby established the reputation of his technology, he had a strong marketing position when he later introduced the technology into the mass market for consumer tape-recording equipment.

Unfortunately, there are no universally applicable rules of thumb for making sound decisions about the sale or production of a technology at this stage. Too many variables enter into the equation: initial development costs, a company's cash position, its other development activities and their requirements, the technology's potential market, the possibilities of market segmentation, and—perhaps most important—the extent to which a technology is perceived as *essential* to a company's present or future activities.

Stage 3: Application Launch

The application launch stage of the TLC corresponds to the first, or "performance maximizing," phase of Abernathy and Utterback,[3] during which a company is likely to be developing its technology further—either through product modification or through application to different or perhaps wider product areas. But if a technology has been developed to the point of product launch without the involvement of potential buyers, decisions on its exploitation become more complex. The originating company, having faced both the high costs of development and of product launch, now confronts a number of issues that work *against* its recovery of some of those costs through license arrangements.

First, there may not be enough companies around with the skill to employ the new technology properly. The hasty sale of licenses could easily damage the reputation of the technology. This factor weighed heavily, for example, in the considerations of the Pilkington Company in exploiting the technology for glass-reinforced concrete.

Pilkington bought the license for this technology from the British Building Research Council with the aim of selling it to individual construction companies. Thus, Pilkington served as middleman between a research-oriented development company and the market because of its experience in license deals and its understanding of glass technology. However, the license process proved very lengthy, for Pilkington found it necessary to restrict the number of buyers by rigorous company appraisal and product inspection in order to maintain high product quality.

Sale of a technology during stage 3 may also be delayed by the long lead times involved in customer purchase of a relatively unproved technology. The purchase may depend on government backing for the buyer, which in turn may depend on a country's industrial policy. In addition, the sale of a technology may be held up or prevented by government restrictions on the seller, especially where the technology has strategic or military implications—as, for example, in such fields as computer networks, high-energy lasers, wide-bodied aircraft, and diffusion bonding. In the United States, the Technology Transfer Ban Act, updated in 1978, prohibits the sale to any communist country—or to any country that fails to impose restrictions on such a sale—of any "signficant" or "critical" technology or product with a potential military or crime control application.

Consider, as well, how a sale of technology affects those technologists who are responsible for development within the purchasing company. They may see a purchase as an indication of failure and therefore may try to delay the decision to buy a technology while pressing for funds to develop their own. The "not invented here" syndrome is rife, although it may be more prevalent in some countries than others. In Japan, for example, the ratio of license revenues to license payments has remained fairly constant at around 1 to 8; in West Germany, the ratio is 1 to 2.5. By contrast, the ratio in the United Kingdom is approximately 1 to 1; in the United States, 10 to 1.

The final market factor working against technology sales at this stage is that customer purchase usually requires major changes in the purchaser's way of doing things. A company may be unwilling to undertake these changes until a technology is proved through more extensive product application or until its own technology is seen to be clearly inadequate.

On the other hand, the originating company itself may now wish to delay the sale of a technology, thinking that its potential value will increase with greater market acceptance. The company may also feel the need to recoup its development costs while taking advantage of the opportunity to skim the market as a monopoly supplier of a possible major technology. Further, it may wish to control the use of the technology in order to use its own production facilities to capacity.

The Swedish ASEA Company, for instance, provides electric locomotives for U.S. railroads. Although the technology involved in electric locomotive construction is relatively well known, the ASEA locomotives have a sophisticated electronic control system that makes them especially attractive to American railroads. Hence, the electric locomotive as a product is literally the vehicle for a technology sale. By tying the technology sale to its own product, ASEA hopes to maximize its revenues at this stage of the TLC.

Stage 4: Application Growth

Until this point in the TLC, the major issue restricting technology sales has been development costs. It is this fourth stage that Abernathy and Utterback call the stage of "sales maximization."[4] As an originating company begins to reap the rewards of increasing product sales, a number of strong reasons *for* technology sales begin to surface. The arguments made within the company, however, are likely to be in favor of delaying any sale. Thus, the crucial issue here is *timing*.

Growth in customer demand usually coincides with great interest in a technology by the developer's competitors. These competitors may well wish to avoid the high costs of developing their own alternative versions of products based on the technology. Therefore, the market value of the technology is probably now at its maximum. Nonetheless, the originating company's success in its own product sales, together with the discomfort of its competitors, is often a persuasive argument against selling the technology. In fact, a decision to sell during stage 4 is one of the most difficult that a company can make.

A technology sale is thus often delayed until later in the TLC when the value of the technology has decreased, both because of lessened customer interest and because of the development of alternative and perhaps improved technologies by competitors. This is often a mistake. A cold assessment of market potential could lead many companies to sell their technologies at the very moment that their own sales are increasing and before their markets are saturated. Such an assessment should include consideration of:

1. *Market size.* A decision to sell a technology through geographically selective license arrangements can lead to increased revenues based

on wider application of the technology. More generally, a company faced with booming or novel market demand for an innovative technology may not be able to generate cash quickly enough to exploit the technology fully through its own production.

2. *Technological leadership.* The willingness of a company to share a technology much in demand can reduce its competitors' incentive to engage in their own technological development. The originator, by investing its additional revenues in further R&D, can better maintain its leadership position. Of course, such an approach must rest on a careful strategic assessment of whether the company's strengths are more in the creation of new ideas or in the reduction of old ideas to practical implementation.[5]

3. *Standardization.* The issue of government and industry standards is often vital in the growth phase of the TLC. The originator of a technology has a clear early advantage: the first product on the market *is* the standard. However, by stage 4 some of the company's competitors may develop alternative technologies and, if they have production advantages, may soon flood the market with their own products.

The active sale of licenses by the originating company will help ensure that its technology is incorporated into the production of as many companies as possible. Different technologies are often incompatible, and thus the first company to have its technology widely adopted may well set the technology standard for all. For example, Philips N.V. successfully achieved such standardization in the market for pocket dictating machine cassettes. Although Philips does not produce all the cassettes for all the machines in the world, most are produced according to its design and are subject to a royalty payment to Philips.

Another example is Ray Dolby's strategy for exploiting his noise reduction technology in the tape-recorder market. Dolby sold his technology to professional users in the form of equipment only (Dolby units) but has not allowed other professional equipment manufacturers to use his technology in their products. The market was small enough for him to do this without provoking competition.

Had he tried the same strategy in the consumer cassette market, which is vast in scale, he would immediately have invited rivalry. His decision there was to offer his technology to all manufacturers on a license basis and to require that licensees display the Dolby name and logo on the front of their equipment. In return for their license fees, manufacturers can submit their new products to Dolby for detailed criticism and advice, and improvements in the Dolby circuitry are made available to them without charge.[6] Even so, standardization has been difficult to achieve. Philips produced and promoted a rival technology system and only later was won over to become a licensee of Dolby.

Exhibit 2 summarizes the crucial factors in stage 4 of the TLC. In general, the best strategy is to seek both wide application and standardization

Exhibit 2.   The Critical Timing Decision During Stage Four

Factors for Early Sale	Factors Against Early Sale
Difficulty of developing new market alone	Low value of technology until proved
Lack of process or support technologies in company	High initial investment by developer
Cash shortage	Need to use production facilities
Importance of achieving standardization	High value added in production
Wide potential application for technology	

of a technology while discouraging other companies from producing substitute technologies. Technology sales have an important part to play. Delay in sales here can mean that the value of the technology decreases, leaving the company to exploit the technology by other means after it has passed its peak value.

Stage 5: Technology Maturity

By the time a technology reaches maturity, it will have been modified and improved, not only by the originator but also by competing companies. No longer is timing of technology sales crucial. Instead, the originating company will be concerned with its production costs, the involvement with buyers that technology sales would now bring, and the relationship between those sales and its own production.

The originator's production will level off or decline as the overall market for products based on the technology stabilizes. The only fresh markets for the technology will now be found in less advanced countries, which are eager to substitute their own production for imports.

Technology transfer to a Third World country often takes place on the basis of standard turnkey deals. However, a number of developing countries have tied the technology seller into ever more complicated arrangements. For example, the Algerians have increasingly sought to transfer technology through *clef en main*, *produit en main*, and *marché en main* purchases (literally, "key in hand," "product in hand," and "market in hand").

In the *clef en main* arrangement, the technology seller's involvement continues past the point of completing a production facility to training of staff. *Produit en main* transactions are not complete until the facility is fully on stream and has delivered products for an extended time. In the *marché en main* arrangement, the technology seller provides both *produit en main* services and a guaranteed market.

Dangers of Technology Transfer.   During stage 5, which corresponds to Abernathy and Utterback's "cost reduction" phase,[7] the originating company must reduce costs to compete in its own markets. Hence, any decision to transfer technology to a low-cost producer must take into account the effects of that transfer on the company's own manufacturing plans. No producer wants to stumble by accident into the kind of competition Fiat now faces in its Western European car markets from its licensees in the Soviet Union and Poland.

In general, developing countries, like those of the Eastern bloc, wish to add value to their natural resources by buying sophisticated process technologies. Brazil, for example, wants to sell steel, not iron ore, and may be able to export steel relatively cheaply because it possesses key raw materials. This need to turn raw materials into finished or semifinished products is good news for companies like Davy International of the United Kingdom, which now has a big Brazilian steel plant under way. But the buy-back and barter arrangements on which such deals often rest make it essential that a technology seller consider the effects of those arrangements on its own plants, work force, and other product areas.

Stage 6: Degraded Technology

The final stage of the TLC occurs when a technology has reached the point of virtually universal exploitation. By this time, license agreements will probably have expired, and the technology will be so well known as to be of little commercial value for direct sale.

However, many older technologies may still have market value in Third World countries. For example, some Middle Eastern countries had to import from Western Europe prefabricated ventilating ducts, which were essentially large boxes of air that were expensive to transport. But imports ceased when old-fashioned spot-welding technology was sold to the importing countries. Similarly, a small British company sold the technology for manufacturing simple wooden school furniture to another Middle Eastern country.

Cyril Hobbs, managing director of R&D at Laing Construction Group (a U.K. company), believes that what these "countries are looking for is basic standard technology. The question is how to identify what to us is old hat but may be just what other countries need. Here it [is] useful to have an outsider looking in. . . . I'm constantly explaining that I'm not selling Britain's seed corn just because technology is involved. We're selling yesterday's and today's know-how to the developing countries. . . it will take most of them 20 years to absorb what we're throwing at them now."[8]

Technology Middlemen. Many transactions, including the two just described, are arranged by one of the growing number of technology middlemen, who are in business to bring together potential buyers and sellers of technology. The number of companies or individuals acting as intermediaries in technology transactions has grown considerably in recent years. They usually operate for a fee paid by the technology seller based on a percentage of royalty or lump-sum revenue.

A member company of the British Technology Transfer Group, which was set up as a nonprofit body by 10 companies that had a wide variety of skills of particular interest to less developed countries, confirms the value of these intermediaries:

"When we were trying to sell our expertise in the Middle East, we found out how difficult it was as an individual company, however well known we were in the U.K. You have two different levels of selling. First you have to convince the technical experts, then they have to persuade the nontechnical people in charge of the purse strings. If you can say you are part of an organization recognized by the British Overseas Trade Board, that is a reference straightaway."[9]

In Conclusion

Fifteen years ago, Theodore Levitt's article on the product life cycle suggested that a company's basic technology should be embodied in a range of products.[10] We argue here that the full exploitation of a company's technology should include not only product applications but also technology sales. The complete marketing of a technology requires at least the following prerequisites:

1. *Development of a coherent strategy for a full portfolio of technologies.* Just as a company analyzes its product portfolio according to the position of its products in their life cycle, so it should pay attention to the TLC positions of its existing product and process technologies. Are its products, although selling well, based on a technology that is now widely available to other, perhaps lower-cost, competitors? Is the company heavily dependent on a single main technology or on vulnerable sources of raw materials?

One British company, a market leader in specialized industrial pumps, reinforced its position with a series of new product introductions, each incorporating refinements on previous products. However, all the company's products were based on a single main technology that was increasingly available to other lower-cost producers. Analysis of the situation led the company to rethink its overall strategy. First, it embarked on a program of license and buy-back arrangements to exploit more fully its existing technology; and second, it changed the direction of its R&D activity away from past over-reliance on a single, widely available technology.

2. *Decisions on acquisition or divestment of individual technologies.* TLC planning involves at the outset clear *marketing* decisions about the whole course of a technology's development. The possibility of license or sale must be built into development plans, which need constant review both before and after application launch.

3. *Awareness of the value of developing technology primarily for direct sale without incorporation into products.* This can occur in the case of technologies which do not fit into a company's main strategy or for which

the company lacks the required production or marketing resources. It is likely that there will be a growth in the number of companies whose sole aim is the development of technologies to the application launch stage for subsequent sale to other companies.

4. *Clear understanding of the relationship between the sale of a technology through license and the sale of products based on that technology.* All too frequently, the licensing of a technology is delayed until the company's product sales and, thus, the market value of the technology start to decline. Full exploitation of a technology frequently involves *earlier* rather than *later* license or sale.

5. *Recognition that a technology buyer often has a better idea of its needs and opportunities than a technology seller.* Most companies find it easier to analyze an inadequacy in their own technology when they know of a product or process innovation elsewhere in use than to assess the value of their own potentially marketable technologies or the appropriate customers, prices, and overall strategies for them.

6. *Reliance on technology marketers.* All too frequently technology sales are the part-time responsibility of top management. The marketing of a technology during all the stages of its TLC requires specialized decisions usually beyond the expertise of top corporate managers as well as conventional product marketers. Our research suggests that this marketing function be separated both from a company's overall strategic planners and from its regular marketing staff. Only after these specialists have carried out detailed analyses of a technology and its potential markets should their work be integrated with that of general strategic planners.

Appendix

Derivation of the Technology Life Cycle

The literature on the product life cycle typically distinguishes between the life cycle of a generic product and that of an individual manufacturer's brand.[11] In the same way, we distinguish between what might be called "major" and "minor" technologies in both products and processes. A major product technology, for example, is the Hovercraft; freeze-drying is a major process technology; and the microcircuit involves both. Major technologies developed by one company may differ in a number of ways from the minor technologies or "brand" variations introduced later by others.

The stages of the technology life cycle are related here to Abernathy and Utterback's model of product and process development within a company, although we are concerned with the relationship between both product and process technology and the *market* that may exist for them.[12] We relate the TLC stages to Abernathy and Utterback's model for two reasons: first, to highlight the different corporate strategies—performance maximization, sales maximization, cost minimization, and so on—that apply at different stages of the TLC; and, second, to stress the importance of appropriate process technologies to the successful exploitation of product technologies.

The TLC approach sheds light both on the changing importance of individual strategies and on the changing decisions that companies face if they are to find the right markets for their technologies. Also, the TLC emphasizes the crucial question of *timing* in any sale of technology.

Notes

1. Theodore Levitt, "Exploit the Product Life Cycle,"*HBR* November–December 1965, p.81. See also Rolando Polli and Victor Cook, "Validity of the Product Life Cycle," *The Journal of Business*, vol. 42, no. 4, October 1969, p.385.

2. See L. Nabseth and G.F. Ray, *The Diffusion of New Industrial Processes* (Cambridge, England: Cambridge University Press, 1974), p.200.

3. William J. Abernathy and J.M. Utterback, "A Dynamic Model of Process and Product Innovation," *Omega*, vol. 3, no. 6, 1975, p.639.

4. Abernathy and Utterback, p.643.

5. H. Igor Ansoff and John M. Stewart, "Strategies for a Technology-based Business," *HBR* November–December 1967, p. 71.

6. See the *Financial Times*, September 11, 1979.

7. Abernathy and Utterback, p. 644.

8. *London Sunday Times*, May 16, 1976.

9. *London Sunday Times*, January 30, 1977.

10. Levitt, p. 81.

11. Polli and Cook, p. 385.

12. Abernathy and Utterback, p. 639.

23

Quality Is More Than Making a Good Product

HIROTAKA TAKEUCHI and JOHN A. QUELCH

Considerations of quality until how have focused on worker motivation and the production process. But even well-designed, defect-free products can fail if they don't fit consumers' perceptions of high quality or if appropriate follow-up service is unavailable. So argue the authors in urging companies to monitor changes in consumers' views of quality and to provide after-sale service for their products. Companies can track public perceptions of quality by surveying existing and potential customers and by keeping a close watch on indicators of public taste. And because servicing needs vary during a product's life, companies must keep in touch with customers to learn which needs are most important.

Before designing a customer service program, managers should conduct a customer service audit, which consists of an evaluation of a company's own services compared with competitors'. With that knowledge, companies can be assured that the services they provide are appropriate.

Corporate executives and consumers have in recent years adopted divergent views of product quality. Several recent surveys indicate how wide the quality perception gap is:

□ Three out of five chief executives of the country's largest 1,300 companies said in a 1981 survey that quality is improving; only 13% said it is declining.[1] Yet 49% of 7,000 consumers surveyed in a separate 1981 study said that the quality of U.S. products had declined in the

---

Published 1983.

past five years. In addition, 59% expected quality to stay down or decline further in the upcoming five years.[2]

☐ Half the executives of major American appliance manufacturers said in a 1981 survey that the reliability of their products had improved in recent years. Only 21% of U.S. consumers expressed that belief.[3]

☐ Executives of U.S. auto manufacturers cite internal records that show quality to be improving each year. "Ford quality improved by 27% in our 1981 models over 1980 models," said a Ford executive.[4] But surveys show that consumers perceive the quality of U.S. cars to be declining in comparison with imported cars, particularly those from Japan.

Mindful of this gap, many U.S. companies have turned to promotional tactics to improve their quality image. Such efforts are evident in two trends. The first is the greater emphasis advertisements place on the word *quality* and on such themes as reliability, durability, and workmanship. Ford, for instance, advertises that "quality is job one," and Levi Strauss proffers the notion that "quality never goes out of style." And many ads now claim that products are "the best" or "better than" competitors'.

The second trend is the move to quality assurance and extended service programs. Chrysler offers a five-year, 50,000 mile warranty; Whirlpool Corporation promises that parts for all models will be available for 15 years; Hewlett-Packard gives customers a 99% uptime service guarantee on its computers; and Mercedes-Benz makes technicians available for roadside assistance after normal dealer service hours.

While these attempts to change customer perceptions are a step in the right direction, a company's or a product's quality image obviously cannot be improved overnight. It takes time to cultivate customer confidence, and promotional tactics alone will not do the job. In fact, they can backfire if the claims and promises do not hold up and customers perceive them as gimmicks.

To ensure delivery of advertising claims, companies must build quality into their products or services. From a production perspective, this means a companywide commitment to eliminate errors at every stage of the product development process—product design, process design, and manufacturing. It also means working closely with suppliers to eliminate defects from all incoming parts.

Equally important yet often overlooked are the marketing aspects of quality-improvement programs. Companies must be sure they are offering the benefits customers seek. Quality should be primarily customer-driven, not technology-driven, production-driven, or competitor-driven.

In developing product quality programs, companies often fail to take into account two basic sets of questions. First, how do customers define quality, and why are they suddenly demanding higher quality than in the past? Second, how important is high quality in customer service, and how can it be ensured after the sale?

As mundane as these questions may sound, the answers provide essential information on how to build an effective customer-driven quality program. We should not forget that customers, after all, serve as the ultimate judge of quality in the marketplace.

The Production–Service Connection

Product performance and customer service are closely linked in any quality program; the greater the attention to product quality in production, the fewer the demands on the customer service operation to correct subsequent problems. Office equipment manufacturers, for example, are designing products to have fewer manual and more automatic controls. Not only are the products easier to operate and less susceptible to misuse but they also require little maintenance and have internal troubleshooting systems to aid in problem identification. The up-front investment in quality minimizes the need for customer service.

Besides its usual functions, customer service can act as an early warning system to detect product quality problems. Customer surveys measuring product performance can also help spot quality control or design difficulties. And of course detecting defects early spares later embarrassment and headaches.

Quality-Improvement Successes

It is relevant at this point to consider two companies that have developed successful customer-driven quality programs: L.L. Bean, Inc. and Caterpillar Tractor Company. Although these two companies are different businesses—L.L. Bean sells outdoor apparel and equipment primarily through mail-order while Caterpillar manufactures earth-moving equipment, diesel engines, and materials-handling devices, which it sells through dealers—both enjoy an enviable reputation for high quality.

Some 96.7% of 3,000 customers L.L. Bean recently surveyed said that quality is the attribute they like most about the company. Bean executes a customer-driven quality program by:

☐ Conducting regular customer satisfaction surveys and sample group interviews to track customer and noncustomer perceptions of the quality of its own and its competitors' products and services.

☐ Tracking on its computer all customer inquiries and complaints and updating the file daily.

☐ Guaranteeing all its products to be 100% satisfactory and providing a full cash refund, if requested, on any returns.

☐ Asking customers to fill out a short, coded questionnaire and explain their reasons for returning the merchandise.

☐ Performing extensive field tests on any new outdoor equipment before listing it in the company's catalogs.

☐ Even stocking extra buttons for most of the apparel items carried years ago, just in case a customer needs one.

Despite recent financial setbacks, Caterpillar continues to be fully committed to sticking with its quality program, which includes:

☐ Conducting two customer satisfaction surveys following each purchase, one after 300 hours of product use and the second after 500 hours of use.

☐ Maintaining a centrally managed list of product problems as identified by customers from around the world.

☐ Analyzing warranty and service reports submitted by dealers, as part of a product improvement program.

☐ Asking dealers to conduct a quality audit as soon as the products are received and to attribute defects to either assembly errors or shipping damages.

☐ Guaranteeing 48-hour delivery of any part to any customer in the world.

☐ Encouraging dealers to establish side businesses in rebuilding parts to reduce costs and increase the speed of repairs.

How Do Customers Define Quality?

To understand how customers perceive quality, both L.L. Bean and Caterpillar collect much information directly from them. Even with such information, though, pinpointing what customers *really* want is no simple task. For one thing, consumers cannot always articulate their quality requirements. They often speak in generalities, complaining, for instance, that they bought "a lemon" or that manufacturers "don't make 'em like they used to."

Consumers' priorities and perceptions also change over time. Taking automobiles as an example, market data compiled by SRI International suggest that consumer priorities shifted from styling in 1970 to fuel economy in 1975 and then to quality of design and performance in 1980.[5] (See Exhibit 1.)

In addition, consumers perceive a product's quality relative to competing products. As John F. Welch, chairman and chief executive of General Electric Company, observed, "The customer . . . rates us better or worse than somebody else. It's not very scientific, but it's disastrous if you score low."[6]

Exhibit 1.   Changes in the Importance to Customers of U.S. Automobile Characteristics

	1970	1975	1980
1	Styling	Fuel economy	Quality
2	Value for money	Styling	How well-made
3	Ease of handling and driving	Prior experience with the make	Fuel economy
4	Fuel economy	Size and weight	Value for money
5	Riding comfort	Ease of handling and driving	Riding comfort

One of the major problems facing U.S. automobile manufacturers is the public perception that imported cars, particularly from Japan, are of higher quality. When a 1981 *New York Times*-CBS News poll asked consumers if they thought that Japanese-made cars are usually better quality than those made here, about the same, or not as good, 34% answered better, 30% said the same, 22% said not as good, and 14% did not know. When the Roper Organization asked the same question in 1977, only 18% said better, 30% said the same, 32% said not as good, and 20% did not know.[7]

Further, consumers are demanding high quality at low prices. When a national panel of shoppers was asked where it would like to see food manufacturers invest more, the highest-rated response was "better quality for the same price."[8] In search of such value, some consumers are even chartering buses to Cohoes Manufacturing Company, an apparel specialty store located in Cohoes, New York that has a reputation for offering high-quality, designer-label merchandise at discount prices.

Consumers' perceptions of product quality are influenced by various factors at each stage of the buying process. Some of the major influences are listed in Exhibit 2.

Watching for Key Trends

What should companies do to improve their understanding of customers' perspectives on quality? We know of no other way than to collect and analyze internal data and to monitor publicly available information.

Internally generated information is obtained principally through customer surveys, interviews of potential customers (such as focus group interviews), reports from salespeople, and field experiments. Recall how L.L. Bean and Caterpillar use these approaches to obtain data on how their current and potential customers rate their products' quality versus those of competitors'.

Publicly available information of a more general nature can be obtained through pollsters, independent research organizations, government agencies, and the news media. Such sources are often helpful in identifying shifts in societal attitudes.

Exhibit 2.   Factors Influencing Consumer Perception of Quality[a]

Before Purchase	At Point of Purchase	After Purchase
Company's brand name and image	Performance specifications	Ease of installation and use
Previous experience	Comments of salespeople	Handling of repairs, claims, warranty
Opinions of friends	Warranty provisions	Spare parts availability
Store reputation	Service and repair policies	Service effectiveness
Published test results	Support programs	Reliability
Advertised price for performance	Quoted price for performance	Comparative performance

[a]Not necessarily in order of importance.

Companies that try to define their customers' attitudes on product and service quality often focus too narrowly on the meaning of quality for their products and services; an understanding of changing attitudes in the broader marketplace can be equally valuable.

Toward the end of the last decade, too many U.S. companies failed to observe that the optimism of the mid-1970s was increasingly giving way to a mood of pessimism and restraint because of deteriorating economic conditions. Several polls taken during the 1970s indicated the nature and extent of this shift[9]; for instance, Gallup polls showed that while only 21% of Americans in the early 1970s believed "next year will be worse than this year," 55% held this pessimistic outlook by the end of the 1970s.

Pessimistic about what the future held, consumers began adjusting their lifestyles. The unrestrained desire during the mid-1970s to buy and own more gave way to more restrained behavior, such as "integrity" buying, "investment" buying, and "life-cycle" buying.

Integrity purchases are those made for their perceived importance to society rather than solely for personal status. Buying a small, energy-efficient automobile, for example, can be a sign of personal integrity. Investment buying is geared toward long-lasting products, even if that means paying a little more. The emphasis is on such values as durability, reliability, craftsmanship, and longevity. In the apparel business, for example, more manufacturers have begun stressing the investment value of clothing. And life-cycle buying entails comparing the cost of buying with the cost of owning. For example, some might see a $10 light bulb, which uses one-third as much electricity and lasts four times as long as a $1 conventional light bulb, as the better deal.

These changes in buying behavior reflect the pessimistic outlook of consumers and their growing emphasis on quality rather than quantity: "If we're going to buy less, let it be better."

By overlooking this fundamental shift in consumer attitudes, companies missed the opportunity to capitalize on it. If they had monitored the information available, managers could have identified and responded to the trends earlier.

Ensuring Quality After the Sale

As we suggested earlier, the quality of customer service after the sale is often as important as the quality of the product itself. Of course, excellent customer service can rarely compensate for a weak product. But poor customer service can quickly negate all the advantages associated with delivering a product of superior quality.

At companies like L.L. Bean and Caterpillar, customer service is not an afterthought but an integral part of the product offering and is subject to the same quality standards as the production process. These companies realize that a top-notch customer service operation can be an effective means of accomplishing the following three objectives:

1. *Differentiating a company from competitors.*   As more customers seek to extend the lives of their durable goods, the perceived quality of customer service becomes an increasingly important factor in the purchase decision. Whirlpool Corporation promises to stand by its products rather than hide behind its distribution channels; it has parlayed a reputation for effective customer service into a distinct competitive advantage that reinforces its image of quality.

2. *Generating new sales leads and discouraging switches to alternative suppliers.*   Keeping in regular contact with customers so as to deliver new information to them and gather suggestions for product improvements can ensure the continued satisfaction of existing customers and improve the chances of meeting the needs of potential purchasers.

3. *Reinforcing dealer loyalty.*   Companies with strong customer service programs can also broaden their distribution channels more easily to include outlets that may not be able to deliver high levels of postpurchase customer service on their own.

The Customer Service Audit

To be effective, a customer service operation requires a marketing plan. Customer services should be viewed as a product line that must be packaged, priced, communicated, and delivered to customers. An evaluation of a company's current customer service operation—a customer service audit—is essential to the development of such a plan.

A customer service audit asks managers the following questions:

What Are Your Customer Service Objectives?   Many companies have not established objectives for their customer service operations and have no concept of the role customer service should play in their business and marketing strategies. Every company should know what percentage of its revenue stream it expects to derive from service sales and whether the goal is to make a profit, break even, or—for reasons of competitive advantage—sustain a loss.

What Services Do You Provide?   It is useful to develop a grid showing which services your company provides or could provide for each of the products in your line. These might include customer education, financing arrangements, order confirmation and tracing, predelivery preparation, spare-parts inventory, repair service, and claims and complaints handling.

How Do You Compare with the Competition?   A similar grid can be used to chart the customer services your competitors provide. Through customer surveys, you can identify those areas of customer service in which your company rates higher or lower than the competition. In areas where your company is weak, can you invest to improve your performance? Where you are strong, how easy is it for competitors to match or exceed your performance?

What Services Do Your Customers Want?   There is little value in developing superior performance in areas of customer service most customers consider only marginally important. An essential ingredient of the audit is, therefore, to understand the relative importance of various customer services to current and potential customers. Distinct customer segments can often be identified according to the priorities they attach to particular services.

What Are Your Customers' Service Demand Patterns?   The level and nature of customer service needed often change over the product's life. Services that are top priority at the time of sale may be less important five years later. Companies must understand the patterns and timing of demand for customer services on each of their products. These they can graph, as Exhibit 3 shows.

Product A in the exhibit is a security control system, an electronics product with few moving parts. A high level of service is needed immediately following installation to train operators and debug the system. Thereafter, the need to service quickly drops to only periodic replacement of mechanical parts, such as frequently used door switches.

Product B is an automobile. Service requirements are significant during the warranty period because of customer sensitivity to any aesthetic and functional defects and also because repairs are free (to the customer). After the warranty period, however, service requirements beyond basic maintenance will be more extensive for B than for A, since there are more mechanical parts to wear out.

Exhibit 3.   Postpurchase Service Demands for Two Products

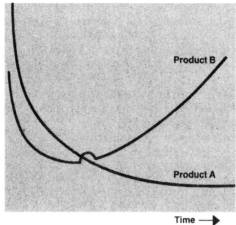

What Trade-Offs Are Your Customers Prepared to Make?   Excellent service can always be extended—at a price. You should know the costs to your company of providing assorted customer services through various delivery systems (an 800 telephone number, a customer service agent, a salesperson) at different levels of performance efficiency. At the same time, you should establish what value your customers place on varying levels of customer service, what level of service quality they are prepared to pay for, and whether they prefer to pay for services separately or as part of the product purchase price.

Customers are likely to differ widely in price sensitivity. A printing press manufacturer, for example, has found that daily newspaper publishers, because of the time sensitivity of their product, are willing to pay a high price for immediate repair service, whereas book publishers, being less time pressured, can afford to be more price conscious.

The Customer Service Program

The success of the marketing program will depend as much on effective implementation as on sound analysis and research. After reviewing several customer service operations in a variety of industries, we believe that managers should concentrate on the following seven guidelines for effective program implementation:

1. *Educate your customers.*   Customers must be taught both how to use and how not to use a product. And through appropriate training programs, companies can reduce the chances of calls for highly trained service personnel to solve simple problems. General Electric recently established a

network of product education centers that purchasers of GE appliances can
call toll free. Many consumer problems during the warranty period can be
handled at a cost of $5 per call rather than the $30 to $50 cost for a service
technician to visit a consumer's home.

2. *Educate your employees.*   In many organizations, employees view
the customer with a problem as an annoyance rather than as a source of
information. A marketing program is often needed to change such negative
attitudes and to convince employees not only that customers are the ultimate
judge of quality but also that their criticisms should be respected and acted
on immediately. The internal marketing program should incorporate detailed
procedures to guide customer-employee interactions.

3. *Be efficient first, nice second.*   Given the choice, most customers
would rather have efficient resolution of their problem than a smiling face.
The two of course are not mutually exclusive, but no company should hesitate to centralize its customer service operation in the interests of efficiency.
Federal Express, for example, recently centralized its customer service function to improve quality control of customer-employee interactions, to more
easily monitor customer service performance, and to enable field personnel
to concentrate on operations and selling. The fear that channeling all calls
through three national centers would depersonalize service and annoy customers used to dealing with a field office sales representative proved
unwarranted.

4. *Standardize service response systems.*   A standard response
mechanism is essential for handling inquiries and complaints. L.L. Bean has
a standard form that customer service personnel use to cover all telephone
inquiries and complaints. As noted earlier, the documented information is
immediately fed into a computer and updated daily to expedite follow-through.
In addition, most companies should establish a response system to handle
customer problems in which technically sophisticated people are called in
on problems not solved within specific time periods by lower-level employees.

5. *Develop a pricing policy.*   Quality customer service does not necessarily mean free service. Many customers even prefer to pay for service
beyond a minimum level. This is why long warranty periods often have
limited appeal; customers recognize that product prices must rise to cover
extra warranty costs, which may principally benefit those customers who
misuse the product.[10] More important to success than free service is the
development of pricing policies and multiple-option service contracts that
customers view as equitable and easy to understand.

Because a separate market exists for postsale service in many product
categories, running the customer service operation as a profit center is increasingly common. But the philosophy of "selling the product cheap and
making money on the service" is likely to be self-defeating over the long
term, since it implicitly encourages poor product quality.

6. *Involve subcontractors, if necessary.*   To ensure quality, most
companies prefer to have all customer services performed by in-house personnel. When effectiveness is compromised as a result, however, the com-

pany must consider subcontracting selected service functions to other members of the distribution channel or to other manufacturers. Otherwise the quality of customer service will decline as an aftermath of cost-cutting or attempts to artificially stimulate demand for customer service to use slack capacity. Docutel, the automated teller manufacturer, for example, transferred responsibility for customer service operations to Texas Instruments because servicing its small base of equipment dispersed nationwide was unprofitable.

7. *Evaluate customer service.* Whether the customer service operation is treated as a cost center of a profit center, quantitative performance standards should be set for each element of the service package. Do an analysis of variances between actual and standard performances. American Airlies and other companies use such variances to calculate bonuses to service personnel. In addition, many companies regularly solicit customers' opinions about service operations and personnel.

In conclusion, we must stress that responsibility for quality cannot rest exclusively with the production department. Marketers must also be active in contributing to perceptions of quality. Marketers have been too passive in managing quality. Successful businesses of today will use marketing techniques to plan, design, and implement quality strategies that stretch beyond the factory floor.

Notes

1. Results of a *Wall Street Journal*-Gallup survey conducted in September 1981, published in the *Wall Street Journal*, October 12, 1981.

2. Results of a survey conducted by the American Society for Quality Control and published in the *Boston Globe*, January 25, 1981.

3. 1981 survey data from *Appliance Manufacturer*, April 1981.

4. John Holusha, "Detroit's New Stress on Quality," *New York Times*, April 30, 1981.

5. Norman B. McEachron and Harold S. Javitz, "Managing Quality: A Strategic Perspective," SRI International Business Intelligence Program Report No. 658 (Stanford, Calif.: 1981).

6. John E. Welch, "Where is Marketing Now That We Really Need It?" a speech presented to the Conference Board's 1981 Marketing Conference, New York City, October 28, 1981.

7. John Holusha, Ibid.

8. Bill Abrams, "Research Suggests Consumers Will Increasingly Seek Quality," *Wall Street Journal*, October 15, 1981.

9. Daniel Yankelovich, *New Rules* (New York: Random House, 1981), p. 182.

10. For evidence of this fact, see John R. Kennedy, Michael R. Pearce, and John A. Quelch, *Consumer Products Warranties: Perspectives, Issues, and Options*, report to the Canadian Ministry of Consumer and Corporate Affairs, 1979.

24
Successful Share-Building Strategies

ROBERT D. BUZZELL and FREDERIK D. WIERSEMA

That an important relationship exists between market share and return on investment is widely accepted by marketers. New research data, drawn from a larger number of companies than have previously been examined, now strengthen the notion of that relationship by specifying those aspects that are most important for market planners. The new data also identify factors that help determine long-term market share, such as levels of new product activity and product quality. The authors conclude by suggesting strategic approaches for strengthening market share.

Market share helps determine business performance. Not only do marketing executives say so but abundant evidence supports the statement.

Past data analyses have consistently demonstrated that most high-share businesses enjoy above-average profit margins and rates of return on investment, while most small-share businesses have below-average margins and ROI.[1] This is true even when allowance is made for other factors that typically accompany high market share, such as above-average product quality, early entry into the market, and broad product lines.

Previous research suggesting the relationship between market share and profitability came from the Profit Impact of Marketing Strategies (PIMS) program sponsored by the Strategic Planning Institute in Cambridge, Massachusetts. Since analyses of those results were first published in the mid-1970s, the PIMS data base has been greatly expanded.

Information is now available for a much larger number of businesses—about 2,000 as of early 1980. The data also cover a longer time span, ranging up to nine years for some of the participants. Moreover, a wider variety of companies and industries are now represented in the data base, including

---

Published 1981.

smaller companies and a significant number of corporations based outside North America. (For further details of the PIMS program, see the Appendix.)

While the PIMS data base has changed considerably since the program's inception in 1972, the relationship between market share and profitability has not. Exhibit 1 shows average pretax rates of ROI for businesses grouped according to increasing market share, based on four-year periods.

The exhibit shows ROI increasing steadily as market share rises. The average rate of return for business units with shares of more than 40% is two-and-a-half times the average for those with shares of 10% or less. Put another way, a difference of 10 points in market share is accompanied, on average, by an increment of about 5 percentage points in ROI.

Within each group, profit variations reflect differences in other factors related to ROI, such as capital intensity, vertical integration, and market growth. Altogether the PIMS statistical models include 28 factors related to profitability, of which market share is only 1. But when all of these effects are taken into account, the net influence of market share remains strong.

The financial advantages of a strong market position make understandable the fact that a common strategic goal is to increase market share. Only market leaders, such as General Motors and IBM, are satisfied just to hold on to their existing market shares. In most markets, the number two and three competitors—the Fords, Millers, and Schlitzes—are aggressively trying to catch the leaders. Except perhaps in embryonic or rapidly expanding

Exhibit 1. Market Share and Return on Investment in Percentages

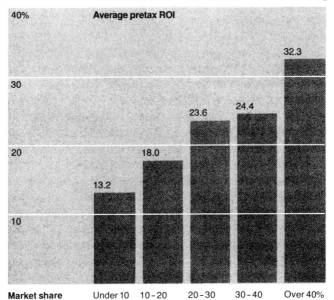

| Market share | Under 10 | 10-20 | 20-30 | 30-40 | Over 40% |

market environments, competitors ranking lower than fourth or fifth must
increase share.

The alternatives are unpalatable: to hang on with an unsatisfactory rate
of ROI often below the cost of capital, or to liquidate.[2] Thus, the vast majority
of businesses would like to increase their market share, and in all likelihood
most are actively trying to do so.

What are the most promising means? In this article, we present some
approaches for increasing market share based on two types of information.
First, we have analyzed the market share changes of more than 1,200 businesses participating in the PIMS program. Second, we have reviewed case
studies, corporate annual reports, and other published accounts of the competitive strategies used to build market share in a wide variety of industries
and product categories. These descriptions add a qualitative dimension to
the standardized financial and market data available from the PIMS program.

Developing a Market Share Model

Market share can be affected by many different aspects of competitive strategy. The concept of the *marketing mix* is based on the working together of
all dimensions of marketing strategy—product policy, pricing, distribution,
sales force efforts, advertising, and promotion—to influence buyer choice.
Not only do management's own policies and programs affect sales, but so
do those of competitors. A realistic approach to explaining market share
change must, therefore, include all of the important elements of marketing
strategy and must somehow relate any single competitor's actions to the
contending moves of rivals.

Since computers first came into general use in marketing research during the 1960s, numerous efforts have been made to develop statistical models
to explain and predict changes in market share. Quite a few of these models
have been described in published accounts; no doubt even more remain in
companies' confidential files. With few exceptions, models of market share
change are designed for single product categories such as beer, cigarettes,
or television sets, and the results are intended to be used only by marketers
of the product studied.

Our analysis of the PIMS data base employed a very different approach:
we related market share changes to competitive strategies for a heteroge-
neous cross section of businesses. We divided the overall sample into three
subgroups—consumer products, raw and semifinished materials, and manufactured industrial products (capital goods, components, and supplies)—
in the belief that major differences would exist among the three in the importance of such strategic factors as pricing and advertising.

No doubt the marketing manager of a producer of ball bearings would
prefer to base decisions on a model of market share change specifically
tailored to that industry. But the data required to develop statistical models

are simply not available for many products. Moreover, one-at-a-time studies of individual markets do not provide a basis for reaching any general conclusions about how market share can be gained or lost—unless, of course, hundreds of similar studies can be assembled and compared. Pending this unlikely occurrence, findings derived from a diverse cross-sectional data base can provide valuable insights into the common denominators of successful share-building strategies.

Measuring Competitive Strategies

For each of the businesses in the PIMS data base, annual information is available on many of the important elements of competitive strategy. These include:

1. *Relative product quality.* This is measured through an index of the quality of each business unit's products or services relative to those of its major competitors (derived from judgmental estimates supplied by line executives and/or planning staff). The judgmental assessments indicate, on an annual basis, what proportion of total sales of products or services was accounted for by each of three categories: those superior to competitors', those of equivalent quality, and those of inferior quality. The index used in our analysis (and in other PIMS research) is computed by subtracting the percentage of inferior quality sales from the percentage of superior quality sales.

2. *Relative new products.* This is the proportion of a business unit's sales accounted for by new products or services—again, relative to major competitors. New products are defined as those introduced during the preceding three years. If a business with 30% of sales in new products were competing with companies estimated to have 20% of new product sales, our index would be 30% minus 20%, or 10%.

3. *Marketing expenditures.* Current outlays for marketing are subdivided into three categories: sales force, media advertising, and sales promotion. Sales promotion costs include contests, premiums, trade shows, distributor and dealer incentives, temporary price reductions, and free goods. To estimate the relationship between marketing effort and market share change, we calculated the percentage change in each type of expenditure and adjusted it for overall market growth. (The nature of these adjustments is explained in a later section.)

4. *Pricing.* Each business unit supplied estimates of its prices relative to competitors', expressed in index form. If prices are equal to competition, the index is set at zero; a 5% premium is expressed as +5, a 5% discount as −5, and so on.

Measuring Market Share Change

Market share can be defined and measured in several ways.[3] When all of the competitors in a market sell a single type of product, like gasoline or soft drinks, their shares of total volume can be calculated in physical units. Most of the business units represented in the PIMS data base, however, produce and market several different types of products or services, as do their competitors. Consequently, the only practical way to measure market share is in terms of monetary value. Each business unit's market share is simply its dollar sales divided by estimated total sales in its served market.

The concept of *served market* also deserves some comment. How should a business define its market for purposes of measuring and tracking market share? Usually more than one definition is possible.[4] Consider, for example, cooking appliances. There are electric ranges, gas ranges, countertop microwave ovens, combination microwave-conventional ranges, and convection ovens. From the viewpoint of, say, Amana, should all of these types of cooking appliances be considered a single market? Or, at the other extreme, should each category be considered a separate market? Also, in view of the substantial quantity of microwave oven imports from Japan, can the United States realistically be viewed as a market unto itself, or is the scope of the market worldwide?

There are no clear-cut answers. In the PIMS program, each business develops its own definition of the served market. The scope of the served market is limited in terms of products, customers, and geography to those sectors or segments within which a business unit actively competes. The market share data reported by the PIMS participants are based on this concept.

The method we have used to measure change in market share also requires a brief explanation. We measure change in terms of average annual percentage rate of increase or decrease in market share. For example, a change of +10% could reflect either of the following situations:

Market Share	Business A	Business B
Year 1	20%	50%
Year 2	22	55
Change	10%	10%

We measure change in market share this way because all our measures of competitive strategy are defined in terms relative both to each business unit's size and also to competitors' activities. For example, our index of new product activity is the percentage of sales accounted for by new products minus the estimated ratio of new products to total sales for major competitors.

Suppose that a business has 20% of its sales in new products. The absolute amount of new product activity that this represents in a given market will depend on the size of the business: it would be twice as great for a business with a 50% market share as for a competitor with a 25% share. Similarly, relative product quality is measured in terms of percentages of a business unit's total sales, and changes in marketing expenditures are measured relative to previous levels of expense, which clearly depend on sales size.

Thus, the amount of effort required to achieve a given increase in market share—in terms of these "relative change" measures—depends on one's starting point. If, for example, a 10% improvement in relative quality on the part of a business with a 50% market share leads to a gain of two points, we would expect the same relative improvement by a competitor with a 25% market share to yield a gain of one point.

We carried out our analysis, then, in terms of percentage rates of change in market share. For each business, an average annual rate of change over a four-year period was calculated by fitting a trend line to the actual year-to-year changes.

Patterns of Change

Using the measures of competitive strategy and market share change just described, we employed a variety of statistical methods to analyze patterns of change among the businesses in the PIMS data base. (While the results are presented in this article in the form of tabulations, our principal method of analysis was multiple regression, in which all of the factors discussed here—and a few others—were simultaneously related to change in market share.) We found that the strategic factors generally involved in market share gains include all of the following:

- [ ] Increase in new product activity.
- [ ] Increase in relative product quality.
- [ ] Increase in expenditures for sales force, advertising, and sales promotion, relative to the growth rate of the served market.

Our analysis also showed that changes in a business unit's market share depend on its competitive position within its market. Specifically, as shown in Exhibit 2, changes in share are related to both market share and market share rank. Because all three types of businesses—consumer products, raw materials, and industrial products—displayed the same basic pattern, they have been combined. The data indicate that businesses with market shares below a certain critical level tend to gain share, while those with shares above that level tend to lose.

A Possible Explanation

Why are changes in market share so strongly related to beginning share level and rank? In a similar study of the PIMS data, we found that the relative sizes of competitors in a market tend to follow a common basic pattern. If the second-ranking competitor is two-thirds as large as the leader, then the third-ranking competitor is about two-thirds as large as the second, and so on down the line.[5]

Exhibit 2. Changes in Market Share Related to Beginning Market Share and Competitive Rank

Market Share at Beginning of Period	Competitive Rank in Market				Average
	No. 1	No. 2	No. 3	No. 4	
	Rate of Change in Share				
Under 10%	[a]	+6.0%	+7.7%	+4.6%	+5.0%
10–20	+3.5%	+3.7	+2.3	−0.8	+2.5
20–30	+4.2	+1.5	−5.4	[a]	+2.3
30–40	+0.4	−3.0	[a]	[a]	−0.6
Over 40	−0.8	[a]	[a]	[a]	−1.0
Average	**+1.2%**	**+2.0%**	**+2.9%**	**+3.8%**	**+2.3%**

[a]Very few or no businesses with these characteristics.

The size ratio that best fits the actual distribution of market share varies from one market to another, but the values for most markets cluster around the overall average of 0.63. The critical levels of market share for each competitive rank are the values 40%, 25%, 15%, and 10%, which form a progression in which each is between 60% and 65% as large as the next highest value.

In a given market, a natural equilibrium exists in terms of the relative sizes of competing businesses. For most markets, a good approximation of the natural structure is one in which the market leader has a 40% share, and numbers 2, 3, and 4 have shares of 25%, 15%, and 10%, respectively. Apart from changes in position caused by major shifts in competitive strategies, each competitor will tend to gain or lose share according to whether it is below or above the natural level.

This may appear to be a rather abstract theory for such a practical matter as change in market share. Most marketing executives probably believe that gains in share must be earned and can be explained sensibly only in terms of tangible advantages in product features, customer service, price, or other specifics. Why should there be any natural tendencies for share to rise or fall?

At present we cannot give a complete explanation of the pattern shown in Exhibit 2, but we are convinced that it is real. While we are not aware of any theory which would have led us to expect such a pattern, we believe that the way changes in share relate to share level and competitive rank reflects powerful forces operating in most markets.

Most of the businesses in the data base enjoyed gains in market share. How can this be? If one competitor gains, must not another lose? Clearly, the PIMS data base does not contain a proportional representation of losers. One reason is that the small-share businesses included only survivors in each marketplace. Some of their gains came at the expense of declining or discontinued businesses, which are less likely to be involved in the PIMS program than those with stable or improving positions.

Influence of New Products

Developing and introducing new products is one important and widely used approach to building market share. Exhibit 3 shows average percentage changes in market share for consumer, raw material, and industrial products businesses as a function of varying levels of new product sales and changes in new product activity. (The data in Exhibits 3, 4, and 5 are based on a sample that excludes businesses which sold most of their output to other units within the same parent corporation. Also excluded are businesses whose ability to gain share was restricted by limitations in plant capacity.)

In general, these data indicate that gains in market share are associated with either a high level of new product activity (relative to competitors) or an increase in new products, or both. Some caution is required in interpreting the pattern shown in Exhibit 3 because the two variables—levels and changes in new products—are inversely related.

For example, industrial product manufacturers that reduced new products relative to competitors gained market share more rapidly (+3.4%) than those that increased their new product activity (+2.9%). But most of the former group started with high proportions of new products to total sales. When we consider both factors in combination, along with all of the other measures of competitive actions, each is significantly related to market share change.

Product innovation is universally recognized as a strategy for building market share—in both mature and expanding markets. Marketers of com-

Exhibit 3. Changes in Market Share and New Product Activity Levels

New Products as a Percent of Sales, Relative to Competitors	Consumer Products	Raw Materials	Industrial Products
	Rate of Change in Share		
At beginning of period:			
Less	+0.0%	−2.5%	+1.5%
Same	+2.4	+0.1	+2.2
More	+1.9	+3.7	+4.5
Change during period:			
Reduced	−1.4	+1.0	+3.4
Same	+2.2	+0.2	+2.4
Increased	+2.8	+2.7	+2.9

Exhibit 4.   Changes in Market Share and Quality Improvement

Change in Relative Quality	Consumer Products	Raw Materials	Industrial Products
	Rate of Change in Share		
Reduced	+2.1%	−0.9%	+0.7%
No change	+0.1	+0.8	+2.5
Increased	+4.0	+2.1	+4.3

puters and semiconductors are continually introducing newer, more powerful, more versatile models. Producers of processed food and personal care
and household products regularly offer "new, improved" formulations, flavors, sizes, and package variations. Even traditionally staid AT&T, faced
with direct competition for the first time in the 1970s, sought to regain lost
market share with a series of new types of telephones and other products.[6]

Influence of Product Quality

A strategy of building market share via new products frequently involves
improvements in the quality of product or service offerings. Sometimes the
quality of established products is upgraded by a more gradual process: au-

Exhibit 5. Changes in Market Share and Changes in Spending for Sales Force, Advertising, and Sales Promotion

Rates of Changes in Expenditures Adjusted for Market Growth	Consumer Products	Raw Materials	Industrial Products
	Rate of Change in Share		
Sales force			
Cut by 5% or more	−3.0%	−0.9%	−2.8%
Steady (±5%)	−0.6	+1.1	+0.7
Increased by 5% or more	+6.6	+1.3	+6.4
Advertising			
Cut by 5% or more	−0.0	+1.9	+0.8
Steady (±5%)	+1.9	+0.2	+3.3
Increased by 5% or more	+3.0	+1.4	+3.2
Promotion			
Cut by 5% or more	−0.2	−2.3	+0.4
Steady (±5%)	−0.5	+0.9	+2.7
Increased by 5% or more	+3.7	+1.9	+4.2

tomobiles are made more fuel efficient, household appliances more compact, industrial machinery simpler to operate.

Whether connected with new product introductions or not, quality improvement is a powerful means of building market share, as shown in Exhibit 4. In all three groups of businesses—consumer products, raw materials, and industrial products—competitors that increased relative quality enjoyed much greater gains in share than those whose quality ratings remained constant or diminished.

Another indication of the importance of product quality is that among business units achieving substantial market share gains (5% or better annual increases), nearly half reported at least moderate improvements in relative quality.

Some recent competitive successes stemming from qualitative factors have been accomplished by Japanese producers of automobiles, cameras, and electronics. A study comparing the U.S. and Japanese color television industries, for example, showed that Japanese-made sets had much lower failure rates. One measure of the difference was that the number of defects per 100 sets shipped by a Motorola plant fell from an average of 165 to 3 or 4 within three years after the plant came under Japanese management.[7] Small wonder, then, that Japanese television producers have enjoyed steady market share gains.

A strategy of building share via quality improvement does not necessarily imply offering deluxe products. We are not suggesting, for example, that Chrysler rebuild its position in the automobile market by emphasizing models more luxurious than Mercedes or Cadillac. Quality, like beauty, is relative; and, in most markets, offering better value—especially in the moderate-priced sector where volume is usually concentrated—is most important.

The spectacular growth of Bic in the ballpoint pen market, beginning in 1958, illustrates the idea. Bic succeeded by providing much better quality at 19 cents than others did at similar or higher prices—not by marketing fancy pens at $5. (Cross pens are also successful and highly profitable, of course, but on a smaller scale.)

Influence of Marketing Budgets

A third major element of share-building strategy is the marketing budget—the amounts spent for sales force, advertising, and sales promotion. Ideally, each category of promotional outlay should be measured relative to spending by competitors. We were unable to do this directly because estimates of competitive expenditures were not available.

Instead, we related changes in each budget category to the concurrent rate of growth or decline in the size of the served market. Specifically, we first calculated percentage rates of change in each category of expenditures; for example, a business that increased sales force spending from $1 million in one year to $1.2 million in the next would be treated as a 20% increase. Next, we computed an average annual rate of change for the entire four-year period and also the rate of change in market share.

The final step was to adjust each business unit's change in marketing expenditures by the rate of growth or decline in its served market. We observed, however, that marketing budgets tend to lag behind gains in sales. We thus analyzed the data base to determine the routine rate of change in each expense category for a given rate of overall market growth. Based on just those businesses whose market share remained essentially unchanged, we found that for each 1% change in the size of the served market, spending on marketing activities changed on average by the following amounts:

	Consumer Products	Raw Materials	Industrial Products
Sales force	0.6%	0.3%	0.6%
Media advertising	0.5	No change	0.3
Sales promotion	0.5	No change	0.5

(We estimated these relationships by a regression analysis in which we used the rate of growth in the served market to predict the rate of growth in each category of expenses. We restricted the sample to businesses with market share gains or losses of less than 5%. Because of this, changes in the size of the market were essentially equal to changes in sales volume for these businesses.)

Such typical relationships between volume change and marketing budget change are of some interest in and of themselves. For one thing, all categories of marketing expense tend to change much less rapidly than sales volume—typically about half as much. The implication is that, with long-term growth in most markets, average ratios of marketing costs to sales should decline. A reason for marketing budgets lagging behind sales growth during the 1970s may have been that rising raw materials costs forced selling prices up faster than the costs of such marketing resources as salespeople's salaries and advertising media. In addition, we suspect that a degree of inertia often interferes with upward adjustment of budgets as sales volume expands, particularly in fast-growing markets.

Marketing budgets are apparently most closely tied to sales variations for consumer products companies and least so for raw materials producers. Indeed, among the latter group only sales force spending displays any systematic relationship to change in volume.

We used the previous relationships to calculate adjusted rates of change in marketing spending. For example, suppose a consumer product business increased its sales force outlays by 15% annually with its market growing by 10%. The normal rate of change would be calculated as follows: 10%

market growth multiplied by 0.6, or 6%, and the adjusted rate of increase for the business is 15% (actual) minus 6% (normal), or 9%. We then related these adjusted rates of change to change in market share. We reasoned that increases greater than normal, based on market growth, usually represented gains in a business unit's share of total marketing effort within its market, while less than normal increases implied spending reductions relative to competition.

Exhibit 5 summarizes the relationships between market share change and adjusted rates of change in marketing expenditures. Clearly, all three forms of promotional effort—personal selling, advertising, and sales promotion—can build market share. Also important, the impact of each type of spending varies considerably among the three types of businesses.

Of all the competitive strategy elements we analyzed, sales force expenditures are most strongly related to market share changes. Intensified selling effort appears to be a common feature of share-building strategies for both consumer and industrial products; its involvement is much less clear for producers of raw materials. Advertising outlays are significant contributors to improvements in market share only for consumer products. Among marketers of industrial products and raw materials, advertising is typically a minor component of the overall marketing budget and presumably has a corresponding small role as a competitive weapon. (There are, of course, exceptions: advertising has apparently been used effectively by some manufacturers of office typewriters, copying machines, and farm equipment.)

Interestingly, changes in sales promotion spending are reasonably important in explaining market share changes for all three types of business. Because the sales promotion category includes a wide variety of competitive activities, the ways in which it is used undoubtedly vary a great deal. For consumer products, temporary price reductions, free samples, and display allowances are widely used forms of promotion, especially in connection with new products. In recent years, durable goods manufacturers have also extensively employed cash rebates. Industrial goods producers use trade shows and exhibits, catalogs, distributor incentive programs, and temporary price reductions as promotional devices.

Efforts to relate changes in sales or market share to marketing expenditures have always been plagued by problems of separating cause from effect. The figures shown in Exhibit 5 are no exception. For example, the data suggest that industrial goods producers which increased sales force budgets by 5% (after adjusting for market growth) enjoyed substantially greater gains in market share than if they had kept their spending in line with the overall market. Did higher outlays on sales force activity cause market share gains, or were budgets expanded in line with growth in sales emanating from other sources?

Our analysis does not permit a clear-cut answer. All that we can say with certainty is that increased outlays on all three categories of marketing expense—and especially on sales force activity—tend to accompany successful share-building strategies. No doubt higher spending levels are usually both causes and effects of sales expansion.

Noninfluence of Pricing

One element of competitive strategy that we found unrelated to change in market share was businesses' price levels relative to competitors. This finding (or nonfinding) will surprise many, especially in view of the emphasis placed on aggressive price-reduction strategies in recent publications on strategic management.

An often-cited example is that of Texas Instruments in the hand-held calculator market in the early 1970s. TI supposedly cut prices in anticipation of cost reductions achieved through a substantial advantage in accumulated volume (or experience).

In much the same way, Japanese producers have established strong positions in U.S. and world markets for motorcycles, cameras, television sets, and audio equipment, among others, partly by pricing at lower levels than established competitors. For that matter, Henry Ford used the same approach to achieve leadership in the automobile industry in the early twentieth century.

These examples illustrate the point that strategies of price reduction are used, sometimes with dramatic effects, to build market share. If this is true, why did we find no relationship between price and market share among the businesses in the PIMS data base? The explanation appears to be that growth via rapid price cutting is not common in mature markets. Most of the PIMS businesses operated in relatively mature competitive environments rather than embryonic industries such as videocassette recorders or electronic word processing systems. Perhaps opportunities to gain volume through aggressive price reduction are rare when technology and marketing practices are well established.

Moreover, price reductions in mature markets by one competitor are likely to be met by rivals, making it more difficult to achieve any advantage in relative price. Whatever the reasons, major changes in price relative to competitors were not common among the businesses in the PIMS data base: fewer than 10% of them either raised or lowered relative prices by as much as 3% per year.

Possible Share-Building Strategies

The experiences of the businesses in the PIMS data base, as summarized in Exhibits 2 through 5, provide useful clues for managers and planners seeking ways to build market share. To recap, the PIMS data show that gains in market share are associated with product quality improvements, new product introductions, and marketing budget increases.

Our analysis also showed that, at least within our sample, price reductions are seldom used as a means of building share. Also, we found that business units tend to gain or lose share depending on whether their market shares are above or below a critical level, which in turn depends on the unit's competitive rank. For example, market leaders tend to lose share if they hold more than 40% of the served market and to gain share if they hold below 40%.

Taken together, the effects of the strategic factors depicted in Exhibits 2 through 5, along with the impact of competitors entering or leaving markets, account for much of the shifting in shares that took place in the markets in which the PIMS businesses participated. We developed statistical models that simultaneously incorporate all of these factors. These models explain about 40% of all the variation in market share changes for consumer products makers and about 30% of the variation for both raw materials and industrial products manufacturers.

While it has provided some clear-cut results concerning factors that affect market share, our analysis failed to isolate certain other forces. Some specific ways of competing are distinctive to particular industries or products and cannot readily be measured and analyzed in a multi-industry program such as PIMS. No doubt, much of the shifting in market position not attributable to changes in quality, new products, or marketing budgets was due to the use of these industry-specific competitive tools.

In addition, enormous differences must exist in the quality of execution of competitive strategies. An increase of 20% in the sales force budget is likely to be much more effective for a business that has well-trained and well-managed salespeople than for a business where the efforts are just as expensive but less adequately executed. It is not surprising, therefore, that our analysis did not explain all of the changes in market share that took place in our sample.

Beyond Statistical Considerations

Based on our review of case studies and other published accounts of share-building strategies, we can add two more guidelines to those derived from a purely statistical analysis:

1. *Successful share-building strategies usually involve a combination of several competitive factors.* The data in Exhibits 3 through 5 show how quality improvements, new products, and marketing expenditures are related to change in market share. This might be interpreted to mean that any one of these elements of competitive strategy could be used independently of others. While situations probably exist in which a single competitive weapon, such as advertising, can be employed to build share without changing anything else, we think they are uncommon. Typically, better results can be obtained by using a balanced, consistent marketing program or a mix of strategic factors.

In fact, among the businesses in the PIMS data base that achieved significant gains in market share, only 17% changed just one of the five strategic factors shown in Exhibits 3 through 5. Most employed two or three factors in combination. For example, quality improvements and new product introductions were almost always accompanied by increases in at least one of the three categories of promotional spending. This pattern is consistent with the notion of the marketing mix, which assumes that all elements of a marketing program are mutually consistent. If any one of these factors changes, it is reasonable that others would need to be changed accordingly.

A classic illustration of the effectiveness of a balanced marketing program is evident in the experience of L'eggs pantyhose.[8] The Hanes Corporation introduced L'eggs in 1971 with a marketing strategy that included several novel elements: a one-size product to fit most users, a new type of package, a special display fixture, a new system of direct-to-the-store distribution, and heavy introductory advertising and promotion.

By 1974, L'eggs was the leading brand in the pantyhose market. While each component of the strategy undoubtedly contributed to the product's success, it also seems clear that the components reinforced each other. For example, heavy advertising and promotion speeded up consumer trial; that facilitated acceptance by retailers; and the system of direct distribution ensured that L'eggs would seldom be out of stock, allowing satisfied buyers to develop steady buying routines.

The value of a balanced marketing program, in which each of several elements plays a part, is hardly a novel idea. But it does merit repeating and is underscored by the experience of most of the PIMS businesses that achieved share gains.

2. *Most successful share-building strategies are based on giving primary emphasis to one or more segments within the served market.* The PIMS data do not break down market volume into segments or submarkets. Yet most markets include several—sometimes many—distinct subdivisions of customer groups, product variations, price versus quality levels, or distribution methods. We are confident that if data on segments within markets were available, they would show that most of the businesses achieving major share gains did so by focusing their efforts on selected segments—often ones that were relatively small at first.

Some of the most dramatic and well-publicized strategic successes of recent years have been based on the principle of segment focus that we advocate. For example, Philip Morris steadily improved its share of the cigarette market throughout the 1970s. Part of the company's success has been due to its heavy support for Merit, a low-tar brand that apparently had special appeal for health-conscious smokers. With similar heavy support, Philip Morris's Miller Beer subsidiary introduced the first successful "light" beer in the mid-1970s. Miller enjoyed substantial gains in market share, thanks in part to aggressive advertising aimed at diet-conscious drinkers.

Honda entered the U.S. motorcycle market in 1959 by offering high-

NOTES357

quality small motorcycles at a time when the established producers regarded such products as toys. Moreover, promotion for Honda was directed to an entirely new type of customer: the suburban, middle-class male. By the mid-1960s Honda's market share was 63%—a position achieved by discovering a new market segment rather than by attempting to compete head-on with the American and British producers that had previously dominated the industry.

Focusing on specific market segments as a growth strategy is not unique to consumer goods markets. Since the mid-1970s, two small companies— Savin and Canon—have successfully challenged Xerox in the office copier market by offering relatively low-priced, small machines suitable both for small users and for decentralized copying services in large organizations.

Savin's low cost—one model was priced almost 50% below the lowest-priced Xerox model—led many users to switch to what might be called "distributed copying" in much the same way that computer terminals and low-priced minicomputers opened the way for distributed computing.[9] Whether Savin planned it that way is unclear, but a small market segment mushroomed—so much so that by 1978 Savin was supposedly selling more copiers than Xerox and IBM combined! (The company's market share measured in dollars, however, was much smaller.) Canon followed essentially the same strategy as Savin during this period and also prospered.

According to Sanford Fox, general manager of Canon's copier division, ". . . we saw an unfilled niche . . . that was created by the strategy of the established companies. The leader—and the followers—hadn't given much attention to 'convenience copiers' . . . we based our strategy on focusing our resources on this slice of the total market."[10]

We believe that most successful share-building strategies, like those of Philip Morris, Miller, Honda, Savin, and Canon, are based both on emphasizing specific market segments and designing products and marketing programs to meet the special needs or interests of these segments. Effective strategies for building market share cannot be reduced to formulas. The trick is to find a segment with sufficient potential for growth that has been neglected. To do so, we suspect, requires substantial creativity or a lot of luck—or both.

Notes

1. For summaries of earlier work, see Sidney Schoeffler, Robert D. Buzzell, and Donald F. Heany, "Impact of Strategic Planning on Profit Performance," *HBR* March-April 1974, p. 137; and Robert D. Buzzell, Bradley T. Gale, and Ralph G.M. Sultan, "Market Share—A Key to Profitability," *HBR* January-February 1975, p. 97.

2. A prominent consultant has suggested that a stable market never has more than three significant competitors. See "The Rule of Three and Four," *Perspectives*, no. 187 (Boston: Boston Consulting Group, 1976).

3. Alfred R. Oxenfeldt, "How to Use Market-Share Measurement," *HBR* January-February 1959, p. 59.

4. The problem of proper market definition has received much attention in connection with the application of strategic management concepts. For a discussion, see Robert D. Buzzell, "Note on Market Definition and Segmentation," no. 9-579-083 (Boston: Intercollegiate Case Clearing House, 1979).

5. Robert D. Buzzell, "Are There Natural Market Structures?" working paper, Harvard Business School, October 1979.

6. "Selling Is No Longer Mickey Mouse at AT&T," *Fortune*, July 17, 1978, p. 98.

7. J.M. Juran, "Japanese and Western Quality: A Contrast in Methods and Results," *Management Review*, November 1978, pp. 27-28, 39-45.

8. Based on F. Stewart DeBruicker and Harvey N. Singer, "L'eggs Products, Inc.," no. 9-575-065 (Boston: Intercollegiate Case Clearing House, 1974).

9. "Savin's Savvy Sell," *Sales and Marketing Management*, October 10, 1977, p. 34.

10. Quoted in an advertisement for the *Wall Street Journal* that appeared in *Advertising Age*, February 11, 1980, p. 15.

Appendix

The PIMS Program

The statistical analyses summarized in the exhibits used the data base of the Profit Impact of Market Strategies (PIMS) program. PIMS is an ongoing program of research and analysis on business strategy conducted by the Strategic Planning Institute in Cambridge, Massachusetts. As of early 1980, more than 200 corporations were participating in the program.

Each company submits financial, market, and competitive information for a number of its divisions and products and receives a variety of diagnostic reports on each business. These reports provide guidelines for explaining current performance and for developing future business strategies.

All of the PIMS data pertain to companies' business divisions, product lines, or other subdivisions within companies that can be distinguished from other parts of companies in terms of several criteria. Ideally, each business unit serves a distinct, well-defined market; has a clearly defined set of competitors; is largely self-sufficient in terms of technology, operations, and marketing; and has, or could have, its own business strategy.

Following these guidelines, the managers and planning specialists of the companies participating in the PIMS program develop their own definitions of businesses, estimates of market size and growth rate, and allocate their own accounting data among businesses as appropriate. The products and industries are not identified in the data base, and all financial data are disguised by applying a common scaling factor to actual monetary amounts.

25
Marketing Intangible Products and Product Intangibles

THEODORE LEVITT

All products, whether they are services or goods, possess a certain amount of intangibility. Services like insurance and transportation, of course, are nearly entirely intangible. And even goods, while they can be seen, often can't be tried out before they are bought. Understanding the degree of a product's intangibility can affect both sales and postsales follow-up strategies. While services are less able to be tested in advance than goods, the intangible factors in both types of products are important for convincing prospective customers to buy. Sellers of services, however, face special problems in making customers aware of the benefits they are receiving. The author considers the intangible factors present in all products and also advises producers of services about how best to hold on to their customers.

Distinguishing between companies according to whether they market services or goods has only limited utility. A more useful way to make the same distinction is to change the words we use. Instead of speaking of *services* and *goods*, we should speak of *intangibles* and *tangibles*. Everybody sells intangibles in the marketplace, no matter what is produced in the factory.

Published 1981.

Author's Note: The current article expands on and further develops some of the concepts I introduced in my last article for *HBR*, "Marketing Success Through Differentiation—Of Anything," which appeared in the January-February 1980 issue. Other articles I have written for *HBR* treat this general subject in yet other ways. These include "The Industrialization of Service" (September-October 1976) and "Production-Line Approach to Service" (September-October 1972). To drive home what I believe is a badly neglected distinction, the present article refers to the role of management in the industrial revolution, a subject more fully developed in my article, "Management and Post Industrial Society," *The Public Interest*, Summer 1976.

The usefulness of the distinction becomes apparent when we consider the question of how the marketing of intangibles differs from the marketing of tangibles. While some of the differences might seem obvious, it is apparent that, along with their differences, there are important commonalities between the marketing of intangibles and tangibles.

Put in terms of our new vocabulary, a key area of similarity in the marketing of intangibles and tangibles revolves around the degree of intangibility inherent in both. Marketing is concerned with getting and keeping customers. The degree of product intangibility has its greatest effect in the process of trying to get customers. When it comes to holding on to customers—to keeping them—highly intangible products run into very special problems.

First, this article identifies aspects of intangibility that affect sales appeal of both intangible and tangible products. And, next, it considers the special difficulties sellers of intangibles face in retaining customers.

Intangibility of All Products

Intangible products—travel, freight forwarding, insurance, repair, consulting, computer software, investment banking, brokerage, education, health care, accounting—can seldom be tried out, inspected, or tested in advance. Prospective buyers are generally forced to depend on surrogates to assess what they're likely to get.

They can look at gloriously glossy pictures of elegant rooms in distant resort hotels set exotically by the shimmering sea. They can consult current users to see how well a software program performs and how well the investment banker or the oil well drilling contractor performs. Or they can ask experienced customers regarding engineering firms, trust companies, lobbyists, professors, surgeons, prep schools, hair stylists, consultants, repair shops, industrial maintenance firms, shippers, franchisers, general contractors, funeral directors, caterers, environmental management firms, construction companies, and on and on.

Tangible products differ in that they can usually, or to some degree, be directly experienced—seen, touched, smelled, or tasted, as well as tested. Often this can be done in advance of buying. You can test-drive a car, smell the perfume, work the numerical controls of a milling machine, inspect the seller's steam-generating installation, pretest an extruding machine.

In practice, though, even the most tangible of products can't be *reliably* tested or experienced in advance. To inspect a vendor's steam-generating plant or computer installation in advance at another location and to have thoroughly studied detailed proposals and designs are not enough. A great deal more is involved than product features and physical installation alone.

Though a customer may buy a product whose generic tangibility (like the computer or the steam plant) is as palpable as primeval rock—and though that customer may have agreed after great study and extensive negotiation to a cost that runs into millions of dollars—the process of getting it built on time, installed, and then running smoothly involves an awful lot more than the generic tangible product itself. Such intangibles can make or break the product's success, even with mature consumer goods like dishwashers, shampoos, and frozen pizza. If a shampoo is not used as prescribed, or a pizza not heated as intended, the results can be terrible.

Similarly, you commonly can't experience in advance moderate-to-low-priced consumer goods such as canned sardines or purchased detergents. To make buyers more comfortable and confident about tangibles that can't be pretested, companies go beyond the literal promises of specifications, advertisements, and labels to provide reassurance.

Packaging is one common tool. Pickles get put into reassuring see-through glass jars, cookies into cellophane-windowed boxes, canned goods get strong appetite-appealing pictures on the labels, architects make elaborately enticing renderings, and proposals to NASA get packaged in binders that match the craftsmanship of Tyrolean leatherworkers. In all cases the idea is to provide reassuring tangible (in these examples, visual) surrogates for what's promised but can't be more directly experienced before the sale.

Hence, it's sensible to say that all products are in some important respects intangible, even giant turbine engines that weigh tons. No matter how diligently designed in advance and carefully constructed, they'll fail or disappoint if installed or used incorrectly. The significance of all this for marketing can be profound.

When prospective customers can't experience the product in advance, they are asked to buy what are essentially promises—promises of satisfaction. Even tangible, testable, feelable, smellable products are, before they're bought, largely just promises.

Buying Promises

Satisfaction in consumption or use can seldom be quite the same as earlier in trial or promise. Some promises promise more than others, depending on product features, design, degree of tangibility, type of promotion, price, and differences in what customers hope to accomplish with what they buy.

Of some products less is expected than what is actually or symbolically promised. The right kind of eye shadow properly applied may promise to transform a woman into an irresistible tigress in the night. Not even the most eager buyer literally believes the metaphor. Yet the metaphor helps make the sale. Neither do you really expect the proposed new corporate headquarters, so artfully rendered by the winning architect, automatically to produce all those cheerfully productive employees lounging with casual elegance at lunch in the verdant courtyard. But the metaphor helps win the assignment.

Thus, when prospective customers can't properly try the promised product in advance, metaphorical reassurances become the amplified necessity of the marketing effort. Promises, being intangible, have to be "tangibilized" in their presentation—hence the tigress and the contented employees. Metaphors and similes become surrogates for the tangibility that cannot be provided or experienced in advance.

This same thinking accounts for the solid, somber Edwardian decor of downtown law offices, the prudentially elegant and orderly public offices of investment banking houses, the confidently articulate consultants in dark vested suits, engineering and project proposals in "executive" typeset and leather bindings, and the elaborate pictorial documentation of the performance virtuosity of newly offered machine controls. It explains why insurance companies pictorially offer "a piece of the rock," put you under a "blanket of protection" or an "umbrella," or place you in "good hands."

Not even tangible products are exempt from the necessity of using symbol and metaphor. A computer terminal has to look right. It has to be packaged to convey an impression of reliable modernity—based on the assumption that prospective buyers will translate appearance into confidence about performance. In that respect, the marketing ideas behind the packaging of a $1 million computer, a $2 million jet engine, and a $.5 million numerically controlled milling machine are scarcely different from the marketing ideas behind the packaging of a $50 electric shaver or a $2.50 tube of lipstick.

Importance of Impressions

Common sense tells us, and research confirms, that people use appearances to make judgments about realities. It matters little whether the products are high priced or low priced, whether they are technically complex or simple, whether the buyers are supremely sophisticated in the technology of what's being considered or just plain ignorant, or whether they buy for themselves or for their employers. Everybody always depends to some extent on both appearances and external impressions.

Nor do impressions affect only the generic product itself—that is, the technical offering, such as the speed, versatility, and precision of the lathe; the color and creaminess of the lipstick; or the appearance and dimensions of the lobster thermidor. Consider, for example, investment banking. No matter how thorough and persuasive a firm's recommendations and assurances about a proposed underwriting and no matter how pristine its reputation for integrity and performance, somehow the financial vice president of the billion-dollar client corporation would feel better had the bank's representative not been quite so youthfully apple-cheeked.

The product will be judged in part by who offers it—not just who the vendor corporation is but also who the corporation's representative is. The vendor and the vendor's representative are both inextricably and inevitably part of the "product" that prospects must judge before they buy. The less tangible the generic product, the more powerfully and persistently the judgment about it gets shaped by the packaging—how it's presented, who presents it, and what's implied by metaphor, simile, symbol, and other surrogates for reality.

So, too, with tangible products. The sales engineers assigned to work with an electric utility company asking for competitive bids on a $100 million steam boiler system for its new plant are as powerfully a part of the offered product (the promise) as is the investment banking firm's partner.

The reason is easy to see. In neither case is there a product until it's delivered. And you won't know how well it performs until it's put to work.

The Ties that Bind

In both investment banking and big boilers, becoming the designated vendor requires successful passage through several consecutive gates, or stages, in the sales process. It is not unlike courtship. Both "customers" know that a rocky courtship spells trouble ahead. If the groom is not sufficiently solicitous during the courtship—if he's insensitive to moods and needs, unresponsive or wavering during stress or adversity—there will be problems in the marriage.

But unlike a real marriage, investment banking and installed boiler systems allow no room for divorce. Once the deal is made, marriage and gestation have simultaneously begun. After that, things are often irreversible. Investment banking may require months of close work with the client organization before the underwriting can be launched—that is, before the baby is born. And the construction of an electric power plant takes years, through sickness and in health. As with babies, birth of any kind presents new problems. Babies have to be coddled to see them through early life. Illness or relapse has to be conscientiously avoided or quickly corrected. Similarly, stocks or bonds should not go quickly to deep discounts. The boiler should not suddenly malfunction after several weeks or months. If it does, it should be rapidly restored to full use. Understandably, the prospective customer will, in courtship, note every nuance carefully, judging always what kind of a husband and father the eager groom is likely to make.

The way the product is packaged (how the promise is presented in brochure, letter, design appearance), how it is personally presented, and by whom—all these become central to the product itself because they are elements of what the customer finally decides to buy or reject.

A product is more than a tangible thing, even a $100 million boiler system. From a buyer's viewpoint, the product is a promise, a cluster of value expectations of which its nontangible qualities are as integral as its tangible parts. Certain conditions must be satisfied before the prospect buys. If they are not satisfied, there is no sale. There would have been no sale in the cases of the investment banker and the boiler manufacturer if, during the prebidding (or courtship) stages of the relationship, their representatives had been improperly responsive to or insufficiently informed about the customer's special situations and problems.

In each case, the promised product—the whole product—would have been unsatisfactory. It is not that it would have been incomplete; it just would not have been right. Changing the salespeople in midstream probably would not have helped, since the selling organization would by then have already "said" the wrong thing about its "product." If, during the courtship, the prospective customer got the impression that there might be aftermarket problems—problems in execution, in timeliness, in the postsale support necessary for smooth and congenial relations—then the customer would have received a clear message that the delivered product would be faulty.

Special Problems for Intangibles

So much, briefly, for making a sale—for getting a customer. *Keeping* a customer is quite another thing, and on that score more pervasively intangible products encounter some distinct difficulties.

These difficulties stem largely from the fact that intangible products are highly people-intensive in their production and delivery methods. Corporate financial services of banks are, in this respect, not so different from hairdressing or consulting. The more people-intensive a product, the more room there is for personal discretion, idiosyncrasy, error, and delay. Once a customer for an intangible product is sold, the customer can easily be unsold as a consequence of the underfulfillment of his expectations. Repeat buying suffers. Conversely, a tangible product, manufactured under close supervision in a factory and delivered through a planned and orderly network, is much more likely than an intangible product to fill the promised expectation. Repeat buying is therefore less easily jeopardized.

A tangible product is usually developed by design professionals working under conditions of benign isolation after receiving guidance from market intelligence experts, scientists, and others. The product will be manufactured by another group of specialists under conditions of close supervision that facilitate reliable quality control. Even installation and use by the customer are determined by a relatively narrow range of possibilities dictated by the product itself.

Intangible products present an entirely different picture. Consider a computer software program. The programmer does the required research directly and generally on the customer's premises, trying to understand complex networks of interconnecting operations. Then that same person designs the system and the software, usually alone. The process of designing is, simultaneously, also the process of manufacturing. Design and manufacturing of intangible products are generally done by the same people—or by one person alone, like a craftsman at a bench.

Moreover, manufacturing an intangible product is generally indistinguishable from its actual delivery. In situations such as consulting, the delivery *is* the manufacturing from the client's viewpoint. Though the consulting study may have been excellent, if the delivery is poor, the study will be viewed as having been badly manufactured. It's a faulty product. So too with the work of all types of brokers, educators and trainers, accounting firms, engineering firms, architects, lawyers, transportation companies, hospitals and clinics, government agencies, banks, trust companies, mutual funds, car rental companies, insurance companies, repair and maintenance operations, and on and on. For each, delivery and production are virtually indistinguishable. The whole difference is nicely summarized by Professor John M. Rathwell of Cornell University: "Goods are produced, services are performed."[1]

Minimizing the Human Factor

Because companies making intangible products are highly people-intensive operations, they have an enormous quality control problem. Quality control on an automobile assembly line is built into the system. If a yellow door is hung on a red car, somebody on the line will quickly ask if that's what was intended. If the left front wheel is missing, the person next in line, whose task is to fasten the lug bolts, will stop the line. But if a commercial banker misses an important feature of a financing package or if she doesn't do it well, it may never be found—or found too late. If the ashtrays aren't cleaned on a rented car, that discovery will annoy or irritate the already committed customer. Repeat business gets jeopardized.

No matter how well trained or motivated they might be, people make mistakes, forget, commit indiscretions, and at times are uncongenial—hence the search for alternatives to dependence on people. Previously in *HBR*, I have suggested a variety of ways to reduce people dependence in the so-called service industries. I called it the *industrialization of service*, which means substituting hard, soft or hybrid technologies for totally people-intensive activities:

☐ *Hard* technologies include automatic telephone dialing for operator assisted dialing, credit cards or repetitive credit checking, and computerized monitoring of industrial processes. And the benefits are considerable. Automatic telephone switching is, for example, not only cheaper than manual switching but far more reliable.

☐ *Soft* technologies are the substitution of division of labor for one-person craftsmanship in production—as, for example, organizing the work force that cleans an office building so that each worker specializes in one or several limited tasks (dusting, waxing, vacuuming, window cleaning) rather than each person doing all these jobs alone. Insurance companies long ago went to extensive division of labor in their applications processing—registering, underwriting, performing actuarial functions, issuing policies.

☐ *Hybrid* technologies combine the soft and the hard. The floor is waxed by a machine rather than by hand. French fries are precut and portion packed in a factory for finishing in a fast-food restaurant in specially designed deep fryers that signal when the food is ready. A computer automatically calculates and makes all entries in an Internal Revenue Service form 1040 after a moderately trained clerk has entered the raw data on a console.

The Managerial Revolution

Industrializing helps control quality and cut costs. Instead of depending on people to work *better*, industrialization redesigns the work so that people work *differently*. Thus, the same modes of managerial rationality are applied to service—the production, creation, and delivery of largely intangible products—that were first applied to production of goods in the nineteenth century. The real significance of the nineteenth century is not the industrial revolution, with its shift from animal to machine power, but rather the managerial revolution, with its shift from the craftsman's functional independence to the manager's rational routines.

In successive waves, the mechanical harvester, the sewing machine, and then the automobile epitomized the genius of the century. Each was rationally designed to become an assembled rather than a constructed machine, a machine that depended not on the idiosyncratic artistry of a single craftsman but on simple, standardized tasks performed on routine specifications by unskilled workers. This required detailed managerial planning to ensure proper design, manufacture, and assembly of interchangeable parts so that the right number of people would be at the right places at the right times to do the right simple jobs in the right ways. Then, with massive output, distribution, and after-marketing training and service, managers had to create and maintain systems to justify the massive output.

On Being Appreciated

What's been largely missing in intangible goods production is the kind of managerial rationality that produced the industrial revolution. That is why the quality of intangibles tends to be less reliable than it might be, costs higher than they should be, and customer satisfaction lower than it need be.

While I have referred to the enormous progress that has in recent years been made on these matters, there is one characteristic of intangible products that requires special attention for holding customers. Unique to intangible products is the fact that the customer is seldom aware of being served well. This is especially so in the case of intangible products that have, for the duration of the contract, constant continuity—that is, you're buying or using or consuming them almost constantly. Such products include certain banking services, cleaning services, freight hauling, energy management, maintenance services, telephones, and the like.

Consider an international banking relationship, an insurance relationship, an industrial cleaning relationship. If all goes well, the customer is virtually oblivious to what he's getting. Only when things don't go well (or a competitor says they don't) does the customer become aware of the product's existence or nonexistence—when a letter of credit is incorrectly drawn, when a competitive bank proposes better arrangements, when the annual insurance premium notice arrives or when a claim is disputed, when the ashtrays aren't cleaned, or when a favorite penholder is missing.

The most important thing to know about intangible products is that the *customers usually don't know what they're getting until they don't get it*. Only then do they become aware of what they bargained for; only on dissatisfaction do they dwell. Satisfaction is, as it should be, mute. Its existence is affirmed only by its absence.

And that's dangerous—because the customers will be aware only of failure and of dissatisfaction, not of success or satisfaction. That makes them terribly vulnerable to the blandishments of competitive sellers. A competitor can always structure a more interesting corporate financing deal, always propose a more imaginative insurance program, always find dust on top of the framed picture in the office, always cite small visible failures that imply big hidden ones.

In getting customers for intangibles it is important to create surrogates, or metaphors, for tangibility—how we dress; how we articulate, write, design, and present proposals; how we work with prospects, respond to inquiries, and initiate ideas; and how well we show we understand the prospect's business. But in keeping customers for intangibles, it becomes important regularly to remind and show them what they're getting so that occasional failures fade in relative importance. If that's not done, the customers will not know. They'll only know when they're *not* getting what they bought, and that's all that's likely to count.

To keep customers for regularly delivered and consumed intangible products, again, they have to be reminded of what they're getting. Vendors must regularly reinstate the promises that were made to land the customer. Thus, when an insurance prospect finally gets "married," the subsequent silence and inattention can be deafening. Most customers seldom recall for long what kind of life insurance package they bought, often forgetting as well the name of both underwriter and agent. To be reminded a year later via a premium notice often brings to mind the contrast between the loving attention of courtship and the cold reality of marriage. No wonder the lapse rate in personal life insurance is so high!

Once a relationship is cemented, the seller has created equity. The seller now has a customer. To help keep the customer, the seller must regularly enhance the equity in that relationship lest it decline and become jeopardized by competitors.

There are innumerable ways to do that strengthening, and some of these can be systematized, or industrialized. Periodic letters or phone calls that remind the customer of how well things are going cost little and are surprisingly powerful equity maintainers. Newsletters or regular visits suggesting new, better, or augmented product features are useful. Even non-business socializing has its value—as is affirmed by corporations struggling in recent years with the IRS about the deductibility of hunting lodges, yachts, clubs, and spouses attending conferences and customer meetings.

Here are some examples of how companies have strengthened their relationships with customers:

☐ An energy management company sends out a periodic "Update Report" on conspicuous yellow paper, advising clients how to discover and correct energy leaks, install improved monitors, and accomplish cost savings.

☐ A computer service bureau organizes its account managers for a two-week series of blitz customer callbacks to "explain casually" the installation of new central processing equipment that is expected to prevent cost increases next year while expanding the customers' interactive options.

☐ A long-distance hauler of high-value electronic equipment (computers, terminals, mail sorters, word processors, medical diagnostic instruments) has instituted quarterly performance reviews with its shippers, some of which include customers who are encouraged to talk about their experiences and expectations.

☐ An insurance company sends periodic one-page notices to policyholders *and* policy beneficiaries. These generally begin with a single-sentence congratulation that policy and coverage remain nicely intact and follow with brief views on recent tax rulings affecting insurance, new notions about personal financial planning, and special protection packages available with other types of insurance.

In all these ways, sellers of intangible products reinstate their presence and performance in the customers' minds, reminding them of their continuing presence and the value of what is constantly, and silently, being delivered.

Making Tangible the Intangible

It bears repeating that all products have elements of tangibility and intangibility. Companies that sell tangible products invariably promise more than the tangible products themselves. Indeed, enormous efforts often focus on the enhancement of the intangibles—promises of bountiful benefits conferred rather than on features offered. To the buyer of photographic film, Kodak promises with unremitting emphasis the satisfactions of enduring remembrance, of memories clearly preserved. Kodak says almost nothing about the superior luminescence of its pictures. The product is thus remembrance, not film or pictures.

The promoted products of the automobile, as everyone knows, are largely status, comfort, and power—intangible things of the mind, rather than tangible things from the factory. Auto dealers, on the other hand, assuming correctly that people's minds have already been reached by the manufacturers' ads, focus on other considerations: deals, availability, and postpurchase servicing. Neither the dealers nor the manufacturers sell the tangible cars themselves. Rather, they sell the intangible benefits that are bundled into the entire package.

If tangible products must be intangibilized to add customer-getting appeal, the intangible products must be tangibilized—what Professor Leonard L. Berry calls "managing the evidence."[2] Ideally, this should be done as a matter of routine on a systematic basis—that is, industrialized. For instance, hotels wrap their drinking glasses in fresh bags or film, put on the toilet seat a "sanitized" paper band, and neatly shape the end piece of the toilet tissue into a fresh-looking arrowhead. All these actions say with silent affirmative clarity that "the room has been specially cleaned for your use and comfort"—yet no words are spoken to say it. Words, in any case, would be less convincing, nor could employees be reliably depended on to say them each time or to say them convincingly. Hotels have thus not only tangibilized their promise, they've also industrialized its delivery.

Or take the instructive case of purchasing house insulation, which most home owners approach with understandable apprehension. Suppose you call two companies to bid on installing insulation in your house. The first insulation installer arrives in a car. After pacing once around the house with measured self-assurance and after quick calculations on the back of an envelope, there comes a confident quote of $2,400 for six-inch fiberglass—total satisfaction guaranteed.

Another drives up in a clean white truck with clipboard in hand and proceeds to scrupulously measure the house dimensions, count the windows, crawl the attic, and consult records from a source book on the area's seasonal temperature ranges and wind velocities. The installer then asks a host of questions, meanwhile recording everything with obvious diligence. There follows a promise to return in three days, which happens at the appointed hour, with a typed proposal for six-inch fiberglass insulation at $2,800—total satisfaction guaranteed. From which company will you buy?

The latter has tangibilized the intangible, made a promise into a credible expectation. Even more persuasive tangible evidence is provided by an insulation supplier whose representative types the relevant information into a portable intelligent printing terminal. The analysis and response are almost instant, causing one user to call it "the most powerful tool ever developed in the insulation industry." If the house owner is head of a project buying team of an electric utility company, the treasurer of a mighty corporation, the materials purchasing agent of a ready-mixed cement company, the transportation manager of a fertilizer manufacturer, or the data processing director of an insurance company, it's almost certain this person will make vendor decisions at work in the same way as around the house. Everybody requires the risk-reducing reassurances of tangibilized intangibles.

Managers can use the practice of providing reassuring ways to render tangible the intangible's promises—even when the generic product is itself tangible. Laundry detergents that claim special whitening capabilities lend credibility to the promise by using "blue whitener beads" that are clearly visible to the user. Procter & Gamble's new decaffeinated instant coffee, "High Points," reinforces the notion of real coffee with luminescent "milled flakes for hearty, robust flavor." You can *see* what the claims promise.

Keeping customers for an intangible product requires constant reselling efforts while things go well lest the customer get lost when things go badly. The reselling requires that tasks be industrialized. The relationship with the customer must be managed much more carefully and continuously in the case of intangibles than of tangible products, though it is vital in both. And it gets progressively more vital for tangible products that are new and especially complex. In such cases, "relationship management" becomes a special art—another topic all its own.

Meanwhile, the importance of what I've tried to say here is emphasized by one overriding fact: a customer is an asset usually more precious than the tangible assets on the balance sheet. Balance sheet assets can generally be bought. There are lots of willing sellers. Customers cannot so easily be bought. Lots of eager sellers are offering them many choices. Moreover, a customer is a double asset. First, the customer is the direct source of cash from the sale and, second, the existence of a solid customer can be used to raise cash from bankers and investors—cash that can be converted into tangible assets.

The old chestnut "nothing happens till you make a sale" is awfully close to an important truth. What it increasingly takes to make and keep that sale is to tangibilize the intangible, restate the benefit and source to the customer, and industrialize the processes.

Notes

1. John M. Rathwell, *Marketing in the Service Sector* (Cambridge, Mass.: Winthrop Publishers, 1974), p. 58.

2. Leonard L. Berry, "Service Marketing Is Different," *Business*, May-June 1980, p. 24. He is with the University of Virginia, Charlottesville.

26
Three Essentials of Product Quality

JACK REDDY and ABE BERGER

Responding to the challenge of superior-quality products from overseas is one of the best ways to improve the effectiveness of any manufacturing organization, the outcome of which reaps benefits far beyond immediate quality improvement to meet foreign competition. Application of an evenhanded response to this challenge requires an understanding of the factors that determine quality and product performance. In this article the authors identify the major areas that provide the leverage for improvement, discuss the significant problems that managers face in making the transition to meet world-class standards, and recommend several courses of action. These quality-enhancing methods clearly apply also to manufacturers in industries where foreign competition is not yet a threat.

Overseas competition is forcing many U.S. manufacturers to meet or surpass new, world standards for quality and product performance. Many foreign companies have mastered the basics of good manufacturing from product design to distribution and are outperforming established U.S. companies.

There are practical courses of action that will enable U.S. manufacturers to meet world-class quality standards. But before taking a look at these successful approaches, let us first clear up three misconceptions about improved performance:

1. *Higher quality and performance goals increase costs.* By focusing on process control and early prevention of defects, a U.S. multinational recently reduced its scrap rates in five plants from about 15% to less than 5%, while simultaneously improving outgoing quality fivefold. Its successful

---

Published 1983.

two-year program to gain industrywide quality leadership resulted in a marked cost reduction.

Competitive manufacturers, both domestic and foreign, know from experience that dedication to higher quality, combined with a thorough understanding of the entire manufacturing process, often results in significant reductions in, for instance, scrap, rework, routine inspection, field costs, and warranty losses.

In short, meeting higher quality and performance goals does not inevitably mean higher costs.

2. *It is necessary to exceed competitive quality by a wide margin.* Japanese automobile manufacturers have gained a substantial market share in the United States largely because of consumer perception that their products are of high quality. The quality superiority of Japanese cars is principally in fit and finish—with sharply reduced warranty work. In the quality dimensions that relate to safety, durability, and corrosion resistance, U.S. manufacturers have maintained superiority. But where customers see a clear-cut quality advantage, they usually favor that product, without trying to weigh all the factors.

It is not necessary to exceed competitive quality by a wide margin, nor is it usually commercially rewarding. Staying ahead of competition, however, does require quantitative measurements of all the major aspects of product quality.

3. *A company must identify and shore up its weak areas.* Recently, a U.S. manufacturer decided on a policy of establishing world-class quality. Although it had worked for many years with top Japanese companies that featured lifelong employment, quality circles, and pay levels based on age and seniority, it decided not to emulate the practices of a foreign culture. Instead, the manufacturer built a successful program by following the axiom of good management: emphasizing and capitalizing on its own particular strengths—product innovation, marketing skills, large-scale organization, and availability of capital.

A corollary of this axiom is that identified weaknesses can endanger a competitive strategy. The need to deal with obvious weaknesses should not distract managers from the main business at hand—marshaling all available resources to achieve a strong competitive edge. (The major issues, and the functional groups that have to work together effectively to resolve them, are shown in Exhibit 1.)

Let us turn now to a discussion of the successful methods of organizing for product assurance, getting relevant quality data, and controlling vendor quality.

Organizing for Product Assurance

A few years ago, a leading auto manufacturer introduced a four-cylinder engine as part of a program to provide customers with an option to improve

Exhibit 1. Managing for World-Class Quality

Major Issue	Prime and Subordinate Responsibilities	Problem	Recommended Approach
Product design	Senior management, marketing, product engineering, and product assurance group	Meeting customer needs and expectations	Innovative design, "extended quality"
Making good on promise to the customer	Senior management, marketing and sales service, and product assurance group	Risk of new product introduction	Getting close to problem Root cause determination Realistic appraisal "Trial horse" standard Buying back product from field Limited, rolling introduction Improved servicing
Resource allocation roadblocks	Senior management, financial staff, and product assurance group	Too much data	Cost of quality plan Product performance standards Verification of competitive standing of audit
Developing a quality commitment at vendors' plants	Buyers and purchasing management, quality control engineers	The squeeze on buyers	Verification of process Capability of vendors Establishing and managing to virtually defect-free product
Establishing and managing to realistic specifications	Engineering management, quality control engineering, and product engineering	Insufficient specifications	Realism in specification Cooperation Improved understanding

373

Exhibit 1. *(Continued)*

Major Issue	Prime and Subordinate Responsibilities	Problem	Recommended Approach
Maintaining the integrity of manufacturing facilities	Plant management, supervisors and maintenance employees	Overadaptation	Product readiness Trial runs

gas mileage. Faced with severe time limitations, plant engineers had not found a satisfactory method for achieving dynamic balance; thus, the engine vibrated excessively under certain conditions. In spite of this unresolved quality problem, the company introduced the engine to the market with the hope that customers who wanted better mileage would tolerate the excessive vibration.

Unfortunately, all testing had been done with one basic sedan model. When customers selected the new engine in the station wagon model, they experienced unacceptable vibration at about 50 mph. During the first production year, dealers "corrected" the problem by refusing to sell the new engine in a station wagon model. Nevertheless, a few hundred station wagons did get to customers. These required engine replacement, and sales of the manufacturer's entire product line fell well below forecast. The engineers eventually found the solution in time for the following year's production run, but the damage to the manufacturer's reputation continued long afterward.

Failing to meet quality standards, particularly when introducing products, carries major risks for organizations. Managers should address such questions as how long a new product will last, how frequently and consistently it will be made, and how effectively it will be serviced.

Independent PA Group

Powerful organizational barriers often prevent the bearers of bad tidings from being heard during the planning phase. An independent product assurance group, with responsibility for evaluating product quality, can deter overenthusiastic attempts to rush new products to market prematurely. Managers should encourage the expression of honest opinions about all critical decisions.

Management makes the final decision about the launch of a product; but its decision should not only be rational, it should appear rational to the staff. There is no substitute for careful, realistic planning which includes an assessment of the validity of estimates. It is only when an independent test group affirms the necessary corrective action by rigorous testing that management can be assured the problem has been solved.

The product assurance group should be staffed by people who have the respect of decision makers in all functional departments. The group's primary responsibility in the sale of products is to determine the cause of actual or potential field problems and to promptly initiate effective corrective action. Changes in design, in the manufacturing process, or in operating procedures may be required to eliminate or substantially reduce the risk of a problem's recurrence.

The reputation of the product assurance group depends on the objectivity with which it proceeds and its skill in finding solutions. The only way to prove that the case has been found and the quality problem corrected is by demonstrating that the problem does not recur under controlled, high-stress conditions.

Usually, a 20% improvement in performance under high-stress test conditions results in considerably more than a 20% reduction in field problems, and often a borderline field problem disappears after only a slight modification in design or manufacture. Any deterioration in performance during high-stress tests requires thorough investigation by the product assurance group.

A demonstrated test improvement does not ensure better performance in the field, of course, because no controlled environment can duplicate field conditions. To safeguard against this kind of error, new designs should always be tested with a standard or "trial horse" as a control. This test standard can be an established product made either by the company or by a competitor. A high-stress test is a cheaper way to avoid risk than overdesign of a product, a practice often favored by design engineers.

With test appraisals by the product assurance group and by careful monitoring of data from field service organizations, management will be able to determine which quality improvements will give customers a better product.

The product assurance group should have funds to buy back samples of products long in service and "lemons" from the field. A small sample of long-service or intensively used products can provide insight into unexpected problems and the effect of unusual environmental conditions. Lemons are very useful for component-search tests. Both kinds of buy-back samples help to identify questionable parts that call for corrective action.

Marketing Dimension

In high-risk situations where evidence of potential design or quality problems exist, or where the time allowed for testing the new product is inadequate, marketing management should consider reducing the risk by introducing a limited quantity.

For example, a leading maker of copiers faced a crisis deadline: its most feared competitor had selected an announcement date for what was thought to be a superior product. Six months ahead of this date, the product assurance group delivered the bad news to senior management: its new copier would not be perfected by the deadline and, worse, an estimated extra year of subassembly engineering would be needed.

By facing the facts squarely, management derived what proved to be a highly successful strategy. Marketing went ahead with a limited introduction, starting in three cities; sales-service people in those cities were given special training on how to manage the product during the critical first year; engineering developed a retrofit program to replace deficient subassemblies; and field staff was increased to reduce the potential damage of a limited introduction of a less-than-perfect product.

A competent sales-service group, given the charter, can develop marketing strategies to improve the servicing of a new product. While its prime objective will always be rapid correction of problems, a secondary goal will be to look for problem patterns that can lead to more effective servicing. With these data, sales-service managers can evaluate repair costs in terms of geographical area, application, and usage. Ineffective repair work will show up either as clusters of repeated service calls or as excessive use of replacement parts. (It is not unusual to find that more than half the parts replaced were not defective. Such a finding warrants investigation.)

Getting Relevant Data

Recently, a large manufacturer pursuing cost reduction switched to an outside supplier for process materials previously made in-house. Raw material costs soon registered predicted savings. Scrap losses soared, however, as a result of incomplete specifications and ambiguous contract definitions. Fortunately, a well-integrated quality-loss report system focused management's attention on the problem, thus limiting the large losses that would have otherwise resulted.

Successful management of quality and product performance requires a coherent hierarchy of reports, covering three main categories of basic information:

1. *Cost of quality data.* Any departure from specs or normal procedures creates extra cost, generally measurable as a tangible loss. It is not true that quality is an elusive, intangible essence that cannot be tracked and managed like product costs and production rates. Management should make it clear that it requires quantitative reports on quality costs that identify even insignificant detail.

2. *Quality and performance audits.* Once management has established the appropriate standards for external product performance and for internal quality costs, a periodic audit for conformance to those standards is a straightforward task.

3. *Product performance in the field.* Management needs to know the extent to which product performance lives up to customer expectations. Any divergence from expected performance creates quantifiable extra costs, ranging from warranty or call-back campaign costs to lost sales over and above anticipated sales-service costs for planned performance.

All large companies prepare reports that provide some relevant information in all three areas. Few companies, however, convert these reports into a coherent whole, equivalent to the bottom line of a financial report. Even fewer make regular use of outside auditing skills to verify the reported figures.

The inevitable result of poorly defined goals, lack of objective measurement, and inadequate reporting of product quality and performance is deterioration of competitive standing. Thus, in the following section, we discuss systems to provide "good quality numbers."

Setting Quality Goals

In the 1950s, Japanese business managers invited American consultants to train them in quality concepts and measurement. The Japanese took the lessons of meaningful quality control seriously and are now harvesting the benefits. The staff and junior managers trained at that time are Japan's senior managers today. While many Americans have had similar training, few U.S. organizations promote senior managers primarily because of their expertise in quality control and product assurance.

A U.S. engine components maker uses inspection procedures for each step of a series of precision machining and treating operations which provide yields of 98% or more acceptable parts per step. As a result of the multiple operations in the process, however, the overall yield is less than 90%. Moreover, the cost of rework and inspection is about 20% of the manufacturing cost. Of even greater importance, the process is unstable and unpredictable; a minor upset at any step can result in a marginally acceptable product.

Major Japanese manufacturers have established clear-cut quality goals; they budget for zero defects and measure discrepancies in parts per million. This approach contrasts sharply with the majority of U.S. manufacturers, who use an "acceptable quality level" system. The AQL approach assumes that a certain small percentage of defective product is inevitable, and that the objective of quality control is to reach the AQL level.

The difficulty with AQL applied to components is that satisfactory performance of an assembly requires that all parts work properly. When building anything as complicated as an automobile (15,000 parts) or a copying machine (1,500 parts), a system that permits any defective parts—even a fraction of one percent—delivers a finished product containing several defective parts. This "allowable defects" approach puts U.S. manufacturers at a significant competitive disadvantage to their Japanese counterparts, who do not knowingly accept any defective parts.

When setting goals of zero defects, U.S. managers need to know what level of quality customers expect and what quality problems they will tolerate. It may not be necessary to acheive an absolute level of zero defects, but management should be aware of the exact standard necessary to meet competition—and then should continually measure actual performance against that standard.

Measuring Quality Performance

By making a considerable effort, a U.S. television set maker had reduced service calls during its 90-day warranty period to 0.8% of the sets produced, or 80 calls per 10,000 sets. But a Japanese competitor continued to increase market share because of a reputation for superior quality. A field auditor of the Japanese sets showed that they required only 60 calls per 10,000 sets during warranty. Many U.S. managers would ignore this small difference as being imperceptible to consumers. But the management of the American company had been educated in the principle of gaining a competitive advantage by making quality a little bit better and, as a result, it set a new goal of 50 calls per 10,000 sets.

Analysis of the reasons for the U.S. manufacturer's service calls found many different causes. A typical plant assembly problem might occur up to ten times in a production day of 10,000 units. How could the company establish as an "unshakable fact" that this particular defect had been reduced to virtually nil? Management instituted a monthly warehouse audit of 15,600 sets to ensure that the process was under control. Monthly audits of this magnitude are costly; but if management is serious about meeting the quality competition, such audits are necessary.

It is important to match actual field performance against goals and to control life-cycle costs. Predicting product performance requires understanding the environmental conditions and stress levels the product will experience. With this information, engineers can construct test conditions that will simulate all the environments at stresses beyond the normal design level. Tests results may be fragmentary, however, and questions may arise as to the accuracy of the simulations and consistency of the results.

Management's role, however, is straightforward. To determine whether product performance is truly competitive, managers should bring together all the data relating to field performance and life-cycle costs and consider them as a whole. Establishing that a product is a little bit better than the competition requires well-designed concepts and refined measurements.

Controlling Vendor Quality

Since most manufacturers purchase more than half their parts from vendors, knowledge of effective approaches for controlling vendor quality is an essential element in the achievement of world-class quality.

In this section, we will discuss two key topics in dealing with vendors: first, the role of the buyer, and second, the management of specifications.

A leading copier manufacturer developed a new machine requiring 1,500 purchased parts, and buyers were given three months to find qualified bidders to supply these parts. In an attempt to obtain the lowest costs and still meet delivery schedules, the buyers selected 500 different vendors. After the buyers had placed the orders, a survey team determined the qualifications of the vendors making the 30 most critical parts and reported that only six vendors could deliver parts consistently manufactured to specification, at the cost quoted. As it turned out, the company required a costly two-year program to correct the problems created during the three-month rush of placing orders without benefit of adequate information about vendor qualifications.

Buyers and purchasing managers are often given unrealistically tight schedules. In addition, they are usually isolated from engineering and quality control staff whose services they frequently need to fulfill their mission of buying at the lowest cost from qualified vendors. Major problems often arise when buyers try to assess a vendor's qualifications. Some of the information needed requires detailed sampling and analysis of the vendor's manufacturing process, and this has to be done by quality control engineers in close cooperation with the vendor's technical personnel at the vendor's plant. Inspecting a few selected pieces at the buyer's receiving dock does not fully describe the consistency of the product or the reliability of the vendor's tooling. Nor does it generate understanding of the vendor's interpretation of the manufacturer's specifications.

Recommended Buyer Approach

Buyers occupy a unique position in the quest to deliver a better product to the customer. Companies that have made the transition to higher quality levels understand that buyers are the key to improved vendor quality through the attitudes they convey to vendors.

A buyer is powerless to effect change unless senior managers have set quality as an overriding goal. The obsession to provide management with reports of money saved, orders placed, or on-time deliveries may overwhelm considerations of quality. However, when top management emphasizes quality as its highest objective, a buyer will not only prepare periodic reports of vendor quality performance but will also insist on appropriate action whenever warranted by performance below, or above, the established norms.

The cost of establishing vendor capability is both high and difficult to predict, as is the cost of handling off-quality or marginal products. Because efficiency goals are important, buyers should concentrate on those vendors and products where cost is an opportunity for improvement at reasonable cost. To set correct priorities, buyers should consult technical staff for advice.

A buyer's approach and style are vitally important. To implement a successful quality-improvement program in a vendor's plant, the buyer should work with the vendor until the parts are effectively defect-free and stress the importance to the vendor of new attitudes toward quality. The buyer should examine and evaluate trade-offs, handle problems of off-specification material in a forceful yet diplomatic manner, and participate in corrective action programs with the vendor. Finally, the buyer should show a high capacity for patience, understanding, and trust. Such skills and attitudes, well appreciated by senior management, are often found in experienced buyers.

One company that embarked on a program of vendor quality improvement reaped some unexpected benefits. It reeducated buyers about the terms of its existing but dormant "preferred vendor" program, and set a goal of doubling the number of preferred vendors from 40 to 80 in one year. Although this effort involved but a small percentage of all the company's vendors, the program resulted in block bids on groups of similar parts from those who had qualified as preferred vendors. When the percentage bought from a preferred vendor increased from 2% to 10%, it became much easier to deal with occasional quality problems and to negotiate favorable prices.

Conformance to Realistic Specs

Clear specifications are the starting point for all quality decisions. Each specification has to make sense at every manufacturing stage from product design to field servicing. Are the specs realistic? Or are they arbitrarily set to a tight limit to protect the designer in case something goes wrong? Can the product be manufactured economically? Can the product be serviced and maintained in the field? These questions are not always easy to answer.

Many Japanese manufacturers have adopted the "slotted hole" approach in dealing with the question of specifications. Rather than trying to ensure a good subassembly by tight control of the specifications of individual parts, they buy wide-tolerance parts that fit loosely and use precise production fixtures to mate the parts and meet exact requirements. Fasteners ensure that the parts stay mated. The service staff is supplied with equivalent production fixturing to align all parts properly during adjustment or repair in the field.

A trial-run program for key products, beginning with those that show quality problems, is a good way to control the product and process. The buyer arranges for a trial run of a small sample of product to ensure that all components of the process are working together to produce the desired quality level. Such a trial run is technically known as a "process capability study."

Detailed review of the results of a trial run may lead to modification of the specs, perhaps changing the limits of acceptability to optimize the commercial trade-offs between cost and quality. On the other hand, analysis of results may bring about a decision to redesign the product to improve manufacture or to review the vendor's capability. The purpose of a trial run is to provide concrete data on which to make such decisions.

Carefully planned process capability studies determine precisely what product quality levels can be attained when both people and equipment operate within the process specifications. Such studies are also valuable for setting achievable goals for the quality and yield of a process.

In most plants, management assumes that specs are correct and that the stated tolerances are necessary. In our experience, this assumption is false; a significant fraction of valuable processing time in plants is inefficiently employed in refining products to unnecessarily tight specifications. Trial runs provide the buyer with data on product performance which often proves that existing specifications and tolerances are unrealistic. The money saved by development of realistic specifications is typically many times the cost of conducting trial runs.

The vendors' managements should set standards of plant performance to reflect buyers' needs for quality products. Interpretation of specifications is always a problem. Where many different parts are supplied by various vendors, there are corresponding misunderstandings about specifications. Even when the specifications are relatively unambiguous, problems arise in methods of measurement and interpretation of the figures.

If the buyer and supplier meet, plan, make trial runs, audit each other's findings, and talk through the differences, many solutions can be found. Management should provide the budget and authorization for its quality engineers to interact with vendors' staff.

A friendly approach is cost effective. For example, one U..S. automobile manufacturer began a program to control vendor quality in the 1960s by adopting regulatory approaches developed by the Department of Defense. The vendors soon learned to conform to specifications, but the auto company had to assign 300 people to administer the program.

A competing company (which enjoyed a well-earned reputation for good management) started a vendor control program somewhat later that was based on a philosophy of establishing a close and cooperative working relationship. This company also made rapid progress in getting vendors to meet specifications but its system required only 75 people to deal with approximately the same number of vendors and workload.

While both systems achieved the same goal of managing vendor conformance to realistic specifications at the desired cost, and both parties made a profit, the administrative cost of the cooperative approach was one-fourth that of the regulatory program.

Setting a Course

Application of an evenhanded management approach to quality requires understanding the factors that determine quality and product performance. We have identified the major areas that provide leverage for improving quality, while meeting long-term goals of profit performance and competitive standing.

Setting a course to meet world-class quality standards requires a commitment by senior management that all functional departments within the organization will take the necessary action steps—creating a successful design, setting realistic specifications, manufacturing the product to specification, buying and inspecting parts, monitoring quality, and servicing the product.

The cost of implementing our recommendations is reasonable, compared with the gains realized. While there are no secrets or insurmountable problems, the approaches require a broad commitment to quality at all levels of the organization. Our experience has been that making quality the organization's most important goal can make work more satisfying for all concerned. The customer receives a better product and, perhaps most important, the manufacturer achieves not only a profitable return on investment but the emotional reward of making a product whose quality is second to none in the world.

Appendix

A Special Concern

To meet production schedules and stay within budget, corporate headquarters often encourages plant managers to tolerate substandard conditions. Forced to adapt, plant managers usually opt for the expedient course, sacrificing long-term objectives in favor of immediate goals. Plant maintenance, quality control, and manufacturing engineering are obvious targets for cuts. The consequences of such shortsighted adaptation tend to accumulate rapidly and can easily degrade a profitable, competitive process into a marginal one, or even a loser. Unfortunately, the underlying cause of the problem—management's sacrifice of principle for expediency—is seldom recognized as the culprit when the search for a scapegoat begins.

The problem usually develops from the forces created by the financial people. The inefficient end-of-the-month push to meet schedules is a common example. Another is the emphasis on annual capital expenditure planning, which encourages short-range thinking and promotes a philosophy of adaptation to inadequate staff, tooling, or equipment.

The solution lies in senior management's recognition of the problem and reallocation of financial resources to meet both the immediate and long-term requirements of the business.

27
Good Product Support Is Smart Marketing

MILIND M. LELE and UDAY S. KARMARKAR

Product support can be as simple as a set of instructions and a throwaway wrench that comes with an assemble-it-yourself child's bicycle or as complicated as warranty programs, service contracts, parts depots, and equipment on loan to replace a defective machine while it is being repaired. All of these constitute product support; they are designed to ensure that customers obtain the most value from use of the product after the sale. Such factors as heightened customer awareness and higher expectations about support levels, reduced ability to perceive product differentiation through superior technology and/or features, and improvements in support methodology have greatly increased the importance of product support in company strategy. The identification of customer expectations regarding product support and the development of cost-effective strategies for meeting those expectations is, these authors demonstrate, a major facet of successful marketing today.

When making purchases, customers often believe they are buying more than the physical item; they also have expectations about the level of postpurchase support the product carries with it. This support can range from simple replacement of a faulty item to complex arrangements designed to meet customer needs over the product's entire useful life. Our investigations show that defining these expectations of support and meeting them effectively can be critical to a successful marketing effort. Consider:

Published 1983.

1. Caterpillar Tractor and John Deere, two companies whose marketing strategies are based on providing superior product support. Over the past quarter century both have concentrated on strengthening their dealers' service capabilities and on upgrading parts availability. They have backed these efforts with extensive service staffs and emergency parts ordering systems. They have directed equipment design to emphasize reliability and serviceability, and to minimize downtime. These two companies have made product support cornerstones of their organizations' corporate cultures and values.[1] This has remained true despite damaging strikes, recession, and acreage taken out of production.

2. The failure of Olivetti to establish itself in the United States, despite considerable investment during the last 15 years, primarily because of poor product support. The company has vacillated in its choice of distribution channels, thereby demoralizing its dealers. Parts and service training support have been inconsistent and usually poor. Initial buyer enthusiasm for new products has been repeatedly dampened by inadequate documentation and user training. As a result, despite excellent products at competitive prices, the company has failed to gain a strong foothold in the U.S. market.

Caterpillar and Deere illustrate the value of using support to improve marketing effectiveness. Product support, however, is an underutilized marketing resource in many companies. Developing and executing support strategies with marketing impact is difficult, and managers frequently do not know where to begin.

To maximize the marketing impact, managers need to have an accurate idea of customer support expectations and how to measure them. They can then use this information to segment existing markets in a new way or, in some cases, even to define new markets.

In developing a support strategy, it is necessary for managers to make trade-offs between effectiveness and cost. Our studies show that these trade-offs are often quite complicated and need to be evaluated carefully. Managers need to understand the nature of each trade-off and to develop a suitable framework for choosing among competing alternatives.

Why Support Fails

To many people, product support means parts, service, and warranty. In the early stages of market growth, customers concentrate more on technology and features and are concerned with only a few aspects of support, such as parts and service. As the market starts to mature, customer needs become more sophisticated. Product support encompasses everything that can help maximize the customer's after-sales satisfaction—parts, service, and warranty plus operator training, maintenance training, parts delivery, reliability engineering, serviceability engineering, and even product design.

In many companies, however, the earlier limited view still holds sway; as a result they separate product support from marketing strategy. In our experience, companies in which this is the case exhibit some or all of the following characteristics:

An Explicit Support Strategy Is Lacking.   The company views product support as a collection of individual tasks—enhanced product and/or service reliability, upgraded parts availability, improved training of service personnel, investment in additional service facilities—without an overall integrating theme. Improving support means "more of the same."

Responsibility for Support Is Diffused.   Many companies do not centralize responsibility for product support; individual departments such as reliability engineering, service administration, and customer relations carry out support tasks. As a result, management receives a disjointed picture of product support and its relation both to the customers' needs and expectations and to the company's overall product design and marketing strategy.

Support Needs Are Considered Late in the Development Cycle.   Managers often fail to contemplate such needs until after the design is frozen and the marketing strategy decisions have been made. Individual departments adopt support strategies that may not be compatible with one another.

Management Focuses on Individual Support Attributes.   Because of the diffusion of responsibility, management tends to focus on internal matters— engineering reliability, parts availability, warranty costs—rather than on customer-oriented measures such as downtime per failure.

Taken together, the foregoing characteristics lead to an often-observed cycle:

1 Top management becomes concerned about customer complaints relating to product support.
2 Individual departments demand more resources to improve customer satisfaction.
3 Lacking an overall strategy, investments in individual areas (e.g., reliability, parts inventories) rapidly reach a point of diminishing returns.
4 Customer complaints continue because basic problems have not been addressed.
5 The cycle repeats.

The net result is a waste of resources and potential or actual loss of market share to competitors with superior support strategies. To break the cycle, managers must first appreciate how customer expectations can affect support and marketing strategies and then learn how to use these expectations constructively.

Segmenting the Market

Customer expectations about product support add a crucial dimension to market segmentation. In most cases the package of support services that must be offered—implicitly or explicitly—changes significantly from one market segment to another. While many companies break down markets in terms of product features and performance, few segment markets on the basis of customers' support expectations. The result is that some support areas are overserviced while others are neglected.

Think of a word processor for a secretarial station. Potential buyers range from small one-secretary offices to large companies. There appear to be two market segments—one needing a basic model at a low price and the other a more comprehensive model at a higher price. Yet when customer expectations about support are analyzed, distinct differences emerge.

In the *one-machine office* the duration of downtime because of failure is crucial. Equipment failure means work virtually ceases, which can be extremely expensive. Disruption costs may be high because a small office cannot spare the people to search for replacements. The customer therefore expects both a low failure rate and minimum downtime per failure. Support costs or maintenance expenses are of secondary importance.

In the *multimachine office* downtime is important but not crucial; another functioning machine can be used to get important work out. Assuming that both the failure rate and downtime per failure are reasonably low, the customer is likely to be more interested in keeping maintenance and repair costs low over the life of the product.

These different expectations regarding support focus on varied attributes—failure frequency and downtime on the one hand, and maintenance and repair costs on the other—that form two distinct support segments. To meet customers' needs in each segment, management can choose a variety of strategies. For the word processor market, a company could (a) design for higher reliability (and charge a premium), (b) provide parts and service support as needed without a fixed-fee service contract, (c) develop a monthly service contract, or (d) use a spare machine on-site and incorporate its cost in the maintenance contract.

Each of these support strategies affects such major elements of marketing as product design and development, production and delivery, sales, and pricing. Choosing the right strategy involves a series of trade-offs such as product cost versus support effectiveness, product cost versus support cost, and support cost versus support effectiveness.

The importance of customer support expectations as an added dimension in market segmentation now becomes evident: different strategies are best for different segments. Ignoring these differences runs the risk of under- or overservicing segments, or under- or overpricing the product and the support services. The three steps involved in developing effective support strategies for a given product are:

1 Defining customer expectations regarding support.
2 Understanding the trade-offs implied in each support strategy.
3 Identifying the strategies that best fit management's objectives.

In planning a support program, however, managers need to be aware of the character of customer expectations, of the limitations of different support strategies, and of the interactions among strategies.

Defining Customer Needs

A major problem in segmenting the market on the basis of customer expectations lies in defining what these expectations are. Unlike product features or performance levels, customer support expectations focus on intangible attributes such as reliability, dependability, or availability. Without a suitable framework, the task of defining support segments is very difficult.

Because these intangible qualities can be viewed as proxies for underlying costs, the life-cycle cost concept used in equipment purchasing decisions can provide the basis for quantifying customer preferences regarding support. The life of a product after it is placed in service can be viewed as a sequence of uptimes and downtimes, terminated eventually by final failure, obsolescence, or sale and replacement. As the product goes through this cycle, customers can incur three types of costs:

1 Fixed costs on each failure occasion, independent of the length of downtime.
2 Variable costs that depend on the length of downtime and whose major component is the value of service lost (opportunity cost).
3 Maintenance costs of the product or service.

Because random events determine some of these costs, and since customers are likely to be risk averse, another factor must also be considered: uncertainty concerning the length and frequency of failure, the time needed for repair, and the magnitude of costs incurred.

To illustrate how underlying costs measure customer expectations, consider a washing machine used by a household and a large crawler tractor used by a builder. If the washing machine breaks, the homeowner incurs a repair bill (the fixed cost of failure). By and large, the homeowner is unwilling to pay a large premium to reduce the downtime (low variable costs of failure).

Other things being equal, the purchaser of a domestic washing machine wants to keep repair costs low (high reliability).

On the other hand, if the crawler tractor breaks, the builder incurs significant fixed costs (of repair) and variable costs (wages paid to crews that sit idle until the tractor is back in action). Very often, the builder pays out more in wages for every hour the tractor is down than for repairs (the variable costs are far higher than the fixed costs). For this reason, the builder wants a tractor with both high reliability and low downtime per failure, and may even trade off reliability for less downtime.

In practice, customers incur fixed, variable, and maintenance costs. They are also risk averse and therefore concerned about uncertainty. Furthermore, as we have observed, in many cases customers do not clarify the relative importance of costs and risks. "I want a dependable product" often describes a wide variety of support needs. To define customer expectations accurately it is therefore necessary to find out which costs and risks customers are likely to be concerned about and then to develop suitable techniques for measuring them.

Measurable Entities

Once the costs and risks of concern to the customer have been identified, managers can single out attributes such as reliability, availability, and dependability, and measure these in such terms as failure frequency, mean time between failures, downtime per failure, and the like.

While conceptually straightforward, translation of expectations into measurable terms is complicated by the fact that many customer expectations regarding support are nonlinear, support effectiveness is measured by many different variables, and statistical averages are misleading.

Nonlinear Expectations.   By and large, we are conditioned to think linearly: if one hour of downtime is bad, two hours are twice as bad. Unfortunately, customer expectations regarding support do not follow this simple logic. Instead, a threshold can be established for each expectation.

During the harvest season, for instance, farmers are extremely sensitive to the length of time a piece of farm equipment is out of commission because of a failure. Their reactions to downtimes lasting a half-day versus a day or more are vastly different. A downtime failure of a combine that can be repaired in four hours or less is tolerable; in fact, it often provides a welcome respite from harvesting. As the length of downtime increases past four to six hours, however, farmers become concerned, and by eight hours or so, they may be frantic. Beyond eight hours, the actual period of downtime is immaterial; farmers will go to almost any lengths to get up and running again—even if it means purchasing a new or used combine.

Farmers appear to have a similar threshold regarding the frequency with which a combine fails. Naturally, they hope it never fails; but, being realists, they're willing to accept an average of one or two failures per season.

Farmers' tolerance of failure decreases very rapidly beyond this point, however, so that a combine design averaging three or four failures per season acquires a poor reputation. This attitude appears to be independent of the downtime duration at each failure; the number of failures is what the farmers remember, not how quickly the repairs were made.

Not all support expectations have clear thresholds. For instance, customers expect gradual improvements in the operational availability of a product or service (i.e., in its effective use during a given period). Since expected life-cycle costs—the purchase costs combined with discounted maintenance and repair costs less discounted salvage value, if any—vary in a smooth progression, expectations about these are predictable and linear. Customer reactions (to operational availability, life-cycle costs, and so on) are proportional to the value of the support variable.

Support Effectiveness.   Only in the case of low-cost household appliances like toasters or alarm clocks does a single variable such as reliability adequately measure support effectiveness. The farmer measures the support provided to his combine or tractor in terms of at least two variables—failure frequency and downtime per failure. The sophisticated purchaser of electronic office equipment weighs the support packages available as well as the training and programming assistance provided.

Moreover, customer preferences are often noncompensatory. Customers rank-order their preferences and do not consider an excess of one type of support as a substitute for deficiencies in another. A contractor buying a bulldozer, for example, wants both high reliability and low downtime per failure. There will be dissatisfaction with any equipment that causes excessive downtime per failure, no matter how infrequently the failure occurs. Similarly, the office equipment buyer wants rapid response, irrespective of how infrequently it may be needed. For both, the risks and requirements of downtime are too high.

Statistical Averages.   One customer may get a dreamboat; another a lemon or a succession of lemons. Parts can be obtained over the counter—right away or ten days later. To cope with random fluctuations, people tend to use the average or the mean: the average weekly sales, the average wage rate, the average time between failures, and so forth.

In our investigations, we found ample evidence that averages are not only misleading but potentially dangerous when measuring support effectiveness. An industrial equipment company, for example, prided itself on the apparently high reliability of its product. Engineering tests indicated that the mean time between failures for its major product line was 400 hours. Since the average annual usage was 600 hours, management felt satisfied; after all, the machine experienced between one and two failures per year.

On conducting a survey of users, however, the company received a rude shock. True enough, the average number of failures was 1.65 per year.

But, more than 40% of the users reported more than two failures a year; and of those, 20% had four or more failures. As the sales vice president put it, "If that's true, over 40% of our customers are not happy with our performance!"

This situation is also true of other support measures such as downtime per failure. These measures tend to be distributed in a skewed fashion, with a significant proportion of them lying well above the mean. For this reason, the mean is an extremely misleading measure. A more appropriate measure is a percentile, such as 80th or 90th percentile of the variable in question. This measure would have shown the industrial equipment company that a large proportion of their users were in fact experiencing more than two failures a year. Similarly, the office equipment company that assured purchasers, "We can usually have a service person out to your location within four to six hours" would have found that response time in the 80th percentile was closer to two working days.

Choosing an Alternative

Having defined customer needs, the company can set about designing suitable support strategies. Normally, the manager can use one of several alternative support approaches. Each meets certain customer needs, such as greater reliability, shorter downtime per failure, or lower repair costs. At the same time, each affects the manufacturer's costs or revenues by creating higher product costs, increasing support costs, or lowering revenues. Choosing an alternative involves a trade-off between the effectiveness in meeting customer needs and impact on costs.

Such trade-offs are complex; neither effectiveness nor cost can be judged in terms of a single variable. Since support strategies meet diverse customer needs and affect the manufacturer's costs in various areas, trade-offs have to be made along several dimensions of effectiveness and cost.

Two additional factors further complicate the process of choosing a support strategy—the limitations of individual strategies and the interactions among strategies.

Limitations of Strategies

The building blocks of any support package are the individual strategies designed to improve reliability, make the design modular, provide equipment on loan, and add diagnostic capabilities. Exhibit 1 lists some typical strategies, together with suppliers' costs and customers' benefits. While the impact of each varies with the technology and the industry, we have observed that all strategies exhibit diminishing returns to the customer, increasing costs to the supplier, and limited areas of impact.

Diminishing Returns. Every support strategy produces diminishing returns with respect to customer benefits; beyond a certain point, further improvements are increasingly ineffective. For example, reliability improvements

Exhibit 1. Support Strategies: Costs and Benefits

Support Strategy	Suppliers' Costs	Customers' Benefits
Improve product	Design, engineering, and manufacturing	Lower rate of failure
Use modular designs, component exchange	Design, engineering, and inventory holding	Less downtime per failure, greater availability
Locate service facilities near markets	Site and facility; transportation and inventory	Faster access, less downtime, greater parts availability
Provide diagnostic equipment	Design, manufacturing, and service training	Faster diagnosis, less downtime, greater parts availability
Provide equipment on loan/standbys	Holding equipment for loan	Less downtime
Offer longer warranty periods and wider coverage	Warranty reserves and repair	Less uncertainty
Use mobile repair units	Transportation, inventory, and personnel	Faster response, improved service availability

that extend the mean time between failures increase the availability of equipment to the customer, but the rate of increase slows down past a saturation point. Customers recognize this phenomenon, and once this point has been reached their focus shifts to other concerns, such as repair time.

Increasing Costs.   The initial improvements in any strategy are the simplest and therefore the cheapest. Succeeding improvements are progressively more expensive. It will cost the manufacturer more to raise the mean time between failure from 100 to 150 hours, for instance, than it did to raise it from 50 to 100 hours.

Limited Impact.   Each of the strategies shown in Exhibit 1 affects only part of the failure and restoration cycle. Diagnostics reduce the time required to locate the failure but do not affect repair time. Providing equipment on loan lowers the variable costs of a failure but does not alter the fixed costs.

Interactions of Strategies

The foregoing limitations require the use of a suitable combination of individual strategies to meet customer needs. In synthesizing an overall strategy, a manager must know how individual strategies interact to ensure that the proposed combination achieves desired levels of customer benefits while keeping supplier costs as low as possible. Specifically, the manager needs to be aware of how strategy interactions can raise or lower overall costs to the supplier, complement benefits, and cause benefits substitution.

Cost Adjustment.   The way in which separate strategies interact affects the overall cost. For example, increasing reliability will lower the cost of supplying equipment on loan. It may, however, raise the cost of warranty repairs because it requires more expensive components.

Benefits Complementarity.   Certain combinations tend to reinforce the benefits of individual strategies. For instance, diagnostics are more effective with modular designs, which, in turn, are more effective when used in conjunction with on-site repair.

Benefits Substitution.   One strategy may serve as a substitute for another in terms of customer benefits. For example, speed of repair is less important when equipment loans are made available; therefore, both diagnostics and to a lesser degree modular design are substitutes for equipment on loan. Modular design reduces the need for large field inventories of spare parts; thus, these two strategies are to a certain extent substitutes for each other.

Developing a Structured Process

The need to use several measures of cost and effectivess and the limitations and interactions of individual strategies make a structured process for choosing support strategy essential. In its absence, a manager may not realize that existing strategies cost more and are less effective than alternatives, may yield to the pressures of individual departments and choose a suboptimal strategy, or may fail to make the decisions needed to stay competitive.

   While situations vary, in general a manager should:

1 *Define suitable measures of cost.*   Life-cycle costs are often appropriate; other measures can also be used.
2 *Categorize all feasible support alternatives.*   Alternatives involv-

ing major design changes should not be excluded as they could be essential to improving support effectiveness.

3 *Develop techniques to evaluate the cost and effectiveness of alternative strategies.* Computer simulation, use of mathematical modeling, or field trials may be useful.

4 *Measure the cost and effectiveness of each alternative.* As measurements will be imprecise, it is necessary to show ranges and estimates of error.

5 *Choose one measure of cost and another of effectiveness and plot the results.* The most important or significant measures should be analyzed in this step; other measures will be checked later.

6 *Identify key strategies.* Some strategies will stand out as superior in cost and effectiveness.

7 *Repeat trade-off analysis using other measures.* Determining if different measures change key strategies is a valuable check.

This process can narrow the options to two or three major choices. The final decision will depend on external factors such as management's preferences, the competitive situation, or other marketing or product concerns.

What to Focus On

Support strategies are not static; a strategy that is effective today will, if unchangeable, become ineffective in meeting future customer needs. Generally, customer satisfaction increases with improvements in one area (e.g., reliability) up to a point. As diminishing returns to the customer set in and the manufacturer's costs increase, companies will need to switch to another, often radically different strategy, like lending equipment. And when customers demand higher levels of satisfaction than can be economically provided with loaners, the company has to switch to still another approach, like improving access to components that fail and thereby reducing repair time.

This pattern appears to be characteristic of product support systems in general. A different, dominant strategy provides the most customer satisfaction at successive stages, and the level of customer satisfaction increases progressively. Each rise in the level of satisfaction raises the manufacturer's costs and accentuates the need for choosing another, more efficient support strategy.

To ensure that their products remain competitive, managers must identify the various stages that exist for their products and market segments. Having chosen a support strategy, they must ascertain their company's and competitors' relative positions, anticipate when customer needs or competitive pressures will require the company to shift to the next stage, and plan for shifts in support strategy.

A manufacturer's relative market position often determines support strategy. If customers and competitors perceive the company as a leader in identifying and meeting support needs, management can set the pace at which support effectiveness is improved. On the other hand, a company that is perceived as an "also ran" has to follow and, if possible, anticipate changes in the strategies of any leaders or in customer expectations.

Since shifting to a new stage raises the level of effectiveness considerably, companies that are slow to react to changes in customer needs and/or the level of support provided by competitors risk being frozen out. Improvements in the level of support given in other industries, raising customers' expectations across the board; pressure on competitors to maintain or increase market share; and introduction of new support techniques—any or all of these could signal the need for a shift. Managers also need to plan for such shifts to ensure that existing support strategies don't box them in.

Designing Support: A Case Study

An industrial equipment manufacturer started to design a new series of industrial tractors to replace its current models in the mid- to late-1980s. The company was aware of customer dissatisfaction regarding existing levels of support, which it had made several efforts to improve. Realizing the value of designing support and product strategies in parallel and recognizing that responsibility for support was fragmented, management appointed a study team reporting to the president. The team's charter was to develop strategies that would profitably deliver superior support for the new series of industrial tractors.

Existing marketing data indicated a number of diverse customer needs regarding product support. Although it identified individual support elements such as greater parts availability, higher reliability, and more service training, the data gave little insight as to how customers measured overall support effectiveness or made purchase decisions.

To determine failure frequency, causes of failure, downtime per failure, and the components of downtime, the study team mailed a survey to the entire user population and received more tham 3,000 responses. In addition, the team used a combination of focus groups and in-field interviews to determine customer preferences and develop measures of support effectiveness.

The team's investigations showed that customers focused on two key factors: the downtime caused by an individual tractor failure and a combination of how often their tractors failed, how much total downtime these failures caused, and the level of regular maintenance required.

The relative importance of these factors in purchase decisions varied. For one customer group, downtime per failure made the greatest impact on purchase decisions, while a second group weighed other factors as well. This suggested the existence of two separate support segments. The team decided to use the following measures of support effectiveness for both segments: the 85th percentile of downtime per failure (i.e., no more than

15% of the failures exceed this level of downtime), and the annual operational availability or ratio of uptime to the sum of uptime, downtime, and maintenance time.

The team felt that the operational availability ratio best captured the effects of improvements in engineering reliability. It also smoothed out random fluctuations in parts availability and showed the impact of improvements and maintainability and serviceability.

When the team analyzed the causes of downtime, it found that parts delay accounted for more than half the total downtime, with repair time taking up a third, and travel time the rest. This fact suggested some alternative strategies: increased dealer-level parts inventories, improved service training, and the use of mobile repair vans. Where downtime was critical, equipment on loan would be furnished, if economical.

When the team analyzed the causes of failures, it discovered that a large number were breakdowns in electrical and hydraulic components. Individually, these failures were easy to repair; their cumulative effect was, however, large. Engine and power-train failures did not have the same impact because, while each failure caused considerable downtime, such failures occurred infrequently. These facts suggested some additional strategies: improved reliability (especially of electrical and hydraulic components) and tractor design to permit modular exchange of defective components in the field.

After identifying all feasible alternatives, summarized in Exhibit 2, the team developed a computer-based simulator, which duplicated as far as

Exhibit 2. Alternative Support Strategies for an Industrial Tractor

Key	Strategy
A	Improve fill rate for parts from 91% to 95%
B	Improve mean time between failures from 350 to 450 hours
C	Develop and install microprocessor-based diagnostic capability in each tractor
D	Provide faster parts service using parts vans
E	Redesign tractor to permit faster modular exchange of electrical and hydraulic components
F	Provide users with tractors on loan during serious failures
G	Redesign tractor for modular exchange of electrical, hydraulic, and engine-driven train components
H	Redesign tractor as in strategy E and provide loaners
I	Redesign tractor as in strategy G and provide loaners
J	Redesign tractor as in strategy C; provide loaners and built-in diagnostics

possible the effects of using a given strategy or combination of strategies in terms of downtime and operational availability. Finally, the team calculated the costs of the various alternatives, using a life-cycle cost model.

Key Trade-Offs

To identify the optimal choices, the team then plotted the costs and effectiveness of the various strategies. Exhibit 3 shows a typical plot. Overall, effectiveness improved substantially (for example, the 85th percentile of downtime was reduced from 45 hours to 10 hours or less. However, support costs increased at least fourfold too). In addition, the analysis showed that:

☐ While parts delay was a significant factor in total downtime, improving parts availability had little impact. This was because most repairs required several parts, and absence of even one part caused at least a one-day delay because of shipping time.

☐ Built-in diagnostics had little impact; in most cases, diagnostic time wasn't important.

☐ Equipment on loan was not economic until overall reliability had reached approximately 400 hours between failures.

☐ Equipment loans and modular exchange were complementary. Loaners reduced customer downtime while modular exchange reduced the number of loaners by allowing rapid in-field repairs.

As shown in Exhibit 3, there were basically three stages—from 50 hours of downtime to 30 hours, from 30 hours to 20 hours, and from 20 hours to 10 hours. In each stage, the most efficient strategy was quite different. In Stage 1, improving reliability was the best strategy. In Stage II, providing loaners was the most efficient, while in Stage III, a combination of modular exchange and loaners was most efficient.

Management's Choices

After reviewing the team's analysis, management decided that under current market conditions, supplying loaners (Strategy F in Exhibit 2) was the most cost-effective. However, loaners would not provide long-term advantages because competitors could easily do the same. Therefore, the company decided to make major changes in its design philosophy and to aim for greater modularization of critical components. A combination of modular exchange and loaners would provide superior support at least cost, while the long lead times required for design changes would ensure long-term competitive advantage. Management therefore decided to proceed as follows:

1 Improve the reliability of its existing design to allow use of equipment on loan.

2 Introduce equipment on loan (Strategy F) in the mid-1980s, or earlier if competitive pressures demanded it.

Exhibit 3. Trade-Off Analysis Plot of Support Strategies

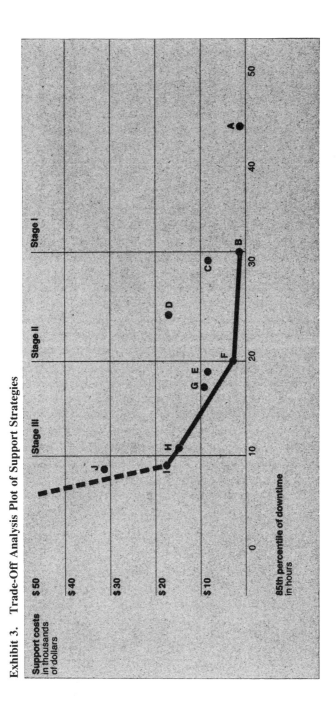

    3 Change its design approach to allow progressive modularization of
        key components.

    4 Switch over to a combination of modular exchange and loans (Strat-
        egies H and I) in the late 1980s.

The industrial equipment manufacturer needed three to five years to
change its design and to modularize its components. Had the company concentrated on improving reliability of its existing product, it would have found
itself locked in and unable to change without incurring large engineering and
tooling costs as well as a premature phase-out of its current designs.

Notes

1. Thomas J. Peters and Robert H. Waterman, Jr., *In Search of Excellence: Lessons from America's Best-Run Companies* (New York: Harper & Row, 1982), and "How Deere Outclasses the Competition," *Forbes*, January 21, 1980, p. 79.

28

Manage Risk In Industrial Pricing

BARBARA BUND JACKSON

In 1974, the world market price of copper reached $1.52 a pound. Soon afterward, the price fell sharply to below 60 cents a pound, and it remained depressed at about that price until early 1978. But one year later copper was up to 95 cents a pound and heading higher. Obviously, such major fluctuations and uncertainties in the prices of metals and other commodities used in manufacturing processes make risk management an important dimension in industrial pricing. This article presents a structured framework for analyzing and evaluating prices in the face of cost uncertainties and for considering and assigning risk in product pricing.

Unpredictable, frequent, or large fluctuations in the prices of commodities—gold, silver, lead, copper, sugar, and so on—pose special problems for companies that use these materials in their production processes. For example, the once-stable price of powder from the metal tantalum rose 300% between mid-1978 and mid-1979. Such fluctuations make cost prediction and management difficult for producers and, as a result, raise pricing problems. Should managers, in facing these decisions:

☐ Hedge by buying futures on commodity exchanges?

☐ Include escalators or de-escalators in their price quotes? If so, how and when should these be calculated?

☐ Publish price lists or just quote on individual orders?

☐ Change their published prices as costs change?

☐ Be willing to write fixed-price contracts for specific time periods?

☐ Set prices to reflect anticipated cost changes or only to mirror past cost changes?

Published 1980.

☐   Invest R&D effort to make more efficient use of commodities?

☐   Invest to find substitutes for the troublesome commodities?

☐   Examine how competitors responded to these problems in the past and how they are likely to respond in the future?

☐   Study what changes are occurring in the circumstances and needs of customers and how those changes might affect pricing choices?

Industrial marketers have a wide variety of answers, reflecting industry traditions, competitive conditions, and changing circumstances. Different industries are coping in different ways; different companies within the same industry have chosen diverse methods.

The fluctuations in commodity prices have increased so much over the past decade that many managers feel they are facing a new type of problem: the experience of managing prices in more stable times does not seem directly applicable to today's situation. And, while many managers have made very sensible responses to these uncertainties, they often feel that they lack a structured framework for informed decision making in dealing with price changes of their raw materials.

This article suggests such an analytic framework in the face of major fluctuations in commodity prices and recognizes that increased uncertainties in costs increase the risks in industrial pricing. The uncertainties make it important for marketers to evaluate regularly and systematically the pricing questions just listed. (Later on in the article, I will use this framework for risk management to show how to address these pricing questions.)

As used here, *risk* means both uncertainty and the results of uncertainty. The term reflects a lack of predictability of results, not the attractiveness or unattractiveness of those results. Thus managers often consider completely predictable cost increases unattractive and predictable cost decreases desirable, but I would call neither "risky."

Risk has negative connotations for many people. It may seem strange to refer to uncertainties about attractive outcomes as risks. But the uncertainty is partly separable from the outcome because, even if the possible outcome is attractive, the uncertainty is often unattractive. If we knew the outcome for sure, we could better plan for it; uncertainty inhibits precise planning, which is important in pricing.

The structured framework presented here allows us to consider differential attitudes toward risk. It assumes, however, that (everything else being equal) we would always rather face less uncertainty.

Risk in Industrial Pricing

To discuss the effects of risk associated with future prices of commodities, I will use a scheme that Benson P. Shapiro and I described in an earlier

HBR article, which outlines a customer-based approach to pricing.[1] We suggested a conceptual formula for analyzing customers' perceptions of benefits and costs: *benefits* minus *costs other than price* equals *highest price the customer will pay*.

In this scheme, benefits and costs are determined within the customer's total usage system. Benefits include the performance of the physical product, the delivery and service provided by the vendor, and the reliability of the product. The importance of each source of benefit depends on the customer's usage system. If a machine is central to one customer's operation, that customer will value reliability of the equipment very highly. If a customer needs corrugated shipping boxes but has very limited storage space, that customer will value prompt and frequent delivery.

Similarly, the costs-other-than-price part of the equation is based on the customer's usage system. Operating costs, maintenance, and risks of failure in use are examples of these costs. Different customers will emphasize different costs. Schematically, Exhibit 1 shows the highest price determined from benefits and nonprice costs. The total in the left-hand column must equal the total in the right-hand column—that is, the highest price can be found by subtracting the costs other than price from the benefits.

Uncertainties in price can be incorporated into this framework. If we assume that risk is undesirable, we can show a decrease in risk by either increasing benefits or decreasing costs other than price. Exhibit 2 shows an increase in customer benefits when prices are made less uncertain (by a long-term fixed-price contract or by any of the other mechanisms described later in this article). Because total customer benefits are higher after risk reduction, with no change in other costs the customer is willing to pay a somewhat higher price.

Similarly, Exhibit 3 shows the reverse situation. The assumption is that originally the customer was quoted fixed prices but now faces increased uncertainty in prices—perhaps through an escalator clause based on the cost of a key raw material in the product. This exhibit depicts the increase in uncertainty as an increase in costs other than price. (Alternatively, it could show a decrease in benefits.) The difference between benefits and costs other than price has decreased, and the highest price the customer is willing to pay for the product is lower.

Thus the amount of risk placed on the customer becomes just one more dimension of product planning and pricing in the industrial marketplace. As such, the question of risk can be analyzed in much the same way as other pricing and product policy decisions. In deciding what features to build into a product, marketers consider the value to the customer compared with the cost of incorporating the features into their products. Similarly, in deciding how to manage risk in industrial pricing, they consider the effects of the risk on themselves and their customers and then decide who should bear how much risk.

Exhibit 1. Industrial Pricing Framework

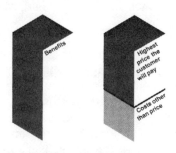

**Exhibit 2. Industrial Pricing Framework
After Price Uncertainty Is Reduced**

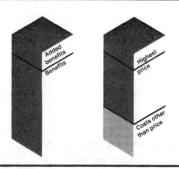

**Exhibit 3. Industrial Pricing Framework
After Risk Is Increased**

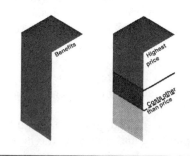

Concept of Risk Management

A simplified industrial marketing chain includes three parts: the commodity producer-seller, the manufacturer who uses the commodity in producing a product, and the purchaser of that product. There can, of course, be other intermediaries in the marketing chain.

Uncertainties in commodity cost are not the only risks in the marketing chain. The possibility of interrupted supplies also raises problems. And there are many other business risks (relating to levels of demand, performance of equipment, quality of raw materials, and numerous other factors) that managers face all the time. But this discussion focuses on risks associated with price changes of raw materials in industrial marketing situations, although managers can apply many of the ideas when the chain is extended to an end consumer.

The basic idea of risk management in pricing is that different stages in the marketing chain can bear the risks of major price fluctuations. Creative risk management first requires that marketing managers determine the degree of risk in each part of the chain and assess the ability and willingness of each chain member to take risks. Next, managers must select mechanisms from two main categories for assigning and managing risk: (1) devices that allow *avoidance* of risk by reducing the total risk in the chain and (2) devices that involve *assignment* of risk to the members of the chain (according to their abilities and willingness to bear risk). Often assignment involves sharing the uncertainty.

Let us consider the management of risk in the manufacturer and purchaser portions of the chain. The commodity producer-seller is treated as the source of uncertainty. This situation raises several basic questions:

- [ ] How much total risk should the manufacturer and purchaser bear?
- [ ] How should any costs of risk reduction be assigned?
- [ ] How should that risk be allocated between them?

Before discussing the specific mechanisms for either avoiding or assigning risk, we must first consider the basis of risk management.

Why Risk Management Makes Sense

Most people in most situations are risk averse. Nevertheless, they regularly bear risks because the potential outcomes of risk-involving activities are attractive. (People go into business because success and profits—not business risks per se—are attractive.) In fact, we are often willing to pay a premium to avoid risk. It is this willingness to pay risk premiums that encourages creative risk management in industrial pricing.

For example, suppose that you are a division manager who has accepted a particular contract. For simplicity, suppose that you believe you will earn either $0 or $10,000 from that contract, the two outcomes being equally likely. Suppose that another company offers to take the contract off your hands. How much would you risk? For many people, the answer would be $5,000, the expected return from the contract. (The expected return is found by averaging the possible outcomes, using probabilities for weights. Here the outcomes of $0 and $10,000 each have a probability of ½. The expected return is $5,000 = ($0)/2 + ($10,000)/2.)

Now suppose instead that your division has a very substantial contract on which you expect to earn either $0 or $10 million, and you again think each outcome is equally likely. How much would you require in return for that contract, with all of its costs and revenues? Would you hold out for $5 million, the expected value? Many managers would not; they would be willing to take a bit less.

For example, you might settle for $3.5 million, arguing that you would accept less than the expected value in exchange for avoiding the possibility of winding up with $0. If so, you would be called *risk averse*. The difference between the expected value ($5 million) and the amount you would accept ($3.5 million) is called your *risk premium*. It is the amount you are willing to give up in exchange for avoiding the uncertainty or risk of a specific situation.

As this simplified example suggests, individuals and corporations generally will pay larger premiums to avoid larger risks. On the other hand, they will generally require larger premiums to induce them to bear larger risks.

The term *larger* here is relative. A risk that is small for a large, diversified manufacturer may seem large to a small customer. In that case, the manufacturer might be much less reluctant than the customer to bear the risk.

Such common properties of individuals' attitudes toward risk form the basis for risk sharing. If we break a specific risk into pieces, with a number of people or organizations bearing parts of the risk, the total of any risk premiums demanded by those people or organizations will often be considerably less than the risk premium needed to convince an individual to bear the total risk. Syndicates formed to undertake risky ventures (such as exploring for oil or marketing an issue of bonds) are based on this concept. In industrial pricing, the concept suggests that manufacturer and purchaser each bear a part of the risk. Escalator and de-escalator clauses that pass part but not all of the risk to the purchaser are among the mechanisms for this purpose.

(The accompanying Appendix describes preference theory, a formalism for expressing and analyzing individuals' attitudes toward risk.)

The differences in risk attitudes of different individuals suggest a related principle for risk sharing. Total risk premiums can be reduced if more risk is assigned to those who are less averse to bearing risk. Negotiation in an industrial purchasing situation can result in risk sharing between buyer and seller, with both better off than if either bore the total risk.

A related concept in evaluating a particular risk is to consider the other risks borne by individuals and companies. The uncertainty to a manufacturer of lead acid batteries caused by changes in the cost of lead to fill one particular contract may be quite small on the scale of the manufacturer's uncertainty about total earnings. Unfortunately for the manufacturer, however, the risk on one contract is closely tied to the risks on all the other battery contracts, each involving fluctuations in lead prices. If lead prices are higher than expected, the total adverse effect on the manufacturer, considering all the contracts, will be great. Then again, lower prices than expected will have a large, favorable effect.

For the purchaser of batteries in one contract, lead risk is not likely to be important. In other words, this risk will probably not be tied to other risks borne by the purchaser. As a result, it is sensible for many battery customers to share the risks rather than for the manufacturer to bear the total risk. In fact, recent instability in prices of lead has caused several battery manufacturers to include this type of sharing (in automatic pass-through clauses) in their contracts.

Avoidance of Risk

Manufacturers have tried several methods of avoiding risk in raw materials price fluctuations. The most common ways include hedging, fixed-price contracts from suppliers, technological advancements, commodity substitution, and shortening the time during which price volatility can occur.

Hedging Contracts

When manufacturers buy futures on commodity exchanges, they reduce the uncertainty in the marketing chain through hedging. A manufacturer of corn syrup might buy corn futures and thereby achieve a firm price for corn. Exhibit 4 shows this situation schematically. Arrows indicate the movement of corn and corn products through the chain. Wide arrows represent more and thin arrows less risk. Over the long run, the manufacturer often expects to pay more for corn with hedging because of the costs of hedging contracts. For the period of those contracts, the company's corn cost is locked in and risk is eliminated. Thus the company pays the hedging costs for (a) the certainty of knowing what corn costs will be and (b) the resulting improvement in its ability to quote firm prices to its customers for finished products to be delivered in the future. In a sense, hedging is like buying insurance.

In terms of industrial pricing, we can think of the corn syrup manufacturer as the purchaser of corn. With hedging the manufacturer's benefits rise but, at the same time, overall costs increase. Hedging is a sensible choice for the company if the rise in benefits is larger than the rise in costs caused by the hedging contracts.

The cost of reducing uncertainty is shared if part of the higher cost is

Exhibit 4.   Hedging Costs Shared by Seller and Buyer

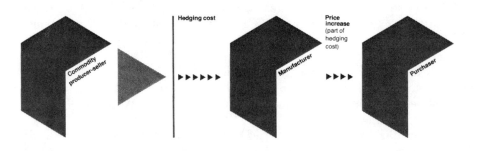

Exhibit 5.   Risk Avoidance Through Advanced Technology

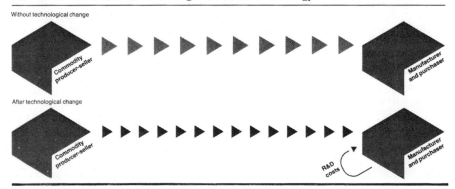

passed on to the customer (Exhibit 4). If hedging by the manufacturer results in more settled prices for the purchaser, the purchaser's benefits will generally increase. Therefore, the customer should be willing to pay a somewhat higher price. The question of just how hedging costs should be allocated between the two is part of the risk-assignment issue that we shall look at later.

Other Methods

When hedging is either unavailable or inappropriate, managers can use other methods to avoid risk. In obtaining fixed-price contracts from their suppliers, manufacturers reduce uncertainty in the marketing chain. Such contracts were common in the past for metal commodities like tantalum but are now becoming rare. Thus manufacturers and purchasers of electrical capacitors made with tantalum today face greater uncertainty than they did in times of relatively stable prices.

Technology can also be used to avoid risk. One company reduced its requirement for tantalum to produce capacitors by applying advanced technology and a higher-than-usual grade of the metal to reduce total use.

Exhibit 5 shows the situation schematically. Without technological change the risk would be higher. Hence the large arrows. After technological change, which cut the amount of tantalum needed, the risk is smaller because the usage is lower. Hence the smaller arrows. The R&D cost is shown in the bottom figure as a separate arrow.

The cost of the R&D effort that reduced the usage was shared between manufacturer and customer. After technological change in this case, part of the risk was avoided. And because there was enough reduction in risk, total manufacturer and purchaser benefits increased more than enough to cover the R&D costs.

In other cases, R&D might find substitute commodities with less volatile prices or might provide flexibility to allow shifts into or out of alternate materials, depending on their prices. After the steep rise in the price of sugar in 1974, a major industrial user of sugar acquired a producer of high fructose corn syrup. It also accelerated development of recipes with alternative sweetener systems for its products so that recipes could be changed in response to the relative price changes of sweeteners.

Risk can also be reduced by shortening the time during which fluctuations can occur. A large food processor required that price quotes be received from bidding manufacturers of corrugated boxes three or four months before the start of a contract period. To protect themselves against possible price rises during that interval, the sellers added safety margins to their bids. By developing a computer program to speed up the evaluation of bids, the purchaser was able to delay the due date for quotes and thus reduce the hedging premium added by the bidding manufacturers.

In all of these cases, risk reduction increases benefits to the manufacturer, the purchaser, or both. The increase in benefits makes one or both parties willing to pay more for the products they buy.

Assignment of Risk

In the assignment of risk between manufacturer and purchaser, pass-through mechanisms transfer the risk to the purchaser. Escalation and de-escalation clauses in contracts or "adders" (surcharges) to published list prices serve this purpose. An example is the use of an adder or factor for the price of zinc in determining prices of zinc-coated (galvanized) steel products. This situation is illustrated in Exhibit 6. The large arrows show how the adder shifts the risk to the purchaser. The small arrows indicate the flow of physical metal separate from the flow of risk.

This situation corresponds to the pricing diagram seen earlier in Exhibit 3. The purchaser's nonprice costs increase with the increase in risk and,

Exhibit 6.   Risk Transferred from Seller to Buyer

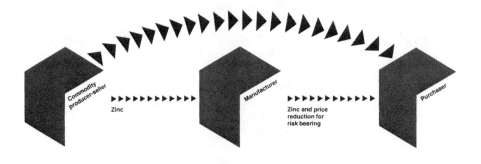

Exhibit 7.   Risk not Transferred from Seller to Buyer

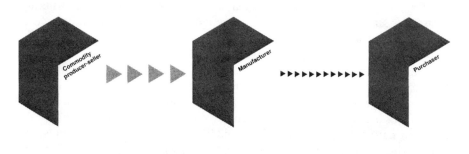

consequently, the purchaser will expect somewhat lower price levels than would be appropriate with less risk. By contrast, Exhibit 7 shows the situation in which the manufacturer absorbs the risk by quoting fixed prices and doing no hedging.

In practice, a variety of mechanisms exists between the extremes of these two situations. Historically, the situation in which the manufacturer absorbed the risk was the rule. Yet there have been exceptions—for example, the price of syrup for Coca-Cola has long been tied to sugar prices, and contracts for cable for residential power distribution have generally included adders for metal prices.

Today, however, the situation of transferring risk from manufacturer to purchaser is becoming far more common. Adders are used for gold, silver, platinum, lead, sugar, copper, and other commodities. In addition, managers use many types of formulas to share risk between buyer and seller.

These mechanisms for sharing risk make sense because of the common attitudes about large versus small risks. The principle can be demonstrated with two different pricing diagrams: one for the manufacturer acting as purchaser of the raw material, the other for the customer buying the manufactured product.

For example, suppose that the manufacturer and the purchaser of electromechanical relays must somehow share the risks caused by fluctuations in gold and silver prices. Exhibit 8 shows the viewpiont of the relay manufacturer acting as a metals purchaser. The metals risk increased the nonprice costs. The exact amount of this change depends on the manufacturer's specific attitude toward risk. Because the benefits column for the manufacturer has not changed, the total height of the costs column also remains unchanged. Therefore, the highest price the manufacturer will pay dcreases when the cost of risk bearing is added.

Similarly, Exhibit 9 reveals the viewpoint of the relay purchaser toward bearing none or all of the metals risk. The physical metal from the situation in Exhibit 8 is included in the relays purchased in Exhibit 9. The purchaser's nonprice costs increases substantially when the metals risk is included. Because the benefits to the purchaser don't change, the highest price decreases to offset the costs of risk bearing. (Note that the nonprice costs for risk

Exhibit 8. Manufacturer's Purchase of Metals

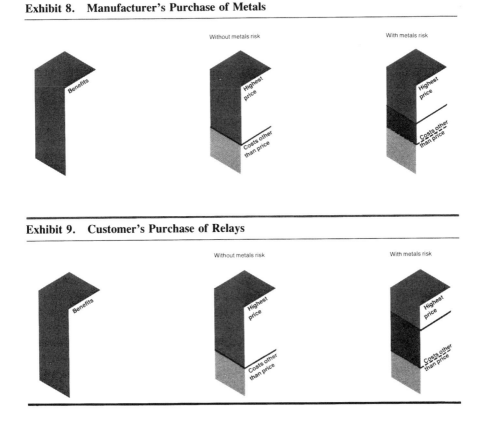

Exhibit 9. Customer's Purchase of Relays

bearing are higher for the purchaser than for the manufacturer; in this case, the purchaser is more risk averse.)

We can also consider a sharing of the metals risk. One possibility is for each party to bear half the risk. That situation is shown in Exhibit 10. Thus the nonprice costs for bearing the full risk for the manufacturer are more than twice those of bearing only half the risk. The same is true for the purchaser. These general relationships reflect the way most people view larger risks as considerably more painful than smaller risks. (The specific amounts of these costs of risk bearing would have to be found by questioning the manufacturer and purchaser.) The benefits to each party have not changed, so the highest prices are decreased to offset the cost increases. Because the cost increases are substantially smaller when the risk is shared, the decreases in highest price are also substantially smaller.

The total nonprice costs for risk bearing are lower than they would be if either the manufacturer or the purchaser bore the entire risk. The reduction will likely be shared between the two parties. For example, the relay price might be less than the full amount the purchaser is willing to pay, leaving the purchaser with an excess of benefits over costs. At the same time the price could more than compensate the manufacturer for bearing half the risk.

Exhibit 10.   Sharing of Risk Caused by Fluctuations in Commodity Prices

I. Manufacturer's purchase of metals

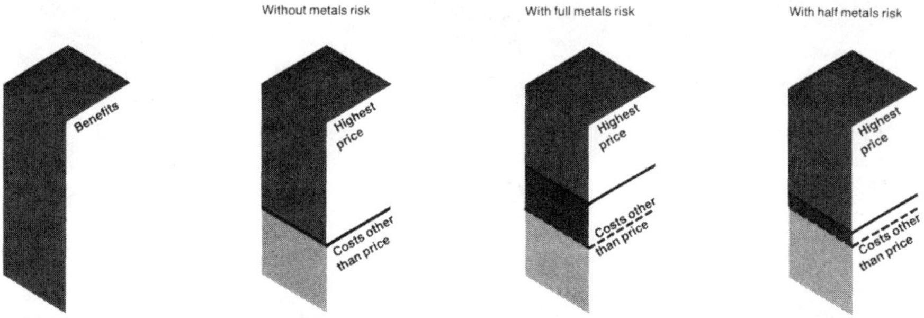

II. Customer's purchase of relays

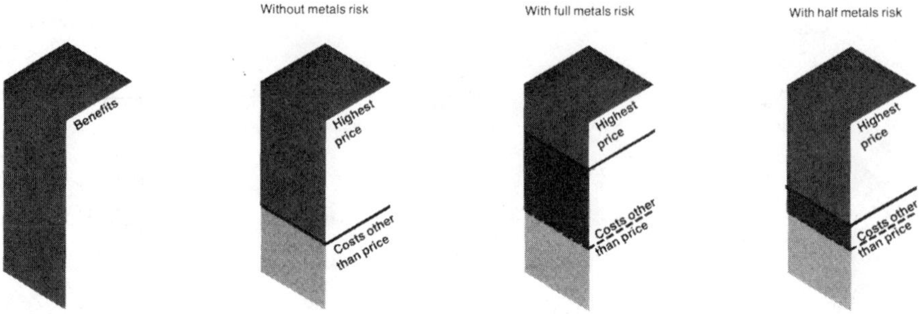

Importance of Timing

In many of these mechanisms for sharing risk, timing is important. Long-term contracts and infrequent price changes place most of the risk on the manufacturer. In contrast, even if announced price lists are used, a manufacturer can pass through much of the risk by changing the lists frequently. During the first 75 days of 1979, one producer of beryllium copper alloys raised prices five times and cut them once to reflect fluctuations in copper prices.

Shorter contract periods also result in more frequent price adjustments. With such mechanisms, the manufacturer bears the risk in between price changes, while the customer assumes the effects of commodity price changes each time the manufacturer changes prices to reflect changes in its costs.

Manufacturers sometimes avoid the position of constantly trying to catch up with ever-increasing costs by pricing in anticipation of future cost increases, not merely in reaction to past changes. In cases of rapidly increasing commodity prices, the financial impact of this choice can be considerable.

Even when escalators and de-escalators are used, timing is important. Managers must decide whether the price is determined at the time of ordering or on delivery of the end product. The difference can be substantial. For example, a product manager for one manufacturer of gold-plated sockets for integrated circuits estimated that calculating a gold adder at the time of product delivery would allow her to price 20% to 30% higher than had she figured the cost at the time of ordering.

Computer technology may be needed to allow some types of risk sharing. The marketing vice president of one electrical connector manufacturer has announced that his company will use a gold adder, figured at the time of delivery, as soon as the computer system needed to administer the addder is completed.

In another case (not involving a commodity), a major industrial insurer cut its underwriting losses by changing from three-year to one-year policies. It adjusted rates annually to reflect more recent experience in the costs of coverage. Technology in the form of computerized help in policy writing and servicing made the more frequent policies practical. On the other hand, insurance firms that have experimented with periods as short as 90 days for automobile insurance policies have found that administrative costs more than outweigh the benefits of frequent price adjustments.

Options for Handling Risk

A seller may offer different risk assignment options to different customers. Manufacturers of underground electrical cable typically include escalator and de-escalator clauses in their contracts with utilities. But in contracts with municipalities, they must quote fixed prices. The fixed prices, therefore, include cushions for changes in metal prices, thus compensating the manufacturers for risk bearing.

Within the same industry, different companies may choose varying mechanisms for handling risk. Fluctuations in the price of gold create risks for sellers and buyers of the sockets that hold integrated circuits. One manufacturer is using tin-alloy plating to replace gold plating, thus dealing with risk by means of substitution.

Another manufacturer has developed a way of placing gold more precisely on the crucial connection point; the new process eliminates the previous practice of spreading the gold more widely to ensure adequate coverage. This manufacturer, which emphasizes the new technology in its advertising, has dealt with risk by means of technology.

Other competitors have instigated price adders to reflect gold costs. Still others have retained fixed-price lists but allow for more frequent revisions. These companies have dealt with the risk problem by means of allocation or assignment.

How a manufacturer chooses to handle the risks of commodity price fluctuations may change as the fluctuations vary in size or in frequency. In any case, good decisions on risk require consideration of:

☐ The attitudes of buyers and sellers toward risk.

☐ The opportunities that exist for risk avoidance and the cost of using those opportunities.

☐ The opportunities for shifting or allocating all or part of the risk to others along the marketing chain.

☐ The methods used by competitors to handle risk problems.

Consider the following four examples for either avoiding or assigning risk in industrial pricing. Suppose that:

1. Your salespeople report that the divisional manager of a customer company is under increasing pressure to provide better forecasts of performance. (His past forecasts have been inaccurate.) In terms of risk, this piece of information says that your customer will likely show increased risk aversion and will be willing to pay somewhat increased premiums to avoid future uncertainty.

Therefore, this customer may find a fixed-price contract extending for a year very attractive, even if the price includes a premium to compensate your company for bearing additional risk. If you are more willing than the customer to bear risk, you may also find such an arrangement attractive.

2. Your manufacturing process uses copper, and you foresee increasing uncertainty in copper prices. Your competitor has the best engineering talent in the industry. The more uncertain the price of copper, the more your competitor is likely to try to engineer away part of the risk. Anticipating

such actions should give you a head start in responding to them. You may try in-house engineering, or you may adopt risk allocation mechanisms.

Alternatively, you may decide to compete in other dimensions and work hard to build your reputation for service so that you differentiate your company through service rather than price. It may then be acceptable for your company to be an imitator rather than an innovator in technological change.

3.   You manage a division of a large corporation with substantial financial resources. Your competitors are small companies with far less financial cushion. Prices for a major commodity input are increasingly uncertain, and your customers find the uncertainty burdensome.

Thus the ability to bear more risk than your competitors may be turned into a strong competitive advantage. If you can convince your corporate management that it should play the long-run averages and bear much of the risk in its marketing chain, you can offer your customers a distinctive pricing policy by offering firm prices (including premiums for risk bearing).

4.   You are a small company supplying a larger one. If uncertainties in the costs of your inputs are increasing, you may try in negotiations to convince the customer to bear most or all of the risk with a pass-through. You can reduce total risk premiums for the chain in this way and can offer the customer somewhat lower base prices in exchange for assuming more risk.

In considering these and similar options for avoidance and assignment of risk, the idea is simply to add the analysis of attitudes toward risk as one more active dimension in considering customer needs and competitor capabilities. Risk bearing also becomes another dimension for manufacturers to understand their own capacities. Just as managers regularly evaluate customer needs and competitive abilities in terms of product features, delivery, and service, they can evaluate others in terms of risk. And just as they evaluate possible changes in product or service offerings in terms of benefits and costs, they can evaluate possible methods of risk avoidance or risk assignment in terms of the costs of implementation and the benefits to the members of the marketing chain.

Analyzing the Pricing Questions

We can use the framework suggested here for managing risk in industrial pricing to analyze the pricing questions raised at the outset:

☐   Hedging makes sense if the hedging cost is lower than the premium the members of the chain would pay to avoid risk.

☐   Escalators and de-escalators transfer risk to the customer. These mechanisms make sense if the customer is less risk averse than the manufacturer with regard to that particular risk.

   ☐ Published prices generally increase price stability. Thus they transfer risk to the producer.

   ☐ Frequent price changes transfer more risk to the purchaser. Infrequent changes place more risk on the manufacturer.

   ☐ Longer-term contracts put more risk on the manufacturer.

   ☐ Setting prices to anticipate cost changes is one way for the manufacturer to cover part of the costs of risk bearing.

   ☐ R&D is potentially attractive if it is likely to cost less than it will save in the costs of risk bearing.

   ☐ Searching for substitutes can be considered a specific type of R&D.

   ☐ The pricing moves of competitors help determine the risk/price trade-offs available to the customer. These also help provide the environment in which the customer evaluates all benefits and costs.

   ☐ As circumstances change, the customer may become more or less risk averse. Accordingly, the manufacturer may want to price so that the customer bears less or more risk.

Managing risk in an industrial marketing chain is most difficult in times of change such as (1) when the level of risk increases, (2) when the attitude of the purchaser shifts for some reason, and (3) when a competitor uses technology to avoid part of a risk.

    Therefore, much of the value of these concepts will come through carefully tracking the environment for changes in levels of risk, in attitudes toward risk, and in potential methods for avoiding or assigning risk. Managers can monitor risk factors in their own companies, in their supplier or customer companies, in competitor companies, and in the environment at large. Doing so allows better planned responses to the problems of industrial pricing in the face of major fluctuations in commodity prices.

Notes

1. "Industrial Pricing to Meet Consumer Needs," HBR November-December 1978, p. 119.

Appendix

Attitudes Toward Risk Sharing

Preference curves provide a formal mechanism for expressing and analyzing attitudes toward risk sharing. *Table A*, an example of a preference curve, shows the criteria of net income along the horizontal axis and the preference values, between 0 and 1, along the vertical axis.

    Suppose that Manager Jones faces an uncertainty that will result in net income of either $120,000 or $170,000. Manager Jones believes there is a .6

Table A.   Manager Jones's Preference Curve

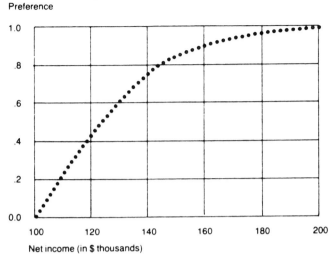

chance of a $120,000 outcome and a .4 chance of $170,000. The preference curve has been constructed so that it can be used to find what is called Jones's certainty equivalent. This quantity is the minimum certain amount Jones would accept in exchange for the uncertainty. In other words, Jones would accept the certainty equivalent and give up the outcome regardless of whether it was $120,000 or $170,000.

The procedure for finding the certainty equivalent is the following:

1. From the table we can find the *preference values* corresponding to the possible outcomes (the values are .46 for $120,000 and .94 for $170,000).

2. We can also find the *expected preference*, which is the average of the two preference values (.46 and .94) adjusted for the probabilities (.6 and .4) that they will occur. Thus .6(.46) + .4(.94) = .65.

3. Now we find the criterion (net income) corresponding to this expected preference of .65. This value is the *certainty equivalent*. For Jones, the certainty equivalent for this risk is $132,000. He would accept $132,000 for sure, instead of bearing the uncertainty of whether the gain will be $120,000 or $170,000.

It is also useful to calculate the *expected value* of the uncertainty. Expected value is defined as the weighted average of the criterion values themselves, with probabilities used as weights. The term represents the amount we would expect to receive, on average, if we faced many separate uncertainties just like the current situation. (In any single uncertainty, however, we will not receive exactly the expected value.)

Here the expected value is .6($120,000) + .4($170,000), or $140,000. In this case, Jones's certainty equivalent is less than the expected value by $8,000. This amount is his *risk premium*. Jones is said to be risk averse. He

416

MANAGE RISK IN INDUSTRIAL PRICING

is willing to pay a premium, compared with the expected value, to avoid uncertainty.*

Allocating Risk with Preference Curves. Assume now that Manager Jones's net income would be $150,000 except for the effect of one particular uncertainty. That uncertainty may raise income by $50,000 or lower it by $50,000; there is a .6 chance of increase and a .4 chance of decrease. The uncertainty is:

Net Income	Probability
$100,000	.4
$200,000	.6

Preference (from Exhibit 9)
0.0
1.0

The expected preference would then be: .6(1.0) + .4(0.0) = .6.

The certainty equivalent is the net income corresponding to preference value .6, or $129,000. Thus the expected income value would be: .6($200,000) + .4($100,000) = $160,000. The risk premium would then be $31,000 (the difference).

We can now consider risk sharing. Suppose that Jones faces the uncertainty cited with .6 and .4 as the probabilities in connection with a sale to customer, Entrepreneur Booth, whose preference curve is shown in Table B. That curve is not as pronounced and shows less risk aversion than Jones's. Suppose that Booth's net income will be $250,000 plus the effect of any of the uncertainty that she shares with Jones. Suppose also that Jones and Booth agree on the probabilities describing the uncertainty.

If Booth bears the entire uncertainty, she will face the following uncertain future:

Net Income	Probability
$200,000	.4
$300,000	.6
Preference	
0.0	
1.0	

The expected preference is .6. Her certainty equivalent is $240,000, and her risk premium is $260,000 − $240,000, or $20,000. Because this premium is

---

*For further discussion, including consideration of how to assess a preference curve, see John S. Hammond III, "Better Decisions with Preference Theory," *HBR* November-December 1967, p. 123.

Table B. Entrepreneur Booth's Preference Curve

Preference

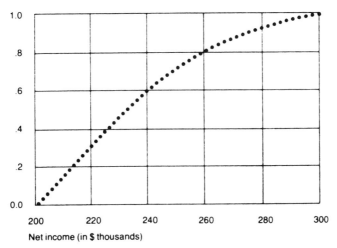

Net income (in $ thousands)

lower than Jones's, it makes sense for Booth to bear the risk in exchange for a payment from Jones. For example, he could pay her $24,000, which is more than her risk premium but less than his. Both parties benefit.

Even better options may exist. Suppose the buyer and seller split the risk evenly. Their uncertain futures, certainly equivalents, and risk premiums would then be found as follows:

Manager Jones

Net Income	Probability
$125,000	.4
$175,000	.6
Expected preference	.6(.95) + .4(.53) = .78
Certainty equivalent	$141,000
Expected net income	$155,000
Risk premium	$ 14,000

Entrepreneur Booth

Net income	Probability
$225,000	.4
$275,000	.6
.6(.9) + .4(.4) = .7	—
$250,000	—
$255,000	—
$ 5,000	—

This arrangement has reduced the total risk premium to $14,000 + $5,000, or $19,000.

We could consider other ways of dividing the risk between Manager Jones and Entrepreneur Booth, as the following results show:

Jones's Fraction of Risk	Booth's Fraction of Risk	Jones's Risk Premium	Booth's Risk Premium	Total Risk Premium
1.0	0.0	$31,000	$ 0	$31,000
¾	¼	21,500	500	22,000
½	½	14,000	5,000	19,000
⅜	⅝	7,250	8,250	15,500
¼	¾	4,500	11,000	15,500
⅛	⅞	2,250	15,750	18,000
0.0	1.0	0	20,000	20,000

It appears that a sharing with a fraction in the range of ¼ to ⅜ of the risk assigned to Jones is optimal, in the sense that it reduces the total risk premium. Booth bears more of the risk because she is less risk averse, but it is still in Jones's favor to bear some of that risk. To induce Booth to bear her part of the risk, Jones could offer her a premium—for example, he could pay her $15,000 to bear ¾ of this risk. Jones is then better off. He has paid $15,000 to reduce his risk premium from $31,000 to $4,500. Booth is also better off because she has received the $15,000 in return for assuming an uncertainty for which her premium is $11,000.

This formal search procedure is often not practical. It requires knowing the preference curves of both buyer and seller. In practice, it is hard enough to evaluate our own preferences and almost impossible to be really precise about those of our customers or competitors. In addition, the problem becomes considerably more difficult because an individual's attitude toward one risk generally depends on how much other risk he or she faces. In this example, we assumed away that "contextual uncertainty" by supposing that Jones and Booth both knew their incomes for the year with the exception of the single risk they were sharing. This asumption is, however, clearly unrealistic.

In some situations, we may want to guess at preference curves for our customers, suppliers, or competitors. We can perform analyses for several possible curves to explore customer, supplier, or competitor behavior. In most cases, managers would not formally assess preference curves but would nevertheless use concepts of risk aversion, risk premiums, and risk sharing to think sensibly about risk management.

PART FOUR

NEW APPROACHES FOR REACHING CUSTOMERS

AN OVERVIEW

Stiffening competition means that sellers must be constantly appraising alternative means for reaching potential buyers. Thanks to newly emerging communications techniques, marketers can choose from an expanding assortment of approaches for selling their products and services.

Benson P. Shapiro and John Wyman provide an overview in their article, "New Ways to Reach Your Customers," of the new tools—including national account management, demonstration centers, industrial stores, telemarketing, and catalog selling—which have replaced traditional selling approaches.

Thomas V. Bonoma suggests in his article, "Major Sales: Who *Really* Does the Buying," that when big-ticket items are being sold, reaching the true buyer can be as challenging as making the appropriate sales pitch. He provides suggestions for accomplishing both tasks.

Similarly, Mr. Bonoma points out in his article, "Get More Out of Your Trade Shows," that there's more than meets the eye in deciding whether or not to display and sell products at such shows. He argues that trade shows should become part of companies' overall marketing strategy and should be assessed with regard to selling and nonselling objectives.

The notion that purchases made via computers and cable television will replace those made at retail stores comes under close scrutiny in "Non-store Marketing: Fast Track or Slow?" by John A. Quelch and Hirotaka

Takeuchi. They conclude that the seeming inevitability of nonstore marketing may be misleading.

One newly emerging marketing tool that is proving itself effective in today's climate is described by John A. Quelch and Kristina Cannon-Bonventre in their article, "Better Marketing at the Point of Purchase." Such devices as store displays and promotions can provide consumer goods manufacturers with a competitive edge, the authors argue.

And an old tool that needs reexamination and rethinking is assessed by John A. Quelch in the article, "It's Time to Make Trade Promotion More Productive." Partly because it has been overused in recent years, trade promotion needs more effective management to once again become a cost-effective means of reaching customers, he argues.

Marketers of industrial products can similarly make more effective use of an old means of reaching customers, maintain James D. Hlavacek and Tommy J. McCuistion in their article, "Industrial Distributors—When, Who, and How?" The key is appropriate matching of products and distributors, they note.

Effectively communicating with customers is a task that all organizations, including nonprofits, must be attuned to, argues Alan R. Andreasen in "Nonprofits: Check Your Attention to Customers." That means adopting a customer orientation rather than a product orientation, he suggests.

Just because the marketing message reaches customers doesn't mean it works as intended, contends Rena Bartos in "Ads That Irritate May Erode Trust in Advertised Brands."

Malcolm A. McNiven suggests in his article, "Plan for More Productive Advertising," that marketers can assess the impact of their ad programs. He offers an approach that allocates advertising costs according to company goals and also helps managers decide which products to advertise through which media.

A final approach for reaching and keeping customers is offered by Robert E. Weigand in his article, " 'Buying In' to Market Control." He concludes that marketers of certain repeat-sales products can entice customers into long-term purchases by offering favorable initial terms.

29

New Ways to Reach Your Customers

BENSON P. SHAPIRO and JOHN WYMAN

Important methods that help marketers communicate more effectively with potential and existing customers have come into wider use over the past decade. These techniques can assist marketers in two ways: first, they allow increased flexibility for devising marketing programs and, second, in an age of escalating selling and media costs, they enable marketers to hold down expenses. The authors describe the evolving techniques and offer guidance for incorporating them into marketing efforts.

From farther back than any of us can remember, personal selling, advertising, and sales promotion have been the essential marketing approaches. But these tested and proved methods for reaaching customers also have their limitations, particularly in the light of two significant changes that have taken place in the business picture over the past decade:

1 The costs of communication climbed radically. Media costs skyrocketed. And the cost of a sales call, as estimated by McGraw-Hill, rose from $49 in 1969 to $137 in 1979.
2 A new set of options evolved, giving marketers a wider array of communications tools.

These developments mean that the marketing manager can make the best use of the newer methods, as well as the older ones, to respond to increasing top management demand for efficient and effective communication. In particular, the evolving options offer opportunities to improve the

Published 1981.

Author's Note: Benson Shapiro and Rowland Moriarty are working on a major research project on national account management, with the support of the Marketing Science Institute.

precision and impact of the marketing program, sometimes at great cost savings over the traditional methods.

There is no need for us to belabor the all too familiar change in communications costs. On the other hand, little note has been made of the newer options. Thus, in the first section of this article, we will focus on them. Then, in the second section, we will provide a four-step approach for developing a marketing program that makes the best use of both the newer and the older communications tools.

Evolving Options

In the past, the marketer's primary communications tools were *media advertising, direct mail advertising, telephone selling, trade shows,* and *face-to-face selling.* These traditional methods differed in impact and cost per message, with media advertising at the low end and personal selling at the high end. Telephone and personal selling offered flexibility in tailoring the message to the target prospect and in having two-way contact but at a substantial cost, particularly for the field sales force. Trade shows added the excitement and impact of product demonstration but were competitive and temporary in nature.

Whereas the opportunities to "mix and match" the five traditional approaches into a coherent, synergistic marketing program were limited, we believe that the increase in the number of available tools gives the marketing manager the ability to develop a more integrated, tailored, and cost-effective communications program than was previously possible.

The newer tools include *national account management, demonstration centers, industrial stores, telemarketing,* and new forms of *catalog selling.* These tools, used together and with the traditional methods, are leading to a new economics of selling. Let us look first at these five evolving options individually and then at the opportunities they offer when combined with the traditional methods.

National Account Management

A few large accounts comprise a disproportionately large percentage of almost any company's sales (industrial as well as consumer goods and services). National account management can often be applied (1) if these large accounts are geographically or organizationally dispersed, (2) if the selling company has many interactions with the buying company's operating units, and (3) if the product and selling process are complex. National account management thus is an extension, improvement, and outgrowth of personal selling. In essence, this method is the ultimate form of both personal selling and management of the personal selling process.

National account management responds to the needs of the customer for a coordinated communications approach while giving the seller a method of coordinating the costs, activities, and objectives of the sales function for its most important accounts. It is expensive, but the value to customer and seller alike is high if the situation is appropriate and the concept well executed.

Many people and companies use other names for this approach. Banks (as well as some other companies) call it *relationship management* because it draws attention to the primary objective of creating and developing an enduring relationship between the selling and buying companies. Others call it *corporate account management* because the accounts are managed at the corporate level, although the customers buy from several divisions in a multidivisional corporation. Yet others prefer the term *international account management* because the relationships transcend national boundaries. We prefer to use *national account management* because it appears to be the most popular and descriptive term.

National account management programs share certain characteristics, depending on the sales situation:

☐ First, the accounts managed are large relative to the rest of the company's accounts, sometimes generating more than $50 million each.

☐ Second, the national account manager is often responsible for co-ordinating people who work in other divisions of the selling company or in other functional areas. (This raises a great many issues of conflicting objectives and priorities.)

☐ Third, the national account manager often has responsibility for a team that includes support and operations people.

☐ Finally, the manager calls on many people in the buying company in addition to those in the formal buying function (e.g., engineering, manufacturing, finance) and often gets involved in highly conceptual, financially oriented systems sales.

The first issue that confronts companies considering national account management is how many accounts to involve. At this point the marketing managers need to understand the difference between "special handling" for a few select accounts and a real national account management program. Almost any company can develop a way to give special attention to a few accounts. But a full-blown national account management program requires fundamental changes in selling philosophy, sales management, and sales organization. Often the special handling of a few select accounts by top-level sales and marketing managers will lead to a formal program because the managers involved cannot find enough time for both the accounts and their regular duties.

Once the program begins, the selection of national accounts is an important phase. American Can Co., for example, found that careful account selection helped to define the nature of the program and to ease its implementation. Many companies, including IBM, separate their programs into different account categories depending on size, geographical dispersion, and servicing needs.

National accounts need special support, as do the managers responsible for them. All of the standard issues of sales management arise: selection, training, supervision, and compensation. The job requires people with both selling and administrative skills. Training and supervision must be keyed to the need for both depth and breadth in skills. And compensation—both amount and form (salary, commission, or both)—becomes important.

But often the most sensitive matter is how to organize. Some companies organize their national account managers with line authority over a large, dispersed sales and support team. Some go so far as to create separate manufacturing operations for each account, and the account team becomes a profit center. Other companies prefer to view the national account managers as coordinators of salespeople who report to different profit centers or divisions. There is a myriad of choices between these two extremes.

Demonstration Centers

Specially designed showrooms, or demonstration centers, allow customers to observe and usually to try out complex industrial equipment. The approach supplements personal selling and works best when the equipment being demonstrated is complex and not portable. Demonstration centers have been used in many industries including telecommunications, data processing, electronic test gear, and machine tools. A variant of the approach is a traveling demonstration center in which the equipment (or process) for sale is mounted in a trailer truck or bus. Rank Xerox, for example, once used a railroad train to demonstrate its equipment all over Europe.

The demonstration center also supplements trade shows, with three major differences between them:

1 The demonstration center is permanent and thus can more easily be fitted in a company's marketing and sales schedule. Trade shows, on the other hand, are temporary and are not scheduled for the convenience of any single company.
2 The company can determine the location of the demonstration center, unlike trade shows.
3 Demonstration centers are designed to provide a competition-free environment for the selling process. Trade shows, of course, are filled with competitors.

But the primary benefit to the seller comes from demonstration—often to high-level executives who are unavailable for standard sales presentations. Demonstration centers in some situations, furthermore, replace months of regular field selling. The economic trade-off then becomes partially a comparison of the cost of the center versus the cost of traveling salespeople. Demonstrating equipment or processes often has more impact than describing them. The most effective demonstration centers relate directly to the customer's needs and include a custom-designed demonstration.

An outstanding example of the concept involved the use of trailer-mounted, demonstration-sized versions of Union Carbide's UNOX waste-water treatment system by the company's Linde division. In the early 1970s, Linde used these models (costing $100,000 each) to demonstrate that its system could handle the wastewater of an industrial plant or even a particular municipality.

Linde had available to it all of the traditional communications approaches. UNOX sales, however, had been slow and difficult. After carefully considering the time and effort involved in selling, Linde executives decided that the demonstration units would speed sales, generate some sales that otherwise would be lost, and save the substantial expense of traditional approaches. And the demonstration units in fact accomplished all these objectives.

Industrial Stores

This approach also involves a demonstration of equipment or a process with the emphasis generally on cost reduction, not the creation of seller benefits. Stores are permanent, but the same concept is used by companies that present customer seminars and demonstrations in hotels, trade shows, or other temporary facilities. Here too the idea is to bring the customer to the salesperson. Boeing Computer Services, for example, has used hotel room demonstrations effectively in selling structural analysis computer time-sharing services to engineering firms. The store approach works well when:

☐ The sale is too small to justify sales calls. A substantial percentage (often as high as two thirds) of industrial salespeople's time is spent traveling and waiting to see customers. If the sale is small, personal selling is not economical. One way around the problem is to ask the prospect to do the traveling. Thus, the customer comes to the sales-person's location, not vice versa.

☐ The product or process is complex and lends itself to demonstration.

☐ The company does not sell many products to the same customer. (If, on the other hand, the company has a large, active account with the same customer, the cost of a sales call can be amortized over the sale of many products.)

The store approach has been successful in the small business computer industry, where Digital Equipment has more than 20 stores in operation and development. IBM uses a similar approach but promotes it differently, using office space instead of retail space and encouraging appointments instead of drop-ins. In November 1980, however, IBM announced a commitment to develop stores more along the evolving concept used by Digital and other competitors. Xerox has made stores a major part of its marketing strategy.

Industrial stores vary widely according to product lines offered and approach used to attract people to visit. Xerox carries a wide variety of items, including many *not* made by Xerox; other stores offer limited lines produced only by the owners. Some, especially those in prime retail locations, can generate walk-in traffic. Others are in more office-oriented settings. For management, the stores certainly raise retail-oriented questions—location, fixtures, sales staffing—concerning their operations. In addition to display and sales service, stores can also provide physical distribution and service facilities to customers.

Economics has played a large part in the development of the store concept. As selling and travel costs escalate, the use of stores will become even more popular.

Telemarketing

Telephone marketing is an important emerging trend that companies can exploit in five ways—as a less costly substitute for personal selling, a supplement to personal selling, a higher-impact substitute for direct-mail and media advertising, a supplement to direct mail and other media, and a replacement for other slower, less convenient communications techniques.

Cost Savings.   Telephone selling has traditionally provided a highly customized means of two-way communication. Greater sophistication in telecommunications equipment and services, new marketing approaches, and broader applications have turned telephone selling into telemarketing. It still does not provide the quality of a personal visit but is much cheaper. While a commercial or industrial salesperson might average perhaps 5 or 6 fast personal sales calls per day, he or she can average perhaps 30 long telephone calls. The costs are much lower because of the lack of travel. Personal sales calls tend to cost upward of $100 each, while normal-length telephone sales calls cost generally under $10 each.

The cost advantage makes telemarketing a good substitute for visits to small accounts. Fieldcrest, for example, has been using telemarketing in conjunction with catalogs to introduce and sell bed and bath fashions to stores in sparsely settled areas.

Supplement to Personal Visits.   Some selling situations require periodic sales visits. Often the cost of the required call frequency is greater than the sales volume justifies and, in these cases, telephone calls can supplement personal visits. The visits might be made two to four times per year and the telephone calls eight to ten times per year for a total frequency of one per month—but at a cost substantially lower than twelve visits. Personal visits would be used for the opening presentation of, say, a new line of apparel or furniture or the sale of equipment, while telephone calls would be used for fill-in orders or supply sales.

Substitute for Direct Mail. Some insurance salespeople who wish to keep in touch with their customers have switched from using direct mail to the telephone, which gives greater impact—at an admittedly higher cost. For the economics to work well, the person called must be either an existing customer or a good prospect, not just a random name from the phone book. Telemarketing has been successful in selling subscription renewals and other continuity sales and could also aid sales of large consumer durables such as automobiles, swimming pools, and appliances. A Cadillac salesperson might, for example, telephone owners of Lincoln Continentals or Mercedes that are a few years old.

As a Supplement. Telemarketing can add to as well as replace direct mail and media advertising. Many companies have effectively used 800 telephone numbers in direct mail, television, and print media advertising. Such a program has three advantages over mail replies: (1) the prospect can make an immediate commitment to purchase while the idea is fresh and the desire for action greatest—and, perhaps more important, he or she can get an immediate reply; (2) it is easier for most people to telephone than to fill in a coupon and mail it; (3) the selling company can become actively involved in supplying product information to aid the customer's decision making, and the customer can also express concerns to be responded to by the telephone salespeople in future media communication or even in later product development.

The combined media/telemarketing approach has been successful for a variety of products, including specialty coffees, smokeless tobacco, books, and records. AT&T uses the approach to sell many of its products and services. An additional advantage is the quick generation of data about media effectiveness. Within a few days a company or its advertising agency can determine the effectiveness of a new advertising campaign. With mail response, the time lag slows the analysis so that a campaign is generally run longer before review.

Customer–Company Coordination. Finally, the telephone can be used as a part of a communications program to tie companies to their constituencies. The responsiveness and convenience of the telephone, combined with its two-way message content, make it particularly appropriate for this use. A dissatisfied customer, for example, can get a quick response to a problem.[1]

Confused customers who need product information can get it when they need it most, thus preventing product misuse and abuse. O.M. Scott & Sons Co. uses this approach to good advantage in its lawn and garden care business. Problems with the product or its distribution become clear to the seller and can be rectified quickly without much loss of the expensive time of dealers and salespeople. A manufacturer can use the telephone to gather information from salespeople or dealers to find, for example, whether a new product is selling well or whether competitors met a price increase.

The use of the telephone in marketing can create junk phone calls much like junk mail in direct mail advertising. For both economic and customer relations reasons, we advocate the use of selective telemarketing, showing good judgment and good taste. Otherwise, the attention-getting quality of the telephone in uncontrolled situations can irritate consumers.

The telephone's particular mix of benefits and growing cost-effectiveness versus other media make it an increasingly important part of the communications mix. Ongoing telephone contact with customers or prospects can produce important information through close communication. And once the line is open, there are every-increasing opportunities to creatively cross sell complementary products and services.

Catalog Selling

An old approach in the consumer goods market, catalog selling is an evolving method in industrial and commercial markets. Companies active in the office- and computer-supply businesses have found catalogs to be an efficient way of generating the relatively small dollar sales typical of their businesses. The Drawing Board, an office supply company in Dallas, apparently relies solely on its catalog for communication with customers.

Wright Line, Inc., a $50 million vendor of computer-related supplies and capital equipment for computer rooms, programmers and analysts, and small businesses, has developed an elaborate communications system that includes personal selling, telemarketing, and catalogs. The 140-person sales force makes visits for the larger capital equipment sales and for developing systems sales. The quarterly catalog generates both fill-in sales of capital equipment and supplies for already-sold systems, as well as orders from customers whose size would not justify a personal call. Customers can place orders by mail, through the salespeople, or by telephone. Most orders come in by telephone and mail. The catalog—a new approach at Wright Line— has improved sales volume more than Wright Line executives had expected.

Wright Line's integrated approach developed through a combination of careful analysis and trial-and-error testing. Management has been willing and able to try new approaches, carefully analyze the results, and commit resources to the successful experiments.

Other industries have also used catalogs, particularly in conjunction with telephone order centers or telemarketing centers. Sigma Chemical Co., for example, uses a catalog to sell enzymes for laboratory use, although competitors generally use sales forces. Other catalog applications include electronic components and industrial supplies. The approach is highly cost-effective in transmitting a great deal of information to selected prospects and customers in a usable, inexpensive format.

It is interesting to relate the development of the five evolving options to the more traditional approaches. Personal selling led to national account management. Demonstration centers and industrial stores are variations on the trade show. Telemarketing developed from telephone selling and the early inside order desks of industrial distributors. And industrial stores and catalog selling are based on retail stores and consumer catalogs, such as those used by Sears, Roebuck and Co., that date from the nineteenth century.

Economics and technology are driving the evolution, and the need for more precise communications programs is encouraging it.

Creating a Program

The newer ways of selling when combined with the traditional communications appproaches, enable marketers to make precise choices in developing their communications programs. Four major steps are necessary for developing an effective program:

☐ Analyze the communications costs.
☐ Specify the communications needs.
☐ Formulate a coherent program.
☐ Monitor the total system.

Analyze Current Costs

The basic device for understanding marketing costs is a marketing-oriented income statement that divides all costs into three primary categories—manufacturing, physical distribution, and communication—and two generally smaller categories—nondivisible overhead and profit (see Exhibit 1).

This income statement differs from the company's income statement. To be useful, it should begin with the price the customer pays. Distributor discounts are allocated to communications cost (the value of the retail and/or wholesale salespeople, display, advertising, trade show attendance) and physical distribution cost (order processing inventory carrying, transportation). If the distributor customizes the product in the field (e.g., adds accessories, cuts to shape, mixes), the cost of doing so should be allocated to the manufacturing task.

A well-designed marketing-oriented income statement helps marketers determine the role of each set of costs (manufacturing, distribution, and communication) in their businesses. Marketers can then ask questions such as:

☐ Where should I concentrate my cost-cutting activities?
☐ What do I get and, more important perhaps, what does my customer get from each of the three functions?
☐ Do the benefits provided by each function justify the costs?

Marketing executives can thus categorize their businesses as communications intensive, distribution intensive, or manufacturing intensive and can then analyze competitors from the same viewpoints. Avon Products, for

Exhibit 1.   A Marketing-Oriented Income Statement

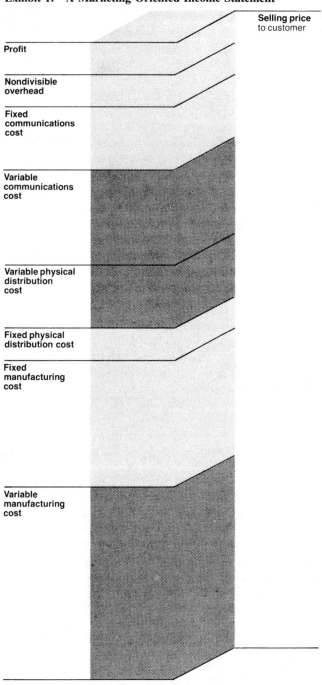

Selling price
to customer

Profit

Nondivisible
overhead

Fixed
communications
cost

Variable
communications
cost

Variable physical
distribution
cost

Fixed physical
distribution cost

Fixed
manufacturing
cost

Variable
manufacturing
cost

example, trades off higher physical distributions costs (sending its cosmetics and toiletries in small packages to its several hundred thousand salespeople) against the higher communications cost of its competitors, which place more emphasis on advertising but use more efficient distribution methods (large sales to supermarket and drug chains that depend on the customer to pick up the order and transport it home).

The marketing-oriented income statement helps to analyze communications costs at a strategic, but not a tactical, level. We cannot consider the detailed costs without first specifying marketers' communications needs or objectives.

Specify Needs

Marketing executives must state precisely the objectives of the communications program and also understand the costs of achieving each objective. There are many different types of communication between a company and its marketing constituencies. Companies may wish to strive for four major goals in specifying their needs.

1. *Persuasive Impact.* Two-way communication is more effective than one-way communication. Media advertising by itself, for example, tends to be one way—from the seller to the buyer—while methods such as telemarketing allow a two-way dialogue.

2. *Customization.* Different people, even within the same buying unit, desire different information, and opportunities for customization vary. Two-way communication, of course, enables the seller to tailor a message to the precise needs of a specific customer at a given moment.

3. *Speed.* Some information is much more time sensitive than others. An order to a commodities broker, for example, is urgent. And because we live in an era that stresses instant gratification, many consumers want to obtain the product as soon as possible after making their choice, even if they have labored over that choice for weeks, months, or even years.

4. *Convenience.* Almost everybody, from a professional purchasing agent to a child buying a stick of bubble gum, wants convenience in making purchases.

Formulate a Program

Marketers can create the most effective communications program only with a complete understanding of the relationships among both the old and the evolving options. Perhaps even more important than the media on their own is their potential for integration into a synergistic system that uses each to its best advantage. Exhibit 2 shows the evolving and traditional options and their varying impact and cost per message.

Combinations are especially powerful because each medium has a different mix of benefits and economics. It is easy to envision a communications system that uses all 10 of the media and combinations listed in Exhibit 2.

Exhibit 2.   Comparing the Evolving and Traditional Options

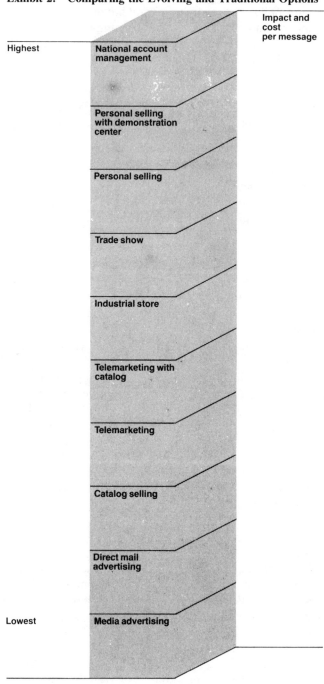

Impact and
cost
per message

Highest

National account
management

Personal selling
with demonstration
center

Personal selling

Trade show

Industrial store

Telemarketing with
catalog

Telemarketing

Catalog selling

Direct mail
advertising

Lowest

Media advertising

To illustrate, media advertising gives broad coverage at a low cost. Direct mail can be used for a somewhat focused message to a specific group of people at a very reasonable cost. Catalog selling provides a great deal of information, particularly for a wide product assortment, to a focused audience. Telemarketing increases the cost relative to options below it but adds a two-way personalized message, convenience, speed, and the best timing.

The combination of catalogs and telemarketing mixes good economics, much information transmittal, and the advantages of the telephone. Industrial stores and trade shows offer the benefits of personal selling with the cost advantages of a stationary sales force. Of course, customer convenience suffers.

Again, personal selling provides important advantages at a high cost. The addition of a demonstration center increases the cost but provides important benefits in major sales. And, finally, national account management provides the ultimate communications medium at the highest cost.

Different approaches can be used for different customers, products, situations, and communications needs. Companies that market many products to many different types of customers will generally need a wider variety of communications modes than companies having a narrower product and customer mix. It should be no surprise that companies such as Digital Equipment and AT&T, with their many products, many types of customers, and new technologies to sell, have been at the forefront of the new approaches. They had little choice.

Time is an important dimension in the development of a synergistic communications program for three major reasons:

1.   First, marketers must plan each communications program with regard to the events of the product's life cycle. The planned introduction of a variation in a product, for example, might require an equally carefully planned change in the communications mix—perhaps to emphasize a new use or a new set of users. Customer knowledge moves through its own life cycle. At some points in a product's life, developing brand awareness among prospects might be particularly important, while at other times the primary emphasis would be on reassuring existing customers.

2.   Second, it takes a long time to implement communications programs. The progression from initial start-up to effective operation of a national account program, for example, can take four to five years. The same is true, but to a lesser extent, of the other media shown in Exhibit 2. It can take a year to develop, test, and carefully execute a good media advertising or catalog sales program. In general, the communications methods with greater impact and higher cost per message in Exhibit 2 require more time to implement than those lower in the hierarchy.

3.   Third, careful planning over time involves the *raison d'être* of all marketing activities—the customer. Customers remember. Thus, frequently changing communications programs is ineffective, inefficient, and confusing.

Customers used to sales calls will not immediately embrace an industrial store or a telemarketing program. All communications programs must reflect a concern for the customer's memory.

The mix-and-match process of developing a program from a set of communications media alternatives has four integral dimensions: market segments, products, media, and time. A lack of concern for any of these elements weakens the whole program.

Monitor the Total System

In some communications-intensive companies the cost of communication can be upward of one fourth of total sales. Obviously, such expenditures warrant careful control.

Wherever possible, managers should gather and analyze all the data related to the communications process. Executives who use industrial stores will have to think as retailers do about such things as traffic (flow of people into the store) and accessibility.

For example, they should monitor the number of visitors to an industrial store, the source of their initial communication, the percentage of "qualified" prospects, and the percentage of sales. Catalog marketers and telemarketers, of course, can monitor such factors as the average size of an order by customer type, the types of products purchased, and frequency of order.

Effectiveness and Efficiency

This article began by discussing reasons for the evolution of newer communications options which, in essence, developed because of cost pressures and the need to accomplish new tasks. The evolving options save costs in three ways:

1. *Greater impact.* A demonstration center, for example, replaces a great deal of traditional personal selling effort. The concept that a smaller amount of high-impact media is more effective than a larger amount of low-impact media is behind a good deal of the evolving options.

2. *Time saving.* Marketers can save time either through the use of the medium with the greatest impact (as in the demonstration center) or through less travel (as in the case of industrial stores, telemarketing, or catalogs).

3. *Greater coordination and closer control.* Marketers can also eliminate waste through greater coordination, as in national account management, or through the closer control possible in industrial stores, telemarketing centers, and catalog operations than in a traditional field sales force.

In summary, then, careful cost analysis, precise needs specification, creative program formulation, and meticulous monitoring will lead to more effective and efficient communication with greater customer impact and lower costs.

Notes

1. For an example of this application, see "Good Listener: At Proctor & Gamble Success Is Largely Due to Heeding Customer," *Wall Street Journal*, April 29, 1980.

30
Major Sales
Who Really Does the Buying?

THOMAS V. BONOMA

When is a buyer not really a buyer? How can the best product at the lowest price turn off buyers? Are there anonymous kingpins who make the real buying decisions? As these questions suggest, the reality of buying and selling is often not what it seems. The psychological and emotional factors that figure strongly in buying and selling usually are unobserved. By overlooking these less tangible aspects of selling, a vendor can lose sales and not even understand why. The author sets up a procedure for analyzing buying decisions and tells sellers how to apply the framework to specific situations. Steps in the procedure include identifying the actual decision makers, determining how they view their self-interests, and using that information to develop an effective sales strategy.

> "You don't understand: Willy was a salesman. . . . He don't put a bolt
> to a nut. He don't tell you the law or give you medicine. He's a man
> way out there in the blue, riding on a smile and a shoeshine. And when
> they start not smiling back—that's an earthquake."
>
> Arthur Miller
> *Death of a Salesman*

Many companies' selling efforts are models of marketing efficiency. Account plans are carefully drawn, key accounts receive special management attention, and substantial resources are devoted to the sales process, from prospect identification to postsale service. Even such well-planned and well-executed selling strategies often fail, though, because management has an incomplete understanding of buying psychology—the human side of selling. Consider the following two examples:

1.   A fast-growing maker and seller of sophisticated graphics computers had trouble selling to potentially major customers. Contrary to the

---

Published 1981.

industry practice of quoting high list prices and giving large discounts to users who bought in quantity, this company priced 10% to 15% lower than competitors and gave smaller quantity discounts. Even though its net price was often the lowest, the company met resistance from buyers. The reason, management later learned, was that purchasing agents measured themselves and were measured by their superiors less by the net price of the sophisticated computers they bought than by the amount deducted from the price during negotiations. This discount had a significance to buyers that sound pricing logic could not predict.

2. Several years ago, at AT&T's Long Lines division, an account manager was competing against a vendor with possibly better technology who threatened to lure away a key account. Among the customer's executives who might make the final decision about whether to switch from Bell were a telecommunications manager who had once been a Bell employee, a vice president of data processing who was known as a "big-name system buster" in his previous job because he had replaced all the IBM computers with other vendors' machines, and an aggressive telecommunications division manager who seemed to be unreachable by the AT&T team.

AT&T's young national account manager was nearly paralyzed by the threat. His team had never seriously considered the power, motivations, or perceptions of the various executives in the customer company, which had been buying from AT&T for many years. Without such analysis, effective and coordinated action on short notice—the usual time available for response to sales threats—was impossible.

Getting at the Human Factors

How can psychology be used to improve sales effectiveness? My contention is that seller awareness of and attention to the human factors in purchasing will produce higher percentages of completed sales and fewer unpleasant surprises in the selling process.

It would be inaccurate to call the human side of selling an emerging sales concern; only the most advanced companies recognize the psychology of buying as a major factor in improving account selection and selling results. Yet in most industries, the bulk of a company's business comes from a small minority of its customers. Retaining these key accounts is getting increasingly difficult as buyers constantly look not only for the best deal but also for the vendor that best understands them and their needs. It is this understanding and the targeted selling that results from it that can most benefit marketing managers.

Buying a Corporate Jet
The personal aspects and their complexities become apparent when one looks closely at an example of the buying process: the purchase of a business

jet, which carries a price tag in excess of $3 million. The business-jet market splits obviously into two segments: those companies that already own or operate a corporate aircraft and those that do not.

In the owner market, the purchase process may be initiated by the chief executive officer, a board member (wishing to increase efficiency or security), the company's chief pilot, or through vendor efforts like advertising or a sales visit. The CEO will be central in deciding whether to buy the jet, but he or she will be heavily influenced by the company's pilot, financial officer, and perhaps by the board itself.

Each party in the buying process has subtle roles and needs. The salesperson who tries to impress, for example, both the CEO with depreciation schedules and the chief pilot with minimum runway statistics will almost certainly not sell a plane if he overlooks the psychological and emotional components of the buying decision. "For the chief executive," observes one salesperson, "you need all the numbers for support, but if you can't find the kid inside the CEO and excite him or her with the raw beauty of the new plane, you'll never sell the equipment. If you sell the excitement, you sell the jet."

The chief pilot, as an equipment expert, often has veto power over purchase decisions and may be able to stop the purchase of one or another brand of jet by simply expressing a negative opinion about, say, the plane's bad weather capabilities. In this sense, the pilot not only influences the decision but also serves as an information "gatekeeper" by advising management on the equipment to select. Though the corporate legal staff will formulate the purchase agreement and the purchasing department will acquire the jet, these parties may have little to say about whether or how the plane will be obtained, and which type. The users of the jet—middle and upper management of the buying company, important customers, and others—may have at least an indirect role in choosing the equipment.

The involvement of many people in the purchase decision creates a group dynamic that the selling company must factor into its sales planning. Who makes up the buying group? How will the parties interact? Who will dominate and who submit? What priorities do the individuals have?

It takes about three months for those companies that already own or operate aircraft to reach a decision. Because even the most successful vendor will sell no more than 90 jets a year, every serious prospect is a key account. The nonowners, not surprisingly, represent an even more complex market, since no precedent or aviation specialists exist.

The buying process for other pieces of equipment and for services will be more or less similar, depending on the company, product, and people involved. The purchase of computer equipment, for example, parallels the jet decision, except that sales prospects are likely to include data processing and production executives and that the market is divided into small and large prospects rather than owners and non-owners. In other cases (such as upgrading the corporate communications network, making a fleet purchase, or launching a plant expansion), the buying process may be very different. Which common factors will reliably steer selling-company management toward those human considerations likely to improve selling effectiveness?

Different buying psychologies exist that make effective selling difficult. On the one hand, companies don't buy, people do. This knowledge drives the seller to analyze who the important buyers are and what they want. On the other hand, many individuals, some of whom may be unknown to the seller, are involved in most major purchases. Even if all the parties are identified, the outcome of their interaction may be unpredictable from knowledge of them as individuals. Effective selling requires usefully combining the individual and group dynamics of buying to predict what the buying "decision-making unit" will do. For this combination to be practical, the selling company must answer four key questions.

Who's in the "Buying Center"?

The set of roles, or social tasks, buyers can assume is the same regardless of the product or participants in the purchase decision. This set of roles can be thought of as a fixed set of behavioral pigeon-holes into which different managers from different functions can be placed to aid understanding. Together, the buying managers who take on these roles can be thought of as a "buying center."

Exhibit 1 shows six buying roles encountered in every selling situation. I have illustrated these roles by using the purchase or upgrading of a telecommunications system as an example. Let's consider each triangle, representing a buying role, in turn.

The *initiator* of the purchase process, whether for a jet, paper towels, or communication services, recognizes that some company problems can be solved or avoided by acquiring a product or service. A company's turboprop aircraft may provide neither the speed nor the range to get top management quickly to and from scattered operations. The prospective buyer of communications equipment may want to take advantage of technological improvements or to reduce costs through owning instead of leasing.

One or more *gatekeepers* are involved in the purchase process. These individuals, who may have the title of buyer or purchasing manager, usually act as problem or product experts. They are paid to keep up on the range of vendor offerings. In the jet example, the chief pilot will ordinarily fill this role. In the telecommunications example given in Exhibit 1, corporate purchasing, the corporate telecommunications staff or, increasingly, data processing experts may be consulted. By controlling (literally keeping the gate open or shut for) information and, sometimes, vendor access to corporate decision makers, the gatekeepers largely determine which vendors get the chance to sell. For some purchases the gatekeeping process is formalized

Exhibit 1. Members of the Buying Center and Their Roles

Initiator	Division general manager proposes to replace the company's telecommunications system
Decider	Vice president of administration selects, with influence from others, the vendor the company will deal with and the system it will buy
Influencers	Corporate telecommunications department and the vice president of data processing have important say about which system and vendor the company will deal with
Purchaser	Corporate purchasing department completes the purchase to specifications by negotiating or bidding
Gatekeeper	Corporate purchasing and corporate telecommunications departments analyze the company's needs and recommend likely matches with potential vendors
Users	All division employees who use the telecommunications equipment

through the use of an approved-vendors list, which constitutes a written statement of who can (and who, by absence, cannot) sell to the company.

Influencers are those who "have a say" in whether a purchase is made and about what is bought. The range of influencers becomes increasingly broad as major purchases are contemplated, because so many corporate resources are involved and so many people affected. In important decisions, board committees, stockholders of a public company, and even "lowly" mechanics can become influencers. One mining-machinery company encountered difficulty selling a new type of machine to its underground-mining customers. It turned out that mine maintenance personnel, who influenced the buying decision, resisted the purchase because they would have to learn to fix the new machine and maintain another stock of spare parts.

The *deciders* are those who say yes or no to the contemplated purchase. Often with major purchases, many of a company's senior managers act together to carry out the decider role. Ordinarily, however, one of these will become champion or advocate of the contemplated purchase and move it to completion. Without such a champion, many purchases would never be made. It is important to point out that deciders often do not "sign off" on purchases, nor do they make them. That is left to others. Though signers often represent themselves as deciders, such representation can be deceptive. It is possible for a vendor with a poor feel for the buying center to *never* become aware of the real movers in the buying company.

The purchase of executive computer work stations clearly illustrates both the importance of the champion and the behind-the-scenes role of the decider. A high-level executive who has become interested in using computers at his or her job after reading a magazine article or after tinkering with a home computer might decide to try out microcomputers or time-sharing terminals. The executive might then ask the company's data processing group—which is likely to be quite resistant and averse to executive meddling—to evaluate available microcomputer equipment. When trial purchases are made, the high-level executive will quietly help steer the system through the proper channels leading to acceptance and further purchases. The vendor, dealing directly with the data processing people, may never be aware that this decider exists.

The *purchaser* and the *user* are those concerned, respectively, with obtaining and consuming the product or service. The corporate purchasing department usually fills the purchaser role. Who fills the user role depends on the product or service.

Remember that I am discussing social roles, not individuals or groups of individuals. As such, the number of managers filling the buying roles varies from 1 to 35. In very trivial situations, such as a manager's purchase of a pocket calculator on a business trip, one person will fill all six roles. The triangles in Exhibit 1 would overlap: the manager initiates (perceives a need), gatekeeps (what brand did I forget at home?), influences himself or herself (this is more than I need, but it's only $39.95), decides, buys, and uses the equipment.

In more important buying situations, the number of managers assuming roles increases. In a study of 62 capital equipment and service acquisitions in 31 companies, Wesley J. Johnston and I quantified the buying center.[1] In the typical capital equipment purchase, an average of four departments (engineering and purchasing were always included), three levels of management hierarchy (for example, manager, regional manager, vice president), and seven different persons filled the six buying roles. For services, the corresponding numbers were four departments, two levels of management, and five managers. As might be expected, the more complex and involved the buying decision, the larger the decision unit and the more careful its decisions. For example, when packing supplies were ordered, little vendor searching or postsale evaluation was involved. When a new boiler was bought, careful vendor comparisons and postsale audits were undertaken.

Who Are the Powerful Buyers?

As useful as the buying-center concept is, it is difficult to apply because managers do not wear tags that say "decision maker" or "unimportant person."[2] The powerful are often invisible, at least to vendor representatives.

Unfortunately, power does not correlate perfectly with organizational rank. As the case of the mine maintenance personnel illustrates, those with little formal power may be able to stop a purchase or hinder its completion. A purchasing manager who will not specify a disfavored vendor or the secretary who screens one vendor's salespeople because of a real or imagined slight also can dramatically change the purchasing outcome. Sales efforts cannot be directed through a simple reading of organizational charts; the selling company must identify the powerful buying-center members.

In Exhibit 2, I outline five major power bases in the corporation. In addition, I have categorized them according to whether their influence is positive (champion power) or negative (veto power).

Reward power refers to a manager's ability to encourage purchases by providing others with monetary, social, political, or psychological benefits. In one small company, for instance, the marketing vice president hoped to improve marketing decisions by equipping the sales force with small data-entry computers. Anticipating objections that the terminals were unnecessary, he felt forced to offer the sales vice president a computer of his own. The purchase was made.

Coercive power refers to a manager's ability to impose punishment on others. Of course, threatening punishment is not the same thing as having the power to impose it. Those managers who wave sticks most vigorously are sometimes the least able to deliver anything beyond a gentle breeze.

Attraction power refers to a person's ability to charm or otherwise persuade people to go along with his or her preferences. Next to the ability to reward and punish, attraction is the most potent power base in managerial

Exhibit 2. Bases of Power

Type of Power	Champion	or Veto
Reward: Ability to provide monetary, social, political, or psychological rewards to others for compliance	√	
Coercive: Ability to provide monetary or other punishments for noncompliance	√	
Attraction: Ability to elicit compliance from others because they like you	√	√
Expert: Ability to elicit compliance because of technical expertise, either actual or reputed		√
Status: Compliance-gaining ability derived from a legitimate position of power in a company		√

Note: These five power bases were originally proposed over 20 years ago by psychologists J.R.P. French, Jr. and Bertram Raven. See "The Bases of Social Power" in D. Cartwright, ed. *Studies in Social Power* (Ann Arbor: University of Michigan Press, 1959).

life. Even CEOs find it difficult to rebut a key customer with whom they have flown for ten years who says, "Joe, as your friend, I'm telling you that buying this plane would be a mistake."

When a manager gets others to go along with his/her judgment because of real or perceived expertise in some area, *expert power* is being invoked. A telecommunications manager will find it difficult to argue with an acknowledged computer expert who contends that buying a particular telephone switching system is essential for the "office of the future"—or that not buying it now eventually will make effective communication impossible. With expert power, the skills need not be real, if by "real" we mean that the individual actually possesses what is attributed to him/her. It is enough that others believe that the expert has special skills or are willing to respect his/her opinion because of accomplishments in a totally unrelated field.

Status power comes from having a high position in the corporation. This notion of power is most akin to what is meant by the word *authority*. It refers to the kind of influence a president has over a first-line supervisor and is more restricted than the other power bases. At first glance, status power might be thought of as similar to reward or coercive power. But it differs in significant ways. First, the major influence activity of those positions of corporate authority is persuasion, not punishment or reward. We jawbone rather than dangle carrots and taunt with sticks because others in the company also have significant power which they could invoke in retaliation.

Second, the high-status manager can exercise his or her status repeatedly only because subordinates allow it. In one heavy-manufacturing division, for example, the continual specification of favored suppliers by a plant manager (often at unfavorable prices) led to a "palace revolt" among other managers whose component cost evaluations were constantly made to look poor. Third, the power base of those in authority is very circumscribed since authority only tends to work in a downward direction on the organization chart and is restricted to specific work-related requests. Status power is one of the weaker power bases.

Buying centers and individual managers usually display one dominant power base in purchasing decisions. In one small company, an important factor is whether the manager arguing a position is a member of the founding family—a kind of status power and attraction power rolled into one. In a large high-technology defense contractor, almost all decisions are made on the basis of real or reputed expertise. This is true even when the issue under consideration has nothing to do with hardware or engineering science.

The key to improved selling effectiveness is in observation and investigation to understand prospects' corporate power culture. The sales team must also learn the type of power key managers in the buying company have or aspire to. Discounts or offers of price reductions may not be especially meaningful to a young turk in the buying company who is most concerned with status power; a visit by senior selling-company management may prove much more effective for flattering the ego and making the sale. Similarly, sales management may wish to make more technical selling appeals to engineers or other buying-company staff who base their power on expertise.

The last two columns of Exhibit 2 show that the type of power invoked may allow the manager to support or oppose a proposal, but not always both. I believe status and expert power are more often employed by their holders to veto decisions with which they do not agree. Because others are often "sold" on the contemplated purchase, vetoing it generally requires either the ability to perceive aspects not seen by the average manager because of special expertise or the broader view that high corporate status is said to provide. Reward and coercive power are more frequently used to push through purchases and the choice of favored vendors. Attraction power seems useful and is used by both champions and vetoers. The central point here is that for many buying-center members, power tends to be unidirectional.

Six Behavioral Clues
Based on the preceding analysis of power centers, I have distilled six clues for identifying the powerful:

1. Though power and formal authority often go together, the correlation between the two is not perfect. The selling company must take into account other clues about where the true buying power lies.

2. One way to identify buying-center powerholders is to observe com-

munications in the buying company. Of course, the powerful are not threatened by others, nor are they often promised rewards. Still, even the most powerful managers are likely to be influenced by others, especially by those whose power is based on attraction or expertise. Those with less power use persuasion and rational argument to try to influence the more powerful. Managers to whom others direct much attention but who receive few offers of rewards or threats of punishment usually possess substantial decision-making power.

    3.   Buying-center decision makers may be disliked by those with less power. Thus, when others express concern about one buying-center member's opinions along with their feelings of dislike or ambivalence, sellers have strong clues as to who the powerful buyer is.

    4.   High-power buyers tend to be one-way information centers, serving as focal points for information from others. The vice president who doesn't come to meetings but who receives copies of all correspondence about a buying matter is probably a central influencer or decider.

    5.   The most powerful buying-center members are probably not the most easily identified or the most talkative members of their groups. Indeed, the really powerful buying group members often send others to critical negotiations because they are confident that little of substance will be made final without their approval.

    6.   No correlation exists between the functional area of a manager and his or her power within a company. It is not possible to approach the data processing department blindly to find decision makers for a new computer system, as many sellers of mainframes have learned. Nor can one simply look to the CEO to find a decision maker for a corporate plane. There is no substitute for working hard to understand the dynamics of the buying company.

What Do They Want?

Diagnosing motivation accurately is one of the easiest management tasks to do poorly and one of the most difficult to do well. Most managers have lots of experience at diagnosing another's wants, but though the admission comes hard, most are just not very accurate when trying to figure out what another person wants and will do. A basic rule of motivation is as follows: All buyers (indeed, all people) act selfishly or try to be selfish but sometimes miscalculate and don't serve their own interests. Thus, buyers attempt to maximize their gains and minimize their losses from purchase situations. How do buyers choose their own self-interest? The following are insights into that decision-making process from research.

    First, buyers act as if a complex product or service were decomposable into various benefits. Examples of benefits might include product features, price, reliability, and so on.

    Second, buyers segment the potential benefits into various categories.

The most common of these are financial, product-service, social-political, and personal. For some buyers, the financial benefits are paramount, while for others, the social-political ones—how others in the company will view the purchase—rank highest. Of course, the dimensions may be related, as when getting the lowest-cost product (financial) results in good performance evaluations and a promotion (social-political).

Finally, buyers ordinarily are not certain that purchasing the product will actually bring the desired benefit. For example, a control computer sold on its reliability and industrial-strength construction may or may not fulfill its promise. Because benefits have value only if they actually are delivered, the buyer must be confident that the selling company will keep its promises. Well-known vendors, like IBM or Xerox, may have some advantage over lesser-known companies in this respect.

As marketers know, not all promised benefits will be equally desired by all customers. All buyers have top-priority benefit classes, or "hot buttons." For example, a telecommunications manager weighing a choice between Bell and non-Bell equipment will find some benefits, like ownership, available only from non-Bell vendors. Other desired benefits, such as reputation for service and reliability, may be available to a much greater degree from Bell. The buyer who has financial priorities as a hot button may decide to risk possible service-reliability problems for the cost-reduction benefits available through ownership. Another manager—one primarily concerned with reducing the social-political risks as a result of service problems—may reach a different decision. Exhibit 3 schematically shows the four classes into which buyers divide benefits; the telecommunications example illustrates each class.

Outlining the buyer's motivation suggests several possible selling approaches. The vendor can try to focus the buyer's attention on benefits not a part of his or her thinking. A magazine sales representative, for instance, devised a questionnaire to help convince an uncertain client to buy advertising space. The questionnaire sought information about the preferred benefits—in terms of reach, audience composition, and cost per thousand readers. When the prospective buyer "played this silly game" and filled out the questionnaire, he convinced himself of the superior worth of the vendor's magazine on the very grounds he was seeking to devalue it.

Conversely, sellers can de-emphasize the buyer's desire for benefits on which the vendor's offering stacks up poorly. For example, if a competing vendor's jet offers better fuel economy, the selling company might attempt to refocus the buyer's attention toward greater speed or lower maintenance costs.

The vendor can also try to increase the buyer's confidence that promised benefits will be realized. One software company selling legal administrative systems, for example, provides a consulting service that remote users can phone if they are having problems, backup copies of its main programs in case users destroy the original, a complete set of input forms to encourage

Exhibit 3. Dominant Motives for Buying a Telecommunications System

| | Benefit Class[a] | | |
Financial	Product or Service	Social or Political	Personal
Absolute cost savings	**Pre- and post-sales service**	Will purchase enhance the buyer's standing with the buying team or top management?	Will purchase increase others' liking or respect for the buyer?
Cheaper than competitive offerings	**Specific features**		
Will provide operating-cost reductions	**Space occupied by unit**		
Economics of leasing versus buying	**Availability**		

[a]The benefits in bold type are more highly valued than the others and represent the company's "hot button"

full data entry, and regular conferences to keep users current on system revisions. These services are designed to bolster the confidence of extremely conservative administrators and lawyers who are shopping for a system.

Finally, vendors often try to change what the buyer wants, or which class of benefits he or she responds to most strongly. My view of motivation suggests that such an approach is almost always unsuccessful. Selling strategy needs to work with the buyer's motivations, not around them.

How Do They Perceive Us?

How buyers perceive the selling company, its products, and its personnel is very important to efficient selling. Powerful buyers invariably have a wide range of perceptions about a vending company. One buyer will have a friend at another company who has used a similar product and claims that "it very nearly ruined us." Another may have talked to someone with a similar product who claimed that the vending company "even sent a guy out on a plane to Hawaii to fix the unit there quickly. These people really care."

One drug company representative relates the story of how the company was excluded from all the major metropolitan hospitals in one city because a single influential physician believed that one of the company's new offerings was implicated in a patient's death. This doctor not only generalized his impressions to include all the company's products but encouraged his friends to boycott the company.

A simple scheme for keeping tabs on how buyers perceive sellers is to ask sales officials to estimate how the important buyers judge the vending company and its actions. This judgment can be recorded on a continuum ranging from negative to positive. If a more detailed judgment is desired,the selling company can place its products and its people on two axes perpendicular to each other, like this:

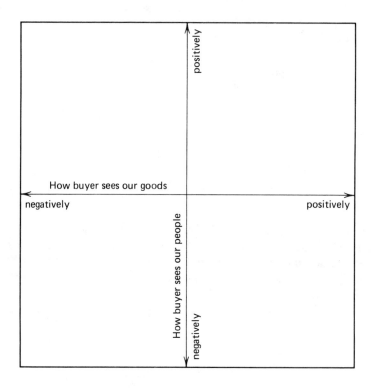

The scarcity of marketing dollars and the effectiveness of champions in the buying process argue strongly for focusing resources where they are likely to do the most good. Marketing efforts should aim at those in the buying company who like the selling company, since they are partially presold. While there is no denying the adage, "It's important to sell everybody," those who diffuse their efforts this way often sell no one.

Gathering Psychological Intelligence

While I would like to claim that some new technique will put sound psychological analyses magically in your sales staff's hands, no such formula exists. But I have used the human-side approach in several companies to increase sales effectiveness, and there are only three guidelines needed to make it work well.

Make Productive Sales Calls a Norm, Not an Oddity

Because of concern about the rapidly rising cost of a sales call, managers are seeking alternative approaches to selling. Sales personnel often do not have a good idea of why they are going on most calls, what they hope to find out, and which questions will give them the needed answers. Sales-call planning is not only a matter of minimizing miles traveled or courtesy calls on unimportant prospects but of determining what intelligence is needed about key buyers and what questions or requests are likely to produce that information.

I recently traveled with a major account representative of a duplication equipment company, accompanying him on the five calls he made during the day. None of the visits yielded even 10% of the potential psychological or other information that the representative could use on future calls, despite the fact that prospects made such information available repeatedly.

At one company, for example, we learned from a talkative administrator that the chairman was a semirecluse who insisted on approving equipment requests himself; that one of the divisional managers had (without the agreement of the executive who was our host) brought in a competitor's equipment to test; and that a new duplicator the vendor had sold to the company was more out of service than in. The salesperson pursued none of this freely offered information, nor did he think any of it important enough to write down or pass on to the sales manager. The call was wasted because the salesperson didn't know what he was looking for or how to use what was offered him.

Exhibit 4 shows a matrix that can be used to capture on a single sheet of paper essential psychological data about a customer. I gave some clues for filling in the matrix earlier in the article, but how sales representatives go about gathering the information depends on the industry, the product, and especially the customer. In all cases, however, key selling assessments involve (1) isolating the powerful buying-center members, (2) identifying what they want in terms of both their hot buttons and specific needs, and (3) assessing their perceptions of the situation. Additionally, gathering psychological information is more often a matter of listening carefully than of asking clever questions during the sales interview.

Listen to the Sales Force

Nothing discourages intelligence gathering as much as the sales force's conviction that management doesn't really want to hear what salespeople know about an account. Many companies require the sales force to file voluminous call reports and furnish other data—which vanish, never to be seen or even referred to again unless a sales representative is to punished for one reason or another.

450

Exhibit 4. Matrix for Gathering Psychological Information.

Who's in the buying center, and what is the base of their power?	Who are the powerful buyers, and what are their priorities?	What specific benefits does each important buyer want?	How do the important buyers see us?	Selling strategy

To counter this potentially fatal impediment, I recommend a sales audit. Evaluate all sales force control forms and call reports and discard any that have not been used by management for planning or control purposes in the last year. This approach has a marvelously uplifting effect all around; it frees the sales force from filling in forms it knows nobody uses, sales management from gathering forms it doesn't know what to do with, and data processing from processing reports no one ever requests. Instead, use a simple, clear, and accurate sales control form of the sort suggested in Exhibit 4—preferably on a single sheet of paper for a particular sales period. These recommendations may sound drastic, but where management credibility in gathering and using sales force intelligence is absent, drastic measures may be appropriate.

Emphasize Homework and Details

Having techniques for acquiring sales intelligence and attending to reports is not enough. Sales management must stress that yours is a company that rewards careful fact gathering, tight analysis, and impeccable execution. This message is most meaningful when it comes from the top.

Cautionary Notes

The group that influences a purchase doesn't call itself a buying center. Nor do decision makers and influencers think of themselves in those terms. Managers must be careful not to mistake the analysis and ordering process for the buyer's actions themselves. In addition, gathering data such as I have recommended is a sensitive issue. For whatever reasons, it is considered less acceptable to make psychological estimates of buyers than economic ones. Computing the numbers without understanding the psychology, however, leads to lost sales. Finally, the notion implicit throughout this article has been that sellers must understand buying, just as buyers must understand selling. When that happens, psychology and marketing begin to come together usefully. Closed sales follow almost as an afterthought.

Notes

1. Wesley J. Johnston and Thomas V. Bonoma, "Purchase Process for Capital Equipment and Services," *Industrial Marketing Management*. 1981, vol. 10, p. 253.

2. In the interest of saving space, I will not substantiate each reference to psychological research. Documentation for my assertions can be found in Thomas V. Bonoma and Gerald Zaltman, *Management Psychology* (Boston: Kent Publishing Company, 1981). See Chapter 8 for the power literature and Chapter 3 for material on motivation.

Get More Out of Your Trade Shows

THOMAS V. BONOMA

In theory, trade shows should be ideal marketing tools. They offer the opportunity of face-to-face contact with both existing and potential customers. Why, then, do managers tend to be unenthusiastic—and even disdainful—about such events? It's partly because the accomplishments of trade shows, unlike other major marketing tools such as advertising and direct sales, cannot be easily measured. Yet managers frequently feel obligated to attend, if only because the marketplace expects them to be present.

The author maintains that executives can gain more from trade shows by understanding the benefits offered and picking the events accordingly. Trade show benefits can be broadly grouped into selling and nonselling categories. The selling opportunities involve, among other things, access to key decision makers, contact with prospects, and the opportunity to service customers. Their non-selling aspects include the availability of intelligence about competitors, the opportunity to upgrade employee morale, and the chance to test new products.

To many managers, trade shows are, at best, a necessary evil, to be endured rather than exploited. Consider these observations:

1. From the senior vice president of a $200 million industrial company: "Trade shows are terribly expensive and of limited value for the business you do versus the dollars spent. Once we did cut out a show, but there was such buyers' remorse that we were forced to reinstate it. Everyone wondered if we were having some financial difficulties and couldn't afford to participate! For us, trade shows are a self-perpetuating problem. If I could just throw that money into operating profit each year, I'd be a superstar. But we go, we go."

Published 1983.

2.   From Burton L. Salomon, president of institutional sales for Manhattan Industries: "Everything nowadays is done for the show management, not for the exhibitors. The only other ones to get anything out of trade shows are the hotels and the prostitutes." Yet Mr. Salomon's group participated in six major and ten small shows in 1980 alone and was planning to continue its participation in these events.

3.   From Kenton E. McElhattan, president and chairman of National Mine Service Company, a sizable producer of underground mining equipment and supplies: "The major reason we go to trade shows is because our competitors are there. Additionally, shows give the junior people in our company exposure to our big accounts, give everyone a crack at new foreign buyers, and give us a chance to introduce major new equipment to the industry. But mostly, it's a matter of image."

Trouble in Showland

When a potentially attractive marketing tool offers face-to-face customer contact coupled with the allure of increased sales, marketers might be expected to embrace it eagerly. They have embraced trade shows, but often come away feeling as if they had been hustled. This is primarily due to four negative aspects of trade show programs:

1   Unknown effectiveness—the marketing return per dollar spent.
2   Difficulty of measuring efficiency—the effectiveness of these events compared with other marketing communications tools, such as selling or advertising.
3   High and rising costs of participation.
4   A growing feeling that shows are boondoggles—more a "perk" for managers and current customers than a sound marketing communications tool.

Because of these problems, little agreement exists as to what trade shows return for the money spent or their proper marketing role. The purpose of this article is to develop an approach for evaluating their benefits.

The Macro Picture

After sales force costs, the trade show is one of the most significant line items in the marketing budget for many companies. While shows usually are associated mainly with industrial companies, often nonindustrial businesses are represented too. For many companies, trade show expenditures are the major—and for more than a few, the only—form of organized marketing communications activity other than efforts by the sales force and distributors.

The trade show is most familiar as an exhibition. Manufacturers, distributors, and other vendors display their products or describe their services to invited persons including current and prospective customers, suppliers, other business associates, and the press. The public usually is excluded. A typical event, such as the International Automotive Services Industries Show or the International Coal Show, runs eight hours a day for three days, plus one or two preview days, and registers 25,000 attendees.[1]

Expositions, on the other hand, are open to the public, usually through the sale of tickets, and fall into two categories: public shows and fairs. Typical public shows feature themes such as home-garden, boat, auto, hi-fi, and antiques; they are often retail-sales oriented and sometimes resemble middle eastern bazaars. Most fairs, by contrast, are rural, run for a week or longer, and only sometimes permit commercial exhibits in addition to their usual displays of community activities and commerce. Of the 431 members listed in the *Directory of the International Association of Fairs and Expositions*, 376 reported 1979 show attendance figures totaling 77.2 million. About 35% of the general population attended one or another kind of exposition in 1979.

A total of 7,857 trade shows with 10 or more booths held in 1979 accounted for an expenditure of $6 billion on such items as space rental, exhibit design and construction, shipping, installation, attendance promotion, and the costs of manning the booths. This investment was greater than that made for magazine, radio, or outdoor advertising during 1979 (the latest year for which figures are available), and was exceeded substantially only by newspaper and television advertising expenditures. The cost of a face-to-face trade show contact—defined as an individual who stops at an exhibitor's booth and requests literature—was estimated at almost $60, compared with nearly $140 for a sales call.

Between 5% and 35% of a company's annual advertising budget may be allocated to trade show expenditures—generally more for industrial businesses and less for consumer goods companies. In terms of the entire marketing budget, the percentages range from 5% to 20%, with 10% to 12% as an average. These percentages, already large, make no attempt to account for the most significant cost of trade show participation—top management time. Although there is no such thing as a typical company or trade show, an estimated $73,000 is allocated for each show, and the median manufacturer, or distributor, attends nine to ten shows annually.

The Micro Picture—Three Programs

How is trade show money spent? A look at three corporate programs gives an idea.

The National Mine Service Company, whose chairman was quoted at the outset, spends approximately 25% of its annual non-sales force marketing budget on trade shows. The company participates in four to six small trade shows each year and allocates a sum annually to a fund to be spent at the industry's major trade exposition, the American Mining Congress International Coal Show. This event is held once every four years. NMS, which has $130 million in annual sales, spent somewhat more than $1 million on its participation in the 1980 Coal Show. That figure includes conservative estimates of the cost of managerial time. The Coal Show, like many other major trade presentations, is a nonselling show, classified as an educational activity by the Internal Revenue Service. At such shows, selling is prohibited. NMS used one Coal Show to introduce a major new piece of mining equipment to the industry and drew some 12,000 visitors to its exhibit at another.

The Spangler Candy Company is a small business producing candy products, including Dum-Dum brand lollipops. Spangler participates in an average of 12 trade shows annually, with its major effort aimed at a national confectioners' show. In contrast to National Mine, Spangler participates exclusively in selling shows where orders are not only expected from distributors and retailers but used also as the primary indicator of trade show effectiveness. Because Spangler expects numerical sales targets to be reached and meetings between its top offices and key customers to occur at trade shows, managers carefully measure show performance on these two variables.

Atlantic Aviation Corporation's trade show program is more akin to that of National Mine than Spangler's. A medium-sized marketer of aircraft and aviation services, Atlantic exhibits at five to seven events a year. Its largest participation is at the National Business Aircraft Association Show, to which it sends 60 to 70 company representatives at a cost of more than $250,000. Unlike Spangler, Atlantic cannot easily assess the impact of the gatherings on sales. According to an Atlantic manager, "We have a difficult time justifying the money that trade shows cost, because no proof exists that a sale was made due to our participation in any given show. The acquisition of a business aircraft is a long process—no one is going to make a $4 million purchase without some long, hard thinking. The trade show may or may not be influential."

Measuring Effectiveness: The Traditional Wisdom

Standards for evaluating trade shows' effectiveness are more available than are standards for assessing their efficiency.

To measure effectiveness, most managers set pre-show objectives; one survey, for example, found that 55% of top managers whose companies participated in trade shows listed specific goals to be attained.[2] These covered such aims as introducing or evaluating new products, generating sales leads and new sales contacts, and soliciting orders at the show. Measures of trade show effectiveness in terms of these objectives included the following:

☐ The number of leads generated from a show.
☐ The quantity of actual sales from these leads.
☐ The cost per lead generated.

☐   The feedback about the show subsequently given to the sales force.

☐   The amount of literature distributed at the show.

While such measures might be appropriate for Spangler Candy's trade shows, they are much harder to apply to those where sales are not allowed such as the affairs attended by NMS and Atlantic Aviation. Many contacts at these type shows are not quantifiable. When displaying expensive mining equipment or a business jet, it is hard to know if a show "looker" is indeed a quality lead. Attendance at a booth may have more to do with the appearance of the exhibit and quantity of food than with any intention to buy.

Clearly, the traditional measures of effectiveness make strong assumptions about what trade shows do. Implicit is the notion that they are more opportunities for direct selling than sales promotion devices.

The emphasis on numbers of contacts, cost per contact, amount of literature distributed, and sales suggests that a majority of managers view shows as an almost straight-line extension of personal selling, done in mass fashion, rather than as a tool to maintain relationships with key customers or to satisfy other needs like competitive intelligence-gathering.

Effective market communications involves objectives other than those that are selling-related. Regular contact between a company and its existing customers, for instance, may be a good way for a company to become aware of service problems before they fester, or to learn about a customer's future plans before they surprise the vendor in some unpleasant way. Yet most trade shows are evaluated for effectiveness on a cost-per-call basis, and other important potential benefits are not addressed.

As for measuring the efficiency of trade shows, there is no traditional wisdom on which a manager can rely. What proportion of the marketing dollar should be allocated to trade shows? Does the type of show make a difference, and should companies take this into account in designing their trade show mix? What indicators tell whether one marketing communications program, including shows, is balanced and another is not?

A Broader Perspective

Most managers struggle with trade show budget allocation and benefit measurement issues without a clear sense of the answers to four questions:

1   What functions should a trade show program perform in the company's overall marketing communications operation?

2   To whom should the marketing effort be directed at trade shows?

3   What is the appropriate show mix for the company? How can the company meet its objectives with it?

4   Considering the rest of the marketing mix, what should the trade show investment-audit policy be? How should audits be carried out?

To answer these questions, we must explore how trade shows and expositions can satisfy complex selling and nonselling marketing communications functions.

Selling Objectives

The selling goals that can be satisfied at a trade show are distinct. Five important selling functions which may be filled by participation in various shows and exhibitions are the following:

- ☐ Identification of prospects.
- ☐ Gaining access to key decision makers in current or potential customer companies.
- ☐ Disseminating facts about vendor products, services, and personnel.
- ☐ Actually selling products.
- ☐ Servicing current accounts' problems through contacts made.

Any given trade show can have a high potential to satisfy one or several of these functional objectives and a low potential to satisfy others. For example, the New England Truck Show (a trade show, not an exposition) mainly satisfies the objectives of prospecting for new leads, gaining access to those who may buy a tractor-trailer or a fleet, and disseminating information on vendor benefits to potential customers. Not much selling per se goes on at a show such as this, except by secondary vendors of add-on equipment or maintenance services.

By contrast, a microcomputer exposition such as the Midwest Computer Show, held for owners of small businesses, or a show organized by a greeting card manufacturers' trade association, is more selling-oriented than identification- and access-oriented. Account servicing generally plays a smaller role at such expositions.

Although every trade show or exposition does not offer the opportunity to fully satisfy all selling objectives, most companies, in my experience, do not take maximum advantage of the possibilities that exist. A prime example is the opportunity for significant account servicing at major trade shows. Cheaply and at one crack, smart managers can learn how already sold products or services are viewed by key accounts and obtain information which would be difficult to get otherwise.

Nonselling Objectives

I have labeled the second marketing communications function served by trade shows as nonselling objectives. These include maintaining the company image with competitors, customers, and the industry generally, plus the press; gathering intelligence on competitors' products, prices, and other important marketing variables; maintaining and enhancing corporate morale; and the product testing-evaluation function cited by so many managers in the survey previously mentioned.

It is hard to know exactly what top managers mean when they talk about the image-maintenance effects of trade show participation, although they refer to this function frequently. The term certainly relates to a company's exhibit and its personnel at important trade shows compared with both previous exhibits and its competitors' efforts. As one chief executive put it to me, "We have to be here to convince our customers and prospects that we are a large, solid, stable force in the industry. That means this big booth, chrome, and plush carpets. If we didn't come here, or came and stood on a single linoleum square handing out suckers, people rightly would wonder if we were in trouble."

Intelligence of all sorts about competitors is freely available at most major trade shows. Shows are one of the cheapest and most reliable ways a company can inform its technical, production, and marketing people about the competition. Even when proprietary components or systems are closely guarded secrets, companies sometimes throw caution to the winds for the benefit of show customers.

At one major trade show I attended last year a new product displayed by one vendor was a high point for competitors' visits. Proprietary solid-state motor controls, usually hidden behind steel panels, were displayed for all to see under Lucite panels. A blueprint for the proprietary cutting head was draped across a table and I was able to photograph it easily. Even though I was wearing a badge which identified me as affiliated with a competitor, a chief design engineer talked freely with me about total R&D costs, development time, and components sources for the new machine. A major trade show represents a three-day college education in competitive strategy and tactics.

An infrequently mentioned, but very important, function of trade shows is to boost the morale of those staff members who are chosen to attend. This morale boost often extends widely, affecting low-level staff (i.e., engineers, shop floor personnel, and sales representatives) and inexperienced managers, as well as the usual array of more senior managers. While most staff members attending trade shows work harder than they do during a comparable period at their usual work, the impression remains that selection to attend a major show is an important privilege. This feeling is especially strong among engineering and R&D department staff who seldom get as much customer contact as they need, and members of the sales force who enjoy the opportunity to rub shoulders with top management.

Finally, a trade show offers a valuable opportunity to introduce products and services and assess preliminary customer reactions. It is an inexpensive test market with a self-selected, invited audience likely to be critical but appreciative. There are dangers, however, in the use of trade shows for market sampling in this way, especially when demonstration of new products reveals too much to competitors that is of a proprietary nature.

Not every show offers all these nonselling benefits to attending businesses. Some minor events, such as regional computer expositions or coal industry safety equipment shows, probably will not offer much in the way of intelligence gathering or morale boosting to participants. Still these can be used to build a company's image ("These guys are at every show there is!" remarks a regular visitor) or test new products out of the limelight of an international exhibition. Other shows may be better for morale building or gathering information on the competition.

Management's first task in evaluating its projected participation in any trade show, then, is to determine how well each contemplated show allows satisfaction of the company's selling and nonselling objectives. A good annual exercise for managers is to choose their most critical objectives, and then to map the trade show investments that best satisfy these. National Mine's objectives, for example, appear to have much more to do with the nonselling objectives of image building and morale boosting for its younger executives, by making them visible to key account personnel, and with the selling objective of account servicing. The heavy equipment manufactured by NMS ranges in price from $60,000 to more than $1 million, so it is unlikely that NMS would make many immediate sales through involvement in selling shows. On the other hand, participation in a nonselling, industry promotion event probably makes less sense for a company producing a full line of low unit-price software for owners of small businesses.

Analyzing Shows

Clarifying and expanding objectives does not alone produce effective trade show programs. To plan communications strategy and measure effectiveness, managers must reach two further decisions about show participation. First, which of its market constituencies is the target? Second, what kinds of show are available for this purpose?

Trade shows can be divided roughly into those where objectives of the selling process are the major focus, and those where satisfaction of nonselling objectives is a likelier consequence of participation. Sometimes these distinctions are formalized by character, as when a primarily educational association holds an industry promotional show. More often, the differences between selling and nonselling shows are more a matter of degree than of kind, and the two types form endpoints for a continuum along which any show can be placed. It is useful for planning purposes to categorize both the trade show program and individual show participations in this manner.

When the type of trade show is matched to market constituency, guidelines result which can help managers plan participations and evaluate effectiveness. The matrix in Exhibit 1 enables us to consider trade shows in terms of primary target audiences of current buyers and potential customers that management hopes to reach.

The upper left quadrant of the matrix outlines the characteristics that exist when a company's main concern is to maintain or enhance relationships

Exhibit 1.   Trade Shows and Market Constituencies

	Selling objectives	Nonselling objectives
Current customers	Maintain relationships Transmit messages to key accounts Remedy service problems Stimulate add-on sales	Maintain image Test products Gather competitive intelligence Widen exposure
Potential customers	Contact prospects Determine needs Transmit messages Commit to callback or sale	Contact prospects Foster image building Test products Gather competitive intelligence

with its current customers, and its major opportunities to do so (whether by choice or show availability) are at selling shows. The criteria by which participation should be evaluated to assess effectiveness in this case include maintenance of contact with accounts, becoming aware of and remedying account problems, and transmitting messages to key accounts. Planning and measuring mechanisms might include the number of meetings with key accounts held at the show, the kind and nature of account problems of which managers become aware, and the kind of customer and competitor intelligence gathered from the event. Because the company's primary motives are account maintenance and enhancement, there should be no attempt to calculating cost per contact or amount of literature distributed.

The lower left quadrant in Exhibit 1 depicts the conditions when a company's primary objective is to acquire new leads and customers from prospects and generate sales or commitments for call-backs at the show. Here the planning and measuring guides would resemble those recommended by traditional wisdom—that is, tabulating such things as meetings with prospects and actual sales. Similar planning-evaluation measures could be constructed for the two nonselling quadrants of the matrix in the exhibit.

The distinctions I have drawn, though arbitrary, make it possible to comment on the effectiveness of trade show participation. If a company chooses current buyers as its primary target and potential customers as a secondary one, for instance, effectiveness measures should be constructed accordingly. Similarly, as in the case of Atlantic Aviation, if the major motivation for attending shows is maintaining image, then effectiveness measures should be derived from the nonselling quadrants of the exhibit.

Gaining Efficiency and Coherence

Once marketing communications objectives have been identified, it is possible to make allocation decisions in terms of selling and nonselling goals.

Selling Variables

From the viewpoint of selling, management must decide how much of its marketing communications budget it wishes to allocate to *getting users* and how much to *keeping users*. To a great degree, this decision will be dictated by the nature of the remainder of the market communications program currently in place, including the sales force, sales promotion, and advertising subfunctions.

A sales force is an excellent tool for keeping customers through selling and account servicing and a poor tool for getting new customers because of the high costs per contact. Advertisements, brochures, and the like are good customer-getting tools and also help with image maintenance. But they are usually ineffective in persuading customers to keep coming back, except in the case of low-priced and simple merchandise. Sales promotions, such as incentives, gifts, or other items given to current and potential customers serve both getting and keeping purposes, depending on the industry. In consumer goods, for example, coupons and other trade promotions help attract new users. For some industrial products, gifts and other promotions can help keep a current user satisfied and generate incremental sales.

In contrast to such specific and targeted marketing communications tools, trade shows can meet a broad range of different objectives simultaneously. Like all multipurpose tools, however, their impact tends to diffuse and lack force if they are not managed closely. For this reason, a company would be wise to use its trade show program as mortar to fill up the chinks in the bricks of its overall advertising, sales force deployment, and sales promotion strategy. If some aspect of the marketing communications mix is weak, managers should employ trade shows to shore it up.

For example, the typical industrial or commercial company spends the bulk of its marketing dollars—often up to 80%—on its sales force, less on sales promotions, and even less on advertising. Such a communications mix is much better at keeping users than at getting new ones. Managers in this case may wish to invest mostly in trade shows that allow maximum satisfaction of lead-generating and prospecting objectives. If they also offer account servicing, so much the better—but this will not be the major reason for participation.

Companies with top-heavy advertising budgets and lower sales force expenditures might want to seek events allowing satisfaction of objectives such as closing sales, servicing accounts, and other customer-keeping activities. Similarly, companies whose greatest marketing strength lies in prospecting and getting trial customers would lean toward account-servicing shows.

Nonselling Variables

Managers must also decide how well nonselling aspects of their marketing communications mix help to maintain corporate image, gather intelligence, boost morale, and allow new-product testing. They must compare trade show opportunities with other aspects of their strategy, such as a corporate communications program directed at image maintenance or a market research program for product testing. A company like Atlantic Aviation, for example, which has an extensive corporate communications program in the form of advertising and is backed by plane manufacturers with extensive market research facilities, needs to spend less on trade shows to satisfy the nonselling functions than does a company like National Mine, which has a low advertising budget and does little formal market research.

Managing Showland

To summarize how trade show budget allocations fit into the broader scope of a company's overall marketing communications program, consider Exhibit 2. It assesses how well a company's current program, without trade shows, meets objectives. Strong areas can include the ability to get customers, keep customers, or satisfy nonselling objectives such as image building, intelligence gathering, and morale boosting. It describes available trade shows in terms of their ability to meet these objectives. The squares in the matrix of Exhibit 2 serve as a rough guide to the amount of funds a company may want to invest in a trade show program under different conditions.

For example, the exhibit recommends a high-profile trade show program to the company whose marketing communications mix is efficient in keeping customers—but inefficient in getting them—if shows are available which potential customers can be expected to attend. If, however, managers suspect that most of what goes on at available shows satisfies the nonselling function and they lack good opportunities for prospecting, the exhibit recommends stopping or at least curtailing trade show appearances.

On the other hand, it recommends a full-bore high-profile show program for companies whose mix is poor for retaining customers although efficient at identifying and selling prospects—when the available shows mainly attract current customers. Many smaller computer companies, such as Apple Computer and Tandy Corporation, face this problem, as they find customers

Exhibit 2. Trade Show Spending Decisions

Trade show strengths	Marketing communications mix strengths		
	Gets customers	Keeps customers	Builds morale, allows testing, gets intelligence, maintains image
Gets customers	Low investment in shows	High investment in shows	Maintenance investment
Keeps customers	High investment in shows	Low investment in shows	Maintenance investment
Builds morale, allows testing, gets intelligence, maintains image	Low or maintenance investment	Maintenance investment	Maintenance investment

easier to come by than to keep a rapidly-changing technological environment that promises a more advanced state of the art with a supplier switch. When available shows signal great opportunities to prospect for new business, such companies should not overlook them. However, they might be better off investing funds in shows that help keep customers.

Establishment or maintenance of a trade show program just for image strengthening or just for intelligence gathering is probably a bad investment. To do so solely in the hope of servicing current accounts or getting new prospects is also a bad investment. Unless management plans its show participation to bolster its selling weaknesses and to satisfy nonselling objectives, it should participate in only a very few trade shows or, perhaps, none at all.

The data for evaluations such as the ones I suggest are readily available to managers from a company's show records and, more importantly, from the "long subjective look" of the communications program recommended by one of the managers quoted previously. Trade shows are an inherently "sloppy" marketing problem. Crisp quantitative decision models will never be available to codify their subtler functions. But that is no reason for marketers to avoid careful thinking and systematizing of their subjective impressions. That, after all, is the essence of management.

Notes

1. The Trade Show Bureau (49 Locust Street, New Canaan, CT 06840) provided some of the statistics. See their *Research Reports* series. Nos. 3, 4, and 5, and their *Trade Show Fact Sheet*.

2. This survey, ''The Exhibitor and His Approach to Trade Shows,'' is available from Exhibits Surveys, Inc., P.O. Box 327, Middletown, NJ 07748.

32

Nonstore Marketing
Fast Track or Slow?

JOHN A. QUELCH and HIROTAKA TAKEUCHI

A decade of impressive growth has convinced many retailers and analysts alike that the prospects for nonstore marketing in the years ahead are virtually unlimited. Not only would the various forms of nonstore sales presently in use continue to increase in volume far faster than retail sales generally; the application of such new marketing technologies as interactive cable television would add yet more support to their current stunning growth rate.

   This optimistic forecast, argue the authors, is simply not borne out by the facts. Though the future of nonstore marketing is indeed promising, the promise is by no means unlimited. Forces already at work will both slow the growth of its established approaches—mail-order catalogs and the like—and will also restrict the immediate usefulness of the newer technologies. In a dispassionate and balanced way, the authors provide a detailed overview of nonstore marketing and a measured estimate of its future prospects.

Will nonstore marketing, sometimes called direct marketing, become the next revolution in retailing? According to several optimistic forecasts, the answer is an unquestionable yes. There is already in place a variety of established selling techniques that permit consumers to purchase products and services without having to visit retail stores, and several new approaches have been made possible by recent technological advances. (The Appendix provides a brief description of both.)

   It is, however, far easier to describe the various types of nonstore marketing than to distinguish it as a whole from other forms of retailing, for the line between in-store and nonstore marketing is fuzzy. Consider, for example, that:

   1.   A consumer may become confident enough to purchase merchandise by mail order only after having shopped at a store several times. Al-

Published 1981.

ternatively, a catalog may interest a consumer in a product that he or she subsequently purchases in a store.

2.   Every year, department and specialty stores with annual sales of $75 million or more generally issue 6 to 20 catalogs with a circulation of from 100,000 to a million each. Among typical department stores, telephone and mail-generated orders account for 15% of total volume during the Christmas season,[1] and old-line retailers such as Sears and Lazarus are experimenting with interactive cable television to sell their products and services.

3.   Mail-order houses like Talbots and Carroll Reed are expanding their retail store networks. As of this writing, Talbots has 16 stores and Carroll Reed, 15 (excluding ski shops).

4.   Manufacturers that traditionally sold their products only through retail outlets are adding direct marketing as an additional mode of distribution. Nearly 50 companies in the *Fortune* "500" have already become members of the Direct Mail/Marketing Association.[2]

5.   Fruit growers, cattle breeders, and cheese producers are discovering the fast-growing mail-order food business. Consumers can now buy "gourmet" foods from some 500 mail-order food houses, which do three quarters of their annual volume during the Christmas season.[3] Conglomerates like Tenneco (House of Almonds), Greyhound (Pfaelzer Brothers steaks), and Metromedia (Figi's cheese) have already entered this high-margin specialty business.

These developments, among others, lead us to agree with the optimistic forecasters that the growth of nonstore marketing in recent years has been impressive and that its promise remains bright. At the same time, however, we do foresee several limits to its unrestrained growth in the future and are, therefore, not convinced that it will soon revolutionize retailing.

Marketing Failure—and Success

Established forms of direct marketing produced mixed results during the 1970s. To understand clearly their future potential, we need to examine the reasons for their past failure and successes.

Grocery Shopping

During the past 10 years, several attempts have been made to automate nonstore grocery shopping. One of the first was launched in San Diego by Telemart Enterprises, Inc. in the fall of 1970. In two weeks of operation, Telemart received some 23,000 orders (with no minimum amount required) and had to close its doors. The warehouse employees who collected ordered items and put them into shopping bags simply could not keep pace: they were able to fill less than one fifth of the orders. Telemart even resorted to shutting off the telephones, but too late.

According to *Computerworld*, the Telemart system worked like this: "A shopper would call in and give his or her credit number. The order taker would interconnect the shopper with a 'talking computer' for a three-way conversation. Using a catalog, the shopper would list the desired items. The computer would record the items ordered, verify that they were in stock, give a verbal response on the price of each item, provide totals, and mention any specials of the day.

"The computer would then print out an optimized collection list for the central distribution center, select the most efficient truck routing for delivery of goods to the customer, maintain all records of accounts payable and receivable, and keep a running tabulation of inventories."[4]

Store-to-Door, a system similar to Telemart's, opened two years later in Sacramento and lasted a little longer—from September 7 to November 4, 1972. In this case, the computer, not overacceptance, was to blame. The system was supposed to handle 3,400 orders a day but actually was able to handle only 500. Although Store-to-Door had promised afternoon delivery on items ordered in the morning and next-morning delivery on items ordered in the afternoon, its delivery times quickly began to slip as a result of delays in computerized order processing and invoice printing.

The next entrant into the field was Call-a-Mart in Louisville, Kentucky, in June 1973. This company folded after 14 months of operation, having disappointed its customers by curtailing its product assortment to about 4,000 items (at the time, supermarkets usually carried about 9,000 items).

Why were these attempts to automate the nonstore purchasing of groceries so short-lived, especially given favorable demographic and lifestyle trends? There are four possible explanations:

1. *Lack of managerial skills.* Each attempt was plagued by a major operational problem. One company could not handle warehousing and logistical problems; another, the computer system; the third, the dynamics of merchandising. The common denominator here is managerial incompetence. These companies simply did not have the managerial skills necessary to run a complex service operation.

2. *Underfinancing.* Each of the companies was seriously underfinanced. Telemart started from an initial investment base of roughly $2 million; the others, less than $1 million. To imagine that they could develop for only $1 million or $2 million a centralized, mechanized, and computerized distribution system with enough left over for inventory and promotion was, at best, wishful thinking.

3. *Failure to satisfy consumer needs.* The service was supposed to free shoppers from time-consuming trips to the store. But they had to spend 10 to 30 minutes, depending on the size of their order, compiling a properly coded grocery list from a catalog (and pulling out old invoices if they wanted to compare prices). They had to spend another 10 to 30 minutes giving their orders to the telephone operators or the "talking computer" and then stay

home waiting for the groceries to be delivered. Next, they had to examine the quality of the goods and, if necessary, send some of them back for redelivery.

4. *Inability to offer low prices.* The companies had intended to pass along to consumers the savings resulting from operating economies (e.g., lower rent, lower utility charges, a more efficient warehouse, lower payroll expenses, lower incidence of checkout errors and shoplifting). In reality, consumers paid competitive prices for the items that they ordered as well as a few extra dollars for membership and delivery. In some cases, the membership fee was as much as $10 and the delivery fee $4 per trip.

Mail-Order Catalogs

In contrast to the abortive attempts at nonstore grocery shopping, selling through mail-order catalogs positively thrived in the 1970s. Americans spent an estimated $26.2 billion on mail-order items in 1978,[5] up from $12 billion in 1975;[6] over the same period, mail-order houses tallied an average after-tax profit of 7%.[7] These figures compare quite favorably with those of the retailing industry as a whole, whose sales grew at less than half the rate and showed less than half the profit margin of mail-order sales.

In recent years, the fastest growing and most profitable part of the whole mail-order business has been the specialty houses like L.L. Bean, which now account for nearly 75% of total mail-order sales.[8] Their success derives in part from the various factors listed in Exhibit 1 and, in part from:

Efficient Operation. To support the 26 million catalogs it mails each year, L.L. Bean, for example, is organized so that customers can telephone orders 24 hours a day, 365 days a year, and can return all merchandise without

Exhibit 1. Factors Contributing to the Success of Mail-Order Catalogs

Socioeconomic Factors	External Factors	Competitive Factors
More women joining the work force	Rising cost of gasoline	Inconvenient store hours
Population growing older	Availability of WATS 800 lines	Unsatisfactory service in stores
Rising discretionary income	Expanded use of credit cards	Difficulty of parking, especially near downtown stores
More single households	Low-cost data processing	"If you can't beat 'em join 'em" approach of traditional retailers
Growth of the "me" generation	Availability of mailing lists	

questions asked. The distribution center processes virtually all mail orders within 72 hours, and the computer maintains a sales record on a customer-by-customer basis.

Strong Financial Backing.   Although L.L. Bean is still owned by the Bean family, in recent years an increasing number of corporations with substantial financial resources—corporations such as ITT, Beatrice Foods, W.R. Grace, General Mills, Quaker Oats, and Tenneco—have acquired mail-order businesses. In the future, each of these companies may own several mail-order businesses. General Mills, for example, owns Talbots (women's sportswear), Eddie Bauer (outdoor clothing), Bowers and Ruddy Galleries (rare coins), H.E. Harris (stamps), and Lee Wards (knitting goods).

Carefully Selected Merchandise.   Because a specialty mail-order house knows in detail who its customers are and what they are looking for, it has to carry only a limited assortment of products. The mail-order catalog, in a sense, shops the market for its customers and edits the offering. Selected merchandise simplifies things for the customer by eliminating the need to sort through an array of products and by reducing the need for assurance of product quality.

Bounded, Not Unbounded, Potential

But will this boom in nonstore marketing last? The loss of consumers' discretionary income and a marked decline in their response rates to direct marketing suggest that the 1980s will not be as fertile a decade for continued growth as some observers believe. In our opinion, four primary factors will restrain the growth rate of established methods of nonstore marketing: reluctant consumers, inappropriate products, cautious manufacturers, and threatened retailers.

Reluctant Consumers

For a family living on Manhattan's East Side—especially a family in which both adults work—shopping may be sufficiently tedious to make direct marketing a great convenience. For the many Americans with increasing leisure time, however, shopping is an important form of entertainment. Browsing through a mail-order catalog is simply not as satisfying as being able to touch, feel, and smell the merchandise.

Many consumers see other values in store shopping, too. It exposes them to an assortment of product alternatives; it facilitates price comparisons and avoids delivery charges; and it permits consumers to deal personally with salespeople. Although the decline in the quality of in-store service is often cited as one reason for the growth of direct marketing, shoppers still appreciate discussions with store personnel as a source of product information as well as for their social value.

Marketers can, of course, segment consumers according to their preferred shopping styles. Some value convenience more than price and thus respond frequently and enthusiastically to direct marketing offers; some are curious enough about certain kinds of merchandise to pay for information in catalog form. According to an Ogilvy & Mather survey in 1978, the 23% of consumers who spent more than $100 apiece in direct marketing purchases during the previous year accounted for a full 83% of total nonstore dollar volume.[9]

The majority of consumers, however, still view mail and telephone ordering as risky. These people, perhaps remembering the unscrupulous practices of an earlier generation of direct marketers, are less interested in convenience than in product quality, reliable delivery, and the ease with which unsatisfactory products can be returned for refund or replacement. In addition, many view the techniques of direct marketing—the unsolicited telephone calls, the "junk" mail, and the trading and renting of mailing lists—as an invasion of privacy.

Inappropriate Products

Not all products lend themselves equally well to direct marketing. Stereo equipment, for example, is an expensive, heavy, bulky item subject to transit damage and high delivery costs. It requires extensive comparison shopping and in-store demonstration. Even someone who has a specific brand of equipment in mind prefers to purchase it in a store because the retail price of stereo equipment is customarily negotiated at the point of sale. And if the equipment must later be returned for exchange or servicing, the typical consumer will perceive a local store as both more convenient and more likely to be responsive than an out-of-state direct marketer.

Nonstore marketers have indeed offered big-ticket luxury items through mail-order catalogs—if only to legitimize in the consumer's mind the idea of purchasing them without visiting a store. A major credit card company, for example, recently offered its cardholders a complete stereo system. Although the system is a well-known brand, recipients of the offer may well have felt that the advertised equipment was shortly to be discontinued or that the credit card company was, at best, a questionable distributor of such equipment. By contrast, when Gulf Oil offers its cardholders a tire inflator, no such doubts or uncertainties exist.

The direct marketing of "collectibles" has enjoyed quite a different consumer response. Collectibles like coins or plates are not especially heavy or bulky, yield high profits relative to transaction and delivery costs, and do not require instructions for use. They are specialty items, often with broad product lines, that by definition are not in wide distribution and sometimes not available at all in stores.

Potential purchasers are price insensitive and lack the strong brand preferences that might prompt extensive comparison shopping. Those direct marketers of collectibles like the Franklin Mint that are able to establish lasting credibility for their company name can significantly reduce a consumer's sense of risk in buying by mail and can therefore amortize the marketing costs of an initial purchase over a sequence of follow-on purchases.

Still other factors can influence the suitability of a product for direct marketing. Health remedies urgently needed by consumers must be distributed through convenience stores; consumers cannot wait for a mail delivery.

Similarly, products that have to be customized do not lend themselves to direct marketing. Neither, of course, do perishable food items. However, these rules do not always hold. Many mail-order companies in Wisconsin market cheeses and cured meats through catalogs because their customers associate the highest quality in cheese with a particular state and are consequently willing to make mail-order purchases to obtain what they obviously view as a specialty item.

From these examples, it should be clear that to date the ideal product for direct marketing has been a small, lightweight yet durable, high-margin specialty item available to consumers only through selective distribution. Direct marketers have with mixed success been attempting to broaden the range of products that consumers are willing to purchase from them by offering free trials, money-back guarantees, and 800-number toll-free complaint "hotlines." They have also been trying to reduce the consumer's perception of risk by associating an image of quality with their company names.

Cautious Manufacturers

Two principal considerations have kept most manufacturers from engaging in direct marketing themselves, even though it might bring them closer to the consumer and give them more control of distribution channels.

1. *Opposition from traditional distributors.* With the exception of stores with their own direct marketing operations, retail outlets might view a manufacturer's direct marketing efforts as likely to cut into their own sales. As a result, they might threaten retaliatory action by delisting products or reducing promotional support.

2. *Limited product lines.* Few manufacturers have sufficiently broad product lines to develop mail-order catalogs of their own. Those manufacturers interested in generating sales through direct marketing, therefore, have to work with a third party. Their products might, say, appear along with those of other manufacturers in a catalog developed by a mail-order house such as Horchow.

If so, however, the manufacturer must be willing both to accept reduced brand-name recognition and to forgo the use of packaging and point-of-sale material to stimulate brand awareness. The manufacturer must also be alert to the threat to its traditional channels of distribution should the direct marketer set a lower price than its retail outlets do.

As a rule, the stronger the manufacturer's relationship with traditional distribution channels and the larger its market share, the less interest the manufacturer will have in nonstore marketing.

Threatened Retailers

As noted previously, direct marketing threatens the sales of traditional retail outlets—especially those that carry high-margin specialty items. Specialty and department stores are not, however, without defense.

Such prestigious department stores as Neiman-Marcus can hedge their bets by becoming direct marketers themselves and thus expand the geographical base of their sales without investing in new stores. They can control the rate at which their nonstore business expands and prevent any reduction in the ROI of their traditional stores.

Chain stores can minimize sales losses by emphasizing personalized in-store service, by extending store hours, by offering in-store boutiques, by developing a specific image for each local outlet, and by competing with the catalogs of direct marketers through newspaper supplement advertising and direct mailings of their own.

Specialty store chains can also compete against direct marketers on the basis of in-store service, convenience, and breadth of assortment. A specialty shoe retailer such as Edison Bros. can offer customers a wide choice of merchandise at different price and quality levels by locating several outlets with different names in a large mall designed for one-stop shopping and by developing more powerful store images through store design and focused product selection.

Because direct marketers require more lead time for product planning than do retailers and because the product mix listed in a catalog cannot be quickly changed, specialty stores that sell fashion-sensitive merchandise are especially well-equipped to compete with direct marketers by emphasizing the up-to-date nature of their product lines.

New Marketing Technologies

For the various reasons mentioned in the preceding sections, we do not foresee as rapid a growth rate during the 1980s for the established techniques of nonstore marketing as some others do. But what will be the impact of the new technologies? Will they really enhance the growth of nonstore marketing by broadening the means by which direct marketers deliver their messages to and accept orders from consumers? In this section, we examine the possibilities opened by three of these new technologies.

Interactive Cable Television

Direct marketers have shown great interest in interactive cable television by purchasing advertising spots and developing new forms of catalog programming. Its appeal to consumers is that it allows them simply to press a key-pad to purchase an item that they see advertised on a commercial spot or catalog program rather than having to telephone an 800 number.

A typical catalog program on a cable channel might consist of a 30-minute "fashion show" of a direct marketer's merchandise. Such programs could be shown to all subscribers as a part of regularly scheduled programming or to individual subscribers on request and at their convenience. In fact, Times-Mirror Cable and Comp-U-Card have recently launched in six metropolitan markets "The Shopping Channel," which is exclusively devoted to catalog programming of this nature.

Recent tests of direct response advertising and catalog programming or interactive cable systems have not, however, been auspicious. Video Communications, Inc. of Tulsa found viewer reaction during a two-hour movie aired on a national cable network to direct response ads for books and furniture to be "practically zero,"[10] and an American Express Co. executive reported that the results of tests of his company's Christmas catalog on the QUBE system "were not overwhelming."[11] Catalog programming on interactive cable television is unlikely either to supplant the printed catalogs used by direct marketers or to emerge in the near future as a significant source of sales revenue for them. There are several reasons for this.

Consumer Barriers. Will people watch catalog programs? Given the range of viewing options, will the drawing power of a catalog program be sufficient to justify both the investment of direct marketers in its production and the investment of cable operators in its transmission? Will consumers be willing to pay more than the regular monthly cable charge for an opportunity to view such programming?

And for those people who do watch a catalog program, what advantages, if any, will it offer them over a printed catalog? Its entertainment value may be high, but will this translate into incremental purchases? Its information value is likely to be higher only when the actual demonstration of a product can add to understanding of its utility.

The printed catalog has several advantages. Readers can put the catalog down or pick it up at any time and can examine some items in detail while skipping others. A consumer often wants to mull over a possible purchase, refer to the catalog entry, and perhaps even discuss it with friends before making a decision.

Such flexibility is less available with catalog programs. If they are a part of regularly scheduled programming, the user must watch them at designated times and make immediate decisions whether to purchase. Not surprisingly, the president of Cable Ad Associates, which recently initiated the development of a national cable catalog, found that "people who didn't have the [printed] catalog wouldn't order. . . . The only way (catalog) marketing on TV will work is through strong print support."

A further deterrent to the purchase of cable-advertised products is the impersonal nature of the transaction. The success of many direct response marketers stems in part from courteous and knowledgeable telephone operators who can respond to questions about the merchandise and in some cases make incremental sales. And though it may eventually be possible for consumers to place an order with a person who will appear on their home TV screen and with whom they can interact directly, such a development is a long way off.

At present, however, even if a shopper is inclined to purchase a cable-advertised item, two other barriers may prevent the transaction from taking place:

First, as with TV advertising, a consumer may be uncertain whether the price of an item is higher than in a store. Some people will be willing to pay more for the convenience of "instant" shopping; others will not. To overcome this price perception problem, many direct marketers indicate in their television advertisements that the products offered are not available in any store.

Second, a consumer may be unwilling to use the electronic funds transfer system (EFTS) that purchasers of catalog program merchandise will use to make payments. With an EFTS, the buyer will not immediately receive a written record of the transaction, will have less opportunity to cancel the transaction than is now possible with payment by check, and will probably lose the advantage of the float. And many people remain concerned about the confidentiality of EFTS transactions and purchases.

Cable Operator Barriers.   Like consumers, cable operators may not be very enthusiastic about catalog programming. There are two principal reasons for their lukewarm enthusiasm.

First, cable operators have traditionally focused on obtaining revenues from subscribers, rather than from advertisers, and have been quite sensitive to potential subscriber resentment about inclusion of advertising—even in the form of catalog programming. The idea is likely to become more acceptable as rising costs require cable operators to choose between raising subscription fees and raising advertising revenues.

The introduction of national cable networks such as CNN and ESPN, which are funded by advertising; the establishment of the Cable Advertising Bureau; the development of audience research for cable stations; the growing interest of advertising representatives in handling cable station clients; and the investment in test campaigns by large national advertisers—all these developments suggest that advertising on both one-way and two-way cable television is likely to increase. But if it does, interest in the untried hybrid form, catalog programming, is likely to decrease among both advertisers and station operators.

Second, the public policymakers usually responsible for awarding cable franchises do not always view catalog programming as a positive addition to a prospective franchisee's programming proposals. Indeed, some policymakers may view catalog programming as socially undesirable because disadvantaged consumers may be drawn into making impulse purchases of goods they cannot afford.

Of the roughly 4,500 cable stations in operation in the United States, very few are interactive systems. Of those not interactive in mode, half cannot be converted; and few of the remainder will be converted because cable station franchisees usually enjoy local monopolies. Therefore, no direct marketer can reach all cable television households with a catalog program and an interactive system.

Cost Barriers. The direct marketers whose products are shown on cable programs will have to bear the costs of producing the catalog programs. Some experimentation will be necessary to establish the optimal program format. Unlike a television advertisement, whose costs can be amortized over many showings, a catalog program must absorb the full costs immediately, for it cannot be shown more than a few times in a single market and still be effective.

Usually, local cable station operators pay cable networks, such as Ted Turner's Cable News Network, for the programming that the networks make available. Payments are made on a per subscriber basis, and the station operators cover these payments through their installation and monthly rental charges.

It seems likely, however, that station operators will view catalog programming as a form of advertising and that, far from agreeing to pay for airing it, they will expect compensation themselves. This compensation could take one of two forms: (1) the direct marketer could buy air time for the catalog program in the same way that sponsors now buy spots on television; or (2) the station operator could receive a percentage of the sales revenue generated by orders transmitted through the interactive system.

Even allowing for gradual consumer acceptance of catalog programming, the costs of generating incremental sales dollars are likely to be greater than with direct mail. The relative profitability of catalog programming becomes more questionable still when we consider its possible effect on direct-mail sales. And no direct marketer simultaneously employing both approaches could get away with charging higher prices on the catalog program than in the printed catalog in order to cover the additional costs of catalog programming.

On balance, then, catalog programming on interactive cable television is not ready for widespread adoption as a new direct marketing technique.

Interactive Information Retrieval

Through either the telephone or a two-way interactive cable system, a consumer can call up information from computer data banks. The information requested will appear on his television screen. This new technology enables the consumer to control the timing, sequencing, and content of information retrieval and to make purchases of products and services through the use of a key-pad, with expenses automatically charged to bank or credit card accounts. Here too, though, several barriers impede the rapid development of a novel approach to direct marketing.

Technological Barriers. At present, alphanumerics and graphics, but not still or moving pictures, can be retrieved from a data bank and displayed on a TV screen. Because the system can transmit only verbal, not visual, information on product attributes, it has a built-in constraint: the range of products that a person is likely to buy solely on the basis of information obtained from the system is rather narrow. Other technical problems remain, including the development of an indexing system so that a shopper can identify quickly and easily the best way to call up desired information.

Consumer Barriers. A mass market of shoppers who are at ease with computers will develop only gradually, as children familiar with home video games and classroom computers enter adulthood. To hasten things along, the French government has initiated a 10-year program to eliminate telephone directories. Users must become familiar with computerized data bases and with calling up desired directory information on a video screen attached to every telephone set. Even with greater familiarity, information retrieval systems will require much planning by individual users because they force consumers to seek out product information before deciding whether to make a purchase.

Cost Barriers. Connecting a household to an information retrieval system is expensive; it requires a decoder, a key-pad, and/or a specially modified TV set. Since either the consumer or the system operator must shoulder the expense, this investment may be a barrier to acceptance. In addition, each time someone uses the data bank, he or she will incur operating costs. So long as these combined costs hinder mass adoption of the system, its user base will probably remain too small to persuade manufacturers and retailers to supply the necessary data or to absorb some of the cost of including their data in the system.

Other constraints abound. Because of the expense to individual households, European marketers, at least, will initially tailor their information retrieval systems for the business community, supplying it with news, stock market reports, and flight schedules—that is, with time-sensitive and continually changing information. Business executives may use the system, for example, to make hotel reservations or to check on availability of crude oil supplies. And since the business market will lead the consumer market in adopting information retrieval systems, product-related data bases supplied by manufacturers and retailers are unlikely to be an early inclusion. This will certainly be the case in those European countries where government agencies have designed and developed the retrieval systems.

Even if limited product information were included in the data base, would a consumer who uses the system be any more likely to make a purchase than one who receives a mailed catalog? If not, manufacturers and retailers have little incentive to take on the costs of supplying information to the data base.

Nor would a consumer, who can use the system to retrieve information on a range of alternatives in a particular product category, be more likely to make an immediate purchase than, information in hand, to shop one or more stores for a preferred brand. Here too, if the purchase is not made via the system, manufacturers have little incentive to supply information.

But what if a shopper could not only request product information but also ascertain which stores in the area carry a particular product or brand and at what price? Price sensitivity in the marketplace would increase, and the price flexibility of both retailers and manufacturers would decline. Yet for durable goods such as cars and appliances, where pre-purchase information might be helpful, price has traditionally been a matter of negotiation between buyer and seller. Thus, it is unlikely to be included in a seller-financed data base. Only those manufacturers and retailers with standardized prices would be prepared to bear the costs of supplying information. Would consumers be willing to pick up the slack?

Videocassettes and Videodiscs

Catalog houses can produce cassettes, or more probably the lower-priced discs, for free distribution or at a nominal charge to households with videocassette recorders or videodisc players. One department store chain has experimented with this approach but has found that it cannot offset the $12 production and delivery costs of a cassette, versus the $2 cost of a printed, mailed catalog, by generating incremental sales.

Because the markets for videocassette recorders and videodisc players now feature several incompatible systems, distribution of a cassette or disc compatible with each consumer's equipment would be a rather complicated process. In addition, high equipment costs, although projected to decline, will delay widespread adoption of this direct marketing system. Standard cassettes and discs might, of course, carry paid commercials as a way of reducing unit costs, but people will probably not enjoy interruptions in their video material and might simply skip the advertisements.

A Word of Advice

We do not think that these new technologies—cable television, interactive information retrieval, and videocassettes and videodiscs—will accelerate the growth of nonstore marketing. There is little reason to suspect that consumers will soon take to them in large numbers, and they offer direct marketers few, if any, usable techniques for making their selling tasks easier.

Nor do we believe that nonstore marketing will soon bring about the predicted revolution in retailing. We do, however, think that the following *evolution* of direct marketing will take place during the next decade:

1. The distinction between in-store and nonstore marketing will become even fuzzier than it is now. We expect nonstore marketers to continue expanding their store networks (Avon, for example, recently acquired Tiffany) and retailers to continue expanding their catalog programs (Bloomingdale's recently began to mail its catalogs on an almost monthly basis).

2. The established methods of nonstore marketing will continue to dominate the sale of products and services to the consumer, but we expect the rapid growth rate enjoyed by these methods in the 1970s to slow down.

3. The actual impact of new technologies on nonstore marketing will be minimal. They will have no major effect on in-home shopping before the year 1990.

As a result, companies already in the direct marketing business, as well as those contemplating entry, should plan to:

4. Keep a long time horizon in mind. Successful direct marketers need time to build and refine their businesses and to earn a decent return. A simulation model developed by an industry source concludes that it would take 10 years for an operator of an automated food-shopping system to reach the break-even point.[12]

5. Consider the "worst case" scenario in planning by analyzing various "what if" questions and creating contingency plans accordingly. Here are some examples of appropriate questions:

☐ What if postal rates double?
☐ What if privacy laws prevent direct marketers from selling or buying mailing lists?
☐ What if a freeze is placed on credit card usage?
☐ What if a reputable competitor files for bankruptcy?
☐ What if consumers mount a revolt against "catalog clutter"?

6. Concentrate on establishing efficient and effective operations. As more and more direct marketers compete for the customer's purse, competitive survival will depend on ease of product ordering, high speed and low expense of delivery, intelligent planning of product assortments, inventory levels, catalog mailings, and the quality of customer interaction with the direct marketer.

7. Beware of overkill. Consumers who think of catalog browsing as a fascinating pastime may become bored if faced with a blizzard of catalogs.

Nonstore marketers would like to believe that a revolution is under way, but it will come, if at all, more slowly than they expect. It will come only if it can truly satisfy the needs and wants of consumers. Revolutions of this sort are made by consumers, not marketers.

Notes

1. Isadore Barmash, "Retailers Plan More Catalogues," *New York Times*, August 10, 1980.

2. Walter McQuade, "There's a Lot of Satisfaction (Guaranteed) in Direct Marketing," *Fortune*, April 21, 1980, p. 124.

3. William Harris, "Christmas Mail Munch," *Forbes*, December 22, 1980, p. 40.

4. "Telemart Failure Laid to Overacceptance," *Computerworld*, October 1970, p. 38.

5. "Socioeconomic Trends Cause High Growth in Nonstore Marketing Field," *Marketing News*, February 8, 1980, p. 1.

6. Sandra Salmans, "The Cataloguers: Santa's Workshop is Really a Warehouse Near a Post Office," *New York Times*, December 7, 1980.

7. *Marketing News*, "Socioeconomic Trends," p. 1.

8. Salmans, "The Cataloguers."

9. Cited in the *New York Times*, March 30, 1979.

10. Quoted in Les Luchter, "The New Cable Networks," *Marketing Communications*, January 1980, p. 53.

11. Quoted in Pat Sloan, "Stores Boost Direct Mail, Eye Cable," *Advertising Age*, May 26, 1980, p. 4.

12. Charles E. Hansen, "Magic Carpet Supermarkets," unpublished report, 1976. Mr. Hansen is CEO of Resource and Technology Management Corporation, Richmond, Virginia.

13. A detailed typology of nonstore retailing approaches is included in William Davidson and Alice Rodgers, "Non-Store Retailing: Its Importance to and Impact on Merchandise Suppliers and Competitive Channels," Management Horizons Inc. working paper, Columbus, Ohio, 1977.

14. "Vending Unit Sales Slide with Economy," *New York Times*, August 8, 1980.

15. Quoted in "Home Video Part 2: What's Its Future as an Ad Medium?" *Marketing and Media Decisions*, March 1980. p. 104.

Appendix

Types of Nonstore Marketing[13]

Established Methods

1. *Mail-order catalogs.* General merchandisers (Sears and J.C. Penney), department stores (Bloomingdale's and Macy's), catalog showrooms (Best Products and Service Merchandise), and specialty merchandisers (L.L. Bean and Horchow) periodically mail catalogs to targeted groups of current

and potential customers. Consumers may respond either by placing a telephone or mail order or, more traditionally, by visiting a retail outlet or a
catalog showroom to make an in-store purchase.

2. *Direct response advertising.* Consumers become aware of a product through print or broadcast advertising or through a telephone call from
a salesperson and may purchase the product by agreeing to the salesperson's
offer, by making a telephone call (usually to a toll-free number), or by
returning an order form through the mail. Frequently, direct response merchandisers who use broadcast advertising pay the station a commission for
each inquiry or order received in lieu of paying for advertising time.

3. *Home selling.* Consumers learn about a product in a face-to-face
meeting with the seller's agent. Fuller Brush and Avon, for example, use
door-to-door salespeople; Stanley Home Products and Tupperware use party
plan selling; and Amway uses a legal "pyramid" selling approach. Although
home selling is an expensive way of delivering product information to consumers, it does allow for product demonstration, personal service, and immediate delivery.

4. *Vending machines.* These machines, which represent a mixture
of in-store and nonstore marketing, enable manufacturers and wholesalers
to increase the intensity of retail distribution and, by extension, the convenience of such buy-on-impulse items as candy, beverages, and cigarettes.
These purchases add up: throughout the United States, consumers drop some
200,000 coins every minute into six million vending machines.[14]

New Technologies

1. *Interactive cable television.* An interactive cable system like the
Warner-Amex Cable Communications QUBE service in Columbus, Ohio,
permits viewers to purchase merchandise displayed on their television screens
and charge the cost to a credit card or bank account by punching a key-pad.
The system offers viewers the convenience of making impulse purchases
from an armchair, without the need for even a telephone call.

2. *Interactive information retrieval.* Systems like Canada's Telidon,
Britain's Prestel, and France's Antiope permit customers to use a computer
data bank by telephone or by a two-way cable system. The desired information appears on the home television screen, which is connected to the
telephone system through a decoder. By operating a key-pad device, a consumer can control the information appearing on the screen. Viewdata Corporation of America, a subsidiary of the Knight-Ridder newspaper chain, is
currently testing such a system in Coral Gables, Florida.

3. *Videocassettes and videodiscs.* These devices, which have to date
been sold principally as a means of enabling consumers to record television
programs that they would otherwise miss, are thought by some to have
significant promise as advertising media. According to direct marketing expert Maxwell Sroge, "Discalogs [videodisc catalogs] will be in the mail within
the next three years."[15]

33

Better Marketing at the Point of Purchase

JOHN A. QUELCH and KRISTINA CANNON-BONVENTRE

Retail stores have become the newest battleground in the war of consumer goods manufacturers to win customers. As advertising costs soar, retail sales efforts deteriorate, and consumers become more discriminating, manufacturers are discovering the need to reach potential buyers directly at the time and place at which the buying decision is made—the point of purchase. Manufacturers are finding that such tools as well-designed displays, distinctive packaging, price and sample promotions, and in-store advertising can provide them with a competitive edge. To make point-of-purchase programs work, manufacturers must be able not only to devise attractive displays but also to tailor them to various kinds of retail outlets. Finally, manufacturers must effectively execute their programs by clearly delineating their responsibilities vis-à-vis those of their retailers and by choosing the best means of servicing them.

The retail point of purchase represents the time and place at which all the elements of the sale—the consumer, the money, and the product—come together. By using various communications vehicles, including displays, packaging, sales promotions, in-store advertising, and salespeople, at the point of purchase (POP), the marketer hopes to influence the consumer's buying decision.

Partly because of the diversity of communications vehicles available and partly because effective POP programs can aid in competing for retailers' support, marketers need to manage their POP programs carefully so as to ensure that both retailers and consumers will see consistency and coordi-

Published 1983.

nation in the programs rather than confusion and contradiction. Recent examples of innovative, well-managed POP programs include:

1.   Atari's Electronic Retail Information Center (ERIC), a computerized display installed in more than 500 stores that is designed to help sell computers. An Atari 800 home computer linked to a videodisc player asks a series of questions to help the retailer determine a customer's level of computer ability and product needs. ERIC then switches on a video disk that plays the most appropriate of 13 messages based on the customer's inputs.[1]

2.   Kodak's Disc Camera, launched in May 1982. A rotating display unit presented the disc story to the consumer without the need for salesperson assistance. In addition to the display unit, the POP program included merchandising aids, sales training and meetings for retail store personnel, film display and dispenser units, giant film cartoons, window streamers, lapel buttons, and cash register display cards.[2]

3.   Ford Motor Company's showroom wine-and-cheese parties, started in Dallas and San Diego in 1982 to provide a "more comfortable [car] buying process for women" and to respond to the fact that 40% of new car purchases (valued at $35 billion) are now made by women. The auto showroom has traditionally been an uncomfortable environment for women, whom salesmen have often patronized or overpowered with technical details. The showroom events represent an effort to manage the point of purchase to attract an increasingly important customer segment.[3]

Innovative management of the point of purchase has been applied to a broad range of consumer product categories, including:

☐   Candy, gum and magazines, which depend on impulse purchases for a large percentage of their sales.

☐   Personal computers and other new technical products that require in-store demonstration.

☐   Pantyhose and vitamins, which because they include multiple items in each brand line must be presented especially clearly to the consumer and efficiently stocked.

☐   Lawn and garden appliances, which are sold through several types of retailers, each of whom requires a different POP program.

☐   Liquor and tobacco, which are prohibited from advertising in some media.

☐   Automobiles and other mature, large-ticket items usually associated with intensive personal selling.

We believe that the expenditures of consumer goods manufacturers on POP communications will increase and that marketers who can manage events at the point of purchase well can gain competitive advantage. In this article we consider why managing the point of purchase is becoming more important, the roles of each element of the POP communications mix, and how consumer goods marketers can improve their management of the point of purchase.

POP's New Importance

POP expenditures are of increasing significance to marketers for three reasons. First, they often prove more productive than advertising and promotion expenditures. Second, the decline in sales support at the store level is stimulating interest among retailers in manufacturers' POP programs. Third, changes in consumers' shopping patterns and expectations, along with an upsurge in impulse buying, mean that the point of purchase is playing a more important role in consumers' decision making than ever before.

For the same reasons, retailers are becoming increasingly receptive to manufacturers' offers of POP merchandising programs. Even K mart stores, long off limits to manufacturers' sales representatives, now allow them to set up displays and offer planograms. The delicate power balance between the manufacturer and the trade is such, however, that retailers will not give up control of the POP readily, particularly at a time when its importance is growing. Moreover, the pressure on retailers to carve out distinctive positionings to survive heightens their determination to control store layouts, space allocations, and POP merchandising.

Hence, at the same time that their interest in manufacturers' POP programs is rising, retailers are becoming more selective than they once were and beginning to impose constraints, such as restricting the height of displays to preserve the vistas in each department and on each floor. To maintain consistency in store formats and to take advantage of volume discounts, Sears, Roebuck and Company recently centralized all fixture ordering at headquarters.

Improving Communications Productivity

Marketers are carefully examining alternatives and supplements to media advertising, which has roughly tripled in cost since 1968. POP programs cannot substitute for media advertising, nor are they as easily controlled in the store since they are implemented on someone else's turf. They can, however, reinforce and remind consumers about the advertising messages they have seen before entering the store. POP programs help improve productivity in the following ways:

Low Cost.   While reaching 1,000 adults through a 30-second network television commercial costs $4.05 to $7.75, the cost per thousand for a store merchandiser or a sign with a one-year life is only 3 cents to 37 cents.[4] These figures reflect the low production and installation costs of POP materials and the fact that the same POP materials are seen repeatedly by consumers and salespeople.

Consumer Focus.   POP programs focus on the consumer but also provide a service to the trade. Because they help move products off the shelves into consumers' hands, POP expenditures are often more productive than off-invoice price reductions to the trade, which risk being pocketed and therefore withheld from the consumer.

Precise Target Marketing.   POP programs can be easily tailored to the needs of local markets or classes of trade in response to marketers' increasing emphasis on region-by-region marketing programs and on account management of key retail customers. In addition. particular consumer segments can be precisely targeted. Revlon's Polished Ambers Dermanesse Skin programmer, a nonelectronic teaching aid used at the point of purchase to suggest appropriate cosmetic combinations to black women, exemplifies a targeted approach that could not be undertaken efficiently via media advertising alone.

Easy Evaluation.   Alternative POP programs can be inexpensively presented in split samples of stores. Stores equipped with checkout scanner systems can quickly provide the sales data needed to evaluate the impact of POP programs for the benefit of both manufacturer and retailer.

Declining Retail Sales Push

Manufacturers are increasingly questioning whether they can rely on retail sales clerks to push their products at the point of purchase. The quality of retail salespeople appears to have declined as their status has diminished. Their high turnover rate (often more than 100% per year) reflects their relatively low educational level and remuneration.

Sales positions are increasingly being viewed as dead-end jobs since more retailers now prefer to hire university-trained managers.

To reduce labor costs and remain price competitive, retailers such as Sears have cut the number of clerks covering the floor in favor of centralized checkouts. Consumers have developed the impression that salespeople are less attentive and knowledgeable when, in fact, they have to cover more shoppers and product lines than before.

To cut costs while extending opening hours, retailers have also shifted to inexperienced and uncommitted part-time salespersons, who often know little about a product's features and cannot demonstrate its use.

Thus, retail salespeople increasingly lack both ability and credibility. Effective POP programs can compensate for such sales weaknesses by enabling the manufacturer to maintain control of the message delivered to the consumer at the place and time of the final purchase decision. Marketers who provide the most attractive, educational, entertaining, and easy-to-use POP programs are likely to win the favor of store management. Their products are also likely to receive more push from overextended retail salespeople because an effective POP program can increase their credibility and facilitate the selling task.

Changing Consumer Expectations

These days consumers are inclined to seek special deals and wait for sales before they buy large ticket items or stock up on small items. As a result, consumer demand for such products as cosmetics and home furnishings fluctuates more widely than ever before. Retailers are interested in POP merchandising techniques and displays that can productively occupy consumers while they are waiting for sales help. For this reason and because of union restrictions on part-time personnel, Bell Phone Centers, for example, offer consumers many POP aids, including demonstration units.

The increasing use of automatic teller machines and vending machines, the expanded use of self-service store formats, and the advent of computerized shopping mall guides all indicate that consumers who value speed and convenience are becoming amenable to helping themselves at the point of purchase. This trend is evident, for example, in hardware stores, where manufacturers such as McCulloch and retail chains such as ServiStar are providing more and more display centers to present their product lines.

Many consumers wish to do their shopping quickly and efficiently; yet, at the same time, the longer they are in a retail store, the more likely they are to buy. Purchases planned least often were, according to one survey, auto supplies (94%), magazines and newspapers (91%), and candy and gum (85%).[5] Drugstore purchases, too, were largely unplanned—60% of them, including 78% of snack food and 69% of cosmetics purchases.[6] An average of 39% of department store purchases were unplanned, ranging from 27% of women's lingerie purchases to 62% of costume jewelry purchases.[7] Effective POP programs not only present useful information efficiently; they can also make shopping entertaining and remove some of its frustration.

The Point-of-Purchase Communications Mix

How can consumer goods marketers address the different—and sometimes conflicting—interests of the manufacturer, the retailer, and the consumer at the point of purchase?

Using Displays Effectively

For one thing, they can use well-designed displays. They attract consumer attention, facilitate product inspection and selection, allow the access of several shoppers at once, inform and entertain, and stimulate unplanned expenditures. Because additional display space can expand sales without any change in retail price, consumer goods marketers increased their spending on POP displays 12% annually between 1980 and 1982. Well-designed displays respond to the needs of both the retailer and the consumer.

They reduce store labor costs by facilitating shelf stocking and inventory control, minimizing out-of-stock items, and lowering the required level of back-room inventory. For example, automatic feed displays such as 7-Up's single-can dispensers eliminate the need for store clerks to realign shelf stock.

Good displays are designed for a particular type of store and often for a specific store department. For example, the Entenmann Division of General Foods realized that its display designs in the bakery sections of supermarkets were not transferable to the cash register areas, where the company wished to sell its new line of snacks, so it developed an additional range of displays.

Good displays reflect the likely level of trade support. There is no point in designing a large display that will not generate the retailer's required level of inventory turnover. Likewise, there is no point in offering the trade a permanent display for a seasonal product. Richardson-Vicks, for example, redesigns its display each year rather than provide a permanent fixture because retailers give floor space to Vicks Cold Centers during the winter months only.

Well-designed displays are versatile and can accommodate new products. Max Factor, for example, provides retailers with a floor-stand display consisting of a series of interchangeable trays and cartridges. New product lines, packed in similar trays, can be easily inserted, while the cartridges can, when removed from the floor stand, double as counter display units.

Manufacturers must, of course, also keep their own interests in mind when they are designing displays. For example, Johnson & Johnson's First Aid Center provides supermarkets and drugstores with a permanent display for more than 30 of its first aid items.[8] By creating a strong visual impact at the point of purchase, the display presents Johnson & Johnson as a large, well-established company that offers consumers the convenience of easy product selection and "one-shelf shopping" for all their first aid needs. It also discourages retailers from stocking only the fastest-moving items. In addition, the display carries the company name and thus prevents the retailers from using the display to stock other products. At the same time, it helps Johnson & Johnson preempt competition in slow-moving product categories in which the retailer can justify stocking only one brand.

While displays such as these are becoming prevalent in self-service environments, other innovative displays are being developed to supplement the efforts of salespeople. For example, Mannington Mills' Compu-Flor, a small computerized display placed in floor covering retail outlets, is programmed to use a potential consumer's answers to eight questions about room decor. The terminal then displays three to ten appropriate Mannington styles for the customer to choose from. When idle, the machine beeps periodically to attract consumers. Mannington had placed the units in 700 stores by the end of 1982 at a cost of $8 million, an amount equal to the company's advertising budget.

Mannington found that Compu-Flor selected styles for customers more efficiently than salespeople (who had trouble remembering all the styles in the product line), encouraged salespeople to push Mannington products rather than those of its two larger competitors (Armstrong and Congoleum), and boosted the number of sales closed on a customer's first store visit.[9]

Compu-Flor is just one of a number of computerized video displays at the point of purchase that provide a standard controllable message from manufacturer to consumer, a way of engaging customers' attention while they are waiting for sales assistance, and entertainment.

A Package Is More Than a Container

Packaging has many functions beyond acting as a container for a product.

Appropriate packaging, of course, attracts attention at the point of purchase. Manufacturers such as Nabisco and Kellogg use the same package design for many items in their product lines to present a highly visible billboard of packages to consumers at the point of purchase. In 1979, Nabisco standardized the package design of its chocolate-covered cookies; the market share for this product rose from 24% to 34% by 1981.[10]

Standardized packaging also permits easy identification of brands, types, and sizes. Private-label suppliers have imitated the color codes used to identify various sizes of disposable diapers made by the brand name manufacturers. Similarly, packaging communicates product benefits and identifies target groups. Contrast the packaging of Marlboro cigarettes, aimed at men, Virginia Slims, targeted at women, and Benson & Hedges Deluxe Ultra Lights, with a silver package designed to appeal to elitists among both men and women.

And the right packaging limits the potential for pilferage of small items. The manufacturer of Fevertest, a plastic strip that, when placed on the forehead, indicates the presence of fever, added size and value to the product by enclosing the strip in a wallet, packaging the wallet in a blister pack, and displaying the item on pegboards at supermarket and drugstore checkout counters.

Consumer and trade expectations of product packaging should not discourage marketers from innovation, though frequent changes in package size and design breed trade resistance, especially when existing shelf configurations cannot easily accommodate the new packages. Reflecting the shift to self-service car maintenance, Kendall and Arco recently began to sell oil in plastic containers with built-in pouring spouts.

Making Shopping Fun

Manufacturers are increasingly using consumer promotions to make shopping exciting. These include premiums, coupons, samples, and refund offers in or on product packages to help them stand out and break through the visual clutter at the point of purchase. Package-delivered promotions have the further advantage of being inexpensive in comparison with consumer promotions offered in magazine advertisements or direct mail campaigns.

Manufacturers are also becoming aware that retailers favor manufacturers whose promotions bring consumers into the store. For example, some sweepstakes promotions, such as Brown Shoe Company's Footworks contest, encourage the consumer to match symbols in an advertisement with those on a store display or package in order to enter the contest. Retailers also like promotions that tie into store merchandising themes and cross-sell other products (promotions built around recipes or complete home decorating services, for instance) and promotions that avoid the use of special price packs that require retailers to replace existing shelf stock and set up new Universal Product Code entries in store computer systems.

In-Store Advertising Media

Manufacturers can extend to retailers a number of innovative approaches for reinforcing brand awareness and delivering advertising messages at the point of purchase. These include:

- [ ] Commercials broadcast over in-store sound systems.
- [ ] Moving message display units with changeable electronic messages.
- [ ] Customer-activated videotapes and videodiscs that show merchandise such as furniture that is too bulky to be displayed on the department floor; the videotapes can also be played in window displays to present, for example, designer fashion shows.
- [ ] Television sets installed over cash registers to show waiting customers commercials for products that are usually available nearby.
- [ ] Advertisements on carts used in supermarkets and other self-service outlets.
- [ ] Danglers and mobile displays that use available air space rather than limited floor space.

Implementation Steps

Recognizing the significance of the point of purchase is not enough. Consumer goods marketers must pay more attention to developing effective POP programs and, even more important, to ensuring that they are properly implemented at the store level.

Before developing a POP program, managers must have a clear understanding of their marketing strategy—which products are being delivered to which markets through which channels of distribution. Given the marketing strategy, marketers should go on to answer such questions as:

- [ ] What must happen at the point of purchase to satisfy consumer needs?
- [ ] Which channel members—manufacturers, retailers, consumers— are willing to perform which functions?

☐ Which members can perform them most cost-effectively?

☐ How should the functions be allocated?

☐ How should the pricing structure for the product (and for the POP program) reflect this allocation of functions?

Program Development

Once they answer these questions, marketers can work out the specifics of the POP program—objectives, vehicles, and budgets. Here are five principles that should guide this process:

1. Integrate all elements of the POP communications mix. The package, for example, cannot be designed independently of the display. All POP vehicles should communicate consistent and mutually reinforcing messages to both the trade and the consumer.

2. Offer the trade a coordinated POP program for an entire product line rather than a collection of POP materials for particular items. To further impress the trade, make sure that the POP program is easy to understand and financially realistic.

3. Link POP assistance to trade performance. High-quality displays, for example, should not be given away to the trade unless linked to a quantity purchase or paid for with cooperative advertising dollars earned on previous purchases.

4. Assume that various POP programs will be necessary for distribution channels. The traditional hardware store and the self-service mass merchandiser, for example, differ both in store environment and in type of customer; the ideal POP program for each will not be the same.

5. Integrate POP communications with non-POP communications. Television advertising should tell consumers in which stores and departments they can find the advertised product and should include shots of product packages and displays to facilitate consumer recall and brand identification at the point of purchase. Sometimes a POP display becomes the basis for a television advertising campaign, as in the case of the Uniroyal POP unit, which invited the consumer to drill a hole in a Royal Seal tire to demonstrate that no air was lost if it was punctured.

Program Execution

Any POP program is only as effective as the quality of its implementation at the store level. Effective implementation requires that managers, first, recognize the execution challenge. Many innovative approaches to managing the point of purchase fail because responsibilities for such tasks as stocking and maintaining displays are not clearly allocated or, once allocated, are not properly performed. Under these circumstances, cooperation between manufacturers and retailers can quickly turn into recrimination.

Consumer goods marketers are often too eager to assume POP responsibilities themselves. To increase their control over the execution of their marketing programs, they might enhance effectiveness and reduce expense to make the programs work by appropriately compensating the retailers.

Two recent examples highlight the risks of ineffective execution at the point of purchase:

☐ General Entertainment Corporation failed in its 1982 attempt to market popular music cassette tapes from floor-stand displays in supermarkets partly because its field sales force could not maintain display inventories of 168 stockkeeping units, many of which changed every few months.

☐ Binney & Smith, manufacturer of Crayola crayons and other arts materials, quickly placed 1,500 special merchandising units called Crayola Fun Centers in a variety of distribution outlets following their introduction in 1980. But efficiently servicing the displays proved difficult, and Binney terminated the contract of the servicing firm handling this task.

In general, the greater the number of stockkeeping units in a display and the greater the diversity of channel environments in which the displays are placed, the more complex and challenging effective execution becomes.

Next, managers must evaluate the execution alternatives. Consumer goods marketers usually have three options for carrying out POP programs—to use their own salespeople, to contract with brokers or service merchandisers, and to rely on the retailer. The evaluation should center on comparative costs, degree of marketers' control over the execution, and the relative importance of effective POP merchandising in leveraging a product's overall marketing program. The more important it is, the more justification the marketer has for using a direct sales force.

One important reason for the success of L'eggs was the company's decision to have its own salespeople deliver the product on consignment to stores and to assume total responsibility for managing the point of purchase. Yet the ability of the L'eggs salespeople to stock product displays efficiently had a negative twist; although it enabled L'eggs to introduce numerous line extensions, their addition complicated the product selection process at the point of purchase and made it seem inconvenient in the minds of many consumers.

To ensure the freshness and integrity of its snacks, Frito-Lay's 9,000 van salespeople visit 300,000 outlets each week. Beyond taking orders, they are trained to advise retailers about how to allocate shelf space in the snack food section according to a six-point space management program. Yet, despite the clout of its sales force, Frito-Lay could not persuade supermarkets to stock its new line of Grandma's cookies at supermarket check-out counters; they are now being displayed in the cookie sections.

These two examples deliver an important message. Even when a company has the sales force to ensure the execution of a POP program, it must never lose sight of the needs of consumers and the trade.

Many consumer goods marketers cannot afford their own sales forces and must rely on brokers or service merchandisers. Both are often unfairly demeaned. A good broker is sometimes more effective than a direct sales force in managing the point of purchase, as many big companies, including H.J. Heinz and Pillsbury, know well. Because they carry a number of non-competing product lines, brokers enjoy economies of scale that enable them to visit retail stores more often than a manufacturer's sales force to check stocks, reset displays, and offer planograms. Brokers can establish close relationships with retailers in their local areas and organize blockbuster promotional events for their principals. For frozen food manufacturers, brokers are especially important to managing the point of purchase. Frequent store visits are essential because freezer space is limited on account of equipment and energy costs, and stores carry little, if any, back-room inventory.

If your company uses brokers or service merchandisers, here are four approaches to ensure that they effectively execute your POP program:

1　Check the size of the broker's sales force against the company's product line commitments. Is the brokerage firm overextended? How important is your business to the firm?

2　Develop a POP program that is creative yet easy to implement. As a result, your company may gain more attention from the broker's salespeople (and, therefore, the trade) than the broker's other principals.

3　Compensate the broker appropriately for the POP tasks you expect him or her to perform. Do you provide bonus incentives to broker salespeople for additional display placements?

4　Evaluate POP performance. Do you buy display audits to compare your share of display space with your market share? Do you occasionally play the customer, visit stores, check displays, and ask sales clerks for information?

These same principles are relevant whether the retailer, a broker, or a direct sales force is responsible for executing the POP program. The most important point for the consumer goods marketer to recognize is that an effective POP program never runs like clockwork. It needs constant attention and reevaluation.

Many consumer goods marketers are increasing their expenditures on POP programs. In 1982, for example, Elizabeth Arden, Inc. raised its POP budget by 40%.[11] What these marketers recognize is the old adage that the difference between success and failure often depends on the last 5% of effort rather than on the 95% that preceded it. In consumer marketing, that last 5% manifests itself at the point of purchase just before consumers choose what to buy.

Notes

1. "Firms Start Using Computers to Take the Place of Salesmen," *Wall Street Journal,* July 15, 1982.

2. "Kodak's Dazzling Disc Introduction," *Marketing Communications,* July 1982, p. 21.

3. "Wine, Baubles, and Glamor Are Used to Help Lure Female Consumers to Ford's Showrooms," *Marketing News,* August 6, 1982, p. 1.

4. "Consumer Product Marketing: The Role of Permanent Point-of-Purchase," *POPAI News,* vol. 6, no. 2, 1982, p. 5.

5. "POPAI/Dupont Consumer Buying Habits Survey," *Chain Store Age/Supermarkets,* December 1978, p. 41.

6. "Drug Store Buying Decisions: 60 Percent In-Store," *POPAI News,* vol. 6, no. 2, 1982, p. 1.

7. D.N. Bellenger, D.H. Robertson, and E.C. Hirschman, "Impulse Buying Varies by Product," *Journal of Advertising Research,* vol. 18, 1978, p. 15.

8. "Marketing Textbook: Case History J&J First Aid Shelf Management System," *POPAI News,* vol. 6, no. 2, 1982, p. 8.

9. Lawrence Stevens, "A Computer to Help Salesmen Sell," *Personal Computing,* November 1982, p. 62.

10. Don Veraska, "More Than One Tough Cookie Wrapped This One Up," *Advertising Age,* August 9, 1982, p. M-14.

11. "A Facelift for Elizabeth Arden," *Business Week,* August 23, 1982, p. 101.

34

It's Time to Make Trade Promotion More Productive

JOHN A. QUELCH

Conceptually, trade promotions seem perfectly sensible. Consumer product manufacturers grant wholesalers and retailers price reductions to encourage special displays and so boost sales of their products. But such deals are subject to abuse by both manufacturers and the trade. For one thing, managers often view deals as an easy way to make their sales and profit targets, losing sight of the role of promotions in their companies' overall marketing strategies. Deals tend to emphasize short-term sales results at the expense of long-term planning. Too much use can dilute their marketing impact.

The fast-increasing costs associated with trade promotions are worrying many manufacturers and causing them to look closely at this marketing activity. They are discovering that reducing or eliminating promotions is easier said than done. The author maintains that manufacturers must view trade promotions from a strategic as well as a tactical perspective and must tailor individual programs to the evolving marketplace.

Trade promotion is supposed to be a cooperative marketing activity. Manufacturers extend promotions, or deals, in the form of temporary price reductions to encourage retailers and wholesalers to increase purchase commitments and build inventories. The trade publicizes these price reductions to consumers, who then step up their purchases. Everyone along the line benefits.

Too often in recent years, though, the arrangement hasn't been working

Published 1983.

as planned. Manufacturers complain that the costs associated with trade promotions are rising too fast and that retailers and wholesalers are failing to deliver on such promises as special in-store displays, feature advertising mentions, and fully-discounted consumer prices. The trade complains that manufacturers are being unreasonable in their expectations. Friction has replaced cooperation.

The following survey findings give an indication of the nature of the problems in trade promotions:

☐ Responding to a 1981 *Chain Store Age* survey, 76.4% of retailers state that they are being offered more promotions than the previous year; 22.2% report fewer deals.[1]

☐ An annual survey of managers in 65 consumer packaged goods companies indicated that 40% of the average 1980 marketing budget was spent on advertising, 35% on trade promotion, and 25% on consumer promotion.[2] Thus, trade promotions comprise a substantial segment of marketing expenses.

☐ Line managers with consumer packaged goods manufacturers responding to a 1981 *Progressive Grocer* survey ranked the total number of trade promotions and their frequency as 2 and 4 in a list of their most important problems; retail line managers ranked these as 30 and 27 respectively.[3] This suggests much disparity in the two groups' perceptions.

☐ In a 1981 survey, managers of marketing services in major consumer packaged good companies cited "effective trade and consumer promotion" more frequently than any other issue as their biggest challenge.[4]

This study reviews ways to improve the productivity and design of trade promotion programs. The analysis and conclusions are based primarily on field interviews conducted during 1981 and 1982 with some 30 line marketing managers and sales promotion specialists. This article is written from the perspective of manufacturers of grocery products, health and beauty aids, and semidurable goods, but has obvious implications for other consumer goods producers.

Diminishing Returns

Trade promotions differ both in role and nature from the two other elements in a typical marketing budget—advertising and consumer promotions. Advertising generally communicates information about brand benefits to emphasize product identity and cement brand loyalty. It usually represents a long-term investment in future sales. Trade promotion, in contrast, is typically viewed as an easily executed means of boosting short-term sales. The emphasis is on price rather than brand benefits. Costs vary directly with unit sales and are therefore incurred on a pay-as-you-go basis at less financial risk than advertising costs. While the effectiveness of both advertising and trade promotion ultimately depends on the level of consumer response, trade promotion requires cooperation between the manufacturer and the trade.

Consumer promotion programs may emphasize either brand image or price. Some, such as a sweepstakes or premium offer, communicate brand benefits directly to the consumer and require little retailer input. Others, such as manufacturers' price reductions and bonus packs, encourage consumers to sample a brand but do nothing to enhance its image.

When manufacturers offer trade promotions, they expect that the financing costs associated with taking on additional inventory will persuade retailers to provide special merchandising support to accelerate product movement. This might include passing the manufacturer's price reduction through to the consumer, featuring this price cut in store advertising, and displaying the product prominently. Manufacturers expect to obtain short-term increases in sales and market share as a result of this support.

But many executives interviewed indicate that trade promotions are no longer meeting these objectives. They mention four main failings:

1. Trade pressure for frequent promotion deals erodes consumer franchises of existing brands, adds to the expense of establishing new brands, and heightens consumer price sensitivity. (A 1981 Needham, Harper & Steers tracking survey found that 58% of women and 65% of men "try to stick to well-known brand names" compared to 74% and 80% in 1975.)[5] In some cases price reductions increase neither market share nor total category demand of products.

2. A trade buyer often responds to promotion deals by purchasing only for normal inventory, because the discount compares favorably with inventory holding costs, the buyer could add to inventories without reducing standard ROI. Frequent discounts facilitate deal-to-deal purchasing that results in uneven factory shipments and increased production costs.

3. Trade buyers often take advantage of discounts but fail to provide merchandising support or pass price reductions through to the consumer even when required to do so by the terms of the transaction. (One study of supermarket purchasing and merchandising decisions found that of 992 deals accepted, 46% received no merchandising support and only one third of total deal allowances were passed through to the consumer.)[6]

4. Some retailers respond to deals by purchasing above their own requirements and reselling or diverting the excess to other retailers at a profit. Diversion of low-bulk, high-margin health and beauty aids is especially widespread.

The severity of these problems varies from one product category to another, and, within a category, from one brand to another. But most managers interviewed consider that their trade promotion expenditures are rising at the same time as their productivity is declining.

A Changing Environment

In explaining these difficulties, managers in grocery-product manufacturing identify three problems. First, some managers emphasize the growing concentration of buying power of the grocery chains relative to that of the manufacturers. Chains can now use electronic scanning systems installed at checkout counters to determine which items should be stocked and promoted. Thus, they are no longer as dependent on manufacturers' salespeople to tell them which items to carry and in what quantity. In addition, retailers are increasingly concerned with protecting the market shares of their own private label and generic brands that have increased at the expense of national brands in many product categories.

A second problem, in the view of other managers, is that the pressure for trade promotions is an inevitable result of heightened retail competition stimulated by a depressed economy, increased consumer price sensitivity, and the emergence of new retail forms such as no-frills warehouse grocery stores. Moreover, the average supermarket at any given time is faced with 1,000 items offered on promotion but has the capacity to set up only about 50 end-of-aisle displays each week. Thus, there are simply too many promotion deals chasing a limited number of special in-store displays and feature spots in retailer advertising.

A third problem, say additional managers, is the manufacturers. These managers argue that manufacturers' salespeople and product managers are too wrapped up in the short term; often they attempt to meet year-end objectives by implementing fourth-quarter promotions that steal from future sales.

Manufacturers' Rationale

Despite increasing dissatisfaction with trade promotions, most manufacturing executives don't consider eliminating this marketing technique and reducing list prices across the board a feasible alternative.

For one reason, promotion deals provide them with the flexibility to adjust to temporary variations in demand and supply and to attract more price-sensitive, less brand-loyal consumers without changing list prices. Moreover, deals allow them to maintain higher list prices than otherwise, thereby protecting their gross margins in the event of any federal price controls.

Many manufacturers, however, would like to reduce their trade promotion expenditures. But those companies that have tried sudden dramatic reductions have experienced unpleasant repercussions. Even large, powerful manufacturers have sustained big market share losses from such efforts— Pillsbury on cake mixes, Philip Morris on 7Up, and Gorham on silver flatware—because wholesalers and retailers retaliated. The trade may respond to trade promotion cutbacks by cutting feature activity on the brand, refusing to carry the full product line, reducing the number of shelf facings, or declining to carry a weak brand sold by the same manufacturer.

Once a product category or an individual brand becomes associated with heavy trade promotion in the minds of manufacturer salespeople, wholesale and retail buyers, and consumers, the situation is hard to reverse. Only if management is prepared to accept a dramatic drop in sales volume is a sudden cutback in trade promotion feasible. A gradual shift of marketing expenditures from trade promotion to consumer promotion and, later, to advertising is less likely to cause sales force resentment or trade retaliation.

Manufacturers can ward off trade pressure for more promotion deals for their premium-priced national brands. One method is the introduction of "fighting brands," such as Colgate-Palmolive's Value Brands and Procter & Gamble's Summit line of paper products priced as much as 20% below the major advertised national brands. Another is comparative advertising of national brands with private labels, such as Charmin bathroom tissue and Ivory dishwashing liquid, to justify their higher prices. Manufacturers can also withdraw or regionalize their weak-selling brands when the cost of maintaining them in nationwide distribution is the offer of deals on their stronger brands.

How to Improve Promotion Management

Because promotion touches many functions in the organization—advertising, sales, production, and finance—managers must commit themselves to improving productivity in this area. The interviews and evaluations lead us to conclude that the commitment must focus on encouraging managers, first to view trade promotions as an integral element of marketing strategy and, second, to improve their design.

Changing the Managerial Orientation

As an initial step in improving promotion management and productivity, managers should evaluate the ability of marketing personnel to handle trade promotions and consider expanding training in this area. This involves assessing the qualifications of in-house sales promotion staff to review brand promotion plans, of product managers to design and execute promotions, and of salespeople to tailor presentations to individual trade accounts and advise buyers on inventory management.

As a part of sales force evaluation, managers should consider changing performance measures. One possibility is shifting to a system that considers profit contribution as well as quantity of cases sold. At PepsiCo, for example, the bonus component of a salesperson's compensation package is based not only on achieving volume targets but also on deal and distribution cost targets negotiated between marketing and sales force managers.

Another method is to set detailed promotion-related objectives for salespeople, particularly those who service stores as well as headquarters accounts. Some manufacturers offer bonuses if a brand's share of feature advertising in a salesperson's territory exceeds the brand's market share and has grown over the preceding period.

Finally, product managers and the sales force can be placed on different time periods for performance measurement purposes to avoid pressure on manufacturing and distribution capacity during the fiscal year's fourth quarter. Lever Brothers, for example, assesses the performance of each of its six regional sales organizations on a different calendar year.

A second step in changing managerial orientation is to recognize that the marketing strategies required for trade accounts differ. To tailor promotion and merchandising efforts, managers must understand each major customer's marketing strategy. This is especially important because the grocery trade is increasingly segmented. There are warehouse stores that purchase most of their merchandise on deal discounts and food emporiums that stress quality and assortment over price.

Salespeople must also understand how the buyers at each trade account are evaluated. Many retailers emphasize deal-to-deal buying and inventory loading and assess their buyers solely on average margins achieved. It can be more useful to evaluate on the basis of ROI, where deal discounts are traded off against inventory-carrying costs.

Managers with a good understanding of their accounts will make more effective presentations and obtain more merchandising support for their brands. Some manufacturers design optimal purchase plans to maximize the ROI of key individual trade accounts based on their forthcoming promotion calendars.

Finally, managers should determine which accounts are not providing the required merchandising support for the allowances they claim. Procter & Gamble, for one, restricts allowances on purchases of company products by warehouse stores. These do not usually advertise specific items or maintain shelf displays regularly so that special merchandising support is rarely given. Interestingly, Procter & Gamble's action is supported by many supermarket chains that compete with warehouse stores and themselves furnish merchandising support for promotion deals. Few manufacturers realize how much respect they can earn from the trade by legitimately enforcing their performance requirements.

Improving Promotion Design

The effectiveness of trade promotions can be increased if product managers spend more time on promotion design. They need to identify and develop promotion objectives consistent with a brand's long-term strategic aims. They must also design promotions in the light of the consumer buying process for the product. Promotions for impulse items, for example, should focus on gaining additional display space at the point of purchase.

To develop profitable promotions, managers should consider the following issues:

Product Range. All sizes in a brand line should be promoted together only when no particular size enjoys sufficient shelf movement to warrant special merchandising support or when individual wholesalers and retailers are themselves pushing different sizes. The trade tends to respond to an across-the-board promotion deal by giving special merchandising support to the one size that is most profitable to them. Product managers should consider promoting their larger sizes more often than smaller ones to accelerate in-home product use and permanently trade consumers up to large-size items.

The complexity of the decision lies in the number of stockkeeping units that comprise the brand. For example, the Hartmann Luggage Company manufactures a multitude of separately priced, hard-sided and soft-sided luggage items. Most of these are made in four fabrics and in men's and women's styles. Should Hartmann promote its entire line, its higher- or lower-priced stock or its more or less popular items? Should it promote the entire range in a single fabric line at the same time or a single size in all four fabrics? Or is the Hartmann quality image such that promotions cheapen the brand and should be avoided altogether?

A brand's trade promotion activity should not be developed piecemeal but should be planned on an annual basis. For example, a product manager of one frozen food brand implemented a balanced portfolio of trade promotion offers during 1980 for the twelve packings (six flavors in two sizes) in his line. He made six trade promotion offers—three at low discount rates on the most popular items and three at higher discount rates on items with growth potential. He divided the offers between the individual-serving size and the larger family-serving size. The brand's profitability rose 45% over the previous year.

Market Scope. When a brand's market share, competitive activity, sales force pressure, retail environment, or trade and consumer responsiveness to promotion offers vary from one marketplace to another, it is inadvisable to offer a single trade promotion program in all market areas. But product managers who design regional trade promotion strategies should keep in mind several limitations to this approach. Because extensive efforts are required not only to plan such programs but also to present them to sales force managements, only the largest companies can afford them. Regional marketing programs also add to distribution costs and trade buyers for national chains do not welcome the complexity of different deal offers for different market entities.

Discount Rates. In setting the discount rate, a product manager should consider how much additional volume is required to break even, whether the discount is so deep it attracts customers who are unlikely to buy again at regular list price, and whether the trade will pass the entire discount through to the customer.

To avoid self-destructive promotion deal wars, product managers should not automatically match or exceed the discount rates offered by competing brands. Leader brands, in particular, should have discount rates below the norm and just above the threshold necessary to stimulate trade interest. However, an unusual competitive threat may require a more aggressive approach. To discourage the eastward advance of Procter & Gamble's Folger's coffee, General Foods offered deep discounts on Maxwell House. P&G retaliated with even heavier spending. The profitability of the Maxwell House division fell sharply, but did General Foods have any option except to discount? Under certain circumstances, promotion deal wars are unavoidable. (General Foods and P&G were able to sustain their deal war partly because each gained market share at the expense of weaker national and regional brands that could not support an equivalent level of deal activity.)[7]

Timing.   The primary timing issues are when, how often, and how long to promote. The timing of deals should not be predictable so that wholesalers, retailers, and consumers will not be able to coordinate their purchase cycles with them.

The frequency and duration of trade promotion offers depend heavily on a brand's importance to the trade. A high-share brand in a high-volume category should be able to get great merchandising support from many trade accounts even if promoted infrequently for only two or three weeks at a time. Such a brand may also be able to command support for an off-season deal. Deals for a low-share brand in a low-volume category should probably be offered more often and for longer periods. It will then be available whenever a trade account has a promotion slot that cannot be filled with a more attractive brand.

Terms.   To decide the details of allowances for any trade promotion offer, the product manager should first rigorously define merchandising performance requirements. For example, the size, location, and timing of both feature advertisements and in-store displays can be specified and related to a sliding scale of allowances for different levels of performance.

Next, the product manager should incorporate multiple options to cater to the different promotion preferences of various classes of wholesalers and retailers. Salespeople and trade buyers can discuss which option is best for each retail account.

Finally, the manager should monitor current trends in the terms of allowances. These include linking off-invoice allowances to minimum purchase requirements, limiting accounts to one order per promotion, avoiding split shipments in all but the most seasonally sensitive product categories, and reducing the number of free goods allowances requiring retailers with scanning systems to post additional computer records.

Integrated Promotions.   To encourage trade buyers to increase their purchases and schedule special merchandising support, trade promotions should
run concurrently with consumer promotions. For example, a widely advertised cash refund offer with a sweepstakes built around a theme relevant to
store merchandisers can often stimulate special store displays for the promoted brand or product line.

Making Informed Decisions

To effectively plan future promotions, managers must be able to evaluate
past campaigns in detail. To do that, certain key questions must be answered,
including the following:

☐   What are the effects, both short and long term, of trade promotions on brand sales, market share, and profits?

☐   What are the design features of profitable trade promotions?

☐   What mix of trade promotions over the course of the annual promotion plan makes most sense?

☐   What is the optimal allocation of marketing expenditures among
trade promotion, consumer promotion, and advertising?

To begin to answer these questions, management needs descriptive
information, including internal data on factory shipments, promotion activity, and price changes, and external data on warehouse withdrawals by the
trade, retail shelf movement, store penetration, feature advertising and display support by the trade, and competitor prices. Display activity is harder
to monitor than advertising features because expensive store visits are required. Moreover, unless store observations are taken each week, special
displays lasting just seven days may be overlooked.

Manufacturers should also consider developing decision support systems for promotion evaluation and planning. At Chesebrough-Pond's, for
example, factory shipments, warehouse withdrawals, retail sales, and other
data for each brand size are merged into a common data base organized by
retail account. As a result, marketers can conduct analyses at various levels
of aggregation—by brand size, by individual account, by class of trade, by
size of account, and by sales territory. In addition, product managers use a
simulation model which can compute the profit impact of past promotions,
in total or by account, and project the profit impact of proposed programs.

Managers should also aim to understand the effects of a promotion on
buying behavior—particularly purchases by such groups as brand switchers,
"deal-prone" consumers who tend to buy whatever brand is on sale, and
loyal users who would have been prepared to pay the regular price. Such
questions can be considered through a study of the diary or scanner system

purchase records of consumer panels. Some companies analyze data in selected markets in conjunction with shipment and account sales data.

Too often, companies reduce the value of trade promotion as a marketing tool by excessive use. The trade as well as manufacturers must realize that if the same national brands are nearly always "on special," consumers will become skeptical.

Manufacturers have to counter this erosion of trade promotion productivity. They can gradually reduce trade promotion expenditures, shifting funds to consumer promotion and advertising that will support brand franchises. In addition, they can increase the productivity of trade promotion expenditures by improving promotion management, promotion design, and promotion evaluation. In either case, effective leadership is essential for successful implementation.

Notes

1. *Chain Store Age*, September 1981, p. 32.

2. Donnelley Marketing, *Third Annual Survey of Promotion Practices*, July 1981, p. 2.

3. "48th Annual Report of the Grocery Industry," *Progressive Grocer*, special issue, April 1981.

4. Temple, Barker & Sloan, Inc., "Findings of Marketing Services Survey of U.S. Packaged Goods Manufacturers," September 1981, p. 9.

5. Reported in Bill Abrams, "Brand Loyalty Rises Slightly, But Increases Could Be a Fluke," *Wall Street Journal*, January 7, 1982, p. 23.

6. See Michel Chevalier and Ronald C. Curhan, "Retail Promotion as a Function of Trade Promotion: A Descriptive Analysis," *Sloan Management Review*, Fall 1976, p. 19.

7. See "FTC Judge OKs GF Defense vs. Folgers," *Advertising Age*, February 8, 1982, p.6.

35

Industrial Distributors
When, Who, and How?

JAMES D. HLAVACEK and TOMMY J. McCUISTION

With the cost of sales calls rising sharply, increasing numbers of industrial product manufacturers are looking to independent distributors for marketing help. Too often, though, the experience with distributors is an unhappy one as sales fail to meet expectations. Complicating the problem, manufacturers may blame product design or price for the disappointing results when the distributor is the culprit. Or they may blame the distributor's efforts when in fact the choice of distributor is at fault.

Dissatisfaction can be avoided, argue the authors, if marketing managers take more seriously the job of directing sales by outsiders. Specifically, the authors advise marketing managers to divide the task of overseeing industrial distributors into three components: selecting the products distributors will sell, choosing the distributors, and evaluating their performances.

Now that the average cost of a direct sales call exceeds $100, more producers are relying on industrial distributors to serve key markets. The distributors are independent firms, usually consisting of only a handful of sales and support people. Unlike manufacturers' representatives, who take on the role of sales representatives and work on a commission basis, industrial distributors take possession of the products they sell and assume the role of partner with manufacturers.

Industrial giants such as 3M, Norton, Pfizer, and Mead Paper make a large portion of their sales through such distributors. To counter competition coming mainly from Japanese photocopy machine manufacturers, both IBM and Xerox recently named independent distributors to market their low-priced copiers and typewriters.

But marketing an industrial product through distributors is risky and complicated. Consider the situation confronting one well-known industrial

Published 1983.

producer that developed what it thought to be a promising product. After placing it with independent distributors, building up substantial inventory, and filling the distributor pipeline, the company finds one year later that the product is selling poorly. Not surprisingly, the general manager and other officials are distressed.

They wonder: "Is this a lousy product? . . . Is it priced too high? . . . Are we doing something wrong in sales? . . . Are the distributors letting us down?" But these could be the wrong questions. Perhaps the product is not suited to this type of sales arrangement. Or maybe the company chose the wrong distributors to market the item. Moreover, like many companies, the organization may have no one person to oversee the process of selling through distributors. In theory, the top marketing or sales executive bears this responsibility, but in practice it tends to be fragmented and neglected.

Many of the mistakes producers make in selecting and using distributors can be avoided or corrected. Companies that want to rely heavily on industrial distributors must first decide if the products are appropriate candidates for this selling approach. If they decide in the affirmative, they must then select the best distributor candidates. Finally, companies must be able to evaluate their distributors' performances.

Is the Product Right?

Products that are suitable for independent distributors usually have the following characteristics:

1. *A large potential customer base.* A distributor is unlikely to do as good a job selling a product with appeal to only a handful of customers as the producer will do. Yet producers often allow custom-tailored products to become distributor items. For example, when distributors sold special metal and rubber gaskets designed to fit customers' requirements, they created virtually no new accounts. After several years, it became clear that the distributors received only repeat orders from accounts originally obtained by the manufacturer's sales people. The broader the customer base with standard requirements, the greater the need for a distributor network.

2. *A stockable item.* Most customer-designed parts, chemicals, or machinery are easily eliminated as possibilities for distributors. The product should be easily stocked and serviced locally, as is a catalog item that is manufactured in large quantities and sold a few at a time.

3. *Small-quantity sales.* Items sold in bulk are usually not sold through distributors. The small quantity sales rule applies especially to heavy equipment items like construction machinery and trucks. The customer buys one or a few at a time and is concerned about the subsequent availability of service and parts. Replacement parts selling for a few dollars each can be sold by distributors.

4. *Low-level customers.* The lower in the organization the responsibility for buying an item, the more likely it will be sold through a distributor.

The flat organizational structure of an owner-operated business has little or no buying specialization and therefore buys often from a distributor. Some products, such as certain aircraft control mechanisms, are bought directly from the producer by high-level managers in the buying company. When designing and producing the mechanisms for a certain airplane, the supplier needs highly skilled engineers working with the customer's design engineers and procurement people.

However, other products being sold to that same airplane builder, such as O-ring seals or fasteners, are standardized and can be sold through distributors to purchasing officials to whom off-the-shelf service is important. During the introductory stages of most industrial products, they are specified by and sold to design engineers. The selling effort often requires engineer-to-engineer type relations. As the product becomes more widely known, the purchasing department assumes the principal buying role.

5. *Rapid delivery and service.* If the product is needed immediately because of an equipment breakdown or an operating supply shortage, speedy replacement is essential. The cost of downtime for an oil drilling rig is more than $100 a minute and the downtime on an automotive engine assembly line is more than $100,000 per hour. Minutes can be a matter of life and death when a hospital operating room needs a small piece of surgical tubing or parts for a life-support machine. In all these situations, the longer the downtime, the more costly the situation and the greater the need for prompt delivery and possibly for technical service by a local distributor.

Selecting Distributors

If a product fails to meet any of the previous five qualifiers, it probably will not succeed as a distributor item. Yet merely meeting them all does not guarantee success. There are many pitfalls to avoid in the selection of distributors.

Think Market Segments

Many industrial producers think primarily in terms of geographic coverage before considering distinct market or customer segments. Such thinking leads to limited sales. For example, parts of the marine- and forest-product industries are located in the Pacific Northwest. But customers in these two markets frequently buy the same product from different distributors in the same region. The marine customer buys mostly from a marine supply distributor, which stocks special products for its customers' needs. Among the needs is having products with U.S. Coast Guard approval for resistance to saltwater corrosion; the lumber and plywood markets don't need that approval.

Also, customers prefer to deal with distributors who know their industry's language. Thus, the wood products customers residing in the same geographic area and buying some of the same products as marine customers use a distributor who serves only the forest products industry. In many cases

the customers and distributors in the two industries do not know of each
other.

Deere employs different distributors to serve the agriculture and construction equipment market segments. Caterpillar uses different distributors
to serve the construction equipment, lift truck, and diesel truck engine markets in the same geographic territories.

The wise producer thinks of different types of distributors to serve
different or specialized market segments. If one manufacturer is already
penetrating a market segment, the second or third entrant to that market
segment should carefully consider the type of distributor the successful first
entrant chose.

Finally, producers should be aware of total market *potentials* for each
market segment and geographic territory. They can then compare the potentials with each distributor's actual sales. This information should help
them develop annual distribution quotas around the local market size and
growth rates. Decisions about directing and adding distributors become easier.

Life Cycle Changes

Many companies fail to recognize that selling requirements for a product
change over its life cycle. The industrial producer that has the wrong distributors for the stage the product is in may make the following observations
of its distributors: "They don't call on the right people. . . . They don't
know how to sell the benefits of the product. . . . The distributor is mostly
filling repeat telephone orders, and delivery is too slow."

A product unknown to the market requires a specialized distributor
that can provide technical assistance as bugs are worked out and new uses
developed with the customer's engineers. To justify all the time spent ed-
ucating prospects, the distributor will probably demand an exclusive territory. As more applications for the product develop, the technical know-how
becomes more widely available in handbooks and manuals until finally it is
common knowledge.

The journey for a given industrial product from innovation to obsolescence ranges from 10 to 50 years. This means that one type of industrial
distributor could be successful with a product for a long period. As the
product matures, becoming more standardized and better known, a diminishing amount of specialized knowledge is needed to sell it. At the point of
maturity in the product's life cycle, off-the-shelf delivery time and price
become more important than the need for specialized knowledge. At this
stage, producers should consider expanding the number of general distributors in nonexclusive territories.

Getting Products Specified

Don't assume that your distributors will get your product specified. Only in
unusual cases does an engineering type of distributor get the specifying job
done, and then only if the specifier and user are in the same geographic area.

If required specification work is not done, the industrial distributor will not receive orders. For example, when building a plant in California, General Motors's headquarters might sign a contract for an automated production line with a machine tool maker in Ohio. A company that wants to sell parts to that supplier must first meet GM's specifications. Without approval from General Motors's corporate headquarters, the distributor cannot serve the machine tool maker.

A solution for producers is to designate a person to do nothing but get the company's products specified or qualified at original equipment manufacturers (OEMs), government agencies, automotive companies, railroads, or wherever. This person may be a product specialist who also knows the industry.

Producer—Distributor Policies

Because industrial distributors channels are outside the company, management policies governing them cannot be routinely developed and administered. Distributors are typically independent entrepreneurs who own 100% of the business; the industrial producer must very carefully develop distribution policies that do not conflict with those of its partners in profit.

Before selecting and franchising distributors for a product, producers should develop policies together with the distributor that address the following areas:

User Information. To formulate future marketing policies, industrial producers must know who their ultimate customers are. Some producers require distributors to report each sale by part number, customer, destination, and place of billing. This in turn helps the producer provide effective market analysis for distributors.

Such information is sometimes available from warranties for equipment that customers fill in and return to the producer. However, for components and consumable industrial or technical products like chemicals, bearings, and surgical supplies, there are no purchaser-warranty feedback information systems. The producer who has an unfavorable reputation for taking distributor-developed accounts away from distributors will understandably have difficulty obtaining such sales information from distributors. For such producers, distributor councils can be a valuable source of information about the marketplace. A meeting with distributors represents contacts with hundreds of ultimate customers.

Serving Large Accounts. When a distributor has developed a large OEM or end-user account, a clear policy is needed to determine whether the account remains with the distributor or is handled directly by the producer. Some companies leave the distributor-developed OEM account alone as long as the account is living up to its potential.

Inventories and Pricing.   Most of a distributor's capital is committed to the producer's inventories. The producer's pricing practices can enhance, protect, or penalize the market value and profit margins on the inventories. One manufacturer whose own regional sales people call on distributors has a policy of paying the sales force based only on what the distributor sells and not on what it buys. This eliminates the temptation to overload the distributor with inventory.

Assessing Qualifications

Producers tend to choose distributors who are already overloaded with products and to shy away from those who are underfinanced. Successful industrial distributors are usually courted by numerous producers and, as a consequence, are probably carrying as many product lines as they can effectively handle. But a technical product usually has to be demonstrated to customers; distributors with few product lines are often best able to provide that concentrated technical assistance.

Industrial companies often err by not choosing the underfinanced newer distributor because the corporate officials caution, "Beware of those who run slim and don't have adequate financial means to carry our inventory or do business with us." This creates a bias toward the more mature and better-financed distributor, which may not be the aggressive and specialized distributor the product requires. The credit rating on the new but aggressive distributor will rarely be something that excites the home office financial people.

The manufacturer may err further by not attempting to help finance or otherwise support the promising distributor. Some producers have allowed new distributors to start up and to eventually buy out the distributorship. A common arrangement is to have a producer's salesperson start a company-owned store, which the employee buys once it becomes profitable.

A single distributor can seldom give a producer the market coverage and penetration needed in large trading regions. Producers must avoid saturating any market with distributors to the extent that the profit potential becomes unattractive for everyone. Thus, industrial producers must continually analyze the market structure and assess the potential in each market segment.

Finally, distributors who are not aggressive enough or are overloaded should be disenfranchised. Industrial products that require much technical selling should be handled by a specialized distributor. Industrial products bought mainly on the basis of price and service should be placed with aggressive general-line distributors.

Distributor Training and Support

Often the distributor's sales representatives are undertrained and undersupported—as some would say, "Franchise them and forget them." Effectively training distributors' sales people to sell a product takes many hours. The producer must demonstrate the product features and benefits for many different situations or applications. The more technical the product, the more time necessary for sales training. Sometimes the producer must train both the distributor and the initial customers.

Manufacturers should also provide distributors with technical field assistance for potential key accounts. Some producers have regional sales people who can accompany distributors on calls and provide technical backup. While the producer sales force may be viewed as a luxury, it can perform such valuable functions as analyzing accounts and getting specified. The payoff may come 6 to 12 months later.

Manufacturers can further support their distributors by supplementing product literature with heavy trade-magazine advertising to generate inquiries and sales leads. When it gets inquiries, the producer must turn them over promptly to the appropriate distributor.

Manuals and handbooks that help people use a product or solve technical problems have also proved to be excellent sales tools. Well-known examples exist in many industries. The "Merck Manual," which first appeared in 1899, was written to help physicians select medications, noting that "memory is treacherous" and that "even the most thoroughly informed physician needs a reminder to enable him to prescribe exactly what is needed for the patient."[1] In 1983, the "Merck Manual" is in the 14th edition; it covers 2,500 pages of disorders and suggested therapies. The "O-Ring Handbook" by Parker Hannifin Corporation helps design engineers specify solutions to prevent leakage in oil systems or air systems. Ingersoll-Rand wrote the "Drill Doctor's Book" to help drillers select the bit, speed, and set-up in various rock- and coal-mining situations.

Evaluating Performance

Once companies have entered an agreement with distributors, manufacturers should periodically review their distributor's performances. Here is one possible assessment approach:

Stage 1: Top-Management Assessment. Management reviews its figures on the sales growth the distributor achieves and compares the market share in the assigned territory with the national average. The district sales manager also ranks distributors as excellent, good, fair, or poor, taking account of attention given to the products, customer service, and the quality of coverage in the assigned area. Combining headquarters data and district managers' judgments, managers can quickly identify the best distributors and mark the doubtful ones for further evaluation.[2]

This assessment can also incorporate the approach used in Exhibit 1. Once the market potentials are known for a product-market segment in each territory, they can be compared with the actual market penetration or market

Exhibit 1. Approach to Evaluating Existing Distributors

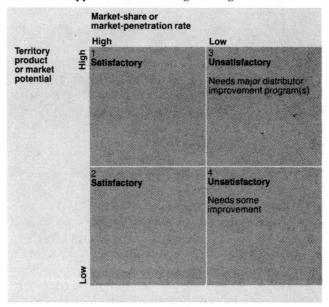

share of the distributor in each territory. A distributor with a product in category 3 or 4 needs improvement—possibly another branch should be opened or maybe the product should be placed with another type of distributor. If a distributor carries multiple lines, the same analysis can be performed in aggregate for each distributor.

Stage 2: Regional-Territory Evaluation. Armed with a detailed headquarters assessment of "problem" distributors, the person responsible for the field evaluation ranks each on 10 criteria:

1 Adequacy of business experience, as reflected in quality of customer service.
2 Coverage of assigned area and time available to seek more business.
3 Competence in managing the business (sales management, financial control, record keeping, warehousing, and inventory control).
4 Historical trend of volume measured against performance requirements established by the company's district sales manager.
5 Share of market in assigned area.
6 Demonstrated willingness to carry a full line of products and to service all customer needs.
7 Annual inventory turns.
8 Efficiency and condition of warehouse facilities and equipment.

9 Financial position (accounts receivable, cash position, outstanding obligations, inventories, fixed assets, and payment record).

10 Ability to grow in the assigned area.

The astute industrial manufacturer periodically faces the task of getting more effort out of certain distributors or of replacing those who consistently perform inadequately. The southeastern area sales manager for a large maker of commercial electrical equipment decided to take a hard look at his distribution network when, after three years, his region's sales declined from third to fifth place among six sales regions. He talked with each of his 30 distributors, analyzed their sales performances over recent years, and sorted them into three categories: (1) distributors whose market shares stood at or above the national average, (2) distributors short of the national average but capable of reaching it, and (3) those for whom the national average seemed hopelessly out of reach.

Complete and periodic distribution evaluations require considerable time and diplomacy. But continual upgrading and strengthening of a distribution network are necessary to manage a distribution channel effectively.

The Payoff

A good distributor network is often the key to market leadership and overall business success. Because it takes many years of continuous attention to develop and maintain, a sound producer-distributor organization is often a high barrier to competitors. Without a solid network, even a manufacturer with a superior product can fail in the marketplace. A producer that recognizes the importance of distributors has a major competitive advantage that can reap attractive profits for itself and its distributors.

Notes

1. "The Merck Manual," published by Merck, Sharp & Dohme Research Laboratories, Division of Merck & Co., Inc., Rahway, New Jersey, 1983.

2. A.L. McDonald, Jr., "Shaping Distributor Channels," *Business Horizons*, Summer 1964, p. 24.

Nonprofits
Check Your Attention to Customers

ALAN R. ANDREASEN

Nonprofit organizations chronically face financial difficulties. Now the situation has worsened because they are being squeezed between the uncertain economic climate and cutbacks in government support. While the managers of these institutions may think that they have already tried everything possible, more than ever they must be innovative in developing additional funding sources. As Mr. Andreasen argues, most nonprofits have failed to exploit marketing techniques which can build support from users or customers that leads to improved cash flow. The author contends that managers of nonprofit organizations focus too closely on their products or services; he admonishes them to give more attention to the needs and wants of their consumers.

☐ The director of an urban art museum describes her marketing strategy as "an educational task." She says: "I assemble the best works available and then display them grouped by period and style so that the museum-goer can readily see the similarities and differences between, say, a Bracque and a Picasso or between a Brancusi and an Arp. Our catalogs and lecture programs are carefully coordinated with this approach to complete our marketing mix."

☐ The public relations manager of a social service agency claims: "We are very marketing oriented. We research our target markets extensively and hire top-flight creative people with strong marketing backgrounds to prepare brochures. They tell our story with a sense of style and graphic innovation that has won us several awards."

☐ A marketing vice president for a charitable foundation ascribes his success to careful, marketing-oriented planning: "Once a year we plan

Published 1982.

the entire year's series of messages, events, and door-to-door solicitation. We emphasize the fine humanitarian work we do, showing and telling potential donors about the real people who have benefited from donations to us. Hardly a week goes by without some warm human-interest story appearing in the local press about our work. The donors just love it!"

These are the kinds of statements one hears from officials of successful nonprofit organizations that are highly respected for their supposedly innovative marketing approaches. The executives have attended courses and seminars on marketing, and their planning documents and speeches are laced with marketing jargon like "benefit segmentation," "product positioning," and "message strategies."

While they believe they are marketing oriented, these organizations actually have a product-oriented or, at best, a selling-oriented marketing approach. They start with their own organizations and services, determine how they want to market them, and *then* turn to customer analysis to achieve their goals. Despite their protestations to the contrary, they do not begin the process with consumers. The distinction is subtle but important. Managers need to adopt a new view of marketing and its role in their organizations. The first step in this learning process is self-awareness—recognizing the underlying product or selling orientation in the approaches they and their institutions use.

Marketing has certainly achieved wide respectability in the nonprofit world. Hospital administrators, college presidents, and theater directors are often as familiar with the writings and speeches of marketing experts as they are with those of the traditional management sages. Yet all too many of these managers have adopted the trappings of marketing without grasping its essence. For this reason, marketing among nonprofit heads may go the way of such fads as motivation research and sensitivity training.

Selling Versus Marketing

While most readers probably well understand the distinction between a selling or product orientation and a marketing orientation, reconsideration of the terms ensures a common starting point for this article. A *product orientation* involves focusing on an organization's basic offering and a belief that the best marketing strategy for increasing sales is to improve this offering's quality. A *selling orientation* equates the marketing task with persuading target audiences that they ought to accept the offering—that it is superior to any alternatives.

The art museum director described at the outset of the article believes she knows what her audience should learn about art; she sees her principal marketing task as "educational." The public relations manager concentrates not just on what she has to say but on how to say it; effective persuasion is the key element in her marketing strategy. And the charitable foundation's director believes his story is one that donors will just love to hear (of course, he also loves to tell it).

These marketers start with what they wish others to know about their organizations and only later think about customers' needs and wants. This is very different from a modern marketing orientation, which espouses the opposite approach. Institutions shouldn't ignore their own goals, preferences, strengths, and weaknesses; nevertheless, these concerns should not outweigh consumers' interests.

To illustrate, let's consider the typical art museum. As indicated in the opening quotation, most art museum directors see their marketing problem as one of assembling the best collections, displaying them well, and notifying the press and public of their availability. This product orientation manifests itself in the labels museums concoct for works of art, which museum directors see as a key marketing tool to get mass audiences to appreciate the artworks.

What information does a label usually include? First, facts about the artist: name, nationality, dates of birth and death. For whom is this information most important? Certainly for the museum director and his or her peers, since it ensures location of the artwork with others created by artists of the same nationality and period. Often labels also relate information about bequests, including donors' names. Of course, this information helps the director secure more donations (admittedly an important marketing task). On the other hand, given limited space, a donor's name is hardly a key piece of data for most museum-goers. Finally, there is usually a catalog (or inventory) number on the bottom of the label that helps the director keep track of the collection, prevent theft, and schedule repairs.

But what information would consumers like to see posted next to each work? If museum directors talked to consumers, as I have, they would discover that there is not one consumer market but three—each with different needs and wants but united against the typical labels. The three groups and their information needs can be defined as follows:

The Aesthetes.   Some viewers are most interested in the aesthetic-artistic properties of each work. They want to know about design, use of materials, color, and techniques. They want to know about anything unusual in the artist's style and about good or bad features of the work. The artwork itself is of key importance to this group.

The Biographers.   These people are fascinated by artists, their lives, their choices of subject matter, and their models. They would like to know how a work fits into the artist's career and what special meaning it has for his or her growth and development. For this group, the key feature is not so much the work but the artist behind it.

The Cultural Historians.   This group usually has had some formal or informal exposure to art or social history. Its members are interested in the work as an element in the sweep of cultural and artistic history. They want to know, for example, why this technique or this subject matter was chosen at this particular time and what the piece tells about the age, the country, and the broader artistic framework. Did the work influence other artists then or later? Does it reflect any of its predecessors? What was the society like that produced this artwork and this artist?

Clearly, three systems—not one—are needed. To some museum directors' surprise, such customer-oriented messages may not only broaden people's appreciation of the arts but also spur museum attendance or even donations. Directors might experience a leap in old-fashioned customer satisfaction, especially among those just beginning to explore museums and the arts.

Key Indicators

How can nonprofit organizations determine whether they have a selling or product orientation rather than a marketing focus? Among the symptoms that I have found to suggest a product or selling mind set are the following:

1. *Seeing the offering as inherently desirable.* Nonprofit heads seldom entertain the possibility that potential consumers may not share their enthusiasm about their offerings. They cannot see why, given a clear description of their institution and what it provides, consumers would not want to respond enthusiastically.

Committed theater managers may find it hard to believe that right-thinking people wouldn't wish to attend a well-acted play; charitable organizations' directors sometimes cannot fathom an unwillingness to give; and those who head up nonprofit special-interest groups often can't see why people won't vote for, say, cleaner air or the ERA. Other nonprofits, including organizations designed to push such health-enhancing notions as wearing seatbelts and quitting smoking, also are surprised that they have difficulty generating a positive response.

One organization that overcame the notion that its offerings are inherently desirable is the National Cancer Institute. Most women, NCI discovered, agreed that practicing breast self-examination was a good thing to do, and many knew how to do it. Yet the majority were not practicing such examination or, at best, did so only rarely. What was the problem? If the examination yielded nothing, the woman would feel a sense of relief the first few times but eventually she would become bored at finding nothing and would stop the procedure. But the prospect of "success" was so frightening that most women never even tried the self-examination or, at any rate, didn't check themselves regularly. It was only when NCI understood these barriers—as perceived by the target audience—to an obviously good practice that it began to develop more user-oriented marketing programs. NCI's new stance, based on assurances that progress is being made against breast cancer (and thus one shouldn't fear discovering lumps), has resulted in increased self-detection.

2. *The notion of consumer ignorance.* Nonprofit managers tend to ascribe any lack of interest to the fact that consumers don't fully appreciate the nature of the offer. Or, if customers do understand, managers just haven't found the right incentives to motivate them.

Again the National Cancer Institute provides a good example of what a change to a marketing orientation can accomplish. For many years, the conventional wisdom among those charged with reducing cigarette consumption was that either smokers didn't believe smoking was bad for them or that they were not motivated enough to quit. But consumer surveys revealed that seven out of eight smokers did believe that smoking was a very bad habit and that many of them had in fact tried to stop. NCI concluded that what smokers needed as part of the marketing mix was a set of clear-cut techniques for quitting and a sense of hope that they might succeed. Because of this new consumer perspective, NCI reoriented its program toward action rather than information.

3. *Overemphasis on promotion.* Many nonprofit organizations place too much stock in advertising and public relations. They are convinced that the director should concentrate on the message and its packaging. (Of course, the message directors usually have in mind is the story they want to tell.)

Many blood-collection agency heads believe that the best way to encourage donations is to tell consumers about the good things donors' blood can do or to stress that giving blood is a civic duty. They believe that people hold back from giving because they don't appreciate the gift's virtues or because they are afraid. Thus, agency heads reason, consumers need to be told about the benefits and assured that the costs are trivial—indeed, that giving can be fun.

While these messages work for some people, important segments respond to far different messages. For example, many men, especially blue-collar workers, can be motivated by challenges to their masculinity. The macho man who can tell his co-workers that he is a 20-gallon donor may feel well rewarded. (Indeed, some pain-and-suffering in the process might enhance the reward.) Thus, campaigns in factories focusing on individual giving records (bar charts or 10- and 20-gallon lapel pins) can be highly effective.

Many social, fraternal, and church group members can be motivated by the let's-all-participate aspects of a bloodmobile visit. They will respond to messages about camaraderie, about feeling left out if you don't join in, or about letting the group down if you don't go. All these messages have little to say about the occasion for the get-together or its value to society.

One blood bank director even uses sexual attraction as a marketing strategy. This director found that a small segment of middle-aged men considered the attentions of the pretty nurses well worth the inconvenience of regular blood donations. This donor center has built a highly loyal following.

The innovative marketer who listens to potential customers can gain surprising insights about what the target audience wants and what will get it to act.

4. *The secondary role of consumer research.* If one "knows" that the problem lies with the consumer and that better promotion is the key to marketing success, the principal role for research is merely to confirm beliefs. Yet, as most profit-sector marketers will attest, research can challenge some managers' most fundamental assumptions about their customers. Take as an example officials of a small midwestern hospital who worried that patients were dissatisfied with some of its recently hired foreign-born doctors. Staff nurses reported frequent patient complaints about the doctors, sometimes because they "couldn't understand" what the doctors were saying. Moreover, different cultural backgrounds appeared to be seriously affecting doctor-patient rapport. The hospital turned to field research to find out how to cope with the problem.

The research indicated, however, that the foreign-doctor problem was not really serious in the eyes of patients or prospective patients. Few interviewees mentioned the issue voluntarily in the field study or scored it as a significant blot on the hospital's image. Doctors instead were rated just as easy to understand as doctors at rival institutions. Indeed many patients, far from complaining, perceived the foreign doctors as more serious and conscientious than their breezy, golf-loving U.S. counterparts. Needless to say, this research saved the hospital from spending many promotional dollars to correct a problem that didn't exist. What was really needed was a marketing program directed toward the hospital staff, especially the nurses and foreign doctors.

5. *One best marketing strategy.* Since the nonprofit administrator is not often in close touch with the market, he or she may view it as monolithic or at least as having only a few crudely defined market segments. Subtle distinctions are played down. As a consequence, most nonprofits tend to develop only one or two marketing strategies, aim them at the most obvious market segments, and then run with them. This climate of managerial certainty precludes experimentation either with alternative strategies or with variations for market subsegments.

Also encouraging this approach is the fact that nonprofit managers often come from nonbusiness backgrounds and may fear taking risks. Personal job survival and slow aggrandizement of the budget and staff are often their paramount objectives. And since such administrators are typically responsible only to a volunteer board—which meets irregularly and sometimes prefers to know little about day-to-day operations—they do their best to keep a low profile and avoid shaking up the board. Finally, since most nonprofits are in fact deficit organizations that make up their losses with fund raising, aggressive marketing strategies are unnecessary. These forces, then, support the typical nonprofit manager's natural inclination to be conventional, not adventuresome.

Yet the opportunities for careful experimentation abound. A case in point is Carleton College.[1] Since 1978, the Northfield, Minnesota, school has systematically explored alternatives to the traditional single-brochure approach. A survey had shown that target high school students saw Minnesota as cold and isolated, Carleton itself as too "cerebral," and the library as too small. The standard brochure was updated to play down the cold weather, point out how easy it is to get to the attractive Twin Cities, and feature a new picture of the library that shows it is really quite large.

More recently, Carleton discovered that regional differences affect perceptions of the college. So the school sends letters to Western students emphasizing outdoor activities and Carleton's informality and to Easterners stressing the school's academic prestige. And, finally, the school now informs those from Minnesota about its financial aid and the fact that Carleton enjoys a significant national, not just regional, reputation.

Since 1978, Carleton has seen its yearly applications increase from 1,470 to 1,875, while the response rate from mailings has jumped from 5.9% to more than 14%. It remains financially solvent and is protecting its reputation as academically selective.

6. *Ignoring generic competition.* While many nonprofit organizations consciously compete—the Heart Fund with the American Cancer Society, the Metropolitan Museum of Art with the Whitney or the Museum of Modern Art—many institutions don't have clear competitors because their services or so-called products are intangible or stress behavior changes. The competitors of those marketing, say, blood donations or forest-fire prevention are not immediately apparent. So it's not surprising that marketers ignore competition at either the product or generic level. But at the product level, blood banks, for example, compete with other charities for donors (who seek dollars, not blood). Even institutions with easily identifiable organizational competitors often face product competition from unlikely quarters. Thus, art museums compete with aquariums for family outings, with books and educational TV for art lovers, and with movies and restaurants as places to socialize.

Nonprofit organizations rarely plan strategies to compete at the product level because they lack a customer perspective. And this failure is even more serious at the nonproduct level. Before people will write their Congressional representatives in support of ERA, for instance, they must give up their long-held ideas and divert their energies to the new cause. Inertia can be a powerful force, but enthusiastic nonprofit marketers tend to ignore it. When they peddle changes in behavior or new ideas, most nonprofits de-emphasize competition from the status quo.

7. *A marketing staff selected for its product knowledge.* In a modern marketing organization, staff members are selected on the basis of their knowledge of customer markets and of marketing research and management techniques. One can learn the key characteristics of a product in a few weeks,

but market awareness and marketing expertise take years to master. Once gained, this expertise can be applied to many product or market contexts.

In many nonprofit organizations, knowledge of the product or service counts most. A preference for marketers with a product orientation prevails in nonprofit organizations because of three factors:

First, since marketing is unfamiliar to many nonprofit heads, they don't know how to evaluate marketing skills (while they can evaluate product know-how).

Second, many top nonprofit administrators accumulated most of their experience using product marketing and so are more comfortable working with people who have that orientation. Many business managers of arts organizations were once active performers or were formally trained in music, theater, design, or museum curatorship. Most hospital administrators have either medical or public health backgrounds, and college presidents usually have PhDs in academic disciplines. Seldom are these administrators selected purely for their management skills.

Finally, the world of nonprofits is a fairly clubby one where key people know other big names around the country; thus, a certain amount of favoritism prevails. A prospective staff member with the proper connections and the right vocabulary stands a much better chance of making it than a total outsider. The marketing professional, who probably doesn't know what "needs assessment" or "audience development" means, is at a disadvantage. This self-reinforcement means that the customer-oriented marketer who wants to come in and turn the organization around will be seen (whether consciously or not) as a threat.

A New Way to Pass the Hat

How, then, can the marketing approaches in such organizations be changed? As noted previously, many nonprofit organizations' leaders are convinced they have already adopted the best marketing approaches. So the first step for concerned administrators is to assess the organization's managerial orientation.

It is also a good idea to start a customer research program. Customer research need not be expensive, and (as corporate marketers know) it is an essential precursor of each year's planning.

Furthermore, managers should rub shoulders with experienced marketers. Staff members can go outside regular channels for exposure to customer-oriented marketing. They might attend seminars, conferences, and courses by for-profit professionals or by academics who espouse customer-centered approaches. The institution can also bring a marketing consultant into the organization to evaluate problems and demonstrate how a modern marketer tries to solve them. And it can seek out one or more marketing professionals for the board of directors and observe how such professionals react to marketing problems.

Remember, the organizational atmosphere must change. Changing it is a straightforward process once nonprofit managers and staff become aware of what is at stake. And, since many not-for-profits are still exploring marketing's potential for helping them, the opportunities for adopting a constructive orientation are much greater than in fields where marketing has a longer history.

Notes

1. "College Learns to Use Fine Art of Marketing," *Wall Street Journal,* February 23, 1981.

37

Ads That Irritate May Erode Trust in Advertised Brands

RENA BARTOS

Conventional wisdom in the advertising industry holds that a certain amount of irritation helps make advertising effective. Conversely, many practitioners believe that if consumers *like* the advertising they see, hear, or read, it may be too "soft" to break through the competitive clutter.

There is clear evidence, however, that dislike of ads correlates with negative attitudes toward the industry. No one has yet examined the effect of such consumer antipathy on the credibility of particular companies' images and brand names. Nevertheless, the inferential evidence is so strong that it would be prudent to heed the warning signals. Until the hypothesis that advertising which a consumer says "insults my intelligence" is proven to have no deleterious effect on brand image and credibility, we should proceed with caution in framing the advertising message.

In 1974 the American Association of Advertising Agencies (AAAA) conducted a study that updated a mid-1960s survey of consumer attitudes toward advertising.[1] Trends showed a decline in the number of people who agree with positive statements about advertising and a rise in the number who think that it often "persuades people to buy things they should not buy" and that most of it "insults the intelligence of the American consumer."

Analysis revealed that if consumers like the ads they see, their opinions of advertising overall improve. And if they feel that most advertising is boring, in poor taste, or insulting to their intelligence, they tend to distrust the advertising industry. These criticisms are linked statistically with skep-

Published 1981.

ticism and distrust. In other words, the criticisms appeared to be manifestations of disbelief in advertising messages.

According to annual lifestyle studies since then by William D. Wells, director of research at the Needham, Harper & Steers agency, advertising is increasingly insulting consumers' intelligence. (See Exhibit 1.)

The erosion of advertising credibility may, in turn, be undermining consumers' trust in advertised brands. The development of brand loyalty is precisely the contribution that advertising has made to marketing. But there are ominous signs that consumers may not remain sold when the credibility or value of a brand image erodes. A disquieting clue emerged from a question in Wells's annual study. As Exhibit 2 indicates, the results of the past two years show a sharp decline in support of branded products.

A panel appointed by the National Advertising Review Board recently commissioned the Gallup Organization for a survey to learn the nature and scope of consumer complaints about advertising. Although half the respondents told Gallup that on at least one occasion in the past year they had wanted to complain about advertising, only 8% of the population actually did register complaints. Most of the unvoiced criticisms concerned taste: the advertising was "insulting to my intelligence," "in poor taste," "offensive," "distasteful," or "too overtly sexual."

Other complaints focused on the intrusiveness of television advertising. Respondents said that commercials are "too long," "too loud," and "repeated too often." According to the panel, objective tests have demonstrated that TV advertising is actually no louder than the programs. So perceptions of intrusiveness may be another facet of consumer irritation or dislike of the execution of the ad. As the report noted, "If a viewer does not like a particular commercial, he may hear it as too loud or too repetitious."

The panel acknowledged the importance of public perception of good taste as an element in the reputations of brands: "Advertisers know that their advertising is often the most visible part of their corporate structure, and they know that they will often be judged by its honesty, accuracy, and good taste as critically as they are judged by the quality of their products."

New Day Coming

News of the new video technology and speculation about its impact on advertising and marketing have dominated the trade press. No one knows

Exhibit 1.   Advertising Insults My Intelligence

Percent Who Agree	1975	1976	1977	1978	1979	1980
Men	61	62	61	64	66	66
Women	60	62	61	61	69	67

Exhibit 2.   "I Try to Stick with Well-Known Brand Names"

Percent Who Agree	1975	1976	1977	1978	1979	1980
Men	80	82	77	75	74	64
Women	72	74	72	72	66	56

which forms will survive or when the revolution will happen. One thing is certain: advertising as we know it may not survive into the next decade.

One fascinating aspect of the change is the choice that consumers will have about when, or even whether, to watch advertising on TV. They will be able to tune the ads out of the programs they choose to view. They will be able to invite advertising into their living rooms for comparison shopping.

When ready to buy, they will instantly obtain comparative information on the relevant product category. This is a dream situation for marketers; they will be in a position to tell their sales stories to target customers in the process of making the purchase decision.

Two-way cable TV also offers the promise of direct selling and consumer feedback on programs and commercials. Advertisers who avail themselves of this powerful response tool will be able to learn directly which advertising persuades consumers and which turns them off.

Another possibility for pay TV is the inclusion of commercials designed for the program in which they will appear. This will be done with full subscriber approval in order to reduce subscription fees. These will be uninvited commercials and, like any uninvited guest, they will have to be tactful and ingratiating to earn their welcome.

When the viewing context changes, viewers can happily zap the commercials they find insulting, irritating, or in poor taste. When advertising comes invited into viewers' homes instead of crashing its way into their consciousness, the industry will be forced to reconsider its criterion of effectiveness that to break through the competitive clutter, advertising has to annoy.

Positive Sales Tool

These days advertised brands are facing a real challenge from unbranded, generic products. The brands that survive this challenge will be the ones that consumers think are unique and of superior quality. According to Wells, negative sell works best on "avoidance products" like household cleansers and odor control products. Ironically, these categories are most susceptible to competition from generics.

A brand image is not a luxury that marketers may indulge in after they have met their need to fight for market share points. Unless they cultivate and nurture their brand image, their advertising may be undermining the very purposes for which they created that brand.

The dimension of brand personality is crucially important to the survival of brand franchises. The evidence is clear that consumers do not relate to or identify with personalities that they find insulting, demeaning, or intensely irritating. These are not friends they would welcome to their homes. Marketers should be on guard to avoid strategies that may result in short-term gains but that will ultimately erode the quality of the images of advertised brands.

A fascinating result of the AAAA study is that liking advertising is relevant to good opinion of this industry. When consumers say a commercial is "funny," "clever," "artistic," or "enjoyable," they have somewhat positive opinions of the advertising industry.

The inferential evidence of a link between "liking" and good opinion is so strong that liking can be the secret weapon in the battle to build the kind of brand personalities that will inspire trust instead of distrust.

An interesting footnote on this subject comes from Great Britain. The low point in British opinion of advertising came in 1966, when only 23% of the British public admitted to liking TV advertising while 32% said they disliked it. These attitudes were reversed during the 1970s. The most recent report, issued in September 1980, tells us that 50% of the people in the United Kingdom like advertising on TV while only 15% said they dislike it. Exhibit 3 shows these results.

Advertising practitioners in the United Kingdom believe there is a clear relationship between enjoyment of advertising and approval of the industry. According to one of them, "People are willing to acknowlege that they quite like advertising: its wit, its subtlety, its cleverness, its use of celebrities. Certainly over the decade there has been a conscious attempt on the part of agencies to make advertising that entertains. So in that respect, our product is more popular and has helped the climate of public opinion."

Ironically, during the same period when confidence in brands and the credibility of advertising have eroded in the United States, our cousins across the Atlantic have recaptured public approval of advertising through the simple strategy of creating advertising that consumers really enjoy.

Actually, we may be rescued by the explosion of change in media technology. Even if advertisers do not respond to the groundswell of con-

Exhibit 3.   Liking and Disliking TV Advertising

Percent Who:	September 1961	August 1966	April 1972	March 1976	September 1980
Like TV advertising	35	23	43	48	50
Dislike TV advertising	29	32	24	16	15

sumer alienation from advertising, developments may force them to woo their customers rather than bludgeon them into buying the products. The dimension of liking could be a crucial criterion of advertising effectiveness.

A happy by-product of the change could be harmony between a corporation's goals and the public's perception of its advertised brands. When positive emotional response becomes an essential sales tool, companies may find that they are not only selling their products but also improving the images of their brands and enhancing their own reputations.

38

Plan for More Productive Advertising

MALCOLM A. McNIVEN

Many managers have the mistaken notion that the productivity of advertising cannot be measured. This author describes a productivity program by which a company can allocate the various costs of advertising in line with company goals and marketing strategy. In addition, he points out areas where opportunities for cost savings may exist.

A major expense for any consumer products company and for most industrial companies is advertising. Considering the financial pressures on businesses today, it is remarkable that the advertising budget has received so little attention and examination by top management.

This is partly due to the fact that many managers accept two basic axioms about advertising: first, that it is a necessary evil in their business expenditures and second, that its effectiveness cannot be measured. Neither of these is true, since advertising—instead of being a financial burden—can provide the means to increase growth and profit if used creatively and wisely. In addition, the productivity of advertising can be measured far more accurately than most managers expect.

In 1977, U.S. businesses spent approximately $44 billion for advertising in the major media, with television accounting for about $9 billion of that. A large proportion of this was spent by the top 100 advertisers, whose individual media budgets varied from $25 million to $400 million. These media expenses were usually equaled by the amount spent on consumer and trade

Published 1980.

promotion. In many cases, the advertising budgets exceeded the profit before tax for those companies, particularly for the packaged consumer goods companies. In most consumer businesses, the only cost that exceeds the advertising and promotion budget is that for ingredients of their products.

Given budgets of these magnitudes, a program of productivity improvement can yield significant payoffs, and, in the case of reductions of advertising expense, the improvements show up directly in net profits.

An advertising and sales promotion (A&SP) productivity program should have two basic parts. The first is strategic, in that it involves establishing a dollar amount for an annual A&SP budget and the way in which that budget should be allocated. The second part involves cost reduction by examining each element of advertising. Let us take the hard part first—the establishment of the advertising budget.

Budget Strategy

Most advertising budgets are developed by means of guidelines that each corporation has established for its different businesses. A common method uses a ratio of advertising and sales promotion expense to gross margin—that is, an advertising budget can be developed by calculating the expected gross margin (mainly a function of volume) for the coming year. One can then allocate a fixed percentage of that gross margin to advertising and sales promotion.

Another method is the "cents per case" system, which considers advertising dollars as a variable expense. To determine an A&SP budget, one simply multiplies a case volume estimate for the coming year by the cents-per-case figure that is right for the business.

A third guideline is the percentage increase method, whereby last year's A&SP budget is increased by a percentage that depends on an arbitrary inflationary figure and the expected growth of the business in the coming year.

While these methods are widely used, they do not offer much hope for improving advertising productivity. The guidelines merely perpetuate a past situation rather than attempt to devise an advertising strategy that might permit a company to break out of its existing cost structure into a more favorable one.

Recent developments have permitted use of a total business approach in place of the guideline methods. The total business approach looks at advertising budgets as part of an advertising strategy that is derived from a marketing strategy which, in turn, is derived from a business strategy. Using this approach, the business manager can strategically coordinate advertising funds with promotion and pricing strategies and can thereby provide objectives with which to evaluate the consequences of those strategies.

When confronted with an advertising budgeting decision, one must first know the potential profitability of that business and its strengths and weaknesses to develop a basic business strategy. Business goals lead to a marketing strategy that capitalizes on strengths and corrects marketing weaknesses. Once marketing objectives are set, it makes sense to focus on advertising in the following three ways:

☐ Develop an advertising strategy to help reach the marketing objectives in the most efficient way.

☐ Establish a money limit for advertising in the annual budget.

☐ Construct a plan to spend that money in the proper place, at the proper time, and with the proper message.

This process can be illustrated by a recent business strategy developed and implemented in Pillsbury's frozen pizza division. The frozen pizza business is characterized by high growth, high volume, many manufacturers, low profits, little advertising, and big trade promotions. Pillsbury wanted to increase both volume (by 30%) and profit (by 100%) for its Totino's frozen pizza. Marketing objectives were established to increase product quality (best-tasting frozen pizza), geographic distribution (expand to Chicago and Phoenix), and consumer brand preference.

Advertising objectives included increased consumer awareness of the brand (over 70%) as well as increased trial (over 20%) and repurchase (over 40%) of the new product. The advertising strategy shifted the emphasis from trade support (case allowances) to television advertising, thereby increasing the dollars available for affecting consumer preferences. That money was allocated for maximum impact, as I will discuss later.

Sales, share, and profit performance were the measures for the strategy, and the outcome was a successful application of a total business approach to advertising. However, planning is easier if you know how your sales respond to advertising.

Advertising Elasticity

It is well known that products in different categories respond differently to advertising. If you have a measure of this responsiveness (called advertising elasticity), you can calculate the amount of advertising that will be required to achieve your marketing goals.

To measure the advertising elasticity of a product, you must be able to determine what change in sales will result from a change in advertising dollars. There are three ways of doing this:

1. *Statistical analysis.* Identify areas of the country or periods of time when the advertising budget was at various levels. Then, using multiple regression or similar techniques, make an estimate of the resulting effect the amount spent had on sales and calculate the advertising elasticity. This can

be done by plotting a simple regression line obtained by comparing the change in advertising dollars and sales dollars over a period of one year (see Exhibit 1).

If the relationship is not clear, other factors (such as number of sales-people and competitive activity) can be used to reduce the variation in the data and thereby show a clearer relationship between advertising and sales.

2. *Computer simulation.* Computer models can simulate various levels of advertising and their effects on sales. These computer model systems are available from software vendors at a cost of $20,000 to $80,000, depending on the complexity of the answer desired. They require information about your sales, advertising, distribution, profits, and consumer brand switching, and they require the same information about your major competitors. My experience has shown these systems to be very helpful and well worth the expense.

3. *Field experiments.* The most accurate way to estimate advertising elasticity is to conduct field experiments by advertising at different levels in different markets and by measuring the resulting sales response. While these tests are expensive ($100,000) and time consuming (six months), they are worthwhile in a relatively stable, highly advertised product class.

An advertising elasticity coefficient will be a fraction or decimal obtained by dividing the resulting change in sales by the actual change in advertising. For example, if a 10% change in advertising results in a 1% change in sales, the advertising elasticity coefficient is .10. This is similar to price elasticities that describe the change in sales as a result of a change in price.

Advertising elasticities can vary widely from one product to another, but they tend to be stable for a mature product over time. Examples of advertising elasticities for six packaged food products in varying product

Exhibit 1.   Effect on Sales of Various Amounts of Advertising

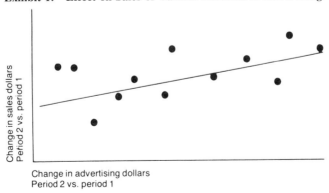

Note: Each point on the plot represents the experience in a given sales area for that period of time.

categories are shown in Exhibit 2. The price elasticities associated with these products are also shown. (Price elasticities are usually negative, since sales volume generally goes down when price goes up.)

Once the advertising elasticity is known for a product, you can estimate the amount that must be spent for advertising to generate the sales required to meet your marketing goals. If the expense of the advertising is too great and will not pay back because of a low advertising elasticity, then you may have to look for marketing forces other than advertising (such as price, distribution, and trade promotion) to help you achieve your objectives for a particular product.

In the Totino's pizza example, if the advertising elasticity were .15, it would require a 40% increase in advertising expense to achieve a 6% increase in sales, with case allowances held even. In the introduction of that new product, we estimated its advertising elasticity by computer models. This made it possible for the Pillsbury Company to set advertising strategy from a knowledge of the expected results which, in turn, gave management the confidence to use much higher levels of advertising for its frozen pizza product category than had been used in the past.

Direct Dollars to Consumers

One of the other major factors that influences advertising budgeting is the question of how much to budget for sales promotion and trade allowances. Specific product classes have established practices concerning the ratio of trade allowances to media advertising expenses. For products like coffee, frozen pizza, paper products, and flour the trade allowances are high; media expenses may represent no more than 10% or 15% of the total A&SP budget. Conversely, health and beauty aids, cigarettes, and soft drinks use a high percentage of media advertising, and trade allowances may be as small as 20% of the A&SP budget.

Since trade allowances do very little to build a brand franchise, the advertiser should be constantly trying to increase the proportion of the A&SP

Exhibit 2. Price and Advertising Elasticities for Various Products

Product	Advertising Elasticity	Price Elasticity
A	.10	-2.10
B	.10	-1.60
C	.15	$-.85$
D	.13	-1.30
E	.20	-1.30
F	.70	-2.80

budget devoted to media advertising, even though the sales force and the trade are usually pushing in the other direction.

Computer programs can now estimate the amount of media advertising and trade allowances required to achieve certain marketing objectives. There are opportunities for productivity increases if one can reduce trade allowances as far as possible and still achieve the distribution and promotional exposure that the product needs. While these estimates need to be tempered by the judgment of the sales force and other knowledgeable persons, they help by providing a quantitative estimate of the trade allowances that would be required by a particular product market.

Two financial ratios that management should monitor for each consumer business are *A&SP ÷ gross margin* and *media ÷ total A&SP*. In packaged foods, *A&SP ÷ GM* runs in the range of 30% to 40%. The size of this ratio indicates the marketing support needed to maintain market share. The lower the ratio, the less competitive the product class. Experience or testing will help establish the minimum A&SP-GM ratio to achieve business goals, but it is important to keep testing new ways to reduce the A & SP-GM ratio without reducing marketing effectiveness.

The media-A&SP ratio should be .5 or above, which would indicate an equal number of dollars spent against the consumer and against the trade. If the ratio falls below .5, then the product will gradually lose market share, or the product class will drop to commodity status with little brand loyalty. The media-A&SP ratio should be increased until the minimum expense for promotional and trade support is determined. This can be estimated by computer models or discerned by actual experimenting in test markets. Careful management of these two ratios can have a very beneficial effect on the productivity of the entire advertising budget.

Making a Test

It makes good sense to test alternative advertising plans by taking one or more local markets and trying media and promotional plans that might work. A company can place different combinations of advertising and promotion into local markets and watch their effects on sales, on trade attitudes, on distribution, and on market share.

A successful testing program depends on keeping track of expenses and resulting profits, market by market. Trained financial and marketing analysts working together can then evaluate the productivity of each marketing strategy by studying test data on advertising levels, media mix, advertising-trade dollar balance, and timing of advertising. By means of these tests it is possible to learn a lot about how advertising works for a company—and how it doesn't.

One Piece at a Time.   The natural variations in a business from market to market provide real opportunities for advertising productivity. In some markets, a brand may be well known and the market share secure; in others, a brand may have stronger competition and consumers may not know the product as well. These two situations require different advertising and marketing strategies. Matching spending patterns to each market's needs will yield more overall mileage from A&SP dollars.

One way to accomplish such a match is through charting for each market the per capita consumption of the product class and the product's market share. You can then determine where you should be advertising to build the market, where you should be advertising to build your market share, and where you shouldn't advertise at all. In Exhibit 3, for example, Seattle is a market where the product is used heavily by consumers but where the market share is low. This calls for a competitive marketing program designed to take share away from competitors. In New York and Los Angeles, however, the product category is used at a high rate by consumers and the market share is high. In these markets, a company would want to maintain its position and would hope to achieve consistently good profit margins.

In Chicago and Atlanta, the product category is not widely used and the market share is very low. In general, it is a good idea to write off markets of this type; they are not productive places to spend time and money.

In Denver, the market share is high but the product category is not widely used. Here a company should undertake market-building efforts to increase consumers' awareness and use of that product category. Business will grow accordingly because of the high market share. It may also help to chart your business by demographic segments, usage segments, and product

Exhibit 3.   Matching Spending with Markets.

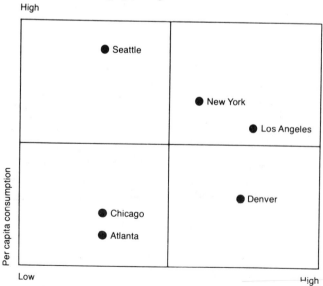

categories. Such a breakdown will allow you to identify the ways in which advertising will be most productive. Strategies of this type use advertising as a strategic weapon and permit greater productivity for each dollar.

Timing Is Everything.   After planning a geographic strategy, a company has another opportunity for productivity in the timing of its advertising. It is important to be sure that advertising appears when consumers are receptive to a message about the particular product. This could be in late evening television when they are relaxed and sitting quietly, or it could be at the end of the week when they are reading their newspapers before going to the supermarket. In other words, a company should know the consumption and buying habits of its customers and should time its advertising accordingly.

Another aspect of timing concerns the strategy of spending the majority of the budget in a few large bursts or choosing a steady but low level of delivery. The approach should differ by type of product, particular marketing problem, and size of advertising budget. In general, a few short bursts are preferable to a steady low level of advertising, but there are many possible combinations of such tactics. For example, you can:

☐ Advertise heavily during your peak sales season only.

☐ Maintain a steady low level all year, plus a major burst during your peak season.

☐ Advertise every other week during your peak season.

☐ Advertise on one specific day all year long.

The volume of advertising is measured by units called gross rating points (GRPs). A GRP equals one advertising exposure to 1% of U.S. homes. Advertising agencies have worked out methods of combining all broadcast media, and in some cases print media, into a combined GRP measure.

It is necessary to determine the GRP level that is correct for a product for each time period. If it appeals to a wide audience (for example, all women 18 to 49 years of age), less than 75 GRPs per week is probably not effective during the main selling period. It would be better to advertise less frequently in order to reach at least a 75 GRP per week level so that the advertising reaches enough potential customers often enough to create an awareness of the product and the desire to buy it.

Reach and Frequency.   One should also set reach (how many people) and frequency (how often) objectives for advertising so that computer media models can be used to calculate the best media schedule. This very complex subject can best be handled by the advertising agency media department. A company should ask for all the help it can get from the media department, since this is one service its commission payments are buying. The media people should show a company several plans at different reach and frequency levels and different dollar levels. If additional dollars do not buy much more reach or frequency, then the company may be overadvertising.

All of the subjects discussed thus far will help increase the productivity of advertising through the establishment of an appropriate advertising budget and the proper allocation of those dollars geographically and over time. Once a company has such programs under way, it must pursue them: advertising productivity is a continuous, regular process.

Cost Reduction

The second major part of an advertising productivity program involves cost reduction in advertising expense without loss of advertising exposure or effectiveness. It is a common practice to cut advertising budgets when a business is not reaching its profit goals. These cuts, however, reduce advertising exposure and thus sales. Because of the complex and poorly understood nature of the advertising industry, normal cost reduction programs often bypass advertising in lieu of something more tangible such as production, distribution, or office expense. However, there are many opportunities to reduce costs in the advertising area. Let us go through a few of those possible ways here, although this list is by no means complete.

Agency Compensation

For many years the normal method of compensation for advertising agencies has been a 15% commission on billings. Although this is still the most common method, advertisers have begun to adopt others because they believe that agency payment should depend on services rendered, which may vary widely depending on the problems involved in the advertising program.

For a company that does a great deal of national television advertising, chances are that a 15% commission is too much. With large amounts of print advertising in small publications or spot television advertising in selected markets it could be that a 15% commission is too little. The commission rate should be consistent with the expense incurred by the agency for the services wanted.

Some advertisers have based their agency fees on hours spent plus a reasonable profit level, and these fees change as assignments change. This arrangement generally results in a better relationship between agency and client. A similar approach is a guaranteed profit level that puts a minimum and maximum profit range on the agency's fee. Both of these systems tend to increase the productivity of advertising dollars, since the compensation to the agency is adjusted to match the services required by the client.

Another method of reducing agency compensation is through establishment of in-house agencies that can buy advertising directly. Media planning and buying can be handled internally by a few media specialists if the media requirements are not too complex. Most large advertisers maintain a small internal media group to supplement the personnel assigned to their account by the agency. Creative advertising development and production can be handled by internal advertising specialists or bought from small agencies called creative boutiques.

It is possible to reduce expense this way, but there is also the risk of reducing the quality of advertising programs. Developing good advertising is a difficult process, so a company that intends to do it internally should hire real experts. Media planning and buying are more easily accomplished internally and are a company's best bet for in-house development.

Commercial Production

A 30-second television commercial currently costs about $45,000 to produce; some cost more than $100,000. Commercial production is a complex field involving sets, studios, actors, and residuals. Only an expert knows whether a company is getting value for its money, and a company should bring in such an expert to set standards for advertising production. The money paid for this advice is a small percentage of the potential savings involved in bringing more sense to production costs without reducing the quality of advertising. A recent example of this is a consultant who was paid $30,000 and who achieved a $50,000 savings for the company in his first year.

Proof of Performance

There are problems inherent in the broadcast media that may cause complete or partial deletion of a commercial from the air when it should have been shown. It is hard to know when this has occurred but, if such a case can be identified, the networks will make good on the time. Monitoring services will discover a large proportion of such broadcast errors and will collect from the networks. These services charge a percentage of the recovery that accrues and thus offer an opportunity for cost savings to the advertiser.

The same monitoring problem occurs with retail customers in their performance on agreed-on promotions. For cooperative advertising and in-store activity, it pays to hire auditors to be sure that customers are delivering on their promises to promote a product. This auditing effort will result in more effective promotions at the retail level and a savings on promotion payments to the trade.

Procurement of Materials

Normal procurement procedures and standards that are applied to purchases of commodities and office supplies should also apply to procurement of advertising materials. Because advertising procurement is a specialized skill, it often does not and probably should not be part of the procurement department. When procurement systems and controls are applied to advertising materials, the savings are substantial.

Advertising materials include forms of printed matter such as direct mail, print ads, point-of-purchase displays, and coupons. In a large consumer products company, the annual budget for such materials can run as high as $30 million. In procuring these materials, it is important to set standards of quality, obtain at least three bids, look for volume discounts, and have the suppliers regularly inventory purchased items. A company should expect efficient procurement of advertising materials as in any other area. The savings will be dramatic.

The areas just described—agency compensation, commercial production, proof of performance, and procurement of materials—are examples of opportunities for cost savings. Many others will appear when a company starts looking at its total advertising operation by examining each element. The objective, then, is not to reduce the quality of advertising but to apply normal good business practices to the advertising area.

Throughout this article I have suggested that experts or consultants of various types be brought in to help in an advertising productivity program. This is necessary because of the specialized nature of some aspects of advertising. Except for very large advertisers, it probably does not pay to maintain a staff of experts on media, production, creative development, or advertising research.

Internal people may be unfamiliar with some aspects of the advertising program, or they may have fallen into a way of operating that is not as productive as it could be. Agencies, however, are usually compensated on a percentage of the total billings and, therefore, have a built-in conflict of interest. Consultants can ensure that everything possible is being done to make the advertising program productive, and they can provide an objective view and fresh ideas that pay their way many times over.

Question of Productivity

An effective way to initiate an advertising productivity program is to ask marketing and agency people several questions:

☐ If we cut out all advertising for product X for one year, what would we lose?

☐ Is it more profitable this year to increase advertising by 25% or to cut it by 25%?

☐ Why don't we shift 20% of our trade allowance dollars into television?

☐ What would we have lost by spending 20% less on our advertising production costs?

☐ Why don't we try to double our advertising in two markets and see what happens?

☐ Do we have to pay our agency 15% of our media budget?

☐ Why do we advertise the same way all over the United States when our business differs so much by area?

☐ Could we buy media ourselves instead of through the agency?

The answers to such questions are not always easy, but they will start a process of thought and experimentation that will result in better allocation of the advertising budget. If a company undertakes the programs described here in a sensible way and commits itself to accomplishing them, it is not unreasonable to expect a 5% to 20% savings in the advertising and sales promotion budget.

Many people will say that it is not feasible to undertake such a program, and others will say that it will harm advertising by stifling creativity. Neither statement is true. Like any other productivity improvement program, it must be carried out with sensitivity and a clear understanding of what is good for the business. In addition to the monetary payoff, the establishment of good business practices in the advertising program will create a discipline and a responsibility that may otherwise be lacking. These added qualities will tend to increase the stature of the advertising function—showing it to be a strategic and tactical tool of tremendous value to any business.

39

"Buying In" to Market Control

ROBERT E. WEIGAND

The ultimate marketing accomplishment for any company is to legally obtain total or near total control of markets. Marketers of certain products and services accomplish this by offering low initial prices or other inducements to tie customers to their suppliers for long-term periods. The author labels attempts by companies to set themselves up as sole suppliers of goods and services "buying in." Most of the companies' profits are made during the "get well" or "follow on" stage. While the financial advantages of the buy-in/get-well sequence are obvious, the approaches to making the practice work and the problems that are frequently encountered in trying it are less obvious. The author describes both the advantages and potential difficulties associated with buying in. He also considers some of the moral and legal issues that the practice may raise.

☐ A Virginia public utility helped pay for underground electric wiring at a large housing development. For all practical purposes, home buyers would have no choice between electricity and gas because the utility and the builder agreed that the homes would be all-electric. The subsidized underground wiring would be paid for—many times over—by the sale of electricity during subsequent years.

☐ Both General Motors and Ovitron Corporation submitted bids to build squad radios for the U.S. Army. GM won the bid, but Ovitron challenged the outcome in court, arguing that GM's bid was below cost. The winner, it argued, would be rewarded by charging a higher price on subsequent contracts for the same product. GM's tactic withstood the legal challenge, thus opening the door to future profitable contracts.

Published 1980.

☐ The city of Oakland built the Oakland-Alameda County Stadium in 1966 so that the Raiders would have a place to play football. The cost was substantial, but the city fathers knew it would be recouped from the rent the team would pay back over the years. However, the stadium could only be paid off if the Raiders remained in Oakland for the long term. When the team wanted to move to Los Angeles recently, the city filed suit. It claimed that the Raiders constitute a public use and necessity. If successful, the city's attorneys will have found a way to link major capital expenditure made many years ago to a flow of revenue that the city and county have enjoyed over many years.

The above vignettes suggest the general character of a practice that is scarcely acknowledged in business literature but is extremely widespread among many industries. The practice is usually called "buying in," with the subsequent practices and profits referred to as "getting well" or the "follow on."

By buying in I mean linking an initial sale—sometimes made at less than satisfactory profits or even losses—to subsequent more lucrative sales of either the same or related goods or services. The initial buy-in sale itself usually generates volume or margins too small to warrant investment. Follow-on sales, in contrast, allow the seller to get well if the stream of revenue from the follow-on product or service is long enough or if margins are high enough.

The practice of buying in has several important characteristics. First, the seller—not the customer—does the buying in. The seller is buying customer patronage at some future time by offering an attractively priced product or service today.

Second, the process consists of a sequence of sales that are in some way tightly linked. The sequence may be as few as two sales, as when an aircraft manufacturer sells two jet aircraft to a small airline and subsequently sells five more to complete the carrier's needs. Or it may consist of an initial sale followed by a stream of sales for quite some time into the future, such as—from the example cited previously—when GM sold squad radios to the Army.

Third, the link between the buy-in and the follow-on sales must be strong if buying in is to succeed. If the first sale does not render follow-on sales a near certainty, the seller has not bought into the future and may simply have spent a lot of money obtaining a low-profit project. Sellers make every effort to solidify the link, while astute customers, rival businesses, and sometimes government agencies attempt to weaken it.

Fourth, the seller must take the view that the profit is to be earned over the life of the products or services. If there is price and profit movement, it will be from low prices and profits during the buy-in to higher prices and profits during the get-well period.

Finally, the customers who are courted and the products or services that are sold during the buy-in may not be the same during the follow-on campaign. For example, the Virginia electric utility mentioned earlier subsidized underground electrical wiring for a major house builder. However, the follow-on sales of electricity were made to those who later bought the houses.

This article focuses on the following: the techniques or methods that managers can use to link a buy-in sale to subsequent get-well sales; the circumstances that should exist and the problems that are created during buy-in situations; and suggestions about how to handle possibly troublesome moral issues that may arise from getting well either too soon or too conspicuously.

Ties that Bind

A seller can use a variety of techniques to encourage a buyer to remain loyal. Strong patents, copyrights, and carefully guarded trade secrets quite obviously act as deterrents to follow-on competition. Polaroid enjoyed a stream of nearly exclusive revenue from instant-picture film sales for more than 30 years, largely because its patents fended off prospective rivals. And anyone who has ever shopped in a large food store knows about encyclopedias. The first volume of a set can be purchased for, say $1.99. This is the buy-in. But the follow-on volumes, available from the same food store, will cost $4.99 or whatever amount it takes to make the entire project profitable. The publisher's copyright, of course, precludes imitators wl.ɔ could break the buy-in.

Less obvious ways are illustrated by the following examples:

1. When Murphy Pacific, a marine salvage company, entered a bid to clear 10 ships from the Suez Canal, it was up against tough bidding from several European companies. The bidding was particularly spirited because the bidders assumed that the winner would be in a unique position to win subsequent dredging and removal contracts—since the company's equipment would already be in place and its engineers would already know the canal's physical charcteristics.

2. The Clean Air Act required America's automobile manufacturers to build cars that would be nearly pollution free for their entire life span—defined as 50,000 miles or five years. But factory-installed catalytic converters were expected to last only about 25,000 miles. So each of the four major car makers told the Environmental Protection Agency that they could assure clean-burning cars only if the replacement converters—installed after about 25,000 miles of driving—were installed by a franchised dealer with genuine factory parts. But independent parts manufacturers and repair shops insisted that this argument was just a ploy to keep them out of the lucrative aftermarket. Since each catalytic converter could cost $100 to $150, access to the follow-on sales was worth arguing about.

The methods for trying the buy-in to follow-on sales fall into five categories:

1. Tying the customer to an operating pattern that encourages continued patronage. For example, Stansaab Elektronik of Sweden successfully beat out such companies as Sperry Rand, IBM, and Raytheon to provide an air traffic control system for seven Soviet airports. The contrast was large—about $72 million—but industry experts say that the follow-on business may be more than 10 times that figure. After all, if the Soviets hope to provide a traffic control system for the entire Soviet Union, its parts must be compatible. Stansaab Elektronik has thus gone a long way toward making follow-on sales.

2. Committing the customer to an inventory of parts and supplies. Airplane manufacturers are among the best illustrations of this approach. Air carriers are anxious to keep the number of engines, tires, light switches, and thousands of other parts to a minimum; they are most likely to do so if they obtain their aircraft fleet from a single manufacturer. Other suppliers of major installations or heavy equipment find making subsequent sales to be much easier than initial ones because customers soon discover how difficult and costly it is to make major changes in inventories of parts and supplies.

3. Committing the customer to the follow-on because a change of suppliers would require retraining employees. Today's managers often view a skilled work force as a fixed asset, much like a piece of equipment. Cost-conscious managers are reluctant to retrain skilled employees unless absolutely necessary. IBM has been accused of preempting commercial markets for computing equipment by seeing to it that employees of prospective customers learned while in college how to operate IBM equipment. IBM accomplished its goal by selling or leasing its equipment to many American colleges and universities at discounts as high as 60% off commercial prices. IBM knew that students who learned computing on its machines would not be likely to prefer a rival's equipment once they started working. Rather than retrain their new employees, employers bought IBM equipment. Under legal pressures during the 1970s, IBM sharply curtailed the heaviest discounting. But even today, many computer companies, including IBM, give modest discounts to educational institutions. Each company hopes that it can buy in educationally and get well commercially.

Airbus Industrie, a French company, faced the obstacle of skilled employees trained on the equipment of other companies when it attempted to sell its Airbus jet to Eastern Airlines. All of Eastern's flight and maintenance personnel had been trained on American-made equipment, and management was understandably reluctant to change the practice. So Airbus promised to teach Eastern's captains, first officers, cabin attendants, and maintenance personnel how to work with the A-300 airplane. Industry observers say that the total training costs—paid for by Airbus—could run into several millions of dollars.

But the buy-in worked. Airbus—with its free training, along with a loan of four aircraft for six months for test purposes and a promise of a well-equipped parts and maintenance depot in Miami—cracked the American market. U.S. aircraft makers, government officials, and others charged Airbus Industrie with unscrupulous tactics. But the buy-in now seems to have withstood the test, and Eastern may buy as many as 50 Airbus planes at $50 million each in the current decade.

4.   Becoming involved in establishing a product's specifications so that the designer is uniquely suited to meet the specifications. This might best be labeled the "sole savior syndrome." Prospective marketers may argue that they only want to help the prospective customer define his or her needs. This may seem charitable until it turns out that the solution can only be provided by a single supplier—naturally, the one who aided in the design.

For example, few American companies make buses, whether for local or intercity transportation. When the Department of Transportation consults with manufacturers before specifying what sorts of buses it will subsidize for urban mass-transport systems, each manufacturer usually attempts to guide the specifications so that it, and it alone, will be the chosen supplier. Allegations of favoritism—and sometimes lawsuits—often follow contract announcements.

Another example is of a major Western European multinational that invested in a Far Eastern country and that, like a good corporate citizen, earned only a modest profit. It warned highly placed individuals in government ministries about unscrupulous companies that might be inclined to sell poor-quality products to the country. Indeed, the European company even helped government officials write an import policy that would minimize such problems. Not surprisingly, the European company is probably the only one in its industry that can meet the standards it helped establish. It is depending on bureaucratic lethargy to keep the standards in place for a long time. And its critics further believe that its low prices and fair-profit stance will not last long.

5.   Withholding information about a buy-in product until the last possible moment before market introduction. Secrecy can act as a significant—although incomplete—barrier to follow-on rivalry. Companies that market safety razors have been known to produce razors that are compatible only with the blades that they market. The specifications of the razors are carefully guarded secrets until the day they are introduced.

Problems of Buying In

Various problems face a company that hopes to buy into a particular market. First, if buying in is to succeed, the tie between the initial and subsequent transactions must be virtually unbreakable. If customers, potential rivals, or government breaks the linkage, both sales volume and gross margins may fall to levels below which it is impossible to recoup the company's initial outlay or bring a satisfactory life-of-the-project return on investment. Each of these three parties has much to gain from making sure that follow-on sales are not monopolized by the original entrant. Some attempts to break the link succeed and some do not, as the following illustrate:

1. Eastman Kodak, easily the dominant company in the photo industry, was accused by Berkey Photo of using its camera trade secrets as a barrier to new competition. By keeping the details of its cameras a secret until introduction day, Kodak had the film sales to itself until prospective rivals could buy the camera and film from the nearest retailer, replicate them, and market them alongside the Kodak brand, which was by then well established. In a lower court, Berkey won the right to compel Kodak to "predisclose" trade secrets about cameras and film far ahead of the introduction date. But Berkey lost its victory in an appeals court, which held that Kodak was entitled to the fruits of its research and was simply "reaping the competitive rewards attributable to its efficient size." Thus the link that Kodak established between its buy-in and its follow-on sales survived Berkey's legal challenge.

2. Public utilities in Pennsylvania, like those in Virginia and nearly everywhere else, often fought hard for new customers, sometimes subsidizing the costs of new household appliances and wiring or piping for housing projects. The utilities knew that they could get well on the subsequent sales of electricity or gas. To stop such practices, the Pennsylvania Public Utility Commission ordered electric and gas utilities in the state to discontinue any practices that would encourage architects, builders, or developers to choose one source of power over another. The consequence of this order is that the initial cost of a home or apartment may be higher by the amount of the utility's previous subsidy, but the buyer may later benefit from lower lighting and heating bills. At the very least, it would seem that those who are not purchasing or renting new homes or apartments will not be obliged to subsidize those who are.

3. Schick began marketing razor blades that would fit both its own Ultrex twin-blade shavors and Gillette's Atra razors. Gillette claimed that Schick had infringed on its patents, so Schick paid Gillette $3 million for the right to market the blades—and not to be sued. But Schick says that once Gillette took the money, it came out with the Atra Invitation, a razor designed to make the original obsolete. Schick sued Gillette in mid-1979, claiming that the changes represented an anticompetitive practice meant to keep Schick out of Gillette's aftermarket sales.

In the automotive industry, the aftermarket for air conditioners, radios, heaters, wire wheels, rustproofing, and a host of other products has traditionally been lucrative. But in recent years, manufacturers have tried to make most of these products standard parts of their automobiles. This means both higher returns to the car manufacturers and smaller shares of after-market sales for independent suppliers. In 1979, GM declared that it would factory-install Delco radios—a GM product—on 13 different models, including its new X-body cars. Dealers could no longer order automobiles without a radio. Eleven independent radio distributors brought legal action through their Custom Automotive Sound Association, claiming that the step would foreclose the independents from a huge car-buyer market. Rather than face trial, GM and the association settled out of court. GM agreed not to make radios standard equipment until the end of 1983. It also agreed to give the association four months' notice of any other changes it might make that would affect the competitive position of its members.

The fundamental issue, of course, is whether a radio is an integral part of an automobile or a separate follow-on commodity. GM's legal position quite obviously would be that an automobile surely includes a body, engine, wheels—and a radio. The trade association would claim that radios are optional and that competition for customer allegiance should be open to all.

American law has generally been sympathetic to the protection of industrial property and the right of owners to exploit subsequent business opportunities. However, others have a corresponding right to demonstrate that a greater good is served by opening up those opportunities to outsiders. In short, for others to pick away at the linkage between the buy-in and follow-on sales is perfectly normal—and sometimes successful.

A second condition for successful buying in is possession of the capacity for fulfilling both the buy-in and follow-on sales. For example, much effort is now going into obtaining contracts to provide telecommunications equipment for developing countries. The largest companies—Western Electric, ITT, Siemens, GTE, L.M. Ericsson, Northern Telecom, Nippon Electric, and Philips—are vying to win the initial bids so that they will be in a position to influence and perhaps win subsequent contracts. Small companies that are unable to provide the full gamut of products and services probably need not apply.

If the company that buys in is unable to follow on with the more lucrative downstream sales, it has done no more than prime the market for others. As I discuss elsewhere (see the ruled insert), franchisors who attempted to be sole suppliers to their franchisees learned in a series of court cases that they were restraining trade. The long and steady stream of revenue that should have derived from their monopoly supplier position just did not materialize. Rivals who weren't invited showed up and proved they could supply products that were as good as anyone's. The courts helped both the franchisees and outside suppliers break the buy-in/get-well link. Thus the franchisors primed the market—for someone else.

A third factor is that buying in generally requires more capital for a longer period than single-product marketing. By definition, the buy-in is made at lower-than-normal profits. Follow-on sales may lag by only a few days, in some instances, but in other cases may be months or years in coming.

This means at the very least that buying in is not generally attractive to the underfinanced company or to the single-product company with stockholders impatient for dividends. The multiproduct company can afford to wait for its revenue from a buy-in situation simply because it has funds coming in from its other products or services. Thus the cost of a buy-in gets subsidized by the revenue generated by the company's high-profit products or services.

Finally, buying in can create internal company squabbles if the buy-in and get-well products come out of different profit centers—that is, if top management is asking the manager of the profitable get-well division to subsidize the manager of the unprofitable division that helps the company buy in. Which division earns a profit is of little concern to top management but of the utmost importance to the division manager who is up for annual review. Most management groups have had enough experience with similar profit-center problems that they are able to cope reasonably well with the buy-in problem. However, when top management does not acknowledge and deal with the issue, it opens the door to serious personnel difficulties.

Dealing with Ethics and Guilt

A successful buy-in is a mixed blessing. On one hand, it virtually assures future profits during the get-well period. But on the other hand, the practice, if crudely managed, contains the potential for generating an uproar in the marketplace. In its worst form, customers see themselves as exploited and locked into a situation from which there is no exit. They may describe businesses as "monopolist" and see themselves as being "over a barrel" or "with a gun to my head," and so on. And that is often the case. Buying in *is* exploitative under certain circumstances. Managers who are sensitive to increasingly astute and critical customers must face the uncomfortable fact that the intent of buying in is to lock a customer into the selling company.

Perhaps the easiest way to minimize customer antagonism and feelings of entrapment is to maintain, during the get-well period, the quality of product or service that the customer has come to expect. This rule, however, is easy to forget, particularly when management is under pressure to increase profits.

There are other less obvious ways—not all equally defensible— that businesses can use to lessen the potential hostility from customers who are more or less beholden to their suppliers:

1. *The full-explanation solution.* During the buy-in period customers should know exactly what their obligations will be and what the seller will deliver during the get-well period. This admonition is easily understood by industrial goods' sellers. Their customers are likely to have engineers who pore over product specifications, attorneys who read the fine print in con-

tracts, accountants who explore every financial option, and so on. Every foreseeable contingency is resolved. In short, when customers put together a buying team that is as astute as the selling team, there are no surprises.

Purchasers of consumer goods, in contrast, are usually less sophisticated. Although they are often shrewd buyers who can carefully weigh the consequences of their decisions, they do not have either the skills or the tools of professional buyers. One example of just how informed (or uninformed) the typical customer can be is provided by the long-standing dispute between Book-of-the-Month Club and the Federal Trade Commission. At issue is whether the company's advertising should make explicit the fact that members must pay handling and shipping charges. The company has argued that a specific statement noting that prices do not include handling and shipping charges is unnecessary because customers expect to pay such charges. However, the FTC has maintained that the fees come as a surprise and that the discount earned by the customer is partly lost when packing and shipping charges are paid. Thus savings are far less than the company's advertising implies, argues the FTC. A forthright explanation of customer rights and obligations in the club's advertising could reduce whatever customer dissatisfaction might exist. But of course it might also make the club's buy-in offer less attractive.

2. *The multicompany get-well solution.*   Companies that have succeeded in buying in can reduce antitrust risks and increase customer satisfaction—without necessarily reducing profits—if rival businesses are allowed to participate in the get-well sales. Multiple licensing of get-well patents is one way of allowing rivals in without necessarily damaging profits. Motives are difficult to discern, but I suspect that part of the reason at least a few companies pick up corporate hitchhikers via licensing is that it reduces prospective antitrust attention and customer animosity. Licensing arrangements among rivals generate profits for the licenser but also give customers at least the illusion—and usually the reality—of choice in the marketplace. Licensing is not popular, presumably because many managements believe that profits from licensing are less than profits from monopoly sales. That may help explain why companies such as Kodak, IBM, and Gillette have been so reluctant to allow others to profit from their buy-in situations.

3. *The sliding-down-the-learning-curve solution.*   It is less a matter of business strategy and more a matter of luck to be in an industry where the learning curve is alive and well. Learning curve theory tells us that cost per unit goes down during a product's life by virtue of the producer's experience with the product. If a product costs, say, $1 per unit to manufacture in 1980, costs may be only 90 cents by 1983. This decline is brought about by production sophistication rather than economies of scale, which may reduce production costs even more.

One industry in which the learning curve is thriving is the semiconductor industry. Producers are far more efficient now than they were just a few years ago, and this experience is reflected in selling prices that have declined dramatically over the years.

Under such conditions, sellers who have bought into a market can earn generous profits while simultaneously maintaining stable prices or perhaps even gradually reducing them. Of course, costs must go down even faster.

4. *The for-the-good-of-the-public solution.* One can argue that businesses which bind customers to purchases that enhance their quality of life are making a positive contribution to consumer welfare. Some psychologists maintain that certain prospective buyers need help in taking the last step toward purchasing products they want. The psychologists contend that many customers are unable to tell a salesperson, "Yes, I'll take it," or cannot bring themselves to sign their name to a mail-order form, even though they know the product will improve their life at least a bit. A tempting buy-in offer made by the seller helps the customer past this mental obstacle.

A formidable problem in persuading hard-to-persuade customers is that they are likely to have substantial postpurchase anxieties about the propriety of their purchases. More than 20 years ago, Leon Festinger pointed out that customers often attempt to provide themselves a comforting rationale for their purchases afterward.[1] They actively seek out and believe information that supports their decision while avoiding or rejecting information that suggests a wrong decision. Festinger's theory explains business strategy that is directed at customers who constitute the follow-on market.

The argument can be made, then, that book clubs use buying in for the public good. Most readers would no doubt accept the argument that a literate public is socially beneficial. So if the psychological theory that people need help overcoming their own purchasing anxieties is right, the clubs that keep sending books unless they are told not to are providing a public service. This presumes, of course, that the money spent on books would otherwise be spent on something of lower social value.

Furthermore, the club managers may have read or even anticipated Festinger's propositions about post-decision dissonance, because their advertising no longer alludes only to the joy of reading. Rather, the advertising also suggests the benefits of owning a collection of fine books. The book clubs learned long ago that while people often buy books to read, they sometimes buy books to leave on their coffee tables and impress their friends. People who buy books but do not read them have their consciences soothed by believing from advertising that ownership of a good book is almost as important as reading it.

5. *The don't-get-well-too-quickly solution.* This strategy consists of realizing gross margins during the follow-on sales that are less than what they might be. The approach works best when the seller has the near certainty of a long string of sales into the future and can enjoy the luxury of watching revenue from follow-on sales come drifting in, slowly but surely.

This approach sounds nearly unassailable, but several caveats are worth mentioning. First, it is based on the premise that the link between the buy-in and get-well sales is so strong that the seller will enjoy sales in perpetuity. But the tendency of companies to develop "new and improved" products suggests that companies which have bought in would rather not simply let things be. Second, low margins may be unnecessary if placating the consumer market is the only objective, since customers often have little or no idea of what constitutes a fair price. In short, getting well by selling products at high gross margins will generate no ill will in the marketplace if customers do not know that the prices they are paying contribute to high margins. This situation exists with many new consumer products that allow the seller much pricing freedom without risking significant customer criticism.

Sellers who face industrial buyers usually have no such leeway. Industrial customers often can reconstruct prices and have a reasonably accurate idea about the seller's profit margins. They know—better than the household buyer—when the seller is getting well too quickly. For such customers, the slower approach to getting well—meaning a lower selling price and lower margin per unit—may mean higher profits over the life of the project. In addition, rivals may lose interest in breaking the buy-in/get-well link if low prices make the get-well profit potential less attractive.

An ironic danger associated with getting well slowly is that low-margin pricing may smack of a monopolistic approach that appears to foreclose the market to would-be rivals. The irony is that low prices make profit margins too small to encourage market entry by other potential suppliers. Crudely stated, high margins attract rivals, while low margins repel them. Federal antitrust officials have given ample attention in the past to sales of such diverse products as linen and office supplies because entrenched suppliers set prices too low rather than too high. Thus getting well so slowly that it preserves the market for a single well-established supplier can be dangerous legally. Consequently the practice must be handled with great care.

6. *The muddy-the-water solution.* This strategy is reserved for those who are morally certain about what they do, though in an open debate the strategy would be hard to defend. One approach consists of separating in the customers' minds the business entity that engages in the buy-in from the one that enjoys the getting well. If enough confusion can be created in the marketing process, customers will not link the two entities and will continue to think well of one unit while any animosity will be directed at the other.

For example, appliance retailers, automobile dealers, and others sell their financing papers via financial institutions. After making a down payment, customers are obligated to a bank or finance company—not to a retailer—for monthly payments. Some retailers have profited rather handsomely by selling get-well financing papers to outside businesses. Some financial institutions, with no reputation to protect, have abused their strong legal position. The retailer in such situations could continue to show much sympathy but give no substantive help to the purchaser. If handled properly, the customer would presumably direct all his or her antagonism toward the financing institution rather than the retailer.

A second and more palatable approach consists of making product design, packaging, or styling changes that hinder comparison with earlier purchases. No seller wants to hear a customer say, "But when I bought this identical product just a year ago it cost me only. . . ." Regular product changes that are announced as improvements are the most common solution, particularly when they are accompanied by style and packaging changes and a phasing out of the older model. Unhappily, business executives may honestly believe that the newer product is a real improvement and that it offers customers more value for their money. But the customers may not notice any real improvement, looking on the changes as purely cosmetic.

In Conclusion

Buying in represents an attempt to monopolize markets. The result, however, is usually far less than a powerful and long-term hold on customer allegiance. Furthermore, most monopolies such as those held in a buy-in/get-well situation are hard to maintain over the years; they tend to deteriorate. This tendency is a tribute to the abilities of customers, government, and rivals to break the link to the get-well stage.

Whatever the effectiveness of buy-in attempts, sensitive executives must not lose sight of the moral issues that buying in may pose. No executive enjoys being in the position of those in the cigarette industry who, until recent years, freely passed out samples of their products on college campuses. Once addicted, the students would pay back the cost of the buy-in many times over. But when the relationship of smoking to health problems became widely known, public criticism forced the companies to stop giving out samples.

Business managers give more attention to buying in than academicians, who would mostly prefer not to acknowledge its importance as a business tool. Even the managers who use the technique often do not use the vocabulary presented here and may not recognize it when they see it in other situations.

Of course, not every product or service is suited to buying in. But the practice occurs often enough, generates serious commercial and legal problems for both seller and buyer, and imposes enough ethical questions that it deserves explicit acknowledgment by both managers and academicians.

Notes

1. Leon Festinger, *A Theory of Cognitive Dissonance* (Stanford, Calif.: Stanford University Press, 1957).

Appendix 1

Small Businesses and Franchisor Buy-Ins

Buying in is largely reserved for well-financed companies, usually those that are able to wait patiently for their profits. However, small businesses often play a central role in breaking the link between the buy-in and the get-well stages that larger companies work so hard to preserve. When smaller rivals succeed, the large company becomes simply another seller on the block peddling its wares.

A conspicuous example of the buy-in/get-well phenomenon in recent years is the supplier-customer relationship that developed during the growth years of franchising. Franchisors sometimes signed up franchisees at attractively low initial contract prices. The franchisees agreed, among other things, to confine their purchases to products supplied by the franchisors, who thus acquired what amounted to a captive list of customers. The franchisors usually argued that the restriction was necessary because they wanted to maintain high and uniform standards of quality among franchisees. Milk shakes, hamburgers, cola drinks, coffee, and so on should taste the same throughout the land, they maintained.

Such restrictive purchasing agreements would have been acceptable among honorable people, but there is ample dispute about whether everyone was entirely honorable. Congressional testimony in 1970 revealed how franchisors added unconscionably large markups to the products that they either manufactured or purchased from others for resale to their captive customers. One franchisor was getting well quickly, buying a spice blend for $3 and wholesaling it to its franchisees for $21.50.

The judicial system has been tough on franchisors who have been getting well via the enforced patronage of their franchisees. Beginning with Chicken Delight in 1970, the courts generally have held that franchisees should be permitted to purchase their materials and supplies from whomever they may choose so long as product quality is not affected. Some court decisions have been carefully tailored to the specific cases. For example, Chock Full O'Nuts won the right to be the sole provider to franchisees of coffee and baked goods, but its outlets were allowed to satisfy their other product needs elsewhere.

The decisions restricting the freedom of franchisors to buy in and get well have aided many small businesses. Independent suppliers of ground beef, milk, paper cups, napkins, spices, restaurant cooking equipment, and everything else necessary to help run a franchise received a marketing boost.

Astute franchisors realized that their earlier practices would not withstand legal challenges and so adjusted their policies to accommodate new suppliers, many of them local or regional companies. In some instances, they permitted their franchisees to buy from any suppliers whose products met quality standards established by the franchisor. For example, one restaurant franchisor has a two-page description of standards for ground beef. Any meat-packer or wholesaler whose beef meets the standards is automatically an eligible supplier. In other cases, franchisees were permitted to purchase from a list of approved suppliers whose products the franchisor had reviewed and found reliable. For example, 1977 court testimony revealed that Kentucky Fried Chicken had nine approved suppliers who were permitted to sell paper products—carryout boxes, napkins, cups, and towe-lettes—to its franchisees; none were related to KFC. Franchisees were promised in their contracts that further approvals of suppliers would not be "unreasonably withheld." Quite obviously, many of the small suppliers that were once foreclosed from the franchise market have now become regular suppliers to the industry.

Appendix 2

Stopping a Buy-In Before It Starts

When the Federal Communications Commission voted last April to encourage American Telephone and Telegraph to become more deeply involved in the computing industry, it recognized the giant company's follow-on potential. It feared that Ma Bell might be able to use its communications strength to gain access to the computing business. To prevent this from happening, the commission argued that all of AT&T's intracorporate dealings must be at arm's length. Each division must stand on its own merits, meaning that the communications people cannot help the computer people find—and hold—customers. So if AT&T's computer division were to go into hand-to-hand combat with IBM, it must do so like any other new rival in the industry. It cannot ride the coattails of an already well-established communications division.

About the Authors

Alan R. Andreasen is visiting professor, Graduate School of Management, UCLA. He has written or edited ten books and monographs and over sixty articles on marketing management, consumer behavior, marketing research, regulation, and nonprofit marketing. His books include The Disadvantaged Consumer *and his articles, "Cost-Conscious Marketing Research," "Consumers Complain—Does Business Respond?," and "Life Status Changes and Changes in Consumer Preferences and Behavior."*

Rena Bartos is a senior vice president and director of communications development at J. Walter Thompson Company. Her major responsibility is tracking social trends and identifying marketing opportunities resulting from social change. She works with all JWT offices in implementing her findings, and she consults with JWT clients throughout the world. Mrs. Bartos is an active spokeswoman for JWT. She represents the Agency on the Research Committee of the American Association of Advertising Agencies, chairs the Subcommittee on Consumer Attitude Research of the 4A's, and has chaired the Subcommittee of the Future of the Advertising Agency Research Function. She also chaired the 1975–76 EFFIE Awards Program for the New York Chapter of the American Marketing Association as well as the Public Policy Statements Committee of the Public Policy Division, American Marketing Association. Mrs. Bartos was one of the first women invited to join the Copy Research Council and also holds memberships in the American Association for Public Opinion Research and the Advertising Women of New York. She was elected a vice president of JWT in 1969, named director of communications research in 1970, and elected a senior vice president in June 1975.

Abe Berger obtained his undergraduate education at New York University and received his doctorate in physical chemistry from the University of Chicago. He carried out physical research for both government and industry

Publisher's Note. Biographical information was not available on all authors at the time of publication.

553

for many years before becoming a consultant. Currently he works with clients to optimize product and process specifications while reducing production costs. He is a co-founder of Reddy, Berger, Rosen and Woods, Inc., with Jack Reddy, and the author of many technical and business publications.

Thomas V. Bonoma *is associate professor in the MBA program at the Harvard Business School. His research interests include directing more academic attention to marketing practice. Other research activities in which he maintains active interest include industrial buying behavior, industrial marketing, and sales management. He also has written on the psychology of management and has been a regular contributor to the social psychology literature. In addition to a marketing implementation course, Professor Bonoma teaches regularly in Harvard's Strategic Marketing Management program for top marketing executives and in HBS' Advanced Management Program and Program for Management Executives. He has taught as well in a number of corporate executive programs on marketing. His recent books include a casebook and instructor's manual on* Managing Marketing, Industrial Buying Behavior, Industrial Market Segmentation, Psychology of Management, Executive Survival Manual, *and* Achieving Marketing Excellence. *Professor Bonoma has contributed a number of articles to the* Harvard Business Review, *to all of marketing's major journals and many of those in the area of management, and to many journals and magazines on psychology. To "relax," he programs a microcomputer and publishes a monthly column in* Microcomputing *magazine. Professor Bonoma consults to a number of major corporations on matters of marketing excellence, major account selling, industrial marketing, and marketing strategy. He sits on the board of directors of three corporations as well. He is a social psychologist by original training specializing in social power, conflict, and influence. He graduated from Ohio University (A.B., Psychology, 1968), the University of Miami (M.S., Social Psychology, 1969), and the State University of New York at Albany (Ph.D., Social Psychology, 1972).*

Albert V. Bruno *is Glenn Klimek Professor of Business at the University of Santa Clara's Leavey School of Business. He has a Ph.D. in industrial administration from the Krannert School at Purdue University. Professor Bruno served as chairman of the Marketing Department at the University of Santa Clara from 1975 to 1983. He recently completed a NSF-funded study of venture capital with Tyzoon T. Tyebjee. Professor Bruno's research interests include marketing strategy, high technology management, entrepreneurship, and technology management.*

Robert D. Buzzell *is Sebastian S. Kresge Professor of Business Administration at Harvard University, Graduate School of Business Administration. A member of the HBS faculty since 1961, Buzzell previously taught at the Ohio State University. Professor Buzzell has been author or co-author of books and articles on a variety of topics related to marketing management, stra-*

tegic planning, marketing research, international marketing, and public policy issues. Articles by Buzzell have appeared in the Harvard Business Review, Journal of Marketing, Journal of Marketing Research, Journal of Advertising Research, *and* Encyclopedia Brittanica Book of the Year. *He has spoken at conferences and seminars conducted by the American Marketing Association, the Conference Board, the Advertising Research Foundation, and other industry and professional associations. From 1968 to 1972, Buzzell was Executive Director of the Marketing Science Institute, a non-profit, industry-supported research organization associated with Harvard Business School. In 1974 he served as Research Director of a major research project at MSI aimed at identifying and measuring the determinants of profits in individual businesses. This project later evolved into an independent organization, the Strategic Planning Institute, which conducts the PIMS research program.*

Kristina Cannon-Bonventre *received her Ph.D. from Harvard University after which she worked in a consulting firm for several years as a research scientist. She also spent two years as a research associate in consumer marketing and retailing at Harvard Business School. She is now an assistant professor of marketing at Northeastern University's College of Business Administration. Her research and other professional activities are in the areas of consumer marketing and relationships between distribution and the economics of demand. Professor Cannon-Bonventre has written a number of business cases for Harvard Business School and for private industry. In addition to her research, teaching, and other activities in marketing, she is active in efforts to place Ph.D.s from the arts and sciences in industry and other nontraditional careers.*

Arnold C. Cooper *is Louis A. Weil, Jr. Professor of Management at the Krannert Graduate School of Management, Purdue University. He is author, co-author, or co-editor of five books and a number of articles on entrepreneurship, strategic planning, and the management of technology. He served on the Federal Advisory Committee on Industrial Innovation and now serves on the Indiana Employment Development Commission. He was chairperson of the Division of Business Policy and Planning of the Academy of Management. He has served on the editorial boards of* The Academy of Management Journal *and* Strategic Management Journal, *as well as the advisory board of The Center for Entrepreneurial Management.*

Harry A. Garfield II *is a partner in the Boston law firm of Berman, DeValerio & Pease, specializing in antitrust and securities law. From 1969 until 1983, Mr. Garfield was an official of the Federal Trade Commission, where he served as assistant director of the Bureau of Competition in Washington and as assistant regional director of the agency's Boston office. Prior to his government service, Mr. Garfield was for many years in private practice in New York City. He graduated from Yale University and from Columbia Law*

School. He also attended the Advance Management Program at the Harvard Business School and teaches Government–Business Relations in the Harvard Extension Program.

Jeff C. Goldsmith *is president, Health Futures, Inc. Formerly he was director, Office of Health and Planning and Health Regulating Affairs at the University of Chicago Medical Center.*

Kathryn Rudie Harrigan, *DBA (Harvard), MBA (Texas), is associate professor of strategic management, Columbia University. Her books include* Strategies for Declining Businesses, Strategies for Vertical Integration, Strategic Flexibility: A Management Guide for Changing Times, *and* Strategies for Joint Ventures. *She is a member of the editorial board and frequent contributor to* Strategic Management Journal, Journal of Business Strategy, *and* Academy of Management Journal; *she also writes for* Long Range Planning *and* Academy of Management Review.

James D. Hlavacek *is professor of management at the Babcock Graduate School of Management at Wake Forest University. Dr. Hlavacek also serves as editor-in-chief of the* Journal of Industrial Marketing. *Professor Hlavacek is the co-author (with B.C. Ames) of two recently published books,* Managerial Marketing for Industrial Firms *and a practitioner's book,* Managerial Marketing: The Ultimate Advantage. *Professor Hlavacek is the author of many articles and is a principal in a firm that specializes in developing and leading in-house executive programs for technical-based corporations.*

Thomas Hout *is vice-president of Boston Consulting Group and has served in BCG's London, Tokyo, and Boston offices. Mr. Hout writes occasional op–ed columns on international business for* The Wall Street Journal *and* The New York Times.

Jack G. Kaikati *is professor of marketing at Southern Illinois University— Edwardsville, where he teaches international business. He has written extensively on questionable overseas payments, the Arab boycott, and international and domestic barter trade. His articles appear in such publications as* Harvard Business Review, Journal of Marketing, Sloan Management Review, California Management Review, Columbia Journal of World Business, Business Horizons, *among others.*

Uday S. Karmarkar *is associate professor of operations management and operations research at the Graduate School of Management, University of Rochester, and director of the Center for Manufacturing and Operations Management. His research interests lie in manufacturing management as well as service issues such as product support, and include cost and performance measurement, organization and incentives. Professor Karmarkar's work has been published in* Management Science, Operations Research, Naval Research Logistics Quarterly, IIE Transactions, Econometrica,

Interfaces, Harvard Business Review, *and* Organizational Behavior and Human Performance. *He is an Associate Editor of* Operations Research *and a former editor of the* Naval Research Logistics Quarterly. *Professor Karmarkar is a member of ORSA, TIMS, OMA, and IIE. He is a co-founder of ORSA's Special Interest Group in Manufacturing. He is a member of the Manufacturing Management Council of the Society for Manufacturing Engineers and an Honorary member of the Rochester APICS chapter. Professor Karmarkar has been involved in consulting, research projects and management seminars with companies such as John Deere and Co., Eastman-Kodak, Motorola, and Xerox.*

Raymond LaGarce *is professor and chairman of marketing at Southern Illinois University–Edwardsville. His current research is in the areas of product management and channel and distribution management.*

Milind M. Lele *is the managing director of SLC Consultants, Inc., a management consulting firm with offices in Chicago, Los Angeles, and New York. Over the past fifteen years he has worked with a number of client firms in a wide variety of industries including agricultural equipment, chemicals, industrial distribution, heavy machinery, telecommunications equipment, and telecommunications services. He advises clients on corporate strategy and marketing issues relating to diversification, identification of new product and market opportunities, new product development, customer service, and product support. In addition to consulting, Dr. Lele is a lecturer in marketing at the University of Chicago's Graduate School of Business. During 1983 he was also a visiting Associate Professor at Northwestern University's Kellogg Graduate School of Management. Dr. Lele obtained undergraduate degrees in physics and electronics in India and his M.S. and Ph.D. in operations research from Harvard University.*

Theodore Levitt *is Edward W. Carter Professor of Business Administration at the Harvard Business School. An economist by training, he was a business consultant in Chicago before coming to Harvard in 1959. He is a four-time winner of McKinsey Awards for best articles in the* Harvard Business Review. *He also holds the record as the most frequently published author in the* Review. *He's the author of eight books, the latest being* The Marketing Imagination. *Professor Levitt is an active consultant to management and on the boards of directors of several companies.*

Tommy J. McCuistion *is executive in residence and senior lecturer, Weatherhead School of Management, Case Western Reserve University. He retired in 1981 as corporate vice president of marketing, planning, economics and acquisitions of Parker Hannifin Corporation. He is a member of the North American Society for Corporation Planning, Inc., and has served on boards of directors of many societies and organizations such as National Fluid Power Association, Sales and Marketing Executives of Cleveland and Los*

Angeles, and Rubber Manufacturer's Association. *His articles have appeared in* Applied Hydraulics, Rubber Age, *and* Industry Week *as well as* HBR.

Shelby H. McIntyre *received a B.S., M.B.A., and Ph.D. from Stanford University. He is the chairman of the Marketing Department at the University of Santa Clara. He is a former employee of the General Electric Company where he held various positions in operations research–related work. He is active in research concerned with computer-based decision support systems, marketing research techniques, and high-tech marketing innovation. His articles have appeared in* Journal of Marketing Research, Management Science, Business Horizons, Journal of Applied Psychology, Academy of Management Journal, Industrial Labor Relations Review, Industrial Marketing, Journal of Retailing, *and* HBR.

Michael E. Porter *is a professor at the Harvard Business School and a leading authority on competitive strategy. He is the author of seven books and over thirty articles. His book* Competitive Strategy: Techniques for Analyzing Industries and Competitors, *is widely recognized as the leading work in its field. His newest book is* Competitive Advantage: Creating and Sustaining Superior Performance. *Professor Porter has served as a counselor on competitive strategy to many leading U.S. and international companies. He has also served as a counselor to governments and was appointed by President Ronald Reagan to the President's Commission on Industrial Competitiveness in 1983 where he was Chairman of the Commission's Strategy Committee. Professor Porter is the recipient of many awards and honors, including the David O. Wells Prize in Economics, the McKinsey Award for the best* Harvard Business Review *article, and the Graham and Dodd Award of the Financial Analysts Federation.*

John A. Quelch *is associate professor of business administration at the Graduate School of Business Administration, Harvard University. A graduate of Oxford, the University of Pennsylvania, and Harvard, he has written extensively on the marketing of consumer products in* Harvard Business Review, Business Horizons, Marketing Science, *and other professional journals. He is the co-author of* Advertising and Promotion Management *and* Cases in Advertising and Promotion Management.

Jack Reddy *holds a B.S. in engineering from Rensselaer Polytechnic Institute and an MBA from Harvard. He is a certified management consultant, a founding member of the IMC, and president and co-founder of Reddy, Berger, Rosen and Woods, Inc., with Abe Berger. He has been active in the development of new statistical and managerial techniques designed for product and profit improvement. He has led hundreds of assignments with major clients in both the U.S. and Europe.*

Chris Ryan *received his undergraduate degree in physics from the University of Hull and his M.Sc. in business studies from the University of Bath. He* *is a marketing manager in the British electronics industry. His earlier career was in research and development of electrical materials and in production management. Mr. Ryan has written many articles in physics, electronics, and management culminating in his book* The Marketing of Technology.

***Benson P. Shapiro** is a well-known authority on marketing, particularly industrial marketing, sales management, pricing, and product policy. He is the author or co-author of six books including* Segmenting the Industrial Market *(with Thomas V. Bonoma) and the three-volume series* Marketing Management *with Robert J. Dolan and John A. Quelch. He has written fourteen* Harvard Business Review *articles and is currently head of the required MBA marketing course at the Harvard Business School.*

***Robert Stobaugh** is the Charles E. Wilson Professor of Business Administration and director of the doctoral programs at the Harvard Business School. He directed the Harvard Business School Energy Project and is a co-author of the best-selling book* Energy Future: Report of the Energy Project at the Harvard Business School. *His teaching activity is in the fields of energy, international business, and technology and production. His most recent book is* Technology Crossing Borders, *which he co-edited with Professor Louis T. Wells, Jr., and which was the first publication of the Harvard Business School Press. Prior to receiving his doctorate from Harvard Business School, he had a career in the international oil and chemical industries.*

***Hirotaka Takeuchi** received his B.A. from International Christian University in Tokyo and his M.B.A. and Ph.D. from the University of California, Berkeley. He has been an assistant professor at the Harvard Business School, where he taught courses in marketing and retailing. He also taught marketing at the University of California, Berkeley for a year prior to joining the Harvard faculty. He currently teaches international marketing strategy at Hitotsubashi University in Tokyo and conducts joint research at Harvard. Professor Takeuchi's current research interests are focused on the role of marketing within a firm's global strategy and the linkage of marketing to R&D and production within the new product development process. His papers on these two topics have been presented at the Harvard Business School's 75th Anniversary Colloquium in March and April 1984. His previous papers have appeared in the* Harvard Business Review, Journal of Retailing, California Management Review, *and others. He has been quoted widely in* Business Week, Wall Street Journal, Time, *and others. His business experience includes management consulting work with McKinsey and Company in Tokyo and marketing research and account service work with McCann-Erickson in San Francisco and Tokyo. He is a consultant to a number of leading multinationals in both the United States and Japan and has been a frequent speaker at management conferences and seminars around the world.*

***Piero Telesio** is a business consultant and currently teaches at the Management Education Institute at Arthur D. Little, Inc. He received his doctorate* *from Harvard Business School and has written on international technology transfer, licensing, and trade. Dr. Telesio has also taught at the Boston University School of Management and the Fletcher School of Law and Diplomacy, Tufts University.*

Tyzoon T. Tyebjee *is associate professor at the University of Santa Clara's Leavey School of Business. He has a Ph.D. in Business Administration from the University of California, Berkeley. His interests are in the areas of marketing strategy, international marketing, new product development and the management of high-technology ventures. He has recently completed a three-year study of venture capital and high-technology startups. Professor Tyebjee is also the director of the International Business Studies program at the University of Santa Clara. He has consulted for a variety of clients including Levi Strauss, Raychem, California Microwave, Stoneware Software, and the California Fresh Market Tomato Advisory Board. His specialty is in the analysis of market survey data and in management training programs for rapidly growing companies.*

Robert E. Weigand *is professor of marketing at The University of Illinois at Chicago where he specializes in channel management and international business operations. His most recent* Harvard Business Review *article deals with investment incentives. He has written sixty articles about marketing and international business and is a co-author of* Basic Retailing. *Weigand earlier taught at DePaul University and holds degrees from The University of Illinois and The University of Notre Dame.*

Frederik D. Wiersema *is vice president of marketing and planning in a rapidly growing high-tech firm. In addition, he is currently doing research on strategic problems faced by new ventures, and is an adjunct professor of management at Simmons College, Graduate School of Management, Boston. He holds a doctorate in business administration from Harvard Business School.*

Aubrey Wilson *was founder and past chairman of Industrial Market Research Limited, London, and is now an independent consultant. He has written nine books on marketing subjects and pioneered the techniques for marketing professional services. Mr. Wilson is a well-known international lecturer and was recently awarded the annual prize of the Association of European Marketing Consultants for his development of the marketing audit technique. He has contributed two articles to the* Harvard Business Review.

Carolyn Y. Woo *is an assistant professor at Purdue University. Her research interests include strategies for low market share businesses and the integration of strategic and financial management issues. Her publications have appeared in the* Harvard Business Review, Management Science, *and* Management Journal. *She also served as a consultant at the Strategic Planning Associates.*

John Wyman is vice president for AT&T Communications. He joined AT&T in 1957 and has gained experience in operations and engineering as well as sales and marketing. He has been a vice president of marketing and a vice president of sales for AT&T Long Lines.

George S. Yip is a senior consultant with the Cambridge office of Management Analysis Center, Inc., an international general management consulting firm. His expertise is in areas of marketing strategy and strategic planning. He has also held sales and business management positions at Data Resources, Inc., the economic information firm, and product and advertising management positions at the Birds Eye Foods and Lintas Advertising divisions of Unilever Ltd. Mr. Yip is the author of one book and several articles on marketing and strategy. He holds masters and doctoral degrees from Cambridge University (England), the Cranfield School of Management (England), and the Harvard Business School.

Author Index

Abernathy, W. J., 264, 326, 329
Amsalem, M. A., 297
Andreasen, A. R., 60, 420
Aries, R. S., 118
Ayoub, S., 21

Banzhaf, J., 53
Barksdale, H. C., 55
Barnet, R., 60
Bartos, R., 6, 13, 420
Baxter, W., 69
Bentham, J., 158
Berger, A., 9, 299
Berlin, I., 20
Berry, L. L., 369
Best, A., 60
Biaggadike, R., 227
Bloom P. N., 6, 13
Bonoma, T. V., 6, 8, 10, 177, 299, 419, 442
Boorstein, D. J., 17
Britten, S., 154
Bruno, A. V., 178
Buzzard, R. D., 282, 300
Buzzell, R. D., 7, 178, 230

Campbell, J., 139–140
Cannon-Bonventre, K., 420
Cho, D., 297
Claybrook, J., 54
Cooper, A. C., 7, 177

De Bodinat, H., 297
Dolby, R., 325
Drucker, P., 29

Ellwood, P. M., Jr., 134, 138
Etzioni, A., 61

Farris, C., 161
Flashner, B., 133
Ford, D., 299
Ford, H., 19
Fox, S., 357
Furness, B., 53

Garfield, H. A., II, 13
Ginzberg, E., 85
Goldsmith, J. C., 14
Green M., 60
Greyser, S. A., 6, 13

Haldeman, H. R., 120
Hall, W. K., 192
Hamermesh, R. G., 192
Harrigan, K. R., 7, 177
Hayes, R. H., 264
Heany, D. F., 230
Henderson, B., 191
Herbert, M. E., 134, 138
Herrmann, R. O., 61
Hirsch, F., 154
Hlavacek, J. D., 420
Hobbs, C., 327
Hout, T., 178

Jackson, B. B., 300
Jefferson, E., 263
Johnston, W. J., 442

Kaikati, J. G., 14
Karmarkar, U. S., 300
Keddie, G. J., 297
Kissinger, H., 30
Kotler, P., 153, 157

La Garce, R., 14
Lawrence, D. H., 154
Lele, M. M., 300
Levitt, T., 1, 6, 7, 9, 13, 141, 178, 187–188, 300, 328

McCarthy, J. O., 56
McCuistion, T. J., 420
McElhattan, K. E., 453
McGill, A., 187
McIntyre, S. H., 178
McNiven, M. A., 420
Miller, J. C., III, 231
Molitor, G., 61
Moriarity, R., 421
Moxon, R. W., 297

Nader, R., 51, 52, 53, 54

Olson, M., 62

Perreault, W., 55
Peterson, E., 53
Pirsig, R., 179, 304
Pomper, C. L., 297
Porter, M. E., 7, 177, 178, 221

Quelch, J. A., 8, 10, 299, 419, 420

Reddy, J., 9, 299
Robinson, P., 161
Ronstadt, R. C., 297
Ryan, C., 299

Schoeffler, S., 230
Scopes, J., 153
Shapiro, B. P., 9, 400, 419, 421
Smith, T., 60
Solomon, B. L., 453
Stobaugh, R. B., 178, 297
Stopes, M., 153

Takeuchi, H., 8, 10, 299, 419–420
Telesio, P., 178, 297
Tyebjee, T. T., 178

Utterback, J. M., 326, 329

Warland, R. H., 61
Watson, C. M., 14
Weigand, R. E., 420
Welch, J. F., Jr., 26, 334
Wells, L. T., Jr., 297
Wells, W. D., 522
West, C., 14
Wiersema, F. D., 300
Wilson, A., 14
Wilson, B. D., 297
Wind, Y., 161
Woo, C. Y., 7, 177
Wyman, J., 9, 419

Yip, G. S., 178

Zald, M. N., 56

Subject Index

Absolute measure, 268
"Acceptable quality level" system, 377
Acquisitions entry, 227–228, 230–231
Advertising, 521–525
  AAAA study, 521–522, 524
  British advertising, public attitudes, 524
  cable television and, 523
  complaints, TV ads, 522
  consumer attitude studies, 521–522
  future trends, 523
  by hospitals, 136–138
  interactive cable television, 472–475
  vs. promotion, 494–495
Advertising and sales promotion (A&SP)
     budget, 527, 530–531
  A&SP-GM ratio, 531
  media-A&SP ratio, 531
Advertising productivity program, 526–537
  budget strategy, 527–534
    advertising elasticity calculation, 528–530
    A&SP-GM ratio, 531
    cents per case system, 527
    gross margin calculation method, 527
    media-A&SP ratio, 531
    percentage increase method, 527
    testing strategies, 531–533
    timing and, 533
    total business approach, 527–528
  cost reduction methods, 534–536
    agency compensation, 534–535
    auditing, 535
    commercial production, 535
    procurement of materials, 535–536
  gross rating points (GRPs), 533
  reach and frequency models, 533–545
Affluent older consumers, 106–107, 109–110
African and Malagasy Industrial Property
     Office, 123

Age, *see* Older consumers
Airbus Industrie, 224
  follow-on sales, 541
Airline industry, marketing territory, 3
Allocation, skills of manager and, 311
American Association of Advertising
     Agencies (AAAA), consumer attitude
     study, 521–522, 524
American Enterprise Institute, 54
American Express, 223
American industry:
  business environment (1970s), 32–33
  diversification, U.S. manufacturing
     industries, 47–48
  foreign competition and, 146–147
    lessons from, 148
  innovations in, 145–146
  scientists/engineers in, 147
  subsidiaries overseas, 148–151
American Motors, Chinese market and, 317
Anchor Health Plan, 140
Anti-Industrialists, consumer organization,
     60–61, 63
Antitrust, 68–81
  dealers, cutting off of, 75
  distribution antitrust, roles for, 69–71
  hierarchy of distribution restraints, 72–75
  interbrand/intraband competition and, 76
  legal challenges, people for, 79–80
  legal development of, 70–71
  market economics, mini-analysis of, 78–79
  motivation, determination of, 76–78
  objectives, determination of, 76
  policy, as barriers to intervention, 230–231
  risks:
    assessment of, 80–81
    levels of, 74
  "rule of reason" test, 71

Armco Steel, 37
  diversification, 47
Art museum, marketing of, 512, 513–515
ASEA Company, technology sale, 324
A&SP, *see* Advertising and sales promotion
      (A&SP) budget
Atlantic Aviation Corporation, trade show,
      455
Attraction power, 442–443
Augmented products, 237–239
Automatic washing machines:
  Hoover, Ltd., failure of, 22–25
  trends in Western Europe, 24
Automobile manufacturers, follow-on sales,
      replacement converters, 540

Babcock & Wilcox, 296
Banking industry, marketing territory, 3
"Banzhaf's Bandits," 53
Barriers to entry, 221–224
  antitrust intervention, 230–231
  position of entrants and, 222
  protective features of, 221–222
  reduction of, 222–224
  vertical integration and, 266
  workings of, 221–222
Bausch & Lomb, competition to, 228
Behavior, buying behavior, 336–337, 501–502
  trade promotions and, 501–502
Beijing Automotive Industrial Corporation,
      317–318
Bethlehem steel, losses for, 36
Bic pens, 351
Bowmar, 264
Brand management, 240
Brand names:
  branded food marketing, 241–242
  counterfeiting of, 116–123
  identification of, 116
British Technology Transfer Group, 327
BSR, competitive strategy of, 256–257
Budgets, advertising, 527–534. *See also*
      Advertising productivity program
Bundespost, 224
"Bunny marketing," 307
Burroughs, bank equipment setup, 321–32
Business environment, United States
      (1970s), 32–33
Business Roundtable, 54
"Buy class," 161
Buyers:
  group dynamics, 437–438
  motivation, analysis of, 445–447
  perceptions of selling company, 447–448

powerful buyers, 442–445
  identification of, 444–445
  quality control of vendors, 379–380, 381
Buying behavior, 336–337
  trade promotions and, 501–502
Buying in, 538–551
  conditions for, 542, 544–545
  customer relations and, 545–549
  examples of, 538–539
  follow-on sales, 540–542
    methods of, 541–542
  franchisors, 550–551
  meaning of, 539–540
  problems of, 542–545
  small businesses and, 549–550
Buying roles, 439–442
  deciders, 441
  gatekeepers, 439
  influences, 441
  initiator, 439
  purchaser/user, 441
Buying style, of women, 97–98
"Buy phase," 161

Cable television, advertising, future trends,
      523. *See also* Interactive cable
      television
CAD/CAM:
  effect of, 30
  small scale manufacturing, 20
Call-a-Mart, 467
Canon, market share strategy, 357
Capital:
  global strategy for, 259
  vertical integration and, 266
Cars, women's role in market, 98–99
Cartier, fake goods, 117, 121
Catalogs
  printed, advantages of, 473
  selling, 428–429
  see also Interactive cable television
Caterpillar Tractor Company, 223, 249–251,
      254–255
  assembly plant locations, 250
  beginnings of globalization, 249
  competition, barriers against, 249–250
  Komatsu as challenger to, 250–251
  product support, 384
  quality program of, 334
  strategic strengths of, 251
  success strategies of, 40
Cents per case system, 527
Certificate of need, hospitals, 127–128
Chrysler, 4

losses for, 35, 36
reinvestment errors of, 46
Cigarettes, global reach of, 17
Cincinnati Milacron, counter competitive
    action, 173
Cluster analysis, 194
Coca-Cola, global reach of, 17
Code-law country, trademarks, 121
Coercive power, 442
Colgate case, 70
Colgate-Palmolive, foreign manufacturing
    plants, 293
Collectibles, nonstore marketing, 470
Comite Colbert, 119
Commercials, production of, 535
Commissions, advertising agencies, 534
Commodity prices, *see* Industrial pricing
Common-law country, trademarks, 121
Compensation, advertising agencies, 534
Competition:
    business in consumerism industry, 65
    conditions of demand, 207–208
    foreign markets, 3–4
    global companies and, 19, 247, 248–249,
        255–257
    hospitals, 126
    increases in, 3–4, 6–7
    new entrants and, 226–227
    nonprofit organizations, 518
    see also Counter competition; Foreign
        competition
Competitive strategies:
    low market share businesses, 200–202
    measurement of, 345
    top manufacturing industries, 39–43
Computers:
    advertising budget, 531
    advertising elasticity measurement, 529
Conoco Inc., Du Pont and, 263
Consumerism, 51–67
    adaptation of organizations, 63–64
    "brands" of consumerism, 52
    business strategies for, 64–66
    consumer protection laws, 53
    current decade, 54–55, 62–63
    during 1970s, 51, 53–54
    during 1960s, 52–53
    "free rider" problem, 62
    future of, 61–62
    organizations, 55–61
        Anti-Industrialists, 60–61
        Coops, 59
        Corporates, 60
        Deregulators, 58

Feds, 56, 58
Locals, 58–59
Nationals, 56
Reindustrialists, 61
participative consumerism, 64
pocketbook consumerism, 64
public discontent with movement, 54, 55
regulatory agencies, reform of, 53
stages of, 52
Consumer Issues Working Group, 54
Consumer Product Safety Act, 53
Consumer research, 517
Consumers:
    intangible products and, 366–368
    nonstore shopping and, 469–470
    older consumers, 104–115
    women's market, 82–103
Consumers Union, 53
Contacts in Consumerism, 54
Contraceptive sheath, marketing of, 165–168
Coops, consumer organization, 59, 63
Corporates, consumer organization, 60, 63
Corporation, power bases in, 442–443
Costs:
    cost containment, hospitals, 128–129
    cost recution advertising, 534–535
    differentiated position leader, 42
    lowering of, internationally, 19
    lowest delivered, cost leader, 39–42
    see also Low-cost strategies
Counter competition, 172–175
    Cincinnati Milacron, 173
    factors for success, 174–175
    General Electric, 173
    IBM and, 172–174
    Intel, 173
    Texas Instruments, 174
Counterfeiting, 116–123
    coalitions against, 119
    foreign fake goods market, 116–117
    imitation, 118
    international agreements, 121–123
    outright piracy, 117–118
        "palming off" fakes, 118
        reasons for, 117
    strategies against, 119–121
        hands-off strategy, 119–120
        prosecuting strategy, 120
        warning strategy, 121
        withdrawal strategy, 120–121
    wholesale piracy, 118
CPI, 225
Customers:
    company relationship with, 368

Customers (*Continued*)
   perceptions of quality, 334–335
   product support and needs of, 387–390
   see also Consumers; Product quality
Customer service audit, 337–338
Customer service program, 339–341

Dart & Kraft, 223
Data base, interactive information retrieval,
   475–477. *See also* PIMS (Profit
   Impact of Market Strategies) data
   base
DCF risk-return analysis, 259
Debt policies, global strategy for, 259
Deciders, buying role of, 441
Declining industries, 205–219
   conditions of demand, 207–208
      demand pockets, nature of, 208
      perceptual factors, 207–208
      rate/pattern of decline, 208
   divestment, 215
   exit barriers, 208–210
      disposition of assets, 212
      high costs, 209–210
      information gaps, 211
      managerial resistance, 211
      reasons for continuing, 210
      social barriers, 211–212
      specialized assets, 209
   focus strategy for, 214–215
   harvest strategy, 216, 215
   leadership strategy for, 212, 214
   strategy for decline, 216–218
Deere & Company, 286
   product support, 384
Demand, declining businesses and, 207–208
Demarketing, unmentionables, 160–161
Demonstration centers, 424–425
Deregulated industries, 3
Deregulators, consumer organization, 58
Diamler Benz, success strategies of, 40
Diamond Reo, losses for, 36, 41
Differentiated position leader, 42
Differentiation, 232–245
   consumer services, 233
   generic products, 233
   products, 233–240
   role of management in, 240–244
   see also Products
Digital Equipment, 38
Direct marketing, *see* Nonstore marketing
Direct response advertising, 480
Disabled, older consumers, 106
Disadvantaged, older consumers, 105–106

Discalogs, 480
Discounts, trade promotions and, 499–500
Displays, point of purchase displays, 485–487
Distribution:
   antitrust:
      laws, development of, 70–71
      rules for, 69–71
   hierarchy of restraints, 72–75
   technology-information revolution and, 5
   see also Antitrust
Distributors:
   assessment approach, 509–511
      management assessment, 509–511
   industrial distributors, 503–511
   products for, 504–505
   regional-territorial evaluation, 510–511
   selection of, 505–509
      life cycle changes in product and, 506
      market segment factors, 505–506
      producer/distributor policies and, 507–508
      product specification and, 506–507
      qualifications assessment, 508
      training/support factors, 508–509
Diversification, U.S. manufacturing
      industries, 47–48
Diversified marketing, 284
Divestment, for declining businesses, 215
Dividend policies, global strategy for, 259
Doctor's emergency officenter, 133
Dolby Laboratories, marketing position,
      322, 325
Du Point, Conoco and, 263

Eastman Kodak, 38
   Berkey photo conflict, 543
   instant picture technology, 317
Economy, changes, marketing and, 2
Elasticity calculation, advertising, 528–530
Electronic Retail Information Center, point
      of purchase program, 482
"Empty promises" marketing, 306–307
End-game, 205–206
Entrepreneurial marketing, 281–282
Entrepreneurship, 4
Entry strategies, 224–229
   acquisition entry, 227–228, 230–231
      negative factors in, 228–229
   competition, avoidance of, 226–227
   lateness, advantages of, 224–225
   negating barriers, 227
   new businesses, weak position of, 222
   technological change and, 225–226
   see also Barriers to entry
Environmental changes, 2–5

competitive marketing environment, 3–4, 6–7
future and, 10–11
management, attitudes about, 4, 7–9
national/international order, 2–3, 5–6
new entrants and, 225–226
technology-information revolution, 4–5, 9–10
Ethernet, 322
Ethnic markets, 20–21
European A300 Airbus, 321
European Common Market, trademark convention, 123
Expected products, 236–237
Expert power, 443
Expositions, 454
Exxon, 224
FTC and, 231

Family, new family structure, 2
Federal agencies, consumer agencies, 56–57
Federal Communications Commission, AT&T computer division, 551
Federal Express, production system, 227
Federal laws, consumer protection laws, 53
Federal Trade Commission, 53
breakfast cereals market investigation, 230
Exxon and, 231
health care industry and, 128
Xerox case, 318
Feds, consumer organization, 56, 58, 63
Females, as target groups, 83, 84. See also Women's market
Field experimentation, advertising elasticity measurement, 529
Fighting brands, 497
Financial management, global companies, 258–259
Financial profile, over-49 group, 113–114
Fixed-price contracts, risk and, 406
Focus strategy, for declining businesses, 214–215
Follow-on sales, 540–542
Ford Motor Company:
competitive positions (1980s), 36
integration technique, 45
point of purchase program, 482
Foreign competition, 3–4, 146–147
counter competition, 172–175
lessons learned from, 148
penetration of, 171–172
U.S. manufacturing industries and, 34
Foreign markets, fake goods, 116–117
Foreign subsidiaries, 148–151

reorganization of, 149–150
usefulness of, 151
Franchisors, buying in, 550–551
"Free rider" problem, marketing and, 62
Freestanding emergency rooms, diversification tactic, 133–134
Freightliner, improvement strategies of, 41
Frito-Lay:
marketing functions, 306
sales force, power of, 490
Functions, of marketing, 304–306

Gatekeepers, buying role of, 439
General Electric, 38
counter competitive action, 173
low cost strategy, 296
sale of fluidics technology, 317
sale of oil digesting companies, 316–317
scale of technologies, 320
General Foods, studies of retailers, 241
General Inter-American Convention for Trademark and Commercial Name Protection, 122
General Motors:
competitive positions (1980s), 36
cost-reduced strategy, 39
Delco radio issue, 544
integration policy, 45
General Tire, 37
diversification, 47
Generic products:
differentiation, 233
meaning of, 235–236
Gillette:
advertising, 306
suit with Schick, 543
Global companies, 16, 17, 246–262
approaches for success, 29
Caterpillar Tractor Company, 249–251
characteristics of, 248
competition and, 247, 248–248, 255–257
definition of, 261–262
financial management, 258–259
allocating capital, 259
debt/dividends, 259
Honda, 252–254
L. M. Ericsson, 251–252
management approaches, 247, 257–258
multidomestic, definition of, 261
multinational, definition of, 261
newly industrializing companies and, 256
organizational structure, 258
scope of knowledge, 20
winning strategies of, 255

Globalization:
  barriers to, 21
  distribution and, 26–27
  economic nationalism and, 28
  economies of scope and, 30–31
  failures in, home laundry equipment,
    22–25
  global *vs.* multinational corporations, 16,
    17, 20, 29–30
  Japanese companies, 18–19
    marketing strategy, 26
  national/local preferences and, 20–21
  standardization of products, 17–21
Goal setting, product quality, 377
Goodrich, diversification, 47
Goodyear, 37
Grocery shopping, nonstore approach,
    466–468
Gross margin calculation method, 527
Gross rating points (GRPs), 533
GTE Sylvania case, 71

Hands-off strategy, counterfeiting, 119–120
Hard technologies, meaning of, 365
Harvest strategy, for declining businesses,
    206, 215
Health care market, 124–143
  competition in, 126
  economic power of physicians and, 126
  health maintenance organization plans,
    127, 134–135
  horizontal integration, 138–139
  new forms of delivery, 126–127
  new organizational strategies, 139–141
  regulatory policies, 127–129
    certificate of need, 127–128
    cost containment, 128–129
    Federal Trade Commission, 128
    health manpower policy, 128
  risks in expansion of, 141
  see also Hospitals
Health maintenance organizations (HMO),
    127, 134–135
Health Professionals Educational Assistance
    Act of 1976, 128
Heavy duty truck manufacturing, evolution
    of, 35–36. *See also* Caterpillar
    Tractor Company
High market share, 191–192
High-value added, low market share
    businesses, 200
Home computers, 5
Homemakers, over-49 group, 108–109, 111,
    112–113

Home selling, 480
Honda, 252–254
  globalization of, 253
  marketing strategies of, 253–254
  market share strategy, 356–357
  use of debt, 259
Hoover, Ltd., failures of, 22–25
Hospitals,
  competitive strategies, 129–138
    advertising, 136–138
    competing for physicians, 129–131
    freestanding emergency rooms, 133–134
    health maintenance organizations,
      134–135
    outpatient care, 131–132
    outpatient surgery, 132–133
    screening programs, 135
    transportation services, 135–136
  organizational strategy, example of,
    139–141
  see also Health care market
Husbands, participation in household, 101
Hybrid technologies, meaning of, 365–366

IBM, 223–224
  counter competitive action, 172–172
  follow-on sales, 541
  manufacturing policies, 290–291
  market management, 242
Implementation, marketing strategy and,
    302–304, 305, 312
Industrialization, benefits of, 366
Industrialization of service, 365
Industrial pricing, 399–418
  analysis of pricing questions, 413–414
  benefits/costs determination, 401
  fluctuations in, 400
  management decisions in, 399–400
  risk in, 400–401
  see also Risk management
Industrial stores, 425–426
Industrial tractors, product support case
    study, 394–398
Influencers, buying role of, 441
Initiators, buying role of, 439
Inland Steel, 37
  integration technique, 45
Intangible products:
  consumer perception of, 366–368
  definition of, 360
  industrialization and, 366
  manufacturing of, 364–365
  problems of, 364–366
  quality control difficulties, 365

strengthening customer relations, 368
tangibility, creation in, 368–370
Integrity buying, 336
Intel, counter competitive action, 173
Interactive cable television, 472–475, 480
cable operator barriers, 474–475
cost barriers, 475
disadvantages to consumer, 473–474
Interactive information retrieval, 475–477,
480
consumer barriers, 476
cost barriers, 476–477
technological barriers, 476
Interactive skills, of manager, 311
International Anticounterfeiting Coalition,
119, 123
International brand piracy, see
Counterfeiting
International Harvester, 4
losses for, 35–36, 41
reinvestment errors of, 46
International order, changes in, 2–3, 5–6
International technology transfer and
production, research project, 296–297
International Union for the Protection of
Industrial Property, 122
Investment buying, 336
Isopropanol, market management process,
242–243

Japanese companies, 4
goal setting, product quality, 377
marketing approach, 26
monetary system and operations in, 31
quality/cost factors, 18–19
rise in market share and, 351, 372
specifications, "slotted hole" approach,
380
SmithKlein Corporation strategy in, 27
Johnson & Johnson First Aid Center, 486
Jones & Laughlin, merger with Youngstorm,
36

Kaiser, losses for, 36
Karmarkar, U.S., 300
Kodak, point of purchase program, 482
Komatsu, 223
as challenger to Caterpillar, 250–251
distribution strategy, 27

Leadership positions, of performance
leaders, 44–45
Leadership strategy, for declining
businesses, 212, 214

L'eggs:
marketing program, 356
success of, 490
Leisure time, over-49 group, 112, 113
Levis Strauss, counterfeiting and, 120
Lexel Corporation, 282
Life-cycle buying, 336
L.L. Bean:
quality program of, 333–334
success of, 468–469
L. M. Ericsson:
as global company, 251–252, 255
innovations of, 252
Locals, consumer organization, 58–59, 63
London Rubber Company, marketing
techniques, 168–170
Louis Vuitton, counterfeiting and, 120–121
Low-cost strategies, 293–296
low-cost inputs, 295–296
low labor costs, 294–295
Otis Elevator Company, 293–294
for production, 44
scale economics, 293–294
Lowest delivered cost leader, 42
Low market share study, 191–204
businesses in, 193
competitive strategy, 200
environmental characteristics of
businesses, 193
high-value added characteristic, 200
poor performers, characteristics of, 202
products, 198–200
levels of, 198–199
purchasing frequency, 199, 200
standardized, 199
types of, 199
profitability and, 202–203
profitable low-share businesses, 195, 198
share building, consequences of, 192
strategies for, 200–202
low total cost, 201–202
pricing, 201
quality of products, 201
strong focus, 200–201, 203

Mack, losses for, 36
Madrid Agreement Concerning the
International Registration of
Trademarks, 122
Magazines:
over-49 group, 110–111
women and, 97
Mail-order catalogs, 470–480

Mail-order catalogs (*Continued*)
  success of, 468–469
  see also Nonstore marketing
Males, as target groups, 83, 84
Management:
  brand, 240
  criticism of American, 4
  effective, issue of, 4, 7–8
  execution skills, 310–311
  global companies, 247, 257–258
  interactive skills, 311
  market, 240
  product, 240
Managers:
  allocation skills, 311
  monitoring skills, 311
  organizing skills, 311
  role in distribution antitrust, 71–73
Mannington Mills, Compu-Flor, 486–487
Manufacturing industries, 32–50
  adverse conditions and, 39
  average returns, 37–38
  competitive positions of, 39–43
  diversification and, 47–48
  external pressures, 33
  failing industries, facts about, 45–46
  foreign competition and, 34
  growth levels, 34
  heavy duty truck manufacturing, 35–36
  intangible products, 364–365
  leadership positions and, 44–45
  maturation of, 33, 48–49
  steel industry, 36
  success strategies, 36, 39–43
Manufacturing policies:
  low-cost strategies, 293–296
  managers role in, 296
  marketing-intensive strategy, 292–293
  technology-driven strategy, 287–292
Market drift, 181–182
Marketing:
  customer service audit, 337–338
  customer service program, 339–341
  declining industries, 205–219
  differentiation and success, 232–245
  environmental changes, 2–5
  family, changing structures and, 2, 6
  functions of, 304–306
    problem areas, 305
  future challenges to, 10–11
  health care market, 124–143
  high-risk situation, example of, 375–376
  nonprofit organizations, 512–520
  nonstore marketing, 465–480

point of purchase programs, 481–482
  product support and, 383–398
  vs. selling, 513–514
  target groups, 83
  technology-information revolution and, 5
  unmentionables, 153–170
  view of society and, 83
  women's market, 82–103
Marketing culture, 309–310
Marketing inertia, 179–190
  areas for change, 184–186
  customer/manager contact and, 187
  distribution channels and, 189
  examples of, 180–181
  found business and, 184
  market drift and, 181–182
  past success and, 182–183
  pricing policy and, 188
  product differentiation and, 187–188
  qualitative monitoring methods and,
    186–187
  success of others and, 183
  treatment for, 186–189
Marketing mix, 344
"Marketing Myopia," (Levitt), 1
Marketing practice, 304–310
  fundamentals of, 304–306
  good practice, characteristics of, 312–313
  managers skills for, 310–311
  policy directives, 309–310
  problems of, 305
  program level, 306–307
  systems level, 307–309
Marketing stages, 280–285
  diversified marketing (stage 4), 284
  entrepreneurial marketing (stage 1),
    281–282
  opportunistic marketing (stage 2), 282–283
  responsive marketing (stage 3), 283–284
Marketing strategies, 301–314
  catalog selling, 428–429
  demonstration centers, 424–425
  diagnosis of problems in, 304
  implementation and, 302–304
  industrial stores, 425–426
  national account management, 422–424
  market-intensive strategy, 292–293
  telemarketing, 426–428
  see also Marketing practice; Nonstore
    marketing
Marketing theme, 309
Market-intensive strategy, 292–293
  product flexibility, 292–293
  response to change and, 292

Market management, 240
  isopropanol, case example, 242–243
Market share, 342–348
  factors for gains in, 347, 348–349
  high, 44, 191–192
  low, 191–204
  marketing budgets and, 351–354
  market share model development, 344–345
  measurement of change, 345–347
  measurement of competitive strategies,
    345
  new businesses, 222
  new products, influence of, 349–350
  relative price levels and, 354
  sales force expenditures and, 353, 355
  share building strategies, factors in,
    355–357
  size of competitors and, 347–348
Media:
  active affluent older consumers and,
    109–110
  active retired group and, 110–111
  over-49 homemakers and, 111
  women's behavior and, 96–97
Medtronic, 225
"Merck Manual," 509
Microprocessors, Teradyne Corporation, 27
Middle Eastern countries, differences in, 21
Mile Square Health Center, 140
Miller Brewing Company, 228
Mitsubishi, Caterpillar and, 251
Modernity, 16
Mohasco, market intensive strategy, 296
Money:
  Japanese operations and, 31
  qualities of, 20
Monitoring skills, of managers, 311
Motivation, of buyers, 445–447
Multidomestics, definition of, 261
Multinational corporation, 16, 17
  definition of, 261
  scope of knowledge, 20
  fixed local preferences, belief in, 21
Murphy Pacific, follow-on sales, 540

"Nader's Raiders," 53
National account management, 422–424
  characteristics of, 423
  "special handling" accounts, 423
National Advertising Review Board,
    consumer complaint survey, 522
National Cancer Institute, marketing
    program, 515–516

National Health Planning and Resource
    Development Act of 1974, 127
National Mine Service Company, trade
    show, 454–455
National order, changes in, 2–3, 6
Nationals, consumer organization, 56
Nestle, baby formula, 3
New businesses:
  barrier reducing factors, 223–224
  marketing stages, 280–285
  weak position of, 222
  see also Barriers to entry; Entry strategies
Newly industrializing countries (NICs), 256
Newspapers:
  over-49 group and, 109
  women and, 97
New York Air, 224, 226
Nonprofit organizations, 512–520
  administrators orientation, 517, 519
  art museum, 512, 513–515
  audience response and, 515–516
  consumer knowledge and, 516
  consumer research, role of, 517
  marketing approaches, examples of,
    512–513
  National Cancer Institute, marketing
    program, 515–516
  promotion and, 516–517
  selling vs. marketing orientation, 513–514,
    515
  staff, 518–519
Nonstore marketing, 465–480
  consumers, reluctance of, 469–470
  established methods of, 479–480
  future and, 478
  grocery shopping, 466–468
    failure of, 467–468
  growth of, 465–466
  interactive cable television, 472–475, 480
  interactive information retrieval, 475–477,
    480
  mail-order catalogs, 468–469
    factors for success, 468
  manufacturers and, 471–472
  products, appropriateness of, 470–471
  retailers and, 472
  videocassettes/videodiscs, 477, 480

Older consumers, 104–115
  active affluent group, 106–107
    media and, 109–110
  active retired group, 107–108
    media and, 110–111
  developing new perspective for, 114–115

Older consumers (*Continued*)
  disabled, 106
  disadvantaged, 105–106
  financial profile of, 113–114
  homemakers, 108–109
    media and, 111
  interests of, 112–113
  as target group, 84
  watershed events of, 105
Opportunistic marketing, 282–283
Organizational structure, global companies, 258
Organizing skills, of managers, 311
Otis Elevator Company, scale-driven strategy, 293–294
Outboard Marine Corporation, distribution overhead, 26–27
Outpatient care, diversification tactic, 131–132
Outpatient surgery, diversification tactic, 132–133

Paccar, competitive positions (1980s), 36
Packaging, 361, 363, 487
"Paris Union," 122
Pennsylvania Public Utility Commission, public utilities practices and, 543
People Express, 224
Pepsi-Cola, global reach of, 17
Percentage increase method, 527
Philip Morris:
  acquisitions entry, 228
  market share approach, 356
  success strategies of, 40
Phillips Petroleum, 37
Physicians:
  economic power of, 126
  recruitment by hospitals, 129–131
Pilkington Company:
  float glass development, 321
  glass technology, 323
Pillsbury, 241
PIMS (Profit Impact of Market Strategies)
    data base, 44, 264, 342–343, 358
  research program, 264, 267–275
    absolute measure in, 268
    elative measure in, 269
    market stability, 274
    materials-costs, 274
    product innovation and, 274–275
    relative vertical integration and profitability, 271
    scale and profitability, 271–273
    value added, definition of, 268

vertical integration and profitability, 269–271
  see also Market share
Point of purchase programs, 481–482
  consumer expectations and, 485
  development of, 489
  displays, use of, 485–487
  examples of, 482
  execution of, 489–491
  expenditures of, 483
  in-store advertising media, 488
  packaging, 487
  productivity improvement, 483–484
  promotions, 487–488
  sales weakness, compensation for, 484–485
  types of products for, 482
Polaroid, instant picture technology, 317
Policy directives, marketing, 309–310
Politicization, problems of, 308
Potential products, 239–240
Preference theory, 404
  attitudes toward risk sharing study, 414–418
Prestel, 224
Price fixing, 79
Pricing:
  low market share businesses, 201
  market share and, 354
  see also Industrial pricing
Process capability study, 380
Procter & Gamble:
  entry strategies, 224
  new products and, 227
Procurement, advertising materials, 535–536
Product innovation, market share and, 349–350
Product management, 240
Product orientation, meaning of, 513
Product quality, 331–341, 372–382
  buyers role, 379–380, 381
  buying behavior and, 336–337
  Caterpillar quality program, 334
  customer's definition of, 334–335
  customer service audit and, 337–338
  customer service program and, 339–341
  customer service, relationship to, 333
  focus for customer studies, 335–336
  goal setting and, 377
  L.L. Bean customer-driven quality program, 333–334
  marketing factors, 375–376
  market share and, 350–351
  misconceptions about increases in, 371–372

perceptions of, 331–332
performance, measurement of, 378
plant conditions and, 382
process capability study, 380
product assurance:
  groups for, 374–375
  organizational factors, 372–376
promotional strategies and, 322
report system and, 376–377
specifications and, 380–381
vendors, quality control of, 378–381
Products, 233–240
  augmented products, 237–239
  "avoidance products," 523
  branded food marketing, 241–242
  components of, 234–235
  customer's perception of, 234–235
  customization of, 19
  expected products, 236–237
  generic products, 235–236
  impressions, importance of, 362–363
  intangible products, 360, 361
    problems of, 364–366
  low market share businesses, 198–199, 201
  packaging of, 361, 363
  potential products, 239–240
  product lines, 19
  promises of, 362–363
  standardization of, 17–21
  tangible products, 360–361, 362, 364
Product strategies:
  low-cost strategies, 293–296
  marketing-intensive strategy, 292–293
  technology-driven strategy, 287–292
Product support, 383–398
  case study, industrial tractors, 394–398
  components of, 384–385
  customer needs and, 387–390
  failure of, factors in, 384–386
  market segments and, 386
  support strategies, 390–392
    considerations in, 392–393
    focus for, 393–394
    interactions of, 392
    limitations of, 390–392
Promotion, 488
  nonprofit organizations, 516–517
  see also Trade promotion
Prosecuting strategy, counterfeiting, 120
Purchasers, buying role of, 441
Purchasing:
  integrity buying, 336
  investment buying, 336
  life-cycle buying, 336

women and, 98–99
see also Buying behavior

Quality:
  cost and, 18
  increasing product quality, 8–9
  Japanese products, 18–19
  see also Product quality
Quality control:
  "acceptable quality level" system, 377
  goal setting and, 377
  intangible products, 365
Questionnaires, Target Group Index, 94

Radio:
  advertisements for unmentionables, 157
  over-49 group, 110–111
  women and, 97
Ralph Nader's Public Citizen, 56
Reach and frequency, advertising, 533–534
Regulation:
  agencies, call for reform, 53
  brand name counterfeiting, 119–123
  hospitals, 127–129
  regulatory changes, new entrants and, 226
Reindustrialists, consumer organization, 61
Relative measure, 269
Reliance Electric Company, 231
Rentokil Company, marketing techniques,
    168–170
Report system, product quality, 376–377
Responsive marketing, 283–284
Retired consumers, 107–108, 110–111
  time factors, 107–108
Revlon, Japanese market and, 26
Reward power, 442
Richardson-Merrill, Inc., 223
Risk management, 403–405
  attitudes and risk, 404
  avoiding risks, 405–407
    fixed-price contracts, 406
    hedging contracts, 405–406
    technology and, 406–407
    time factors and, 407
  risk assignment options, 411–413
  risk averse, 404
  risk premium, 404
  sharing risk, 407–411
    attitudes toward, 414–418
    escalators/de-escalators and, 407, 411
    metals risk, example, 409–410
    timing in, 411
"Rule of reason" test, 71

Rush-Presbyterian-St. Luke's Hospital and
    Medical Center, organizational
    strategy of, 139–141

Safeway, 18
Sales force expenditures, market share and,
    353, 355
Samaritan Health Services, 134, 136
Sanitac service, marketing techniques,
    168–170
Sanitary napkin disposal service, marketing
    of, 168–170
Savin, market share strategy, 357
Scale driven strategies, 293–294
Schick, suit with Gillette, 543
Schwinn case, 71
Screening programs, hospitals, 135
Selected Business Ventures, 320
Self-concept, women, 96
Selling:
    buying group and, 437–438
    buying roles and, 439–442
    cost analysis in, 429, 431
    vs. marketing, 513–514
    needs of customer and, 431
    program development for, 429–434
    sales audit, 451
    sales calls, 449
    synergistic communications program,
        development of, 431, 433–434
    trade shows, 452–463
    see also Marketing strategies
Selling orientation, meaning of, 513
Served market, 346
Service, industrialization of, 365
Share/growth matrices, 44
Shasta, distribution, 227
Showrooms, demonstration centers, 424–425
Siemen, Bazil operation, 256
Sinclair radionics, flat screen technology, 317
Singer sewing machines, fake goods, 116
Small businesses, buying in, 549–550
SmithKlein Corporation, Japanese market,
    strategy for, 27
Social movement organizations, "free rider"
    problem, 62
Soft-drink industry, distribution, 227
Soft technologies, meaning of, 365
Southland, 18
Spangler Candy company, trade show, 455
Specialization, vertical integration and, 267
Specifications:
    product quality and, 380–381
    "slotted hole" approach, 380

Standardization of products, 17–21
    global competitor and, 19
    lowering costs internationally, 19
    product lines, 19
    quality/cost and, 18–19
Stansaab Elektronik, follow-on sales, 541
Statistical analysis, advertising elasticity,
    528–529
Status power, 443
Steel industry, losses in, 36
Stoneware, 283
Store-to-Door, 467
Success, strategies for, U.S. manufacturing
    industries, 36, 39–43
SWECO, 225
Synergistic communications program, 431,
    433–434
    time, importance of, 433
Systems, marketing, 307–309

Tangible products, 362, 364
    definition of, 360–361
Tappan, reinvestment errors of, 46
Target Group Index, 94
Target groups, 83
    bachelors, 84
    girls, 83
    housewives, 83
    male head of household, 83
    older population as, 84
    see also Women's market
Technological change, new entrants and,
    225–226
Technologies:
    factors in marketing of, 328–329
    hard, 365
    hybrid, 365–366
    market size and, 324–325
    rationale for sale of, 316–318
    risk avoidance and, 406–407
    sale of, 323
        sale of licenses, 322, 325
        standardization and, 325
        technological leadership and, 325
        technology life cycle and, 324
    soft, 365
    vertical integration and, 266
Technology-driven strategy, 287–292
    facilities abroad, 290–291
    IBM and, 290–291
    management of technology, 291–292
Technology-information revolution, 4–5,
    9–10
    distribution of products and, 5

home computers, 5
marketing implications, 5
Technology life cycle, 316, 318–328
application growth, 324–326
application launch stage, 322–324
degraded technology phase, 327–328
development of, 329–330
selling/licensing decisions, 322
selling technologies and, 320–321
staffing and, 321
technology application stage, 321–322
technology development stage, 318–321
technology maturity stage, 326–327
Technology Transfer Ban Act, 323
Telemark Enterprises, 466–467
Telemarketing, 426–428
cost savings of, 426
customer/company coordination and,
427–428
supplementary functions of, 426–427
vs. direct mail, 427
Telephone systems, L. M. Ericsson,
251–252
Television:
over-49 group and, 110–111
women and, 97
Teradyne Corporation, organizing
marketing, 27
Terrorism, international, 2–3
Texas Instruments, 38
counter competitive action, 174
forward integration, 264
Third World markets, 3
Time factors, advertising, 533
"TI Shows U.S. Industry How to Compete
in the 1980's," 38
Total business approach, advertising budget,
527–528
Trademarks:
code-law country, 121
common law country, 121
Trademark Registration Treaty, 122
counterfeiting, 116–123
Trade promotion, 493–502
vs. advertising, 494–495
buying behavior and, 501–502
improvements for, 497–502
discounts, 499–500
management, 497–498
market scope, 499
product range, 499
promotion design, 498
terms, 500–501
timing, 500

problems in, 494, 495–496
reasons for, 496–497
Trade shows, 452–463
costs involved, examples, 454–455
expositions, 454
managers' perceptions of, 452–453
measuring effectiveness of, 455–456,
459–461
morale boost and, 458
negative aspects of, 453
nonselling objectives, 457–459
nonselling variables, 462
selling objectives, 457
selling variables, 461–462
Transportation services, hospitals, 135–136
Travel market:
over-49 group, 113
women in, 99
Truck manufacturing, Caterpillar, 249–251
Truth in Lending Act, 53
Truth in Packaging Act, 53

Uniroyal, losses for, 36
United Auto Workers, 26
United Steelworkers of America, 26
United Technologies, 38
Unmentionables, 153–170
contraceptive sheath, 165–168
demarketing, 160–161
desirable/undesirable products, 157–158
desirable unmentionable, marketing of,
164–170
effect of time/place on, 156
groups of, 155–156
marketing mix, 162–163
marketing process and, 154
market segments and, 162
meaning of, 155, 156
product mix, 163–164
radio advertisements of, 157
sanitary napkin disposal service, 168–170
scale of unmentionability, 158–160
UNOX, demonstration centers and, 425
Utterback, J. M., 326, 329

Value added, definition of, 268
Vending machines, 480
Vendors:
buyers and, 379–380, 381
controlling quality of, 378–381
Versatec, 226
Vertical integration of, 45, 263–279
benefits of, 265–266
cost reduction, 265

Vertical integration of (*Continued*)
    entry barriers, 266
    improved coordination, 265–266
    supply assurance, 265
    technological capabilities, 266
  definition of, 265
  examples of, 263–264
  guidelines for evaluation benefits/risks,
    276–277
  PIMS research program, 264, 267–275
  profitability of, 267–268, 275
  risks of, 266–267
    capital, 266
    lessened flexibility, 267
    scale requirements, 266–267
    specialization losses, 267
    see also PIMS (Profit Impact of
    Marketing Strategies) data base
    research program
Videocassettes/videodiscs, catalogs on, 477,
  480
Vienna Diplomatic Conference on Property,
  122

Warning strategy, counterfeiting, 121
Warwick Electronics, 286–287
White Motor:
  losses for, 36, 41
  reinvestment errors of, 46
Widows, 109
Withdrawal strategy, counterfeiting, 120–121
Women's market, 82–103

basic assumptions about, 84–85
buying style of, 97–98
cars and, 98–99
housewife market, 85–86, 88
  demographic differences, 94, 96
  over-49 homemakers, 108–109, 111
  types of women, 93–94
husbands and, 101
life cycle and, 89, 99
media behavior, 96–97
purchasing behavior, 98–99
redefinition of, 101, 102–103
self-concepts, types of women, 96
travel related items, 99
women as head of household, 86, 88
working women, 85, 89, 92–93
  economic necessity and, 89
  motivational factors, 92
  professional fulfillment and, 92–93
  second paycheck and, 89, 92
widows, 109
World Intellectual Property Organization,
  122–123
Wright Line, Inc., catalog selling, 428

Xerox, 38, 224
  Ethernert system, 322
  FTC charges, 318
  market management, 242

Zero defects goal, 377